- **Dynamic Study Modules**—help students learn the language of MIS by continuously assessing their activity and performance in real time by adapting to the student's **knowledge** and confidence on each concept. These are available as graded assignments prior to class, and accessible on smartphones, tablets, and computers.

- **Learning Catalytics™**—is an interactive, student response tool that uses students' smartphones, tablets, or laptops to engage them in more sophisticated tasks and **critical thinking** as well as **collaboration** with other class members. Included with MyLab with eText, Learning Catalytics enables you to generate classroom discussion, guide your lecture, and promote peer-to-peer learning with real-time analytics.

- **Reporting Dashboard**—View, analyze, and report learning outcomes clearly and easily, and get the information needed to keep students on track throughout the course with the new Reporting Dashboard. Available via the MyLab Gradebook and fully mobile-ready, the Reporting Dashboard presents student performance data at the class, section, and program levels in an accessible, visual manner.

- **Enhanced eText**—keeps students engaged in learning on their own time, while helping them achieve greater conceptual understanding of course material. The embedded videos, simulations, and activities bring learning to life. to apply the very concepts they are reading about. Combining resources that illuminate content with accessible self-assessment, MyLab with Enhanced eText provides students with a complete digital learning experience—all in one place.

- **Accessibility (ADA)**—Pearson is working toward WCAG 2.0 Level AA and Section 508 standards, as expressed in the **Pearson Guidelines for Accessible Educational Web Media.** Moreover, our products support customers in meeting their obligation to comply with the Americans with Disabilities Act (ADA) by providing access to learning technology programs for users with disabilities.

  Please email our Accessibility Team at **disability.support@pearson.com** for the most up-to-date information.

- **LMS Integration**—You can now link from Blackboard Learn, Brightspace by D2L, Canvas, or Moodle to MyISLab. Professors can acess assignments, rosters, and resources, and synchronize grades with your LMS gradebook.
  Single sign-on provides students access to all the personalized learning resources that make studying more efficient and effective.

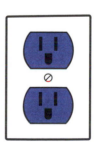

ALWAYS LEARNING

MANAGEMENT INFORMATION SYSTEMS

MANAGING THE DIGITAL FIRM

FIFTEENTH EDITION

Kenneth C. Laudon

New York University

Jane P. Laudon

Azimuth Information Systems

330 Hudson Street, NY NY 10013

VP Editorial Director: Andrew Gilfillan
Senior Portfolio Manager: Samantha Lewis
Content Development Team Lead: Laura Burgess
Program Monitor: Ann Pulido/SPi Global
Editorial Assistant: Michael Campbell
Product Marketing Manager: Kaylee Carlson
Project Manager: Katrina Ostler/Cenveo® Publisher Services
Text Designer: Cenveo® Publisher Services
Cover Designer: Brian Malloy/Cenveo® Publisher Services
Cover Art: Aleksandarvelasevic/DigitalVision Vectors/
   Getty Images

Full-Service Project Management:
   Cenveo® Publisher Services
Composition: Cenveo® Publisher Services
Printer/Binder: LSC Communications/Kendallville
Cover Printer: Pheonix Color
Text Font: 10.5/13 ITC Veljovic
Unattributed Figures and Chapter Opener Diagrams:
   Kenneth C. Laudon, Jane P. Laudon, Management
   Information Systems, 15 Ed., © 2018, Pearson
   Education, Inc., New York, NY.

Library of Congress Cataloging-in-Publication Information
Laudon, Kenneth C., 1944- author. | Laudon, Jane P. (Jane Price),
   author.
Management information systems : managing the digital firm / Kenneth
   C. Laudon, New York University, Jane P. Laudon, Azimuth Information
   Systems.
Fifteenth Edition. | Hoboken : Pearson, [2018] | Revised edition
   of the authors' Management information systems, [2016]
LCCN 2016048325| ISBN 0134639715 | ISBN 9780134639710
LCSH: Management information systems.
LCC T58.6 .L376 2018 | DDC 658.4/038011—dc23
LC record available at https://lccn.loc.gov/2016048325

2   17

ISBN-13: 978-0-13-463971-0
ISBN-10: 0-13-463971-5

About the Authors

Kenneth C. Laudon is a Professor of Information Systems at New York University's Stern School of Business. He holds a B.A. in Economics from Stanford and a Ph.D. from Columbia University. He has authored 12 books dealing with electronic commerce, information systems, organizations, and society. Professor Laudon has also written more than 40 articles concerned with the social, organizational, and management impacts of information systems, privacy, ethics, and multimedia technology.

Professor Laudon's current research is on the planning and management of large-scale information systems and multimedia information technology. He has received grants from the National Science Foundation to study the evolution of national information systems at the Social Security Administration, the IRS, and the FBI. Ken's research focuses on enterprise system implementation, computer-related organizational and occupational changes in large organizations, changes in management ideology, changes in public policy, and understanding productivity change in the knowledge sector.

Ken Laudon has testified as an expert before the United States Congress. He has been a researcher and consultant to the Office of Technology Assessment (United States Congress), the Department of Homeland Security, and the Office of the President, several executive branch agencies, and Congressional Committees. Professor Laudon also acts as an in-house educator for several consulting firms and as a consultant on systems planning and strategy to several Fortune 500 firms.

At NYU's Stern School of Business, Ken Laudon teaches courses on Managing the Digital Firm, Information Technology and Corporate Strategy, Professional Responsibility (Ethics), and Electronic Commerce and Digital Markets. Ken Laudon's hobby is sailing.

Jane Price Laudon is a management consultant in the information systems area and the author of seven books. Her special interests include systems analysis, data management, MIS auditing, software evaluation, and teaching business professionals how to design and use information systems.

Jane received her Ph.D. from Columbia University, her M.A. from Harvard University, and her B.A. from Barnard College. She has taught at Columbia University and the New York University Graduate School of Business. She maintains a lifelong interest in Oriental languages and civilizations.

The Laudons have two daughters, Erica and Elisabeth, to whom this book is dedicated.

Brief Contents

Complete Contents

Chapter 4 Ethical and Social Issues in Information Systems 122

Chapter 8   Securing Information Systems   292

PART THREE   Key System Applications for the Digital Age   335

Chapter 15   Managing Global Systems   560

Business Cases And Interactive Sessions

Here are some of the business firms you will find described in the cases and Interactive Sessions of this book:

We wrote this book for business school students who wanted an in-depth look at how today's business firms use information technologies and systems to achieve corporate objectives. Information systems are one of the major tools available to business managers for achieving operational excellence, developing new products and services, improving decision making, and achieving competitive advantage. Students will find here the most up-to-date and comprehensive overview of information systems used by business firms today. After reading this book, we expect students will be able to participate in, and even lead, management discussions of information systems for their firms.

When interviewing potential employees, business firms often look for new hires who know how to use information systems and technologies for achieving bottom-line business results. Regardless of whether you are an accounting, finance, management, operations management, marketing, or information systems major, the knowledge and information you find in this book will be valuable throughout your business career.

What's New in This Edition

Currency

The 15th edition features all new opening, closing, and Interactive Session cases. The text, figures, tables, and cases have been updated through September 2016 with the latest sources from industry and MIS research.

New Features

- **New Conceptual Videos** collection includes 45 conceptual videos of 3 to 5 minutes in length. Ken Laudon walks students through three of the most important concepts in each chapter using a contemporary animation platform. Available only in the MyMISLab digital edition
- **New Video Cases** collection: 36 video cases (two or more per chapter) and 10 additional instructional videos covering key concepts and experiences in the MIS world. Video Cases are listed at the beginning of each chapter.
- **Learning Tracks:** 47 Learning Tracks in MyMISLab for additional coverage of selected topics.

New Topics

- **Big Data and the Internet of Things:** In-depth coverage of big data, big data analytics, and the Internet of Things (IoT) in Chapters 1, 6, 7, and 12. Includes big data analytics, analyzing IoT data streams, Hadoop, in-memory computing, non-relational databases, and analytic platforms.

- **Cloud Computing:** Updated and expanded coverage of cloud computing in Chapter 5 (IT infrastructure) with more detail on types of cloud services, private and public clouds, hybrid clouds, managing cloud services, and a new Interactive Session on using cloud services. Cloud computing also covered in Chapter 6 (databases in the cloud), Chapter 8 (cloud security), Chapter 9 (cloud-based CRM and ERP), Chapter 10 (e-commerce), and Chapter 13 (cloud-based systems development).
- **Social, Mobile, Local:** New e-commerce content in Chapter 10 describing how social tools, mobile technology, and location-based services are transforming marketing and advertising.
- **Social Business:** Expanded coverage of social business, introduced in Chapter 2 and discussed in throughout the text. Detailed discussions of enterprise (internal corporate) social networking as well as social networking in e-commerce.
- BYOD and mobile device management
- Smart products
- DevOps
- Zero-day vulnerabilities
- Machine learning
- Chatbots
- Near field communication (NFC)
- Native advertising
- Windows 10
- Microsoft Office 365
- Zero-day vulnerabilities
- Platforms
- Software-defined storage (SDS)

The 15th Edition: The Comprehensive Solution for the MIS Curriculum

Since its inception, this text has helped to define the MIS course around the globe. This edition continues to be authoritative but is also more customizable, flexible, and geared to meeting the needs of different colleges, universities, and individual instructors. Many of its learning tools are now available in digital form. This book is now part of a complete learning package that includes the core text, Video Case Package, and Learning Tracks.

The core text consists of 15 chapters with hands-on projects covering the most essential topics in MIS. An important part of the core text is the Video Case Study and Instructional Video Package: 36 video case studies (two to three per chapter) plus 10 instructional videos that illustrate business uses of information systems, explain new technologies, and explore concepts. Videos are keyed to the topics of each chapter.

In addition, for students and instructors who want to go deeper into selected topics, there are 47 Learning Tracks in MyMISLab that cover a variety of MIS topics in greater depth.

The CORE Text

The core text provides an overview of fundamental MIS concepts using an integrated framework for describing and analyzing information systems. This framework shows information systems composed of management, organization, and technology elements and is reinforced in student projects and case studies.

Chapter Organization

Each chapter contains the following elements:

- A Chapter Outline based on Learning Objectives
- Lists of all the Case Studies and Video Cases for each chapter
- A chapter-opening case describing a real-world organization to establish the theme and importance of the chapter
- A diagram analyzing the opening case in terms of the management, organization, and technology model used throughout the text
- Two Interactive Sessions with Case Study Questions
- A Review Summary keyed to the Student Learning Objectives
- A list of Key Terms that students can use to review concepts
- Review questions for students to test their comprehension of chapter material
- Discussion questions raised by the broader themes of the chapter
- A series of Hands-on MIS Projects consisting of two Management Decision Problems, a hands-on application software project, and a project to develop Internet skills
- A Collaboration and Teamwork Project to develop teamwork and presentation skills with options for using open source collaboration tools
- A chapter-ending case study for students to apply chapter concepts
- Two assisted-graded writing questions with prebuilt grading rubrics
- Chapter references

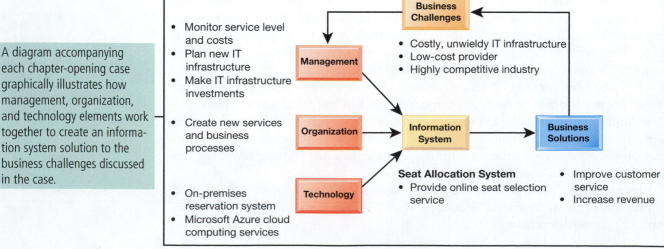

A diagram accompanying each chapter-opening case graphically illustrates how management, organization, and technology elements work together to create an information system solution to the business challenges discussed in the case.

Key Features

We have enhanced the text to make it more interactive, leading edge, and appealing to both students and instructors. The features and learning tools are described in the following sections.

Business-Driven with Real-World Business Cases and Examples

The text helps students see the direct connection between information systems and business performance. It describes the main business objectives driving the use of information systems and technologies in corporations all over the world: operational excellence, new products and services, customer and supplier intimacy, improved decision making, competitive advantage, and survival. In-text examples and case studies show students how specific companies use information systems to achieve these objectives.

We use only current (2016) examples from business and public organizations throughout the text to illustrate the important concepts in each chapter. All the case studies describe companies or organizations that are familiar to students, such as Nike, the San Francisco Giants, Facebook, Walmart, Google, Macy's, and GE.

Interactivity

There's no better way to learn about MIS than by doing MIS! We provide different kinds of hands-on projects where students can work with real-world business scenarios and data and learn firsthand what MIS is all about. These projects heighten student involvement in this exciting subject.

- **Online Video Case Package.** Students can watch short videos online, either in-class or at home or work, and then apply the concepts of the book to the analysis of the video. Every chapter contains at least two business video cases that explain how business firms and managers are using information systems and explore concepts discussed in the chapter. Each video case consists of one or more videos about a real-world company, a background text case, and case study questions. These video cases enhance students' understanding of MIS topics and the relevance of MIS to the business world. In addition, there are 10 Instructional Videos that describe developments and concepts in MIS keyed to respective chapters.

- **Online Conceptual Videos [the digital edition only].** Forty-five video animations where the authors walk students through three concepts from each chapter.

- **Interactive Sessions.** Two short cases in each chapter have been redesigned as Interactive Sessions to be used in the classroom (or on Internet discussion boards) to stimulate student interest and active learning. Each case concludes with case study questions. The case study questions provide topics for class discussion, Internet discussion, or written assignments.

- **Hands-On MIS Projects.** Every chapter concludes with a Hands-On MIS Projects section containing three types of projects: two Management Decision Problems; a hands-on application software exercise using Microsoft Excel, Access, or web page and blog creation tools; and a project that develops Internet business skills. A Dirt Bikes USA running case in MyMISLab provides additional hands-on projects for each chapter.

Each chapter contains two Interactive Sessions on Management, Organizations, or Technology using real-world companies to illustrate chapter concepts and issues.

Case Study Questions encourage students to apply chapter concepts to real-world companies in class discussions, student presentations, or writing assignments.

---

396 Part Three Key System Applications for the Digital Age

INTERACTIVE SESSION: TECHNOLOGY

Getting Social with Customers

Businesses of all sizes are finding Facebook, Twitter, and other social media to be powerful tools for engaging customers, amplifying product messages, discovering trends and influencers, building brand awareness, and taking action on customer requests and recommendations. Half of all Twitter users recommend products in their tweets.

About 1.6 billion people use Facebook, and more than 30 million businesses have active brand pages, enabling users to interact with the brand through blogs, comment pages, contests, and offerings on the brand page. The "like" button gives users a chance to share with their social network their feelings about content and other objects they are viewing and websites they are visiting. With like buttons on millions of websites, Facebook can track user behavior on other sites and then sell this information to marketers. Facebook also sells display ads to firms that show up in the right column of users' home pages and most other pages in the Facebook interface such as photos and apps.

Twitter has developed many new offerings to interest advertisers, like "promoted tweets" and "promoted trends." These features give advertisers the ability to have their tweets displayed more prominently when Twitter users search for certain keywords. Many big advertisers are using Twitter's Vine service, which allows users to share short, repeating videos with a mobile-phone app or post them on other platforms such as Facebook.

Lowe's is using Facebook mobile video and Snapchat image messaging to help first-time millennial home buyers learn home improvement skills. The home improvement retailer launched a new series of social videos in April 2016 to showcase spring cleaning and do-it-yourself projects. Lowe's believes this is a more immediate and interactive way to reach

Lowe's "In-a-Snap" Snapchat series tries to inspire young homeowners and renters to undertake simple home improvement projects such as installing shelves to build a study nook. During the Lowe's Snapchat story, users can tap on the screen to put a nail in a wall or chisel off an old tile. Lowe's is working on another series of video tutorials on Facebook and Instagram called "Home School" that uses drawings from chalk artists to animate maintenance projects.

Lowe's social media activities have helped increase brand engagement. Although the company's social campaigns are designed to teach first-time homeowners or young renters about home improvement, the company is also hoping they will encourage consumers to think differently about the brand beyond its products and services. Management believes millennials who are becoming first-time homeowners want to know the deeper meaning of what a company is trying to stand for, not just the products and services it offers.

An estimated 90 percent of customers are influenced by online reviews, and nearly half of U.S. social media users actively seek customer service through social media. As a result, marketing is now placing much more emphasis on customer satisfaction and customer service. Social media monitoring helps marketers and business owners understand more about likes, dislikes, and complaints concerning products, additional products or product modifications customers want, and how people are talking about a brand (positive or negative sentiment).

General Motors (GM) has 26 full-time social media customer care advisers for North America alone, covering more than 150 company social channels from GM, Chevrolet, Buick, GMC, and Cadillac, and approximately 85 sites such as automotive enthusiast

CASE STUDY QUESTIONS

1. Assess the management, organization, and technology issues for using social media technology to engage with customers.

2. What are the advantages and disadvantages of using social media for advertising, brand building, market research, and customer service?

3. Give an example of a business decision in this case study that was facilitated by using social media to interact with customers.

4. Should all companies use social media technology for customer service and marketing? Why or why not? What kinds of companies are best suited to use these platforms?

- **Collaboration and Teamwork Projects.** Each chapter features a collaborative project that encourages students working in teams to use Google Drive, Google Docs, or other open source collaboration tools. The first team project in Chapter 1 asks students to build a collaborative Google site.

Assessment and AACSB Assessment Guidelines

The Association to Advance Collegiate Schools of Business (AACSB) is a not-for-profit corporation of educational institutions, corporations, and other organizations that seeks to improve business education primarily by accrediting university business programs. As a part of its accreditation activities, the AACSB has

Management Decision Problems

11-8 U.S. Pharma Corporation is headquartered in New Jersey but has research sites in Germany, France, the United Kingdom, Switzerland, and Australia. Research and development of new pharmaceuticals is key to ongoing profits, and U.S. Pharma researches and tests thousands of possible drugs. The company's researchers need to share information with others within and outside the company, including the U.S. Food and Drug Administration, the World Health Organization, and the International Federation of Pharmaceutical Manufacturers & Associations. Also critical is access to health information sites, such as the U.S. National Library of Medicine, and to industry conferences and professional journals. Design a knowledge portal for U.S. Pharma's researchers. Include in your design specifications relevant internal systems and databases, external sources of information, and internal and external communication and collaboration tools. Design a home page for your portal.

11-9 Canadian Tire is one of Canada's largest companies, with 50,000 employees and 1,100 stores and gas bars (gas stations) across Canada selling sports, leisure, home products, apparel, and financial services as well as automotive and petroleum products. The retail outlets are independently owned and operated. Canadian Tire has been using daily mailings and thick product catalogs to inform its dealers about new products, merchandise setups, product ordering, and problem resolution, and it is looking for a better way to provide employees with human resources and administrative documents. Describe the problems created by this way of doing business and how knowledge management systems might help.

Two real-world business scenarios per chapter provide opportunities for students to apply chapter concepts and practice management decision making.

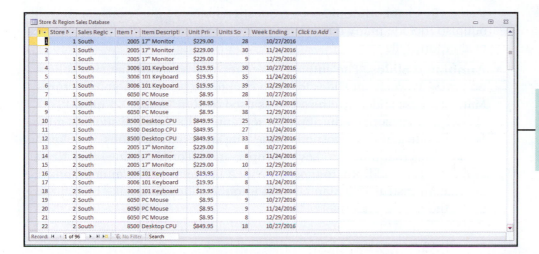

Students practice using software in real-world settings for achieving operational excellence and enhancing decision making.

Improving Decision Making: Using Web Tools to Configure and Price an Automobile

Software skills: Internet-based software
Business skills: Researching product information and pricing

3-11 In this exercise, you will use software at car websites to find product information about a car of your choice and use that information to make an important purchase decision. You will also evaluate two of these sites as selling tools.

You are interested in purchasing a new Ford Escape (or some other car of your choice). Go to the website of CarsDirect (www.carsdirect.com) and begin your investigation. Locate the Ford Escape. Research the various Escape models, and choose one you prefer in terms of price, features, and safety ratings. Locate and read at least two reviews. Surf the website of the manufacturer, in this case Ford (www.ford.com). Compare the information available on Ford's website with that of CarsDirect for the Ford Escape. Try to locate the lowest price for the car you want in a local dealer's inventory. Suggest improvements for CarsDirect.com and Ford.com.

Each chapter features a project to develop Internet skills for accessing information, conducting research, and performing online calculations and analysis.

developed an Assurance of Learning Program designed to ensure that schools do in fact teach students what they promise. Schools are required to state a clear mission, develop a coherent business program, identify student learning objectives, and then prove that students do in fact achieve the objectives.

We have attempted in this book to support AACSB efforts to encourage assessment-based education. The back end papers of this edition identify student learning objectives and anticipated outcomes for our Hands-On MIS projects. The authors will provide custom advice on how to use this text in colleges with different missions and assessment needs. Please e-mail the authors or contact your local Pearson representative for contact information.

For more information on the AACSB Assurance of Learning Program and how this text supports assessment-based learning, please visit the website for this book.

Customization and Flexibility: Learning Track Modules

Our Learning Tracks feature gives instructors the flexibility to provide in-depth coverage of the topics they choose. There are 47 Learning Tracks in MyMISLab available to instructors and students. This supplementary content takes students deeper into MIS topics, concepts, and debates; reviews basic technology concepts in hardware, software, database design, telecommunications, and other areas.

Author-Certified Test Bank and Supplements

- **Author-Certified Test Bank.** The authors have worked closely with skilled test item writers to ensure that higher-level cognitive skills are tested. Test bank multiple-choice questions include questions on content but also include many questions that require analysis, synthesis, and evaluation skills.

- **Annotated Slides.** The authors have prepared a comprehensive collection of 50 PowerPoint slides for each chapter to be used in your lectures. Many of these slides are the same as used by Ken Laudon in his MIS classes and executive education presentations. Each of the slides is annotated with teaching suggestions for asking students questions, developing in-class lists that illustrate key concepts, and recommending other firms as examples in addition to those provided in the text. The annotations are like an Instructor's Manual built into the slides and make it easier to teach the course effectively.

Student Learning-Focused

Student Learning Objectives are organized around a set of study questions to focus student attention. Each chapter concludes with a Review Summary and Review Questions organized around these study questions, and each major chapter section is based on a Learning Objective.

Career Resources

The Instructor Resources for this text include extensive Career Resources, including job-hunting guides and instructions on how to build a Digital Portfolio demonstrating the business knowledge, application software proficiency, and Internet skills acquired from using the text. The portfolio can be included in a resume or job application or used as a learning assessment tool for instructors.

Instructor Resources

At the Instructor Resource Center, www.pearsonhighered.com/irc, instructors can easily register to gain access to a variety of instructor resources available with this text in downloadable format. If assistance is needed, our dedicated technical support team is ready to help with the media supplements that accompany this text. Visit http://247.pearsoned.com for answers to frequently asked questions and toll-free user support phone numbers.

The following supplements are available with this text:

- Instructor's Resource Manual
- Test Bank

- TestGen® Computerized Test Bank
- PowerPoint Presentation
- Image Library
- Lecture Notes

Video Cases and Instructional Videos

Instructors can download step-by-step instructions for accessing the video cases from the Instructor Resources Center. Video Cases and Instructional Videos are listed at the beginning of each chapter as well as in the Preface.

Learning Tracks Modules

There are 47 Learning Tracks in MyMISLab providing additional coverage topics for students and instructors. See page xxvi for a list of the Learning Tracks available for this edition.

Video Cases and Instructional Videos

Chapter	Video
Chapter 1: Information Systems in Global Business Today	Business in the Cloud: Facebook and eBay Data Centers UPS Global Operations with the DIAD Instructional Video: Tour IBM's Raleigh Data Center
Chapter 2: Global E-business and Collaboration	Walmart's Retail Link Supply Chain CEMEX: Becoming a Social Business Instructional Video: US Foodservice Grows Market with Oracle CRM on Demand
Chapter 3: Information Systems, Organizations, and Strategy	GE Becomes a Digital Firm: The Emerging Industrial Internet National Basketball Association: Competing on Global Delivery with Akamai OS Streaming
Chapter 4: Ethical and Social Issues in Information Systems	What Net Neutrality Means for You Facebook and Google Privacy: What Privacy? The United States v. Terrorism: Data Mining for Terrorists and Innocents Instructional Video: Viktor Mayer Schönberger on the Right to Be Forgotten
Chapter 5: IT Infrastructure and Emerging Technologies	Rockwell Automation Fuels the Oil and Gas Industry with the Internet of Things (IoT) ESPN.com: The Future of Sports Broadcasting in the Cloud Netflix: Building a Business in the Cloud
Chapter 6: Foundations of Business Intelligence: Databases and Information Management	Dubuque Uses Cloud Computing and Sensors to Build a Smarter City Brooks Brothers Closes in on Omnichannel Retail Maruti Suzuki Business Intelligence and Enterprise Databases
Chapter 7: Telecommunications, the Internet, and Wireless Technology	Telepresence Moves out of the Boardroom and into the Field Virtual Collaboration with IBMSametime
Chapter 8: Securing Information Systems	Stuxnet and Cyberwarfare Cyberespionage: The Chinese Threat Instructional Video: Sony PlayStation Hacked; Data Stolen from 77 Million Users Instructional Video: Meet the Hackers: Anonymous Statement on Hacking SONY
Chapter 9: Achieving Operational Excellence and Customer Intimacy: Enterprise Applications	Life Time Fitness Gets in Shape with Salesforce CRM Evolution Homecare Manages Patients with Microsoft CRM Instructional Video: GSMS Protects Products and Patients by Serializing Every Bottle of Drugs
Chapter 10: E-commerce: Digital Markets, Digital Goods	Walmart Takes on Amazon: A Battle of IT and Management Systems Groupon: Deals Galore Etsy: A Marketplace and Community Instructional Video: Walmart's eCommerce Fulfillment Center Network Instructional Video: Behind the Scenes of an Amazon Warehouse
Chapter 11: Managing Knowledge	How IBM's Watson Became a Jeopardy Champion Alfresco: Open Source Document Management and Collaboration
Chapter 12: Enhancing Decision Making	PSEG Leverages Big Data and Business Analytics Using GE's PREDIX Platform FreshDirect Uses Business Intelligence to Manage Its Online Grocery. Business Intelligence Helps the Cincinnati Zoo Work Smarter

Video Cases and Instructional Videos (Continued)

Chapter	Video
Chapter 13 Building Information Systems	IBM: Business Process Management in a SaaS Environment IBM Helps the City of Madrid with Real-Time BPM Software Instructional Video: BPM: Business Process Management Customer Story Instructional Video: Workflow Management Visualized
Chapter 14 Managing Projects	Blue Cross Blue Shield: Smarter Computing Project NASA Project Management Challenges
Chapter 15 Managing Global Systems	Daum Runs Oracle Apps on Linux Lean Manufacturing and Global ERP: Humanetics and Global Shop

Learning Tracks

Chapter	Learning Tracks
Chapter 1: Information Systems in Global Business Today	How Much Does IT Matter? Information Systems and Your Career The Mobile Digital Platform
Chapter 2: Global E-business and Collaboration	Systems From a Functional Perspective IT Enables Collaboration and Teamwork Challenges of Using Business Information Systems Organizing the Information Systems Function Occupational and Career Outlook for Information Systems Majors 2014–2020
Chapter 3: Information Systems, Organizations, and Strategy	The Changing Business Environment for IT
Chapter 4: Ethical and Social Issues in Information Systems	Developing a Corporate Code of Ethics for IT
Chapter 5: IT Infrastructure and Emerging Technologies	How Computer Hardware Works How Computer Software Works Service Level Agreements The Open Source Software Initiative Comparing Stages in IT Infrastructure Evolution Cloud Computing
Chapter 6: Foundations of Business Intelligence: Databases and Information Management	Database Design, Normalization, and Entity-Relationship Diagramming Introduction to SQL Hierarchical and Network Data Models
Chapter 7: Telecommunications, the Internet, and Wireless Technology	Broadband Network Services and Technologies Cellular System Generations Wireless Applications for Customer Relationship Management, Supply Chain Management, and Healthcare Introduction to Web 2.0 LAN Topologies
Chapter 8: Securing Information Systems	The Booming Job Market in IT Security The Sarbanes-Oxley Act Computer Forensics General and Application Controls for Information Systems Management Challenges of Security and Control Software Vulnerability and Reliability
Chapter 9: Achieving Operational Excellence and Customer Intimacy: Enterprise Applications	SAP Business Process Map Business Processes in Supply Chain Management and Supply Chain Metrics Best-Practice Business Processes in CRM Software
Chapter 10: E-commerce: Digital Markets, Digital Goods	E-commerce Challenges: The Story of Online Groceries Build an E-commerce Business Plan Hot New Careers in E-Commerce E-commerce Payment Systems Building an E-commerce Website
Chapter 11: Managing Knowledge	Challenges of Knowledge Management Systems
Chapter 12: Enhancing Decision Making	Building and Using Pivot Tables

Chapter	Learning Tracks
Chapter 13: Building Information Systems	Unified Modeling Language Primer on Business Process Design and Documentation Primer on Business Process Management Fourth-Generation Languages
Chapter 14: Managing Projects	Capital Budgeting Methods for Information Systems Investments Enterprise Analysis (Business Systems Planning) and Critical Success Factors Information Technology Investments and Productivity

MyMISLab

Available in MyMISLab

- MIS Video Exercises - Videos illustrating MIS concepts, paired with brief quizzes
- MIS Decision Simulations - interactive exercises allowing students to play the role of a manager and make business decisions
- Auto-Graded writing exercises - taken from the end of chapter
- Assisted-Graded writing exercises - taken from the end of chapter, with a rubric provided
- Chapter Warm Ups, Chapter Quizzes - objective-based quizzing to test knowledge
- Discussion Questions - taken from the end of chapter
- Dynamic Study Modules - on the go adaptive quizzing, also available on a mobile phone
- Learning Catalytics - bring-your-own-device classroom response tools
- Enhanced eText - an accessible, mobile-friendly eText with Conceptual Animations, which walk students through key concepts in the chapter by making figures come to life
- Excel & Access Grader Projects - live in the application auto-graded Grader projects provided inside MyMISLab to support classes covering Office tools

Acknowledgments

The production of any book involves valued contributions from a number of persons. We would like to thank all of our editors for encouragement, insight, and strong support for many years. We thank our editor Samantha McAfee Lewis and project manager Katrina Ostler for their role in managing the project.

Our special thanks go to our supplement authors for their work, including the following MyLab content contributors: John Hupp, Columbus State University; Robert J. Mills, Utah State University; John P. Russo, Wentworth Institute of Technology; and Michael L. Smith, SUNY Oswego. We are indebted to Robin Pickering for her assistance with writing and to William Anderson and Megan Miller for their help during production. We thank Diana R. Craig for her assistance with database and software topics.

Special thanks to colleagues at the Stern School of Business at New York University; to Professor Werner Schenk, Simon School of Business, University of Rochester; to Professor Mark Gillenson, Fogelman College of Business and Economics, University of Memphis; to Robert Kostrubanic, Indiana-Purdue University Fort Wayne; to Professor Lawrence Andrew of Western Illinois

University; to Professor Detlef Schoder of the University of Cologne; to Professor Walter Brenner of the University of St. Gallen; to Professor Lutz Kolbe of the University of Gottingen; to Professor Donald Marchand of the International Institute for Management Development; and to Professor Daniel Botha of Stellenbosch University who provided additional suggestions for improvement. Thank you to Professor Ken Kraemer, University of California at Irvine, and Professor John King, University of Michigan, for more than a decade-long discussion of information systems and organizations. And a special remembrance and dedication to Professor Rob Kling, University of Indiana, for being our friend and colleague over so many years.

We also want to especially thank all our reviewers whose suggestions helped improve our texts. Reviewers for Managing the Digital Firm include:

Charles Wankel, St. John's University
Ahmed Kamel, Concordia College
Deborah E Swain, North Carolina Central University
Jigish Zaveri, Morgan State University
Robert Gatewood, Mississippi College
James Drogan, SUNY Maritime College
Amiya Samantray, Marygrove College
John Miles, Keuka College
Werner Schenk, University of Rochester
Shuyuan Mary Ho, Florida State University
Brian Jones, Tennessee Technological University
Robert Fulkerth, Golden Gate University
Osman Guzide, Shepherd University

K.C.L.
J.P.L.

Organizations, Management, and the Networked Enterprise

PART ONE introduces the major themes of this book, raising a series of important questions: What is an information system, and what are its management, organization, and technology dimensions? Why are information systems so essential in businesses today? Why are systems for collaboration and social business so important? How can information systems help businesses become more competitive? What broader ethical and social issues are raised by widespread use of information systems?

Information Systems in Global Business Today

Learning Objectives

After reading this chapter, you will be able to answer the following questions:

1-1 How are information systems transforming business, and why are they so essential for running and managing a business today?

1-2 What is an information system? How does it work? What are its management, organization, and technology components? Why are complementary assets essential for ensuring that information systems provide genuine value for organizations?

1-3 What academic disciplines are used to study information systems, and how does each contribute to an understanding of information systems?

MyMISLab™

Visit **mymislab.com** for simulations, tutorials, and end-of-chapter problems.

CHAPTER CASES

The Grocery Store of the Future: Look at Kroger
The Mobile Pocket Office
UPS Competes Globally with Information Technology
Are Farms Becoming Digital Firms?

VIDEO CASES

Business in the Cloud: Facebook and eBay Data Centers
UPS Global Operations with the DIAD
Instructional Video:
Tour IBM's Raleigh Data Center

The Grocery Store of the Future: Look at Kroger

If you were to step into the grocery store of the future, what would it look like? Well, you can get a glimpse by visiting a Kroger supermarket. Kroger Company, headquartered in Cincinnati, Ohio, is the largest U.S. supermarket chain by revenue (with fiscal 2015 sales of $109.8 billion) and the second-largest general retailer (after Walmart). Kroger operates 2,800 supermarkets and multi-department stores in 34 states. It's also a leading-edge user of information systems.

Every time you walk into a Kroger store, infrared sensors note your arrival. Kroger uses its knowledge of how many customers are in that store to predict when long lines will pop up and where cashiers should be allocated to prevent pileups from happening. Data collected over time about customer shopping patterns, purchase transactions, staffing levels, and store layouts are fed into analytics software to help Kroger predict what is likely to happen on certain days of the week or month and how many registers should be open. For example, a Saturday afternoon shopper is likely to spend a longer amount of time in the store than someone shopping at 5:30 on a Wednesday evening. A screen at the front of the store lets employees know when to open up or close down an additional lane. This system, called QueVision, has cut the average wait

©Turgaygundogdu/Shutterstock

time at a Kroger store from four minutes to less than 30 seconds. The sensors do not photograph or identify shoppers, and they are only located at checkout lines and store entrances—not throughout the entire store.

Kroger also uses temperature sensors to monitor cold food storage temperature changes. The company equipped refrigerated containers with sensors that check temperatures every 30 minutes and alert store managers and facilities engineers if temperatures hit unsafe levels for cold storage. A typical Kroger store temperature monitoring system has more than 220 radio frequency identification (RFID) tags connected to a wireless network. Before sensors were installed, Kroger employees had to manually check food storage thermometers twice a day. This process ran up costs if food spoiled or staff made measurement mistakes. The new sensor-based system for reporting temperature changes cuts down on the number of cold products that go bad and have to be thrown out, reduces labor, and saves energy.

Kroger started its own online ordering service called Click List, which allows customers to order groceries online, then pay for and collect their goods at a pickup window at an appointed time without having to leave their car. The fee for this service is $4.95. Traditional e-commerce services tend to attract shoppers purchasing just a few items, but Kroger's service appeals to convenience-minded customers purchasing many grocery items at once as a means of speeding up their regular shopping trips.

Kroger also found that customers wanted to integrate their mobile devices into their shopping experience to view store maps, create grocery lists, pay for goods, and earn loyalty points. Kroger developed a mobile app that features localized shopping lists, targeted ads, and, in select areas, the ability to scan and bag items while shopping. This app has been downloaded 9 million times.

According to Brett Bonner, Kroger's senior director of research and development, the key business metric is higher customer satisfaction levels. Kroger surveys have found that what bothers people the most about grocery shopping is the dreaded wait at the checkout line. Technology is eliminating that problem at Kroger stores and providing customers with a better shopping experience. The grocery business is extremely competitive and low-margin, with profits of only a few cents per dollar. Customer loyalty is especially critical, and Kroger's systems for making shopping easier and more pleasant are a major source of competitive advantage.

With mobile and online e-commerce tools, will there even be grocery stores in the future, or will everyone just order online? Experts feel that grocery stores won't disappear. Shoppers like to see and feel products before they buy. But expect more stores to follow Kroger's lead and more technology innovation from Krogers to keep ahead of the pack.

Sources: www.thekrogerco.com, accessed April 2, 2016; Demitrios Kalogeropoulos, "How Kroger Co. Plans to Spend $4 Billion This Year," *Fox Business,* March 10, 2016; Kate Taylor, "Kroger Is Building the Grocery Store of the Future," *Business Insider,* November 8, 2015; Tom Kaneshige, "The Internet of Things Now Includes the Grocer's Frozen Food Aisle," *CIO,* July 31, 2015; and Laurianne McLaughlin, "Kroger Solves Top Customer Issue: Long Lines," *Information Week,* April 2, 2014.

The challenges facing Kroger show why information systems are so essential today. Kroger operates in a highly competitive industry with ultra-thin profit margins of only 1 or 2 percent. There is a limit to the number of customers each Kroger store can handle at one time, and long checkout lines will appear if there are too many people and too few available registers. Surveys have shown that eliminating long checkout lines makes customers very happy and is the best predictor of whether they will return and purchase again. Kroger used leading-edge information systems to shorten checkout lines, reduce food spoilage costs, and make the customer buying experience more pleasant and convenient. The use of networked sensors linked to the Internet (known as the Internet of Things) and powerful analytics to drive business operations and management decisions are key topics today in the MIS world and will be discussed throughout this text.

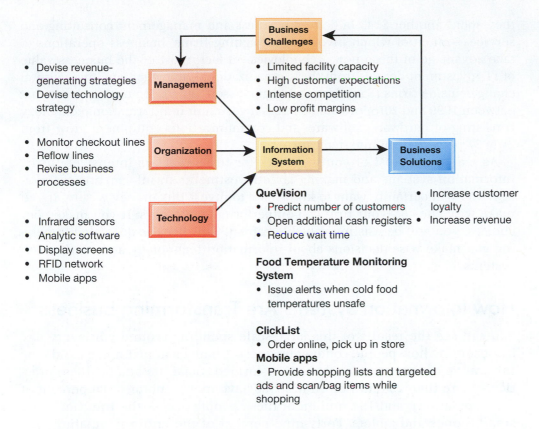

- Devise revenue-generating strategies
- Devise technology strategy

Management

Business Challenges
- Limited facility capacity
- High customer expectations
- Intense competition
- Low profit margins

- Monitor checkout lines
- Reflow lines
- Revise business processes

Organization

Information System

Business Solutions
- Increase customer loyalty
- Increase revenue

- Infrared sensors
- Analytic software
- Display screens
- RFID network
- Mobile apps

Technology

QueVision
- Predict number of customers
- Open additional cash registers
- Reduce wait time

Food Temperature Monitoring System
- Issue alerts when cold food temperatures unsafe

ClickList
- Order online, pick up in store

Mobile apps
- Provide shopping lists and targeted ads and scan/bag items while shopping

The chapter-opening diagram calls attention to important points raised by this case and this chapter. To remain profitable in a hypercompetitive industry, Kroger management chose to use information technology to improve the customer experience. Kroger stores use infrared sensors, wireless networks, and powerful analytic software to predict customer levels, calculate checkout times, and provide information on when and where to open additional checkout stations to reduce waiting times and checkout lines. Kroger also uses wireless sensor systems to monitor the status of cold food storage devices as well as mobile technology to help customers plan for and expedite their shopping.

It is also important to note that deploying these new information systems has changed the way Kroger runs its business. To effectively use its sensor-driven and mobile systems, Kroger had to redesign jobs and procedures for allocating checkout lines, bagging groceries, and monitoring food temperatures. These changes had to be carefully planned to make sure they enhanced service, efficiency, and profitability.

Here are some questions to think about: How are information systems improving operations and customer service at Kroger stores? Give examples of two management decisions that are facilitated by Kroger's information systems. How much of an advantage does Kroger have over its competitors?

1-1 How are information systems transforming business, and why are they so essential for running and managing a business today?

It's not business as usual in America or the rest of the global economy anymore. In 2015, American businesses spent about $1 trillion on information systems hardware, software, and telecommunications equipment. In addition, they spent another $143 billion on business and management consulting and services—much of which involves redesigning firms' business operations to take advantage of these new technologies. In fact, most of the business value of IT investment derives from these organizational, management, and cultural changes inside firms (Saunders and Brynjolfsson, 2016). Figure 1.1 shows that between 1999 and 2015, private business investment in information technology consisting of hardware, software, and communications equipment grew from 21 to 37 percent of all invested capital.

As managers, most of you will work for firms that are intensively using information systems and making large investments in information technology. You will certainly want to know how to invest this money wisely. If you make wise choices, your firm can outperform competitors. If you make poor choices, you will be wasting valuable capital. This book is dedicated to helping you make wise decisions about information technology and information systems.

How Information Systems Are Transforming Business

You can see the results of this large-scale spending around you every day by observing how people conduct business. Changes in technology and new innovative business models have transformed social life and business practices. More than 258 million Americans have mobile phones (80 percent of the population), and 194 million of these people access the Internet using smartphones and tablets. Forty-nine percent of the entire population now uses tablet computers, whose sales have soared. One hundred eighty million Americans use online social networks; 157 million use Facebook, while 53 million use Twitter. Smartphones, social networking, texting, e-mailing, and webinars have all become essential tools of business because that's

FIGURE 1.1 **INFORMATION TECHNOLOGY CAPITAL INVESTMENT**

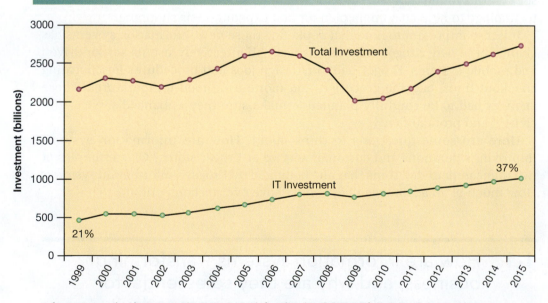

Information technology capital investment, defined as hardware, software, and communications equipment, grew from 21 to 37 percent of all invested capital between 1999 and 2015.

Source: Based on data in U.S. Department of Commerce, Bureau of Economic Analysis, *National Income and Product Accounts*, Table 5.3.6. Real Private Fixed Investment by Type, Chained Dollars (2016).

where your customers, suppliers, and colleagues can be found (eMarketer Chart, 2016).

By June 2015, more than 150 million businesses worldwide had dot-com Internet sites registered (Curtis, 2015). Today, 205 million Americans shop online, and 171 million will purchase online. Every month about 219 million Americans go online to research a product or service. In 2015, FedEx moved about 11.5 million packages daily in 220 countries and territories around the world, mostly overnight, and the United Parcel Service (UPS) moved more than 18 million packages daily. Businesses are using information technology to sense and respond to rapidly changing customer demand, reduce inventories to the lowest possible levels, and achieve higher levels of operational efficiency. Supply chains have become more fast-paced, with companies of all sizes depending on just-in-time inventory to reduce their overhead costs and get to market faster.

As newspaper print readership continues to decline, in 2015 more than 180 million people read a newspaper online, and millions more read other news sites (Conaghan, 2015). Online digital newspaper readership is growing at 10 percent annually, about twice as fast as the Internet itself. About 90 million people watch a video online every day, 80 million read a blog, and 28 million post to blogs, creating an explosion of new writers and new forms of customer feedback that did not exist five years ago (eMarketer, 2016). Social networking site Facebook attracted 156 million monthly visitors in 2015 in the United States and more than 1.4 billion worldwide. Businesses are using social networking tools to connect their employees, customers, and managers worldwide. Most *Fortune* 500 companies now have Facebook pages, Twitter accounts, and Tumblr sites.

E-commerce and Internet advertising continue to expand. Google's online ad revenues surpassed $67 billion in 2015, and Internet advertising continues to grow at more than 15 percent a year, reaching more than $58 billion in revenues in 2015 (eMarketer, 2015).

New federal security and accounting laws requiring many businesses to keep e-mail messages for five years, coupled with existing occupational and health laws requiring firms to store employee chemical exposure data for up to 60 years, are spurring the annual growth of digital information at the estimated rate of 5 exabytes annually, equivalent to 37,000 new Libraries of Congress.

What's New in Management Information Systems

Plenty. In fact, there's a whole new world of doing business using new technologies for managing and organizing. What makes the MIS field the most exciting area of study in schools of business is the continuous change in technology, management, and business processes. Five changes are of paramount importance.

IT Innovations. A continuing stream of information technology innovations is transforming the traditional business world. Examples include the emergence of cloud computing, the growth of a mobile digital business platform based on smartphones and tablet computers, big data, business analytics, and the use of social networks by managers to achieve business objectives. Most of these changes have occurred in the past few years. These innovations are enabling entrepreneurs and innovative traditional firms to create new products and services, develop new business models, and transform the day-to-day conduct of business. In the process, some old businesses, even industries, are being destroyed while new businesses are springing up.

New Business Models. For instance, the emergence of online video services like Netflix for streaming, Apple iTunes, Amazon, and many others for downloading video has forever changed how premium video is distributed and even created. Netflix in 2016 attracted more than 75 million subscribers worldwide to what it calls the "Internet TV" revolution." Netflix has moved into premium TV show production with 30 original shows such as *Fast and Furious, No Country For Old Men, House of Cards, and Orange Is the New Black*, challenging cable and broadcast producers of TV shows, and potentially disrupting cable network dominance of TV show production. Apple's iTunes now accounts for 67 percent of movie and TV show downloads and has struck deals with major Hollywood studios for recent movies and TV shows. A growing trickle of viewers are unplugging from cable and using only the Internet for entertainment.

E-commerce Expanding. E-commerce generated about $600 billion in revenues in 2016 and is estimated to grow to nearly $900 billion by 2020. E-commerce is changing how firms design, produce, and deliver their products and services. E-commerce has reinvented itself again, disrupting the traditional marketing and advertising industry and putting major media and content firms in jeopardy. Facebook and other social networking sites such as YouTube, Twitter, and Tumblr along with Netflix, Apple Beats music service, and many other media firms exemplify the new face of e-commerce in the twenty-first century. They sell services. When we think of e-commerce, we tend to think of selling physical products. While this iconic vision of e-commerce is still very powerful and the fastest-growing form of retail in the United States, growing up alongside is a whole new value stream based on selling services, not goods. It's a services model of e-commerce. Growth in social commerce is spurred by powerful growth of the mobile platform: 80 percent of Facebook's users access the service from mobile phones and tablets. Information systems and technologies are the foundation of this new services-based e-commerce. Mobile e-commerce hit $130 billion in 2016 and is growing at more than 30 percent a year.

Management Changes. The management of business firms has changed: With new mobile smartphones, high-speed wireless Wi-Fi networks, and tablets, remote salespeople on the road are only seconds away from their managers' questions and oversight. Business is going mobile, along with consumers. Managers on the move are in direct, continuous contact with their employees. The growth of enterprise-wide information systems with extraordinarily rich data means that managers no longer operate in a fog of confusion but instead have online, nearly instant access to the really important information they need for accurate and timely decisions. In addition to their public uses on the web, wikis and blogs are becoming important corporate tools for communication, collaboration, and information sharing.

Changes in Firms and Organizations. Compared to industrial organizations of the previous century, new fast-growing twenty-first-century business firms put less emphasis on hierarchy and structure and more emphasis on employees taking on multiple roles and tasks and collaborating with others on a team.

INTERACTIVE SESSION: MANAGEMENT

The Mobile Pocket Office

Can you run your company out of your pocket? Perhaps not entirely, but there are many business functions today that can be performed using an iPhone, iPad, or Android mobile handheld device. The smartphone has been called the "Swiss Army knife of the digital age." A flick of the finger turns it into a web browser, a telephone, a camera, a music or video player, an e-mail and messaging machine, and, increasingly, a gateway into corporate systems. New software applications for document sharing, collaboration, sales, order processing, inventory management, and production monitoring make these devices even more versatile business tools. Mobile pocket offices that fit into a purse or coat pocket are helping to run companies large and small.

Sonic Automotive is one of the largest automotive retailers in the United States with more than 100 dealerships in 14 states. Every year Sonic sells 250,000 new and used cars from approximately 25 different automotive brands, and it also sells auto parts and maintenance, warranty, collision, and vehicle financing services. Sonic Automotive managers and employees do much of their work on the iPhone and iPad.

Sonic developed several custom iPhone and iPad applications to speed up sales and service. Virtual Lot, a dealer inventory app, lets sales associates quickly search for vehicles held in inventory by all Sonic dealerships. They have immediate access to vehicle information, pricing, trade-in values, interest rates, special promotions, financing, and what competitors are charging for identical vehicles. The associates can quickly find the best selection for each customer and often offer far more choices than the competition. Dealers are not limited to selling only their own inventory.

A mobile app called the Sonic Inventory Management System (SIMS) has speeded up and simplified trade-in appraisals and pricing. Sonic staff use their iPhones or iPads to take photos of a car, input the vehicle identification number (VIN) and mileage, and note any issues. The data are transmitted to corporate headquarters, which can quickly appraise the car. A Service Pad app simplifies the steps in repair and warranty work. In the past, customers with cars requiring repairs had to go inside the dealership and sit at a desk with a Sonic staff member who wrote up the repair order by hand. Now the Sonic staff members go outside to the customer's vehicle and enter the repair order on an iPad on the spot.

SKF is a global engineering company headquartered in Gothenburg, Sweden, with 140 manufacturing sites in 32 countries and 48,500 employees worldwide. SKF produces bearings, seals, lubrication systems, and services used in more than 40 industries, including mining, transportation, and manufacturing. SKF has developed more than 30 custom iPhone and iPad applications for streamlining workflows and accessing critical corporate data from anywhere in the world.

For example, a virtual reality app uses the iPhone or iPad camera to identify a factory machine and produce a 3-D overlay of the SKF parts it contains. A sensor-driven app called Shaft Align is used by SKF service teams and customers in the field. Shaft Align connects via wireless Bluetooth sensors to a piece of machinery such as a motor-driven fan to ensure that the drive shaft is running in proper alignment. If not, the app generates step-by-step instructions and a 3-D rendering to show how to manually align the motor. Then it checks the work and produces a report.

A mobile app called MOST enables factory operators to monitor some SKF factory production lines. MOST links to the back-end systems running the machinery and provides operators with key pieces of data. Operators using this mobile app are able to use secure instant messaging to communicate with managers and each other, update maintenance logs, and track products in real time as they move through the factory line.

SKF's Shelf mobile app allows sales engineers and customers to access on demand more than 5,000 pieces of product literature, catalogs, product specifications, and interactive marketing materials. Sales teams can use Shelf to create custom "shelves" to organize, annotate, and share materials with customers right from their iPhones or iPads. The iPhone, iPad, and Shelf app save company sales engineers as much as 25 minutes per day on processes and paperwork, freeing them up to spend more time in the field supporting customers. This increase in productivity is equivalent to putting 200 more sales engineers in the field.

SKF auditors perform about 60 audits per year, and each audit used to take more than a month to complete. With the SKF Data Collect app, auditors are able to use their iPads to collect data and present customers with detailed reports instantly.

SKF Seals offers specifications and information about SKF's machined and injection-molded seals and plastic parts, while the Seal Select app helps users select seals and accessories using several different input parameters to find the right solution for their needs.

Sources: "Sonic Automotive: Driving Growth with iPhone and iPad" and "Driving Innovation in the Factory and in the Field with iOS," iPhone in Business, www.apple.com, accessed March 31, 2016; www.skf.com, accessed March 31, 2016; www.sonicautomotive.com, accessed March 31, 2016; and "Why the Mobile Pocket Office Is Good For Business," ITBusinesEdge.com, accessed March 6, 2015.

CASE STUDY QUESTIONS

1. What kinds of applications are described here? What business functions do they support? How do they improve operational efficiency and decision making?

2. Identify the problems that businesses in this case study solved by using mobile digital devices.

3. What kinds of businesses are most likely to benefit from equipping their employees with mobile digital devices such as iPhones and iPads?

4. One company deploying iPhones has said, "The iPhone is not a game changer, it's an industry changer. It changes the way that you can interact with your customers" and "with your suppliers." Discuss the implications of this statement.

They put greater emphasis on competency and skills rather than position in the hierarchy. They emphasize higher speed and more accurate decision making based on data and analysis. They are more aware of changes in technology, consumer attitudes, and culture. They use social media to enter into conversations with consumers and demonstrate a greater willingness to listen to consumers, in part because they have no choice. They show better understanding of the importance of information technology in creating and managing business firms and other organizations. To the extent organizations and business firms demonstrate these characteristics, they are twenty-first-century digital firms.

iPhone and iPad Applications for Business

1. Salesforce1
2. Cisco WebEx Meetings
3. SAP Business One
4. iWork
5. Evernote
6. Adobe Acrobat Reader
7. Oracle Business Intelligence Mobile
8. Dropbox

Whether it's attending an online meeting, checking orders, working with files and documents, or obtaining business intelligence, Apple's iPhone and iPad offer unlimited possibilities for business users. A stunning multi-touch display, full Internet browsing, and capabilities for messaging, video and audio transmission, and document management make each an all-purpose platform for mobile computing.

© STANCA SANDA/Alamy Stock Photo

You can see some of these trends at work in the Interactive Session on Management. Millions of managers rely heavily on the mobile digital platform to coordinate suppliers and shipments, satisfy customers, and manage their employees. A business day without these mobile devices or Internet access would be unthinkable.

Globalization Challenges and Opportunities: A Flattened World

In 1492, Columbus reaffirmed what astronomers were long saying: the world was round and the seas could be safely sailed. As it turned out, the world was populated by peoples and languages living in isolation from one another, with great disparities in economic and scientific development. The world trade that ensued after Columbus's voyages has brought these peoples and cultures closer. The "industrial revolution" was really a worldwide phenomenon energized by expansion of trade among nations and the emergence of the first global economy.

In 2005, journalist Thomas Friedman wrote an influential book declaring the world was now "flat," by which he meant that the Internet and global communications had greatly reduced the economic and cultural advantages of developed countries. Friedman argued that the United States and European countries were in a fight for their economic lives, competing for jobs, markets, resources, and even ideas with highly educated, motivated populations in low-wage areas in the less developed world (Friedman, 2007). This "globalization" presents both challenges and opportunities for business firms.

A significant percentage of the economy of the United States and other advanced industrial countries in Europe and Asia depends on imports and exports. In 2015, about 30 percent of the $19 trillion U.S. economy resulted from foreign trade, both imports and exports. In Europe and Asia, the number exceeded 50 percent. Many *Fortune* 500 U.S. firms derive more than half their revenues from foreign operations. Tech companies are particularly dependent on offshore revenue: 85 percent of Intel's revenues in 2015 came from overseas sales of its microprocessors, while Apple got 60 percent of its revenue outside of the United States. Eighty percent of the toys sold in the United States are manufactured in China, while about 90 percent of the PCs manufactured in China use American-made Intel or Advanced Micro Design (AMD) chips. The microprocessor chips are shipped from the United States to China for assembly into devices.

It's not just goods that move across borders. So too do jobs, some of them high-level jobs that pay well and require a college degree. In the past decade, the United States lost several million manufacturing jobs to offshore, low-wage producers. But manufacturing is now a very small part of U.S. employment (less than 12 percent of the labor force and declining). In a normal year, about 300,000 service jobs move offshore to lower-wage countries. Many of the jobs are in less-skilled information system occupations, but some are "tradable service" jobs in architecture, financial services, customer call centers, consulting, engineering, and even radiology.

On the plus side, the U.S. economy creates more than 3.5 million new jobs in a normal, non-recessionary year. Although only 1.1 million private sector jobs were created due to slow recovery in 2011, by 2015 the U.S. economy was adding more than 2 million new jobs annually for the third straight year. Employment in information systems and the other service occupations is expanding, and wages are stable. Outsourcing may have accelerated the development of new systems in the United States and worldwide as new systems could be maintained and developed in low-wage countries. In part this explains why the job market for MIS and computer science graduates is growing rapidly in the United States.

The challenge for you as a business student is to develop high-level skills through education and on-the-job experience that cannot be outsourced. The challenge for your business is to avoid markets for goods and services that can be produced offshore much less expensively. The opportunities are equally immense. Throughout this book, you will find examples of companies and individuals who either failed or succeeded in using information systems to adapt to this new global environment.

What does globalization have to do with management information systems? That's simple: everything. The emergence of the Internet into a full-blown international communications system has drastically reduced the costs of operating and transacting on a global scale. Communication between a factory floor in Shanghai and a distribution center in Rapid City, South Dakota, is now instant and virtually free. Customers can now shop in a worldwide marketplace, obtaining price and quality information reliably 24 hours a day. Firms producing goods and services on a global scale achieve extraordinary cost reductions by finding low-cost suppliers and managing production facilities in other countries. Internet service firms, such as Google and eBay, are able to replicate their business models and services in multiple countries without having to redesign their expensive fixed-cost information systems infrastructure. Briefly, information systems enable globalization.

The Emerging Digital Firm

All of the changes we have just described, coupled with equally significant organizational redesign, have created the conditions for a fully digital firm. A digital firm can be defined along several dimensions. A **digital firm** is one in which nearly all of the organization's *significant business relationships* with customers, suppliers, and employees are digitally enabled and mediated. *Core business processes* are accomplished through digital networks spanning the entire organization or linking multiple organizations.

Business processes refer to the set of logically related tasks and behaviors that organizations develop over time to produce specific business results and the unique manner in which these activities are organized and coordinated. Developing a new product, generating and fulfilling an order, creating a marketing plan, and hiring an employee are examples of business processes, and the ways organizations accomplish their business processes can be a source of competitive strength.(A detailed discussion of business processes can be found in Chapter 2.)

Key corporate assets—intellectual property, core competencies, and financial and human assets—are managed through digital means. In a digital firm, any piece of information required to support key business decisions is available at any time and anywhere in the firm.

Digital firms sense and respond to their environments far more rapidly than traditional firms, giving them more flexibility to survive in turbulent times. Digital firms offer extraordinary opportunities for more flexible global organization and management. In digital firms, both time shifting and space shifting are the norm. *Time shifting* refers to business being conducted continuously, 24/7, rather than in narrow "work day" time bands of 9 a.m. to 5 p.m. *Space shifting* means that work takes place in a global workshop as well as within national boundaries. Work is accomplished physically wherever in the world it is best accomplished.

Many firms, such as Cisco Systems, 3M, and GE (see the Chapter 12 ending case), are close to becoming digital firms, using the Internet to drive every aspect of their business. Most other companies are not fully digital, but they are moving toward close digital integration with suppliers, customers, and employees.

Strategic Business Objectives of Information Systems

What makes information systems so essential today? Why are businesses investing so much in information systems and technologies? In the United States, more than 57 million managers and 120 million workers in the information and knowledge sectors in the labor force rely on information systems to conduct business. Information systems are essential for conducting day-to-day business in the United States and most other advanced countries as well as achieving strategic business objectives.

Entire sectors of the economy are nearly inconceivable without substantial investments in information systems. E-commerce firms such as Amazon, eBay, Google, and E*Trade simply would not exist. Today's service industries—finance, insurance, and real estate as well as personal services such as travel, medicine, and education—could not operate without information systems. Similarly, retail firms such as Walmart and Sears and manufacturing firms such as General Motors and GE require information systems to survive and prosper. Just as offices, telephones, filing cabinets, and efficient tall buildings with elevators were once the foundations of business in the twentieth century, information technology is a foundation for business in the twenty-first century.

There is a growing interdependence between a firm's ability to use information technology and its ability to implement corporate strategies and achieve corporate goals (see Figure 1.2). What a business would like to do in five years often depends on what its systems will be able to do. Increasing market share, becoming the high-quality or low-cost producer, developing new products, and

FIGURE 1.2   THE INTERDEPENDENCE BETWEEN ORGANIZATIONS AND INFORMATION SYSTEMS

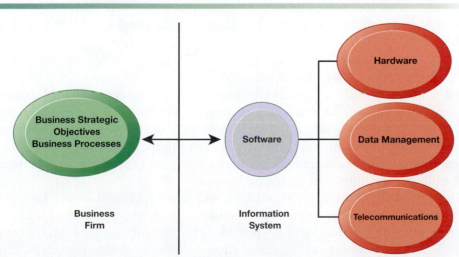

In contemporary systems, there is a growing interdependence between a firm's information systems and its business capabilities. Changes in strategy, rules, and business processes increasingly require changes in hardware, software, databases, and telecommunications. Often, what the organization would like to do depends on what its systems will permit it to do.

increasing employee productivity depend more and more on the kinds and quality of information systems in the organization. The more you understand about this relationship, the more valuable you will be as a manager.

Specifically, business firms invest heavily in information systems to achieve six strategic business objectives: operational excellence; new products, services, and business models; customer and supplier intimacy; improved decision making; competitive advantage; and survival.

Operational Excellence

Businesses continuously seek to improve the efficiency of their operations in order to achieve higher profitability. Information systems and technologies are some of the most important tools available to managers for achieving higher levels of efficiency and productivity in business operations, especially when coupled with changes in business practices and management behavior.

Walmart, the largest retailer on earth, exemplifies the power of information systems coupled with state of the art business practices and supportive management to achieve world-class operational efficiency. In fiscal year 2016, Walmart achieved $499 billion in sales—nearly one-tenth of retail sales in the United States—in large part because of its Retail Link system, which digitally links its suppliers to every one of Walmart's stores. As soon as a customer purchases an item, the supplier monitoring the item knows to ship a replacement to the shelf. Walmart is the most efficient retail store in the industry, achieving sales of more than $600 per square foot, compared with its closest competitor, Target, at $425 a square foot and other large general merchandise retail firms producing less than $200 a square foot.

New Products, Services, and Business Models

Information systems and technologies are a major enabling tool for firms to create new products and services as well as entirely new business models. A **business model** describes how a company produces, delivers, and sells a product or service to create wealth.

Today's music industry is vastly different from the industry a decade ago. Apple Inc. transformed an old business model of music distribution based on vinyl records, tapes, and CDs into an online, legal distribution model based on its own iPod technology platform. Apple has prospered from a continuing stream of innovations, including the iTunes music service, the iPad, and the iPhone.

Customer and Supplier Intimacy

When a business really knows its customers and serves them well, the customers generally respond by returning and purchasing more. This raises revenues and profits. Likewise with suppliers, the more a business engages its suppliers, the better the suppliers can provide vital inputs. This lowers costs. How to really know your customers or suppliers is a central problem for businesses with millions of offline and online customers.

The Mandarin Oriental in Manhattan and other high-end hotels exemplify the use of information systems and technologies to achieve customer intimacy. These hotels use computers to keep track of guests' preferences, such as their preferred room temperature, check-in time, frequently dialed telephone numbers, and television programs, and store these data in a large data repository. Individual rooms in the hotels are networked to a central network server computer so that they can be remotely monitored and controlled. When a customer arrives at one of these hotels, the system automatically changes the room conditions, such as dimming the lights, setting the room temperature, or selecting appropriate music, based on the customer's digital profile. The hotels also analyze their customer data to identify their best customers and to develop individualized marketing campaigns based on customers' preferences.

JCPenney exemplifies the benefits of information systems–enabled supplier intimacy. Every time a dress shirt is bought at a JCPenney store in the United States, the record of the sale appears immediately on computers in Hong Kong at the TAL Apparel Ltd. supplier, a contract manufacturer that produces one in eight dress shirts sold in the United States. TAL runs the numbers through a computer model it developed and then decides how many replacement shirts to make and in what styles, colors, and sizes. TAL then sends the shirts to each JCPenney store, bypassing completely the retailer's warehouses. In other words, JCPenney's shirt inventory is near zero, as is the cost of storing it.

Improved Decision Making

Many business managers operate in an information fog bank, never really having the right information at the right time to make an informed decision. Instead, managers rely on forecasts, best guesses, and luck. The result is over- or underproduction of goods and services, misallocation of resources, and poor response times. These poor outcomes raise costs and lose customers. In the past decade, information systems and technologies have made it possible for managers to use real-time data from the marketplace when making decisions.

For instance, Verizon Corporation, one of the largest telecommunications companies in the United States, uses a web-based digital dashboard to provide managers with precise real-time information on customer complaints, network performance for each locality served, and line outages or storm-damaged lines. Using this information, managers can immediately allocate repair resources to affected areas, inform consumers of repair efforts, and restore service fast.

Competitive Advantage

When firms achieve one or more of these business objectives—operational excellence; new products, services, and business models; customer/supplier intimacy; and improved decision making—chances are they have already achieved a competitive advantage. Doing things better than your competitors, charging less for superior products, and responding to customers and suppliers in real time all add up to higher sales and higher profits that your competitors cannot match. Apple Inc., Walmart, and UPS, described later in this chapter, are industry leaders because they know how to use information systems for this purpose.

Survival

Business firms also invest in information systems and technologies because they are necessities of doing business. Sometimes these "necessities" are driven by industry-level changes. For instance, after Citibank introduced the first automated teller machines (ATMs) in the New York region in 1977 to attract customers through higher service levels, its competitors rushed to provide ATMs to their customers to keep up with Citibank. Today, virtually all banks in the United States have regional ATMs and link to national and international ATM networks, such as CIRRUS. Providing ATM services to retail banking customers is simply a requirement of being in and surviving in the retail banking business.

There are many federal and state statutes and regulations that create a legal duty for companies and their employees to retain records, including digital records. For instance, the Toxic Substances Control Act (1976), which regulates the exposure of U.S. workers to more than 75,000 toxic chemicals, requires firms to retain records on employee exposure for 30 years. The Sarbanes-Oxley Act (2002), which was intended to improve the accountability of public firms and their auditors, requires certified public accounting firms that audit public companies to retain audit working papers and records, including all e-mails, for five years. The Dodd-Frank Wall Street Reform and Consumer Protection Act (2010), which was intended to strengthen regulation of the banking industry, requires firms to retain all records for 10 years. Many other pieces of federal and state legislation in health care, financial services, education, and privacy protection impose significant information retention and reporting requirements on U.S. businesses. Firms turn to information systems and technologies to provide the capability to respond to these challenges.

1-2   What is an information system? How does it work? What are its management, organization, and technology components? Why are complementary assets essential for ensuring that information systems provide genuine value for organizations?

So far we've used *information systems* and *technologies* informally without defining the terms. **Information technology (IT)** consists of all the hardware and software that a firm needs to use in order to achieve its business objectives. This includes not only computer machines, storage devices, and handheld mobile devices but also software, such as the Windows or Linux operating systems, the Microsoft Office desktop productivity suite, and the many thousands of computer programs that can be found in a typical large firm. "Information systems" are more complex and can be best understood by looking at them from both a technology and a business perspective.

What Is an Information System?

An **information system** can be defined technically as a set of interrelated components that collect (or retrieve), process, store, and distribute information to support decision making and control in an organization. In addition to supporting decision making, coordination, and control, information systems may also help managers and workers analyze problems, visualize complex subjects, and create new products.

Information systems contain information about significant people, places, and things within the organization or in the environment surrounding it. By **information** we mean data that have been shaped into a form that is meaningful and useful to human beings. **Data**, in contrast, are streams of raw facts representing events occurring in organizations or the physical environment before they have been organized and arranged into a form that people can understand and use.

A brief example contrasting information and data may prove useful. Supermarket checkout counters scan millions of pieces of data from bar codes, which describe each product. Such pieces of data can be totaled and analyzed to provide meaningful information, such as the total number of bottles of dish detergent sold at a particular store, which brands of dish detergent were selling the most rapidly at that store or sales territory, or the total amount spent on that brand of dish detergent at that store or sales region (see Figure 1.3).

FIGURE 1.3   DATA AND INFORMATION

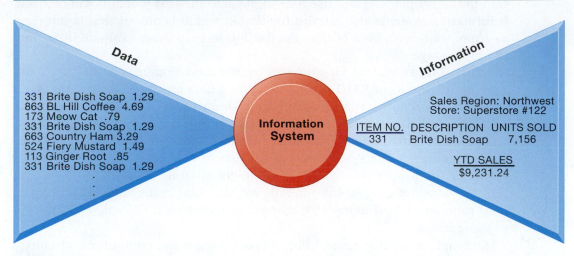

Raw data from a supermarket checkout counter can be processed and organized to produce meaningful information, such as the total unit sales of dish detergent or the total sales revenue from dish detergent for a specific store or sales territory.

Three activities in an information system produce the information that organizations need to make decisions, control operations, analyze problems, and create new products or services. These activities are input, processing, and output (see Figure 1.4). **Input** captures or collects raw data from within the organization or from its external environment. **Processing** converts this

FIGURE 1.4   FUNCTIONS OF AN INFORMATION SYSTEM

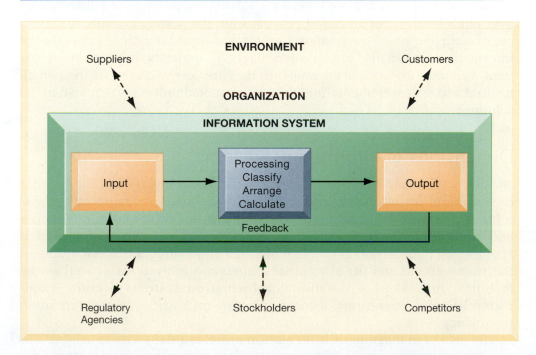

An information system contains information about an organization and its surrounding environment. Three basic activities—input, processing, and output—produce the information organizations need. Feedback is output returned to appropriate people or activities in the organization to evaluate and refine the input. Environmental actors, such as customers, suppliers, competitors, stockholders, and regulatory agencies, interact with the organization and its information systems.

raw input into a meaningful form. **Output** transfers the processed information to the people who will use it or to the activities for which it will be used. Information systems also require **feedback**, which is output that is returned to appropriate members of the organization to help them evaluate or correct the input stage.

In the Kroger system for monitoring cold food storage temperatures, the raw input consists of RFID sensor–generated data on stored food items, such as the item's identification number, item description, storage location, temperature, and time of day. Computers store these data and process them to calculate how much each food item registers above or below its ideal storage temperature. The system output consists of indicators flagging items not stored at the proper temperature that might spoil or be damaged. The system provides meaningful information, such as food items flagged for storage, total number of food items with storage temperature problems, and location of those items.

Although computer-based information systems use computer technology to process raw data into meaningful information, there is a sharp distinction between a computer and a computer program on the one hand and an information system on the other. Computers and related software programs are the technical foundation, the tools and materials, of modern information systems. Computers provide the equipment for storing and processing information. Computer programs, or software, are sets of operating instructions that direct and control computer processing. Knowing how computers and computer programs work is important in designing solutions to organizational problems, but computers are only part of an information system.

A house is an appropriate analogy. Houses are built with hammers, nails, and wood, but these do not make a house. The architecture, design, setting, landscaping, and all of the decisions that lead to the creation of these features are part of the house and are crucial for solving the problem of putting a roof over one's head. Computers and programs are the hammers, nails, and lumber of computer-based information systems, but alone they cannot produce the information a particular organization needs. To understand information systems, you must understand the problems they are designed to solve, their architectural and design elements, and the organizational processes that lead to the solutions.

Dimensions of Information Systems

To fully understand information systems, you must understand the broader organization, management, and information technology dimensions of systems (see Figure 1.5) and their power to provide solutions to challenges and problems in the business environment. We refer to this broader understanding of information systems, which encompasses an understanding of the management and organizational dimensions of systems as well as the technical dimensions of systems, as **information systems literacy**. **Computer literacy**, in contrast, focuses primarily on knowledge of information technology.

The field of **management information systems (MIS)** tries to achieve this broader information systems literacy. MIS deals with behavioral issues as well as technical issues surrounding the development, use, and impact of information systems used by managers and employees in the firm.

Let's examine each of the dimensions of information systems—organizations, management, and information technology.

FIGURE 1.5   INFORMATION SYSTEMS ARE MORE THAN COMPUTERS

Using information systems effectively requires an understanding of the organization, management, and information technology shaping the systems. An information system creates value for the firm as an organizational and management solution to challenges posed by the environment.

Organizations

Information systems are an integral part of organizations. Indeed, for some companies, such as credit reporting firms, there would be no business without an information system. The key elements of an organization are its people, structure, business processes, politics, and culture. We introduce these components of organizations here and describe them in greater detail in Chapters 2 and 3.

Organizations have a structure that is composed of different levels and specialties. Their structures reveal a clear-cut division of labor. Authority and responsibility in a business firm are organized as a hierarchy, or a pyramid structure. The upper levels of the hierarchy consist of managerial, professional, and technical employees, whereas the lower levels consist of operational personnel.

Senior management makes long-range strategic decisions about products and services as well as ensures financial performance of the firm. **Middle management** carries out the programs and plans of senior management, and **operational management** is responsible for monitoring the daily activities of the business. **Knowledge workers**, such as engineers, scientists, or architects, design products or services and create new knowledge for the firm, whereas **data workers**, such as secretaries or clerks, assist with scheduling and communications at all levels of the firm. **Production or service workers** actually produce the product and deliver the service (see Figure 1.6).

Experts are employed and trained for different business functions. The major **business functions**, or specialized tasks performed by business organizations, consist of sales and marketing, manufacturing and production, finance and accounting, and human resources (see Table 1.1). Chapter 2 provides more detail on these business functions and the ways in which they are supported by information systems.

An organization coordinates work through its hierarchy and through its *business processes*. Most organizations' business processes include formal rules

FIGURE 1.6   LEVELS IN A FIRM

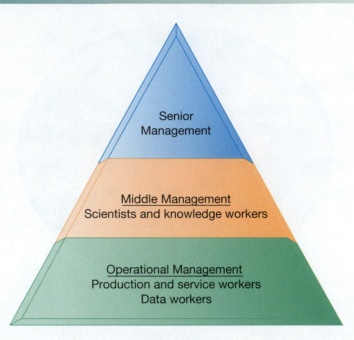

Business organizations are hierarchies consisting of three principal levels: senior management, middle management, and operational management. Information systems serve each of these levels. Scientists and knowledge workers often work with middle management.

that have been developed over a long time for accomplishing tasks. These rules guide employees in a variety of procedures, from writing an invoice to responding to customer complaints. Some of these business processes have been written down, but others are informal work practices, such as a requirement to return telephone calls from coworkers or customers, that are not formally documented. Information systems automate many business processes. For instance, how a customer receives credit or how a customer is billed is often determined by an information system that incorporates a set of formal business processes.

Each organization has a unique **culture**, or fundamental set of assumptions, values, and ways of doing things, that has been accepted by most of its members. You can see organizational culture at work by looking around your university or college. Some bedrock assumptions of university life are that professors know more than students, that the reason students attend college is to learn, and that classes follow a regular schedule.

TABLE 1.1 MAJOR BUSINESS FUNCTIONS

FUNCTION	PURPOSE
Sales and marketing	Selling the organization's products and services
Manufacturing and production	Producing and delivering products and services
Finance and accounting	Managing the organization's financial assets and maintaining the organization's financial records
Human resources	Attracting, developing, and maintaining the organization's labor force; maintaining employee records

Parts of an organization's culture can always be found embedded in its information systems. For instance, UPS's first priority is customer service, which is an aspect of its organizational culture that can be found in the company's package tracking systems, which we describe later in this section.

Different levels and specialties in an organization create different interests and points of view. These views often conflict over how the company should be run and how resources and rewards should be distributed. Conflict is the basis for organizational politics. Information systems come out of this cauldron of differing perspectives, conflicts, compromises, and agreements that are a natural part of all organizations.In Chapter 3, we examine these features of organizations and their role in the development of information systems in greater detail.

Management

Management's job is to make sense out of the many situations faced by organizations, make decisions, and formulate action plans to solve organizational problems. Managers perceive business challenges in the environment, they set the organizational strategy for responding to those challenges, and they allocate the human and financial resources to coordinate the work and achieve success. Throughout, they must exercise responsible leadership. The business information systems described in this book reflect the hopes, dreams, and realities of real-world managers.

But managers must do more than manage what already exists. They must also create new products and services and even re-create the organization from time to time. A substantial part of management responsibility is creative work driven by new knowledge and information. Information technology can play a powerful role in helping managers design and deliver new products and services and redirecting and redesigning their organizations.Chapter 12 treats management decision making in detail.

Information Technology

Information technology is one of many tools managers use to cope with change. **Computer hardware** is the physical equipment used for input, processing, and output activities in an information system. It consists of the following: computers of various sizes and shapes (including mobile handheld devices); various input, output, and storage devices; and telecommunications devices that link computers together.

Computer software consists of the detailed, preprogrammed instructions that control and coordinate the computer hardware components in an information system.Chapter 5 describes the contemporary software and hardware platforms used by firms today in greater detail.

Data management technology consists of the software governing the organization of data on physical storage media.More detail on data organization and access methods can be found in Chapter 6.

Networking and telecommunications technology, consisting of both physical devices and software, links the various pieces of hardware and transfers data from one physical location to another. Computers and communications equipment can be connected in networks for sharing voice, data, images, sound, and video. A **network** links two or more computers to share data or resources, such as a printer.

The world's largest and most widely used network is the **Internet**. The Internet is a global "network of networks" that uses universal standards (described in Chapter 7) to connect millions of networks in more than 230 countries around the world.

The Internet has created a new "universal" technology platform on which to build new products, services, strategies, and business models. This same technology platform has internal uses, providing the connectivity to link different systems and networks within the firm. Internal corporate networks based on Internet technology are called **intranets**. Private intranets extended to authorized users outside the organization are called **extranets**, and firms use such networks to coordinate their activities with other firms for making purchases, collaborating on design, and other interorganizational work. For most business firms today, using Internet technology is both a business necessity and a competitive advantage.

The **World Wide Web** is a service provided by the Internet that uses universally accepted standards for storing, retrieving, formatting, and displaying information in a page format on the Internet. Web pages contain text, graphics, animations, sound, and video and are linked to other web pages. By clicking on highlighted words or buttons on a web page, you can link to related pages to find additional information and links to other locations on the web. The web can serve as the foundation for new kinds of information systems such as UPS's web-based package tracking system described in the following Interactive Session.

All of these technologies, along with the people required to run and manage them, represent resources that can be shared throughout the organization and constitute the firm's **information technology (IT) infrastructure**. The IT infrastructure provides the foundation, or *platform*, on which the firm can build its specific information systems. Each organization must carefully design and manage its IT infrastructure so that it has the set of technology services it needs for the work it wants to accomplish with information systems.Chapters 5 through 8 of this book examine each major technology component of information technology infrastructure and show how they all work together to create the technology platform for the organization.

The Interactive Session on Technology describes some of the typical technologies used in computer-based information systems today. UPS invests heavily in information systems technology to make its business more efficient and customer oriented. It uses an array of information technologies, including bar code scanning systems, wireless networks, large mainframe computers, hand-held computers, the Internet, and many different pieces of software for tracking packages, calculating fees, maintaining customer accounts, and managing logistics.

Let's identify the organization, management, and technology elements in the UPS package tracking system we have just described. The organization element anchors the package tracking system in UPS's sales and production functions (the main product of UPS is a service—package delivery). It specifies the required procedures for identifying packages with both sender and recipient information, taking inventory, tracking the packages en route, and providing package status reports for UPS customers and customer service representatives.

The system must also provide information to satisfy the needs of managers and workers. UPS drivers need to be trained in both package pickup and delivery procedures and in how to use the package tracking system so that they can work efficiently and effectively. UPS customers may need some training to use UPS in-house package tracking software or the UPS website.

UPS's management is responsible for monitoring service levels and costs and for promoting the company's strategy of combining low cost and superior service. Management decided to use computer systems to increase the ease of sending a package using UPS and of checking its delivery status, thereby reducing delivery costs and increasing sales revenues.

INTERACTIVE SESSION: TECHNOLOGY

UPS Competes Globally with Information Technology

United Parcel Service (UPS) started out in 1907 in a closet-sized basement office. Jim Casey and Claude Ryan—two teenagers from Seattle with two bicycles and one phone—promised the "best service and lowest rates." UPS has used this formula successfully for more than a century to become the world's largest ground and air package-delivery company. It's a global enterprise with nearly 444,000 employees, 104,398 vehicles, and the world's ninth-largest airline.

Today UPS delivers 18.3 million packages and documents each day in the United States and more than 220 other countries and territories. The firm has been able to maintain leadership in small-package delivery services despite stiff competition from FedEx and DHL by investing heavily in advanced information technology. UPS spends more than $1 billion each year to maintain a high level of customer service while keeping costs low and streamlining its overall operations.

It all starts with the scannable bar-coded label attached to a package, which contains detailed information about the sender, the destination, and when the package should arrive. Customers can download and print their own labels using special software provided by UPS or by accessing the UPS website. Before the package is even picked up, information from the "smart" label is transmitted to one of UPS's computer centers in Mahwah, New Jersey, or Alpharetta, Georgia, and sent to the distribution center nearest its final destination.

Dispatchers at this center download the label data and use special routing software called ORION to create the most efficient delivery route for each driver that considers traffic, weather conditions, and the location of each stop. Each UPS driver makes an average of 120 stops per day. In a network with 55,000 routes in the United States alone, shaving even one mile off each driver's daily route translates into big savings: $50 million per year. These savings are critical as UPS tries to boost earnings growth as more of its business shifts to less-profitable e-commerce deliveries. UPS drivers who used to drop off several heavy packages a day at one retailer now make several stops scattered across residential neighborhoods, delivering one lightweight package per household. The shift requires more fuel and more time, increasing the cost to deliver each package.

The first thing a UPS driver picks up each day is a handheld computer called a Delivery Information Acquisition Device (DIAD), which can access a wireless cell phone network. As soon as the driver logs on, his or her day's route is downloaded onto the handheld. The DIAD also automatically captures customers' signatures along with pickup and delivery information. Package tracking information is then transmitted to UPS's computer network for storage and processing. From there, the information can be accessed worldwide to provide proof of delivery to customers or to respond to customer queries. It usually takes less than 60 seconds from the time a driver presses "complete" on the DIAD for the new information to be available on the web.

Through its automated package tracking system, UPS can monitor and even reroute packages throughout the delivery process. At various points along the route from sender to receiver, bar code devices scan shipping information on the package label and feed data about the progress of the package into the central computer. Customer service representatives are able to check the status of any package from desktop computers linked to the central computers and respond immediately to inquiries from customers. UPS customers can also access this information from the company's website using their own computers or mobile phones. UPS now has mobile apps and a mobile website for iPhone, BlackBerry, and Android smartphone users.

Anyone with a package to ship can access the UPS website to track packages, check delivery routes, calculate shipping rates, determine time in transit, print labels, and schedule a pickup. The data collected at the UPS website are transmitted to the UPS central computer and then back to the customer after processing. UPS also provides tools that enable customers, such Cisco Systems, to embed UPS functions, such as tracking and cost calculations, into their own websites so that they can track shipments without visiting the UPS site.

A web-based Post Sales Order Management System (OMS) manages global service orders and inventory for critical parts fulfillment. The system enables high-tech electronics, aerospace, medical equipment, and other companies anywhere in the world that ship critical parts to quickly assess their critical parts inventory, determine the most optimal routing strategy to meet customer needs, place orders online, and track parts from the warehouse to the end user. An automated e-mail or fax feature keeps customers informed of each shipping milestone and can provide notification of any changes to flight schedules for commercial airlines carrying their parts.

UPS is now leveraging its decades of expertise managing its own global delivery network to manage logistics and supply chain activities for other companies. It created a UPS Supply Chain Solutions division that provides a complete bundle of standardized services to subscribing companies at a fraction of what it would cost to build their own systems and infrastructure. These services include supply chain design and management, freight forwarding, customs brokerage, mail services, multimodal transportation, and financial services in addition to logistics services.

For example, UPS handles fulfillment and distribution for Plasticard Locktech International (PLI), the world's largest manufacturer of key cards, including hotel key cards, gift cards, and customer loyalty program cards. PLI's customers require quick delivery. Although PLI had no problem fulfilling orders, shipping internationally from its Asheville, North Carolina, manufacturing and distribution location was too costly. PLI now stores inventory at UPS locations in Canada, the United Arab Emirates, and the Netherlands and will soon ship from a Hong Kong facility as well. It would have cost PLI millions to provide its own services for opening a warehouse, staffing, insurance, and logistics. In addition to reducing international shipping costs, PLI realized savings of $200,000 per year by switching to UPS Customs Brokerage Services.

Sources: www.ups.com, accessed March 25, 2016; Steven Rosenbush and Laura Stevens, "At UPS, Algorithm Is the Driver," *Wall Street Journal,* February 16, 2015; and "Keys to Success," UPS Compass, Winter 2015.

CASE STUDY QUESTIONS

1. What are the inputs, processing, and outputs of UPS's package tracking system?

2. What technologies are used by UPS? How are these technologies related to UPS's business strategy?

3. What strategic business objectives do UPS's information systems address?

4. What would happen if UPS's information systems were not available?

The technology supporting this system consists of handheld computers, bar code scanners, desktop computers, wired and wireless communications networks, UPS's data center, storage technology for the package delivery data, UPS in-house package tracking software, and software to access the World Wide Web. The result is an information system solution to the business challenge of providing a high level of service with low prices in the face of mounting competition.

It Isn't Just Technology: A Business Perspective on Information Systems

Managers and business firms invest in information technology and systems because they provide real economic value to the business. The decision to build or maintain an information system assumes that the returns on this investment will be superior to other investments in buildings, machines, or other assets. These superior returns will be expressed as increases in productivity, as increases in revenues (which will increase the firm's stock market value), or perhaps as superior long-term strategic positioning of the firm in certain markets (which produce superior revenues in the future).

We can see that from a business perspective, an information system is an important instrument for creating value for the firm. Information systems

© Bill Aron/PhotoEdit.Inc

Using a handheld computer called a Delivery Information Acquisition Device (DIAD), UPS drivers automatically capture customers' signatures along with pickup, delivery, and time card information. UPS information systems use these data to track packages while they are being transported.

enable the firm to increase its revenue or decrease its costs by providing information that helps managers make better decisions or that improves the execution of business processes. For example, the information system for analyzing supermarket checkout data illustrated in Figure 1.3 can increase firm profitability by helping managers make better decisions as to which products to stock and promote in retail supermarkets.

Every business has an information value chain, illustrated in Figure 1.7, in which raw information is systematically acquired and then transformed through various stages that add value to that information. The value of an information system to a business, as well as the decision to invest in any new information system, is, in large part, determined by the extent to which the system will lead to better management decisions, more efficient business processes, and higher firm profitability. Although there are other reasons why systems are built, their primary purpose is to contribute to corporate value.

The business perspective calls attention to the organizational and managerial nature of information systems. An information system represents an organizational and management solution, based on information technology, to a challenge or problem posed by the environment.Every chapter in this book begins with a short case study that illustrates this concept. A diagram at the beginning of each chapter illustrates the relationship between a business challenge and resulting management and organizational decisions to use IT as a solution to challenges generated by the business environment. You can use this diagram as a starting point for analyzing any information system or information system problem you encounter.

Review the diagram at the beginning of this chapter. The diagram shows how Kroger's systems solved the business problem presented by the need to retain customers and generate revenue in a highly competitive industry with razor-thin profit margins. These systems provided a solution that takes advantage of opportunities provided by new digital technology and the Internet. They opened up new channels for selling goods, increased quality, and improved the customer buying experience. These systems have been essential in improving

FIGURE 1.7 THE BUSINESS INFORMATION VALUE CHAIN

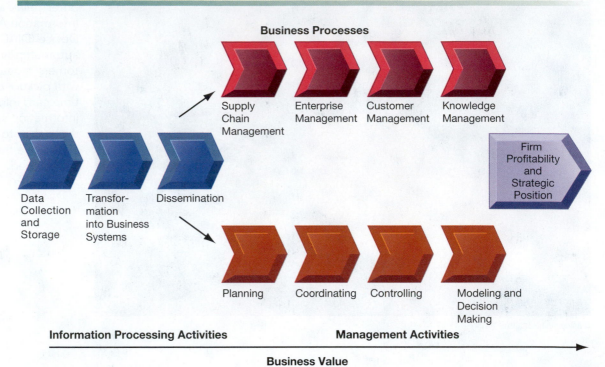

From a business perspective, information systems are part of a series of value-adding activities for acquiring, transforming, and distributing information that managers can use to improve decision making, enhance organizational performance, and, ultimately, increase firm profitability.

Kroger's overall business performance. The diagram also illustrates how management, technology, and organizational elements work together to create the systems.

Complementary Assets: Organizational Capital and the Right Business Model

Awareness of the organizational and managerial dimensions of information systems can help us understand why some firms achieve better results from their information systems than others. Studies of returns from information technology investments show that there is considerable variation in the returns firms receive (see Figure 1.8). Some firms invest a great deal and receive a great deal (quadrant 2); others invest an equal amount and receive few returns (quadrant 4). Still other firms invest little and receive much (quadrant 1), whereas others invest little and receive little (quadrant 3). This suggests that investing in information technology does not by itself guarantee good returns. What accounts for this variation among firms?

The answer lies in the concept of complementary assets. Information technology investments alone cannot make organizations and managers more effective unless they are accompanied by supportive values, structures, and behavior patterns in the organization and other complementary assets. Business firms need to change how they do business before they can really reap the advantages of new information technologies.

Complementary assets are those assets required to derive value from a primary investment (Teece, 1998). For instance, to realize value from automobiles

FIGURE 1.8   VARIATION IN RETURNS ON INFORMATION TECHNOLOGY INVESTMENT

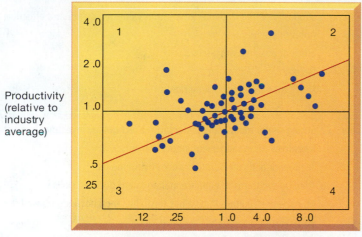

IT Capital Stock (relative to industry average)

Although, on average, investments in information technology produce returns far above those returned by other investments, there is considerable variation across firms.

Source: Based on Brynjolfsson and Hitt (2000).

requires substantial complementary investments in highways, roads, gasoline stations, repair facilities, and a legal regulatory structure to set standards and control drivers.

Research indicates that firms that support their technology investments with investments in complementary assets, such as new business models, new business processes, management behavior, organizational culture, or training, receive superior returns, whereas those firms failing to make these complementary investments receive less or no returns on their information technology investments (Brynjolfsson, 2005; Brynjolfsson and Hitt, 2000; Laudon, 1974). These investments in organization and management are also known as **organizational and management capital**.

Table 1.2 lists the major complementary investments that firms need to make to realize value from their information technology investments. Some of this investment involves tangible assets, such as buildings, machinery, and tools. However, the value of investments in information technology depends to a large extent on complementary investments in management and organization.

Key organizational complementary investments are a supportive business culture that values efficiency and effectiveness, an appropriate business model, efficient business processes, decentralization of authority, highly distributed decision rights, and a strong information system (IS) development team.

Important managerial complementary assets are strong senior management support for change, incentive systems that monitor and reward individual innovation, an emphasis on teamwork and collaboration, training programs, and a management culture that values flexibility and knowledge.

Important social investments (not made by the firm but by the society at large, other firms, governments, and other key market actors) are the Internet and the supporting Internet culture, educational systems, network and computing standards, regulations and laws, and the presence of technology and service firms.

Throughout the book we emphasize a framework of analysis that considers technology, management, and organizational assets and their interactions.

TABLE 1.2   COMPLEMENTARY SOCIAL, MANAGERIAL, AND ORGANIZATIONAL ASSETS REQUIRED TO OPTIMIZE RETURNS FROM INFORMATION TECHNOLOGY INVESTMENTS

Organizational assets	Supportive organizational culture that values efficiency and effectiveness
	Appropriate business model
	Efficient business processes
	Decentralized authority
	Distributed decision-making rights
	Strong IS development team
Managerial assets	Strong senior management support for technology investment and change
	Incentives for management innovation
	Teamwork and collaborative work environments
	Training programs to enhance management decision skills
	Management culture that values flexibility and knowledge-based decision making.
Social assets	The Internet and telecommunications infrastructure
	IT-enriched educational programs raising labor force computer literacy
	Standards (both government and private sector)
	Laws and regulations creating fair, stable market environments
	Technology and service firms in adjacent markets to assist implementation

Perhaps the single most important theme in the book, reflected in case studies and exercises, is that managers need to consider the broader organization and management dimensions of information systems to understand current problems as well as to derive substantial above-average returns from their information technology investments. As you will see throughout the text, firms that can address these related dimensions of the IT investment are, on average, richly rewarded.

1-3   What academic disciplines are used to study information systems, and how does each contribute to an understanding of information systems?

The study of information systems is a multidisciplinary field. No single theory or perspective dominates. Figure 1.9 illustrates the major disciplines that contribute problems, issues, and solutions in the study of information systems. In general, the field can be divided into technical and behavioral approaches. Information systems are sociotechnical systems. Though they are composed of machines, devices, and "hard" physical technology, they require substantial social, organizational, and intellectual investments to make them work properly.

Technical Approach

The technical approach to information systems emphasizes mathematically based models to study information systems as well as the physical technology

FIGURE 1.9   CONTEMPORARY APPROACHES TO INFORMATION SYSTEMS

The study of information systems deals with issues and insights contributed from technical and behavioral disciplines.

and formal capabilities of these systems. The disciplines that contribute to the technical approach are computer science, management science, and operations research.

Computer science is concerned with establishing theories of computability, methods of computation, and methods of efficient data storage and access. Management science emphasizes the development of models for decision-making and management practices. Operations research focuses on mathematical techniques for optimizing selected parameters of organizations, such as transportation, inventory control, and transaction costs.

Behavioral Approach

An important part of the information systems field is concerned with behavioral issues that arise in the development and long-term maintenance of information systems. Issues such as strategic business integration, design, implementation, utilization, and management cannot be explored usefully with the models used in the technical approach. Other behavioral disciplines contribute important concepts and methods.

For instance, sociologists study information systems with an eye toward how groups and organizations shape the development of systems and also how systems affect individuals, groups, and organizations. Psychologists study information systems with an interest in how human decision makers perceive and use formal information. Economists study information systems with an interest in understanding the production of digital goods, the dynamics of digital markets, and how new information systems change the control and cost structures within the firm.

The behavioral approach does not ignore technology. Indeed, information systems technology is often the stimulus for a behavioral problem or issue. But the focus of this approach is generally not on technical solutions. Instead, it concentrates on changes in attitudes, management and organizational policy, and behavior.

Approach of This Text: Sociotechnical Systems

Throughout this book you will find a rich story with four main actors: suppliers of hardware and software (the technologists); business firms making investments and seeking to obtain value from the technology; managers and employees seeking to achieve business value (and other goals); and the contemporary legal, social, and cultural context (the firm's environment). Together these actors produce what we call *management information systems*.

The study of management information systems (MIS) arose to focus on the use of computer-based information systems in business firms and government agencies. MIS combines the work of computer science, management science, and operations research with a practical orientation toward developing system solutions to real-world problems and managing information technology resources. It is also concerned with behavioral issues surrounding the development, use, and impact of information systems, which are typically discussed in the fields of sociology, economics, and psychology.

Our experience as academics and practitioners leads us to believe that no single approach effectively captures the reality of information systems. The successes and failures of information systems are rarely all technical or all behavioral. Our best advice to students is to understand the perspectives of many disciplines. Indeed, the challenge and excitement of the information systems field are that it requires an appreciation and tolerance of many different approaches.

The view we adopt in this book is best characterized as the **sociotechnical view** of systems. In this view, optimal organizational performance is achieved by jointly optimizing both the social and technical systems used in production.

Adopting a sociotechnical systems perspective helps to avoid a purely technological approach to information systems. For instance, the fact that information technology is rapidly declining in cost and growing in power does not necessarily or easily translate into productivity enhancement or bottom-line profits. The fact that a firm has recently installed an enterprise-wide financial reporting system does not necessarily mean that it will be used, or used effectively. Likewise, the fact that a firm has recently introduced new business procedures and processes does not necessarily mean employees will be more productive in the absence of investments in new information systems to enable those processes.

In this book, we stress the need to optimize the firm's performance as a whole. Both the technical and behavioral components need attention. This means that technology must be changed and designed in such a way as to fit organizational and individual needs. Sometimes, the technology may have to be "de-optimized" to accomplish this fit. For instance, mobile phone users adapt this technology to their personal needs, and as a result manufacturers quickly seek to adjust the technology to conform with user expectations. Organizations and individuals must also be changed through training, learning, and planned organizational change to allow the technology to operate and prosper. Figure 1.10 illustrates this process of mutual adjustment in a sociotechnical system.

FIGURE 1.10   A SOCIOTECHNICAL PERSPECTIVE ON INFORMATION SYSTEMS

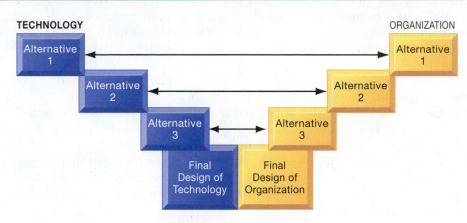

In a sociotechnical perspective, the performance of a system is optimized when both the technology and the organization mutually adjust to one another until a satisfactory fit is obtained.

Review Summary

1-1 *How are information systems transforming business, and why are they essential for running and managing a business today?*

E-mail, online conferencing, smartphones, and tablet computers have become essential tools for conducting business. Information systems are the foundation of fast-paced supply chains. The Internet allows many businesses to buy, sell, advertise, and solicit customer feedback online. Organizations are trying to become more competitive and efficient by digitally enabling their core business processes and evolving into digital firms. The Internet has stimulated globalization by dramatically reducing the costs of producing, buying, and selling goods on a global scale. New information system trends include the emerging mobile digital platform, big data, and cloud computing.

Information systems are a foundation for conducting business today. In many industries, survival and the ability to achieve strategic business goals are difficult without extensive use of information technology. Businesses today use information systems to achieve six major objectives: operational excellence; new products, services, and business models; customer/supplier intimacy; improved decision making; competitive advantage; and day-to-day survival.

1-2 *What is an information system? How does it work? What are its management, organization, and technology components? Why are complementary assets essential for ensuring that information systems provide genuine value for organizations?*

From a technical perspective, an information system collects, stores, and disseminates information from an organization's environment and internal operations to support organizational functions and decision making, communication, coordination, control, analysis, and visualization. Information systems transform raw data into useful information through three basic activities: input, processing, and output.

From a business perspective, an information system provides a solution to a problem or challenge facing a firm and represents a combination of management, organization, and technology elements. The management dimension of information systems involves issues such as leadership, strategy, and management behavior. The technology dimension consists of computer hardware, software, data management technology, and networking/telecommunications technology (including the Internet). The organization dimension of information systems involves issues such as the organization's hierarchy, functional specialties, business processes, culture, and political interest groups.

In order to obtain meaningful value from information systems, organizations must support their technology investments with appropriate complementary investments in organizations and management. These complementary assets include new business models and business processes, supportive organizational culture and management behavior, and appropriate technology standards, regulations, and laws. New information technology investments are unlikely to produce high returns unless businesses make the appropriate managerial and organizational changes to support the technology.

1-3 *What academic disciplines are used to study information systems, and how does each contribute to an understanding of information systems?*
The study of information systems deals with issues and insights contributed from technical and behavioral disciplines. The disciplines that contribute to the technical approach focusing on formal models and capabilities of systems are computer science, management science, and operations research. The disciplines contributing to the behavioral approach focusing on the design, implementation, management, and business impact of systems are psychology, sociology, and economics. A sociotechnical view of systems considers both technical and social features of systems and solutions that represent the best fit between them.

Key Terms

Business functions, 19
Business model, 14
Business processes, 12
Complementary assets, 26
Computer hardware, 21
Computer literacy, 18
Computer software, 21
Culture, 20
Data, 16
Data management technology, 21
Data workers, 19
Digital firm, 12
Extranets, 22
Feedback, 18
Information, 16
Information system, 16
Information systems literacy, 18
Information technology (IT), 16

Information technology (IT) infrastructure, 22
Input, 17
Internet, 21
Intranets, 22
Knowledge workers, 19
Management information systems (MIS), 18
Middle management, 19
Network, 21
Networking and telecommunications
    technology, 21
Operational management, 19
Organizational and management capital, 27
Output, 18
Processing, 17
Production or service workers, 19
Senior management, 19
Sociotechnical view, 30
World Wide Web, 22

MyMISLab

To complete the problems marked with the MyMISLab, go to the EOC Discussion Questions in MyMISLab.

Review Questions

1-1 How are information systems transforming business, and why are they so essential for running and managing a business today?

- Describe how information systems have changed the way businesses operate and their products and services.

- Identify three major new information system trends.

- Describe the characteristics of a digital firm.

- Describe the challenges and opportunities of globalization in a "flattened" world.

- List and describe six reasons why information systems are so important for business today.

1-2 What is an information system? How does it work? What are its management, organization, and technology components? Why are complementary assets essential for ensuring that information systems provide genuine value for organizations?

- Define an information system and describe the activities it performs.

- List and describe the organizational, management, and technology dimensions of information systems.

- Distinguish between data and information and between information systems literacy and computer literacy.

- Explain how the Internet and the World Wide Web are related to the other technology components of information systems.

- Define complementary assets and describe their relationship to information technology.

- Describe the complementary social, managerial, and organizational assets required to optimize returns from information technology investments.

1-3 What academic disciplines are used to study information systems, and how does each contribute to an understanding of information systems?

- List and describe each discipline that contributes to a technical approach to information systems.

- List and describe each discipline that contributes to a behavioral approach to information systems.

- Describe the sociotechnical perspective on information systems.

Discussion Questions

1-4 Information systems are too important to be MyMISLab left to computer specialists. Do you agree? Why or why not?

1-5 If you were setting up the website for a Major MyMISLab League Baseball team, what management, organization, and technology issues might you encounter?

1-6 What are some of the organizational, manage- MyMISLab rial, and social complementary assets that help make UPS's information systems so successful?

Hands-On MIS Projects

The projects in this section give you hands-on experience in analyzing financial reporting and inventory management problems, using data management software to improve management decision making about increasing sales, and using Internet software for researching job requirements. Visit MyMISLab's Multimedia Library to access this chapter's Hands-On MIS Projects.

Management Decision Problems

1-7 Snyders of Hanover, which sells about 80 million bags of pretzels, snack chips, and organic snack items each year, had its financial department use spreadsheets and manual processes for much of its data gathering and reporting. Hanover's financial analyst would spend the entire final week of every month collecting spreadsheets from the heads of more than 50 departments worldwide. She would then consolidate and reenter all the data into another spreadsheet, which would serve as the company's monthly profit-and-loss statement. If a department needed to update its data after submitting the spreadsheet to the main office, the analyst had to return the original spreadsheet, then wait for the department to resubmit its data before finally submitting the updated data in the consolidated document. Assess the impact of this situation on business performance and management decision making.

1-8 Dollar General Corporation operates deep-discount stores offering housewares, cleaning supplies, clothing, health and beauty aids, and packaged food, with most items selling for $1. Its business model calls for keeping costs as low as possible. The company has no automated method for keeping track of inventory at each store. Managers know approximately how many cases of a particular product the store is supposed to receive when a delivery truck arrives, but the stores lack technology for scanning the cases or verifying the item count inside the cases. Merchandise losses from theft or other mishaps have been rising and now represent more than 3 percent of total sales. What decisions have to be made before investing in an information system solution?

Improving Decision Making: Using Databases to Analyze Sales Trends

Software skills: Database querying and reporting
Business skills: Sales trend analysis

1-9 In this project, you will start out with raw transactional sales data and use Microsoft Access database software to develop queries and reports that help managers make better decisions about product pricing, sales promotions, and inventory replenishment. In MyMISLab, you can find a Store and Regional Sales Database developed in Microsoft Access. The database contains raw data on weekly store sales of computer equipment in various sales regions. The database includes fields for store identification number, sales region, item number, item description, unit price, units sold, and the weekly sales period when the sales were made. Use Access to develop some reports and queries to make this information more useful for running the business. Sales and production managers want answers to the following questions:

- Which products should be restocked?
- Which stores and sales regions would benefit from a promotional campaign and additional marketing?
- When (what time of year) should products be offered at full price, and when should discounts be used?

You can easily modify the database table to find and report your answers. Print your reports and results of queries.

Improving Decision Making: Using the Internet to Locate Jobs Requiring Information Systems Knowledge

Software skills: Internet-based software
Business skills: Job searching

1-10 Visit a job-posting website such as Monster.com. Spend some time at the site examining jobs for accounting, finance, sales, marketing, and human resources. Find two or three descriptions of jobs that require some information systems knowledge. What information systems knowledge do these jobs require? What do you need to do to prepare for these jobs? Write a one- to two-page report summarizing your findings.

Collaboration and Teamwork Project

Selecting Team Collaboration Tools

1-11 Form a team with three or four classmates and review the capabilities of Google Drive and Google Sites for your team collaboration work. Compare the capabilities of these two tools for storing team documents, project announcements, source materials, work assignments, illustrations, electronic presentations, and web pages of interest. Learn how each works with Google Docs. Explain why Google Drive or Google Sites is more appropriate for your team. If possible, use Google Docs to brainstorm and develop a presentation of your findings for the class. Organize and store your presentation using the Google tool you have selected.

Are Farms Becoming Digital Firms?

CASE STUDY

Ohio farmer Mark Bryant raises corn, soybeans, and soft red winter wheat on 12,000 acres. But you'll hardly ever see him on a tractor because that isn't how farms work anymore. Bryant spends most of his time monitoring dashboards full of data gathered from the 20 or so iPhones and five iPads he has supplied to employees who report on his acreage in real time. Using software from a Google-funded startup called Granular, Bryant analyzes the data along with data gathered from aircraft, self-driving tractors, and other forms of automated and remote sensors for yield, moisture, and soil quality.

Tractors themselves have been morphed into pieces of intelligent equipment, and are now much smarter. Many tractors and combines today are guided by Global Positioning System (GPS) satellite-based navigation systems. The GPS computer receives signals from earth-orbiting satellites to track each piece of equipment's location and where it has gone. The system helps steer the equipment so farmers are able to monitor progress on iPads and other tablet computers in their tractor cabs.

The world's largest producer of autonomous four-wheeled vehicles isn't Tesla or Google, it's John Deere. The cab of one of Deere's self-driving tractors is now so full of screens and tablets that it looks like the cockpit of a jet airplane. John Deere and its competitors aren't just turning out tractors, combines, and trucks that can drive themselves, they are also turning out wirelessly connected sensors that map every field as well as planting and spraying machines that can use computerized instructions to apply seed and nutrients to a field.

Deere & Co. has embedded information technology in all of its farming equipment, creating an eco-system for controlling sprayers, balers, and planters. Deere products include AutoTrac GPS-controlled assisted-steering systems, which allow equipment operators to take their hands off the wheel; JDLink, which enables machinery to automatically upload data about fields to a remote computer center and farmers to download planting or fertilizing instructions; and John Deere Machine Sync, which uses GPS data to create maps based on aerial or satellite photos to improve planting, seeding, spraying, and nutrient application.

Deere now ranks among the leading companies offering tools for farmers to practice what is known as precision agriculture. Managing fields with this level of computerized precision means farmers need to use fewer loads of fertilizer, potentially saving an individual farmer tens of thousands of dollars. Some also see precision agriculture as the solution to feeding the world's exploding population. By 2050, the world's population is predicted to be 9.2 billion people, 34 percent higher than today. More people will have the means to purchase food that requires more land, water, and other resources to produce. To keep up with rising populations and income growth, global food production must increase by 70 percent and precision agriculture could make this possible. Farmers using fertilizer, water, and energy to run equipment more precisely are less wasteful, and this also promotes the health of the planet.

Other large agricultural companies like Monsanto and Dupont are big precision agriculture players, providing data analysis and planting recommendations to farmers who use their seeds, fertilizers, and herbicides. Because adjustments in planting depth or the distance between crop rows can make a big difference in crop yields, these companies want their computers to analyze the data generated during computerized planting work to show farmers how to further increase their crop output.

The farmer provides data on his or her farm's field boundaries, historic crop yields, and soil conditions to these companies or another agricultural data analysis company, which analyzes the data along with other data it has collected about seed performance and soil types in different areas. The company doing the data analysis then sends a computer file with recommendations back to the farmer, who uploads the data into computerized planting equipment. The farmer's planting equipment follows the recommendations as it plants fields. For example, the recommendations might tell an Iowa corn farmer to lower the number of seeds planted per acre or to plant more seeds per acre in specified portions of the field capable of growing more corn. The farmer might also receive advice on the exact type of seed to plant in different areas. The data analysis company monitors weather and other factors to advise farmers how to manage crops as they grow.

A software application developed by Monsanto called FieldScripts takes into account variables such as the amount of sunlight and shade and variations in soil nitrogen and phosphorous content down to an area as small as a 10-meter-by-10-meter grid. Monsanto analyzes the data in conjunction with the genetic properties of its seeds, combines all this information with climate predictions, and delivers precise planting instructions or "scripts" to iPads connected to planting equipment in the field. Tools such as FieldScripts would allow farmers to pinpoint areas that need more or less fertilizer, saving them the cost of spreading fertilizer everywhere while boosting their yields in areas that have performed more poorly and reducing the amount of excess fertilizer that enters the water table—good for the environment.

Prescriptive planting could help raise the average corn harvest to more than 200 bushels an acre from the current 160 bushels, some experts say. On a larger scale, according to Monsanto, the world's largest seed company, data-driven planting advice to farmers could increase worldwide crop production by about $20 billion a year. So far, output from prescriptive planting systems has not achieved those spectacular levels.

Is there a downside to all of this? For small farmers, the answer may be yes. The costs of investing in the new technology and vendor service fees for some of these tools such as FieldScripts can amount to more than what many small farmers can earn in extra yield from their farms. According to Sara Olson of Lux Research Inc., the problem with precision agriculture is the diminishing returns that come along with costly technologies on smaller farms. That means that only the really big farms are likely to benefit.

Monsanto estimates that FieldScripts will improve yields by five to 10 bushels per acre. With corn at about $4 per bushel, that's an increase of $20 to $40 per acre. A small farm of about 500 acres could get anywhere from $10,000 to $20,000 in extra revenue. Monsanto charges around $10 per acre for the service, so the farm will wind up paying about $5,000—in addition to paying tens of thousands of dollars to either retrofit its existing planting equipment or buy more modern tractors that include the electronics gear that syncs the "scripts" provided by the Monsanto online service with the planter's onboard navigation systems. Monsanto also charges an extra $15 per acre for its local climate prediction service. A small farm will most likely lose money or break even for the first two years of using a service like Field-Scripts, according to Olson.

For a large farm of about 5,000 acres, FieldScripts could increase revenues by between $100,000 and $200,000. With Monsanto's service costing about $50,000, that farm's total profits will run between $50,000 to $150,000, more than sufficient to offset the cost of updating farm machinery. Whether a farm is big or small, the impact of FieldScripts would be minimal in good years because yields would be high regardless. The technology is likely to have a bigger impact in years when conditions aren't so propitious. A spokesperson for Monsanto stated that the outcome of its prescriptive planting system is less about the size of the farm and more about the farmer's technology know-how. According to Michael Cox, codirector of investment research at securities firm Piper Jaffray Cos., revenue from FieldScripts and other technology-driven products and services could account for 20 percent of Monsanto's projected growth in per-share earnings by 2018.

Although some farmers have embraced prescriptive planting, others are critical. Many farmers are suspicious about what Monsanto and DuPont might do with the data collected about them. Others worry about seed prices rising too much because the big companies that developed prescriptive planting technology are the same ones that sell seeds. (There has been a surge in seed prices during the past 15 years as the biggest companies increased their market share. Monsanto and DuPont now sell about 70 percent of all corn seed in the United States.) Farmers also fear that rivals could use the data to their own advantage. For instance, if nearby farmers saw crop-yield information, they might rush to rent farmland, pushing land and other costs higher. Other farmers worry that Wall Street traders could use the data to make bets on futures contracts. If such bets push futures-contract prices lower early in the growing season, it might squeeze the profits farmers might lock in for their crops by selling futures.

There are not yet any publicly known examples where a farmer's prescriptive-planting information has been misused. Monsanto and DuPont officials say the companies have no plans to sell data gathered from farmers. Monsanto has stated that it supports industrywide standards for managing information collected from fields and that it wouldn't access the data without permission from farmers. Deere & Co., which has been working with DuPont and Dow Chemical Co. to formulate specialized seed-planting recommendations based on data from its tractors, combines, and other machinery, says it obtains consent from customers before sharing any of their data.

Some farmers have discussed aggregating planting data on their own so they could decide what information to sell and at what price. Others are working with smaller technology companies that are trying to keep agricultural giants from dominating the prescriptive-planting business. Startups such as Farmobile LLC, Granular Inc., and Grower Information Services Cooperative are developing information systems that will enable farmers to capture data streaming from their own tractors and combines, store the data in their own remote data centers, and market the data to seed, pesticide, and equipment companies or futures traders if they so choose. Such platforms could help farmers wring larger profits from precision farming and give them more control over the information generated on their fields.

Sources: "Precision Agriculture," www.research.ibm.com, accessed April 4, 2016; Matthew J. Grassi, "Agrible Launches Nutrient Forecasting, Spray Smart Features," PrecisionAg, March 9, 2016; www.monsanto.com, accessed April 4, 2016; Jacob Bunge, "On the Farm: Startups Put Data in Farmers' Hands," *Wall Street Journal,*

August 31, 2015; Mary K. Pratt, "How Technology Is Nourishing the Food Chain," *Computerworld,* August 18, 2015; and Michael Hickins, "For Small Farmers, Big Data Adds Modern Problems to Ancient Ones," *Wall Street Journal,* February 25, 2014.

CASE STUDY QUESTIONS

1-12 List and describe the technologies used in this case study.

1-13 In what sense are U.S. farms now digital firms? Explain your answer.

1-14 How is information technology changing the way farmers run their business?

1-15 How do the systems described in this case improve farming operations?

1-16 How do precision agriculture systems support decision making? Identify three different decisions that can be supported.

1-17 How helpful is precision agriculture to individual farmers and the agricultural industry? Explain your answer.

MyMISLab

Go to the Assignments section of MyMISLab to complete these writing exercises.

1-18 What are the strategic objectives that firms try to achieve by investing in information systems and technologies? For each strategic objective, give an example of how a firm could use information systems to achieve the objective.

1-19 Describe the complementary assets that firms need in order to optimize returns from their information system investments. For each type of complementary asset, give an example of a specific asset a firm should have.

Chapter 1 References

Brynjolfsson, Erik and Lorin M. Hitt. "Beyond Computation: Information Technology, Organizational Transformation, and Business Performance." *Journal of Economic Perspectives* 14, No. 4 (2000).

Brynjolfsson, Erik. "VII Pillars of IT Productivity." *Optimize* (May 2005).

Bureau of Economic Analysis. *National Income and Product Accounts*. www.bea.gov, accessed April 19, 2016.

Carr, Nicholas. "IT Doesn't Matter." *Harvard Business Review* (May 2003).

Chae, Ho-Chang, Chang E. Koh, and Victor Prybutok. "Information Technology Capability and Firm Performance: Contradictory Findings and Their Possible Causes." *MIS Quarterly* 38, No. 1 (March 2014).

Conaghan, Jim. "Newspaper Digital Audience Grew Twice as Fast as the Internet in the Past 12 Months." Newspaper Association of America (October 9, 2015).

Curtis, Sophie. "Dot-com at 30: Will the World's Best-Known Web Domain Soon Be Obsolete?" Telegraph.co.uk (March 15, 2015).

Dedrick, Jason, Vijay Gurbaxani, and Kenneth L. Kraemer. "Information Technology and Economic Performance: A Critical Review of the Empirical Evidence." Center for Research on Information Technology and Organizations, University of California, Irvine (December 2001).

eMarketer. "eMarketer Numbers for: Blogging, 2014–2018." *eMarketer* (2016).

eMarketer. "US Adults Spend 5.5 Hours with Video Content Each Day." *eMarketer* (April 16, 2015).

eMarketer Chart. "US Digital Ad Spending, 2013–2019" (March 2015).

FedEx Corporation. "SEC Form 10-K for the Fiscal Year Ended May 31, 2015."

Friedman, Thomas. *The World Is Flat.* New York: Picador (2007).

Garretson, Rob. "IT Still Matters." *CIO Insight* 81 (May 2007).

Hughes, Alan and Michael S. Scott Morton. "The Transforming Power of Complementary Assets." *MIT Sloan Management Review* 47. No. 4 (Summer 2006).

Lamb, Roberta, Steve Sawyer, and Rob Kling. "A Social Informatics Perspective of Socio-Technical Networks." http://lamb.cba.hawaii.edu/pubs (2004).

Laudon, Kenneth C. *Computers and Bureaucratic Reform.* New York: Wiley (1974).

Lev, Baruch. "Intangibles: Management, Measurement, and Reporting." The Brookings Institution Press (2001).

McKinsey Global Institute. "Digital America: A Tale of the Haves and Have-Mores (December 2015).

Mithas, Sunil and Roland T. Rust, "How Information Technology Strategy and Investments Influence Firm Performance: Conjecture and Empirical Evidence." *MIS Quarterly* (March 2016).

Nevo, Saggi and Michael R. Wade. "The Formation and Value of IT-Enabled Resources: Antecedents and Consequences of Synergistic Relationships." *MIS Quarterly* 34, No. 1 (March 2010).

Otim, Samual, Kevin E. Dow, Varun Grover, and Jeffrey A. Wong. "The Impact of Information Technology Investments on Downside Risk of the Firm: Alternative Measurement of the Business Value of IT." *Journal of Management Information Systems* 29, No. 1 (Summer 2012).

Ren, Fei and Sanjeev Dewan. "Industry-Level Analysis of Information Technology Return and Risk: What Explains the Variation?" *Journal of Management Information Systems* 21, No. 2 (2015).

Ross, Jeanne W. and Peter Weill. "Four Questions Every CEO Should Ask About IT." *Wall Street Journal* (April 25, 2011).

Sabherwal, Rajiv and Anand Jeyaraj. "Information Technology Impacts on Firm Performance: An Extension of Kohli and Devaraj (2003)." *MIS Quarterly* (December 2015).

Sampler, Jeffrey L., and Michael J. Earl. "What's Your Information Footprint?" *MIT Sloan Management Review* (Winter 2014).

Saunders, Adam and Erik Brynjolfsson. "Valuing Information Technology Related Intangible Assets." *MIS Quarterly* (March 2016).

Shanks, Ryan, Sunit Sinha and Robert J. Thomas. "Managers and Machines, Unite!" Accenture (2015).

Stats-Wordpress. "Wordpress Global Statistics," https://wordpress.com, accessed April 22, 2016.

Teece, David. *Economic Performance and Theory of the Firm*: *The Selected Papers of David Teece.* London: Edward Elgar Publishing (1998).

U.S. Bureau of Labor Statistics. *Occupational Outlook Handbook*. (December 17, 2015).

Weill, Peter and Jeanne Ross. *IT Savvy: What Top Executives Must Know to Go from Pain to Gain*. Boston: Harvard Business School Press (2009).

2

Global E-business and Collaboration

Learning Objectives

After reading this chapter, you will be able to answer the following questions:

2-1 What are business processes? How are they related to information systems?

2-2 How do systems serve the different management groups in a business, and how do systems that link the enterprise improve organizational performance?

2-3 Why are systems for collaboration and social business so important, and what technologies do they use?

2-4 What is the role of the information systems function in a business?

MyMISLab™

Visit **mymislab.com** for simulations, tutorials, and end-of-chapter problems.

CHAPTER CASES

Enterprise Social Networking Helps ABB Innovate and Grow
New Systems Help Plan International Manage Its Human Resources
Cisco IX5000: What State-of-the-Art Telepresence Can Do for Collaboration
Social Business: Full Speed Ahead or Proceed with Caution?

VIDEO CASES

Walmart's Retail Link Supply Chain
CEMEX: Becoming a Social Business
Instructional Video:
US Foodservice Grows Market with Oracle CRM on Demand

Enterprise Social Networking Helps ABB Innovate and Grow

ABB, headquartered in Zurich, Switzerland, is a global supplier of power grids, industrial motors and drives, and generators for industrial, commercial, and utility operations. The company has about 135,000 employees in 100 countries around the world and is noted for its innovations in ship propulsion and power transmission. Collaboration, sharing information, and ongoing innovation are essential for ABB's growth and business success.

ABB had a corporate intranet, but management believed it was too static and outmoded to meet its current needs for empowering and energizing employees. The intranet had poor capabilities for searching for information, and information was often added instead of changed. This often created two or more different versions of the same content. ABB employees were storing information in wikis, local file servers, and other knowledge platforms besides the intranet, adding to the confusion and inefficiency. There were nine different platforms employees might need to access to do their work. Additionally, the intranet lacked tools to help staff have dialogues, share ideas, and work with other members of the company, including people that they might not know.

© Andrey Popov/Shutterstock

What ABB needed was a central resource that would support dynamic knowledge sharing. The entire staff would be able to easily locate information about the company as well as updates on the latest developments of current initiatives and projects. Tools that would help employees work more closely together—including the ability to locate employees in other parts of the company who were experts in specific subjects—would help streamline operations and speed up key business functions.

ABB replaced its outmoded intranet with one called Inside+ that is more dynamic and socially enabled. Inside+ provides ABB employees with a single entry point to all the information and tools they need for their jobs. These include Microsoft Yammer, Office 365, and Sharepoint.

Yammer is an enterprise social networking platform used by more than 200,000 organizations worldwide. Yammer enables employees to create groups to collaborate on projects and share and edit documents and includes a news feed to find out what's happening within the company. Yammer can be accessed through the web and desktop and mobile devices and can be integrated with other systems such as Microsoft SharePoint and Office 365 to make other applications more "social." SharePoint is Microsoft's platform for collaboration, document sharing, and document management. Office 365 is Microsoft's online service for its Office productivity applications (word processing, spreadsheet, electronic presentations, data management). Its mail service works seamlessly with an online meeting and videoconferencing service, simplifying online meetings.

Inside+ integrates all the key internal platforms that employees use for their work. Individualized Yammer feeds occupy the left half of the landing page. An employee's Yammer feed displays e-mail messages and updates to documents that person has been working on. Conversations on Yammer are archived and searchable. Employees can access Microsoft SharePoint from their Inside+ toolbar, and Office 365 applications are also seamlessly linked to Yammer. This enterprise social network is now used by 50,000 ABB employees-nearly one-third of the company's global workforce.

How has ABB benefited from becoming more "social"? Employees are using Yammer and Inside+ to collaborate on projects, share ideas, and discover people in other departments with useful expertise that could help them in their work. Moving conversations from e-mail to Yammer has made discussions more productive with better employee engagement. Some ABB teams report that their e-mail messages have shrunk by 50 percent. Staff can be productive anytime and anywhere because they are able to access Inside+ from smartphones and tablets. More than half the comments employees post come from mobile devices. The company is also saving on conference costs. For example, instead of flying 100 employees to Zurich for an annual communications conference in 2012 and 2013, the company ran the conference online with all discussion housed and archived on Yammer. Many more employees feel closely involved with the business as a whole—something that could not have been achieved with the old system.

Sources: Adam Bonefeste, "ABB Reinvents Its Intranet with Social Networking Technology," www.yammer.com, January 28, 2015; Rachel Miller, "ABB Employees Have 50,000 Reasons to Discover Yammer," allthingsic.com, accessed March 8, 2016; and www.abb.com, accessed March 14, 2016.

ABB's experience illustrates how much organizations today rely on information systems to improve their performance and remain competitive. It also shows how much systems supporting collaboration and teamwork make a difference in an organization's ability to innovate, execute, and grow profits.

The chapter-opening diagram calls attention to important points raised by this case and this chapter. ABB itself is a knowledge-intensive company that prizes innovation, but it was hampered by outdated processes and tools for managing information that prevented employees and managers from working efficiently and effectively. This affected the company's ability to create and deliver new leading-edge products and services.

ABB management decided that the best solution was to deploy new technology to move from a static corporate knowledge and work environment to one

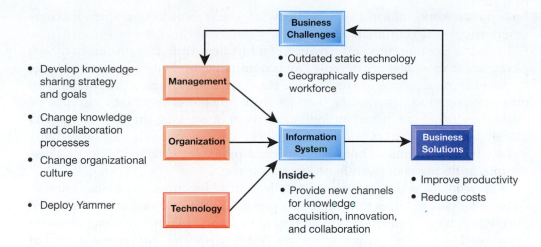

- Develop knowledge-
  sharing strategy
  and goals

- Change knowledge
  and collaboration
  processes

- Change organizational
  culture

- Deploy Yammer

**Business
Challenges**

- Outdated static technology
- Geographically dispersed
  workforce

Management

Organization

Technology

**Information
System**

Inside+

- Provide new channels
  for knowledge
  acquisition, innovation,
  and collaboration

**Business
Solutions**

- Improve productivity
- Reduce costs

that actively engaged employees and enabled them to obtain more knowledge from colleagues. The company consolidated its multiple knowledge platforms so that all employees would use Inside+ as a single entry point into ABB's systems for knowledge sharing and collaboration. ABB took advantage of Microsoft Yammer's social tools to increase employee collaboration and engagement. Inside+ integrates all of the ways employees share knowledge. There is more effective sharing of institutional knowledge, and the company has become more innovative and efficient.

New technology alone would not have solved ABB's problem. To make the solution effective, ABB had to change its organizational culture and business processes for knowledge dissemination and collaborative work, and the new technology made these changes possible.

Here are some questions to think about: How are collaboration and employee engagement keeping ABB competitive? How did using Yammer change the way work was performed at ABB?

2-1 What are business processes? How are they related to information systems?

In order to operate, businesses must deal with many different pieces of information about suppliers, customers, employees, invoices, and payments, and of course their products and services. They must organize work activities that use this information to operate efficiently and enhance the overall performance of the firm. Information systems make it possible for firms to manage all their information, make better decisions, and improve the execution of their business processes.

Business Processes

Business processes, which we introduced in Chapter 1, refer to the manner in which work is organized, coordinated, and focused to produce a valuable product or service. Business processes are the collection of activities required to produce a product or service. These activities are supported by flows of material, information, and knowledge among the participants in business processes. Business processes also refer to the unique ways in which organizations coordinate work, information, and knowledge and the ways in which management chooses to coordinate work.

To a large extent, the performance of a business firm depends on how well its business processes are designed and coordinated. A company's business processes can be a source of competitive strength if they enable the company to innovate or to execute better than its rivals. Business processes can also be liabilities if they are based on inefficient ways of working that impede organizational responsiveness and efficiency. The chapter-opening case describing ABB's improvements in knowledge-sharing processes clearly illustrates these points, as do many of the other cases in this text.

Every business can be seen as a collection of business processes, some of which are part of larger encompassing processes. For instance, uses of mentoring, wikis, blogs, and videos are all part of the overall knowledge management process. Many business processes are tied to a specific functional area. For example, the sales and marketing function is responsible for identifying customers, and the human resources function is responsible for hiring employees. Table 2.1 describes some typical business processes for each of the functional areas of business.

Other business processes cross many different functional areas and require coordination across departments. For instance, consider the seemingly simple business process of fulfilling a customer order (see Figure 2.1). Initially, the sales department receives a sales order. The order passes first to accounting to ensure the customer can pay for the order either by a credit verification or request for immediate payment prior to shipping. Once the customer credit is established, the production department pulls the product from inventory or produces the product. Then the product is shipped (and this may require working with a logistics firm, such as UPS or FedEx). A bill or invoice is generated by the accounting department, and a notice is sent to the customer indicating that the product has shipped. The sales department is notified of the shipment and prepares to support the customer by answering calls or fulfilling warranty claims.

What at first appears to be a simple process, fulfilling an order, turns out to be a very complicated series of business processes that require the close coordination of major functional groups in a firm. Moreover, to efficiently perform all these steps in the order fulfillment process requires a great deal of information.

TABLE 2.1 EXAMPLES OF FUNCTIONAL BUSINESS PROCESSES

FUNCTIONAL AREA	BUSINESS PROCESS
Manufacturing and production	Assembling the product Checking for quality Producing bills of materials
Sales and marketing	Identifying customers Making customers aware of the product Selling the product
Finance and accounting	Paying creditors Creating financial statements Managing cash accounts
Human resources	Hiring employees Evaluating employees' job performance Enrolling employees in benefits plans

FIGURE 2.1   THE ORDER FULFILLMENT PROCESS

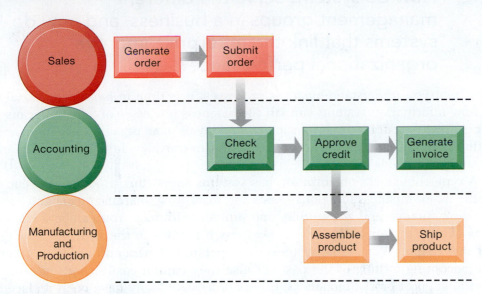

Fulfilling a customer order involves a complex set of steps that requires the close coordination of the sales, accounting, and manufacturing functions.

The required information must flow rapidly within the firm from one decision maker to another; with business partners, such as delivery firms; and with the customer. Computer-based information systems make this possible.

How Information Technology Improves Business Processes

Exactly how do information systems improve business processes? Information systems automate many steps in business processes that were formerly performed manually, such as checking a client's credit or generating an invoice and shipping order. But today, information technology can do much more. New technology can actually change the flow of information, making it possible for many more people to access and share information, replacing sequential steps with tasks that can be performed simultaneously, and eliminating delays in decision making. New information technology frequently changes the way a business works and supports entirely new business models. Downloading a Kindle e-book from Amazon, buying a computer online at Best Buy, and downloading a music track from iTunes are entirely new business processes based on new business models that would be inconceivable without today's information technology.

That's why it's so important to pay close attention to business processes, both in your information systems course and in your future career. By analyzing business processes, you can achieve a very clear understanding of how a business actually works. Moreover, by conducting a business process analysis, you will also begin to understand how to change the business by improving its processes to make it more efficient or effective. Throughout this book, we examine business processes with a view to understanding how they might be improved by using information technology to achieve greater efficiency, innovation, and customer service.

2-2 How do systems serve the different management groups in a business, and how do systems that link the enterprise improve organizational performance?

Now that you understand business processes, it is time to look more closely at how information systems support the business processes of a firm. Because there are different interests, specialties, and levels in an organization, there are different kinds of systems. No single system can provide all the information an organization needs.

A typical business organization has systems supporting processes for each of the major business functions—sales and marketing, manufacturing and production, finance and accounting, and human resources. You can find examples of systems for each of these business functions in the Learning Tracks for this chapter. Functional systems that operate independently of each other are becoming a thing of the past because they cannot easily share information to support cross-functional business processes. Many have been replaced with large-scale cross-functional systems that integrate the activities of related business processes and organizational units. We describe these integrated cross-functional applications later in this section.

A typical firm also has different systems supporting the decision-making needs of each of the main management groups we described in Chapter 1. Operational management, middle management, and senior management each use systems to support the decisions they must make to run the company. Let's look at these systems and the types of decisions they support.

Systems for Different Management Groups

A business firm has systems to support different groups or levels of management. These systems include transaction processing systems and systems for business intelligence.

Transaction Processing Systems

Operational managers need systems that keep track of the elementary activities and transactions of the organization, such as sales, receipts, cash deposits, payroll, credit decisions, and the flow of materials in a factory. **Transaction processing systems (TPS)** provide this kind of information. A transaction processing system is a computerized system that performs and records the daily routine transactions necessary to conduct business, such as sales order entry, hotel reservations, payroll, employee record keeping, and shipping.

The principal purpose of systems at this level is to answer routine questions and to track the flow of transactions through the organization. How many parts are in inventory? What happened to Mr. Smith's payment? To answer these kinds of questions, information generally must be easily available, current, and accurate.

At the operational level, tasks, resources, and goals are predefined and highly structured. The decision to grant credit to a customer, for instance, is made by a lower-level supervisor according to predefined criteria. All that must be determined is whether the customer meets the criteria.

FIGURE 2.2   A PAYROLL TPS

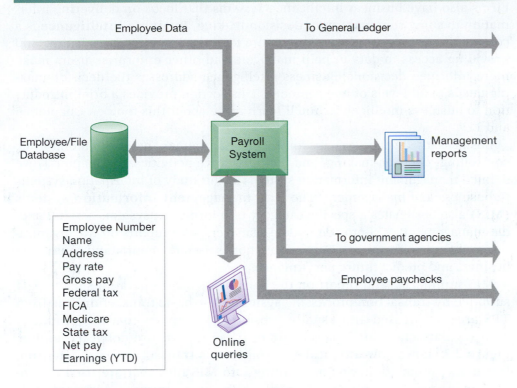

A TPS for payroll processing captures employee payment transaction data (such as a time card). System outputs include online and hard-copy reports for management and employee paychecks.

Figure 2.2 illustrates a TPS for payroll processing. A payroll system keeps track of money paid to employees. An employee time sheet with the employee's name, social security number, and number of hours worked per week represents a single transaction for this system. Once this transaction is input into the system, it updates the system's master file (or database—see Chapter 6) that permanently maintains employee information for the organization. The data in the system are combined in different ways to create reports of interest to management and government agencies and to send paychecks to employees.

Managers need TPS to monitor the status of internal operations and the firm's relations with the external environment. TPS are also major producers of information for the other systems and business functions. For example, the payroll system illustrated in Figure 2.2, along with other accounting TPS, supplies data to the company's general ledger system, which is responsible for maintaining records of the firm's income and expenses and for producing reports such as income statements and balance sheets. It also supplies employee payment history data for insurance, pension, and other benefits calculations to the firm's human resources function and employee payment data to government agencies such as the U.S. Internal Revenue Service and Social Security Administration.

Transaction processing systems are often so central to a business that TPS failure for a few hours can lead to a firm's demise and perhaps that of other firms linked to it. Imagine what would happen to UPS if its package tracking system was not working! What would the airlines do without their computerized reservation systems?

Systems for Business Intelligence

Firms also have business intelligence systems that focus on delivering information to support management decision making. **Business intelligence** is a contemporary term for data and software tools for organizing, analyzing, and providing access to data to help managers and other enterprise users make more informed decisions. Business intelligence addresses the decision-making needs of all levels of management. This section provides a brief introduction to business intelligence. You'll learn more about this topic in Chapters 6 and 12.

Business intelligence systems for middle management help with monitoring, controlling, decision-making, and administrative activities. In Chapter 1, we defined management information systems as the study of information systems in business and management. The term **management information systems (MIS)** also designates a specific category of information systems serving middle management. MIS provide middle managers with reports on the organization's current performance. This information is used to monitor and control the business and predict future performance.

MIS summarize and report on the company's basic operations using data supplied by transaction processing systems. The basic transaction data from TPS are compressed and usually presented in reports that are produced on a regular schedule. Today, many of these reports are delivered online. Figure 2.3 shows how a typical MIS transforms transaction-level data from inventory, production, and accounting into MIS files that are used to provide managers with reports. Figure 2.4 shows a sample report from this system.

MIS typically provide answers to routine questions that have been specified in advance and have a predefined procedure for answering them. For instance, MIS reports might list the total pounds of lettuce used this quarter by a fast-food chain or, as illustrated in Figure 2.4, compare total annual sales figures for

FIGURE 2.3   HOW MANAGEMENT INFORMATION SYSTEMS OBTAIN THEIR DATA FROM THE ORGANIZATION'S TPS

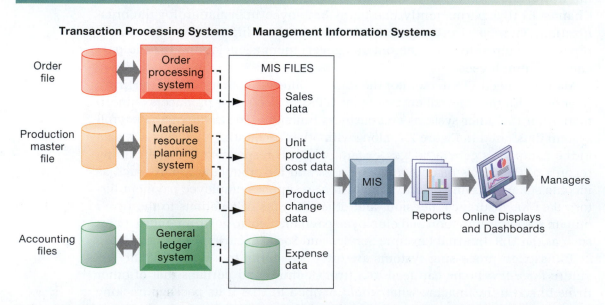

In the system illustrated by this diagram, three TPS supply summarized transaction data to the MIS reporting system at the end of the time period. Managers gain access to the organizational data through the MIS, which provides them with the appropriate reports.

FIGURE 2.4   SAMPLE MIS REPORT

Consolidated Consumer Products Corporation Sales by Product and Sales Region: 2017

PRODUCT CODE	PRODUCT DESCRIPTION	SALES REGION	ACTUAL SALES	PLANNED	ACTUAL versus PLANNED
4469	Carpet Cleaner	Northeast	4,066,700	4,800,000	0.85
		South	3,778,112	3,750,000	1.01
		Midwest	4,867,001	4,600,000	1.06
		West	4,003,440	4,400,000	0.91
	TOTAL		16,715,253	17,550,000	0.95
5674	Room Freshener	Northeast	3,676,700	3,900,000	0.94
		South	5,608,112	4,700,000	1.19
		Midwest	4,711,001	4,200,000	1.12
		West	4,563,440	4,900,000	0.93
	TOTAL		18,559,253	17,700,000	1.05

This report, showing summarized annual sales data, was produced by the MIS in Figure 2.3.

specific products to planned targets. These systems generally are not flexible and have little analytical capability. Most MIS use simple routines, such as summaries and comparisons, as opposed to sophisticated mathematical models or statistical techniques.

Other types of business intelligence systems support more non-routine decision making. **Decision-support systems (DSS)** focus on problems that are unique and rapidly changing, for which the procedure for arriving at a solution may not be fully predefined in advance. They try to answer questions such as these: What would be the impact on production schedules if we were to double sales in the month of December? What would happen to our return on investment if a factory schedule were delayed for six months?

Although DSS use internal information from TPS and MIS, they often bring in information from external sources, such as current stock prices or product prices of competitors. These systems are employed by "super-user" managers and business analysts who want to use sophisticated analytics and models to analyze data.

An interesting, small, but powerful DSS is the voyage-estimating system of a large global shipping company that transports bulk cargoes of coal, oil, ores, and finished products. The firm owns some vessels, charters others, and bids for shipping contracts in the open market to carry general cargo. A voyage-estimating system calculates financial and technical voyage details. Financial calculations include ship/time costs (fuel, labor, capital), freight rates for various types of cargo, and port expenses. Technical details include a myriad of factors, such as ship cargo capacity, speed, port distances, fuel and water consumption, and loading patterns (location of cargo for different ports).

The system can answer questions such as the following: Given a customer delivery schedule and an offered freight rate, which vessel should be assigned at what rate to maximize profits? What is the optimal speed at which a particular vessel can optimize its profit and still meet its delivery schedule? What is the optimal loading pattern for a ship bound for the U.S. West Coast from Malaysia?

FIGURE 2.5 **VOYAGE-ESTIMATING DECISION-SUPPORT SYSTEM**

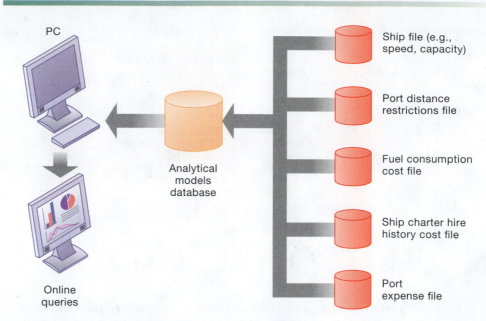

This DSS operates on a powerful PC. It is used daily by managers who must develop bids on shipping contracts.

Figure 2.5 illustrates the DSS built for this company. The system operates on a powerful desktop personal computer, providing a system of menus that makes it easy for users to enter data or obtain information.

The voyage-estimating DSS we have just described draws heavily on models. Other business intelligence systems are more data-driven, focusing instead on extracting useful information from very large quantities of data. For example, large ski resort companies such as Intrawest and Vail Resorts collect and store large amounts of customer data from call centers, lodging and dining reservations, ski schools, and ski equipment rental stores. They use special software to analyze these data to determine the value, revenue potential, and loyalty of each customer to help managers make better decisions about how to target their marketing programs.

Business intelligence systems also address the decision-making needs of senior management. Senior managers need systems that focus on strategic issues and long-term trends, both in the firm and in the external environment. They are concerned with questions such as: What will employment levels be in five years? What are the long-term industry cost trends? What products should we be making in five years?

Executive support systems (ESS) help senior management make these decisions. They address nonroutine decisions requiring judgment, evaluation, and insight because there is no agreed-on procedure for arriving at a solution. ESS present graphs and data from many sources through an interface that is easy for senior managers to use. Often the information is delivered to senior executives through a **portal**, which uses a web interface to present integrated personalized business content.

ESS are designed to incorporate data about external events, such as new tax laws or competitors, but they also draw summarized information from internal MIS and DSS. They filter, compress, and track critical data, displaying the data of greatest importance to senior managers. Increasingly, such systems include

A digital dashboard delivers comprehensive and accurate information for decision making, often using a single screen. The graphical overview of key performance indicators helps managers quickly spot areas that need attention.

business intelligence analytics for analyzing trends, forecasting, and "drilling down" to data at greater levels of detail.

For example, the chief operating officer (COO) and plant managers at Valero, the world's largest independent petroleum refiner, use a Refining Dashboard to display real-time data related to plant and equipment reliability, inventory management, safety, and energy consumption. With the displayed information, the COO and his team can review the performance of each Valero refinery in the United States and Canada in terms of how each plant is performing compared to the production plan of the firm. The headquarters group can drill down to from executive level to refinery level and individual system-operator level displays of performance. Valero's Refining Dashboard is an example of a **digital dashboard**, which displays on a single screen graphs and charts of key performance indicators for managing a company. Digital dashboards are becoming an increasingly popular tool for management decision makers.

The Interactive Session on Organizations describes real-world examples of several of these types of systems used by an organization with employees and staff members working all over the world. Note the types of systems illustrated by this case and the role they play in improving both operations and decision making.

Systems for Linking the Enterprise

Reviewing all the different types of systems we have just described, you might wonder how a business can manage all the information in these different systems. You might also wonder how costly it is to maintain so many different systems. And you might wonder how all these different systems can share

INTERACTIVE SESSION: ORGANIZATIONS

New Systems Help Plan International Manage Its Human Resources

Founded in 1937, Plan International is one of the oldest and largest children's development organizations in the world, promoting rights and opportunities for children in need. With global headquarters in Surrey, UK, the organization has operations in more than 70 countries (including 51 developing nations in Africa, Asia, and the Americas), and worked with 81.5 million children in more than 86,676 communities in 2014. Plan International has grown steadily over the years and has more than 1,200 paid staff members and more than 9,000 volunteers.

Plan International is not affiliated with any religious or political group or government. It obtains about half of its funding from donations from corporations, governments, and trusts and the rest from individuals willing to sponsor a child.

Plan International works with children, families, communities, and local governments to bring about positive change for children in health, education, water and sanitation, protection, economic security, and coping with catastrophes such as wars, floods, earthquakes, and other natural disasters. For example, Plan has sent workers to help children affected by the 2013 Typhoon Haiyan in the Philippines and the Ebola virus outbreak in West Africa. In addition to coordinating emergency response efforts, Plan runs public health information campaigns and trains health and aid workers.

Plan's objective is to reach as many disadvantaged children as possible, and this requires a highly coordinated approach. When an emergency strikes, Plan must locate and deploy the most appropriate resources wherever they are required. To accomplish this a disaster relief team at Plan's head office must sift through data on all of its 10,000 aid workers in 70 countries to see which people have the appropriate skills and experience in medical aid, child protection, education, and shelter management to provide the necessary services. Typically the people chosen to respond to a specific emergency will have a variety of skills, including frontline workers with knowledge of the language and the local area. Plan now has the ability see data about all of its workers' skills the moment an emergency occurs, so it can respond immediately with the right team of people.

Plan is now able to instantly assemble pertinent information about its workers because of its new human resources (HR) systems. The human resources systems allow Plan to track not only the skills people bring when they are hired but also any additional training or experience they have acquired for disaster response emergencies while working for Plan.

The human resources systems also help Plan manage the grants and donations it receives. When a donation first comes in, it is sent to Plan's London headquarters and allocated from there. If, for example, Plan receives a $40 million grant to use in Sierra Leone, Plan will need different people to manage that grant for Plan. Plan needs to be able to scan the organization globally to find the right people.

Before the new human resources systems were implemented, Plan was working with very outdated decentralized systems that were partially manual. The organization had to keep track of employees using a patchwork of 30 different human resources systems, spreadsheets, and documents.

It could take weeks to locate people with the right language skills, disaster experience, and medical training. When a massive earthquake struck Haiti in 2010, Plan had to email everyone asking if staff knew any people who could speak French, had the appropriate disaster management skills, and were available to help.

In 2012 Plan began looking for a human resources system that could handle its growing global workforce, support common processes across all regions, and deliver information on a secure mobile platform in regions where technology infrastructure was not well developed. The organization selected a cloud-based HR system from SAP's SuccessFactors as well as on-premises software from SAP, which satisfied these requirements and are integrated with one another. Implementation of the new system began in May 2013. It took only 16 weeks to implement a fully working system at Plan's international headquarters, and all of Plan's international regions were brought onto the system by 2014.

The cloud-based SuccessFactors system runs in remote computer centers managed by SuccessFactors and is accessible to users via the Internet. The system provides a centralized employee profile with a comprehensive view of employee skill sets, expertise, experience, and career interests. Through an intuitive interface, employees can update their own information, creating an easily searchable directory that every employee can access. Plan uses SuccessFactors software modules for recruiting, performance and goals, succession and development, compensation, and learning. Plan also implemented SuccessFactors Workforce Planning and on-premises SAP Personnel Administration and Organization Management software. Workforce planning entails systematic identification and analysis of what an organization is going to need in terms of the size, type, experience, knowledge, skills, and quality of its workforce to achieve its business objectives. SAP's Personnel Administration software manages employee recordkeeping and organizational data concerning the recruitment, selection, retention, development, and assessment of personnel. SAP's Organization Management software enables organizations to depict and analyze their organizational and reporting structures.

The new human resources systems provide a bird's-eye view of the entire Plan workforce, showing immediately how many people work for Plan, where they are located, what skills they possess, their job responsibilities, and their career paths. Plan's central human resources staff spend much less time chasing information. For example, assembling and analyzing data from employee performance reviews, including

performance-based salary calculations, used to take up to six months. Now all it takes is the push of a button. Employees are able to access their human resources records online and update information such as address, family details, and emergency contacts. By enabling employees to perform these tasks themselves, Plan saves valuable human resources staff time, which can be directed toward more value-adding work. Plan is also able to show its donors exactly how their contributions were spent and the results.

Using SuccessFactors and SAP human resources software, Plan staff are able to identify and dispatch relief workers to disaster areas within hours. When Typhoon Haiyan struck the Philippines in November 2013, Plan specialists were on the scene within 72 hours. Being able to deploy staff to emergencies so rapidly has saved more lives. What's more, Plan's improved response time has helped it secure new sources of funding by giving it more credibility with governments, corporations, and other sources of grants and donations.

Sources: Lauren Bonneau, "Customer Snapshot: Changing Lives and Creating Self-Sufficient Communities—One Child at a Time," www.sap.com, accessed March 10, 2016; "Better Planning for Plan International: The Life-Saving Power of Improved Data Visibility," SAP Insider Profiles, January 1, 2015; and www.plan-international. org, accessed March 10, 2016.

CASE STUDY QUESTIONS

1. Describe the problem faced by Plan International. What management, organization, and technology factors contributed to this problem?

2. Describe the system solution to this problem. Describe the types of systems used for the solution.

3. Why is human resources so important at Plan International?

4. How did these systems improve operational efficiency?

5. How did these systems improve decision making? Give examples of two decisions improved by Plan's new systems.

information and how managers and employees are able to coordinate their work. In fact, these are all important questions for businesses today.

Enterprise Applications

Getting all the different kinds of systems in a company to work together has proven a major challenge. Typically, corporations are put together both through normal "organic" growth and through acquisition of smaller firms. Over a period of time, corporations end up with a collection of systems, most of them older, and face the challenge of getting them all to "talk" with one another and work together as one corporate system. There are several solutions to this problem.

One solution is to implement **enterprise applications**, which are systems that span functional areas, focus on executing business processes across the business firm, and include all levels of management. Enterprise applications help businesses become more flexible and productive by coordinating their business processes more closely and integrating groups of processes so they focus on efficient management of resources and customer service.

There are four major enterprise applications: enterprise systems, supply chain management systems, customer relationship management systems, and knowledge management systems. Each of these enterprise applications integrates a related set of functions and business processes to enhance the performance of the organization as a whole. Figure 2.6 shows that the architecture for these enterprise applications encompasses processes spanning the entire organization and, in some cases, extending beyond the organization to customers, suppliers, and other key business partners.

Enterprise Systems Firms use **enterprise systems**, also known as enterprise resource planning (ERP) systems, to integrate business processes in manufacturing and production, finance and accounting, sales and marketing, and human resources into a single software system. Information that was previously fragmented in many different systems is stored in a single

FIGURE 2.6 ENTERPRISE APPLICATION ARCHITECTURE

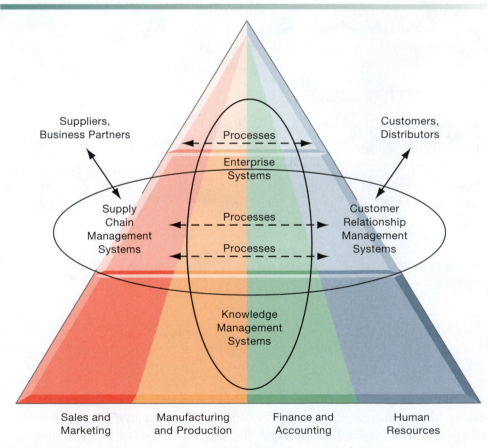

Enterprise applications automate processes that span multiple business functions and organizational levels and may extend outside the organization.

comprehensive data repository where it can be used by many different parts of the business.

For example, when a customer places an order, the order data flow automatically to other parts of the company that are affected by them. The order transaction triggers the warehouse to pick the ordered products and schedule shipment. The warehouse informs the factory to replenish whatever has been depleted. The accounting department is notified to send the customer an invoice. Customer service representatives track the progress of the order through every step to inform customers about the status of their orders. Managers are able to use firmwide information to make more precise and timely decisions about daily operations and longer-term planning.

Supply Chain Management Systems Firms use **supply chain management (SCM) systems** to help manage relationships with their suppliers. These systems help suppliers, purchasing firms, distributors, and logistics companies share information about orders, production, inventory levels, and delivery of products and services so they can source, produce, and deliver goods and services efficiently. The ultimate objective is to get the right amount of their products from their source to their point of consumption in the least amount of time and at the lowest cost. These systems increase firm profitability by lowering the costs of moving and making products and by enabling managers to make better decisions about how to organize and schedule sourcing, production, and distribution.

Supply chain management systems are one type of **interorganizational system** because they automate the flow of information across organizational boundaries. You will find examples of other types of interorganizational information systems throughout this text because such systems make it possible for firms to link digitally to customers and to outsource their work to other companies.

Customer Relationship Management Systems Firms use **customer relationship management (CRM) systems** to help manage their relationships with their customers. CRM systems provide information to coordinate all of the business processes that deal with customers in sales, marketing, and service to optimize revenue, customer satisfaction, and customer retention. This information helps firms identify, attract, and retain the most profitable customers; provide better service to existing customers; and increase sales.

Knowledge Management Systems Some firms perform better than others because they have better knowledge about how to create, produce, and deliver products and services. This firm knowledge is unique, is difficult to imitate, and can be leveraged into long-term strategic benefits. **Knowledge management systems (KMS)** enable organizations to better manage processes for capturing and applying knowledge and expertise. These systems collect all relevant knowledge and experience in the firm and make it available wherever and whenever it is needed to improve business processes and management decisions. They also link the firm to external sources of knowledge.

We examine enterprise systems and systems for supply chain management and customer relationship management in greater detail in Chapter 9. We discuss collaboration systems that support knowledge management in this chapter and cover other types of knowledge management applications in Chapter 11.

Intranets and Extranets

Enterprise applications create deep-seated changes in the way the firm conducts its business, offering many opportunities to integrate important business data into a single system. They are often costly and difficult to implement. Intranets and extranets deserve mention here as alternative tools for increasing integration and expediting the flow of information within the firm and with customers and suppliers.

Intranets are simply internal company websites that are accessible only by employees. The term *intranet* refers to an internal network, in contrast to the Internet, which is a public network linking organizations and other external networks. Intranets use the same technologies and techniques as the larger Internet, and they often are simply a private access area in a larger company website. Likewise with extranets, which are company websites that are accessible to authorized vendors and suppliers and are often used to coordinate the movement of supplies to the firm's production apparatus.

For example, Six Flags, which operates 18 theme parks throughout North America, maintains an intranet for its 1900 full-time employees that provides company-related news and information on each park's day-to-day operations, including weather forecasts, performance schedules, and details about groups and celebrities visiting the parks. The company also uses an extranet to broadcast information about schedule changes and park events to its 30,000 seasonal employees. We describe the technology for intranets and extranets in more detail in Chapter 7.

E-business, E-commerce, and E-government

The systems and technologies we have just described are transforming firms' relationships with customers, employees, suppliers, and logistic partners into digital relationships using networks and the Internet. So much business is now enabled by or based upon digital networks that we use the terms *electronic business* and *electronic commerce* frequently throughout this text.

Electronic business, or **e-business**, refers to the use of digital technology and the Internet to execute the major business processes in the enterprise. E-business includes activities for the internal management of the firm and for coordination with suppliers and other business partners. It also includes **electronic commerce**, or **e-commerce**.

E-commerce is the part of e-business that deals with the buying and selling of goods and services over the Internet. It also encompasses activities supporting those market transactions, such as advertising, marketing, customer support, security, delivery, and payment.

The technologies associated with e-business have also brought about similar changes in the public sector. Governments on all levels are using Internet technology to deliver information and services to citizens, employees, and businesses with which they work. **E-government** refers to the application of the Internet and networking technologies to digitally enable government and public sector agencies' relationships with citizens, businesses, and other arms of government.

In addition to improving delivery of government services, e-government makes government operations more efficient and also empowers citizens by giving them easier access to information and the ability to network electronically with other citizens. For example, citizens in some states can renew their driver's licenses or apply for unemployment benefits online, and the Internet has become a powerful tool for instantly mobilizing interest groups for political action and fund-raising.

2-3   Why are systems for collaboration and social business so important, and what technologies do they use?

With all these systems and information, you might wonder how is it possible to make sense of them. How do people working in firms pull it all together, work toward common goals, and coordinate plans and actions? Information systems can't make decisions, hire or fire people, sign contracts, agree on deals, or adjust the price of goods to the marketplace. In addition to the types of systems we have just described, businesses need special systems to support collaboration and teamwork.

What Is Collaboration?

Collaboration is working with others to achieve shared and explicit goals. Collaboration focuses on task or mission accomplishment and usually takes place in a business or other organization and between businesses. You collaborate with a colleague in Tokyo having expertise on a topic about which you know nothing. You collaborate with many colleagues in publishing a company blog. If you're in a law firm, you collaborate with accountants in an accounting firm in servicing the needs of a client with tax problems.

Collaboration can be short-lived, lasting a few minutes, or longer term, depending on the nature of the task and the relationship among participants. Collaboration can be one-to-one or many-to-many.

Employees may collaborate in informal groups that are not a formal part of the business firm's organizational structure, or they may be organized into formal teams. **Teams** have a specific mission that someone in the business assigned to them. Team members need to collaborate on the accomplishment of specific tasks and collectively achieve the team mission. The team mission might be to "win the game" or "increase online sales by 10 percent." Teams are often short-lived, depending on the problems they tackle and the length of time needed to find a solution and accomplish the mission.

Collaboration and teamwork are more important today than ever for a variety of reasons.

- *Changing nature of work.* The nature of work has changed from factory manufacturing and pre-computer office work where each stage in the production process occurred independently of one another and was coordinated by supervisors. Work was organized into silos. Within a silo, work passed from one machine tool station to another, from one desktop to another, until the finished product was completed. Today, jobs require much closer coordination and interaction among the parties involved in producing the service or product. A report from the consulting firm McKinsey & Company estimated that 41 percent of the U.S. labor force is now composed of jobs where interaction (talking, e-mailing, presenting, and persuading) is the primary value-adding activity. Even in factories, workers today often work in production groups, or pods.

- *Growth of professional work.* "Interaction" jobs tend to be professional jobs in the service sector that require close coordination and collaboration. Professional jobs require substantial education and the sharing of information and opinions to get work done. Each actor on the job brings specialized expertise to the problem, and all the actors need to take one another into account in order to accomplish the job.

- *Changing organization of the firm.* For most of the industrial age, managers organized work in a hierarchical fashion. Orders came down the hierarchy, and responses moved back up the hierarchy. Today, work is organized into groups and teams, and the members are expected to develop their own methods for accomplishing the task. Senior managers observe and measure results but are much less likely to issue detailed orders or operating procedures. In part, this is because expertise and decision-making power have been pushed down in organizations.

- *Changing scope of the firm.* The work of the firm has changed from a single location to multiple locations—offices or factories throughout a region, a nation, or even around the globe. For instance, Henry Ford developed the first mass-production automobile plant at a single Dearborn, Michigan, factory. In 2015, Ford employed 199,000 people at about 67 plants worldwide. With this kind of global presence, the need for close coordination of design, production, marketing, distribution, and service obviously takes on new importance and scale. Large global companies need to have teams working on a global basis.

- *Emphasis on innovation.* Although we tend to attribute innovations in business and science to great individuals, these great individuals are most likely working with a team of brilliant colleagues. Think of Bill Gates and Steve Jobs (founders of Microsoft and Apple), both of whom are highly regarded innovators and both of whom built strong collaborative teams to nurture and support innovation in their firms. Their initial innovations derived from close collaboration with colleagues and partners. Innovation, in other words, is a group and social process, and most innovations derive from collaboration among individuals in a lab, a business, or government agencies. Strong collaborative practices and technologies are believed to increase the rate and quality of innovation.

- *Changing culture of work and business.* Most research on collaboration supports the notion that diverse teams produce better outputs faster than individuals working on their own. Popular notions of the crowd ("crowdsourcing" and the "wisdom of crowds") also provide cultural support for collaboration and teamwork.

What Is Social Business?

Many firms today enhance collaboration by embracing **social business**—the use of social networking platforms, including Facebook, Twitter, and internal corporate social tools—to engage their employees, customers, and suppliers. These tools enable workers to set up profiles, form groups, and "follow" each other's status updates. The goal of social business is to deepen interactions with groups inside and outside the firm to expedite and enhance information sharing, innovation, and decision making.

A key word in social business is *conversations*. Customers, suppliers, employees, managers, and even oversight agencies continually have conversations about firms, often without the knowledge of the firm or its key actors (employees and managers).

Supporters of social business argue that, if firms could tune into these conversations, they would strengthen their bonds with consumers, suppliers, and employees, increasing their emotional involvement in the firm.

All of this requires a great deal of information transparency. People need to share opinions and facts with others quite directly, without intervention from executives or others. Employees get to know directly what customers and other employees think, suppliers will learn very directly the opinions of supply chain partners, and even managers presumably will learn more directly from their

TABLE 2.2 APPLICATIONS OF SOCIAL BUSINESS

SOCIAL BUSINESS APPLICATION	DESCRIPTION
Social networks	Connect through personal and business profiles
Crowdsourcing	Harness collective knowledge to generate new ideas and solutions
Shared workspaces	Coordinate projects and tasks; co-create content
Blogs and wikis	Publish and rapidly access knowledge; discuss opinions and experiences
Social commerce	Share opinions about purchasing or purchase on social platforms
File sharing	Upload, share, and comment on photos, videos, audio, text documents
Social marketing	Use social media to interact with customers; derive customer insights
Communities	Discuss topics in open forums; share expertise

employees how well they are doing. Nearly everyone involved in the creation of value will know much more about everyone else.

If such an environment could be created, it is likely to drive operational efficiencies, spur innovation, and accelerate decision making. If product designers can learn directly about how their products are doing in the market in real time, based on consumer feedback, they can speed up the redesign process. If employees can use social connections inside and outside the company to capture new knowledge and insights, they will be able to work more efficiently and solve more business problems.

Table 2.2 describes important applications of social business inside and outside the firm. This chapter focuses on enterprise social business—its internal corporate uses. Chapters 7 and 10 describe social business applications relating to customers and suppliers outside the company.

Business Benefits of Collaboration and Social Business

Although many articles and books have been written about collaboration, nearly all of the research on this topic is anecdotal. Nevertheless, there is a general belief among both business and academic communities that the more a business firm is "collaborative," the more successful it will be, and that collaboration within and among firms is more essential than in the past. A global survey of business and information systems managers found that investments in collaboration technology produced organizational improvements that returned more than four times the amount of the investment, with the greatest benefits for sales, marketing, and research and development functions (Frost and Sullivan, 2009). McKinsey & Company consultants predict that social technologies used within and across enterprises could potentially raise the productivity of interaction workers by 20 to 25 percent (McKinsey Global Institute, 2012).

Table 2.3 summarizes some of the benefits of collaboration and social business that have been identified. Figure 2.7 graphically illustrates how collaboration is believed to affect business performance.

Building a Collaborative Culture and Business Processes

Collaboration won't take place spontaneously in a business firm, especially if there is no supportive culture or business processes. Business firms, especially large firms, had a reputation in the past for being "command and control"

TABLE 2.3 BUSINESS BENEFITS OF COLLABORATION AND SOCIAL BUSINESS

BENEFIT	RATIONALE
Productivity	People interacting and working together can capture expert knowledge and solve problems more rapidly than the same number of people working in isolation from one another. There will be fewer errors.
Quality	People working collaboratively can communicate errors and corrective actions faster than if they work in isolation. Collaborative and social technologies help reduce time delays in design and production.
Innovation	People working collaboratively can come up with more innovative ideas for products, services, and administration than the same number working in isolation from one another. Advantages to diversity and the "wisdom of crowds."
Customer service	People working together using collaboration and social tools can solve customer complaints and issues faster and more effectively than if they were working in isolation from one another.
Financial performance (profitability, sales, and sales growth)	As a result of all of the above, collaborative firms have superior sales, sales growth, and financial performance.

FIGURE 2.7   REQUIREMENTS FOR COLLABORATION

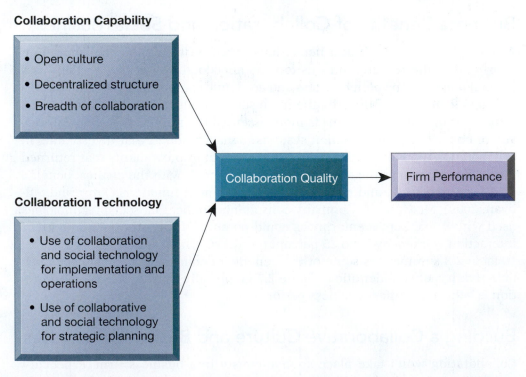

Successful collaboration requires an appropriate organizational structure and culture along with appropriate collaboration technology.

organizations where the top leaders thought up all the really important matters and then ordered lower-level employees to execute senior management plans. The job of middle management supposedly was to pass messages back and forth, up and down the hierarchy.

Command and control firms required lower-level employees to carry out orders without asking too many questions, with no responsibility to improve processes, and with no rewards for teamwork or team performance. If your work group needed help from another work group, that was something for the bosses to figure out. You never communicated horizontally, always vertically, so management could control the process. Together, the expectations of management and employees formed a culture, a set of assumptions about common goals and how people should behave. Many business firms still operate this way.

A collaborative business culture and business processes are very different. Senior managers are responsible for achieving results but rely on teams of employees to achieve and implement the results. Policies, products, designs, processes, and systems are much more dependent on teams at all levels of the organization to devise, to create, and to build. Teams are rewarded for their performance, and individuals are rewarded for their performance in a team. The function of middle managers is to build the teams, coordinate their work, and monitor their performance. The business culture and business processes are more "social." In a collaborative culture, senior management establishes collaboration and teamwork as vital to the organization, and it actually implements collaboration for the senior ranks of the business as well.

Tools and Technologies for Collaboration and Social Business

A collaborative, team-oriented culture won't produce benefits without information systems in place to enable collaboration and social business. Currently there are hundreds of tools designed to deal with the fact that, in order to succeed in our jobs, we are all much more dependent on one another, our fellow employees, customers, suppliers, and managers. Some of these tools are expensive, but others are available online for free (or with premium versions for a modest fee). Let's look more closely at some of these tools.

E-mail and Instant Messaging (IM)

E-mail and instant messaging (including text messaging) have been major communication and collaboration tools for interaction jobs. Their software operates on computers, mobile phones, and other wireless devices and includes features for sharing files as well as transmitting messages. Many instant messaging systems allow users to engage in real-time conversations with multiple participants simultaneously. In recent years, e-mail use has declined, with messaging and social media becoming preferred channels of communication.

Wikis

Wikis are a type of website that makes it easy for users to contribute and edit text content and graphics without any knowledge of web page development or programming techniques. The most well-known wiki is Wikipedia, the largest collaboratively edited reference project in the world. It relies on volunteers, makes no money and accepts no advertising.

Wikis are very useful tools for storing and sharing corporate knowledge and insights. Enterprise software vendor SAP AG has a wiki that acts as a base of information for people outside the company, such as customers and software developers who build programs that interact with SAP software. In the past, those people asked and sometimes answered questions in an informal way on SAP online forums, but that was an inefficient system, with people asking and answering the same questions over and over.

Virtual Worlds

Virtual worlds, such as Second Life, are online 3-D environments populated by "residents" who have built graphical representations of themselves known as avatars. Companies like IBM, Cisco, and Intel Corporations use the online world for meetings, interviews, guest speaker events, and employee training. Real-world people represented by avatars meet, interact, and exchange ideas at these virtual locations using gestures, chat box conversations, and voice communication.

Collaboration and Social Business Platforms

There are now suites of software products providing multifunction platforms for collaboration and social business among teams of employees who work together from many different locations. The most widely used are Internet-based audio conferencing and video conferencing systems, cloud collaboration services such as Google's online services and tools, corporate collaboration systems such as Microsoft SharePoint and IBM Notes, and enterprise social networking tools such as Salesforce Chatter, Microsoft Yammer, Jive, Facebook at Work, and IBM Connections.

Virtual Meeting Systems In an effort to reduce travel expenses and enable people in different locations to meet and collaborate, many companies, both large and small, are adopting videoconferencing and web conferencing technologies. Companies such as Heinz, GE, and PepsiCo are using virtual meeting systems for product briefings, training courses, strategy sessions, and even inspirational chats.

A videoconference allows individuals at two or more locations to communicate simultaneously through two-way video and audio transmissions. High-end videoconferencing systems feature **telepresence** technology, an integrated audio and visual environment that allows a person to give the appearance of being present at a location other than his or her true physical location (see the Interactive Session on Technology). Free or low-cost Internet-based systems such as Skype group videoconferencing, Google+ Hangouts, Zoom, and ooVoo are of lower quality, but still useful for smaller companies. Apple's FaceTime is useful for one-to-one videoconferencing. Some of these tools are available on mobile devices.

Companies of all sizes are finding web-based online meeting tools such as Cisco WebEx, Skype for Business, and Adobe Connect especially helpful for training and sales presentations. These products enable participants to share documents and presentations in conjunction with audioconferencing and live video via webcam.

Cloud Collaboration Services Google offers many online tools and services, and some are suitable for collaboration. They include Google Drive, Google Docs, Google Apps, Google Sites, and Google+. Most are free of charge.

INTERACTIVE SESSION: TECHNOLOGY

Cisco IX5000: What State-of-the-Art Telepresence Can Do for Collaboration

When it comes to collaboration, the fastest-growing requirement is for video-enabled business applications. In the past, videoconferencing was limited to very largest companies that could afford dedicated videoconference rooms and expensive networking and software for this purpose. Today, videoconferencing has been democratized. There's something for everyone.

The cost of the technology has radically fallen, global Internet and desktop transmission of video and audio data is inexpensive and available using standard corporate IT infrastructure, and, importantly, it can be integrated into mobile and desktop tools that are powerful, inexpensive, and ubiquitous. Now, for the first time, it's possible for most employees and professionals in a firm to use videoconferencing and telepresence tools to manage business processes and connect and collaborate with others, even customers, around the globe.

The current generation of telepresence platforms provide much more than video collaboration, with the ability coordinate multiple rich data streams that integrate mobile, desktop, and video streams of digital information, create a collaborative environment, and move the information to where managers and professionals are making decisions.

On the high end, let's look at Cisco's IX5000 immersive telepresence system. It offers leading-edge telepresence, but it's much more affordable and easier to use than in the past. It is sleekly sculpted, with three 4K ultra-high-definition cameras clustered discreetly above three 70-inch LCD screens. The cameras provide crisp, high-definition video. Theater-quality sound emanates from 18 custom speakers and one powerful subwoofer, creating a high-quality lifelike collaboration experience for 8 to 18 people. Video and other content can move across any of the screens. The camera and graphic processors are able to capture the whole room in fine detail, so you can stand up and move around or go the whiteboard. Using the 4K cameras, the IX 5000 creates an image four times larger than what's actually needed to fill the system's three screens. The images can be cropped down to show participants seated behind their tables, but when someone stands up, the crop is removed to show both standing and sitting participants.

The IX5000 is so intuitive that you can make that first call without looking at a manual or calling the information systems department. To install the IX500 system, no special changes to a room are required. And it needs only half the power, installation time, and data transmission capacity (bandwidth) as its previous telepresence systems. How much does all this cost? A six-seat IX5000 studio lists for $299,000, while the 18-seat studio costs $339,000.

The first company to deploy the IX5000 system was Produban, Grupo Santander's technology company specializing in the continuous design and operation of IT infrastructures. Grupo Santander is a Spanish banking group and one of the largest banks in the world in terms of market capitalization. The group has expanded since 2000 through a number of acquisitions, with operations across Europe, Latin America, North America, Africa, and Asia. Santander now has 185,000 employees serving 107 million customers through 13,067 branches. Grupo Santander is noted for innovation and has pioneered in many new digital products and services for online banking, mobile banking, mobile wallet, and digital payments. It is currently in the midst of an intense digital transformation to help it anticipate innovative and attractive solutions for customers' new needs.

Produban is responsible for the entire IT infrastructure of this sprawling global company. With more than 5,500 employees working in nine different countries, Produban services more than 120 companies in areas such as data center design and operation, IT infrastructure design and operation as a service, IT platform design and operation as a service, technology risk management and business continuity, and management of end user computing mobility and self-service management. The company is dedicated to technology innovation and continuous improvement.

Video collaboration helps Produban bring people together to make better decisions faster, which is why over the years it has invested in 76 Cisco TelePresence rooms worldwide. One reason this company is using IX500 technology is its lower total cost of ownership. As you will learn in Chapter 5, total cost of ownership (TCO) includes not only the purchase price of computer hardware, software, and networking equipment but also costs for ongoing maintenance, technical support, training, and utility and real estate costs for housing the technology. The IX5000 Series can be installed into a space as small as 19 feet by 14 feet. With 50 percent less power usage, 50 percent less data transmission capacity, and half the installation time of earlier systems (only eight hours), the IX5000 reduces TCO by 30 percent over three years.

Lower TCO will enable Produban to set up video rooms in more locations, so more teams can benefit. Produban is intent on using videoconferencing throughout the entire corporation. For locations where an IX5000 installation is not feasible, Cisco TelePresence meetings can be extended to users of Cisco WebEx, Cisco's low-cost web-based system for online meetings and application sharing. Remote attendees can join through the Cisco WebEx Meeting Center and receive video, audio, and other digital content from the Cisco TelePresence system. Meetings become even easier to stage among different groups and locations and are more productive.

Sources: Snorre Kjesbu, "The Most Sophisticated Collaboration Experience on the Planet," "'Less Is More' as Cisco Completely Reimagines Flagship Three-Screen Video Conferencing Technology," and "Cisco Telepresence IX5000 Series," www.cisco.com, accessed March 12, 2016; www.produban.com, accessed March 13, 2016; and Brian Riggs, "Immersive Telepresence: New Systems for a Declining Market," NoJitter, March 2, 2015.

CASE STUDY QUESTIONS

1. Describe the capabilities of Cisco's IX5000 telepresence system. How do they promote collaboration and innovation?

2. Why would a company like Produban want to invest in a telepresence system such as Cisco's

IX5000? How are videoconferencing technology and telepresence related to Produban's business model and business strategy?

3. What kinds of other companies might benefit from a telepresence service such as IX5000? Why?

Google Drive is a file storage and synchronization service for cloud storage, file sharing, and collaborative editing. Such web-based online file-sharing services allow users to upload files to secure online storage sites from which the files can be shared with others. Microsoft OneDrive and Dropbox are other leading cloud storage services. They feature both free and paid services, depending on the amount of storage space and administration required. Users are able to synchronize their files stored online with their local PCs and other kinds of devices with options for making the files private or public and for sharing them with designated contacts.

Google Drive and Microsoft OneDrive are integrated with tools for document creation and sharing. OneDrive provides online storage for Microsoft Office documents and other files and works with Microsoft Office apps, both installed and on the web. It can share to Facebook as well. Google Drive is integrated with Google Docs, a suite of productivity applications that offer collaborative editing on documents, spreadsheets, and presentations. Google's cloud-based productivity suite for businesses (word processing, spreadsheets, presentations, calendars, and mail) called Google Apps for Business also works with Google Drive.

Google Sites allows users to quickly create online team-oriented sites where multiple people can collaborate and share files. Google + is Google's effort to make these tools and other products and services it offers more "social" for both consumer and business use. Google + users can create a profile as well as "Circles" for organizing people into specific groups for sharing and collaborating. "Hangouts" enable people to engage in group video chat, with a maximum of 10 people participating at any point in time.

Microsoft SharePoint and IBM Notes Microsoft SharePoint is a browser-based collaboration and document management platform, combined with a powerful search engine that is installed on corporate servers. SharePoint has a web-based interface and close integration with productivity tools such as Microsoft Office, including Office 365, Microsoft's online web-based version of these tools offered as a subscription service. SharePoint software makes it possible for employees to share their documents and collaborate on projects using Office documents as the foundation.

SharePoint can be used to host internal websites that organize and store information in one central workspace to enable teams to coordinate work activities, collaborate on and publish documents, maintain task lists, implement workflows, and share information via wikis and blogs. Users are able to control versions of documents and document security. Because SharePoint stores and organizes information in one place, users can find relevant information quickly and efficiently while working together closely on tasks, projects, and documents. Enterprise search tools help locate people, expertise, and content. SharePoint now features social tools.

Southern Valve & Fitting USA (SVF) provides wholesalers with plumbing, irrigation, and utility valves and fittings. The company had initially used EMC Documentum eRoom and Google Docs for document sharing but encountered integration problems. SVF ported its documents and team sites to Microsoft SharePoint Online, which is integrated with Office 365. This solution combines multiple programs for communication and collaboration into a single online service. Employees can access documents from anywhere in the world using a standard Internet connection and make light edits to documents using Microsoft Office 365 productivity tools. Everything is accessed from a single platform. An order placed in China is handled as a SharePoint project, and all the sales order data and paperwork are shared throughout company (Microsoft Corporation, 2015).

IBM Notes (formerly Lotus Notes) is a collaborative software system with capabilities for sharing calendars, e-mail, messaging, collective writing and editing, shared database access, and online meetings. Notes software installed on desktop or laptop computers obtains applications stored on an IBM Domino server. Notes is web-enabled and offers an application development environment so that users can build custom applications to suit their unique needs. Notes has also added capabilities for blogs, microblogs, wikis, RSS aggregators, help desk systems, voice and video conferencing, and online meetings. IBM Notes promises high levels of security and reliability and the ability to retain control over sensitive corporate information.

Enterprise Social Networking Tools The tools we have just described include capabilities for supporting social business, but there are also more specialized social tools for this purpose, such as Salesforce Chatter, Microsoft Yammer, Jive, and IBM Connections. Enterprise social networking tools create business value by connecting the members of an organization through profiles, updates, and notifications similar to Facebook features but tailored to internal corporate uses. Table 2.4 provides more detail about these internal social capabilities.

Although companies have benefited from enterprise social networking, internal social networking has not caught on as quickly as consumer uses of Facebook, Twitter, and other public social networking products. The chapter-ending case study addresses this topic.

Checklist for Managers: Evaluating and Selecting Collaboration and Social Software Tools

With so many collaboration and social business tools and services available, how do you choose the right collaboration technology for your firm? To answer this question, you need a framework for understanding just what problems

TABLE 2.4 ENTERPRISE SOCIAL NETWORKING SOFTWARE CAPABILITIES

SOCIAL SOFTWARE CAPABILITY	DESCRIPTION
Profiles	Ability to set up member profiles describing who individuals are, educational background, interests. Includes work-related associations and expertise (skills, projects, teams).
Content sharing	Share, store, and manage content including documents, presentations, images, and videos.
Feeds and notifications	Real-time information streams, status updates, and announcements from designated individuals and groups.
Groups and team workspaces	Establish groups to share information, collaborate on documents, and work on projects with the ability to set up private and public groups and to archive conversations to preserve team knowledge.
Tagging and social bookmarking	Indicate preferences for specific pieces of content, similar to the Facebook Like button. Tagging lets people add keywords to identify content they like.
Permissions and privacy	Ability to make sure private information stays within the right circles, as determined by the nature of relationships. In enterprise social networks, there is a need to establish who in the company has permission to see what information.

these tools are designed to solve. One framework that has been helpful for us to talk about collaboration tools is the time/space collaboration and social tool matrix developed in the early 1990s by a number of collaborative work scholars (Figure 2.8).

The time/space matrix focuses on two dimensions of the collaboration problem: time and space. For instance, you need to collaborate with people in

FIGURE 2.8 THE TIME/SPACE COLLABORATION AND SOCIAL TOOL MATRIX

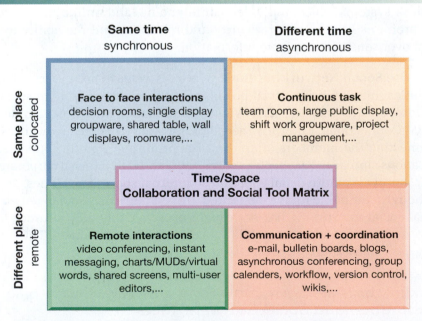

Collaboration and social technologies can be classified in terms of whether they support interactions at the same or different time or place and whether these interactions are remote or colocated.

different time zones, and you cannot all meet at the same time. Midnight in New York is noon in Bombay, so this makes it difficult to have a videoconference (the people in New York are too tired). Time is clearly an obstacle to collaboration on a global scale.

Place (location) also inhibits collaboration in large global or even national and regional firms. Assembling people for a physical meeting is made difficult by the physical dispersion of distributed firms (firms with more than one location), the cost of travel, and the time limitations of managers.

The collaboration and social technologies we have just described are ways of overcoming the limitations of time and space. Using this time/space framework will help you to choose the most appropriate collaboration and teamwork tools for your firm. Note that some tools are applicable in more than one time/place scenario. For example, Internet collaboration suites such as IBM Notes have capabilities for both synchronous (instant messaging, meeting tools) and asynchronous (e-mail, wikis, document editing) interactions.

Here's a "to-do" list to get started. If you follow these six steps, you should be led to investing in the correct collaboration software for your firm at a price you can afford and within your risk tolerance.

1. What are the collaboration challenges facing the firm in terms of time and space? Locate your firm in the time/space matrix. Your firm can occupy more than one cell in the matrix. Different collaboration tools will be needed for each situation.

2. Within each cell of the matrix where your firm faces challenges, exactly what kinds of solutions are available? Make a list of vendor products.

3. Analyze each of the products in terms of its cost and benefits to your firm. Be sure to include the costs of training in your cost estimates and the costs of involving the information systems department, if needed.

4. Identify the risks to security and vulnerability involved with each of the products. Is your firm willing to put proprietary information into the hands of external service providers over the Internet? Is your firm willing to expose its important operations to systems controlled by other firms? What are the financial risks facing your vendors? Will they be here in three to five years? What would be the cost of making a switch to another vendor in the event the vendor firm fails?

5. Seek the help of potential users to identify implementation and training issues. Some of these tools are easier to use than others.

6. Make your selection of candidate tools, and invite the vendors to make presentations.

2-4 What is the role of the information systems function in a business?

We've seen that businesses need information systems to operate today and that they use many different kinds of systems. But who is responsible for running these systems? Who is responsible for making sure the hardware, software, and other technologies used by these systems are running properly and are up-to-date? End users manage their systems from a business standpoint, but managing the technology requires a special information systems function.

The Information Systems Department

In all but the smallest of firms, the **information systems department** is the formal organizational unit responsible for information technology services. The information systems department is responsible for maintaining the hardware, software, data storage, and networks that comprise the firm's IT infrastructure. We describe IT infrastructure in detail in Chapter 5.

The information systems department consists of specialists, such as programmers, systems analysts, project leaders, and information systems managers. **Programmers** are highly trained technical specialists who write the software instructions for computers. **Systems analysts** constitute the principal liaisons between the information systems groups and the rest of the organization. It is the systems analyst's job to translate business problems and requirements into information requirements and systems. **Information systems managers** are leaders of teams of programmers and analysts, project managers, physical facility managers, telecommunications managers, or database specialists. They are also managers of computer operations and data entry staff. Also, external specialists, such as hardware vendors and manufacturers, software firms, and consultants, frequently participate in the day-to-day operations and long-term planning of information systems.

In many companies, the information systems department is headed by a **chief information officer (CIO)**. The CIO is a senior manager who oversees the use of information technology in the firm. Today's CIOs are expected to have a strong business background as well as information systems expertise and to play a leadership role in integrating technology into the firm's business strategy. Large firms today also have positions for a chief security officer, chief knowledge officer, chief data officer, and chief privacy officer, all of whom work closely with the CIO.

The **chief security officer (CSO)** is in charge of information systems security for the firm and is responsible for enforcing the firm's information security policy (see Chapter 8). (Sometimes this position is called the chief information security officer [CISO] where information systems security is separated from physical security.) The CSO is responsible for educating and training users and information systems specialists about security, keeping management aware of security threats and breakdowns, and maintaining the tools and policies chosen to implement security.

Information systems security and the need to safeguard personal data have become so important that corporations collecting vast quantities of personal data have established positions for a **chief privacy officer (CPO)**. The CPO is responsible for ensuring that the company complies with existing data privacy laws.

The **chief knowledge officer (CKO)** is responsible for the firm's knowledge management program. The CKO helps design programs and systems to find new sources of knowledge or to make better use of existing knowledge in organizational and management processes.

The **chief data officer (CDO)** is responsible for enterprise-wide governance and utilization of information to maximize the value the organization can realize from its data. The CDO ensures that the firm is collecting the appropriate data to serve its needs, deploying appropriate technologies for analyzing the data, and using the results to support business decisions. This position arose to deal with the very large amounts of data organizations are now generating and collecting (see Chapter 6).

End users are representatives of departments outside of the information systems group for whom applications are developed. These users are playing an increasingly large role in the design and development of information systems.

In the early years of computing, the information systems group was composed mostly of programmers who performed highly specialized but limited technical functions. Today, a growing proportion of staff members are systems analysts and network specialists, with the information systems department acting as a powerful change agent in the organization. The information systems department suggests new business strategies and new information-based products and services and coordinates both the development of the technology and the planned changes in the organization.

In the next eight years to 2024, IS/MIS will add about 500,000 jobs and will grow 50 percent faster than the average job growth for the economy as a whole. Out of 114 occupations, MIS is ranked 15th in terms of salaries. In 2016 the median wage for IT/MIS jobs is about $80,000, twice the level for all occupations. While all IT/IS occupations show above-average growth, the fastest-growing occupations are computer support specialists (12 percent), database administrators (11 percent), systems analysts (21 percent), information security analysts (18 percent), software engineers (17 percent), and information systems managers (15 percent) (Bureau of Labor Statistics, 2015). Unexpectedly, computer programmers will lose 8 percent in this period, in part because the process of creating computer programs is becoming increasingly efficient with the growth of online software services and cloud computing. In general, the management of IT occupations IS showing faster expansion than the technical occupations in IT. With businesses and government agencies increasingly relying on the Internet for computing and communication, system and network security management positions are especially in demand. See the Learning Track for this chapter titled "Occupational and Career Outlook for Information Systems Majors 2012–2018" for more details on IS job opportunities.

Organizing the Information Systems Function

There are many types of business firms, and there are many ways in which the IT function is organized within the firm. A very small company will not have a formal information systems group. It might have one employee who is responsible for keeping its networks and applications running, or it might use consultants for these services. Larger companies will have a separate information systems department, which may be organized along several different lines, depending on the nature and interests of the firm. Our Learning Track describes alternative ways of organizing the information systems function within the business.

The question of how the information systems department should be organized is part of the larger issue of IT governance. **IT governance** includes the strategy and policies for using information technology within an organization. It specifies the decision rights and framework for accountability to ensure that the use of information technology supports the organization's strategies and objectives. How much should the information systems function be centralized? What decisions must be made to ensure effective management and use of information technology, including the return on IT investments? Who should make these decisions? How will these decisions be made and monitored? Firms with superior IT governance will have clearly thought out the answers.

Review Summary

2-1 *What are business processes? How are they related to information systems?*

A business process is a logically related set of activities that defines how specific business tasks are performed, and it represents a unique way in which an organization coordinates work, information, and knowledge. Managers need to pay attention to business processes because they determine how well the organization can execute its business, and they may be a source of strategic advantage. There are business processes specific to each of the major business functions, but many business processes are cross-functional. Information systems automate parts of business processes, and they can help organizations redesign and streamline these processes.

2-2 *How do systems serve the different management groups in a business, and how do systems that link the enterprise improve organizational performance?*

Systems serving operational management are transaction processing systems (TPS), such as payroll or order processing, that track the flow of the daily routine transactions necessary to conduct business. Management information systems (MIS) produce reports serving middle management by condensing information from TPS, and these are not highly analytical. Decision-support systems (DSS) support management decisions that are unique and rapidly changing using advanced analytical models. All of these types of systems provide business intelligence that helps managers and enterprise employees make more informed decisions. These systems for business intelligence serve multiple levels of management and include executive support systems (ESS) for senior management that provide data in the form of graphs, charts, and dashboards delivered via portals using many sources of internal and external information.

Enterprise applications are designed to coordinate multiple functions and business processes. Enterprise systems integrate the key internal business processes of a firm into a single software system to improve coordination and decision making. Supply chain management systems help the firm manage its relationship with suppliers to optimize the planning, sourcing, manufacturing, and delivery of products and services. Customer relationship management (CRM) systems coordinate the business processes surrounding the firm's customers. Knowledge management systems enable firms to optimize the creation, sharing, and distribution of knowledge. Intranets and extranets are private corporate networks based on Internet technology that assemble information from disparate systems. Extranets make portions of private corporate intranets available to outsiders.

2-3 *Why are systems for collaboration and social business so important, and what technologies do they use?*

Collaboration is working with others to achieve shared and explicit goals. Social business is the use of internal and external social networking platforms to engage employees, customers, and suppliers, and it can enhance collaborative work. Collaboration and social business have become increasingly important in business because of globalization, the decentralization of decision making, and growth in jobs where interaction is the primary value-adding activity. Collaboration and social business enhance innovation, productivity, quality, and customer service. Tools for collaboration and social business include e-mail and instant messaging, wikis, virtual meeting systems, virtual worlds, cloud-based file-sharing services, corporate collaboration systems such as Microsoft SharePoint and IBM Notes, and enterprise social networking tools such as Chatter, Yammer, Jive, and IBM Connections.

2-4 *What is the role of the information systems function in a business?*

The information systems department is the formal organizational unit responsible for information technology services. It is responsible for maintaining the hardware, software, data storage, and networks that comprise the firm's IT infrastructure. The department consists of specialists, such as programmers, systems analysts, project leaders, and information systems managers, and is often headed by a CIO.

Key Terms

Business intelligence, 48
Chief data officer (CDO), 68
Chief information officer (CIO), 68
Chief knowledge officer (CKO), 68
Chief privacy officer (CPO), 68
Chief security officer (CSO), 68
Collaboration, 57
Customer relationship management (CRM) systems, 55
Decision-support systems (DSS), 49
Digital dashboard, 51
Electronic business (e-business), 56
Electronic commerce (e-commerce), 56
E-government, 56
End users, 68
Enterprise applications, 54
Enterprise systems, 54

Executive support systems (ESS), 50
Information systems department, 68
Information systems managers, 68
Interorganizational system, 55
IT governance, 69
Knowledge management systems (KMS), 55
Management information systems (MIS), 48
Portal, 50
Programmers, 68
Social business, 58
Supply chain management
   (SCM) systems, 55
Systems analysts, 68
Teams, 57
Telepresence, 62
Transaction processing systems (TPS), 46

MyMISLab

To complete the problems marked with the MyMISLab, go to the EOC Discussion Questions in MyMISLab.

Review Questions

2-1 What are business processes? How are they related to information systems?

- Define business processes and describe the role they play in organizations.
- Describe the relationship between information systems and business processes.

2-2 How do systems serve the different management groups in a business, and how do systems that link the enterprise improve organizational performance?

- Describe the characteristics of transaction processing systems (TPS) and the roles they play in a business.
- Describe the characteristics of management information systems (MIS) and explain how MIS differ from TPS and from DSS.
- Describe the characteristics of decision-support systems (DSS) and how they benefit businesses.
- Describe the characteristics of executive support systems (ESS) and explain how these systems differ from DSS.
- Explain how enterprise applications improve organizational performance.
- Define enterprise systems, supply chain management systems, customer relationship management systems, and knowledge

management systems and describe their business benefits.

- Explain how intranets and extranets help firms integrate information and business processes

2-3 Why are systems for collaboration and social business so important and what technologies do they use?

- Define collaboration and social business and explain why they have become so important in business today.
- List and describe the business benefits of collaboration and social business.
- Describe a supportive organizational culture and business processes for collaboration.
- List and describe the various types of collaboration and social business tools.

2-4 What is the role of the information systems function in a business?

- Describe how the information systems function supports a business.
- Compare the roles played by programmers, systems analysts, information systems managers, the chief information officer (CIO), the chief security officer (CSO), the chief data officer (CDO), and the chief knowledge officer (CKO).

Discussion Questions

2-5 How could information systems be used to support the order fulfillment process illustrated in Figure 2.1? What are the most important pieces of information these systems should capture? Explain your answer.

2-6 Identify the steps that are performed in the process of selecting and checking out a book from your college library and the information that flows among these activities. Diagram the process. Are there any ways this process could be changed to improve the performance of your library or your school? Diagram the improved process.

2-7 Use the time/space collaboration and social tool matrix to classify the collaboration and social technologies used by ABB.

Hands-On MIS Projects

The projects in this section give you hands-on experience analyzing opportunities to improve business processes with new information system applications, using a spreadsheet to improve decision making about suppliers, and using Internet software to plan efficient transportation routes. Visit MyMISLab's Multimedia Library to access this chapter's Hands-On MIS Projects.

Management Decision Problems

2-8 Don's Lumber Company on the Hudson River features a large selection of materials for flooring, decks, moldings, windows, siding, and roofing. The prices of lumber and other building materials are constantly changing. When a customer inquires about the price on prefinished wood flooring, sales representatives consult a manual price sheet and then call the supplier for the most recent price. The supplier in turn uses a manual price sheet, which has been updated each day. Often, the supplier must call back Don's sales reps because the company does not have the newest pricing information immediately on hand. Assess the business impact of this situation, describe how this process could be improved with information technology, and identify the decisions that would have to be made to implement a solution.

2-9 Henry's Hardware is a small family business in Sacramento, California. The owners, Henry and Kathleen, must use every square foot of store space as profitably as possible. They have never kept detailed inventory or sales records. As soon as a shipment of goods arrives, the items are immediately placed on store shelves. Invoices from suppliers are only kept for tax purposes. When an item is sold, the item number and price are rung up at the cash register. The owners use their own judgment in identifying items that need to be reordered. What is the business impact of this situation? How could information systems help Henry and Kathleen run their business? What data should these systems capture? What decisions could the systems improve?

Improving Decision Making: Using a Spreadsheet to Select Suppliers

Software skills: Spreadsheet date functions, data filtering, DAVERAGE function
Business skills: Analyzing supplier performance and pricing

2-10 In this exercise, you will learn how to use spreadsheet software to improve management decisions about selecting suppliers. You will filter transactional data on suppliers based on several different criteria to select the best suppliers for your company.

You run a company that manufactures aircraft components. You have many competitors who are trying to offer lower prices and better service to customers, and you are trying to determine whether you can benefit from better supply chain management. In MyMISLab, you will find a spreadsheet file that contains a list of all of the items that your firm has ordered from its suppliers during the past three months. The fields in the spreadsheet file include vendor name, vendor identification number, purchaser's order number, item identification number and item description (for each item ordered from the vendor), cost per item, number of units of the item ordered (quantity), total cost of each order, vendor's accounts payable terms, order date, and actual arrival date for each order.

Prepare a recommendation of how you can use the data in this spreadsheet database to improve your decisions about selecting suppliers. Some criteria to consider for identifying preferred suppliers include the supplier's track record for on-time deliveries, suppliers offering the best accounts payable terms, and suppliers offering lower pricing when the same item can be provided by multiple suppliers. Use your spreadsheet software to prepare reports to support your recommendations.

Achieving Operational Excellence: Using Internet Software to Plan Efficient Transportation Routes

Software skills: Internet-based software
Business skills: Transportation planning

2-11 In this exercise, you will use MapQuest software to map out transportation routes for a business and select the most efficient route.

You have just started working as a dispatcher for Cross-Country Transport, a new trucking and delivery service based in Cleveland, Ohio. Your first assignment is to plan a delivery of office equipment and furniture from Elkhart, Indiana (at the corner of E. Indiana Ave. and Prairie Street), to Hagerstown, Maryland (corner of Eastern Blvd. N. and Potomac Ave.). To guide your trucker, you need to know the most efficient route between the two cities. Use MapQuest to find the route that is the shortest distance between the two cities. Use MapQuest again to find the route that takes the least time. Compare the results. Which route should Cross-Country use?

Collaboration and Teamwork Project

Identifying Management Decisions and Systems

2-12 With a team of three or four other students, find a description of a manager in a corporation in *Business Week, Forbes, Fortune,* the *Wall Street Journal,* or another business publication or do your research on the web. Gather information about what the manager does and the role he or she plays in the company. Identify the organizational level and business function where this manager works. Make a list of the kinds of decisions this manager has to make and the kind of information the manager would need for those decisions. Suggest how information systems could supply this information. If possible, use Google Docs and Google Drive or Google Sites to brainstorm, organize, and develop a presentation of your findings for the class.

Social Business: Full Speed Ahead or Proceed with Caution?

CASE STUDY

Many of today's employees are already well versed in the basics of public social networking using tools such as Facebook, Twitter, and Instagram. Larry Ellison, head of the giant software firm Oracle, even went so far as to declare that social networking should be the backbone of business applications and that Facebook is a good model for how business users should interact with software.

According to Gartner, Inc., 50 percent of large organizations will soon have internal Facebook-like social networks, and 30 percent of these will be considered as essential as e-mail and telephones are today. Enterprise social networks will become the primary communications channels for noticing, deciding on, or acting on information relevant to carrying out work. However, Gartner also notes that through 2015, 80 percent of social business efforts will not achieve the intended benefits due to inadequate leadership and an overemphasis on technology.

Social initiatives in a business are different from other technology deployments. For example, implementations of enterprise resource planning or customer relationship management systems are top-down: Workers are trained in the application and expected to use it. In contrast, social business tools require more of a "pull" approach, one that engages workers and offers them a significantly better way to work. In most cases, they can't be forced to use social apps.

When firms introduce new social media technology (as well as other technologies), employees often resist the new tools, clinging to old ways of working, such as e-mail, because they are more familiar and comfortable. There are companies where employees have duplicated communication on both social media and e-mail, increasing the time and cost of performing their jobs. BASF, the world's largest chemical producer with <u>subsidiaries</u> and <u>joint ventures</u> in more than 80 countries, prohibited some project teams from using e-mail to encourage employees to use new social media tools.

Social business requires a change in thinking, including the ability to view the organization in a flatter and more horizontal way. A social business is much more open to everyone's ideas. A secretary, assembly line worker, or sales clerk might be the source of the next big idea.

Social media's key capabilities for managing social networks and sharing digital content can help or hurt an organization. Social networks can provide rich and diverse sources of information that enhance organizational productivity, efficiency, and innovation, or they can be used to support preexisting groups of like-minded people which are reluctant to communicate and exchange knowledge with outsiders. Productivity and morale will fall if employees use internal social networks to criticize others or pursue personal agendas.

Social business applications modeled on consumer-facing platforms such as Facebook and Twitter will not necessarily work well in an organization that has different objectives. Will the firm use social business for operations, human resources, or innovation? The social media platform that will work best depends on its specific business purpose.

This means that instead of focusing on the technology, businesses should first identify how social initiatives will actually improve work practices for employees and managers. They need a detailed understanding of social networks: how people are currently working, with whom they are working, what their needs are, and measures for overcoming employee biases and resistance.

A successful social business strategy requires leadership and behavioral changes. Just sponsoring a social project is not enough—managers need to demonstrate their commitment to a more open, transparent work style. Employees who are used to collaborating and doing business in more traditional ways need an incentive to use social software. Changing an organization to work in a different way requires enlisting those most engaged and interested in helping and designing and building the right workplace environment for using social technologies.

Management needs to ensure that the internal and external social networking efforts of the company are providing genuine value to the business. Content on the networks needs to be relevant, up-to-date, and easy to access; users need to be able to connect to people who have the information they need and who would otherwise be out of reach or difficult to reach. Social business tools should be appropriate for the tasks at hand and the organization's business processes, and users need to understand how and why to use them. For example, in 2012 NASA's Goddard Space Flight Center had to abandon a custom-built enterprise social network called Spacebook because no one knew how its social tools would help people do their jobs. Spacebook was designed to help small teams collaborate without e-mailing larger groups, but very few users adopted it.

Despite the challenges associated with launching an internal social network, there are companies using these networks successfully. For example, Bayer Material Sciences, the $11.8 billion material sciences division of Bayer, made social collaboration a success by making the tools more accessible, demonstrating the value of these tools in pilot projects, employing a reverse mentoring program for senior executives, and training employee experts to spread know-how of the new social tools and approaches within the company and demonstrate their usefulness.

Bayer Material Sciences chose IBM Connections for its social business toolset. IBM Connections is a social platform for collaboration, cooperation, and consolidation typically used in a centralized enterprise social network. Featured are tools for employee profiles; communities of people with common interests and expertise; blogs; wikis; viewing, organizing, and managing tasks; forums for exchanging ideas with others; and polls and surveys of customers and fellow employees along with a home page for each user to see what is happening across that person's social network and access important social data.

A year after the new collaboration tools were introduced, adoption had plateaued. Working with company information technology and business leaders, management established an ambitious set of goals for growing social business along with seven key performance indicators (KPIs) to measure success. The goals included fostering global collaboration, creating stronger networks across regions and departments, creating a less hierarchical culture of sharing, and reducing the confusion of which tools are intended for which job.

These efforts are now paying off: 50 percent of employees are now routinely active in the company's enterprise social network. Although ROI on social business initiatives has been difficult to measure, Bayer Material Sciences has benefited from faster knowledge flows, increased efficiency, and lower operating costs.

Another company that has made social business work is Carlo's Bake Shop, an old family-owned business that is the star of the *Cake Boss* reality television series on the cable television network TLC. The company has 10 locations in New Jersey, New York, and Las Vegas, and people can order custom cakes from its website. Thanks to the popularity of *Cake Boss*, which created a huge upsurge in demand for Carlo's products, the firm is looking to create a national presence over the next few years.

However, store operations were holding the company back. Carlo's was heavily paper-based, and the mountain of paperwork wasted employee time and led to errors, which sometimes resulted in a need to fix or remake cakes or offer partial or total refunds to customers. Custom orders were on paper and carbon paper, order forms were misplaced or lost, and people couldn't read the handwriting from the order taker.

In the latter half of 2012, Carlo's implemented Salesforce CRM with the Salesforce social networking tool Chatter as a solution. Some employees and members of Carlo's management team initially resisted the new system. They believed that because they already used e-mail, Facebook, and Twitter, they didn't need another social tool. The company was able to demonstrate the benefits of social business, and bakers and Chatter changed the way they worked.

Carlo's produces a very large volume of custom cakes from a 75,000-square-foot commissary in Jersey City operating around the clock. Chatter is now the de facto standard for internal communication

from order to delivery. If a key cake decorator is away, that person is still included in the communication and discussion process. Upon returning, the decorator can view any changes in color, shape, or design.

Because Carlo's employees now work more socially, errors are down by more than 30 percent, and crews are able to produce cakes and other custom products more rapidly and efficiently. Managers have access to a data and analytics dashboard that allows them to instantly view store performance and which products are hot and which are not. They can see sales and transaction patterns in depth. As Carlo's expands nationally and perhaps globally, the ability to connect people and view order streams is critical. Social business tools have transformed an organization that was gradually sinking under the weight of paper into a highly efficient digital business.

Sources: Samuel Greengard, "Changing Your Business into a Social Business," Baseline, June 18, 2015; Cordelia Kroob, "The Growth of an Enterprise Social Network at BASF," www.simply-communicate.com, accessed March 12, 2016; Gerald C. Kane, "Enterprise Social Media: Current Capabilities and Future Possibilities," *MIS Quarterly Executive,* March 2015; Dion Hinchcliffe, "In Europe's Biggest Firms, Social Business Is All Grown Up," Enterprise Web 2.0, February 12, 2015; Margaret Jones, "Top Four Social Collaboration Software Fails," http://searchmobilecoputing.techtarget.com, accessed March 17, 2016; Gartner Inc., "Gartner Says 80 Percent of Social Business Efforts Will Not Achieve Intended Benefits Through 2015," January 29, 2013; and Michael Healey, "Why Enterprise Social Networking Falls Short," *Information Week,* March 4, 2013.

CASE STUDY QUESTIONS

2-13 Identify the management, organization, and technology factors responsible for impeding adoption of internal corporate social networks.

2-14 Compare the experiences implementing internal social networks of the two organizations described in this case. Why were they successful? What role did management play in this process?

2-15 Should all companies implement internal enterprise social networks? Why or why not?

MyMISLab

Go to the Assignments section of MyMISLab to complete these writing exercises.

2-16 Identify and describe the capabilities of enterprise social networking software. Describe how a firm could use each of these capabilities.

2-17 Describe the systems used by various management groups within the firm in terms of the information they use, their outputs, and groups served.

Chapter 2 References

Aral, Sinan, Erik Brynjolfsson, and Marshall Van Alstyne. "Productivity Effects of Information Diffusion in Networks," MIT Center for Digital Business (July 2007).

Banker, Rajiv D., Nan Hu, Paul A. Pavlou, and Jerry Luftman. "CIO Reporting Structure, Strategic Positioning, and Firm Performance." *MIS Quarterly* 35, No. 2 (June 2011).

Bernoff, Josh and Charlene Li. "Harnessing the Power of Social Applications." *MIT Sloan Management Review* (Spring 2008).

Boughzala, Imed and Gert-Jan De Vreede. "Evaluating Team Collaboration Quality: The Development and Field Application of a Collaboration Maturity Model." Journal of Management Information Systems 32 No. 3 (2015).

Bughin, Jacques, Michael Chui, and Martin Harrysson. "How Social Tools Can Reshape the Organization." McKinsey Global Institute (May 2016).

Bureau of Labor Statistics. "Occupational Outlook Handbook." Bureau of Labor Statistics (December 2015).

Compare Products. "Videoconferencing Trends of 2016." (2015).

Dimension Data. "2016 Connected Enterprise Report." (2016).

Forrester Consulting. "Total Economic Impact of IBM Social Collaboration Tools" (September 2010).

Forrester Research. "Social Business: Delivering Critical Business Value" (April 2012).

Frenkel, Karen A. "How the CIO's Role Will Change by 2018." *CIO Insight* (January 31, 2014).

Frost and Sullivan. "Meetings Around the World II: Charting the Course of Advanced Collaboration." (October 14, 2009).

Gast, Arne, and Raul Lansink. "Digital Hives: Creating a Surge Around Change." *McKinsey Quarterly* (April 2015).

Greengard, Samuel. "Collaboration: At the Center of Effective Business." *Baseline* (January 24, 2014).

_____. "The Social Business Gets Results." *Baseline* (June 19, 2014).

Guillemette, Manon G. and Guy Pare. "Toward a New Theory of the Contribution of the IT Function in Organizations." *MIS Quarterly* 36, No. 2 (June 2012).

Johnson, Bradford, James Manyika, and Lareina Yee. "The Next Revolution in Interactions," *McKinsey Quarterly* No. 4 (2005).

Kane, Gerald C. "Enterprise Social Media: Current Capabilities and Future Possibilities." *MIS Quarterly Executive* 14, No. 1 (2015).

Kane, Gerald C., Doug Palmer, Anh Nguyen Phillips, and David Kiron. "Finding the Value in Social Business. *MIT Sloan Management Review* 55, No. 3 (Spring 2014).

Kiron, David, Doug Palmer, Anh Nguyen Phillips, and Nina Kruschwitz. "What Managers Really Think About Social Business." *MIT Sloan Management Review* 53, No. 4 (Summer 2012).

Kolfschoten, Gwendolyn L., Fred Niederman, Robert O. Briggs, and Gert-Jan De Vreede. "Facilitation Roles and Responsibilities for Sustained Collaboration Support in Organizations." *Journal of Management Information Systems* 28, No. 4 (Spring 2012).

Li, Charlene. "Making the Business Case for Enterprise Social Networks." Altimeter Group (February 22, 2012).

Malone, Thomas M., Kevin Crowston, Jintae Lee, and Brian Pentland. "Tools for Inventing Organizations: Toward a Handbook of Organizational Processes." *Management Science* 45, No. 3 (March 1999).

Maruping, Likoebe M. and Massimo Magni. "Motivating Employees to Explore Collaboration Technology in Team Contexts." *MIS Quarterly* 39, No.1 (March 2015).

McKinsey & Company. "Transforming the Business Through Social Tools." (2015).

McKinsey Global Institute. "The Social Economy: Unlocking Value and Productivity Through Social Technologies." McKinsey & Company (July 2012).

Microsoft Corporation. "Customer Stories: Southern Valve." (January 18, 2015).

Mortensen, Mark. "Technology Alone Won't Solve Our Collaboration Problems." *Harvard Business Review* (March 26, 2015).

Poltrock, Steven and Mark Handel. "Models of Collaboration as the Foundation for Collaboration Technologies." *Journal of Management Information Systems* 27, No. 1 (Summer 2010).

Ricards, Tuck, Kate Smaje, and Vik Sohoni. "'Transformer in Chief': The New Chief Digital Officer." *McKinsey Digital* (September 2015).

Saunders, Carol, A. F. Rutkowski, Michiel van Genuchten, Doug Vogel, and Julio Molina Orrego. "Virtual Space and Place: Theory and Test." *MIS Quarterly* 35, No. 4 (December 2011).

Siebdrat, Frank, Martin Hoegl, and Holger Ernst. "How to Manage Virtual Teams." *MIT Sloan Management Review* 50, No. 4 (Summer 2009).

Tallon, Paul P., Ronald V.Ramirez, and James E. Short. "The Information Artifact in IT Governance: Toward a Theory of Information Governance." *Journal of Management Information Systems* 30, No. 3 (Winter 2014).

Violino, Bob. "What Is Driving the Need for Chief Data Officers?" *Information Management* (February 3, 2014).

Weill, Peter and Jeanne W. Ross. *IT Governance*. Boston: Harvard Business School Press (2004).

3

Information Systems, Organizations, and Strategy

Learning Objectives

After reading this chapter, you will be able to answer the following questions:

3-1 Which features of organizations do managers need to know about to build and use information systems successfully?

3-2 What is the impact of information systems on organizations?

3-3 How do Porter's competitive forces model, the value chain model, synergies, core competencies, and network economics help companies develop competitive strategies using information systems?

3-4 What are the challenges posed by strategic information systems, and how should they be addressed?

MyMISLab™

Visit **mymislab.com** for simulations, tutorials, and end-of-chapter problems.

CHAPTER CASES

Verizon or AT&T: Which Company Has the Best Digital Strategy?
Can Technology Replace Managers?
Smart Products, Smart Companies
Can Technology Save Sears?

VIDEO CASES

GE Becomes a Digital Firm: The Emerging Industrial Internet
National Basketball Association: Competing on Global Delivery with Akamai OS Streaming

Verizon or AT&T: Which Company Has the Best Digital Strategy?

Verizon and AT&T are the two largest telecommunications companies in the United States. Today their customers do much more than make phone calls. They use their wireless and landline networks to watch high-definition (HD) TV; surf the Internet; send e-mail, text, and video messages; share photos; listen to music; watch videos; and conduct video-conferences around the globe. All of these products and services are digital.

Competition in this industry is unusually intense. Both companies are trying to outflank one another by expanding the range of digital products and services offered to customers. But there are differences. AT&T is making a bet on satellite-based television, having purchased DirecTV in July 2015. Verizon is focusing more on wireless and recently launched its own standalone wireless video service.

AT&T hopes to profit by merging its U-verse suite of TV, Internet, and phone service based on a high-speed network into a common service and offering bundled satellite-cable TV and wireless services that rivals won't be able to match. It also

© Gajus/Fotolia

hopes to work out good deals with content companies, such as its multiyear agreement with Viacom for providing programming content for U-Verse and DirecTV. AT&T still needs its consumer wireless business (and is investing in upgrading its high-speed networks), but this part of the business is sagging because of increased competition. (T-Mobile US has lured away many customers with its low prices.) If AT&T's strategy works, it will become a computing company that manages all sorts of digital things—wireless phones, satellite television, and huge volumes of data—using software in remote online cloud computing centers.

Verizon is continuing to focus on its wireless business, in which it has been a leader for a number of years. Verizon has tried to blunt competition by boasting that its wireless network is the largest and most reliable in the United States. Now it is offering its own standalone wireless video service, which will help it generate revenue from mobile ads and video.

Although the smartphone market is peaking, users are spending more time on these mobile devices—about three hours per day for U.S. adults, according to eMarketer. Verizon sees mobile ads and video as an investment in the future and is beefing up its advertising and media business. It bought AOL, which has a digital ad business as well as web content sites such as Huffington Post, and it also purchased Go90, a free mobile video service that offers full episodes of TV shows such as *The Daily Show*, sports, news, and online video. Verizon hopes to generate revenue from mobile video by selling customers larger data packages to handle the data-intensive video. Verizon will also be able to capitalize on "pay-per-view" opportunities such as sports events and concerts and on targeted advertising using its ability to track what customers watch and read on their smartphones. By combining customer data from smartphones with advertising on AOL, Verizon may even be able to assemble an online advertising technology platform that competes with web giants such as Google and Facebook.

Sources: Ryan Knutson, "Verizon Swings to a Profit, but Pace of Growth Slows," *Wall Street Journal,* January 21, 2016; Douglas MacMillan and Ryan Knutson, "Verizon Tops Pack of Suitors Chasing Yahoo," *New York Times,* April 17, 2016; Thomas Gryta, "Verizon, AT&T Chart Different Paths," *Wall Street Journal,* October 19, 2015; eMarketer, "Growth of Time Spent on Mobile Devices Slows," October 7, 2015; and Tali Arbel, "Wireless Carrier Verizon Is Also in the Market for Eyeballs," Associated Press, October 20 2015.

The story of Verizon and AT&T illustrates some of the ways that information systems help businesses compete and also the challenges of sustaining a competitive advantage. The industry in which both companies operate is extremely crowded and competitive, with traditional telecommunications companies vying with cable companies, Internet services, mobile services, and each other to provide a wide array of digital services and content. To meet the challenges of surviving and prospering in this environment, each of these companies has adopted a different competitive strategy using information technology.

The chapter-opening diagram calls attention to important points raised by this case and this chapter. Both companies saw there were opportunities to use information technology to offer new products and services. AT&T forged a strategy based on combining satellite, high-speed cable TV, Internet, and wireless services to provide a superior package of services and content. Verizon is putting its money on mobile ads and video, with more emphasis on mining its customer data.

This case study also shows that it is difficult to sustain a competitive advantage. The market for online video is close to saturation, and Verizon's plan to track customers has been criticized by privacy advocates for its use of personal customer data. It is unclear how much low-cost rivals in the wireless market will lure away AT&T's and Verizon's customers.

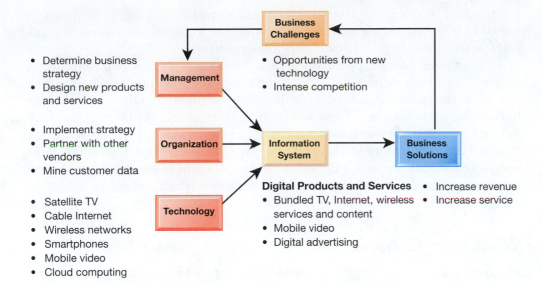

3-1 Which features of organizations do managers need to know about to build and use information systems successfully?

Information systems and organizations influence one another. Information systems are built by managers to serve the interests of the business firm. At the same time, the organization must be aware of and open to the influences of information systems to benefit from new technologies.

The interaction between information technology and organizations is complex and is influenced by many mediating factors, including the organization's structure, business processes, politics, culture, surrounding environment, and management decisions (see Figure 3.1). You will need to understand how

FIGURE 3.1   THE TWO-WAY RELATIONSHIP BETWEEN ORGANIZATIONS AND INFORMATION TECHNOLOGY

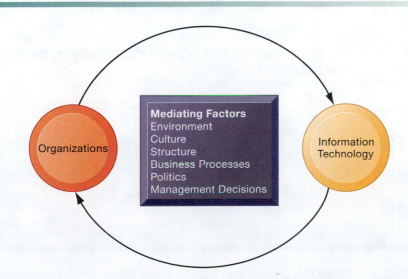

This complex two-way relationship is mediated by many factors, not the least of which are the decisions made—or not made—by managers. Other factors mediating the relationship include the organizational culture, structure, politics, business processes, and environment.

information systems can change social and work life in your firm. You will not be able to design new systems successfully or understand existing systems without understanding your own business organization.

As a manager, you will be the one to decide which systems will be built, what they will do, and how they will be implemented. You may not be able to anticipate all of the consequences of these decisions. Some of the changes that occur in business firms because of new information technology (IT) investments cannot be foreseen and have results that may or may not meet your expectations. Who would have imagined 15 years ago, for instance, that e-mail and instant messaging would become a dominant form of business communication and that many managers would be inundated with more than 200 e-mail messages each day?

What Is an Organization?

An **organization** is a stable, formal social structure that takes resources from the environment and processes them to produce outputs. This technical definition focuses on three elements of an organization. Capital and labor are primary production factors provided by the environment. The organization (the firm) transforms these inputs into products and services in a production function. The products and services are consumed by environments in return for supply inputs (see Figure 3.2).

An organization is more stable than an informal group (such as a group of friends that meets every Friday for lunch) in terms of longevity and routineness. Organizations are formal legal entities with internal rules and procedures that must abide by laws. Organizations are also social structures because they are a collection of social elements, much as a machine has a structure—a particular arrangement of valves, cams, shafts, and other parts.

This definition of organizations is powerful and simple, but it is not very descriptive or even predictive of real-world organizations. A more realistic behavioral definition of an organization is a collection of rights, privileges, obligations, and responsibilities delicately balanced over a period of time through conflict and conflict resolution (see Figure 3.3).

In this behavioral view of the firm, people who work in organizations develop customary ways of working; they gain attachments to existing relationships;

FIGURE 3.2   THE TECHNICAL MICROECONOMIC DEFINITION OF THE ORGANIZATION

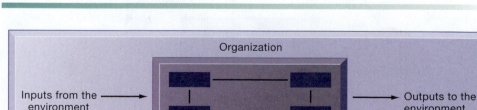

In the microeconomic definition of organizations, capital and labor (the primary production factors provided by the environment) are transformed by the firm through the production process into products and services (outputs to the environment). The products and services are consumed by the environment, which supplies additional capital and labor as inputs in the feedback loop.

FIGURE 3.3   THE BEHAVIORAL VIEW OF ORGANIZATIONS

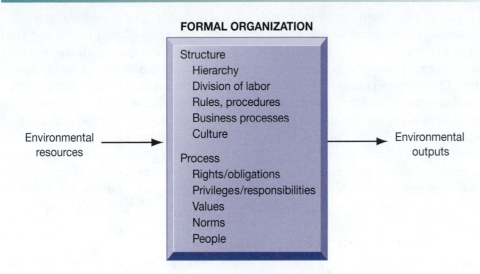

FORMAL ORGANIZATION

Structure
  Hierarchy
  Division of labor
  Rules, procedures
  Business processes
  Culture

Process
  Rights/obligations
  Privileges/responsibilities
  Values
  Norms
  People

Environmental resources →   → Environmental outputs

The behavioral view of organizations emphasizes group relationships, values, and structures.

and they make arrangements with subordinates and superiors about how work will be done, the amount of work that will be done, and under what conditions work will be done. Most of these arrangements and feelings are not discussed in any formal rulebook.

How do these definitions of organizations relate to information systems technology? A technical view of organizations encourages us to focus on how inputs are combined to create outputs when technology changes are introduced into the company. The firm is seen as infinitely malleable, with capital and labor substituting for each other quite easily. But the more realistic behavioral definition of an organization suggests that building new information systems, or rebuilding old ones, involves much more than a technical rearrangement of machines or workers—that some information systems change the organizational balance of rights, privileges, obligations, responsibilities, and feelings that have been established over a long period of time.

Changing these elements can take a long time, be very disruptive, and requires more resources to support training and learning. For instance, the length of time required to implement a new information system effectively is much longer than usually anticipated simply because there is a lag between implementing a technical system and teaching employees and managers how to use the system.

Technological change requires changes in who owns and controls information, who has the right to access and update that information, and who makes decisions about whom, when, and how. This more complex view forces us to look at the way work is designed and the procedures used to achieve outputs.

The technical and behavioral definitions of organizations are not contradictory. Indeed, they complement each other: The technical definition tells us how thousands of firms in competitive markets combine capital, labor, and information technology, whereas the behavioral model takes us inside the individual firm to see how that technology affects the organization's inner workings. Section 3-2 describes how each of these definitions of organizations can help explain the relationships between information systems and organizations.

Features of Organizations

All modern organizations share certain characteristics. They are bureaucracies with clear-cut divisions of labor and specialization. Organizations arrange specialists in a hierarchy of authority in which everyone is accountable to someone and authority is limited to specific actions governed by abstract rules or procedures. These rules create a system of impartial and universal decision making. Organizations try to hire and promote employees on the basis of technical qualifications and professionalism (not personal connections). The organization is devoted to the principle of efficiency: maximizing output using limited inputs. Other features of organizations include their business processes, organizational culture, organizational politics, surrounding environments, structure, goals, constituencies, and leadership styles. All of these features affect the kinds of information systems used by organizations.

Routines and Business Processes

All organizations, including business firms, become very efficient over time because individuals in the firm develop **routines** for producing goods and services. Routines—sometimes called *standard operating procedures*—are precise rules, procedures, and practices that have been developed to cope with virtually all expected situations. As employees learn these routines, they become highly productive and efficient, and the firm is able to reduce its costs over time as efficiency increases. For instance, when you visit a doctor's office, receptionists have a well-developed set of routines for gathering basic information from you, nurses have a different set of routines for preparing you for an interview with a doctor, and the doctor has a well-developed set of routines for diagnosing you. *Business processes*, which we introduced in Chapters 1 and 2, are collections of such routines. A business firm, in turn, is a collection of business processes (Figure 3.4).

Organizational Politics

People in organizations occupy different positions with different specialties, concerns, and perspectives. As a result, they naturally have divergent viewpoints about how resources, rewards, and punishments should be distributed. These differences matter to both managers and employees, and they result in political struggle for resources, competition, and conflict within every organization. Political resistance is one of the great difficulties of bringing about organizational change—especially the development of new information systems. Virtually all large information systems investments by a firm that bring about significant changes in strategy, business objectives, business processes, and procedures become politically charged events. Managers who know how to work with the politics of an organization will be more successful than less-skilled managers in implementing new information systems. Throughout this book, you will find many examples where internal politics defeated the best-laid plans for an information system.

Organizational Culture

All organizations have bedrock, unassailable, unquestioned (by the members) assumptions that define their goals and products. Organizational culture encompasses this set of assumptions about what products the organization should produce, how it should produce them, where, and for whom. Generally, these cultural assumptions are taken totally for granted and are rarely publicly announced or discussed. Business processes—the actual way business firms produce value—are usually ensconced in the organization's culture.

FIGURE 3.4   ROUTINES, BUSINESS PROCESSES, AND FIRMS

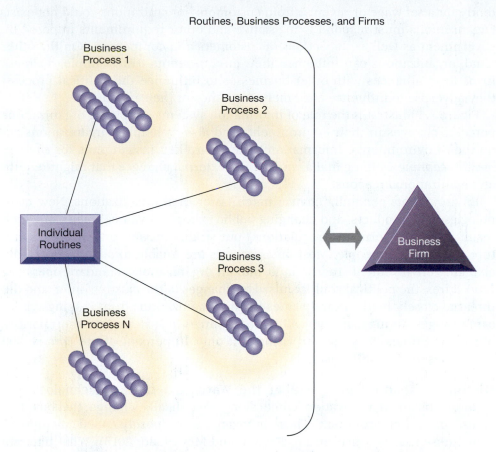

Routines, Business Processes, and Firms

All organizations are composed of individual routines and behaviors, a collection of which make up a business process. A collection of business processes make up the business firm. New information system applications require that individual routines and business processes change to achieve high levels of organizational performance.

You can see organizational culture at work by looking around your university or college. Some bedrock assumptions of university life are that professors know more than students, the reason students attend college is to learn, and classes follow a regular schedule. Organizational culture is a powerful unifying force that restrains political conflict and promotes common understanding, agreement on procedures, and common practices. If we all share the same basic cultural assumptions, agreement on other matters is more likely.

At the same time, organizational culture is a powerful restraint on change, especially technological change. Most organizations will do almost anything to avoid making changes in basic assumptions. Any technological change that threatens commonly held cultural assumptions usually meets a great deal of resistance. However, there are times when the only sensible way for a firm to move forward is to employ a new technology that directly opposes an existing organizational culture. When this occurs, the technology is often stalled while the culture slowly adjusts.

Organizational Environments

Organizations reside in environments from which they draw resources and to which they supply goods and services. Organizations and environments have a reciprocal relationship. On the one hand, organizations are open to and dependent on the social and physical environment that surrounds them. Without financial and human resources—people willing to work reliably and consistently for a set wage or revenue from customers—organizations could not exist. Organizations must respond to legislative and other requirements imposed by government as well as the actions of customers and competitors. On the other hand, organizations can influence their environments. For example, business firms form alliances with other businesses to influence the political process; they advertise to influence customer acceptance of their products.

Figure 3.5 illustrates the role of information systems in helping organizations perceive changes in their environments and also in helping organizations act on their environments. Information systems are key instruments for *environmental scanning*, helping managers identify external changes that might require an organizational response.

Environments generally change much faster than organizations. New technologies, new products, and changing public tastes and values (many of which result in new government regulations) put strains on any organization's culture, politics, and people. Most organizations are unable to adapt to a rapidly changing environment. Inertia built into an organization's standard operating procedures, the political conflict raised by changes to the existing order, and the threat to closely held cultural values inhibit organizations from making significant changes. Young firms typically lack resources to sustain even short periods of troubled times. It is not surprising that only 10 percent of the *Fortune* 500 companies in 1919 still exist today.

Disruptive Technologies: Riding the Wave Sometimes a technology and resulting business innovation come along to radically change the business landscape and environment. These innovations are loosely called "disruptive" (Christensen, 2003; Christensen, Raynor, and McDonald, 2015). What makes a

FIGURE 3.5   ENVIRONMENTS AND ORGANIZATIONS HAVE A RECIPROCAL RELATIONSHIP

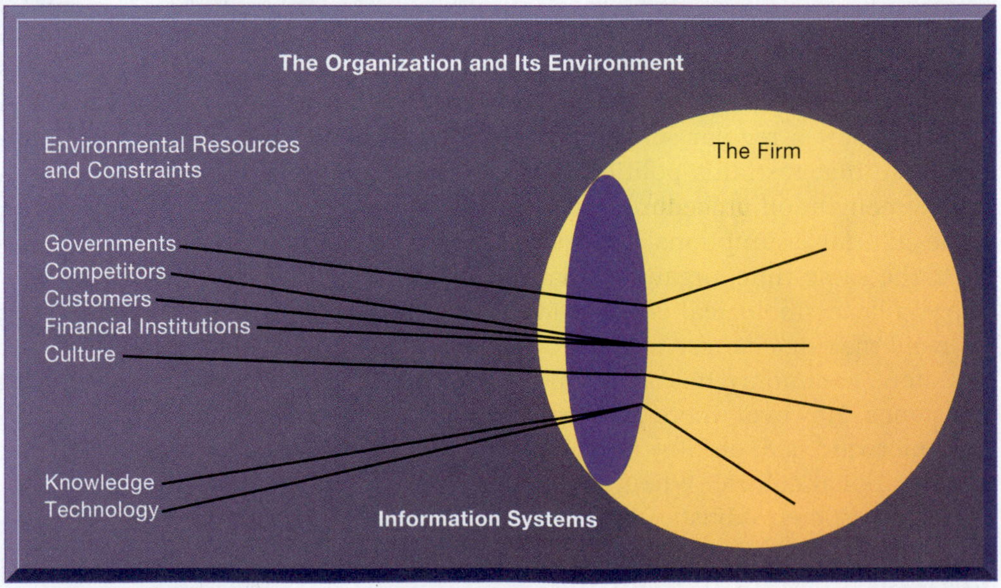

Environments shape what organizations can do, but organizations can influence their environments and decide to change environments altogether. Information technology plays a critical role in helping organizations perceive environmental change and in helping organizations act on their environment.

technology disruptive? In some cases, **disruptive technologies** are substitute products that perform as well as or better (often much better) than anything currently produced. The car substituted for the horse-drawn carriage, the word processor for typewriters, the Apple iPod for portable CD players, and digital photography for process film photography. Table 3.1 describes just a few disruptive technologies from the past.

In these cases, entire industries were put out of business. In other cases, disruptive technologies simply extend the market, usually with less functionality and much less cost than existing products. Eventually they turn into low-cost competitors for whatever was sold before. Disk drives are an example: Small hard disk drives used in PCs extended the market for disk drives by offering cheap digital storage for small files. Eventually, small PC hard disk drives became the largest segment of the disk drive marketplace.

Some firms are able to create these technologies and ride the wave to profits; others learn quickly and adapt their business; still others are obliterated because their products, services, and business models become obsolete. They may be very efficient at doing what no longer needs to be done! There are also cases where no firms benefit and all the gains go to consumers (firms fail to capture any profits). Moreover, not all change or technology is disruptive (King and Baatartogtokh, 2015). Managers of older businesses often do make the right decisions and find ways to continue competing. Disruptive technologies are tricky. Firms that invent disruptive technologies as "first movers" do not always benefit if they lack the resources to exploit the technology or fail to see the opportunity. The MITS Altair 8800 is widely regarded as the first PC, but its inventors did not take advantage of their first mover status. Second movers, so-called "fast

TABLE 3.1 DISRUPTIVE TECHNOLOGIES: WINNERS AND LOSERS

TECHNOLOGY	DESCRIPTION	WINNERS AND LOSERS
Microprocessor chips (1971)	Thousands and eventually millions of transistors on a silicon chip	Microprocessor firms win (Intel, Texas Instruments), while transistor firms (GE) decline.
Personal computers (1975)	Small, inexpensive, but fully functional desktop computers	PC manufacturers (HP, Apple, IBM) and chip manufacturers prosper (Intel), while mainframe (IBM) and minicomputer (DEC) firms lose.
Digital photography (1975)	Using CCD (charge-coupled device) image sensor chips to record images	CCD manufacturers and traditional camera companies win; manufacturers of film products lose.
World Wide Web (1989)	A global database of digital files and "pages" instantly available	Owners of online content and news benefit, while traditional publishers (newspapers, magazines, and broadcast television) lose.
Internet music, video, TV services (1998)	Repositories of downloadable music, video, TV broadcasts on the web	Owners of Internet platforms, telecommunications providers owning Internet backbone (ATT, Verizon), and local Internet service providers win, while content owners and physical retailers (Tower Records, Blockbuster) lose.
PageRank algorithm	A method for ranking web pages in terms of their popularity to supplement web search by key terms	Google is the winner (it owns the patent), while traditional key word search engines (Alta Vista) lose.
Software as web service	Using the Internet to provide remote access to online software	Online software services companies (Salesforce.com) win, while traditional "boxed" software companies (Microsoft, SAP, Oracle) lose.

followers," such as IBM and Microsoft, reaped the rewards. Citibank's ATMs revolutionized retail banking, but they were copied by other banks. Now all banks use ATMs, with the benefits going mostly to the consumers.

Organizational Structure

All organizations have a structure or shape. Mintzberg's classification, described in Table 3.2, identifies five basic kinds of organizational structure (Mintzberg, 1971).

The kind of information systems you find in a business firm—and the nature of problems with these systems—often reflects the type of organizational structure. For instance, in a professional bureaucracy such as a hospital, it is not unusual to find parallel patient record systems operated by the administration, another by doctors, and another by other professional staff such as nurses and social workers. In small entrepreneurial firms, you will often find poorly designed systems developed in a rush that often quickly outgrow their usefulness. In huge multidivisional firms operating in hundreds of locations, you will often find there is not a single integrating information system, but instead each locale or each division has its set of information systems.

Other Organizational Features

Organizations have goals and use different means to achieve them. Some organizations have coercive goals (e.g., prisons); others have utilitarian goals (e.g., businesses). Still others have normative goals (universities, religious groups). Organizations also serve different groups or have different constituencies, some primarily benefiting their members, others benefiting clients, stockholders, or the public. The nature of leadership differs greatly from one organization to another—some organizations may be more democratic or authoritarian than others. Another way organizations differ is by the tasks they perform and the technology they use. Some organizations perform primarily

TABLE 3.2 ORGANIZATIONAL STRUCTURES

ORGANIZATIONAL TYPE	DESCRIPTION	EXAMPLES
Entrepreneurial structure	Young, small firm in a fast-changing environment. It has a simple structure and is managed by an entrepreneur serving as its single chief executive officer.	Small start-up business
Machine bureaucracy	Large bureaucracy existing in a slowly changing environment, producing standard products. It is dominated by a centralized management team and centralized decision making.	Midsize manufacturing firm
Divisionalized bureaucracy	Combination of multiple machine bureaucracies, each producing a different product or service, all topped by one central headquarters.	*Fortune* 500 firms, such as General Motors
Professional bureaucracy	Knowledge-based organization where goods and services depend on the expertise and knowledge of professionals. Dominated by department heads with weak centralized authority.	Law firms, school systems, hospitals
Adhocracy	Task force organization that must respond to rapidly changing environments. Consists of large groups of specialists organized into short-lived multidisciplinary teams and has weak central management.	Consulting firms, such as the Rand Corporation

routine tasks that can be reduced to formal rules that require little judgment (such as manufacturing auto parts), whereas others (such as consulting firms) work primarily with nonroutine tasks.

3-2   What is the impact of information systems on organizations?

Information systems have become integral, online, interactive tools deeply involved in the minute-to-minute operations and decision making of large organizations. Over the past decade, information systems have fundamentally altered the economics of organizations and greatly increased the possibilities for organizing work. Theories and concepts from economics and sociology help us understand the changes brought about by IT.

Economic Impacts

From the point of view of economics, IT changes both the relative costs of capital and the costs of information. Information systems technology can be viewed as a factor of production that can be substituted for traditional capital and labor. As the cost of information technology decreases, it is substituted for labor, which historically has been a rising cost. Hence, information technology should result in a decline in the number of middle managers and clerical workers as information technology substitutes for their labor.

As the cost of information technology decreases, it also substitutes for other forms of capital such as buildings and machinery, which remain relatively expensive. Hence, over time we should expect managers to increase their investments in IT because of its declining cost relative to other capital investments.

IT also affects the cost and quality of information and changes the economics of information. Information technology helps firms contract in size because it can reduce transaction costs—the costs incurred when a firm buys on the marketplace what it cannot make itself. According to **transaction cost theory**, firms and individuals seek to economize on transaction costs, much as they do on production costs. Using markets is expensive because of costs such as locating and communicating with distant suppliers, monitoring contract compliance, buying insurance, obtaining information on products, and so forth (Coase, 1937; Williamson, 1985). Traditionally, firms have tried to reduce transaction costs through vertical integration, by getting bigger, hiring more employees, and buying their own suppliers and distributors, as both General Motors and Ford used to do.

Information technology, especially the use of networks, can help firms lower the cost of market participation (transaction costs), making it worthwhile for firms to contract with external suppliers instead of using internal sources. As a result, firms can shrink in size (numbers of employees) because it is far less expensive to outsource work to a competitive marketplace rather than hire employees.

For instance, by using computer links to external suppliers, automakers such as Chrysler, Toyota, and Honda can achieve economies by obtaining more than 70 percent of their parts from the outside. Information systems make it possible for companies such as Cisco Systems and Dell Inc. to outsource their production to contract manufacturers such as Flextronics instead of making their products themselves.

As transaction costs decrease, firm size (the number of employees) should shrink because it becomes easier and cheaper for the firm to contract for the purchase of goods and services in the marketplace rather than to make the product or offer the service itself. Firm size can stay constant or contract even as the company increases its revenues. For example, when Eastman Chemical Company split off from Kodak in 1994, it had $3.3 billion in revenue and 24,000 full-time employees. In 2015, it generated more than $9.6 billion in revenue with only 15,000 employees.

Information technology also can reduce internal management costs. According to **agency theory**, the firm is viewed as a "nexus of contracts" among self-interested individuals rather than as a unified, profit-maximizing entity (Jensen and Meckling, 1976). A principal (owner) employs "agents" (employees) to perform work on his or her behalf. However, agents need constant supervision and management; otherwise, they will tend to pursue their own interests rather than those of the owners. As firms grow in size and scope, agency costs or coordination costs rise because owners must expend more and more effort supervising and managing employees.

Information technology, by reducing the costs of acquiring and analyzing information, permits organizations to reduce agency costs because it becomes easier for managers to oversee a greater number of employees. By reducing overall management costs, information technology enables firms to increase revenues while shrinking the number of middle managers and clerical workers. We have seen examples in earlier chapters where information technology expanded the power and scope of small organizations by enabling them to perform coordinating activities such as processing orders or keeping track of inventory with very few clerks and managers.

Because IT reduces both agency and transaction costs for firms, we should expect firm size to shrink over time as more capital is invested in IT. Firms should have fewer managers, and we expect to see revenue per employee increase over time.

Organizational and Behavioral Impacts

Theories based in the sociology of complex organizations also provide some understanding about how and why firms change with the implementation of new IT applications.

IT Flattens Organizations

Large, bureaucratic organizations, which primarily developed before the computer age, are often inefficient, slow to change, and less competitive than newly created organizations. Some of these large organizations have downsized, reducing the number of employees and the number of levels in their organizational hierarchies.

Behavioral researchers have theorized that information technology facilitates flattening of hierarchies by broadening the distribution of information to empower lower-level employees and increase management efficiency (see Figure 3.6). IT pushes decision-making rights lower in the organization because lower-level employees receive the information they need to make decisions without supervision. (This empowerment is also possible because of higher educational levels among the workforce, which give employees the capabilities to make intelligent decisions.) Because managers now receive so much more accurate information on time, they become much faster at making decisions, so fewer managers are required. Management costs decline as a percentage of revenues, and the hierarchy becomes much more efficient.

These changes mean that the management span of control has also been broadened, enabling high-level managers to manage and control more workers

FIGURE 3.6   FLATTENING ORGANIZATIONS

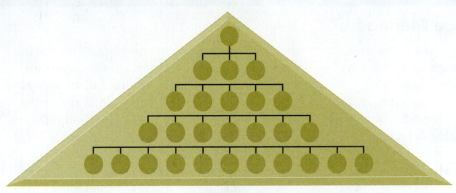

A traditional hierarchical organization with many levels of management

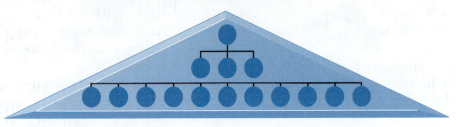

An organization that has been "flattened" by removing layers of management

Information systems can reduce the number of levels in an organization by providing managers with information to supervise larger numbers of workers and by giving lower-level employees more decision-making authority.

spread over greater distances. Many companies have eliminated thousands of middle managers as a result of these changes.

Postindustrial Organizations

Postindustrial theories based more on history and sociology than economics also support the notion that IT should flatten hierarchies. In postindustrial societies, authority increasingly relies on knowledge and competence and not merely on formal positions. Hence, the shape of organizations flattens because professional workers tend to be self-managing, and decision making should become more decentralized as knowledge and information become more widespread throughout the firm.

Information technology may encourage task force–networked organizations in which groups of professionals come together—face-to-face or electronically— for short periods of time to accomplish a specific task (e.g., designing a new automobile); once the task is accomplished, the individuals join other task forces. The global consulting service Accenture is an example. Many of its 373,000 employees move from location to location to work on projects at client locations in more than 56 different countries.

Who makes sure that self-managed teams do not head off in the wrong direction? Who decides which person works on which team and for how long? How can managers evaluate the performance of someone who is constantly rotating from team to team? How do people know where their careers are headed? New approaches for evaluating, organizing, and informing workers are required, and not all companies can make virtual work effective, as described in the Interactive Session on Management.

INTERACTIVE SESSION: MANAGEMENT

Can Technology Replace Managers?

Start-up companies are known for being innovative, and one of those innovations appears to be the way they are being managed. A number of these new firms are trying to minimize headcount and maximize agility by eliminating management hierarchy. In place of managers, they're turning to technology, including user-friendly software and low-cost web-based services such as Amazon.com's Redshift for storing corporate data, analyzing the data, and presenting the results in the form of dashboards that anyone in the firm can use. In the past such data were difficult to obtain, required more senior managers to organize and interpret, or could not be analyzed without expensive business intelligence systems costing millions of dollars. Today even small start-ups can afford to store and manipulate nearly limitless pools of data in near real time.

For example, Chubbies, a rapidly growing clothing start-up targeting college fraternities, doesn't have a CEO. Instead, it has four co-CEOs, each in charge of his or her own business function. This structure is repeated all the way down the company's hierarchy. All Chubbies employees have access to the same data as its top managers. According to Tom Montgomery, one of the Chubbies co-CEOs, when you don't have a traditional CEO and final decision maker, you have to trust people to make the right decisions based on the information they see. Although it takes time to build up that trust, once you do, the company can move much more quickly.

Montgomery points out that in the past, an associate specializing in events for clients might report to a manager in the marketing department in charge of thinking about why the company should be throwing events in the first place. Today, the event planner working alone can use an array of dashboards to determine exactly how many Facebook likes, Instagram posts, and sales arose from a particular event, and she is able to decide on her own whether future events should be scheduled. With the right data and tools to back up her decision, she doesn't need a manager to validate her choices.

Web retailer Zappos.com Inc. announced in 2013 that it was eliminating managers in order to keep the 1,500-person company from becoming too rigid, too unwieldy, and too bureaucratic as it grows. Zappos adopted a "holocracy" model in which workers manage themselves without the aid of middle managers. In contrast to a traditional corporate chain of command, holocracy organizes the business as a series of overlapping, self-governing "circles." Instead of having jobs, holocracies have "roles." Each role belongs to a circle rather than a department. The circles overlap, and individuals hold many different roles. Individuals assigned roles in these circles work together, and their meeting outcomes are recorded using web-based software called Glass Frog. This system allows anyone in the company to view who's responsible for what role and what they're working on. Glass Frog provides a "to-do" list that teams use to define the work they're supposed to be doing and to hold themselves accountable for those tasks.

Although Zappos CEO Tony Hsieh continues to trumpet self-management, it is unclear if employees widely share his enthusiasm. Some employees welcomed the opportunity for more independence. With experience and expertise downplayed, less senior employees with fresh ideas receive more attention. Introverts have benefited from the expectation that everybody speak in meetings. Other employees were confused and frustrated by numerous mandates, endless meetings, and uncertainty about who did what. To whom would they report to if there were no bosses? What was expected of them if they did not have a job title, and how would they be compensated? Within weeks after Zappos embraced holocracy, about 14 percent of employees had left the company. The employee exodus has continued. Zappos's turnover rate for 2015 was 30 percent, 10 percentage points above its typical annual attrition rate.

Treehouse Island Inc., a Portland, Oregon, online coding school, also had a flat organization. Staff worked four-day weeks, worked only on projects they liked, rarely had to send e-mail, and had no direct bosses. However, the business grew, with about 100,000 students enrolled in its online courses and 100 employees. Some projects weren't being completed, and employees were unsure of their responsibilities. Treehouse wasn't burdened by bureaucracy, but work still stalled nevertheless. Without managers to coordinate projects and supervise and encourage workers, Treehouse employees weren't as productive as they could have been. According to Treehouse founder Ryan Carson, there was no real reason to work hard because no one knew about it. Some of Treehouse's best employees started believing that not as much was expected of them.

Questions about which subjects to teach would spark much analysis and chatter but resulted in few answers or plans. Michael Watson, who headed Treehouse finance and operations, estimated that decisions about matters such as Treehouse's website design took twice as long as they should have.

Treehouse partially reversed course in the spring of 2015. Employees still work four-day weeks, but they now have managers. Since that change was made, revenue has increased along with the number of minutes of video courses the company produces. The time required for customer support employees to respond to students who have questions has dropped to three and a half hours from seven

hours. With roles now clearly defined and managers tracking assignments, e-mail is actually enhancing productivity.

According to Quy Huy, professor of strategy at the Singapore campus of the prestigious graduate business school Insead, middle managers are often vilified as symptoms of corporate bloat, but things fall apart without them.

Sources: David Gelles, "The Zappos Exodus Continues After a Radical Management Experiment," *New York Times*, January 13, 2016; Bourree Lam, "Why Are So Many Zappos Employees Leaving?" *The Atlantic*, January 15, 2016; Christopher Mims, "Data Is the New Middle Manager," *Wall Street Journal*, April 19, 2015; and Rachel Feintzeig, "Radical Idea at the Office: Middle Managers," *Wall Street Journal*, April 18, 2015.

CASE STUDY QUESTIONS

1. How do flat organizations differ from traditional bureaucratic hierarchies?

2. How has information technology made it possible to eliminate middle manager positions?

3. What management, organization, and technology issues would you consider if you wanted to move

from a traditional bureaucracy to a flatter organization?

4. Can technology replace managers? Explain your answer.

Understanding Organizational Resistance to Change

Information systems inevitably become bound up in organizational politics because they influence access to a key resource—namely, information. Information systems can affect who does what to whom, when, where, and how in an organization. Many new information systems require changes in personal, individual routines that can be painful for those involved and require retraining and additional effort that may or may not be compensated. Because information systems potentially change an organization's structure, culture, business processes, and strategy, there is often considerable resistance to them when they are introduced.

There are several ways to visualize organizational resistance. Research on organizational resistance to innovation suggests that four factors are paramount: the nature of the IT innovation, the organization's structure, the culture of people in the organization, and the tasks affected by the innovation (see Figure 3.7). Here, changes in technology are absorbed, interpreted, deflected, and defeated by organizational task arrangements, structures, and people. In this model, the only way to bring about change is to change the technology, tasks, structure, and people simultaneously. Other authors have spoken about the need to "unfreeze" organizations before introducing an innovation, quickly implementing it, and "refreezing" or institutionalizing the change (Kolb and Frohman, 1970).

Because organizational resistance to change is so powerful, many information technology investments flounder and do not increase productivity. Indeed, research on project implementation failures demonstrates that the most common reason for failure of large projects to reach their objectives is not the

FIGURE 3.7   ORGANIZATIONAL RESISTANCE TO INFORMATION SYSTEM INNOVATIONS

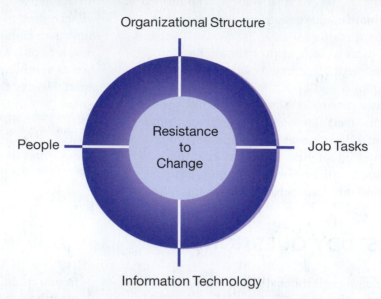

Implementing information systems has consequences for task arrangements, structures, and people. According to this model, to implement change, all four components must be changed simultaneously.

failure of the technology but organizational and political resistance to change. Chapter 14 treats this issue in detail. Therefore, as a manager involved in future IT investments, your ability to work with people and organizations is just as important as your technical awareness and knowledge.

The Internet and Organizations

The Internet, especially the World Wide Web, has an important impact on the relationships between many firms and external entities and even on the organization of business processes inside a firm. The Internet increases the accessibility, storage, and distribution of information and knowledge for organizations. In essence, the Internet is capable of dramatically lowering the transaction and agency costs facing most organizations. For instance, brokerage firms and banks in New York can now deliver their internal operating procedures manuals to their employees at distant locations by posting them on the corporate website, saving millions of dollars in distribution costs. A global sales force can receive nearly instant product price information updates using the web or instructions from management sent by e-mail or text messaging on smartphones or mobile laptops. Vendors of some large retailers can access retailers' internal websites directly to find up-to-the-minute sales information and to initiate replenishment orders instantly.

Businesses are rapidly rebuilding some of their key business processes based on Internet technology and making this technology a key component of their IT infrastructures. If prior networking is any guide, one result will be simpler business processes, fewer employees, and much flatter organizations than in the past.

Implications for the Design and Understanding of Information Systems

To deliver genuine benefits, information systems must be built with a clear understanding of the organization in which they will be used. In our experience, the central organizational factors to consider when planning a new system are the following:

- The environment in which the organization must function
- The structure of the organization: hierarchy, specialization, routines, and business processes
- The organization's culture and politics
- The type of organization and its style of leadership
- The principal interest groups affected by the system and the attitudes of workers who will be using the system
- The kinds of tasks, decisions, and business processes that the information system is designed to assist

3-3 How do Porter's competitive forces model, the value chain model, synergies, core competencies, and network economics help companies develop competitive strategies using information systems?

In almost every industry you examine, you will find that some firms do better than most others. There's almost always a standout firm. In the automotive industry, Toyota is considered a superior performer. In pure online retail, Amazon is the leader; in off-line retail, Walmart, the largest retailer on earth, is the leader. In online music, Apple's iTunes is considered the leader with more than 60 percent of the downloaded music market, and in the related industry of digital music players, the iPod is the leader. In web search, Google is considered the leader.

Firms that "do better" than others are said to have a competitive advantage over others: They either have access to special resources that others do not, or they are able to use commonly available resources more efficiently—usually because of superior knowledge and information assets. In any event, they do better in terms of revenue growth, profitability, or productivity growth (efficiency), all of which ultimately in the long run translate into higher stock market valuations than their competitors.

But why do some firms do better than others, and how do they achieve competitive advantage? How can you analyze a business and identify its strategic advantages? How can you develop a strategic advantage for your own business? And how do information systems contribute to strategic advantages? One answer to that question is Michael Porter's competitive forces model.

Porter's Competitive Forces Model

Arguably, the most widely used model for understanding competitive advantage is Michael Porter's **competitive forces model** (see Figure 3.8). This model provides a general view of the firm, its competitors, and the firm's environment. Earlier in this chapter, we described the importance of a firm's environment and the dependence of firms on environments. Porter's model is all about the firm's general business environment. In this model, five competitive forces shape the fate of the firm.

FIGURE 3.8   PORTER'S COMPETITIVE FORCES MODEL

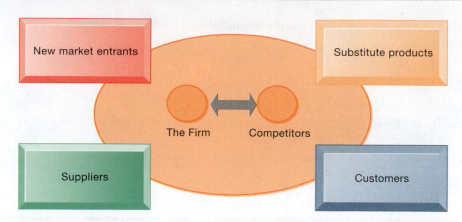

In Porter's competitive forces model, the strategic position of the firm and its strategies are determined not only by competition with its traditional direct competitors but also by four other forces in the industry's environment: new market entrants, substitute products, customers, and suppliers.

Traditional Competitors

All firms share market space with other competitors who are continuously devising new, more efficient ways to produce by introducing new products and services, and attempting to attract customers by developing their brands and imposing switching costs on their customers.

New Market Entrants

In a free economy with mobile labor and financial resources, new companies are always entering the marketplace. In some industries, there are very low barriers to entry, whereas in other industries, entry is very difficult. For instance, it is fairly easy to start a pizza business or just about any small retail business, but it is much more expensive and difficult to enter the computer chip business, which has very high capital costs and requires significant expertise and knowledge that are hard to obtain. New companies have several possible advantages: They are not locked into old plants and equipment, they often hire younger workers who are less expensive and perhaps more innovative, they are not encumbered by old worn-out brand names, and they are "more hungry" (more highly motivated) than traditional occupants of an industry. These advantages are also their weakness: They depend on outside financing for new plants and equipment, which can be expensive; they have a less-experienced workforce; and they have little brand recognition.

Substitute Products and Services

In just about every industry, there are substitutes that your customers might use if your prices become too high. New technologies create new substitutes all the time. Ethanol can substitute for gasoline in cars; vegetable oil for diesel fuel in trucks; and wind, solar, coal, and hydro power for industrial electricity generation. Likewise, Internet and wireless telephone service can substitute for traditional telephone service. And, of course, an Internet music service that allows you to download music tracks to an iPod or smartphone has become a substitute for CD-based music stores. The more substitute products and services in your industry, the less you can control pricing and the lower your profit margins.

Customers

A profitable company depends in large measure on its ability to attract and retain customers (while denying them to competitors) and charge high prices. The power of customers grows if they can easily switch to a competitor's products and services or if they can force a business and its competitors to compete on price alone in a transparent marketplace where there is little **product differentiation** and all prices are known instantly (such as on the Internet). For instance, in the used college textbook market on the Internet, students (customers) can find multiple suppliers of just about any current college textbook. In this case, online customers have extraordinary power over used-book firms.

Suppliers

The market power of suppliers can have a significant impact on firm profits, especially when the firm cannot raise prices as fast as can suppliers. The more different suppliers a firm has, the greater control it can exercise over suppliers in terms of price, quality, and delivery schedules. For instance, manufacturers of laptop PCs almost always have multiple competing suppliers of key components, such as keyboards, hard drives, and display screens.

Information System Strategies for Dealing with Competitive Forces

What is a firm to do when it is faced with all these competitive forces? And how can the firm use information systems to counteract some of these forces? How do you prevent substitutes and inhibit new market entrants? There are four generic strategies, each of which often is enabled by using information technology and systems: low-cost leadership, product differentiation, focus on market niche, and strengthening customer and supplier intimacy.

© Betty LaRue/Alamy Stock Photo

Supermarkets and large retail stores such as Walmart use sales data captured at the checkout counter to determine which items have sold and need to be reordered. Walmart's continuous replenishment system transmits orders to restock directly to its suppliers. The system enables Walmart to keep costs low while fine-tuning its merchandise to meet customer demands.

Low-Cost Leadership

Use information systems to achieve the lowest operational costs and the lowest prices. The classic example is Walmart. By keeping prices low and shelves well stocked using a legendary inventory replenishment system, Walmart became the leading retail business in the United States. Walmart's continuous replenishment system sends orders for new merchandise directly to suppliers as soon as consumers pay for their purchases at the cash register. Point-of-sale terminals record the bar code of each item passing the checkout counter and send a purchase transaction directly to a central computer at Walmart headquarters. The computer collects the orders from all Walmart stores and transmits them to suppliers. Suppliers can also access Walmart's sales and inventory data using web technology.

Because the system replenishes inventory with lightning speed, Walmart does not need to spend much money on maintaining large inventories of goods in its own warehouses. The system also enables Walmart to adjust purchases of store items to meet customer demands. Competitors, such as Sears, have been spending 24.9 percent of sales on overhead. But by using systems to keep operating costs low, Walmart pays only 16.6 percent of sales revenue for overhead. (Operating costs average 20.7 percent of sales in the retail industry.)

Walmart's continuous replenishment system is also an example of an **efficient customer response system**. An efficient customer response system directly links consumer behavior to distribution and production and supply chains. Walmart's continuous replenishment system provides such an efficient customer response.

Product Differentiation

Use information systems to enable new products and services or greatly change the customer convenience in using your existing products and services. For instance, Google continuously introduces new and unique search services on its website, such as Google Maps. By purchasing PayPal, an electronic payment system, in 2003, eBay made it much easier for customers to pay sellers and expanded use of its auction marketplace. Apple created the iPod, a unique portable digital music player, plus iTunes, an online music store where songs can be purchased for $0.69 to $1.29 each. Apple has continued to innovate with its multimedia iPhone, iPad tablet computer, and iPod video player.

Manufacturers and retailers are using information systems to create products and services that are customized and personalized to fit the precise specifications of individual customers. For example, Nike sells customized sneakers through its NIKEiD program on its website. Customers are able to select the type of shoe, colors, material, outsoles, and even a logo of up to eight characters. Nike transmits the orders via computers to specially equipped plants in China and Korea. The sneakers take about three weeks to reach the customer. This ability to offer individually tailored products or services using the same production resources as mass production is called **mass customization**.

Table 3.3 lists a number of companies that have developed IT-based products and services that other firms have found difficult to copy—or at least taken a long time to copy.

Focus on Market Niche

Use information systems to enable a specific market focus and serve this narrow target market better than competitors. Information systems support this strategy by producing and analyzing data for finely tuned sales and

TABLE 3.3   IT-ENABLED NEW PRODUCTS AND SERVICES PROVIDING COMPETITIVE ADVANTAGE

Amazon: One-click shopping	Amazon holds a patent on one-click shopping that it licenses to other online retailers.
Online music: Apple iPod and iTunes	The iPod is an integrated handheld player backed up with an online library of more than 43 million songs.
Golf club customization: Ping	Customers can select from more than 1 million different golf club options; a build-to-order system ships their customized clubs within 48 hours.
Online person-to-person payment: PayPal	PayPal enables the transfer of money between individual bank accounts and between bank accounts and credit card accounts.

marketing techniques. Information systems enable companies to analyze customer buying patterns, tastes, and preferences closely so that they efficiently pitch advertising and marketing campaigns to smaller and smaller target markets.

The data come from a range of sources—credit card transactions, demographic data, purchase data from checkout counter scanners at supermarkets and retail stores, and data collected when people access and interact with websites. Sophisticated software tools find patterns in these large pools of data and infer rules from them to guide decision making. Analysis of such data drives one-to-one marketing that creates personal messages based on individualized preferences. For example, Hilton Hotels' OnQ system analyzes detailed data collected on active guests in all of its properties to determine the preferences of each guest and each guest's profitability. Hilton uses this information to give its most profitable customers additional privileges, such as late checkouts. Contemporary customer relationship management (CRM) systems feature analytical capabilities for this type of intensive data analysis (see Chapters 2 and 9).

Credit card companies are able to use this strategy to predict their most profitable cardholders. The companies gather vast quantities of data about consumer purchases and other behaviors and mine these data to construct detailed profiles that identify cardholders who might be good or bad credit risks. We discuss the tools and technologies for data analysis in Chapters 6 and 12.

Strengthen Customer and Supplier Intimacy

Use information systems to tighten linkages with suppliers and develop intimacy with customers. Chrysler Corporation uses information systems to facilitate direct access by suppliers to production schedules and even permits suppliers to decide how and when to ship supplies to Chrysler factories. This allows suppliers more lead time in producing goods. On the customer side, Amazon keeps track of user preferences for book and CD purchases and can recommend titles purchased by others to its customers. Strong linkages to customers and suppliers increase **switching costs** (the cost of switching from one product to a competing product) and loyalty to your firm.

Table 3.4 summarizes the competitive strategies we have just described. Some companies focus on one of these strategies, but you will often see companies pursuing several of them simultaneously. For example, Starbucks, the world's largest specialty coffee retailer, offers unique high-end specialty coffees and beverages but is also trying to compete by lowering costs.

TABLE 3.4 FOUR BASIC COMPETITIVE STRATEGIES

STRATEGY	DESCRIPTION	EXAMPLE
Low-cost leadership	Use information systems to produce products and services at a lower price than competitors while enhancing quality and level of service	Walmart
Product differentiation	Use information systems to differentiate products, and enable new services and products	Uber, Nike, Apple
Focus on market niche	Use information systems to enable a focused strategy on a single market niche; specialize	Hilton Hotels, Harrah's
Customer and supplier intimacy	Use information systems to develop strong ties and loyalty with customers and suppliers	Toyota Corporation, Amazon

The Internet's Impact on Competitive Advantage

Because of the Internet, the traditional competitive forces are still at work, but competitive rivalry has become much more intense (Porter, 2001). Internet technology is based on universal standards that any company can use, making it easy for rivals to compete on price alone and for new competitors to enter the market. Because information is available to everyone, the Internet raises the bargaining power of customers, who can quickly find the lowest-cost provider on the web. Profits have been dampened. Table 3.5 summarizes some of the potentially negative impacts of the Internet on business firms identified by Porter.

The Internet has nearly destroyed some industries and has severely threatened more. For instance, the printed encyclopedia industry and the travel agency industry have been nearly decimated by the availability of substitutes over the Internet. Likewise, the Internet has had a significant impact on the

TABLE 3.5   IMPACT OF THE INTERNET ON COMPETITIVE FORCES AND INDUSTRY STRUCTURE

COMPETITIVE FORCE	IMPACT OF THE INTERNET
Substitute products or services	Enables new substitutes to emerge with new approaches to meeting needs and performing functions
Customers' bargaining power	Availability of global price and product information shifts bargaining power to customers
Suppliers' bargaining power	Procurement over the Internet tends to raise bargaining power over suppliers; suppliers can also benefit from reduced barriers to entry and from the elimination of distributors and other intermediaries standing between them and their users
Threat of new entrants	Internet reduces barriers to entry, such as the need for a sales force, access to channels, and physical assets; it provides a technology for driving business processes that makes other things easier to do
Positioning and rivalry among existing competitors	Widens the geographic market, increasing the number of competitors and reducing differences among competitors; makes it more difficult to sustain operational advantages; puts pressure to compete on price

retail, music, book, retail brokerage, software, telecommunications, and newspaper industries.

However, the Internet has also created entirely new markets; formed the basis for thousands of new products, services, and business models; and provided new opportunities for building brands with very large and loyal customer bases. Amazon, eBay, iTunes, YouTube, Facebook, Travelocity, and Google are examples. In this sense, the Internet is "transforming" entire industries, forcing firms to change how they do business.

Smart Products and the Internet of Things

The growing use of sensors in industrial and consumer products, often called the Internet of Things (IoT), is an excellent example of how the Internet is changing competition within industries and creating new products and services. Nike, Under Armour, Gatorade, and many other sports and fitness companies are pouring money into wearable health trackers and fitness equipment that use sensors to report users' activities to remote corporate computing centers where the data can be analyzed (see the Interactive Session on Technology). John Deere tractors are loaded with field radar, GPS transceivers, and hundreds of sensors keeping track of the equipment, as described in the Chapter 1 ending case. GE is creating a new business out of helping its aircraft and wind turbine clients improve operations by examining the data generated from the many thousands of sensors in the equipment (see the Chapter 12 ending case). The result is what are referred to as "smart products"—products that are a part of a larger set of information-intensive services sold by firms (Gandhi and Gervet, 2016; Davis, 2015; Porter and Heppelmann, 2014; Iansiti and Lakhani, 2014).

The impact of smart, Internet-connected products is just now being understood. Smart products offer new functionality, greater reliability, and more intense use of products while providing detailed information that can be used to improve both the products and the customer experience. They expand opportunities for product and service differentiation. When you buy a wearable digital health product, you not only get the product itself, you also get a host of services available from the manufacturer's cloud servers. Smart products increase rivalry among firms that will either innovate or lose customers to competitors. Smart products generally raise switching costs and inhibit new entrants to a market because existing customers are trapped in the dominant firm's software environment. Finally, smart products may decrease the power of suppliers of industrial components if, as many believe, the physical product becomes less important than the software and hardware that make it run.

The Business Value Chain Model

Although the Porter model is very helpful for identifying competitive forces and suggesting generic strategies, it is not very specific about what exactly to do, and it does not provide a methodology to follow for achieving competitive advantages. If your goal is to achieve operational excellence, where do you start? Here's where the business value chain model is helpful.

The **value chain model** highlights specific activities in the business where competitive strategies can best be applied (Porter, 1985) and where information systems are most likely to have a strategic impact. This model identifies specific, critical leverage points where a firm can use information technology most effectively to enhance its competitive position. The value chain model views the firm as a series or chain of basic activities that add a margin of value

INTERACTIVE SESSION: TECHNOLOGY

Smart Products, Smart Companies

If you don't use a smart product yet, you soon will. Your shoes, your clothing, your watch, your water bottle, and even your toothbrush are being redesigned to incorporate sensors and metering devices connected to the Internet so that their performance can be monitored and analyzed.

What difference does that make? Take Nike, the world's biggest sports footwear and apparel company. Nike has created a series of information technology–based products and an ecosystem of gadgets and services built around measurable personal improvement through exercise. The Nike + ecosystem links Nike's corporate computer system to smart devices such as the Nike + SportWatch GPS, the Nike + FuelBand, and the Nike + Running App on Apple and Android mobile devices. This enables Nike to analyze individual performance and activity data collected by the devices to help users train and work out more effectively. It also adds value to Nike products and a reason to stay with the brand.

The Nike + SportWatch GPS keeps track of your location, pace, distance, laps, calories burned, and (with the Polar Wearlink +) heart rate. The Nike + Running App tracks your route, distance, pace, calories burned, and time using your phone or another Nike-partnered device, giving you audio feedback as you run. The Nike + FuelBand activity tracker is worn on the wrist and used with an Apple iPhone or iPad. The FuelBand enables wearers to track their physical activity, steps taken daily, and amount of calories burned. The information it collects is integrated into the Nike + online community and phone application, allowing wearers to set their own fitness goals, monitor their progress on the device LED display, and compare themselves to others within the Nike community.

Nike's proprietary software turns all tracked movement from Nike's smart devices into NikeFuel points, which can show achievements, can be shared with friends, or can be used to engage others in competition. NikeFuel is Nike's universal way for measuring movement for all kinds of activities using a metric that enables comparisons—no matter what height, weight, gender, or activity—to past performance, another person, or a daily average (which Nike defines as 2,000 Fuel points.) Users of multiple Nike + devices can visit the nikeplus.com site to access all their data—including lifetime NikeFuel points accumulated from all their Nike + devices.

Nike is developing other fitness technology products to integrate with Nike + . The more people measure their activity with NikeFuel, the more they are locked in to the Nike ecosystem and the harder it will be to switch to other companies' products. Nike's integration of information and technology into its products keeps people coming back to Nike's own website and apps.

Nike believes technology is revolutionizing its relationship with consumers, turning it into a company that provides services as well as products. In the past, when you bought a product, that was the end of the relationship with the company. Now, the purchase of any Nike product has become the beginning of the company's relationship with the consumer. The deeper the relationship, the more consumers will embrace and stay loyal to the Nike brand.

Under Armour, noted for performance clothing using technologically advanced material, is making its products smarter as well. The company has spent $710 million to scoop up mobile apps such as MyFitnessPal, MapMyFitness, and Endomondo, which enable it to tap into the world's largest digital health and fitness community. Under Armour can generate revenue from in-app ads, including ads from other companies, and purchases from app users referred to its products. The platform delivers unprecedented depth of information and insight about fitness-and health-oriented consumers, creating numerous opportunities for Under Armour and other brands to engage with potential and existing customers. For example, MapMyFitness collects data about a user's name, e-mail address, birth date, location, performance, and profile if the user connects to the app using social media. Under Armour does not sell identifiable personal data about individuals to third parties but does provide advertisers with aggregate information about app users. Under Armour is hoping that daily use of its smartphone apps will build stronger ties to customers that will lead to stronger sales of its own apparel, footwear, and other athletic gear.

Under Armour has teamed up with e-commerce retailer Zappos to send users a pop-up notification when their sneakers need replacement, based on workout data logged in MapMyFitness apps. Under

Armour sees clothes themselves eventually becoming the means to track movement and biorhythms. Under Armour developed its own smart footwear called UA SpeedForm Gemini 2 Record Equipped, which tracks a runner's time and date, duration, distance, and splits without the need for other devices. The company also partnered with HTC to develop UA HealthBox, a $400 red box that includes a Wi-Fi scale (for measuring weight and body fat), a heart rate chest strap and removable sensor, and a shower-proof dimpled fitness band to track workouts and sleep. The data these devices collect are stored on an Under Armor Record app on an iPhone or Android phone.

Gatorade, with a 78 percent share of the $7.21 billion sports-drinks market, is developing a microchip-fitted "smart cap" bottle that communicates digitally with a bandage-like sweat patch to provide athletes and fitness buffs constant updates on how much they should drink. According to Gatorade, individual hydration needs differ, with sweat loss ranging from half a liter to more than two liters per hour of exercise. The company is planning to launch as many as a dozen different formulas for electrolytes and carbohydrates in small pods that snap on to bottles.

Gatorade began testing the smart-cap bottle with Brazil's national soccer team ahead of the 2014 World Cup and is testing a new version with the Boston Celtics basketball team and FC Barcelona soccer squad. In the field-tested prototypes, flashing lights tell players when they need to hydrate. Users can customize the smart caps with their name, team logo, and number.

According to Xavi Cortadellas, Gatorade senior director of global innovation and design, personalized nutrition and integrating technology in sports are the next frontier of performance. Gatorade's parent company, PepsiCo, is actively attempting to expand into areas outside of sugary sodas, and such technology-enabled products provide opportunities.

Sources: Kate Taylor, "Gatorade Is Developing a 'Smart Cap' That Keeps Track of Hydration," *Business Insider*, March 21, 2016; Mike Esterl, "Gatorade Sets Its Sights on Digital Fitness," *Wall Street Journal*, March 10, 2016; Edward C. Baig, "Under Armour and HTC Team Up on Connected Fitness," *USA Today*, January 5, 2016; www.underarmour.com, accessed April 20, 2016; www.nike.com, accessed April 19, 2016; John Kell, "Why Under Armour Is Making a Costly Bet on Connected Fitness," *Fortune*, April 21, 2016; and Jared Linzdon, "The Rise and Fall of Wearable Fitness Trackers," *The Globe and Mail*, January 5, 2015.

CASE STUDY QUESTIONS

1. What competitive strategies are the companies discussed in this case pursuing?
2. How are information technology and smart products related to these strategies? Describe the role of information technology in these products.
3. Are there any ethical issues raised by these smart products such as their impact on consumer privacy? Explain your answer.

to a firm's products or services. These activities can be categorized as either primary activities or support activities (see Figure 3.9).

Primary activities are most directly related to the production and distribution of the firm's products and services, which create value for the customer. Primary activities include inbound logistics, operations, outbound logistics, sales and marketing, and service. Inbound logistics includes receiving and storing materials for distribution to production. Operations transforms inputs into finished products. Outbound logistics entails storing and distributing finished products. Sales and marketing includes promoting and selling the firm's products. The service activity includes maintenance and repair of the firm's goods and services.

Support activities make the delivery of the primary activities possible and consist of organization infrastructure (administration and management), human resources (employee recruiting, hiring, and training), technology (improving products and the production process), and procurement (purchasing input).

FIGURE 3.9 THE VALUE CHAIN MODEL

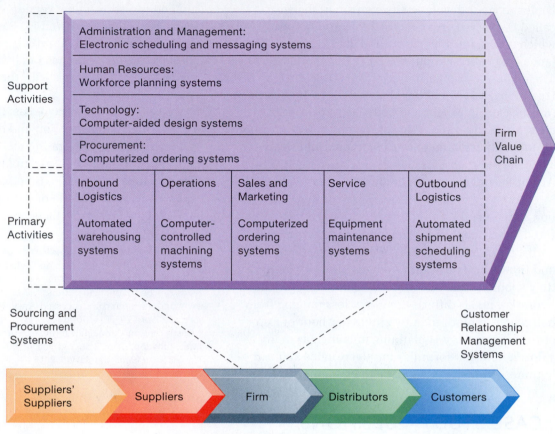

This figure provides examples of systems for both primary and support activities of a firm and of its value partners that can add a margin of value to a firm's products or services.

Now you can ask at each stage of the value chain, "How can we use information systems to improve operational efficiency and improve customer and supplier intimacy?" This will force you to critically examine how you perform value-adding activities at each stage and how the business processes might be improved. You can also begin to ask how information systems can be used to improve the relationship with customers and with suppliers who lie outside the firm's value chain but belong to the firm's extended value chain where they are absolutely critical to your success. Here, supply chain management systems that coordinate the flow of resources into your firm and customer relationship management systems that coordinate your sales and support employees with customers are two of the most common system applications that result from a business value chain analysis. We discuss these enterprise applications in detail later in Chapter 9.

Using the business value chain model will also cause you to consider benchmarking your business processes against your competitors or others in related industries and identifying industry best practices. **Benchmarking** involves comparing the efficiency and effectiveness of your business processes against strict standards and then measuring performance against those standards. Industry **best practices** are usually identified by consulting companies, research organizations, government agencies, and industry associations as the most successful solutions or problem-solving methods for consistently and effectively achieving a business objective.

Once you have analyzed the various stages in the value chain at your business, you can come up with candidate applications of information systems. Then, once you have a list of candidate applications, you can decide which to develop first. By making improvements in your own business value chain that your competitors might miss, you can achieve competitive advantage by attaining operational excellence, lowering costs, improving profit margins, and forging a closer relationship with customers and suppliers. If your competitors are making similar improvements, then at least you will not be at a competitive disadvantage—the worst of all cases!

Extending the Value Chain: The Value Web

Figure 3.9 shows that a firm's value chain is linked to the value chains of its suppliers, distributors, and customers. After all, the performance of most firms depends not only on what goes on inside a firm but also on how well the firm coordinates with direct and indirect suppliers, delivery firms (logistics partners, such as FedEx or UPS), and, of course, customers.

How can information systems be used to achieve strategic advantage at the industry level? By working with other firms, industry participants can use information technology to develop industrywide standards for exchanging information or business transactions electronically, which force all market participants to subscribe to similar standards. Such efforts increase efficiency, making product substitution less likely and perhaps raising entry costs—thus discouraging new entrants. Also, industry members can build industrywide, IT-supported consortia, symposia, and communications networks to coordinate activities concerning government agencies, foreign competition, and competing industries.

Looking at the industry value chain encourages you to think about how to use information systems to link up more efficiently with your suppliers, strategic partners, and customers. Strategic advantage derives from your ability to relate your value chain to the value chains of other partners in the process. For instance, if you are Amazon.com, you want to build systems that:

- Make it easy for suppliers to display goods and open stores on the Amazon site
- Make it easy for customers to pay for goods
- Develop systems that coordinate the shipment of goods to customers
- Develop shipment tracking systems for customers

Internet technology has made it possible to create highly synchronized industry value chains called value webs. A **value web** is a collection of independent firms that use information technology to coordinate their value chains to produce a product or service for a market collectively. It is more customer driven and operates in a less linear fashion than the traditional value chain.

Figure 3.10 shows that this value web synchronizes the business processes of customers, suppliers, and trading partners among different companies in an industry or in related industries. These value webs are flexible and adaptive to changes in supply and demand. Relationships can be bundled or unbundled in response to changing market conditions. Firms will accelerate time to market and to customers by optimizing their value web relationships to make quick decisions on who can deliver the required products or services at the right price and location.

FIGURE 3.10 THE VALUE WEB

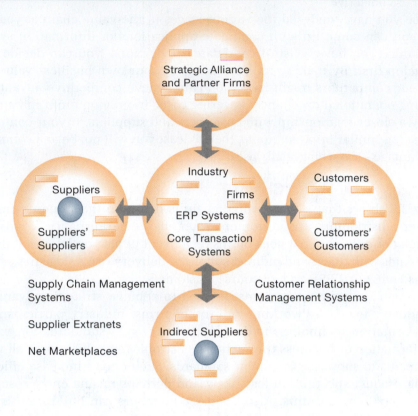

The value web is a networked system that can synchronize the value chains of business partners within an industry to respond rapidly to changes in supply and demand.

Synergies, Core Competencies, and Network-Based Strategies

A large corporation is typically a collection of businesses. Often, the firm is organized financially as a collection of strategic business units and the returns to the firm are directly tied to the performance of all the strategic business units. Information systems can improve the overall performance of these business units by promoting synergies and core competencies.

Synergies

The idea of synergies is that when the output of some units can be used as inputs to other units or two organizations pool markets and expertise, these relationships lower costs and generate profits. Bank and financial firm mergers such as the merger of JPMorgan Chase and Bank of New York as well as Bank of America and Countrywide Financial Corporation occurred precisely for this purpose.

One use of information technology in these synergy situations is to tie together the operations of disparate business units so that they can act as a whole. For example, acquiring Countrywide Financial enabled Bank of America to extend its mortgage lending business and to tap into a large pool of new customers who might be interested in its credit card, consumer banking, and other financial products. Information systems would help the merged companies consolidate operations, lower retailing costs, and increase cross-marketing of financial products.

Enhancing Core Competencies

Yet another way to use information systems for competitive advantage is to think about ways that systems can enhance core competencies. The argument is that the performance of all business units will increase insofar as these business units develop, or create, a central core of competencies. A **core competency** is an activity for which a firm is a world-class leader. Core competencies may involve being the world's best miniature parts designer, the best package delivery service, or the best thin-film manufacturer. In general, a core competency relies on knowledge that is gained over many years of practical field experience with a technology. This practical knowledge is typically supplemented with a long-term research effort and committed employees.

Any information system that encourages the sharing of knowledge across business units enhances competency. Such systems might encourage or enhance existing competencies and help employees become aware of new external knowledge; such systems might also help a business leverage existing competencies to related markets.

For example, Procter & Gamble, a world leader in brand management and consumer product innovation, uses a series of systems to enhance its core competencies. An intranet called InnovationNet helps people working on similar problems share ideas and expertise. InnovationNet connects those working in research and development (R&D), engineering, purchasing, marketing, legal affairs, and business information systems around the world, using a portal to provide browser-based access to documents, reports, charts, videos, and other data from various sources. It includes a directory of subject matter experts who can be tapped to give advice or collaborate on problem solving and product development and links to outside research scientists and entrepreneurs who are searching for new, innovative products worldwide.

Network-Based Strategies

The availability of Internet and networking technology has inspired strategies that take advantage of firms' abilities to create networks or network with each other. Network-based strategies include the use of network economics, a virtual company model, and business ecosystems.

Network Economics **Network economics** refers to market situations where the economic value being produced depends on the number of people using a product. For certain products and markets, the real economic value comes from the fact that other people use the product. In these situations, "network effects" are at work. For instance, what's the value of a telephone if it is not connected to millions of others? Email has value because it allows us to communicate with millions of others. Business models which are based on network effects have been highly successful on the Internet, including social networks, software, messaging apps, and on-demand companies like Uber and Airbnb.

In traditional economics—the economics of factories and agriculture—production experiences diminishing returns. The more any given resource is applied to production, the lower the marginal gain in output, until a point is reached where the additional inputs produce no additional outputs. This is the law of diminishing returns, and it is the foundation for most of modern economics.

In some situations, the law of diminishing returns does not work. For instance, in a network, the marginal costs of adding another participant are about zero, whereas the marginal gain is much larger. The larger the number of subscribers in a telephone system or the Internet, the greater the value to all participants because each user can interact with more people. It is not much more expensive to operate a television station with 1,000 subscribers than with 10 million subscribers. The value of a community of people grows with size, whereas the cost of adding new members is inconsequential. The value of Facebook to users increases greatly as more people use the social network.

From this network economics perspective, information technology can be strategically useful. Internet sites can be used by firms to build communities of users—like-minded customers who want to share their experiences. This builds customer loyalty and enjoyment and builds unique ties to customers. eBay, the giant online auction site, is an example. This business is based on a network of millions of users, and has built an online community by using the Internet. The more people offering products on eBay, the more valuable the eBay site is to everyone because more products are listed, and more competition among suppliers lowers prices. Network economics also provides strategic benefits to commercial software vendors. The value of their software and complementary software products increases as more people use them, and there is a larger installed base to justify continued use of the product and vendor support.

Virtual Company Model Another network-based strategy uses the model of a virtual company to create a competitive business. A **virtual company**, also known as a virtual organization, uses networks to link people, assets, and ideas, enabling it to ally with other companies to create and distribute products and services without being limited by traditional organizational boundaries or physical locations. One company can use the capabilities of another company without being organizationally tied to that company. The virtual company model is useful when a company finds it cheaper to acquire products, services, or capabilities from an external vendor or when it needs to move quickly to exploit new market opportunities and lacks the time and resources to respond on its own.

Fashion companies, such as GUESS, Ann Taylor, Levi Strauss, and Reebok, enlist Hong Kong–based Li & Fung to manage production and shipment of their garments. Li & Fung handles product development, raw material sourcing, production planning, quality assurance, and shipping. Li & Fung does not own any fabric, factories, or machines, outsourcing all of its work to a network of more than 15,000 suppliers in 40 countries all over the world. Customers place orders with Li & Fung over its private extranet. Li & Fung then sends instructions to appropriate raw material suppliers and factories where the clothing is produced. The Li & Fung extranet tracks the entire production process for each order. Working as a virtual company keeps Li & Fung flexible and adaptable so that it can design and produce the products ordered by its clients in short order to keep pace with rapidly changing fashion trends.

Business Ecosystems and Platforms The Internet and the emergence of digital firms call for some modification of the industry competitive forces model. The traditional Porter model assumes a relatively static industry environment; relatively clear-cut industry boundaries; and a relatively stable set of suppliers, substitutes, and customers, with the focus on industry players in a market environment. Instead of participating in a single industry, some of today's firms are much more aware that they participate in industry sets—collections of industries that provide related services and products (see Figure 3.11). **Business ecosystem** is another term for these loosely coupled but interdependent networks of suppliers, distributors, outsourcing firms, transportation service firms, and technology manufacturers (Iansiti and Levien, 2004).

FIGURE 3.11 AN ECOSYSTEM STRATEGIC MODEL

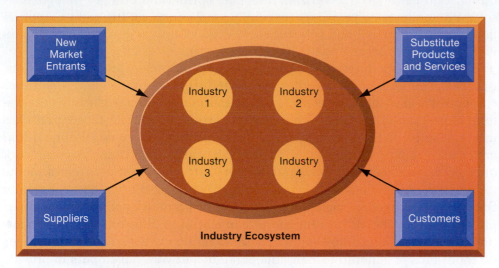

The digital firm era requires a more dynamic view of the boundaries among industries, firms, customers, and suppliers, with competition occurring among industry sets in a business ecosystem. In the ecosystem model, multiple industries work together to deliver value to the customer. IT plays an important role in enabling a dense network of interactions among the participating firms.

The concept of a business ecosystem builds on the idea of the value web described earlier, the main difference being that cooperation takes place across many industries rather than many firms. For instance, both Microsoft and Facebook provide **platforms** composed of information systems, technologies, and services that thousands of other firms in different industries use to enhance their own capabilities (Van Alstyne et al., 2016).

Microsoft has estimated that more than 40,000 firms use its Windows platform to deliver their own products, support Microsoft products, and extend the value of Microsoft's own firm. Facebook is a platform used by billions of people and millions of businesses to interact and share information as well as to buy, market, and sell numerous products and services. Business ecosystems can be characterized as having one or a few keystone firms that dominate the ecosystem and create the platforms used by other niche firms. Keystone firms in the Microsoft ecosystem include Microsoft and technology producers such as Intel and IBM. Niche firms include thousands of software application firms, software developers, service firms, networking firms, and consulting firms that both support and rely on the Microsoft products.

Information technology plays a powerful role in establishing business ecosystems. Obviously, many firms use information systems to develop into keystone firms by building IT-based platforms that other firms can use. In the digital firm era, we can expect greater emphasis on the use of IT to build industry ecosystems because the costs of participating in such ecosystems will fall and the benefits to all firms will increase rapidly as the platform grows.

Individual firms should consider how their information systems will enable them to become profitable niche players in larger ecosystems created by keystone firms. For instance, in making decisions about which products to build or which services to offer, a firm should consider the existing business ecosystems related to these products and how it might use IT to enable participation in these larger ecosystems.

A powerful, current example of a rapidly expanding ecosystem is the mobile Internet platform. In this ecosystem there are four industries: device makers

(Apple iPhone, Samsung Galaxy, Motorola, LG, and others), wireless telecommunication firms (AT&T, Verizon, T-Mobile, Sprint, and others), independent software applications providers (generally small firms selling games, applications, and ring tones), and Internet service providers (who participate as providers of Internet service to the mobile platform).

Each of these industries has its own history, interests, and driving forces. But these elements come together in a sometimes cooperative and sometimes competitive new industry we refer to as the mobile digital platform ecosystem. More than other firms, Apple has managed to combine these industries into a system. It is Apple's mission to sell physical devices (iPhones) that are nearly as powerful as yesterday's supercomputers. These devices work only with a high-speed broadband network supplied by the wireless phone carriers. In order to attract a large customer base, the iPhone had to be more than just a cell phone. Apple differentiated this product by making it a "smart phone," one capable of running more than a million different, useful applications. Apple could not develop all these applications itself. Instead, it relies on thousands of generally small, independent software developers to provide these applications, which can be purchased at the iTunes store. In the background is the Internet service provider industry, which makes money whenever iPhone users connect to the Internet. These four different industries together form an ecosystem, creating value for consumers that none of them could acting alone.

3-4 What are the challenges posed by strategic information systems, and how should they be addressed?

Strategic information systems often change the organization as well as its products, services, and operating procedures, driving the organization into new behavioral patterns. Successfully using information systems to achieve a competitive advantage is challenging and requires precise coordination of technology, organizations, and management.

Sustaining Competitive Advantage

The competitive advantages that strategic systems confer do not necessarily last long enough to ensure long-term profitability. Because competitors can retaliate and copy strategic systems, competitive advantage is not always sustainable. Markets, customer expectations, and technology change; globalization has made these changes even more rapid and unpredictable. The Internet can make competitive advantage disappear very quickly because virtually all companies can use this technology. Classic strategic systems, such as American Airlines's SABRE computerized reservation system, Citibank's ATM system, and FedEx's package tracking system, benefited by being the first in their industries. Then rival systems emerged. Amazon was an e-commerce leader but now faces competition from eBay, Walmart, and Google. Information systems alone cannot provide an enduring business advantage. Systems originally intended to be strategic frequently become tools for survival, required by every firm to stay in business, or they may inhibit organizations from making the strategic changes essential for future success.

Aligning IT with Business Objectives

The research on IT and business performance has found that (a) the more successfully a firm can align information technology with its business goals, the more profitable it will be, and (b) only one-quarter of firms achieve alignment of IT with the business. About half of a business firm's profits can be explained by alignment of IT with business (Luftman, 2003).

Most businesses get it wrong: Information technology takes on a life of its own and does not serve management and shareholder interests very well. Instead of businesspeople taking an active role in shaping IT to the enterprise, they ignore it, claim not to understand IT, and tolerate failure in the IT area as just a nuisance to work around. Such firms pay a hefty price in poor performance. Successful firms and managers understand what IT can do and how it works, take an active role in shaping its use, and measure its impact on revenues and profits.

Management Checklist: Performing a Strategic Systems Analysis

To align IT with the business and use information systems effectively for competitive advantage, managers need to perform a strategic systems analysis. To identify the types of systems that provide a strategic advantage to their firms, managers should ask the following questions:

1. What is the structure of the industry in which the firm is located?

   - What are some of the competitive forces at work in the industry? Are there new entrants to the industry? What is the relative power of suppliers, customers, and substitute products and services over prices?
   - Is the basis of competition quality, price, or brand?
   - What are the direction and nature of change within the industry? From where are the momentum and change coming?
   - How is the industry currently using information technology? Is the organization behind or ahead of the industry in its application of information systems?

2. What are the business, firm, and industry value chains for this particular firm?

   - How is the company creating value for the customer—through lower prices and transaction costs or higher quality? Are there any places in the value chain where the business could create more value for the customer and additional profit for the company?
   - Does the firm understand and manage its business processes using the best practices available? Is it taking maximum advantage of supply chain management, customer relationship management, and enterprise systems?
   - Does the firm leverage its core competencies?
   - Is the industry supply chain and customer base changing in ways that benefit or harm the firm?
   - Can the firm benefit from strategic partnerships, value webs, ecosystems, or platforms?
   - Where in the value chain will information systems provide the greatest value to the firm?

3. Have we aligned IT with our business strategy and goals?

   - Have we correctly articulated our business strategy and goals?
   - Is IT improving the right business processes and activities to promote this strategy?
   - Are we using the right metrics to measure progress toward those goals?

Managing Strategic Transitions

Adopting the kinds of strategic systems described in this chapter generally requires changes in business goals, relationships with customers and suppliers, and business processes. These sociotechnical changes, affecting both social and technical elements of the organization, can be considered **strategic transitions**—a movement between levels of sociotechnical systems.

Such changes often entail blurring of organizational boundaries, both external and internal. Suppliers and customers must become intimately linked and may share each other's responsibilities. Managers will need to devise new business processes for coordinating their firms' activities with those of customers, suppliers, and other organizations. The organizational change requirements surrounding new information systems are so important that they merit attention throughout this text. Chapter 14 examines organizational change issues in more detail.

Review Summary

3-1   *Which features of organizations do managers need to know about to build and use information systems successfully?*

All modern organizations are hierarchical, specialized, and impartial, using explicit routines to maximize efficiency. All organizations have their own cultures and politics arising from differences in interest groups, and they are affected by their surrounding environment. Organizations differ in goals, groups served, social roles, leadership styles, incentives, types of tasks performed, and type of structure. These features help explain differences in organizations' use of information systems. Information systems and the organizations in which they are used interact with and influence each other.

3-2   *What is the impact of information systems on organizations?*

The introduction of a new information system will affect organizational structure, goals, work design, values, competition between interest groups, decision making, and day-to-day behavior. At the same time, information systems must be designed to serve the needs of important organizational groups and will be shaped by the organization's structure, business processes, goals, culture, politics, and management. Information technology can reduce transaction and agency costs, and such changes have been accentuated in organizations using the Internet. New systems disrupt established patterns of work and power relationships, so there is often considerable resistance to them when they are introduced.

3-3   *How do Porter's competitive forces model, the value chain model, synergies, core competencies, and network economics help companies develop competitive strategies using information systems?*

In Porter's competitive forces model, the strategic position of the firm and its strategies are determined by competition with its traditional direct competitors, but they are also greatly affected by new market entrants, substitute products and services, suppliers, and customers. Information systems help companies compete by maintaining low costs, differentiating products or services, focusing on market niche, strengthening ties with customers and suppliers, and increasing barriers to market entry with high levels of operational excellence.

The value chain model highlights specific activities in the business where competitive strategies and information systems will have the greatest impact. The model views the firm as a series of primary and support activities that add value to a firm's products or services. Primary activities are directly related to production and distribution, whereas support activities make the delivery of primary activities possible. A firm's value chain can be linked to the value chains of its suppliers, distributors, and customers. A value web consists of information systems that enhance competitiveness at the industry level by promoting the use of standards and industrywide consortia and by enabling businesses to work more efficiently with their value partners.

Because firms consist of multiple business units, information systems achieve additional efficiencies or enhance services by tying together the operations of disparate business units. Information systems help businesses leverage their core competencies by promoting the sharing of knowledge across business units. Information systems facilitate business models based on large networks of users or subscribers that take advantage of network economics. A virtual company strategy uses networks to link to other firms so that a company can use the capabilities of other companies to build, market, and distribute products and services. In business ecosystems, multiple industries work together to deliver value to the customer. Information systems support a dense network of interactions among the participating firms.

3-4 *What are the challenges posed by strategic information systems, and how should they be addressed?*

Implementing strategic systems often requires extensive organizational change and a transition from one sociotechnical level to another. Such changes are called strategic transitions and are often difficult and painful to achieve. Moreover, not all strategic systems are profitable, and they can be expensive to build. Many strategic information systems are easily copied by other firms so that strategic advantage is not always sustainable.

Key Terms

Agency theory, 90
Benchmarking, 104
Best practices, 104
Business ecosystem, 108
Competitive forces model, 95
Core competency, 107
Disruptive technologies, 87
Efficient customer response system, 98
Mass customization, 98
Network economics, 107
Organization, 82

Platform, 109
Primary activities, 103
Product differentiation, 97
Routines, 84
Strategic transitions, 112
Support activities, 103
Switching costs, 99
Transaction cost theory, 89
Value chain model, 101
Value web, 105
Virtual company, 108

MyMISLab

To complete the problems with the MyMISLab, go to the EOC Discussion Questions in MyMISLab.

Review Questions

3-1 Which features of organizations do managers need to know about to build and use information systems successfully?

- Define an organization and compare the technical definition of organizations with the behavioral definition.
- Identify and describe the features of organizations that help explain differences in organizations' use of information systems.

3-2 What is the impact of information systems on organizations?

- Describe the major economic theories that help explain how information systems affect organizations.
- Describe the major behavioral theories that help explain how information systems affect organizations.

- Explain why there is considerable organizational resistance to the introduction of information systems.
- Describe the impact of the Internet and disruptive technologies on organizations.

3-3 How do Porter's competitive forces model, the value chain model, synergies, core competencies, and network economics help companies develop competitive strategies using information systems?

- Define Porter's competitive forces model and explain how it works.
- Describe what the competitive forces model explains about competitive advantage.
- List and describe four competitive strategies enabled by information systems that firms can pursue.
- Describe how information systems can support each of these competitive strategies and give examples.
- Explain why aligning IT with business objectives is essential for strategic use of systems.
- Define and describe the value chain model.
- Explain how the value chain model can be used to identify opportunities for information systems.

- Define the value web and show how it is related to the value chain.
- Explain how the value web helps businesses identify opportunities for strategic information systems.
- Describe how the Internet has changed competitive forces and competitive advantage.
- Explain how information systems promote synergies and core competencies.
- Describe how promoting synergies and core competencies enhances competitive advantage.
- Explain how businesses benefit by using network economics and ecosystems.
- Define and describe a virtual company and the benefits of pursuing a virtual company strategy.

3-4 What are the challenges posed by strategic information systems, and how should they be addressed?

- List and describe the management challenges posed by strategic information systems.
- Explain how to perform a strategic systems analysis.

Discussion Questions

3-5 It has been said that there is no such thing as a sustainable strategic advantage. Do you agree? Why or why not?

MyMISLab

3-6 It has been said that the advantage that leading-edge retailers such as Dell and Walmart have over their competition isn't

MyMISLab

technology; it's their management. Do you agree? Why or why not?

3-7 What are some of the issues to consider in determining whether the Internet would provide your business with a competitive advantage?

MyMISLab

Hands-On MIS Projects

The projects in this section give you hands-on experience identifying information systems to support a business strategy and to solve a customer retention problem, using a database to improve decision making about business strategy, and using web tools to configure and price an automobile. Visit MyMISLab's Multimedia Library to access this chapter's Hands-On MIS Projects.

Management Decision Problems

3-8 Macy's, Inc., through its subsidiaries, operates approximately 840 department stores in the United States. Its retail stores sell a range of merchandise, including apparel, home furnishings, and housewares. Senior management has decided that Macy's needs to tailor merchandise more to local tastes and that the colors, sizes, brands, and styles of clothing and other merchandise should be based on the sales patterns in each individual Macy's store. How could information systems help Macy's management implement this new strategy? What pieces of data should these systems collect to help management make merchandising decisions that support this strategy?

3-9 T-Mobile has launched aggressive campaigns to attract customers with lower mobile phone prices, and it has added to its customer base. However, management wants to know if there are other ways of luring and keeping customers. Are customers concerned about the level of customer service, uneven network coverage, or data plans? How can the company use information systems to help find the answer? What management decisions could be made using information from these systems?

Improving Decision Making: Using a Database to Clarify Business Strategy

Software skills: Database querying and reporting; database design
Business skills: Reservation systems; customer analysis

3-10 In this exercise, you will use database software to analyze the reservation transactions for a hotel and use that information to fine-tune the hotel's business strategy and marketing activities.

In MyMISLab, you will find a database for hotel reservation transactions developed in Microsoft Access with information about the President's Inn in Cape May, New Jersey. At the Inn, 10 rooms overlook side streets, 10 rooms have bay windows that offer limited views of the ocean, and the remaining 10 rooms in the front of the hotel face the ocean. Room rates are based on room choice, length of stay, and number of guests per room. Room rates are the same for one to four guests. Fifth and sixth guests must pay an additional $20 charge each per person per day. Guests staying for seven days or more receive a 10 percent discount on their daily room rates.

The owners currently use a manual reservation and bookkeeping system, which has caused many problems. Use the database to develop reports on average length of stay, average visitors per room, base revenue per room (i.e., length of visit multiplied by the daily rate), and strongest customer base. After answering these questions, write a brief report about the Inn's current business situation and suggest future strategies.

Improving Decision Making: Using Web Tools to Configure and Price an Automobile

Software skills: Internet-based software
Business skills: Researching product information and pricing

3-11 In this exercise, you will use software at car websites to find product information about a car of your choice and use that information to make an important purchase decision. You will also evaluate two of these sites as selling tools.

You are interested in purchasing a new Ford Escape (or some other car of your choice). Go to the website of CarsDirect (www.carsdirect.com) and begin your investigation. Locate the Ford Escape. Research the various Escape models, and choose one you prefer in terms of price, features, and safety ratings. Locate and read at least two reviews. Surf the website of the manufacturer, in this case Ford (www.ford.com). Compare the information available on Ford's website with that of CarsDirect for the Ford Escape. Try to locate the lowest price for the car you want in a local dealer's inventory. Suggest improvements for CarsDirect.com and Ford.com.

Collaboration and Teamwork Project

Identifying Opportunities for Strategic Information Systems

3-12 With your team of three or four other students, select a company described in the *Wall Street Journal, Fortune, Forbes,* or another business publication or do your research on the web. Visit the company's website to find additional information about that company and to see how the firm is using the web. On the basis of this information, analyze the business. Include a description of the organization's features, such as important business business processes, culture, structure, and environment as well as its business strategy. Suggest strategic information systems appropriate for that particular business, including those based on Internet technology, if appropriate. If possible, use Google Docs and Google Drive or Google Sites to brainstorm, organize, and develop a presentation of your findings for the class.

Can Technology Save Sears?
CASE STUDY

Sears, Roebuck used to be the largest retailer in the United States, with sales representing 1 to 2 percent of the U.S. gross national product for almost 40 years after World War II. Since then, Sears has steadily lost ground to discounters such as Walmart and Target and to competitively priced specialty retailers such as Home Depot and Lowe's. Even the merger with Kmart in 2005 to create Sears Holding Company failed to stop the downward spiral in sales and market share.

Over the years, Sears had invested heavily in information technology. At one time it spent more on information technology and networking than all other noncomputer firms in the United States except the Boeing Corporation. The company was noted for its extensive customer databases of 60 million past and present Sears credit card holders, which it used to target groups such as tool buyers, appliance buyers, and gardening enthusiasts with special promotions. For example, Sears would mail customers who purchased a washer and dryer an offer for a maintenance contract and follow up with annual contract renewal forms. These efforts did not translate into competitive advantage because Sears's cost structure was one of the highest in its industry.

In 1993, under the leadership of Arthur Martinez, Sears embarked on a $4 billion five-year store renovation program to make stores more efficient, attractive, and convenient by bringing all transactions closer to the sales floor and centralizing every store's general offices, cashiers, customer services, and credit functions. New point-of-sale (POS) terminals allowed sales staff to issue new credit cards, accept charge card payments, issue gift certificates, and report account information to card holders. The POS devices provided information such as the status of orders and availability of products, allowing associates to order out-of-stock goods directly from the sales floor. Some stores installed ATMs to give customers cash advances against their Sears credit cards. Sears also moved its suppliers to an electronic ordering system. By linking its computerized ordering system directly to that of each supplier, Sears hoped to eliminate paper throughout the order process and expedite the flow of goods into its stores.

Sears was among the first major retailers to change the way it sold based on shifting consumer habits. For example, Sears introduced a service that lets shoppers buy online and pick up their goods in stores in 2001—well ahead of competitors Walmart in 2007 and Target Corp. in 2013.

Despite these improvements, Sears has lagged in reducing operating costs, keeping pace with current merchandising trends, and remodeling its 1,725 stores, many of which are run-down and in undesirable locations. It is still struggling to find a viable business strategy that will pull it out of its rut. The Sears company has continued to use technology strategies to revive flagging sales: online shopping, mobile apps, and an Amazon.com-like marketplace with other vendors for 18 million products, along with heavy in-store promotions. So far, these efforts have not paid off, and sales have declined since the 2005 merger with Kmart.

Sears continued to pin its hopes on technology, aiming for even more intensive use of technology and mining of customer data. The expectation was that deeper knowledge of customer preferences and buying patterns would make promotions, merchandising, and selling much more effective. Customers would flock to Sears stores because they would be carrying exactly what they want.

A customer loyalty program called Shop Your Way Rewards promises customers generous free deals for repeat purchases if they agree to share their personal shopping data with the company. Sears would not disclose how many customers signed up for Shop Your Way Rewards, but Shop Your Way generates a bigger share of sales every year.

The data Sears is collecting are changing how its sales floors are arranged and how promotions are designed to attract shoppers. For example, work wear has been moved closer to where tools are sold. After data analysis showed that many jewelry customers were men who bought tools, the company created a special Valentine's Day offer for Shop Your Way Rewards members that offered $100 credit for $400 spent on jewelry.

Sears wanted to personalize marketing campaigns, coupons, and offers down to the individual customer, but its legacy systems were incapable of supporting that level of activity. In order to use complex analytic models on large data sets, Sears revamped its data management technology. It used to take Sears six weeks to analyze marketing campaigns for loyalty club members using a traditional large mainframe computer and Teradata data warehouse software. With new technology called Hadoop for managing very large datasets (see Chapter 6), the processing can be completed weekly. Certain online and mobile commerce analyses can be performed daily, and targeting is much more precise, in some cases down to the individual customer.

Sears's old models were able to use 10 percent of available data, but the new models are able to work with 100 percent. In the past, Sears was only able to retain data from 90 days to two years, but with the new "big data" management technology, it can keep everything, increasing its chances of finding more meaningful patterns in the data. Hadoop processing is about one-third the cost of conventional relational databases. With Hadoop's massively parallel processing power, processing 2 billion records takes Sears little more than one minute longer than processing 100 million records.

Sears spent several hundred million dollars improving its stores in 2011, including technological enhancements. Workers use iPads and iPod Touches to access online reviews for customers and check whether items are in stock. Working with McKinsey & Co. consultants, Sears opened a test store in 2009 called Mygofer in Joliet, Ilinois. Mygofer was touted as a revolutionary combination that would meld the convenience of the Internet with the instant gratification of a brick-and-mortar store. The company gutted an 80,000-square-foot Kmart, but the store did not stock items for sale. The idea was to have shoppers place their orders at computers in the front of the store, then pick up their goods at a delivery bay out back. Sears Holdings CEO hoped to roll out hundreds of Mygofer stores if the experiment succeeded. However, some days, more people returned goods than bought them. Shoppers didn't like the fact that they couldn't see and touch things. Sears management had projected that over four years Mygofer would eventually generate $8 million in annual sales. Annual sales struggled to top $1 million. CEO Eddie Lampert stated that going to a store with no products may have been weird for shoppers, but the idea was ahead of its time.

Experts believe that experiments like Mygofer are a diversion from Sears's overarching problems: a deteriorating store network and a brand image that doesn't resonate with today's consumers. Other retailers like Macy's and Nordstrom are also struggling to keep relevant in a world where shopping is steadily moving to the web. But Macy's and Nordstrom are still profitable. Sears Holdings spends nearly $1.90 a square foot on Sears stores and roughly 60 cents a square foot on Kmart stores, according to Matt McGinley, an analyst with Evercore ISI Institutional Equities. That compares with $9.70 a square foot spent by Walmart and $5.75 by Macy's. While Sears spent more than $1 million setting up the Mygofer store in Joliet, the company was starving a profitable crosstown Kmart.

Lampert wants to focus on technology projects that he hopes will turn Sears around, acknowledging that that today's shoppers are less likely to browse and buy in stores. One new service lets Sears customers browse for shoes and apparel online and then reserve items to try on in physical stores. Sears is also creating digital displays for products that are more likely to engage customers with reviews, instructional videos, and *Consumer Reports* ratings.

A service called In-Vehicle Pickup lets customers order goods online and have them delivered to them while they wait in their cars. Sears's In-Vehicle Return/Exchange in Five enables customers to return or exchange purchases in the parking lot within a guaranteed time period of five minutes. Sears improved its online ordering system so that orders could be shipped more quickly and economically by using Sears physical stores as well as distribution centers to fulfill them.

Sears is refashioning its consumer electronic departments as Connected Solutions shops that sell "smart home" devices like a garage door that can be opened or closed remotely with a smartphone, smart thermostats and remotely controlled air conditioners, smart water heaters, home security, and baby monitors. Other "smart home" devices include a wireless-enabled steerable riding mower that indicates when it needs a tuneup and features an app with videos to show you how to do the maintenance yourself along with a smart battery charger and maintainer that monitors voltage and keeps a car battery charged. The company has assembled a first-rate team of tech talent in Seattle to beef up capabilities for diagnosing appliance problems remotely.

Sears is also piloting radio frequency ID (RFID) tags in 15 stores in the hope of increasing sales and margins by giving a more accurate picture of the merchandise stores have in stock. Management said this fall that initiatives like digital signs and radio tags on inventory could bring in $500 million a year in savings and increased sales.

Sears has made some headway with e-commerce. Customers appreciate the in-store pickup for online orders. Shop Your Way, considered a leader in creating personalized offers, is driving more business. Tech should be a bright spot for Sears. But what good is that if no one wants to buy what Sears has to offer? For example *Fortune* reported a January 2016 survey by Prosper Analytics & Insights that found women preferred Goodwill stores over Sears when shopping for clothing. Net losses in the past five years have totaled $8 billion. The company's annual comparable sales have not grown since Sears and Kmart merged in 2005.

Analysts say Sears is reaping what it sowed from years of underinvestment in stores and uninspired merchandising. The struggling retailer spent much of 2015 selling off valuable assets like Lands' End and its stake in Sears Canada along with hundreds of other stores to avoid a cash crunch. Another 50 stores went up for sale in 2016. Sears management says these moves will give the company the financial resources to speed up its transformation into a more tech-driven retailer. More likely according to critics, Sears and CEO Lampert are in a race against time, trying to modernize retailing as sales crater. Lampert continues in the Sears tradition of trying to solve problems by ramping up new technologies while at the same time curtailing some of the mundane investments needed to keep the giant retailer generating sales. By all accounts, Sears remains a fading brand saddled with too many nonperforming physical stores in undesirable locations.

Even with better data analytics, knowledge of customers, loyalty programs, and e-commerce innovations, the question still lingers about whether Sears is effectively using technology to solve its enormous business problems. Is it truly able to offer customers personalized promotions, and are they working? What is the business impact? Where are the numbers to show that Sears's big bet on technology is making the company more profitable? Will Sears's technological forays be able to halt its downward spiral?

Sources: Phil Wahba, "Sears Hedge Fund Manager CEO Calls Criticism of Faltering Retailer 'Unfair,'" *Fortune*, February 25, 2016; "Sears Ranks Below Goodwill Among Women Shoppers," *Fortune*, February 5, 2016; Andrew Gebhart, "Sears Smart Home Lineup Isn't Sexy but Could Be Quite Useful," *CNET*, April 20, 2016; "Sears Holdings," www.fortune.com, accessed April 20, 2016; www. sears.com, accessed April 23, 2016; Steven Russolillo, "Sears's Retooling Can't Fix Everything," *Wall Street Journal*, December 2, 2015; and Suzanne Kapner, "Sears Bets Big on Technology," *Wall Street Journal*, December 16, 2014.

CASE STUDY QUESTIONS

3-13 Analyze Sears using the competitive forces and value chain models. What are Sears's strengths? What are its weaknesses?

3-14 What was the problem facing Sears? What management, organization, and technology factors contributed to this problem?

3-15 What solution did Sears select? What was the role of technology in this solution?

3-16 How effective was the solution selected by Sears? Explain your answer.

MyMISLab

Go to the Assignments section of MyMISLab to complete these writing exercises.

3-17 Describe the impact of the Internet on each of the five competitive forces.

3-18 What are the main factors that mediate the relationship between information technology and organizations and that managers need to take into account when developing new information systems? Give a business example of how each factor would influence the development of new information systems.

Chapter 3 References

Amladi, Pradip. "The Digital Economy: How It Will Transform Your Products and Your Future." *Big Data Quarterly* (March 25, 2016).

Attewell, Paul, and James Rule. "Computing and Organizations: What We Know and What We Don't Know." *Communications of the ACM* 27, No. 12 (December 1984).

Bernstein, Ethan, John Bunch, Niko Canner, and Michael Lee."Beyond the Holocracy Hype." *Harvard Business Review* (July–August 2016).

Bresnahan, Timothy F., Erik Brynjolfsson, and Lorin M. Hitt, "Information Technology, Workplace Organization, and the Demand for Skilled Labor." *Quarterly Journal of Economics* 117 (February 2002).

Cash, J. I., and Benn R. Konsynski. "IS Redraws Competitive Boundaries." *Harvard Business Review* (March–April 1985).

Ceccagnoli, Marco, Chris Forman, Peng Huang, and D. J. Wu. "Cocreation of Value in a Platform Ecosystem: The Case of Enterprise Software. *MIS Quarterly* 36, No. 1 (March 2012).

Chen, Daniel Q., Martin Mocker, David S. Preston, and Alexander Teubner. "Information Systems Strategy: Reconceptualization, Measurement, and Implications." *MIS Quarterly* 34, No. 2 (June 2010).

Christensen, Clayton M. *The Innovator's Dilemma: The Revolutionary Book That Will Change the Way You Do Business.* New York: HarperCollins (2003).

Christensen, Clayton. "The Past and Future of Competitive Advantage." *Sloan Management Review* 42, No. 2 (Winter 2001).

Christensen, Clayton M., Michael E. Raynor, and Rory McDonald. "What Is Disruptive Innovation?" *Harvard Business Review* (December 2015).

Clemons, Eric. "The Power of Patterns and Pattern Recognition When Developing Information-Based Strategy. *Journal of Management Information Systems* 27, No. 1 (Summer 2010).

Coase, Ronald H. "The Nature of the Firm." (1937). In Putterman, Louis and Randall Kroszner. *The Economic Nature of the Firm: A Reader.* Cambridge University Press, 1995.

Davis, Euan. "The Rise of the Smart Product Economy." Cognizant (2015).

Drucker, Peter. "The Coming of the New Organization." *Harvard Business Review* (January–February 1988).

Feintzeig, Rachel." So Busy at Work, No Time to Do the Job." *Wall Street Journal* (June 28, 2016).

Gandhi, Suketo and Eric Gervet. "Now That Your Products Can Talk, What Will They Tell You?" *MIT Sloan Management Review* (Spring 2016).

Gurbaxani, V. and S. Whang, "The Impact of Information Systems on Organizations and Markets." *Communications of the ACM* 34, No. 1 (January 1991).

Hagiu, Andrei and Simon Rothman. "Network Effects Aren't Enough." *Harvard Business Review* (April 2016).

Hitt, Lorin M. "Information Technology and Firm Boundaries: Evidence from Panel Data." *Information Systems Research* 10, No. 2 (June 1999).

Hitt, Lorin M., and Erik Brynjolfsson. "Information Technology and Internal Firm Organization: An Exploratory Analysis." *Journal of Management Information Systems* 14, No. 2 (Fall 1997).

Iansiti, Marco and Karim R. Lakhani. "Digital Ubiquity: How Connections, Sensors, and Data Are Revolutionizing Business." *Harvard Business Review* (November 2014).

Iansiti, Marco, and Roy Levien. "Strategy as Ecology." *Harvard Business Review* (March 2004).

Jensen, M. C. and W. H. Meckling. "Specific and General Knowledge and Organizational Science." *In Contract Economics*, edited by L. Wetin and J. Wijkander. Oxford: Basil Blackwell (1992).

Jensen, Michael C. and William H. Meckling. "Theory of the Firm: Managerial Behavior, Agency Costs, and Ownership Structure." *Journal of Financial Economics* 3 (1976).

Kane, Gerald C., Doug Palmer, Anh Nguyen Phillips, and David Kiron. "Is Your Business Ready for a Digital Future?" *MIT Sloan Management Review* (Summer 2015).

Karimi, Jahangir and Zhiping Walter. "The Role of Dynamic Capabilities in Responding to Digital Disruption: A Factor-Based Study of the Newspaper Industry." *Journal of Management Information Systems* 32, No. 1 (2015).

Kauffman, Robert J. and Yu-Ming Wang. "The Network Externalities Hypothesis and Competitive Network Growth." *Journal of Organizational Computing and Electronic Commerce* 12, No. 1 (2002).

King, Andrew A. and Baljir Baatartogtokh. "How Useful Is the Theory of Disruptive Innovation?" *MIT Sloan Management Review* (Fall 2015).

King, J. L., V. Gurbaxani, K. L. Kraemer, F. W. McFarlan, K. S. Raman, and C. S. Yap. "Institutional Factors in Information Technology Innovation." *Information Systems Research* 5, No. 2 (June 1994).

Kling, Rob. "Social Analyses of Computing: Theoretical Perspectives in Recent Empirical Research." *Computing Survey* 12, No. 1 (March 1980).

Kolb, D. A., and A. L. Frohman. "An Organization Development Approach to Consulting." *Sloan Management Review* 12, No. 1 (Fall 1970).

Kraemer, Kenneth, John King, Debora Dunkle, and Joe Lane. *Managing Information Systems.* Los Angeles: Jossey-Bass (1989).

Lamb, Roberta and Rob Kling. "Reconceptualizing Users as Social Actors in Information Systems Research." *MIS Quarterly* 27, No. 2 (June 2003).

Laudon, Kenneth C. "A General Model of the Relationship Between Information Technology and Organizations." Center for Research on Information Systems, New York University. Working paper, National Science Foundation (1989).

_____. "Environmental and Institutional Models of Systems Development." *Communications of the ACM* 28, No. 7 (July 1985).

_____. *Dossier Society: Value Choices in the Design of National Information Systems.* New York: Columbia University Press (1986).

Laudon, Kenneth C. and Kenneth L. Marr, "Information Technology and Occupational Structure." (April 1995).

Leavitt, Harold J. "Applying Organizational Change in Industry: Structural, Technological, and Humanistic Approaches." In *Handbook of Organizations*, edited by James G. March. Chicago: Rand McNally (1965).

Leavitt, Harold J. and Thomas L. Whisler. "Management in the 1980s." *Harvard Business Review* (November–December 1958).

Ling Xue, Gautam Ray, and Vallabh Sambamurthy. "Efficiency or Innovation: How Do Industry Environments Moderate the Effects of Firms' IT Asset Portfolios." *MIS Quarterly* 36, No. 2 (June 2012).

Luftman, Jerry. *Competing in the Information Age: Align in the Sand* (2nd ed.). Oxford University Press USA (August 6, 2003).

March, James G. and Herbert A. Simon. *Organizations*. New York: Wiley (1958).

McAfee, Andrew and Erik Brynjolfsson. "Investing in the IT That Makes a Competitive Difference." *Harvard Business Review* (July/August 2008).

McFarlan, F. Warren. "Information Technology Changes the Way You Compete." *Harvard Business Review* (May–June 1984).

McLaren, Tim S., Milena M. Head, Yufei Yuan, and Yolande E. Chan. "A Multilevel Model for Measuring Fit Between a Firm's Competitive Strategies and Information Systems Capabilities." *MIS Quarterly* 35, No. 4 (December 2011).

Mintzberg, Henry. "Managerial Work: Analysis from Observation." *Management Science* 18 (October 1971).

Piccoli, Gabriele and Blake Ives. "Review: IT-Dependent Strategic Initiatives and Sustained Competitive Advantage: A Review and Synthesis of the Literature." *MIS Quarterly* 29, No. 4 (December 2005).

Porter, Michael E. *Competitive Advantage*. New York: Free Press (1985).

_____. *Competitive Strategy*. New York: Free Press (1980).

_____. "Strategy and the Internet." *Harvard Business Review* (March 2001).

_____. "The Five Competitive Forces That Shape Strategy." *Harvard Business Review* (January 2008).

Porter, Michael E. and James E. Heppelmann. "How Smart, Connected Products Are Transforming Competition." *Harvard Business Review* (November 2014).

Porter, Michael E. and Scott Stern. "Location Matters." *Sloan Management Review* 42, No. 4 (Summer 2001).

Shapiro, Carl and Hal R. Varian. *Information Rules*. Boston, MA: Harvard Business School Press (1999).

Starbuck, William H. "Organizations as Action Generators." *American Sociological Review* 48 (1983).

Tallon, Paul P. "Value Chain Linkages and the Spillover Effects of Strategic Information Technology Alignment: A Process-Level View." *Journal of Management Information Systems* 28, No. 3 (Winter 2014).

Van Alstyne, Marshall W., Geoffrey G. Parer, and Sangeet Paul Choudary. "Pipelines, Platforms, and the New Rules of Strategy." *Harvard Business Review* (April 2016).

Tushman, Michael L. and Philip Anderson. "Technological Discontinuities and Organizational Environments." *Administrative Science Quarterly* 31 (September 1986).

Weber, Max. *The Theory of Social and Economic Organization*. Translated by Talcott Parsons. New York: Free Press (1947).

Williamson, Oliver E. *The Economic Institutions of Capitalism*. New York: Free Press, (1985).

Zhu, Feng and Nathan Furr. "Products to Platforms: Making the Leap." *Harvard Business Review* (April 2016).

4 Ethical and Social Issues in Information Systems

Learning Objectives

After reading this chapter, you will be able to answer the following questions:

4-1 What ethical, social, and political issues are raised by information systems?

4-2 What specific principles for conduct can be used to guide ethical decisions?

4-3 Why do contemporary information systems technology and the Internet pose challenges to the protection of individual privacy and intellectual property?

4-4 How have information systems affected laws for establishing accountability and liability and the quality of everyday life?

MyMISLab™

Visit **mymislab.com** for simulations, tutorials, and end-of-chapter problems.

CHAPTER CASES

The Dark Side of Big Data

Volkswagen Pollutes Its Reputation with Software to Cheat Emissions Testing

Are We Relying Too Much on Computers to Think for Us?

Facebook Privacy: What Privacy?

VIDEO CASES

What Net Neutrality Means for You

Facebook and Google Privacy: What Privacy?

United States v. Terrorism: Data Mining for Terrorists and Innocents

Instructional Video:

Viktor Mayer Scöhnberger on the Right to Be Forgotten

The Dark Side of Big Data

Organizations today are furiously mining big data, looking for ways to benefit from this technology. There are many big data success stories. For example, the Berg biopharmaceutical company is mining big data on patient tissue samples, clinical history, and demographic characteristics to pinpoint potential biomarkers for pancreatic cancer so that it can be detected much earlier and treated more effectively. The city of Barcelona has reduced its annual water bill by 25 percent by analyzing data from sensors installed in local parks to monitor soil moisture.

But there's a dark side to big data, and it has to do with privacy. We can now collect or analyze data on a much larger scale than ever before and use what we have learned about individuals in ways that may be harmful to them. The following are some examples.

Predictive policing In February 2014, the Chicago Police Department sent uniformed officers to make custom notification visits to individuals—especially gang members—whom a computer system had identified as likely to commit a crime in the future. The intent was to prevent crime by providing the targeted individuals with information about job training programs or informing them about increased penalties for people with certain backgrounds. Many community groups protested the practice as another form of racial profiling.

Insurance rates Auto insurance companies such as Progressive offer a small device to install in your car to analyze your driving habits, ostensibly to give you a better insurance rate. However, some of the criteria for lower auto insurance rates

are considered discriminatory. For example, insurance companies like people who don't drive late at night and don't spend much time in their cars. However, poorer people are more likely to work a late shift and to have longer commutes to work, which would increase their auto insurance rates.

Deloitte Consulting LLP developed a predictive modeling system for insurance applicants that predicts life expectancy by using data about individual consumers' buying habits as well as their personal and family medical histories. The company claims it can accurately predict whether people have any 1 of 17 diseases, including diabetes, tobacco-related cancer, cardiovascular disease, and depression, by analyzing their buying habits. What you pick up at the drugstore might increase your health insurance rates.

Computerized hiring   More and more companies are turning to computerized systems to filter and hire job applicants, especially for lower-wage, service-sector jobs. The algorithms these systems use to evaluate job candidates may be preventing qualified applicants from obtaining these jobs. For example, some of these algorithms have determined that, statistically, people with shorter commutes are more likely to stay in a job longer than those with longer commutes or less reliable transportation or those who haven't been at their address for very long. If asked, "How long is your commute?" applicants with long commuting times will be scored lower for the job. Although such considerations may be statistically accurate, is it fair to screen job applicants this way?

Targeting financially vulnerable individuals   Data brokers have been around for decades, but their tools for collecting and finely analyzing huge quantities of personal data grow ever more powerful. These data brokers now sell reports that specifically highlight and target financially vulnerable individuals. For example, a data broker might provide a report on retirees with little or no savings to a company offering reverse mortgages, high-cost loans, or other financially risky products. Very few rules or regulations exist to prevent targeting of vulnerable groups. Privacy laws and regulations haven't caught up with big data technology.

Sources: Brian Brinkmann, "Big Data Privacy: What Privacy?" Business2Community, March 2, 2016; Bernard Marr, "The 5 Scariest Ways Big Data Is Used Today," *DataInformed*, May 20, 2015; Victoria Craig, "Berg Hopes Big Data Will Lead to Breakthrough for Pancreatic Cancer, *Fox Business*, June 11, 2015; and "Police Gang-warning Tactic of 'Custom Notifications' Is Working," *Chicago Sun-Times*, March 27, 2014.

The challenges of big data to privacy described in the chapter-opening case show that technology can be a double-edged sword. It can be the source of many benefits, including the ability to combat disease and crime and to achieve major cost savings and efficiencies for business. At the same time, digital technology creates new opportunities for invading your privacy and using information that could cause you harm.

The chapter-opening diagram calls attention to important points this case and this chapter raise. Developments in data management technology and analytics have created opportunities for organizations to use big data to improve operations and decision making. One popular use of big data analysis is for predictive modeling—sifting through data to identify how specific individuals will behave and react in the future. The organizations described here are benefiting from using predictive modeling to fight crime, select the best employees, and

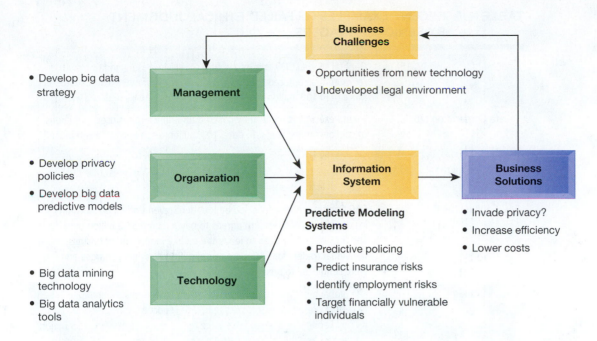

- Develop big data strategy

Management

Business Challenges

- Opportunities from new technology
- Undeveloped legal environment

- Develop privacy policies
- Develop big data predictive models

Organization

Information System

Business Solutions

Predictive Modeling Systems

- Predictive policing
- Predict insurance risks
- Identify employment risks
- Target financially vulnerable individuals

- Invade privacy?
- Increase efficiency
- Lower costs

- Big data mining technology
- Big data analytics tools

Technology

lower insurance and credit lending risks. However, their use of big data is also taking benefits away from individuals. Individuals might be subject to job discrimination, racial profiling, or higher insurance rates because organizations have new tools to assemble and analyze huge quantities of data about them. New privacy protection laws and policies need to be developed to keep up with the technologies for assembling and analyzing big data.

This case illustrates an ethical dilemma because it shows two sets of interests at work, the interests of organizations that have raised profits or even helped many people with medical breakthroughs and those who fervently believe that businesses and public organizations should not use big data analysis to invade privacy or harm individuals. As a manager, you will need to be sensitive to both the positive and negative impacts of information systems for your firm, employees, and customers. You will need to learn how to resolve ethical dilemmas involving information systems.

Here are some questions to think about: Does analyzing big data about people create an ethical dilemma? Why or why not? Should there be new privacy laws to protect individuals from being targeted by companies analyzing big data? Why or why not?

4-1 What ethical, social, and political issues are raised by information systems?

In the past 10 years, we have witnessed, arguably, one of the most ethically challenging periods for U.S. and global business. Table 4.1 provides a small sample of recent cases demonstrating failed ethical judgment by senior and middle managers. These lapses in ethical and business judgment occurred across a broad spectrum of industries.

In today's new legal environment, managers who violate the law and are convicted will most likely spend time in prison. U.S. federal sentencing guidelines adopted in 1987 mandate that federal judges impose stiff sentences on

TABLE 4.1 RECENT EXAMPLES OF FAILED ETHICAL JUDGMENT BY SENIOR MANAGERS

General Motors Inc. (2015)	General Motors CEO admits the firm covered up faulty ignition switches for more than a decade, resulting in the deaths of at least 114 customers. More than 100 million vehicles worldwide need to be replaced.
Takata Corporation (2015)	Takata executives admit they covered up faulty airbags used in millions of cars over many years. To date, 100 million cars need airbags replaced.
Citigroup, JPMorgan Chase, Barclays, UBS (2012)	Four of the largest money center banks in the world plead guilty to criminal charges that they manipulated the LIBOR interest rate used to establish loan rates throughout the world.
SAC Capital (2013)	SAC Capital, a hedge fund led by founder Steven Cohen, pleads guilty to insider trading charges and agrees to pay a record $1.2 billion penalty. The firm was also forced to leave the money management business. Individual traders for SAC were found guilty of criminal charges and were sentenced to prison.
GlaxoSmithKline LLC (2012)	The global healthcare giant admitted to unlawful and criminal promotion of certain prescription drugs, its failure to report certain safety data, and its civil liability for alleged false price reporting practices. Fined $3 billion, the largest healthcare fraud settlement in U.S. history and the largest payment ever by a drug company.
McKinsey & Company (2012)	CEO Rajat Gupta heard on tapes leaking insider information. The former CEO of prestigious management consulting firm McKinsey & Company was found guilty in 2012 and sentenced to two years in prison.
Bank of America (2012)	Federal prosecutors accused Bank of America and its affiliate, Countrywide Financial, of defrauding government-backed mortgage agencies by churning out loans at a rapid pace without proper controls. Prosecutors sought $1 billion in penalties from the bank as compensation for the behavior that they say forced taxpayers to guarantee billions in bad loans.

business executives based on the monetary value of the crime, the presence of a conspiracy to prevent discovery of the crime, the use of structured financial transactions to hide the crime, and failure to cooperate with prosecutors (U.S. Sentencing Commission, 2004).

Although business firms would, in the past, often pay for the legal defense of their employees enmeshed in civil charges and criminal investigations, firms are now encouraged to cooperate with prosecutors to reduce charges against the entire firm for obstructing investigations. These developments mean that, more than ever, as a manager or an employee, you will have to decide for yourself what constitutes proper legal and ethical conduct.

Although these major instances of failed ethical and legal judgment were not masterminded by information systems departments, information systems were instrumental in many of these frauds. In many cases, the perpetrators of these crimes artfully used financial reporting information systems to bury their decisions from public scrutiny in the vain hope they would never be caught.

We deal with the issue of control in information systems in Chapter 8. In this chapter, we will talk about the ethical dimensions of these and other actions based on the use of information systems.

Ethics refers to the principles of right and wrong that individuals, acting as free moral agents, use to make choices to guide their behaviors. Information systems raise new ethical questions for both individuals and societies because they create opportunities for intense social change and, thus, threaten existing distributions of power, money, rights, and obligations. Like other technologies, such as steam engines, electricity, the telephone, and the radio, information technology can be used to achieve social progress, but it can also be used to commit crimes and threaten cherished social values. The development of information technology will produce benefits for many and costs for others.

Ethical issues in information systems have been given new urgency by the rise of the Internet and e-commerce. Internet and digital firm technologies make it easier than ever to assemble, integrate, and distribute information, unleashing new concerns about the appropriate use of customer information, the protection of personal privacy, and the protection of intellectual property.

Other pressing ethical issues that information systems raise include establishing accountability for the consequences of information systems, setting standards to safeguard system quality that protects the safety of the individual and society, and preserving values and institutions considered essential to the quality of life in an information society. When using information systems, it is essential to ask, "What is the ethical and socially responsible course of action?"

A Model for Thinking About Ethical, Social, and Political Issues

Ethical, social, and political issues are closely linked. The ethical dilemma you may face as a manager of information systems typically is reflected in social and political debate. One way to think about these relationships is shown in Figure 4.1. Imagine society as a more or less calm pond on a summer day,

FIGURE 4.1 THE RELATIONSHIP BETWEEN ETHICAL, SOCIAL, AND POLITICAL ISSUES IN AN INFORMATION SOCIETY

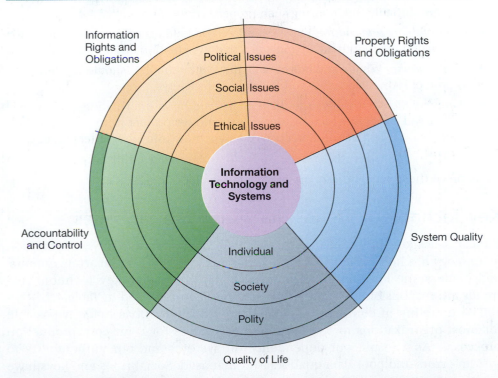

The introduction of new information technology has a ripple effect, raising new ethical, social, and political issues that must be dealt with on the individual, social, and political levels. These issues have five moral dimensions: information rights and obligations, property rights and obligations, system quality, quality of life, and accountability and control.

a delicate ecosystem in partial equilibrium with individuals and with social and political institutions. Individuals know how to act in this pond because social institutions (family, education, organizations) have developed well-honed rules of behavior, and these are supported by laws developed in the political sector that prescribe behavior and promise sanctions for violations. Now toss a rock into the center of the pond. What happens? Ripples, of course.

Imagine instead that the disturbing force is a powerful shock of new information technology and systems hitting a society more or less at rest. Suddenly, individual actors are confronted with new situations often not covered by the old rules. Social institutions cannot respond overnight to these ripples—it may take years to develop etiquette, expectations, social responsibility, politically correct attitudes, or approved rules. Political institutions also require time before developing new laws and often require the demonstration of real harm before they act. In the meantime, you may have to act. You may be forced to act in a legal gray area.

We can use this model to illustrate the dynamics that connect ethical, social, and political issues. This model is also useful for identifying the main moral dimensions of the information society, which cut across various levels of action—individual, social, and political.

Five Moral Dimensions of the Information Age

The major ethical, social, and political issues that information systems raise include the following moral dimensions.

- *Information rights and obligations* What **information rights** do individuals and organizations possess with respect to themselves? What can they protect?

- *Property rights and obligations* How will traditional intellectual property rights be protected in a digital society in which tracing and accounting for ownership are difficult and ignoring such property rights is so easy?

- *Accountability and control* Who can and will be held accountable and liable for the harm done to individual and collective information and property rights?

- *System quality* What standards of data and system quality should we demand to protect individual rights and the safety of society?

- *Quality of life* What values should be preserved in an information- and knowledge-based society? Which institutions should we protect from violation? Which cultural values and practices does the new information technology support?

We explore these moral dimensions in detail in Section 4.3.

Key Technology Trends that Raise Ethical Issues

Ethical issues long preceded information technology. Nevertheless, information technology has heightened ethical concerns, taxed existing social arrangements, and made some laws obsolete or severely crippled. Five key technological trends are responsible for these ethical stresses, summarized in Table 4.2.

The doubling of computing power every 18 months has made it possible for most organizations to use information systems for their core production processes. As a result, our dependence on systems and our vulnerability to system errors and poor data quality have increased. Social rules and laws have not yet adjusted to this dependence. Standards for ensuring the accuracy and reliability of information systems (see Chapter 8) are not universally accepted or enforced.

TABLE 4.2 TECHNOLOGY TRENDS THAT RAISE ETHICAL ISSUES

TREND	IMPACT
Computing power doubles every 18 months	More organizations depend on computer systems for critical operations and become more vulnerable to system failures.
Data storage costs rapidly decline	Organizations can easily maintain detailed databases on individuals. There are no limits on the data collected about you.
Data analysis advances	Companies can analyze vast quantities of data gathered on individuals to develop detailed profiles of individual behavior. Large-scale population surveillance is enabled.
Networking advances	The cost of moving data and making it accessible from anywhere falls exponentially. Access to data becomes more difficult to control.
Mobile device growth impact	Individual cell phones may be tracked without user consent or knowledge. The always-on device becomes a tether.

Advances in data storage techniques and rapidly declining storage costs have been responsible for the multiplying databases on individuals—employees, customers, and potential customers—maintained by private and public organizations. These advances in data storage have made the routine violation of individual privacy both inexpensive and effective. Enormous data storage systems for terabytes and petabytes of data are now available on-site or as online services for firms of all sizes to use in identifying customers.

Advances in data analysis techniques for large pools of data are another technological trend that heightens ethical concerns because companies and government agencies can find out highly detailed personal information about individuals. With contemporary data management tools (see Chapter 6), companies can assemble and combine the myriad pieces of information about you stored on computers much more easily than in the past.

Think of all the ways you generate digital information about yourself—credit card purchases; telephone calls; magazine subscriptions; video rentals; mail-order purchases; banking records; local, state, and federal government records (including court and police records); and visits to websites. Put together and

© Andriy Popov/123RF

Credit card purchases can make personal information available to market researchers, telemarketers, and direct mail companies. Advances in information technology facilitate the invasion of privacy.

mined properly, this information could reveal not only your credit information but also your driving habits, your tastes, your associations, what you read and watch, and your political interests.

Companies purchase relevant personal information from these sources to help them more finely target their marketing campaigns. Chapters 6 and 12 describe how companies can analyze large pools of data from multiple sources to identify buying patterns of customers rapidly and suggest individual responses. The use of computers to combine data from multiple sources and create digital dossiers of detailed information on individuals is called **profiling**.

For example, several thousand of the most popular websites allow Double-Click (owned by Google), an Internet advertising broker, to track the activities of their visitors in exchange for revenue from advertisements based on visitor information DoubleClick gathers. DoubleClick uses this information to create a profile of each online visitor, adding more detail to the profile as the visitor accesses an associated DoubleClick site. Over time, DoubleClick can create a detailed dossier of a person's spending and computing habits on the web that is sold to companies to help them target their web ads more precisely.

LexisNexis Risk Solutions (formerly ChoicePoint) gathers data from police, criminal, and motor vehicle records, credit and employment histories, current and previous addresses, professional licenses, and insurance claims to assemble and maintain dossiers on almost every adult in the United States. The company sells this personal information to businesses and government agencies. Demand for personal data is so enormous that data broker businesses such as Risk Solutions are flourishing. The two largest credit card networks, Visa Inc. and MasterCard Inc., have agreed to link credit card purchase information with consumer social network and other information to create customer profiles that could be sold to advertising firms.

A data analysis technology called **nonobvious relationship awareness (NORA)** has given both the government and the private sector even more powerful profiling capabilities. NORA can take information about people from many disparate sources, such as employment applications, telephone records, customer listings, and wanted lists, and correlate relationships to find obscure connections that might help identify criminals or terrorists (see Figure 4.2).

NORA technology scans data and extracts information as the data are being generated so that it could, for example, instantly discover a man at an airline ticket counter who shares a phone number with a known terrorist before that person boards an airplane. The technology is considered a valuable tool for homeland security but does have privacy implications because it can provide such a detailed picture of the activities and associations of a single individual.

Finally, advances in networking, including the Internet, promise to reduce greatly the costs of moving and accessing large quantities of data and open the possibility of mining large pools of data remotely by using small desktop machines, mobile devices, and cloud servers, permitting an invasion of privacy on a scale and with a precision heretofore unimaginable.

4-2 What specific principles for conduct can be used to guide ethical decisions?

Ethics is a concern of humans who have freedom of choice. Ethics is about individual choice: When faced with alternative courses of action, what is the correct moral choice? What are the main features of ethical choice?

FIGURE 4.2 NONOBVIOUS RELATIONSHIP AWARENESS (NORA)

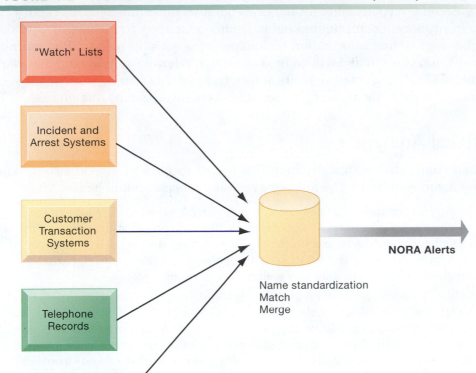

NORA technology can take information about people from disparate sources and find obscure, nonobvious relationships. It might discover, for example, that an applicant for a job at a casino shares a telephone number with a known criminal and issue an alert to the hiring manager.

Basic Concepts: Responsibility, Accountability, and Liability

Ethical choices are decisions made by individuals who are responsible for the consequences of their actions. **Responsibility** is a key element of ethical action. Responsibility means that you accept the potential costs, duties, and obligations for the decisions you make. **Accountability** is a feature of systems and social institutions; it means that mechanisms are in place to determine who took action and who is responsible. Systems and institutions in which it is impossible to find out who took what action are inherently incapable of ethical analysis or ethical action. **Liability** extends the concept of responsibility further to the area of laws. Liability is a feature of political systems in which a body of laws is in place that permits individuals to recover the damages done to them by other actors, systems, or organizations. **Due process** is a related feature of law-governed societies and is a process in which laws are known and understood, and ability exists to appeal to higher authorities to ensure that the laws are applied correctly.

These basic concepts form the underpinning of an ethical analysis of information systems and those who manage them. First, information technologies are filtered through social institutions, organizations, and individuals. Systems do not have impacts by themselves. Whatever information system effects exist are products of institutional, organizational, and individual actions and behaviors. Second, responsibility for the consequences of technology falls clearly on the institutions, organizations, and individual managers who choose to use the technology. Using information technology in a socially responsible manner means that you can and will be held accountable for the consequences of your actions. Third, in an ethical, political society, individuals and others can recover damages done to them through a set of laws characterized by due process.

Ethical Analysis

When confronted with a situation that seems to present ethical issues, how should you analyze it? The following five-step process should help.

1. *Identify and describe the facts clearly* Find out who did what to whom and where, when, and how. In many instances, you will be surprised at the errors in the initially reported facts, and often you will find that simply getting the facts straight helps define the solution. It also helps to get the opposing parties involved in an ethical dilemma to agree on the facts.

2. *Define the conflict or dilemma and identify the higher-order values involved* Ethical, social, and political issues always reference higher values. The parties to a dispute all claim to be pursuing higher values (e.g., freedom, privacy, protection of property, and the free enterprise system). Typically, an ethical issue involves a dilemma: two diametrically opposed courses of action that support worthwhile values. For example, the chapter-opening case study illustrates two competing values: the need to make organizations more efficient and cost-effective and the need to respect individual privacy.

3. *Identify the stakeholders* Every ethical, social, and political issue has stakeholders: players in the game who have an interest in the outcome, who have invested in the situation, and usually who have vocal opinions. Find out the identity of these groups and what they want. This will be useful later when designing a solution.

4. *Identify the options that you can reasonably take* You may find that none of the options satisfy all the interests involved but that some options do a better job than others. Sometimes arriving at a good or ethical solution may not always be a balancing of consequences to stakeholders.

5. *Identify the potential consequences of your options* Some options may be ethically correct but disastrous from other points of view. Other options may work in one instance but not in similar instances. Always ask yourself, "What if I choose this option consistently over time?"

Candidate Ethical Principles

Once your analysis is complete, what ethical principles or rules should you use to make a decision? What higher-order values should inform your judgment? Although you are the only one who can decide which among many ethical principles you will follow, and how you will prioritize them, it is helpful to consider some ethical principles with deep roots in many cultures that have survived throughout recorded history.

1. Do unto others as you would have them do unto you (the **Golden Rule**). Putting yourself in the place of others, and thinking of yourself as the object of the decision, can help you think about fairness in decision making.

2. If an action is not right for everyone to take, it is not right for anyone (**Immanuel Kant's categorical imperative**). Ask yourself, "If everyone did this, could the organization, or society, survive?"

3. If an action cannot be taken repeatedly, it is not right to take at all. This is the **slippery slope rule**: An action may bring about a small change now that is acceptable, but if it is repeated, it would bring unacceptable changes in the long run. In the vernacular, it might be stated as "once started down a slippery path, you may not be able to stop."

4. Take the action that achieves the higher or greater value (**utilitarian principle**). This rule assumes you can prioritize values in a rank order and understand the consequences of various courses of action.

5. Take the action that produces the least harm or the least potential cost (**risk aversion principle**). Some actions have extremely high failure costs of very low probability (e.g., building a nuclear generating facility in an urban area) or extremely high failure costs of moderate probability (speeding and automobile accidents). Avoid actions which have extremely high failure costs; focus on reducing the probability of accidents occurring.

6. Assume that virtually all tangible and intangible objects are owned by someone else unless there is a specific declaration otherwise. (This is the **ethical no-free-lunch rule**.) If something someone else has created is useful to you, it has value, and you should assume the creator wants compensation for this work.

Actions that do not easily pass these rules deserve close attention and a great deal of caution. The appearance of unethical behavior may do as much harm to you and your company as actual unethical behavior.

Professional Codes of Conduct

When groups of people claim to be professionals, they take on special rights and obligations because of their special claims to knowledge, wisdom, and respect. Professional codes of conduct are promulgated by associations of professionals such as the American Medical Association (AMA), the American Bar Association (ABA), the Association of Information Technology Professionals (AITP), and the Association for Computing Machinery (ACM). These professional groups take responsibility for the partial regulation of their professions by determining entrance qualifications and competence. Codes of ethics are promises by professions to regulate themselves in the general interest of society. For example, avoiding harm to others, honoring property rights (including intellectual property), and respecting privacy are among the General Moral Imperatives of the ACM's Code of Ethics and Professional Conduct.

Some Real-World Ethical Dilemmas

Information systems have created new ethical dilemmas in which one set of interests is pitted against another. For example, many companies use voice recognition software to reduce the size of their customer support staff by enabling computers to recognize a customer's responses to a series of computerized questions. Many companies monitor what their employees are doing on the Internet to prevent them from wasting company resources on nonbusiness activities. Facebook monitors its subscribers and then sells the information to advertisers and app developers (see the chapter-ending case study).

In each instance, you can find competing values at work, with groups lined up on either side of a debate. A company may argue, for example, that it has a right to use information systems to increase productivity and reduce the size of its workforce to lower costs and stay in business. Employees displaced by information systems may argue that employers have some responsibility for their welfare. Business owners might feel obligated to monitor employee e-mail and Internet use to minimize drains on productivity. Employees might believe they should be able to use the Internet for short personal tasks in place of the telephone. A close analysis of the facts can sometimes produce compromised solutions that give each side half a loaf. Try to apply some of the principles of ethical analysis described to each of these cases. What is the right thing to do?

4-3 Why do contemporary information systems technology and the Internet pose challenges to the protection of individual privacy and intellectual property?

In this section, we take a closer look at the five moral dimensions of information systems first described in Figure 4.1. In each dimension, we identify the ethical, social, and political levels of analysis and use real-world examples to illustrate the values involved, the stakeholders, and the options chosen.

Information Rights: Privacy and Freedom in the Internet Age

Privacy is the claim of individuals to be left alone, free from surveillance or interference from other individuals or organizations, including the state. Claims to privacy are also involved at the workplace. Millions of employees are subject to digital and other forms of high-tech surveillance. Information technology and systems threaten individual claims to privacy by making the invasion of privacy cheap, profitable, and effective.

The claim to privacy is protected in the United States, Canadian, and German constitutions in a variety of ways and in other countries through various statutes. In the United States, the claim to privacy is protected primarily by the First Amendment guarantees of freedom of speech and association, the Fourth Amendment protections against unreasonable search and seizure of one's personal documents or home, and the guarantee of due process.

Table 4.3 describes the major U.S. federal statutes that set forth the conditions for handling information about individuals in such areas as credit reporting, education, financial records, newspaper records, and electronic and digital communications. The Privacy Act of 1974 has been the most important of these laws, regulating the federal government's collection, use, and disclosure of information. At present, most U.S. federal privacy laws apply only to the federal government and regulate very few areas of the private sector. There were 20 major privacy bills before Congress in 2015, although few of them are likely to be passed in the near future (Kosseff, 2014).

Most American and European privacy law is based on a regime called **Fair Information Practices (FIP)** first set forth in a report written in 1973 by a federal government advisory committee and updated most recently in 2010 to take into account new privacy-invading technology (Federal Trade Commission [FTC], 2010; U.S. Department of Health, Education, and Welfare, 1973). FIP is a set of principles governing the collection and use of information about individuals. FIP principles are based on the notion of a mutuality of interest between the record holder and the individual. The individual has an interest in engaging in a transaction, and the record keeper—usually a business or government

TABLE 4.3 FEDERAL PRIVACY LAWS IN THE UNITED STATES

GENERAL FEDERAL PRIVACY LAWS	PRIVACY LAWS AFFECTING PRIVATE INSTITUTIONS
Freedom of Information Act of 1966 as Amended (5 USC 552)	Fair Credit Reporting Act of 1970
Privacy Act of 1974 as Amended (5 USC 552a)	Family Educational Rights and Privacy Act of 1974
Electronic Communications Privacy Act of 1986	Right to Financial Privacy Act of 1978
Computer Matching and Privacy Protection Act of 1988	Privacy Protection Act of 1980
Computer Security Act of 1987	Cable Communications Policy Act of 1984
Federal Managers Financial Integrity Act of 1982	Electronic Communications Privacy Act of 1986
Driver's Privacy Protection Act of 1994	Video Privacy Protection Act of 1988
E-Government Act of 2002	The Health Insurance Portability and Accountability Act (HIPAA) of 1996 Childrens Online Privacy Protection Act (COPPA) of 1998 Financial Modernization Act (Gramm-Leach-Bliley Act) of 1999

agency—requires information about the individual to support the transaction. After information is gathered, the individual maintains an interest in the record, and the record may not be used to support other activities without the individual's consent. In 1998, the Federal Trade Commission (FTC) restated and extended the original FIP to provide guidelines for protecting online privacy. Table 4.4 describes the FTC's Fair Information Practice principles.

The FTC's FIP principles are being used as guidelines to drive changes in privacy legislation. In July 1998, the U.S. Congress passed the Children's Online Privacy Protection Act (COPPA), requiring websites to obtain parental permission before collecting information on children under the age of 13. The FTC has recommended additional legislation to protect online consumer privacy in

TABLE 4.4 FEDERAL TRADE COMMISSION FAIR INFORMATION PRACTICE PRINCIPLES

Notice/awareness (core principle). Websites must disclose their information practices before collecting data. Includes identification of collector; uses of data; other recipients of data; nature of collection (active/inactive); voluntary or required status; consequences of refusal; and steps taken to protect confidentiality, integrity, and quality of the data.

Choice/consent (core principle). A choice regime must be in place allowing consumers to choose how their information will be used for secondary purposes other than supporting the transaction, including internal use and transfer to third parties.

Access/participation. Consumers should be able to review and contest the accuracy and completeness of data collected about them in a timely, inexpensive process.

Security. Data collectors must take responsible steps to ensure that consumer information is accurate and secure from unauthorized use.

Enforcement. A mechanism must be in place to enforce FIP principles. This can involve self-regulation, legislation giving consumers legal remedies for violations, or federal statutes and regulations.

advertising networks that collect records of consumer web activity to develop detailed profiles, which other companies then use to target online ads. In 2010, the FTC added three practices to its framework for privacy. Firms should adopt privacy by design, building products and services that protect privacy, firms should increase the transparency of their data practices, and firms should require consumer consent and provide clear options to opt out of data collection schemes (FTC, 2012). Other proposed Internet privacy legislation focuses on protecting the online use of personal identification numbers, such as social security numbers; protecting personal information collected on the Internet that deals with individuals not covered by COPPA; and limiting the use of data mining for homeland security.

In 2012, the FTC extended its FIP doctrine to address the issue of behavioral targeting. The FTC held hearings to discuss its program for voluntary industry principles for regulating behavioral targeting. The online advertising trade group Network Advertising Initiative (discussed later in this section), published its own self-regulatory principles that largely agreed with the FTC. Nevertheless, the government, privacy groups, and the online ad industry are still at loggerheads over two issues. Privacy advocates want both an opt-in policy at all sites and a national Do Not Track list. The industry opposes these moves and continues to insist that an opt-out capability is the only way to avoid tracking. Nevertheless, there is an emerging consensus among all parties that greater transparency and user control (especially making opting out of tracking the default option) is required to deal with behavioral tracking. Public opinion polls show an ongoing distrust of online marketers. Although there are many studies of privacy issues at the federal level, there has been no significant legislation in recent years. A 2016 survey by the Pew Research Center found 91 percent of Americans feel consumers have lost control of their personal information online and 86 percent have taken steps to protect their information online.

Privacy protections have also been added to recent laws deregulating financial services and safeguarding the maintenance and transmission of health information about individuals. The Gramm-Leach-Bliley Act of 1999, which repeals earlier restrictions on affiliations among banks, securities firms, and insurance companies, includes some privacy protection for consumers of financial services. All financial institutions are required to disclose their policies and practices for protecting the privacy of nonpublic personal information and to allow customers to opt out of information-sharing arrangements with nonaffiliated third parties.

The Health Insurance Portability and Accountability Act (HIPAA) of 1996, which took effect on April 14, 2003, includes privacy protection for medical records. The law gives patients access to their personal medical records that healthcare providers, hospitals, and health insurers maintain and the right to authorize how protected information about themselves can be used or disclosed. Doctors, hospitals, and other healthcare providers must limit the disclosure of personal information about patients to the minimum amount necessary to achieve a given purpose.

The European Directive on Data Protection

In Europe, privacy protection is much more stringent than in the United States. Unlike the United States, European countries do not allow businesses to use personally identifiable information without consumer's prior consent. On October 25, 1998, the European Commission's Directive on Data Protection went into effect, broadening privacy protection in the European Union (EU) nations. The directive requires companies to inform people when they collect information about them and disclose how it will be stored and used. Customers must provide their **informed consent** before any company can legally use data about them, and they have the right to access that information, correct it, and request that no further data be collected. Informed consent can be defined as consent given with knowledge of all the facts needed to make a rational decision. EU member nations must translate these principles into their own laws and cannot transfer personal data to countries, such as the United States, that do not have similar privacy protection regulations. In 2009, the European Parliament passed new rules governing the use of third-party cookies for behavioral tracking purposes. These new rules were implemented in May 2011 and require website visitors to give explicit consent to be tracked by cookies. Websites will be required to have highly visible warnings on their pages if third-party cookies are being used (European Parliament, 2009).

In January 2012, the EU issued significant proposed changes to its data protection rules, the first overhaul since 1995. The new rules would apply to all companies providing services in Europe and require Internet companies such as Amazon, Facebook, Apple, Google, and others to obtain explicit consent from consumers about the use of their personal data, delete information at the user's request (based on the right to be forgotten), and retain information only as long as absolutely necessary. In 2014, the European Parliament gave strong support to significant changes in privacy policies by extending greater control to users of the Internet. Although the privacy policies of United States firms (in contrast to the government's) are largely voluntary, in Europe, corporate privacy policies are mandated and more consistent across jurisdictions.

Among the changes being discussed are a requirement for firms to inform users before collecting data, every time they collect data, and how it will be used. Users would have to give consent to any data collection. Other proposals call for users to have a right of access to personal data, and the right to be forgotten. The right to be forgotten was upheld by a European Union court in 2014, and since then, Google has had to respond to more than 200,000 requests to remove personal information from its search engine.

Working with the European Commission, the U.S. Department of Commerce developed a safe harbor framework for U.S. firms. A **safe harbor** is a private, self-regulating policy and enforcement mechanism that meets the objectives of government regulators and legislation but does not involve government regulation or enforcement. U.S. businesses would be allowed to use personal data from EU countries if they develop privacy protection policies that meet EU standards. Enforcement would occur in the United States by using self-policing, regulation, and government enforcement of fair trade statutes. However, in October 2015, Europe's highest court struck down the safe harbor agreement entirely, in large part due to the revelations by Edward Snowden that Facebook had shared personal information on European citizens with the NSA and therefore violated the terms of the agreement. In 2016 a new agreement was reached that allows European regulators to monitor American use of European private information.

Internet Challenges to Privacy

Internet technology has posed new challenges for the protection of individual privacy. Information sent over this vast network of networks may pass through many computer systems before it reaches its final destination. Each of these systems is capable of monitoring, capturing, and storing communications that pass through it.

Websites track searches that have been conducted, the websites and web pages visited, the online content a person has accessed, and what items that person has inspected or purchased over the web. This monitoring and tracking of website visitors occurs in the background without the visitor's knowledge. It is conducted not just by individual websites but by advertising networks such as Microsoft Advertising, Yahoo, and Google's DoubleClick that are capable of tracking personal browsing behavior across thousands of websites. Both website publishers and the advertising industry defend tracking of individuals across the web because doing so allows more relevant ads to be targeted to users, and it pays for the cost of publishing websites. In this sense, it's like broadcast television: advertiser-supported content that is free to the user. The commercial demand for this personal information is virtually insatiable. However, these practices also impinge on individual privacy. **Cookies** are small text files deposited on a computer hard drive when a user visits websites. Cookies identify the visitor's web browser software and track visits to the website. When the visitor returns to a site that has stored a cookie, the website software searches the visitor's computer, finds the cookie, and knows what that person has done in the past. It may also update the cookie, depending on the activity during the visit. In this way, the site can customize its content for each visitor's interests. For example, if you purchase a book on Amazon.com and return later from the same browser, the site will welcome you by name and recommend other books of interest based on your past purchases. DoubleClick, described earlier in this chapter, uses cookies to build its dossiers with details of online purchases and examine the behavior of website visitors. Figure 4.3 illustrates how cookies work.

Websites using cookie technology cannot directly obtain visitors' names and addresses. However, if a person has registered at a site, that information can be combined with cookie data to identify the visitor. Website owners can also combine the data they have gathered from cookies and other website monitoring tools with personal data from other sources, such as offline data collected from surveys or paper catalog purchases, to develop very detailed profiles of their visitors.

FIGURE 4.3   HOW COOKIES IDENTIFY WEB VISITORS

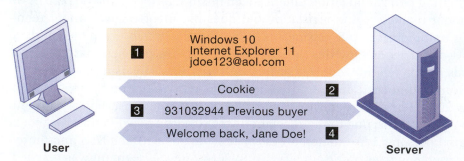

1. The Web server reads the user's web browser and determines the operating system, browser name, version number, Internet address, and other information.
2. The server transmits a tiny text file with user identification information called a cookie, which the user's browser receives and stores on the user's computer hard drive.
3. When the user returns to the website, the server requests the contents of any cookie it deposited previously in the user's computer.
4. The Web server reads the cookie, identifies the visitor, and calls up data on the user.

Cookies are written by a website on a visitor's hard drive. When the visitor returns to that website, the web server requests the ID number from the cookie and uses it to access the data stored by that server on that visitor. The website can then use these data to display personalized information.

There are now even more subtle and surreptitious tools for surveillance of Internet users. So-called super cookies or Flash cookies cannot be easily deleted and can be installed whenever a person clicks a Flash video. Flash uses these so-called local shared object files to play videos and puts them on the user's computer without his or her consent. Marketers use web beacons as another tool to monitor online behavior. **Web beacons**, also called *web bugs* (or simply tracking files), are tiny software programs that keep a record of users' online clickstreams. They report this data back to whomever owns the tracking file invisibly embedded in e-mail messages and web pages that are designed to monitor the behavior of the user visiting a website or sending e-mail. Web beacons are placed on popular websites by third-party firms who pay the websites a fee for access to their audience. So how common is web tracking? In a path-breaking series of articles in the *Wall Street Journal*, researchers examined the tracking files on 50 of the most popular U.S websites. What they found revealed a very widespread surveillance system. On the 50 sites, they discovered 3,180 tracking files installed on visitor computers. Only one site, Wikipedia, had no tracking files. Two-thirds of the tracking files came from 131 companies whose primary business is identifying and tracking Internet users to create consumer profiles that can be sold to advertising firms looking for specific types of customers. The biggest trackers were Google, Microsoft, and Quantcast, all of whom are in the business of selling ads to advertising firms and marketers. A follow-up study found tracking on the 50 most popular sites had risen nearly fivefold due to the growth of online ad auctions where advertisers buy the data about users' web-browsing behavior.

Other **spyware** can secretly install itself on an Internet user's computer by piggybacking on larger applications. Once installed, the spyware calls out to websites to send banner ads and other unsolicited material to the user, and it can report the user's movements on the Internet to other computers. More information is available about intrusive software in Chapter 8.

Nearly 80 percent of global Internet users use Google Search and other Google services, making Google the world's largest collector of online user data. Whatever Google does with its data has an enormous impact on online privacy. Most experts believe that Google possesses the largest collection of personal information in the world—more data on more people than any government agency. The nearest competitor is Facebook.

After Google acquired the advertising network DoubleClick in 2007, Google began using behavioral targeting to help it display more relevant ads based on users' search activities and to target individuals as they move from one site to another to show them display or banner ads. Google allows tracking software on its search pages, and using DoubleClick, it can track users across the Internet. One of its programs enables advertisers to target ads based on the search histories of Google users, along with any other information the user submits to Google such as age, demographics, region, and other web activities (such as blogging). Google's AdSense program enables Google to help advertisers select keywords and design ads for various market segments based on search histories such as helping a clothing website create and test ads targeted at teenage females. A recent study found that 88 percent of 400,000 websites had at least one Google tracking bug.

Google also scans the contents of messages users receive of its free web-based e-mail service called Gmail. Ads that users see when they read their e-mail are related to the subjects of these messages. Profiles are developed on individual users based on the content in their e-mail. Google now displays targeted ads on YouTube and Google mobile applications, and its DoubleClick ad network serves up targeted banner ads.

The United States has allowed businesses to gather transaction information generated in the marketplace and then use that information for other marketing purposes without obtaining the informed consent of the individual whose information is being used. These firms argue that when users agree to the sites' terms of service, they are also agreeing to allow the site to collect information about their online activities. An **opt-out** model of informed consent permits the collection of personal information until the consumer specifically requests the data not to be collected. Privacy advocates would like to see wider use of an **opt-in** model of informed consent in which a business is prohibited from collecting any personal information unless the consumer specifically takes action to approve information collection and use. Here, the default option is no collection of user information.

The online industry has preferred self-regulation to privacy legislation for protecting consumers. The online advertising industry formed the Online Privacy Alliance to encourage self-regulation to develop a set of privacy guidelines for its members. The group promotes the use of online seals, such as that of TRUSTe, certifying websites adhering to certain privacy principles. Members of the advertising network industry, including Google's DoubleClick, have created an additional industry association called the Network Advertising Initiative (NAI) to develop its own privacy policies to help consumers opt out of advertising network programs and provide consumers redress from abuses.

Individual firms such as Microsoft, Mozilla Foundation, Yahoo, and Google have recently adopted policies on their own in an effort to address public concern about tracking people online. Microsoft's Internet Explorer 11 web browser was released in 2015 with the opt-out option as the default, but by 2016 Microsoft removed this feature in large part because most websites ignore the request to opt out. Other browsers have opt-out options, but users need to turn them on, and most users fail to do this. AOL established an opt-out policy that allows users of its site to choose not to be tracked. Yahoo follows NAI guidelines and allows opt-out for tracking and web beacons (web bugs). Google has reduced retention time for tracking data.

In general, most Internet businesses do little to protect the privacy of their customers, and consumers do not do as much as they should to protect themselves. For commercial websites that depend on advertising to support themselves, most revenue derives from selling customer information. Of the companies that do post privacy policies on their websites, about half do not monitor their sites to ensure that they adhere to these policies. The vast majority of online customers claim they are concerned about online privacy, but fewer than half read the privacy statements on websites. In general, website privacy policies require a law degree to understand and are ambiguous about key terms (Laudon and Traver, 2015). In 2016, what firms such as Facebook and Google call a privacy policy is in fact a data use policy. The concept of privacy is associated with consumer rights, which firms do not wish to recognize. A data use policy simply tells customers how the information will be used without any mention of rights.

In one of the more insightful studies of consumer attitudes toward Internet privacy, a group of Berkeley students conducted surveys of online users and of complaints filed with the FTC involving privacy issues. Some of their results show that people feel they have no control over the information collected about them, and they don't know who to complain to. Websites collect all this information but do not let users have access, the website policies are unclear, and they share data with affiliates but never identify who the affiliates are and how many there are. Web bug trackers are ubiquitous, and users are not informed of trackers on the pages they visit. The results of this study and others suggest that consumers are not saying, "Take my privacy, I don't care, send me the service for free." They are saying, "We want access to the information, we want some controls on what can be collected, what is done with the information, the ability to opt out of the entire tracking enterprise, and some clarity on what the policies really are, and we don't want those policies changed without our participation and permission." (The full report is available at knowprivacy.org.)

Technical Solutions

In addition to legislation, there are a few technologies that can protect user privacy during interactions with websites. Many of these tools are used for encrypting e-mail, for making e-mail or surfing activities appear anonymous, for preventing client computers from accepting cookies, or for detecting and eliminating spyware. For the most part, technical solutions have failed to protect users from being tracked as they move from one site to another.

Because of growing public criticism of behavioral tracking, targeting of ads, and the failure of industry to self-regulate, attention has shifted to browsers. Many browsers have Do Not Track options. For users who have selected the Do Not Track browser option, their browser will send a request to websites requesting the user's behavior not be tracked, but websites are not obligated to honor their visitors' requests not to be tracked. There is no online advertising industry agreement on how to respond to Do Not Track requests nor, currently, any legislation requiring websites to stop tracking. Private browser encryption software or apps on mobile devices provide consumers a powerful opportunity to at least keep their messages private.

Property Rights: Intellectual Property

Contemporary information systems have severely challenged existing laws and social practices that protect **intellectual property**. Intellectual property is considered to be tangible and intangible products of the mind created by individuals or corporations. Information technology has made it difficult to protect intellectual property because computerized information can be so easily copied or distributed on networks. Intellectual property is subject to a variety of protections under three legal traditions: trade secrets, copyright, and patent law.

Trade Secrets

Any intellectual work product—a formula, device, pattern, or compilation of data—used for a business purpose can be classified as a **trade secret**, provided it is not based on information in the public domain. Protections for trade secrets vary from state to state. In general, trade secret laws grant a monopoly on the ideas behind a work product, but it can be a very tenuous monopoly.

Software that contains novel or unique elements, procedures, or compilations can be included as a trade secret. Trade secret law protects the actual ideas in a work product, not only their manifestation. To make this claim, the creator or owner must take care to bind employees and customers with nondisclosure agreements and prevent the secret from falling into the public domain.

The limitation of trade secret protection is that, although virtually all software programs of any complexity contain unique elements of some sort, it is difficult to prevent the ideas in the work from falling into the public domain when the software is widely distributed.

Copyright

Copyright is a statutory grant that protects creators of intellectual property from having their work copied by others for any purpose during the life of the author plus an additional 70 years after the author's death. For corporate-owned works, copyright protection lasts for 95 years after their initial creation. Congress has extended copyright protection to books, periodicals, lectures, dramas, musical compositions, maps, drawings, artwork of any kind, and motion pictures. The intent behind copyright laws has been to encourage creativity and authorship by ensuring that creative people receive the financial and other benefits of their work. Most industrial nations have their own copyright laws, and there are several international conventions and bilateral agreements through which nations coordinate and enforce their laws.

In the mid-1960s, the Copyright Office began registering software programs, and in 1980, Congress passed the Computer Software Copyright Act, which clearly provides protection for software program code and copies of the original sold in commerce; it sets forth the rights of the purchaser to use the software while the creator retains legal title.

Copyright protects against copying entire programs or their parts. Damages and relief are readily obtained for infringement. The drawback to copyright protection is that the underlying ideas behind a work are not protected, only their manifestation in a work. A competitor can use your software, understand how it works, and build new software that follows the same concepts without infringing on a copyright.

Look-and-feel copyright infringement lawsuits are precisely about the distinction between an idea and its expression. For instance, in the early 1990s, Apple Computer sued Microsoft Corporation and Hewlett-Packard for infringement of the expression of Apple's Macintosh interface, claiming that the defendants copied the expression of overlapping windows. The defendants countered that the idea of overlapping windows can be expressed only in a single way and, therefore, was not protectable under the merger doctrine of copyright law. When ideas and their expression merge, the expression cannot be copyrighted.

In general, courts appear to be following the reasoning of a 1989 case—*Brown Bag Software v. Symantec Corp*—in which the court dissected the elements of software alleged to be infringing. The court found that similar concept, function, general functional features (e.g., drop-down menus), and colors are not protectable by copyright law (*Brown Bag Software v. Symantec Corp.,* 1992).

Patents

A **patent** grants the owner an exclusive monopoly on the ideas behind an invention for 20 years. The congressional intent behind patent law was to ensure that inventors of new machines, devices, or methods receive the full financial and other rewards of their labor and yet make widespread use of the invention possible by providing detailed diagrams for those wishing to use the idea under license from the patent's owner. The granting of a patent is determined by the United States Patent and Trademark Office and relies on court rulings.

The key concepts in patent law are originality, novelty, and invention. The Patent Office did not accept applications for software patents routinely until a 1981 Supreme Court decision that held that computer programs could be part of a patentable process. Since that time, hundreds of patents have been granted, and thousands await consideration.

The strength of patent protection is that it grants a monopoly on the underlying concepts and ideas of software. The difficulty is passing stringent criteria of nonobviousness (e.g., the work must reflect some special understanding and contribution), originality, and novelty as well as years of waiting to receive protection.

In what some call the patent trial of the century, in 2011, Apple sued Samsung for violating its patents for iPhones, iPads, and iPods. On August 24, 2012, a California jury in federal district court delivered a decisive victory to Apple and a stunning defeat to Samsung. The jury awarded Apple $1 billion in damages. The decision established criteria for determining just how close a competitor can come to an industry-leading and standard-setting product like Apple's iPhone before it violates the design and utility patents of the leading firm. The same court ruled that Samsung could not sell its new tablet computer (Galaxy 10.1) in the United States. In a later patent dispute, Samsung won an infringement case against Apple. In June 2013, the United States International Trade Commission issued a ban for a handful of older iPhone and iPad devices because they violated Samsung patents from years ago. In 2014, Apple sued Samsung again, claiming infringement of five patents. The patents cover hardware and software techniques for handling photos, videos, and lists used on the popular Galaxy 5. Apple sought $2 billion in damages. In 2015, the U.S. Court of Appeals reaffirmed that Samsung had copied specific design patents, but dropped the damages Apple was granted to $930 million.

To make matters more complicated, Apple has been one of Samsung's largest customers for flash memory processors, graphic chips, solid-state drives, and display parts that are used in Apple's iPhones, iPads, iPod Touch devices, and MacBooks. The Samsung and Apple patent cases are indicative of the complex relationships among the leading computer firms.

Challenges to Intellectual Property Rights

Contemporary information technologies, especially software, pose severe challenges to existing intellectual property regimes and, therefore, create significant ethical, social, and political issues. Digital media differ from books, periodicals, and other media in terms of ease of replication; ease of transmission; ease of alteration; compactness—making theft easy; and difficulties in establishing uniqueness.

The proliferation of digital networks, including the Internet, has made it even more difficult to protect intellectual property. Before widespread use of networks, copies of software, books, magazine articles, or films had to be stored on physical media, such as paper, computer disks, or videotape, creating some hurdles to distribution. Using networks, information can be more widely reproduced and distributed. The BSA Global Software Survey conducted by International Data Corporation and The Software Alliance (also known as BSA) reported that the rate of global software piracy was 39 percent in 2015 (The Software Alliance, 2016).

The Internet was designed to transmit information freely around the world, including copyrighted information. You can easily copy and distribute virtually anything to millions of people worldwide, even if they are using different types of computer systems. Information can be illicitly copied from one place and distributed through other systems and networks even though these parties do not willingly participate in the infringement.

Individuals have been illegally copying and distributing digitized music files on the Internet for several decades. File-sharing services such as Napster and, later, Grokster, Kazaa, Morpheus, Megaupload, and The Pirate Bay sprang up to help users locate and swap digital music and video files, including those protected by copyright. Illegal file sharing became so widespread that it threatened the viability of the music recording industry and, at one point, consumed 20 percent of Internet bandwidth. The recording industry won several legal battles for shutting these services down, but it has not been able to halt illegal file sharing entirely. The motion picture and cable television industries are waging similar battles. Several European nations have worked with U.S. authorities to shut down illegal sharing sites, with mixed results.

As legitimate online music stores such as the iTunes Store expanded, some forms of illegal file sharing have declined. Technology has radically altered the prospects for intellectual property protection from theft, at least for music, videos, and television shows (less so for software). The Apple iTunes Store legitimated paying for music and entertainment and created a closed environment from which music and videos could not be easily copied and widely distributed unless played on Apple devices. Amazon's Kindle also protects the rights of publishers and writers because its books cannot be copied to the Internet and distributed. Streaming of Internet radio, on services such as Pandora and Spotify, and Hollywood movies (at sites such as Hulu and Netflix) also inhibits piracy because the streams cannot be easily recorded on separate devices, and videos can be downloaded so easily. Despite these gains in legitimate online music platforms, Apple's iTunes based on downloads of singles and streaming services' unwillingness to pay labels and artists a reasonable fee for playing have resulted in a 50 percent decline in record industry revenues since 2000 and the loss of thousands of jobs.

The **Digital Millennium Copyright Act (DMCA)** of 1998 also provides some copyright protection. The DMCA implemented a World Intellectual Property Organization Treaty that makes it illegal to circumvent technology-based protections of copyrighted materials. Internet service providers (ISPs) are required to take down sites of copyright infringers they are hosting when the ISPs are notified of the problem. Microsoft and other major software and information content firms are represented by the Software and Information Industry Association (SIIA), which lobbies for new laws and enforcement of existing laws to protect intellectual property around the world. The SIIA runs an antipiracy hotline for individuals to report piracy activities, offers educational programs to help organizations combat software piracy, and has published guidelines for employee use of software.

4-4 How have information systems affected laws for establishing accountability and liability and the quality of everyday life?

Along with privacy and property laws, new information technologies are challenging existing liability laws and social practices for holding individuals and institutions accountable. If a person is injured by a machine controlled, in part, by software, who should be held accountable and, therefore, held liable? Should a social network site like Facebook or Twitter be held liable and accountable for the posting of pornographic material or racial insults, or should they be held harmless against any liability for what users post (as is true of common carriers, such as the telephone system)? What about the Internet? If you outsource your information processing to the cloud, and the cloud provider fails to provide adequate service, what can you do? Cloud providers often claim the software you are using is the problem, not the cloud servers.

Computer-Related Liability Problems

In late 2013 hackers obtained credit card, debit card, and additional personal information about 70 to 110 million customers of Target, one of the largest U.S. retailers. Target's sales took an immediate hit from which it has still not completely recovered. Target says it has spent over $60 million to strengthen its systems. In 2015, Target agreed to pay $10 million to customers and $19 million to MasterCard. It has paid an even greater price through the loss of sales and trust.

Who is liable for any economic harm caused to individuals or businesses whose credit cards were compromised? Is Target responsible for allowing the breach to occur despite efforts it did make to secure the information? Or is this just a cost of doing business in a credit card world where customers and businesses have insurance policies to protect them against losses? Customers, for instance, have a maximum liability of $50 for credit card theft under federal banking law.

Are information system managers responsible for the harm that corporate systems can do? Beyond IT managers, insofar as computer software is part of a machine, and the machine injures someone physically or economically, the producer of the software and the operator can be held liable for damages. Insofar as the software acts like a book, storing and displaying information, courts have been reluctant to hold authors, publishers, and booksellers liable for contents (the exception being instances of fraud or defamation); hence, courts have been wary of holding software authors liable for software.

In general, it is very difficult (if not impossible) to hold software producers liable for their software products that are considered to be like books, regardless of the physical or economic harm that results. Historically, print publishers of books and periodicals have not been held liable because of fears that liability claims would interfere with First Amendment rights guaranteeing freedom of expression. The kind of harm software failures causes is rarely fatal and typically inconveniences users but does not physically harm them (the exception being medical devices).

What about software as a service? ATMs are a service provided to bank customers. If this service fails, customers will be inconvenienced and perhaps harmed economically if they cannot access their funds in a timely manner. Should liability protections be extended to software publishers and operators of defective financial, accounting, simulation, or marketing systems?

Software is very different from books. Software users may develop expectations of infallibility about software; software is less easily inspected than a book, and it is more difficult to compare with other software products for quality; software claims to perform a task rather than describe a task, as a book does; and people come to depend on services essentially based on software. Given the centrality of software to everyday life, the chances are excellent that liability law will extend its reach to include software even when the software merely provides an information service.

Telephone systems have not been held liable for the messages transmitted because they are regulated common carriers. In return for their right to provide telephone service, they must provide access to all, at reasonable rates, and achieve acceptable reliability. Likewise, cable networks are considered private networks not subject to regulation, but broadcasters using the public air waves are subject to a wide variety of federal and local constraints on content and facilities. In the United States, with few exceptions, websites are not held liable for content posted on their sites regardless of whether it was placed there by the website owners or users.

System Quality: Data Quality and System Errors

White Christmas turned into a blackout for millions of Netflix customers and social network users on December 24, 2012. The blackout was caused by the failure of Amazon's cloud computing service (AWS), which provides storage and computing power for all kinds of websites and services, including Netflix. The loss of service lasted for a day. Amazon blamed it on elastic load balancing, a software program that balances the loads on all its cloud servers to prevent overload. Amazon's cloud computing services have had several subsequent outages, although not as long-lasting as the Christmas Eve outage. In September 2015 AWS experienced a major outage again. Outages at cloud computing services are rare but recurring. These outages have called into question the reliability and quality of cloud services. Are these outages acceptable?

The debate over liability and accountability for unintentional consequences of system use raises a related but independent moral dimension: What is an acceptable, technologically feasible level of system quality? At what point should system managers say, "Stop testing, we've done all we can to perfect this software. Ship it!" Individuals and organizations may be held responsible for avoidable and foreseeable consequences, which they have a duty to perceive and correct. The gray area is that some system errors are foreseeable and correctable only at very great expense, expense so great that pursuing this level of perfection is not feasible economically—no one could afford the product.

For example, although software companies try to debug their products before releasing them to the marketplace, they knowingly ship buggy products because the time and cost of fixing all minor errors would prevent these products from ever being released. What if the product was not offered on the marketplace? Would social welfare as a whole falter and perhaps even decline? Carrying this further, just what is the responsibility of a producer of computer services—should it withdraw the product that can never be perfect, warn the user, or forget about the risk (let the buyer beware)?

Three principal sources of poor system performance are (1) software bugs and errors, (2) hardware or facility failures caused by natural or other causes, and (3) poor input data quality. A Chapter 8 Learning Track discusses why zero defects in software code of any complexity cannot be achieved and why the seriousness of remaining bugs cannot be estimated. Hence, there is a technological barrier to perfect software, and users must be aware of the potential for catastrophic failure. The software industry has not yet arrived at testing standards for producing software of acceptable but imperfect performance.

Although software bugs and facility catastrophes are likely to be widely reported in the press, by far the most common source of business system failure is data quality. Few companies routinely measure the quality of their data, but individual organizations report data error rates ranging from 0.5 to 30 percent.

Quality of Life: Equity, Access, and Boundaries

The negative social costs of introducing information technologies and systems are beginning to mount along with the power of the technology. Many of these negative social consequences are not violations of individual rights or property crimes. Nevertheless, they can be extremely harmful to individuals, societies, and political institutions. Computers and information technologies potentially can destroy valuable elements of our culture and society even while they bring us benefits. If there is a balance of good and bad consequences of using information systems, who do we hold responsible for the bad consequences? Next, we briefly examine some of the negative social consequences of systems, considering individual, social, and political responses.

Balancing Power: Center Versus Periphery

An early fear of the computer age was that huge, centralized mainframe computers would centralize power in the nation's capital, resulting in a Big Brother society, as was suggested in George Orwell's novel *1984*. The shift toward highly decentralized client–server computing, coupled with an ideology of empowerment of Twitter and social media users, and the decentralization of decision making to lower organizational levels, up until recently reduced the fears of power centralization in government institutions. Yet much of the empowerment described in popular business magazines is trivial. Lower-level employees may be empowered to make minor decisions, but the key policy decisions may be as centralized as in the past. At the same time, corporate Internet behemoths such as Google, Apple, Yahoo, Amazon, and Microsoft have come to dominate the collection and analysis of personal private information of all citizens. Since the terrorist attacks against the United States on September 11, 2001, the federal government has greatly expanded its use of this private sector information under the authority of the Patriot Act of 2001 and subsequent and secret executive orders. In this sense, power has become more centralized in the hands of a few private oligopolies and large government agencies.

Rapidity of Change: Reduced Response Time to Competition

Information systems have helped to create much more efficient national and international markets. Today's more efficient global marketplace has reduced the normal social buffers that permitted businesses many years to adjust to competition. Time-based competition has an ugly side; the business you work for may not have enough time to respond to global competitors and may be wiped out in a year along with your job. We stand the risk of developing a just-in-time society with just-in-time jobs and just-in-time workplaces, families, and vacations. One impact of Uber (see Chapter 10) and other on-demand services firms is to create just-in-time jobs with no benefits or insurance for employees.

Maintaining Boundaries: Family, Work, and Leisure

Parts of this book were produced on trains and planes as well as on vacations and during what otherwise might have been family time. The danger to ubiquitous computing, telecommuting, nomad computing, mobile computing, and the do-anything-anywhere computing environment is that it is actually coming true. The traditional boundaries that separate work from family and just plain leisure have been weakened.

Although authors have traditionally worked just about anywhere, the advent of information systems, coupled with the growth of knowledge-work occupations, means that more and more people are working when traditionally they would have been playing or communicating with family and friends. The work umbrella now extends far beyond the eight-hour day into commuting time, vacation time, and leisure time. The explosive growth and use of smartphones have only heightened the sense of many employees that they are never away from work.

Even leisure time spent on the computer threatens these close social relationships. Extensive Internet and cell phone use, even for entertainment or recreational purposes, takes people away from their family and friends. Among middle school and teenage children, it can lead to harmful antisocial behavior, such as the recent upsurge in cyberbullying.

Although some people enjoy the convenience of working at home, the do-anything-anywhere computing environment can blur the traditional boundaries between work and family time.

© Hongqi Zhang/123RF

Weakening these institutions poses clear-cut risks. Family and friends historically have provided powerful support mechanisms for individuals, and they act as balance points in a society by preserving private life, providing a place for people to collect their thoughts, think in ways contrary to their employer, and dream.

Dependence and Vulnerability

Today, our businesses, governments, schools, and private associations, such as churches, are incredibly dependent on information systems and are, therefore, highly vulnerable if these systems fail. Secondary schools, for instance, increasingly use and rely on educational software. Test results are often stored off campus. If these systems were to shut down, there is no backup educational structure or content that can make up for the loss of the system. With systems now as ubiquitous as the telephone system, it is startling to remember that there are no regulatory or standard-setting forces in place that are similar to telephone, electrical, radio, television, or other public utility technologies. The absence of standards and the criticality of some system applications will probably call forth demands for national standards and perhaps regulatory oversight.

Computer Crime and Abuse

New technologies, including computers, create new opportunities for committing crime by creating new, valuable items to steal, new ways to steal them, and new ways to harm others. **Computer crime** is the commission of illegal acts by using a computer or against a computer system. Simply accessing a computer system without authorization or with intent to do harm, even by accident, is now a federal crime. The most frequent types of incidents comprise a greatest hits list of cybercrime: malware, phishing, network interruption, spyware, and denial of service attacks. (PwC, 2015). The true cost of all computer crime is unknown, but it is estimated to be in the billions of dollars. You can find a more detailed discussion of computer crime in Chapter 8.

Computer abuse is the commission of acts involving a computer that may not be illegal but are considered unethical. The popularity of the Internet and e-mail has turned one form of computer abuse—spamming—into a serious problem for both individuals and businesses. Originally, **spam** was junk e-mail an organization or individual sent to a mass audience of Internet users who had expressed no interest in the product or service being marketed. However, as cell phone use has mushroomed, spam was certain to follow. Identity and financial-theft cybercriminals are turning their attention to smartphones as users check e-mail, do online banking, pay bills, and reveal personal information. Cell phone spam usually comes in the form of SMS text messages, but increasingly, users are receiving spam in their Facebook Newsfeed and messaging service as well. Spammers tend to market pornography, fraudulent deals and services, outright scams, and other products not widely approved in most civilized societies. Some countries have passed laws to outlaw spamming or restrict its use. In the United States, it is still legal if it does not involve fraud and the sender and subject of the e-mail are properly identified.

Spamming has mushroomed because it costs only a few cents to send thousands of messages advertising wares to Internet users. The percentage of all e-mail that is spam was estimated at around 65 percent in 2015 (Kaspersky, 2015). Most spam originates from bot networks, which consist of thousands of captured PCs that can initiate and relay spam messages. Spam volume has declined somewhat since authorities took down the Rustock botnet in 2011. Spam costs for businesses are very high (estimated at more than $50 billion per year) because of the computing and network resources billions of unwanted e-mail messages and the time required to deal with them consume.

ISPs and individuals can combat spam by using spam filtering software to block suspicious e-mail before it enters a recipient's e-mail inbox. However, spam filters may block legitimate messages. Spammers know how to skirt filters by continually changing their e-mail accounts, by incorporating spam messages in images, by embedding spam in e-mail attachments and digital greeting cards, and by using other people's computers that have been hijacked by botnets (see Chapter 8). Many spam messages are sent from one country although another country hosts the spam website.

Spamming is more tightly regulated in Europe than in the United States. In 2002, the European Parliament passed a ban on unsolicited commercial messaging. Digital marketing can be targeted only to people who have given prior consent.

The U.S. CAN-SPAM Act of 2003, which went into effect in 2004, does not outlaw spamming but does ban deceptive e-mail practices by requiring commercial e-mail messages to display accurate subject lines, identify the true senders, and offer recipients an easy way to remove their names from e-mail lists. It also prohibits the use of fake return addresses. A few people have been prosecuted under the law, but it has had a negligible impact on spamming in large part because of the Internet's exceptionally poor security and the use of offshore servers and botnets. Most large-scale spamming has moved offshore to Russia and Eastern Europe where hackers control global botnets capable of generating billions of spam messages. The largest spam network in recent years was the Russian network Festi based in St. Petersburg. Festi is best known as the spam generator behind the global Viagra-spam industry, which stretches from Russia to Indian pharmaceutical firms selling counterfeit Viagra.

For a many years automobile manufacturers around the globe have tried to find ways of manipulating mileage and emissions tests to produce more favorable results on paper than what actually takes place on the road. The use of software for this purpose recently came to light with revelations that Volkswagen Group installed "cheating" software in some of its car models to violate the U.S. Clean Air Act, as described in the Interactive Session on Technology.

INTERACTIVE SESSION: TECHNOLOGY

Volkswagen Pollutes Its Reputation with Software to Cheat Emissions Testing

Volkswagen Group AG tried to aim high by embarking on a strategy to bypass Toyota as the world's largest automaker. One part of that strategy called for tripling U.S. sales in a decade by promoting "clean" diesel-powered cars promising low emissions and high mileage without sacrificing performance. It turned out that about 580,000 cars in the United States and almost 10.5 million more clean diesel models sold worldwide by VW under its VW, Audi, and Porsche brands weren't really "green" at all.

On September 18, 2015, the U.S. Environmental Protection Agency (EPA) issued a notice of violation of the Clean Air Act to the Volkswagen Group after finding that Volkswagen had intentionally programmed turbocharged direct injection diesel engines to activate certain emissions controls only during laboratory emissions testing. The programming caused the vehicle's nitrogen oxide (NOx) output to meet U.S. standards during regulatory testing but emit up to 40 times more NOx when the cars were actually driven on the road. Volkswagen put this software in about 11 million cars worldwide, and in 500,000 in the United States, during model years 2009 through 2015.

Volkswagen was able to get away with cheating on emissions tests for years because it was hidden in lines of software code. Only after investigations by environmental groups and independent researchers did Volkswagen's deception come to light. Many functions in today's automobiles are controlled by millions of lines of software program code, including monitoring carbon monoxide and nitrogen oxide levels to help a car control the amount of pollutants it emits. Diesel engines don't emit much carbon monoxide, but they generally emit a greater amount of nitrogen oxide (NOx), a component in low-atmosphere ozone and acid rain. The United States has tougher NOx standards than Europe, where diesel cars are more common.

Diesel-powered cars use sensors and engine-management software to monitor and limit emission levels. The software can control how much NOx is produced during combustion by regulating the car's mix of diesel fuel and oxygen or by deploying NOx traps to capture the pollutant and catalysts to clean emissions. However, these pollution-reducing measures also reduce fuel economy.

VW did not identify the software or engine component that was used to falsify emissions test results. Experts believe that by examining data on steering, tire rotation, and accelerator use, a software program would be able to determine whether a car was being actually driven on the road or on an emissions-testing bed and adjust engine performance and emissions to pass the test.

In 2007 Volkswagen decided to abandon a pollution-control technology developed by Mercedes-Benz and Bosch and instead used its own internally developed technology. This took place at the same time that VW's hard-driving chief executive Martin Winterkorn started pressuring his managers with much higher growth targets for the U.S. car market. In order to increase market share, VW needed to build the larger cars favored by Americans—and it also had to comply with the Obama administration's toughening standards on mileage. All automakers developed strategies to meet the new mileage rules, and VW's focused on diesel. However, diesel engines, while offering better mileage, also emit more smog-forming pollutants than conventional engines. VW strategy came up against American air pollution standards, which are stricter than those in Europe. Cheating on emissions tests solved multiple problems. Cars equipped with the "cheating" software were able to deliver better mileage and performance while VW avoided having to pay for expensive and cumbersome pollution-control systems.

VW started installing the software to cheat emissions tests in 2008 after learning that its new diesel engine, developed at great expense for its growth strategy, could not meet pollution standards in the U.S. and other countries. Rather than halt production and discard years of research and development, VS decided the best course of action was to game the system. It is unclear who in VW management was responsible for this decision. Lawsuits by New York, Maryland, and Massachusetts have charged that dozens of engineers and managers, including VW's chief executive, were involved.

Volkswagen's cheating on auto emissions tests is not an isolated incident. The entire automobile industry has a history of trying to rig emissions and mileage data, which began as soon as governments began regulating automotive emissions in the early

1970s. Ford was fined $7.8 million in 1998 for using defeat devices enabling Econoline vans to reduce emissions to pass testing and then to exceed pollution limits when driving at highway speeds. General Motors paid $11 million in fines in 1995 for the defeat devices that secretly overrode the emissions control system at times on some of its Cadillac cars. Caterpillar, Volvo, Renault, and other manufacturers were fined $83.4 million in 1998 for using defeat devices. Auto manufacturers have also used other ploys to demonstrate better performance and gas mileage, such as taping cars doors and grilles to improve aerodynamics or making test vehicles lighter by removing the back seats.

The emissions scandal has shaken not just Volkswagen but the entire auto industry. Volkswagen became the target of regulatory investigations in multiple countries, and Volkswagen's stock price fell in value by a third in the days immediately following the cheating revelation. Chief executive Winterkorn resigned, and the head of brand development Heinz-Jakob Neusser, Audi research and development head Ulrich Hackenberg, and Porsche research and development head Wolfgang Hatz were suspended. Volkswagen announced plans to spend $7.3 billion, later raised to $18.32 billion, on rectifying the emissions issues and planned to refit the affected vehicles as part of a recall campaign. The scandal raised awareness of the higher levels of pollution being emitted by all vehicles built by a wide range of car makers, including Volvo, Renault, Jeep, Hyondai, and Fiat, which under real-world driving conditions are prone to exceed legal emission limits.

The emissions crisis has also sparked discussions about how to deal with other kinds of software-controlled machinery besides automobiles. It is believed that such machines will generally be prone to cheating and that their software source code should be made accessible to the public.

Sources: Jack Ewing and Hiroko Tabuchi, "Volkswagen Scandal Reaches All the Way to the Top, Lawsuits Say," *New York Times*, July 19, 2016; Geoffrey Smith and Roger Parloff. "Hoaxwagen," *Fortune*, March 15 2016; Associated Press, "German Prosecutors Investigating Missing Data in VW Scandal," June 9, 2016; Zeynep Turfekci, "Volkswagen and the Era of Cheating Software," *New York Times,* September 23, 2015; Danny Hakim and Hiroko Tabuchi, "Volkswagen Test Rigging Follows a Long Auto Industry Pattern," *New York Times*, September 23, 2015; Danny Hakim, Aaron M. Kessler, and Jack Ewing, " As Volkswagen Pushed to Be No. 1, Ambitions Fueled a Scandal," *New York Times*, September 26, 2015; and Jack Ewing, "Volkswagen Engine-Rigging Scheme Said to Have Begun in 2008," *New York Times*, October 4, 2015.

CASE STUDY QUESTIONS

1. Does the Volkswagen emission cheating crisis pose an ethical dilemma? Why or why not? If so, who are the stakeholders?

2. Describe the role of management, organization, and technology factors in creating VW's software cheating problem. To what extent was management responsible? Explain your answer.

3. Should all software-controlling machines be available for public inspection? Why or why not?

Employment: Trickle-Down Technology and Reengineering Job Loss

Reengineering work is typically hailed in the information systems community as a major benefit of new information technology. It is much less frequently noted that redesigning business processes has caused millions of mid-level factory managers and clerical workers to lose their jobs. Several economists have sounded new alarms about information and computer technology threatening middle-class, white-collar jobs (in addition to blue-collar factory jobs). Erik Brynjolfsson and Andrew P. McAfee argue that the pace of automation has picked up in recent years because of a combination of technologies, including robotics, numerically controlled machines, computerized inventory control, pattern recognition, voice recognition, and online commerce. One result is that machines can now do a great many jobs heretofore reserved for humans, including tech support, call center work, X-ray examination, and even legal document review (Brynjolfsson and McAfee, 2011). These views contrast with earlier assessments by economists that both labor and capital would receive stable shares of income and that new technologies created as many or more new jobs as they destroyed old ones. However, there is no guarantee this will happen in the future, and the income wealth share of labor may continue to fall relative to capital, resulting in a loss of high-paying jobs and further declines in wages.

Other economists are much more sanguine about the potential job losses. In some cases, employment has grown or remained unchanged in industries where investment in IT capital is highest. These economists also believe that bright, educated workers who are displaced by technology will move to better jobs in fast-growth industries. Missing from this equation are unskilled, blue-collar workers and older, less well-educated middle managers. It is not clear that these groups can be retrained easily for high-quality, high-paying jobs.

Equity and Access: Increasing Racial and Social Class Cleavages

Does everyone have an equal opportunity to participate in the digital age? Will the social, economic, and cultural gaps that exist in the United States and other societies be reduced by information systems technology? Or will the cleavages be increased, permitting the better off to become even more better off relative to others?

These questions have not yet been fully answered because the impact of systems technology on various groups in society has not been thoroughly studied. What is known is that information, knowledge, computers, and access to these resources through educational institutions and public libraries are inequitably distributed along ethnic and social class lines, as are many other information resources. Several studies have found that poor and minority groups in the United States are less likely to have computers or online Internet access even though computer ownership and Internet access have soared in the past five years. Although the gap in computer access is narrowing, higher-income families in each ethnic group are still more likely to have home computers and broadband Internet access than lower-income families in the same group. Moreover, the children of higher-income families are far more likely to use their Internet access to pursue educational goals, whereas lower-income children are much more likely to spend time on entertainment and games. This is called the "time-wasting" gap.

Left uncorrected, this **digital divide** could lead to a society of information haves, computer literate and skilled, versus a large group of information have-nots, computer illiterate and unskilled. Public interest groups want to narrow this digital divide by making digital information services—including the Internet—available to virtually everyone, just as basic telephone service is now.

Health Risks: RSI, CVS, and Cognitive Decline

A common occupational disease today is **repetitive stress injury (RSI)**. RSI occurs when muscle groups are forced through repetitive actions often with high-impact loads (such as tennis) or tens of thousands of repetitions under low-impact loads (such as working at a computer keyboard). The incidence of RSI is estimated to be as much as one-third of the labor force and accounts for one-third of all disability cases.

The single largest source of RSI is computer keyboards. The most common kind of computer-related RSI is **carpal tunnel syndrome (CTS)**, in which pressure on the median nerve through the wrist's bony structure, called a carpal tunnel, produces pain. The pressure is caused by constant repetition of keystrokes: in a single shift, a word processor may perform 23,000 keystrokes. Symptoms of CTS include numbness, shooting pain, inability to grasp objects, and tingling. Millions of workers have been diagnosed with CTS. It affects an estimated 3 percent to 6 percent of the workforce (LeBlanc and Cestia, 2011).

INTERACTIVE SESSION: ORGANIZATIONS

Are We Relying Too Much on Computers to Think for Us?

Does our ever–burgeoning dependence on computers foster complacency, suppressing our ability to marshal our mental faculties when required? Although computerization has undoubtedly mitigated malfunctions, work stoppages, and breakdowns, are we concurrently losing our ability to assess alternatives independently and make optimal choices?

At least one technology writer is sure this is exactly what is happening. Nicholas Carr's book, *The Glass Cage: Automation and Us*, lays out the case that our overreliance on computers has dulled our reflexes and eroded expertise. Two cognitive failures undermine performance. Complacency—overconfidence in the computer's ability—causes our attention to wander. Bias—overconfidence in the accuracy of the data we are receiving from the computer—causes us to disregard outside data sources, including conflicting sensory stimuli.

When pilots, soldiers, doctors, or even factory managers lose focus and lack situational awareness, they ignore both suspect data coming from the computer and the external cues that would refute it. The results can be catastrophic. In two instances in 2009, commercial airplane pilots misinterpreted the signals when their autopilot controls disconnected after receiving warnings that the aircraft would stall. Rather than pushing the yoke forward to gain velocity, both pilots heeded faulty control panel data while ignoring environmental cues and pulled back on the yoke, lifting the plane's nose and decreasing airspeed—the exact opposite of what was required. Loss of automation triggered confusion and panic. Sharply curtailed hands-on flight experience (on a typical passenger flight today, a human pilot mans the controls for just three minutes) resulted in stalled aircraft plunging to earth. Fifty died in Buffalo, New York; 228 perished in the Atlantic Ocean en route to Paris from Rio de Janeiro. The Federal Aviation Administration (FAA) is now pressing airlines to adopt stricter requirements for manual flying hours to offset the risks posed by complacency and bias.

Carr's critics point out that air travel is now safer than ever, with accidents and deaths steadily declining over decades and fatal airline crashes exceedingly rare. Carr concedes this point but still worries that pilots have come to rely so much on computers that they are forgetting how to fly. Andrew McAfee, a researcher at the MIT Sloan School of Management, points out that people have lamented the loss of

skills due to technology for many centuries, but on balance, automation has made the world better off. There may be a high-profile crash, but he believes greater automation, not less, is the solution.

Although humans have historically believed that allocating tasks to machines liberates us from the mundane and enables us to pursue the extraordinary, computers have ushered in an altogether different era. Massive data compilation and complex analytical capabilities now mean that decision making, heretofore the sole province of the human brain, is increasingly being accomplished by computers. Offloading tasks to computers liberates us from complex thinking while requiring us to pursue mundane tasks such as inputting data, observing output, and absentmindedly awaiting equipment failure.

Complacency and bias-induced errors are piling up. For example, computer programs now highlight suspect spots on mammograms. With the compulsion to examine images scrupulously relieved, radiologists are now missing some early-stage tumors not flagged by the program. Australian researchers found that accountants at two international firms using advanced auditing software had a significantly weaker understanding of the different types of risk than did those at a firm using simpler software that required them to make risk assessment decisions themselves. Even the most rudimentary tasks, such as editing and spell checking, are now performed differently. Rather than actively participating, we are observers, waiting to be told to correct an error. Are such short-term efficiencies worth the long-term loss of knowledge and expertise?

What's more, software programs are shouldering ever more capabilities heretofore thought to be the exclusive domain of the human brain. Sensory assessment, environmental awareness, coordinated movement, and conceptual knowledge are included in programming that has enabled Google to begin testing its driverless cars on public roads. Some argue that this is precisely the direction in which we should be going: autonomous computers with no human oversight or intervention at all. The solution to pilot error during automation failures? A wholly autonomous autopilot. The solution to doctors' declining diagnostic skills due to complacency and bias? Cut doctors out of the equation altogether.

Carr sees two problems with this thinking. First, complex computer systems require complex interdependencies among databases, algorithms, sensors, software, and hardware. The more mutually dependent elements there are in a system, the greater the potential points of failure and the more difficult they are to find. Second, we have known for more than three decades that humans are spectacularly bad at precisely the job that increased computerization has relegated to them: passive observation. When not actively engaged, our minds tend to drift off to any topic other than the one we are supposed to be monitoring. What's more, because we now know that "use it or lose it" applies to flying airplanes, diagnosing illnesses, spell-checking, and everything in between, restricting humans to observation reduces experts to rookies, escalating the risk of improper responses to malfunctions.

One solution is to design programs that promote engagement and learning, for example, by returning control to the operator at frequent, but irregular, intervals or by ensuring that challenging tasks are included. If operators must perform and repeat complex manual and mental tasks, the generation effect will be reinforced. Unfortunately, introducing these changes necessarily includes software slowdown and productivity decline. Businesses are unlikely to value long-term expertise preservation and development over short-term profits. Who does this technology benefit in the long run?

Sources: Patrick Smith, "Why Pilots Still Matter," *New York Times*, April 10, 2015; Nicholas Carr, "All Can Be Lost: The Risk of Putting Our Knowledge in the Hands of Machines," *Atlantic*, October 23, 2013; John Preston, "Review of Nicholas Carr's *The Glass Cage: Where Automation Is Taking Us*," *Telegraph*, January 11, 2015; Daniel Menaker, " Review of Nicholas Carr's *The Glass Cage*," *New York Times Book Review*, November 7, 2014; John Jones, "The Technophobe's Dilemma: Nicholas Carr's *The Glass Cage*," *DML Central*, November 10, 2014; Maria Bustillos, "Nicholas Carr's Latest Anti-technology Rant, *The Glass Cage*," *LA Times*, September 19, 2014; Carol Callwaladr, "*The Glass Cage: Where Automation Is Taking Us* Review: On Course for Disaster," *Guardian*, January 19, 2015; Daniel J. Levitin, "Book Review: *The Glass Cage* by Nicholas Carr," *Wall Street Journal*, October 10, 2014.

CASE STUDY QUESTIONS

1. Identify the problem described in this case study. In what sense is it an ethical dilemma?

2. Should more tasks be automated? Why or why not? Explain your answer.

3. Can the problem of automation reducing cognitive skills be solved? Explain your answer.

RSI is avoidable. Designing workstations for a neutral wrist position (using a wrist rest to support the wrist), proper monitor stands, and footrests all contribute to proper posture and reduced RSI. Ergonomically correct keyboards are also an option. These measures should be supported by frequent rest breaks and rotation of employees to different jobs.

RSI is not the only occupational illness computers cause. Back and neck pain, leg stress, and foot pain also result from poor ergonomic designs of workstations. **Computer vision syndrome (CVS)** refers to any eyestrain condition related to display screen use in desktop computers, laptops, e-readers, smartphones, and handheld video games. CVS affects about 90 percent of people who spend three hours or more per day at a computer. Its symptoms, which are usually temporary, include headaches, blurred vision, and dry and irritated eyes.

In addition to these maladies, computer technology may be harming our cognitive functions or at least changing how we think and solve problems. Although the Internet has made it much easier for people to access, create, and use information, some experts believe that it is also preventing people from focusing and thinking clearly. They argue that exposure to computers reduces intelligence and actually makes people dumb. One MIT scholar believes exposure to computers discourages drawing and encourages looking up answers rather than engaging in real problem solving. Students, in this view, don't learn much surfing the web or answering e-mail when compared to listening, drawing, arguing, looking, and

Repetitive stress injury (RSI) is a leading occupational disease today. The single largest cause of RSI is computer keyboard work.

© Donna Cuic/Shuttertock

exploring (Henry, 2011). The Interactive Session on Organizations describes a related concern: that automation is de-skilling people by removing opportunities to learn important tasks and impairing their ability to think on their own.

The computer has become part of our lives—personally as well as socially, culturally, and politically. It is unlikely that the issues and our choices will become easier as information technology continues to transform our world. The growth of the Internet and the information economy suggests that all the ethical and social issues we have described will be heightened further as we move further into the first digital century.

Review Summary

4-1 *What ethical, social, and political issues are raised by information systems?*

Information technology is introducing changes for which laws and rules of acceptable conduct have not yet been developed. Increasing computing power, storage, and networking capabilities—including the Internet—expand the reach of individual and organizational actions and magnify their impacts. The ease and anonymity with which information is now communicated, copied, and manipulated in online environments pose new challenges to the protection of privacy and intellectual property. The main ethical, social, and political issues information systems raise center on information rights and obligations, property rights and obligations, accountability and control, system quality, and quality of life.

4-2 *What specific principles for conduct can be used to guide ethical decisions?*

Six ethical principles for judging conduct include the Golden Rule, Immanuel Kant's categorical imperative, the slippery slope rule, the utilitarian principle, the risk aversion principle, and the ethical no-free-lunch rule. These principles should be used in conjunction with an ethical analysis.

4-3 *Why do contemporary information systems technology and the Internet pose challenges to the protection of individual privacy and intellectual property?*

Contemporary data storage and data analysis technology enable companies to gather personal data from many sources easily about individuals and analyze these data to create detailed digital profiles about individuals and their behaviors. Data flowing over the Internet can be monitored at many points. Cookies and other web monitoring tools closely track the activities of website visitors. Not all websites have strong privacy protection policies, and they do not always allow for informed consent regarding the use of personal information. Traditional copyright laws are insufficient to protect against software piracy because digital material can be copied so easily and transmitted to many locations simultaneously over the Internet.

4-4   *How have information systems affected laws for establishing accountability and liability and the quality of everyday life?*

New information technologies are challenging existing liability laws and social practices for holding individuals and institutions accountable for harm done to others. Although computer systems have been sources of efficiency and wealth, they have some negative impacts. Computer errors can cause serious harm to individuals and organizations. Poor data quality is also responsible for disruptions and losses for businesses. Jobs can be lost when computers replace workers or tasks become unnecessary in reengineered business processes. The ability to own and use a computer may be exacerbating socioeconomic disparities among different racial groups and social classes. Widespread use of computers increases opportunities for computer crime and computer abuse. Computers can also create health and cognitive problems such as repetitive stress injury, computer vision syndrome, and the inability to think clearly and perform complex tasks.

Key Terms

Accountability, 131
Carpal tunnel syndrome (CTS), 152
Computer abuse, 149
Computer crime, 149
Computer vision syndrome (CVS), 154
Cookies, 138
Copyright, 142
Digital divide, 153
Digital Millennium Copyright Act (DMCA), 145
Due process, 131
Ethical no-free-lunch rule, 133
Ethics, 126
Fair Information Practices (FIP), 134
Golden Rule, 132
Immanuel Kant's categorical imperative, 132
Information rights, 128
Informed consent, 137
Intellectual property, 141

Liability, 131
Nonobvious relationship awareness (NORA), 130
Opt-in, 140
Opt-out, 140
Patent, 142
Privacy, 134
Profiling, 130
Repetitive stress injury (RSI), 152
Responsibility, 131
Risk aversion principle, 133
Safe harbor, 137
Slippery slope rule, 133
Spam, 149
Spyware, 139
Trade secret, 141
Utilitarian principle, 133
Web beacons, 139

MyMISLab

To complete the problems with the MyMISLab, go to the EOC Discussion Questions in MyMISLab.

Review Questions

4-1   What ethical, social, and political issues are raised by information systems?

- Explain how ethical, social, and political issues are connected and give some examples.

- List and describe the key technological trends that heighten ethical concerns.

- Differentiate between responsibility, accountability, and liability.

4-2 What specific principles for conduct can be used to guide ethical decisions?

- List and describe the five steps in an ethical analysis.
- Identify and describe six ethical principles.

4-3 Why do contemporary information systems technology and the Internet pose challenges to the protection of individual privacy and intellectual property?

- Define privacy and Fair Information Practices.
- Explain how the Internet challenges the protection of individual privacy and intellectual property.
- Explain how informed consent, legislation, industry self-regulation, and technology tools help protect the individual privacy of Internet users.

- List and define the three regimes that protect intellectual property rights.

4-4 How have information systems affected laws for establishing accountability and liability and the quality of everyday life?

- Explain why it is so difficult to hold software services liable for failure or injury.
- List and describe the principal causes of system quality problems.
- Name and describe four quality of life impacts of computers and information systems.
- Define and describe computer vision syndrome and repetitive stress injury (RSI) and explain their relationship to information technology.

Discussion Questions

4-5 Should producers of software-based services, such as ATMs, be held liable for economic injuries suffered when their systems fail?
MyMISLab

4-6 Should companies be responsible for unemployment their information systems cause? Why or why not?
MyMISLab

4-7 Discuss the pros and cons of allowing companies to amass personal data for behavioral targeting.
MyMISLab

Hands-On MIS Projects

The projects in this section give you hands-on experience in analyzing the privacy implications of using online data brokers, developing a corporate policy for employee web usage, using blog creation tools to create a simple blog, and analyzing web browser privacy. Visit MyMISLab's Multimedia Library to access this chapter's Hands-On MIS Projects.

Management Decision Problems

4-8 InfoFree's website is linked to massive databases that consolidate personal data on millions of people. Users can purchase marketing lists of consumers broken down by location, age, gender, income level, home value, and interests. One could use this capability to obtain a list, for example, of everyone in Peekskill, New York, making $150,000 or more per year. Do data brokers such as InfoFree raise privacy issues? Why or why not? If your name and other personal information were in this database, what limitations on access would you want to preserve your privacy? Consider the following data users: government agencies, your employer, private business firms, other individuals.

4-9 As the head of a small insurance company with six employees, you are concerned about how effectively your company is using its networking and human resources. Budgets are tight, and you are struggling to meet payrolls because employees are reporting many overtime hours. You do not believe that the employees have a sufficiently heavy workload to warrant working longer hours and are looking into the amount of time they spend on the Internet.

Each employee uses a computer with Internet access on the job. Review a sample of your company's weekly report of employee web usage, which can be found in MyMISLab.

- Calculate the total amount of time each employee spent on the web for the week and the total amount of time that company computers were used for this purpose. Rank the employees in the order of the amount of time each spent online.

- Do your findings and the contents of the report indicate any ethical problems employees are creating? Is the company creating an ethical problem by monitoring its employees' use of the Internet?
- Use the guidelines for ethical analysis presented in this chapter to develop a solution to the problems you have identified.

Achieving Operational Excellence: Creating a Simple Blog

Software skills: Blog creation
Business skills: Blog and web page design

4-10 In this project, you'll learn how to build a simple blog of your own design using the online blog creation software available at Blogger.com. Pick a sport, hobby, or topic of interest as the theme for your blog. Name the blog, give it a title, and choose a template for the blog. Post at least four entries to the blog, adding a label for each posting. Edit your posts if necessary. Upload an image, such as a photo from your hard drive or the web, to your blog. Add capabilities for other registered users, such as team members, to comment on your blog. Briefly describe how your blog could be useful to a company selling products or services related to the theme of your blog. List the tools available to Blogger that would make your blog more useful for business and describe the business uses of each. Save your blog and show it to your instructor.

Improving Decision Making: Analyzing Web Browser Privacy

Software Skills: Web browser software
Business Skills: Analyzing web browser privacy protection features

4-11 This project will help develop your Internet skills for using the privacy protection features of leading web browser software.

Examine the privacy protection features and settings for two leading web browsers such as Internet Explorer, Mozilla Firefox, or Google Chrome. Make a table comparing the features of two of these browsers in terms of functions provided and ease of use.

- How do these privacy protection features protect individuals?
- How do these privacy protection features affect what businesses can do on the Internet?
- Which does the best job of protecting privacy? Why?

Collaboration and Teamwork Project

Developing a Corporate Code of Ethics

4-12 With three or four of your classmates, develop a corporate ethics code on privacy that addresses both employee privacy and the privacy of customers and users of the corporate website. Be sure to consider e-mail privacy and employer monitoring of worksites as well as corporate use of information about employees concerning their off-the-job behavior (e.g., lifestyle, marital arrangements, and so forth). If possible, use Google Docs and Google Drive or Google Sites to brainstorm, organize, and develop a presentation of your findings for the class.

Business Problem-Solving Case

FACEBOOK PRIVACY: WHAT PRIVACY?

In less than a decade, Facebook has morphed from a small, niche networking site for mostly Ivy League college students into a publicly traded company with a market worth of $338 billion in 2016. Facebook boasts that it is free to join and always will be, so where's the money coming from to service 1.65 billion worldwide subscribers? Just like its fellow tech titan and rival Google, Facebook's revenue comes almost entirely from advertising. Facebook does not have a diverse array of hot new gadgets like Apple does, a global network of brick-and-mortar retail outlets like Walmart does, or a full inventory of software for sale. All Facebook has to sell is your personal information and the information of hundreds of millions of others with Facebook accounts.

Advertisers have long understood the value of Facebook's unprecedented trove of personal information. They can serve ads using highly specific details such as relationship status, location, employment status, favorite books, movies, or TV shows and a host of other categories. For example, an Atlanta woman who posts that she has become engaged might be offered an ad for a wedding photographer on her Facebook page. When advertisements are served to finely targeted subsets of users, the response is much more successful than traditional types of advertising.

A growing number of companies both big and small have taken notice. In 2015, Facebook generated $17.9 billion in revenue, 94 percent of which ($16.8 billion) was from selling ads and the remainder from selling games and virtual goods. Facebook's revenues in 2015 grew by 43 percent over the previous year, driven mostly by adding new users and showing 40 percent more ads than a year earlier. A major contributor to revenue growth in 2015 is ads sold in the mobile News Feed.

That was good news for Facebook, which is expected to continue to increase its revenue in coming years, but is it good news for you, the Facebook user? More than ever, companies such as Facebook and Google, which made approximately $67 billion in advertising revenue in 2015, are using your online activity to develop a frighteningly accurate picture of your life. Facebook's goal is to serve advertisements that are more relevant to you than anywhere else on the web, but the personal information it gathers about you both with and without your consent can also be used against you in other ways.

Facebook has a diverse array of compelling and useful features. Facebook's partnership with the Department of Labor helps connect job seekers and employers; Facebook has helped families find lost pets; Facebook allows active-duty soldiers to stay in touch with their families; it gives smaller companies a chance to further their e-commerce efforts and larger companies a chance to solidify their brands; and, perhaps most obviously, Facebook allows you to keep in touch with your friends, relatives, local restaurants,

and in short, just about all things you are interested in more easily. These are the reasons so many people use Facebook—it provides value to users.

However, Facebook's goal is to get its users to share as much data as possible because the more Facebook knows about you, the more accurately it can serve relevant advertisements to you. Facebook CEO Mark Zuckerberg often says that people want the world to be more open and connected. It's unclear whether that is truly the case, but it is certainly true that Facebook wants the world to be more open and connected because it stands to make more money in that world. Critics of Facebook are concerned that the existence of a repository of personal data of the size that Facebook has amassed requires protections and privacy controls that extend far beyond those that Facebook currently offers.

Facebook wanting to make more money is understandable, but the company has a checkered past of privacy violations and missteps that raise doubts about whether it should be responsible for the personal data of hundreds of millions of people. There are no laws in the United States that give consumers the right to know what data companies like Facebook have compiled. You can challenge information in credit reports, but you can't even see what data Facebook has gathered about you, let alone try to change it. It's different in Europe: you can request Facebook to turn over a report of all the information it has about you.

More than ever, your every move, every click, on social networks is being used by outside entities to assess your interests and behavior and then pitch you an ad based on this knowledge. Law enforcement agencies use social networks to gather evidence on tax evaders and other criminals; employers use social networks to make decisions about prospective candidates for jobs; and data aggregators are gathering as much information about you as they can sell to the highest bidder. Facebook has admitted that it uses a software bug or code to track users across the Internet even if they are not using Facebook.

Think you own your face? Febook's newest privacy issue involves its facial recognition software used for photo tagging of users. This "tag suggestions" feature is automatically on when you sign up, and there is no user consent. A federal court in 2016 allowed a lawsuit to go forward contesting Facebook's right to photo tag without user consent. This feature is in violation of several state laws that seek to secure the privacy of biometric data.

A recent Consumer Reports study found that of 150 million Americans on Facebook, ever day, at least 4.8 million are willingly sharing information that could be used against them in some way. That includes plans to travel on a particular day, which burglars could use to time robberies, or Liking a page about a particular health condition or treatment, which insurers could use to deny coverage. Thirteen million users have never adjusted Facebook's privacy controls, which allow friends using Facebook applications to transfer your data unwittingly to a third party without your knowledge.

Credit card companies and similar organizations have begun engaging in weblining, taken from the phrase redlining, by altering their treatment of you based on the actions of other people with profiles similar to yours. Employers can assess your personality and behavior by using your Facebook likes. In one survey, 93 percent of people polled believe that Internet companies should be forced to ask for permission before using your personal information, and 72 percent want the ability to opt out of online tracking.

Why, then, do so many people share sensitive details of their life on Facebook? Often it's because users do not realize that their data are being collected and transmitted in this way. A Facebook user's friends are not notified if information about them is collected by that user's applications. Many of Facebook's features and services are enabled by default when they are launched without notifying users, and a study by Siegel+Gale found that Facebook's privacy policy is more difficult to comprehend than government notices or typical bank credit card agreements, which are notoriously dense. Did you know that whenever you log into a website using Facebook, Facebook shares some personal information with that site, and can track your movements in that site. Next time you visit Facebook, click Privacy Settings and see whether you can understand your options.

Facebook's value and growth potential are determined by how effectively it can leverage the personal data it aggregated about its users to attract advertisers. Facebook also stands to gain from managing and avoiding the privacy concerns its users and government regulators raise. For Facebook users who value the privacy of their personal data, this situation appears grim, but there are some signs that Facebook might become more responsible with its data collection processes, whether by its own volition or because it is forced to do so. As a publicly traded company, Facebook now invites more scrutiny from investors and regulators because, unlike in the past, its balance sheets, assets, and financial reporting documents are readily available.

In August 2012, Facebook settled a lawsuit with the Federal Trade Commission (FTC) in which it was barred from misrepresenting the privacy or security of users' personal information. Facebook was charged with deceiving its users by telling them they could keep their information on Facebook private but then repeatedly allowing it to be shared and made public. Facebook agreed to obtain user consent before making any change to that user's privacy preferences and to submit to biannual privacy audits by an independent firm for the next 20 years.

Privacy advocate groups such as the Electronic Privacy Information Center (EPIC) want Facebook to restore its more robust privacy settings from 2009 as well as to offer complete access to all data it keeps about its users. Facebook has also come under fire from EPIC for collecting information about users who are not even logged on to Facebook or may not even have accounts on Facebook. Facebook keeps track of activity on other sites that have Like buttons or recommendations widgets and records the time of your visit and your IP address when you visit a site with those features, regardless of whether you click them.

Although U.S. Facebook users have little recourse to access data that Facebook has collected on them, users from other countries have made inroads in this regard. In Europe, over 100,000 Facebook users have already requested their data, and European law requires Facebook to respond to these requests within 40 days. Government privacy regulators from France, Spain, Italy, Germany, Belgium, and the Netherlands have been actively investigating Facebook's privacy controls as the European Union pursues more stringent privacy protection legislation, In June 2015, Belgium's data-protection watchdog sued Facebook over privacy practices such as how Facebook tracks users across the web through Like and Share buttons on external websites.

In January 2014, Facebook shut down its Sponsored Stories feature, which served advertisements in the user's news feed highlighting products and businesses that Facebook friends were using. Sponsored Stories had been one of the most effective forms of advertising on Facebook because they don't seem like advertisements at all to most users. However, this feature triggered many lawsuits, attempted settlements, and criticism from privacy groups, the FTC, and annoyed parents whose children's photos were being used throughout Facebook to sell products.

Although Facebook has shut down one of its more egregious privacy-invading features, the company's Data Use policies make it very clear that, as a condition of using the service, users grant the company wide latitude in using their information in advertising. This includes a person's name, photo, comments, and other information. Facebook's existing policies make clear that users are required to grant the company wide permission to use their personal information in advertising as a condition of using the service. This includes social advertising, by which your personal information is broadcast to your friends and, indeed, the entire Facebook service if the company sees fit. Although users can limit some uses, an advanced degree in Facebook data features is required.

Ad-based firms like Facebook, and hundreds of others, including Google, justify their collection of personal information by arguing that consumers, by virtue of using the service, implicitly know about the data collection efforts and the role of advertisers in paying for the service and must, therefore, believe they are receiving real economic value from ads. This line of reasoning received a blow when in June 2015, researchers at the Annenberg School of Communication at the University of Pennsylvania found that 65 percent of Americans feel they have lost control over their information to advertisers, 84 percent want to control their information, and 91 percent do not believe it is fair for companies to offer discounts or coupons in exchange for their personal information without their knowledge.

In June 2015, Facebook held its first ever privacy conference as part of a growing effort to convince users it really is concerned about privacy and aware of public criticism of the firm. It has hired more than 50 privacy experts focused on Facebook's privacy practices. Critics asked Facebook why it doesn't offer an ad-free service—like music streaming sites—for a monthly fee. Others wanted to know why Facebook does not allow users just to opt out of tracking. But these kinds of changes would be very difficult for Facebook because its business model depends entirely on the unfettered use of its users' personal private information, just like it declares in its data use policy. That policy declares very openly that if you use Facebook, you don't have any privacy with respect to any data you provide to it.

Sources: "'Privacy Shield,' the New Deal Governing How Europe's User Data Is Sent to the US," *Reuters,* February 29, 2016; Katie Collins, "Facebook's Newest Privacy Problem: 'Faceprint' Data," *CNET,* May 16, 2016; United States District Court Northern District of California in Re Facebook Biometric Information Privacy Litigation. Case No. 15-cv-03747-JD Order Re Motion to Dismiss and Summary Judgment, May 6, 2016; Jessica Guynn, "Facebook to Face Privacy Lawsuit over Photo Tagging," *USA Today*, May 6, 2016; Natasha Singer, "Sharing Data, but Not Happily," *New York Times*, June 4, 2015; Sam Schechner and Natalia Drozdiak, "Belgium Takes Facebook to Court over Privacy, User Tracking," *Wall Street Journal*, June 16, 2015; Deepa Seetharaman, "At Facebook Summit, Little Consensus on Privacy," *New York Times*, June 4, 2015; Zeynep Tufecki, "Let Me Pay for Facebook," *New York Times*, June, 4, 2015; IBM, "IBM and Facebook Team Up to Deliver Personalized Brand Experiences through People-Based Marketing," press release, May 6, 2015; Lisa Fleisher, "Admitting Tracking Bug, Facebook Defends European Privacy Practices," *Wall Street Journal*, April 9, 2015; Facebook, Inc., SEC Form 10K filed with the Securities and Exchange Commission for the fiscal year ending December 31, 2014, January 29, 2015; Anna North, "How Your Facebook Likes Could Cost You a Job," *New York Times*, January 20, 2015; Natasha Singer, "Didn't Read Those Terms of Service? Here's What You Agreed to Give Up," *New York Times*, April 28, 2014; Vindu Goel and Edward Wyatt, "Facebook Privacy Change Is Subject of F.T.C. Inquiry," *New York Times*, September 11, 2013; Sarah Perez, "Facebook Graph Search Didn't Break Your Privacy Settings, It Only Feels Like That," *TechCrunch*, February 4, 2013.

CASE STUDY QUESTIONS

4-13 Perform an ethical analysis of Facebook. What is the ethical dilemma presented by this case?

4-14 What is the relationship of privacy to Facebook's business model?

4-15 Describe the weaknesses of Facebook's privacy policies and features. What people, organization, and technology factors have contributed to those weaknesses?

4-16 Will Facebook be able to have a successful business model without invading privacy? Explain your answer. Could Facebook take any measures to make this possible?

MyMISLab

Go to the Assignments section of MyMISLab to complete these writing exercises.

4-17 What are the five principles of Fair Information Practices? For each principle, describe a business situation in which the principle comes into play and how you think managers should react.

4-18 What are five digital technology trends in American business today that raise ethical issues for business firms and managers? Provide an example from business or personal experience when an ethical issue resulted from each of these trends.

Chapter 4 References

Aeppel, Timothy. "What Clever Robots Mean for Jobs." *Wall Street Journal* (February 24, 2015).

Belanger, France and Robert E. Crossler. "Privacy in the Digital Age: A Review of Information Privacy Research in Information Systems." *MIS Quarterly* 35, No. 4 (December 2011).

Bernstein, Amy and Anand Raman. "The Great Decoupling: An Interview with Erik Brynjolfsson and Andrew McAfee." *Harvard Business Review* (June 2015).

Bernstein, Ethan, Saravanan Kesavan, and Bradley Staats. "How to Manage Scheduling Software Fairly." *Harvard Business Review* (December 2014).

Bertolucci, Jeff. "Big Data Firm Chronicles Your Online, Offline Lives." *Information Week* (May 7, 2013).

Bilski v. Kappos, 561 US (2010).

Brown Bag Software vs. Symantec Corp. 960 F2D 1465 (Ninth Circuit, 1992).

Brynjolfsson, Erik and Andrew McAfee. *Race Against the Machine.* Digital Frontier Press (2011).

Chan, Jason, Anindya Ghose, and Robert Seamans. "The Internet and Racial Hate Crimes: Offline Spillovers from Online Access." *MIS Quarterly* 40, No. 2 (June 2016).

Clemons, Eric K. and Joshua S. Wilson. "Family Preferences Concerning Online Privacy, Data Mining, and Targeted Ads: Regulatory Implications." *Journal of Management Information Systems* 32, No. 2 (2015).

Culnan, Mary J. and Cynthia Clark Williams. "How Ethics Can Enhance Organizational Privacy." *MIS Quarterly* 33, No. 4 (December 2009).

Davenport, Thomas H. and Julia Kirby. "Beyond Automation." *Harvard Business Review* (June 2015).

European Parliament. "Directive 2009/136/EC of the European Parliament and of the Council of November 25, 2009." European Parliament (2009).

Federal Trade Commission. "Protecting Consumer Privacy in an Era of Rapid Change." Washington, DC. (2012).

Goldfarb, Avi and Catherine Tucker. "Why Managing Consumer Privacy Can Be an Opportunity." *MIT Sloan Management Review* 54, No. 3 (Spring 2013).

Henry, Patrick. "Why Computers Make Us Stupid." *Slice of MIT* (March 6, 2011).

Hsieh, J. J. Po-An, Arun Rai, and Mark Keil. "Understanding Digital Inequality: Comparing Continued Use Behavioral Models of the Socio-Economically Advantaged and Disadvantaged." *MIS Quarterly* 32, No. 1 (March 2008).

Hutter, Katja, Johann Fuller, Julia Hautz, Volker Bilgram, and Kurt Matzler. "Machiavellianism or Morality: Which Behavior Pays Off In Online Innovation Contests?" *Journal of Management Information Systems* 32, No. 3 (2015).

Kaspersky Lab. "Spam and Phishing Statistics Report Q1-2015." (2015).

Kosseff, Joseph. "Twenty Privacy Bills to Watch in 2014." (January 15, 2014).

Laudon, Kenneth C. and Carol Guercio Traver. *E-Commerce 2016: Business, Technology, Society (12th ed.).* Upper Saddle River, NJ: Prentice-Hall (2017).

Laudon, Kenneth C. *Dossier Society: Value Choices in the Design of National Information Systems.* New York: Columbia University Press (1986).

Leblanc, K. E., and W. Cestia. "Carpal Tunnel Syndrome." *American Family Physician, 83,* No. 8 (2011).

Lee, Dong-Joo, Jae-Hyeon Ahn, and Youngsok Bang. "Managing Consumer Privacy Concerns in Personalization: A Strategic Analysis of Privacy Protection." *MIS Quarterly* 35, No. 2 (June 2011).

MacCrory, Frank, George Westerman, Erik Brynjolfsson, and Yousef Alhammadi. "Racing with and Against the Machine: Changes in Occupational Skill Composition in an Era of Rapid Technological Advance." (2014).

PwC. "US State of Cybercrime Survey 2015." (June 2015),

Pew Research Center. "The State of Privacy in America." (January 20, 2016).

Robinson, Francis. "EU Unveils Web-Privacy Rules." *Wall Street Journal* (January 26, 2012).

Smith, H. Jeff. "The Shareholders vs. Stakeholders Debate." *MIS Sloan Management Review* 44, No. 4 (Summer 2003).

Sojer, Manuel, Oliver Alexy, Sven Kleinknecht, and Joachim Henkel. "Understanding the Drivers of Unethical Programming Behavior: The Inappropriate Reuse of Internet-Accessible Code." *Journal of Management Information Systems* 31, No. 3 (Winter 2014).

Tarafdar. Monideepa, John D'Arcy, Ofir Turel, and Ashish Gupta. "The Dark Side of Information Technology." *MIT Sloan Management Review* 56, No. 2 (Winter 2015).

The Software Alliance. "BSA Global Software Survey 2016." (May 2016).

United States Department of Health, Education, and Welfare. *Records, Computers, and the Rights of Citizens.* Cambridge: MIT Press (1973).

U.S. Senate. "Do-Not-Track Online Act of 2011." Senate 913 (May 9, 2011).

U.S. Sentencing Commission. "Sentencing Commission Toughens Requirements for Corporate Compliance Programs." (April 13, 2004).

Information Technology Infrastructure

PART TWO provides the technical foundation for understanding information systems by examining hardware, software, database, and networking technologies along with tools and techniques for security and control. This part answers questions such as: What technologies do businesses today need to accomplish their work? What do I need to know about these technologies to make sure they enhance the performance of the firm? How are these technologies likely to change in the future? What technologies and procedures are required to ensure that systems are reliable and secure?

5 IT Infrastructure and Emerging Technologies

Learning Objectives

After reading this chapter, you will be able to answer the following questions:

5-1 What is IT infrastructure, and what are the stages and drivers of IT infrastructure evolution?

5-2 What are the components of IT infrastructure?

5-3 What are the current trends in computer hardware platforms?

5-4 What are the current computer software platforms and trends?

5-5 What are the challenges of managing IT infrastructure and management solutions?

MyMISLab™

Visit **mymislab.com** for simulations, tutorials, and end-of-chapter problems.

CHAPTER CASES

EasyJet Flies High with Cloud Computing
Wearable Computers Change How We Work
Computing Takes Off in the Cloud
BYOD: Business Opportunity or Big Headache?

VIDEO CASES

Rockwell Automation Fuels the Oil and Gas Industry with the Internet of Things (IoT)
ESPN.com: The Future of Sports Broadcasting in the Cloud
Netflix: Building a Business in the Cloud

EasyJet Flies High with Cloud Computing

EasyJet is the largest airline in the United Kingdom and the second-largest short-haul airline carrier in the world (behind Ryanair) with more than 800 domestic and international routes in 32 countries. Based in Luton, England, EasyJet has expanded rapidly since its founding in 1995, propelled by a series of acquisitions as well as fulfilling an important market need for low-cost airline services. EasyJet carries more than 70 million passengers per year. Obviously, having a reliable and robust system for booking and managing reservations while keeping costs low is a key business requirement.

EasyJet's customers, like those of other airlines, like the idea of being able to select their seats on a given flight when they made their reservations online. However, EasyJet's existing reservation system did not have the capability to add this new feature, which required investing in an additional computer center and modifying its IT infrastructure.

EasyJet's IT department found a better solution. It retained the core reservation system as is and hosted the seat allocation service in the cloud using Microsoft's Azure cloud service. EasyJet had tried other public cloud computing platforms, but Microsoft's offered a better integration of on-premises and cloud services. EasyJet had used the Microsoft Azure cloud service to build services that communicate wirelessly at airports without running up major airport charges for new services desks.

Microsoft's Azure cloud enabled EasyJet's information system developers to write their own software program code for seat allocation and use as much or as little processing power as needed to test the service. It then turned out to be much faster and cost-effective to have the public cloud actually host the new seat allocation service rather than use EasyJet's internal IT infrastructure.

EasyJet is adopting a hybrid cloud strategy. It is not moving its entire IT infrastructure to the cloud, only specific functions that its internal IT infrastructure can't easily handle. The new capabilities are integrated with the company's existing IT Infrastructure. By enhancing its systems by adding new features in the cloud, the company is able to get more value out of its earlier IT investments, which amounted to many millions of dollars.

© CPC Collection/Alamy Stock Photo

When an EasyJet customer books a reservation, EasyJet's information systems integrate three different technologies. EasyJet's web servers handle the process of customers entering their desired travel dates and destinations for flight bookings. The company's reservation system residing in a different computer center presents data on alternative times and prices of flights for customers to choose from. Finally, the aircraft diagram where users can select their seats is fully hosted on Microsoft's Azure cloud service. The entire experience appears seamless to users.

By enhancing its systems to offer allocated seating, EasyJet was able to increase customer satisfaction by 5 percent and add 7 percent to its revenue growth according to the company's 2013 annual earnings report. In the following two years, the company increased customer conversion to its website by 13 percent. Selecting seats and boarding flights have become much more pleasant.

EasyJet's management believes that good customer experience combined with low prices clearly differentiates the company from competitors. The business benefits of offering online seat selection using cloud computing services have made it possible for EasyJet to continue this strategy because it can keep operating costs low while offering customers top-notch services in searching for and booking flights. Airlines on average spend 2 percent of their revenue on IT infrastructure; EasyJet spends only half a percent of its revenue on IT.

What if the new seat allocation system enhancement had failed to improve customer service and revenue? EasyJet could have easily turned off the cloud service for online seat selection if it so chose. It is much easier to eliminate a cloud service than to remove the functionality from the company's core internal system.

Sources: "Leading European Airline Improves Service and Scalability with Hybrid Cloud Solution," www.microsoft.com, accessed February 9, 2016; www.easyjet.com, accessed May 1, 2016; Clare McDonald, "How EasyJet Uses Digital to Drive Competitive Advantage," *Computer Weekly,* October 13, 2015; and "EasyJet Raises Customer Satisfaction with Hybrid IT," *Computer Weekly*, September 23–29, 2014.

The experience of EasyJet illustrates the importance of information technology infrastructure in running a business today. The right technology at the right price will improve organizational performance. EasyJet was saddled with an outdated IT infrastructure that was far too costly and unwieldy for adding new services, such as online passenger seat selection, that were being offered by competitors. This caused EasyJet to lose customers and prevented the company from operating as efficiently and effectively as it could have.

The chapter-opening case diagram calls attention to important points raised by this case and this chapter. As a low-cost carrier, EasyJet is under pressure to keep costs down, but it still must offer services such as online seat selection that are provided by competing airlines. Management had to find a low-cost solution that enabled the company to remain competitive. It decided to develop and run the new seat selection service on Microsoft's Azure cloud computing platform, where the hardware is located in remote computing centers accessed via the Internet. The seat selection capability is integrated with EasyJet's internal reservation system, which is maintained on premises. This is an example of a hybrid cloud strategy, where an organization maintains part of its

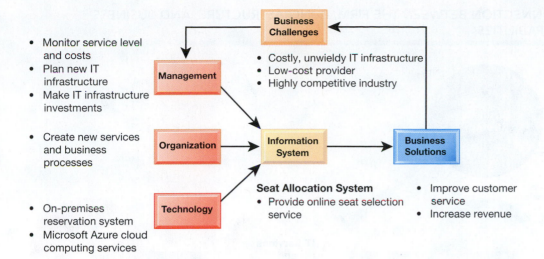

- Monitor service level and costs
- Plan new IT infrastructure
- Make IT infrastructure investments

- Create new services and business processes

- On-premises reservation system
- Microsoft Azure cloud computing services

Business Challenges
- Costly, unwieldy IT infrastructure
- Low-cost provider
- Highly competitive industry

Management

Organization

Technology

Information System

Business Solutions

Seat Allocation System
- Provide online seat selection service

- Improve customer service
- Increase revenue

IT infrastructure itself and part using cloud computing services. Using cloud computing for part of its IT infrastructure enables EasyJet to expand and offer new services at very affordable prices. The company pays for only the computing capacity it actually uses on an as-needed basis and did not have to make extensive and costly new infrastructure investments.

Here are some questions to think about: How did EasyJet's hardware and software technology affect the company's ability to operate? What were the business benefits of using cloud computing?

5-1 What is IT infrastructure, and what are the stages and drivers of IT infrastructure evolution?

In Chapter 1, we defined *information technology (IT) infrastructure* as the shared technology resources that provide the platform for the firm's specific information system applications. An IT infrastructure includes investment in hardware, software, and services—such as consulting, education, and training—that are shared across the entire firm or across entire business units in the firm. A firm's IT infrastructure provides the foundation for serving customers, working with vendors, and managing internal firm business processes (see Figure 5.1).

Supplying firms worldwide with IT infrastructure (hardware and software) in 2016 is estimated to be a $3.5 trillion industry when telecommunications, networking equipment, and telecommunications services (Internet, telephone, and data transmission) are included. Investments in infrastructure account for between 25 and 50 percent of information technology expenditures in large firms, led by financial services firms where IT investment is well over half of all capital investment.

Defining IT Infrastructure

An IT infrastructure consists of a set of physical devices and software applications that are required to operate the entire enterprise. But IT infrastructure also includes a set of firmwide services budgeted by management and composed of both human and technical capabilities. These services include the following:

FIGURE 5.1   CONNECTION BETWEEN THE FIRM, IT INFRASTRUCTURE, AND BUSINESS CAPABILITIES

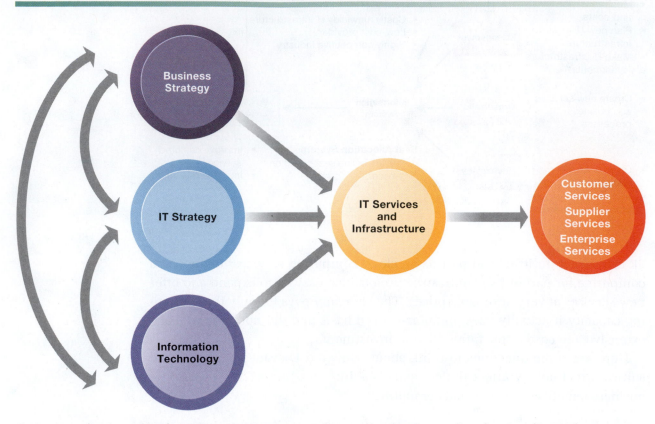

The services a firm is capable of providing to its customers, suppliers, and employees are a direct function of its IT infrastructure. Ideally, this infrastructure should support the firm's business and information systems strategy. New information technologies have a powerful impact on business and IT strategies as well as the services that can be provided to customers.

- Computing platforms used to provide computing services that connect employees, customers, and suppliers into a coherent digital environment, including large mainframes, midrange computers, desktop and laptop computers, and mobile handheld and remote cloud computing services

- Telecommunications services that provide data, voice, and video connectivity to employees, customers, and suppliers

- Data management services that store and manage corporate data and provide capabilities for analyzing the data

- Application software services, including online software services, that provide enterprise-wide capabilities such as enterprise resource planning, customer relationship management, supply chain management, and knowledge management systems that are shared by all business units

- Physical facilities management services that develop and manage the physical installations required for computing, telecommunications, and data management services

- IT management services that plan and develop the infrastructure, coordinate with the business units for IT services, manage accounting for the IT expenditure, and provide project management services

- IT standards services that provide the firm and its business units with policies that determine which information technology will be used, when, and how

- IT education services that provide training in system use to employees and offer managers training in how to plan for and manage IT investments

- IT research and development services that provide the firm with research on potential future IT projects and investments that could help the firm differentiate itself in the marketplace

This "service platform" perspective makes it easier to understand the business value provided by infrastructure investments. For instance, the real business value of a fully loaded personal computer operating at 3.5 gigahertz that costs about $1,000 and a high-speed Internet connection is hard to understand without knowing who will use it and how it will be used. When we look at the services provided by these tools, however, their value becomes more apparent: The new PC makes it possible for a high-cost employee making $100,000 a year to connect to all the company's major systems and the public Internet. The high-speed Internet service saves this employee about an hour per day in reduced wait time for Internet information. Without this PC and Internet connection, the value of this one employee to the firm might be cut in half.

Evolution of IT Infrastructure

The IT infrastructure in organizations today is an outgrowth of more than 50 years of evolution in computing platforms. There have been five stages in this evolution, each representing a different configuration of computing power and infrastructure elements (see Figure 5.2). The five eras are general-purpose mainframe and minicomputer computing, personal computers, client/server networks, enterprise computing, and cloud and mobile computing.

Technologies that characterize one era may also be used in another time period for other purposes. For example, some companies still run traditional mainframe systems or use mainframe computers as servers supporting large websites and corporate enterprise applications.

General-Purpose Mainframe and Minicomputer Era (1959 to Present)

The introduction of the IBM 1401 and 7090 transistorized machines in 1959 marked the beginning of widespread commercial use of **mainframe** computers. In 1965, the mainframe computer truly came into its own with the introduction of the IBM 360 series. The 360 was the first commercial computer that could provide time sharing, multitasking, and virtual memory in more advanced models. IBM has dominated mainframe computing from this point on. Mainframe computers became powerful enough to support thousands of online remote terminals connected to the centralized mainframe using proprietary communication protocols and proprietary data lines.

The mainframe era was a period of highly centralized computing under the control of professional programmers and systems operators (usually in a corporate data center), with most elements of infrastructure provided by a single vendor, the manufacturer of the hardware and the software.

This pattern began to change with the introduction of **minicomputers** produced by Digital Equipment Corporation (DEC) in 1965. DEC minicomputers (PDP-11 and later the VAX machines) offered powerful machines at far lower prices than IBM mainframes, making possible decentralized computing, customized to the specific needs of individual departments or business units rather than time sharing on a single huge mainframe. In recent years, the minicomputer has evolved into a midrange computer or midrange server and is part of a network.

FIGURE 5.2 **ERAS IN IT INFRASTRUCTURE EVOLUTION**

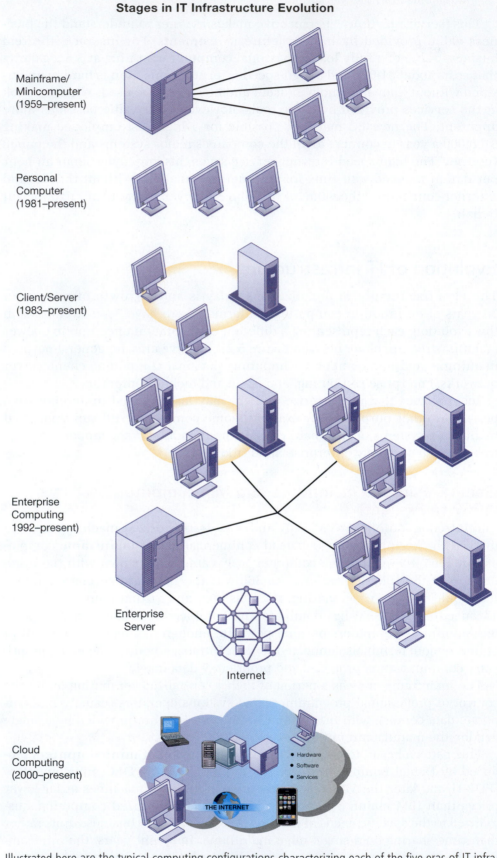

Stages in IT Infrastructure Evolution

Mainframe/
Minicomputer
(1959–present)

Personal
Computer
(1981–present)

Client/Server
(1983–present)

Enterprise
Computing
1992–present)

Enterprise
Server

Internet

Cloud
Computing
(2000–present)

- Hardware
- Software
- Services

THE INTERNET

Illustrated here are the typical computing configurations characterizing each of the five eras of IT infrastructure evolution.

Personal Computer Era (1981 to Present)

Although the first truly personal computers (PCs) appeared in the 1970s (the Xerox Alto, the MITS Altair 8800, and the Apple I and II, to name a few), these machines had only limited distribution to computer enthusiasts. The appearance of the IBM PC in 1981 is usually considered the beginning of the PC era because this machine was the first to be widely adopted by American businesses. At first using the DOS operating system, a text-based command language, and later the Microsoft Windows operating system, the **Wintel PC** computer (Windows operating system software on a computer with an Intel microprocessor) became the standard desktop personal computer. Worldwide PC shipments have declined more than 10 percent because of the popularity of tablets and smartphones, but the PC is still a popular tool for business. About 289 million new PCs were sold worldwide in 2015 (Gartner, Inc., 2016). Approximately 87 percent are thought to run a version of Windows, and about 4 percent run a version of Mac OS. The Wintel dominance as a computing platform is receding as iPhone and Android device sales increase. About 2 billion people worldwide own smartphones, and most of these users access the Internet with their mobile devices.

Proliferation of PCs in the 1980s and early 1990s launched a spate of personal desktop productivity software tools—word processors, spreadsheets, electronic presentation software, and small data management programs—that were very valuable to both home and corporate users. These PCs were stand-alone systems until PC operating system software in the 1990s made it possible to link them into networks.

Client/Server Era (1983 to Present)

In **client/server computing**, desktop or laptop computers called **clients** are networked to powerful **server** computers that provide the client computers with a variety of services and capabilities. Computer processing work is split between these two types of machines. The client is the user point of entry, whereas the server typically processes and stores shared data, serves up web pages, or manages network activities. The term *server* refers to both the software application and the physical computer on which the network software runs. The server could be a mainframe, but today, server computers typically are more powerful versions of personal computers, based on inexpensive chips and often using multiple processors in a single computer box or in server racks.

The simplest client/server network consists of a client computer networked to a server computer, with processing split between the two types of machines. This is called a *two-tiered client/server architecture*. Whereas simple client/server networks can be found in small businesses, most corporations have more complex, **multitiered** (often called **N-tier**) **client/server architectures** in which the work of the entire network is balanced over several different levels of servers, depending on the kind of service being requested (see Figure 5.3).

For instance, at the first level, a **web server** will serve a webpage to a client in response to a request for service. Web server software is responsible for locating and managing stored webpages. If the client requests access to a corporate system (a product list or price information, for instance), the request is passed along to an **application server**. Application server software handles all application operations between a user and an organization's back-end business systems. The application server may reside on the same computer as the web server or on its own dedicated computer. Chapters 6 and 7 provide more detail on other pieces of software that are used in multitiered client/server architectures for e-commerce and e-business.

FIGURE 5.3   A MULTITIERED (N-TIER) CLIENT/SERVER NETWORK

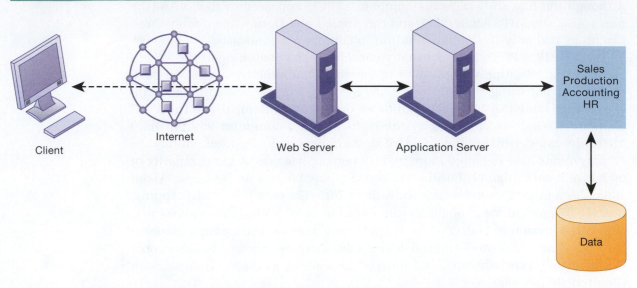

In a multitiered client/server network, client requests for service are handled by different levels of servers.

Client/server computing enables businesses to distribute computing work across a series of smaller, inexpensive machines that cost much less than centralized mainframe systems. The result is an explosion in computing power and applications throughout the firm.

Novell NetWare was the leading technology for client/server networking at the beginning of the client/server era. Today, Microsoft is the market leader with its **Windows** operating systems (Windows Server, Windows 10, Windows 8, and Windows 7).

Enterprise Computing Era (1992 to Present)

In the early 1990s, firms turned to networking standards and software tools that could integrate disparate networks and applications throughout the firm into an enterprise-wide infrastructure. As the Internet developed into a trusted communications environment after 1995, business firms began seriously using the *Transmission Control Protocol/Internet Protocol (TCP/IP)* networking standard to tie their disparate networks together. We discuss TCP/IP in detail in Chapter 7.

The resulting IT infrastructure links different pieces of computer hardware and smaller networks into an enterprise-wide network so that information can flow freely across the organization and between the firm and other organizations. It can link different types of computer hardware, including mainframes, servers, PCs, and mobile devices, and it includes public infrastructures such as the telephone system, the Internet, and public network services. The enterprise infrastructure also requires software to link disparate applications and enable data to flow freely among different parts of the business, such as enterprise applications (see Chapters 2 and 9) and web services (discussed in Section 5-4).

Cloud and Mobile Computing Era (2000 to Present)

The growing bandwidth power of the Internet has pushed the client/server model one step further, toward what is called the "cloud computing model." **Cloud computing** refers to a model of computing that provides access to a shared pool of computing resources (computers, storage, applications, and services) over the network, often the Internet. These "clouds" of computing resources can be accessed on an as-needed basis from any connected device and location.

Cloud computing is now the fastest growing form of computing. According to the International Data Corporation (IDC), worldwide spending on public cloud services is growing at a 19.4 percent compound annual growth rate, nearly six times the rate of overall IT spending growth—from nearly $70 billion in 2015 to more than $141 billion in 2019 (International Data Corporation, 2016).

Thousands or even hundreds of thousands of computers are located in cloud data centers, where they can be accessed by desktop computers, laptop computers, tablets, entertainment centers, smartphones, and other client machines linked to the Internet. Amazon, Google, IBM, and Microsoft operate huge, scalable cloud computing centers that provide computing power, data storage, and high-speed Internet connections to firms that want to maintain their IT infrastructures remotely. Firms such as Google, Microsoft, SAP, Oracle, and Salesforce.com sell software applications as services delivered over the Internet.

We discuss cloud and mobile computing in more detail in Section 5-3. The Learning Tracks include a table titled "Comparing Stages in IT Infrastructure Evolution," which compares each era on the infrastructure dimensions introduced.

Technology Drivers of Infrastructure Evolution

The changes in IT infrastructure we have just described have resulted from developments in computer processing, memory chips, storage devices, telecommunications and networking hardware and software, and software design that have exponentially increased computing power while exponentially reducing costs. Let's look at the most important developments.

Moore's Law and Microprocessing Power

In 1965, Gordon Moore, the director of Fairchild Semiconductor's Research and Development Laboratories, wrote in *Electronics* magazine that since the first microprocessor chip was introduced in 1959, the number of components on a chip with the smallest manufacturing costs per component (generally transistors) had doubled each year. This assertion became the foundation of **Moore's Law**. Moore later reduced the rate of growth to a doubling every two years.

There are at least three variations of Moore's Law, none of which Moore ever stated: (1) the power of microprocessors doubles every 18 months, (2) computing power doubles every 18 months, and (3) the price of computing falls by half every 18 months.

Figure 5.4 illustrates the relationship between number of transistors on a microprocessor and millions of instructions per second (MIPS), a common measure of processor power. Figure 5.5 shows the exponential decline in the cost of transistors and rise in computing power. For instance, in 2016, you could buy an Intel i7 quad-core processor chip with 2.5 billion transistors for about one ten-millionth of a dollar per transistor.

Exponential growth in the number of transistors and the power of processors coupled with an exponential decline in computing costs may not be able to continue much longer. Chip manufacturers continue to miniaturize components. Today's transistors should no longer be compared to the size of a human hair but rather to the size of a virus. Within the next five years or so, chip makers may reach the physical limits of semiconductor size. At that point they may need to use alternatives to fashioning chips from silicon or finding other ways to make computers more powerful (Markoff, 2016).

FIGURE 5.4   MOORE'S LAW AND MICROPROCESSOR PERFORMANCE

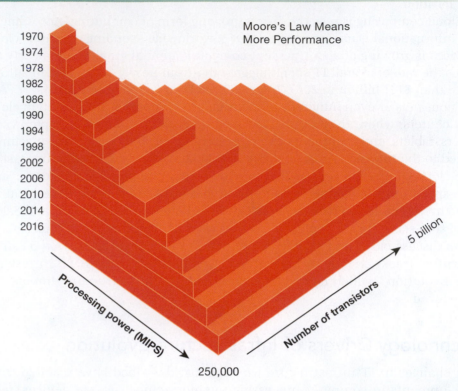

Packing more than 5 billion transistors into a tiny microprocessor has exponentially increased processing power. Processing power has increased to more than 250,000 MIPS (about 2.6 billion instructions per second).

Source: Authors' estimate.

FIGURE 5.5   FALLING COST OF CHIPS

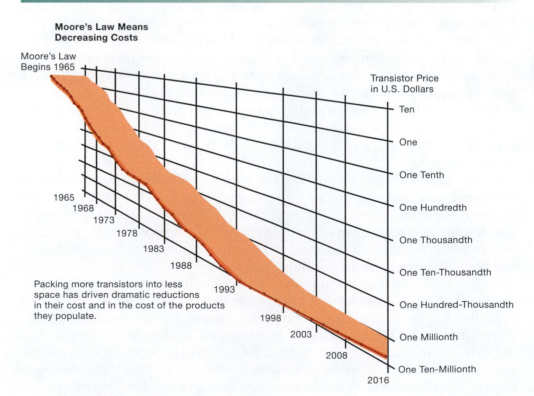

Source: Authors' estimate.

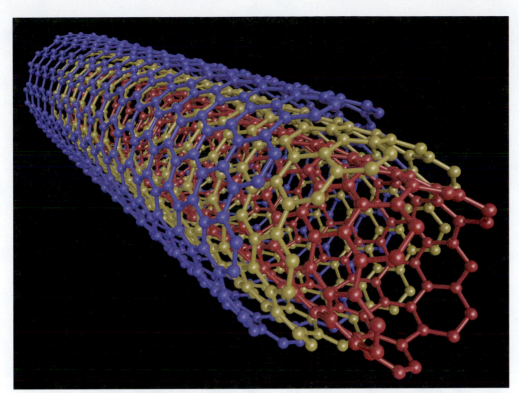

Nanotubes are tiny tubes about 10,000 times thinner than a human hair. They consist of rolled-up sheets of carbon hexagons and have potential use as minuscule wires or in ultrasmall electronic devices and are very powerful conductors of electrical current.

© Owen Thomas/123RF

Chip manufacturers can shrink the size of transistors down to the width of several atoms by using nanotechnology. **Nanotechnology** uses individual atoms and molecules to create computer chips and other devices that are thousands of times smaller than current technologies permit. Chip manufacturers are trying to develop a manufacturing process to produce nanotube processors economically. Stanford University scientists have built a nanotube computer.

The Law of Mass Digital Storage

A second technology driver of IT infrastructure change is the Law of Mass Digital Storage. The amount of digital information is roughly doubling every year Lyman and Varian, 2003). Fortunately, the cost of storing digital information is falling at an exponential rate of 100 percent a year. Figure 5.6 shows that the number of megabytes that can be stored on magnetic media for $1 from 1950 to the present roughly doubled every 15 months. In 2016, a 500 gigabyte hard disk drive sells at retail for about $50.

Metcalfe's Law and Network Economics

Moore's Law and the Law of Mass Digital Storage help us understand why computing resources are now so readily available. But why do people want more computing and storage power? The economics of networks and the growth of the Internet provide some answers.

Robert Metcalfe—inventor of Ethernet local area network technology—claimed in 1970 that the value or power of a network grows exponentially as a function of the number of network members. Metcalfe and others point to the *increasing returns to scale* that network members receive as more and more people join the network. As the number of members in a network grows linearly, the value of the entire system grows exponentially and continues to grow as members increase. Demand for information technology has been driven by the social and business value of digital networks, which rapidly multiply the number of actual and potential links among network members.

FIGURE 5.6 THE AMOUNT OF STORAGE PER DOLLAR RISES EXPONENTIALLY, 1950–2016

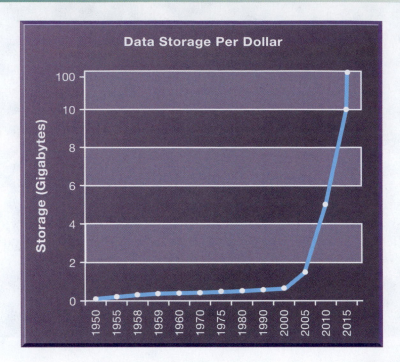

Cloud storage services like Google Drive provide 100 gigabytes of storage for $1.99 per month.

Source: Authors' estimates.

Declining Communications Costs and the Internet

A fourth technology driver transforming IT infrastructure is the rapid decline in the costs of communication and the exponential growth in the size of the Internet. Today there are more than 3.5 billion Internet users worldwide (Internetlivestats.com, 2016). Figure 5.7 illustrates the exponentially declining cost of communication both over the Internet and over telephone networks (which increasingly are based on the Internet). As communication costs fall toward a very small number and approach zero, utilization of communication and computing facilities explode.

To take advantage of the business value associated with the Internet, firms must greatly expand their Internet connections, including wireless connectivity, and greatly expand the power of their client/server networks, desktop clients, and mobile computing devices. There is every reason to believe these trends will continue.

Standards and Network Effects

Today's enterprise infrastructure and Internet computing would be impossible—both now and in the future—without agreements among manufacturers and widespread consumer acceptance of **technology standards**. Technology standards are specifications that establish the compatibility of products and the ability to communicate in a network.

Technology standards unleash powerful economies of scale and result in price declines as manufacturers focus on the products built to a single standard. Without these economies of scale, computing of any sort would be far more expensive than is currently the case. Table 5.1 describes important standards that have shaped IT infrastructure.

FIGURE 5.7 **EXPONENTIAL DECLINES IN INTERNET COMMUNICATIONS COSTS**

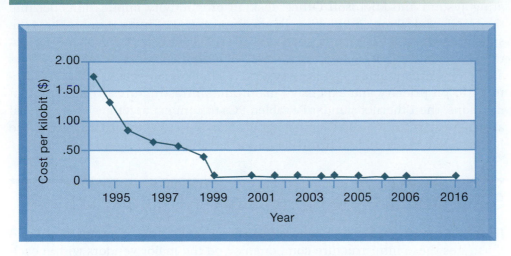

Verizon FiOS (fiber to the home) delivers 1 kilobit of data for a retail price less than 2 thousandths of a penny.

Source: Authors.

TABLE 5.1 **SOME IMPORTANT STANDARDS IN COMPUTING**

STANDARD	SIGNIFICANCE
American Standard Code for Information Interchange (ASCII) (1958)	Made it possible for computer machines from different manufacturers to exchange data; later used as the universal language linking input and output devices such as keyboards and mice to computers. Adopted by the American National Standards Institute in 1963.
Common Business Oriented Language (COBOL) (1959)	An easy-to-use software language that greatly expanded the ability of programmers to write business-related programs and reduced the cost of software. Sponsored by the Defense Department in 1959.
Unix (1969–1975)	A powerful multitasking, multiuser, portable operating system initially developed at Bell Labs (1969) and later released for use by others (1975). It operates on a wide variety of computers from different manufacturers. Adopted by Sun, IBM, HP, and others in the 1980s, it became the most widely used enterprise-level operating system.
Transmission Control Protocol/Internet Protocol (TCP/IP) (1974)	Suite of communications protocols and a common addressing scheme that enables millions of computers to connect together in one giant global network (the Internet). Later, it was used as the default networking protocol suite for local area networks and intranets. Developed in the early 1970s for the U.S. Department of Defense.
Ethernet (1973)	A network standard for connecting desktop computers into local area networks that enabled the widespread adoption of client/server computing and local area networks and further stimulated the adoption of personal computers.
IBM/Microsoft/Intel Personal Computer (1981)	The standard Wintel design for personal desktop computing based on standard Intel processors and other standard devices, Microsoft DOS, and later Windows software. The emergence of this standard, low-cost product laid the foundation for a 25-year period of explosive growth in computing throughout all organizations around the globe. Today, more than 1 billion PCs power business and government activities every day.
World Wide Web (1989–1993)	Standards for storing, retrieving, formatting, and displaying information as a worldwide web of electronic pages incorporating text, graphics, audio, and video enables creation of a global repository of billions of webpages.

Beginning in the 1990s, corporations started moving toward standard computing and communications platforms. The Wintel PC with the Windows operating system and Microsoft Office desktop productivity applications became the standard desktop and mobile client computing platform. (It now shares the spotlight with other standards, such as Apple's iOS and Macintosh operating systems and the Android operating system.) Widespread adoption of Unix-Linux as the enterprise server operating system of choice made possible the replacement of proprietary and expensive mainframe infrastructures. In telecommunications, the Ethernet standard enabled PCs to connect together in small local area networks (LANs; see Chapter 7), and the TCP/IP standard enabled these LANs to be connected into firmwide networks, and ultimately, to the Internet.

5-2 What are the components of IT infrastructure?

IT infrastructure today is composed of seven major components. Figure 5.8 illustrates these infrastructure components and the major vendors within each component category. These components constitute investments that must be coordinated with one another to provide the firm with a coherent infrastructure.

FIGURE 5.8 THE IT INFRASTRUCTURE ECOSYSTEM

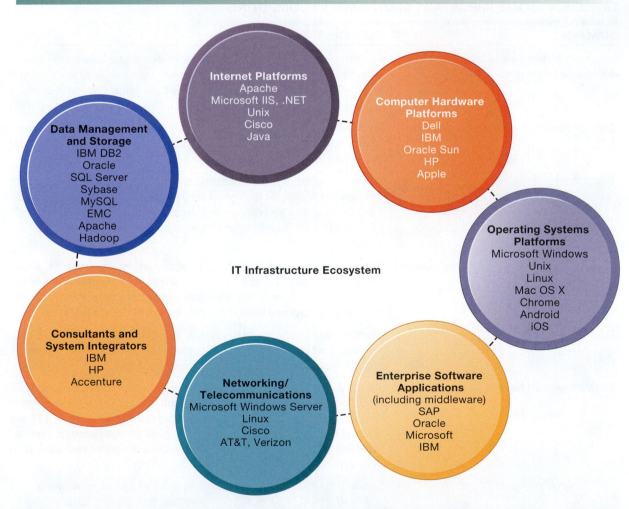

There are seven major components that must be coordinated to provide the firm with a coherent IT infrastructure. Listed here are major technologies and suppliers for each component.

In the past, technology vendors supplying these components offered purchasing firms a mixture of incompatible, proprietary, partial solutions that could not work with other vendor products. Increasingly, vendor firms have been forced to cooperate in strategic partnerships with one another in order to keep their customers. For instance, a hardware and services provider such as IBM cooperates with all the major enterprise software providers, has strategic relationships with system integrators, and promises to work with whichever data management products its client firms wish to use (even though it sells its own database management software called DB2).

Another big change is that companies are moving more of their IT infrastructure to the cloud or to outside services, owning and managing much less on their premises. According to International Data Corporation, by 2020, business spending on cloud infrastructure will account for roughly half of the total computing resources budget. Firms' IT infrastructures will increasingly be an amalgam of components and services that are partially owned, partially rented or licensed, partially located on site, and partially supplied by external vendors or cloud services.

Computer Hardware Platforms

Firms worldwide are expected to spend $626 billion on computer hardware devices in 2016, including mainframes, servers, PCs, tablets, and smartphones. All these devices constitute the computer hardware platform for corporate (and personal) computing worldwide.

Most business computing takes place using microprocessor "chips" manufactured or designed by Intel Corporation and, to a lesser extent, AMD Corporation. Intel and AMD processors are often referred to as "i86" processors because the original IBM PCs used an Intel 8086 processor and all the Intel (and AMD) chips that followed are downward compatible with this processor. (For instance, you should be able to run a software application designed 10 years ago on a new PC you bought yesterday.)

The computer platform changed dramatically with the introduction of mobile computing devices, from the iPod in 2001 to the iPhone in 2007 and the iPad in 2010. Worldwide, 2 billion people use smartphones. You can think of these devices as a second computer hardware platform, one that is consumer device–driven.

The computers with Intel microprocessors in the first computer hardware platform use complex instruction set computing (CISC) with several thousand instructions built into the chip. This requires a considerable number of transistors per processor, consumes power, and generates heat. Mobile devices in the second computer hardware platform are not required to perform as many tasks as computers in the first computer hardware platform. They are able to use reduced instruction set computing (RISC), which contains a smaller set of instructions, consumes less power, and generates less heat. RISC processors for mobile devices are manufactured by a wide range of firms, including Apple, Samsung, and Qualcomm, using an architecture designed by ARM Holdings.

Mainframes have not disappeared. They continue to be used to reliably and securely handle huge volumes of transactions, for analyzing very large quantities of data, and for handling large workloads in cloud computing centers. The mainframe is still the digital workhorse for banking and telecommunications networks that are often running software programs that are older and require a specific hardware platform. Currently, mainframes process 30 billion business transactions per day, and 80 percent of the world's corporate data also originates on the mainframe (ITBusinessEdge.com, 2015).

However, the number of providers has dwindled to one: IBM. IBM has also repurposed its mainframe systems so they can be used as giant servers for enterprise networks and corporate websites. A single IBM mainframe can run thousands of instances of Linux or Windows Server software and is capable of replacing thousands of smaller servers (see the discussion of virtualization in Section 5-3).

Operating System Platforms

The leading operating systems for corporate servers are Microsoft Windows Server, **Unix**, and **Linux**, an inexpensive and robust open source relative of Unix. Microsoft Windows Server is capable of providing enterprise-wide operating system and network services and appeals to organizations seeking Windows-based IT infrastructures. Unix and Linux are scalable, reliable, and much less expensive than mainframe operating systems. They can also run on many different types of processors. The major providers of Unix operating systems are IBM, HP, and Oracle-Sun, each with slightly different and partially incompatible versions.

At the client level, 81 percent of PCs use some form of the Microsoft Windows **operating system** (such as Windows 10, Windows 8, or Windows 7) to manage the resources and activities of the computer. However, there is now a much greater variety of client operating systems than in the past, with new operating systems for computing on handheld mobile digital devices or cloud-connected computers.

Google's **Chrome OS** provides a lightweight operating system for cloud computing using a web-connected computer. Programs are not stored on the user's computer but are used over the Internet and accessed through the Chrome web browser. User data reside on servers across the Internet. **Android** is an open source operating system for mobile devices such as smartphones and tablet computers developed by the Open Handset Alliance led by Google. It has become the most popular smartphone platform worldwide, competing with iOS, Apple's mobile operating system for the iPhone, iPad, and iPod Touch. Android is installed on more than half the tablets, smartphones, and portable computers in use globally.

Conventional client operating system software is designed around the mouse and keyboard but increasingly is becoming more natural and intuitive by using touch technology. **iOS**, the operating system for the phenomenally popular Apple iPad, iPhone, and iPod Touch, features a **multitouch** interface, where users employ one or more fingers to manipulate objects on a screen without a mouse or keyboard. Microsoft's **Windows 10** and Windows 8, which run on tablets as well as PCs, have multitouch capabilities, as do many Android devices.

Enterprise Software Applications

Firms worldwide are expected to spend about $321 billion in 2016 on software for enterprise applications that are treated as components of IT infrastructure. We introduced the various types of enterprise applications in Chapter 2, and Chapter 9 provides a more detailed discussion of each.

The largest providers of enterprise application software are SAP and Oracle. Also included in this category is middleware software supplied by vendors such as IBM and Oracle for achieving firmwide integration by linking the firm's existing application systems. Microsoft is attempting to move into the lower ends of this market by focusing on small and medium-sized businesses.

Data Management and Storage

Enterprise database management software is responsible for organizing and managing the firm's data so that they can be efficiently accessed and used. Chapter 6 describes this software in detail. The leading database software providers are IBM (DB2), Oracle, Microsoft (SQL Server), and Sybase (Adaptive Server Enterprise). MySQL is a Linux open source relational database product now owned by Oracle Corporation, and Apache Hadoop is an open source software framework for managing very large data sets (see Chapter 6). The physical data storage market for large-scale systems is dominated by EMC Corporation.

Networking/Telecommunications Platforms

Companies worldwide are expected to spend $1.44 trillion for telecommunications services in 2016 (Gartner, Inc., 2016). Windows Server is predominantly used as a local area network operating system, followed by Linux and Unix. Large, enterprise-wide area networks use some variant of Unix. Most local area networks, as well as wide area enterprise networks, use the TCP/IP protocol suite as a standard (see Chapter 7).

Cisco and Juniper Networks are leading networking hardware providers. Telecommunications platforms are typically provided by telecommunications/telephone services companies that offer voice and data connectivity, wide area networking, wireless services, and Internet access. Leading telecommunications service vendors include AT&T and Verizon. This market is exploding with new providers of cellular wireless, high-speed Internet, and Internet telephone services.

Internet Platforms

Internet platforms include hardware, software, and management services to support a firm's website, including web hosting services, routers, and cabling or wireless equipment. A **web hosting service** maintains a large web server, or series of servers, and provides fee-paying subscribers with space to maintain their websites.

The Internet revolution created a veritable explosion in server computers, with many firms collecting thousands of small servers to run their Internet operations. There has been a steady push to reduce the number of server computers by increasing the size and power of each and by using software tools that make it possible to run more applications on a single server. The Internet hardware server market has become increasingly concentrated in the hands of IBM, Dell, Oracle, and HP, as prices have fallen dramatically.

The major web software application development tools and suites are supplied by Microsoft (Microsoft Visual Studio and the Microsoft .NET family of development tools), Oracle-Sun (Sun's Java is the most widely used tool for developing interactive web applications on both the server and client sides), and a host of independent software developers, including Adobe (Creative Suite). Chapter 7 describes the components of the firm's Internet platform in greater detail.

Consulting and System Integration Services

Today, even a large firm does not have the staff, the skills, the budget, or the necessary experience to deploy and maintain its entire IT infrastructure. Implementing a new infrastructure requires (as noted in Chapters 13 and 14) significant changes in business processes and procedures, training and education, and software integration. Leading consulting firms providing this expertise include Accenture, IBM Global Business Services, HP, Infosys, and Wipro Technologies.

Software integration means ensuring the new infrastructure works with the firm's older, so-called legacy systems and ensuring the new elements of the infrastructure work with one another. **Legacy systems** are generally older transaction processing systems created for mainframe computers that continue to be used to avoid the high cost of replacing or redesigning them. Replacing these systems is cost prohibitive and generally not necessary if these older systems can be integrated into a contemporary infrastructure.

5-3 What are the current trends in computer hardware platforms?

The exploding power of computer hardware and networking technology has dramatically changed how businesses organize their computing power, putting more of this power on networks and mobile handheld devices. We look at seven hardware trends: the mobile digital platform, consumerization of IT and BYOD, quantum computing, virtualization, cloud computing, green computing, and high-performance/power-saving processors.

The Mobile Digital Platform

Chapter 1 pointed out that new mobile digital computing platforms have emerged as alternatives to PCs and larger computers. The iPhone and Android smartphones have taken on many functions of PCs, including transmitting data, surfing the web, transmitting e-mail and instant messages, displaying digital content, and exchanging data with internal corporate systems. The new mobile platform also includes small, lightweight netbooks optimized for wireless communication and Internet access, **tablet computers** such as the iPad, and digital e-book readers such as Amazon's Kindle with some web access capabilities.

Smartphones and tablet computers are increasingly used for business computing as well as for consumer applications. For example, senior executives at General Motors are using smartphone applications that drill down into vehicle sales information, financial performance, manufacturing metrics, and project management status.

Wearable computing devices are a recent addition to the mobile digital platform. These include smartwatches, smart glasses, smart ID badges, and activity trackers. Wearable computing technology has business uses, and it is changing the way firms work, as described in the Interactive Session on Technology.

INTERACTIVE SESSION: TECHNOLOGY

Wearable Computers Change How We Work

It looks like wearable computing is taking off. Smartwatches, smart glasses, smart ID badges, and activity trackers promise to change how we go about each day and the way we do our jobs. According to an April 2015 report surveying 2,400 U.S. CIOs by IT staffing firm Robert Half Technology, 81 percent expect wearable computing devices such as watches and glasses to become common workplace tools.

Doctors and nurses are using smart eyewear for hands-free access to patients' medical records. Oil rig workers sport smart helmets to connect with land-based experts, who can view their work remotely and communicate instructions. Warehouse managers are able to capture real-time performance data using a smartwatch to better manage distribution and fulfillment operations. Wearable computing devices improve productivity by delivering information to workers without requiring them to interrupt their tasks, which in turn empowers employees to make more informed decisions more quickly.

Although primarily consumer devices, smartwatches are being used for business. The Apple Watch, for example, has a number of features to make employees more productive. It can take phone calls and accept voice commands. It will display an important message, e-mail, or calendar appointment on your wrist. Instead of buzzing loudly and with every e-mail, text message, and calendar alert you receive, the watch uses subtle, discreet vibrations that won't be a distraction in the middle of a meeting. There are Apple Watch versions of Evernote (note taking), PowerPoint (electronic presentations), and Invoice2go, which will automatically prompt you to start logging your work time as soon as you arrive at a job site, send basic invoices, and receive alerts when they're paid.

Salesforce.com has developed several enterprise applications for the Apple Watch. Salesforce1 for Apple Watch delivers instant notifications to salespeople, service agents, and other business users to help speed up their work. For example, sales managers can receive a discount approval request and take action right from the watch. Customer service managers can receive alerts if a critical case requires immediate attention or call wait times are about to exceed thresholds. Digital marketers can be alerted when a marketing campaign surpasses a goal. Salesforce Analytics for Apple Watch enables Salesforce

customers to use analytics data delivered to their smartwatches to view performance metrics, uncover new insights, and take action with dashboards. Users will also be able to query via Voice Search to access a report, view a dashboard, or find other information.

Global logistics company DHL worked with Ricoh, the imaging and electronics company, and Ubimax, a wearable computing services and solutions company, to implement "vision picking" in its warehouse operations. Location graphics are displayed on smartglasses guiding staffers through the warehouse to both speed the process of finding items and reduce errors. The company says the technology delivered a 25 percent increase in efficiency.

Right now, vision picking gives workers locational information about the items they need to retrieve and allows them to automatically scan retrieved items. Future enhancements will enable the system to plot optimal routes through the warehouse, provide pictures of items to be retrieved (a key aid in case an item has been misplaced on the warehouse shelves), and instruct workers on loading carts and pallets more efficiently.

Southern Co., an Atlanta-based energy company, is experimenting with several different wearables in its power plants and its power distribution and transmission pipeline. Southern recently deployed both head-mounted and wrist-mounted computers and performed several "proofs of concept" with Google Glass, Apple Watch, and the Moto 360 Android Wear device. The proofs of concept focused on enhancing plant workers' ability to follow documented procedures more accurately and to document adherence to those procedures. The company also piloted Bluetooth video cameras worn on the head for documenting work processes and for videoconferencing between field personnel and central office personnel. Southern Co. now uses head-worn cameras in some plants and field locations.

At Walt Disney World Resort in Orlando, Florida, guests are issued a MagicBand, a radio frequency identification (RFID) wristband, which serves as their hotel room key and park entrance ticket and can be assigned a PIN and linked to a credit card to make purchases. The wristband is also used to link photos to guest accounts and will soon connect to a vacation-planning system. Staff are equipped with long-range RFID readers so they can personally greet guests. Aggregated RFID data will be used to minimize attraction wait times. Messages entice guests to relocate to less busy areas of the park. FastPass +, Disney's ride reservation system, allocates guests to the most popular attractions by assigning one-hour return windows for express entrance.

The value of wearable computing devices isn't from transferring the same information from a laptop or smartphone to a smartwatch or eyeglass display. Rather, it's about finding ways to use wearables to augment and enhance business processes. Successful adoption of wearable computing depends not only on cost effectiveness but on the development of new and better apps and integration with existing IT infrastructure and the organization's tools for managing and securing mobile devices (see the chapter-ending case study.)

Sources: Mary K. Pratt, "Wearables in the Enterprise? Yes, Really!" *Computerworld,* February 24, 2016; www.salesforce.com, accessed May 5, 2016; Bob Violino, "Wearables in the Workplace: Potential and Pitfalls," *Baseline,* September 9, 2015; Brett Nuckles, "Apple Watch: Is It Good for Business?" *Business News Daily,* May 12, 2015; Dennis McCafferty, "Why Wearable Tech Needs Killer Business Apps," *CIO Insight,* May 1, 2015; and Daisuke Wakabayashi, "What Exactly Is an Apple Watch For?" *Wall Street Journal,* February 16, 2015.

CASE STUDY QUESTIONS

1. Wearables have the potential to change the way organizations and workers conduct business. Discuss the implications of this statement.

2. How would a business process such as ordering a product for a customer in the field be changed if the salesperson was wearing a smartwatch equipped with Salesforce software?

3. What management, organization, and technology issues would have to be addressed if a company was thinking of equipping its workers with a wearable computing device?

4. What kinds of businesses are most likely to benefit from wearable computers? Select a business and describe how a wearable computing device could help that business improve operations or decision making.

Consumerization of IT and BYOD

The popularity, ease of use, and rich array of useful applications for smartphones and tablet computers have created a groundswell of interest in allowing employees to use their personal mobile devices in the workplace, a phenomenon popularly called *"bring your own device" (BYOD)*. **BYOD** is one aspect of the **consumerization of IT**, in which new information technology that first emerges in the consumer market spreads into business organizations. Consumerization of IT includes not only mobile personal devices but also business uses of software services that originated in the consumer marketplace as well, such as Google and Yahoo search, Gmail, Google Apps, Dropbox, and even Facebook and Twitter.

Consumerization of IT is forcing businesses to rethink the way they obtain and manage information technology equipment and services. Historically, at least in large firms, the IT department was responsible for selecting and managing the information technology and applications used by the firm and its employees. It furnished employees with desktops or laptops that were able to access corporate systems securely. The IT department maintained control over the firm's hardware and software to ensure that the business was being protected and that information systems served the purposes of the firm and its management. Today, employees and business departments are playing a much larger role in technology selection, in many cases demanding that employees be able to use their own personal computers, smartphones, and tablets to access the corporate network. It is more difficult for the firm to manage and control these consumer technologies and make sure they serve the needs of the business. The chapter-ending case study explores some of these management challenges created by BYOD and IT consumerization.

Quantum Computing

Quantum computing is an emerging technology with the potential to dramatically boost computer processing power to find answers to problems that would take conventional computers many years to solve. **Quantum computing** uses the principles of quantum physics to represent data and perform operations on these data. While conventional computers handle bits of data either as 0 or 1 but not both, quantum computing can process bits as 0, 1, or both simultaneously. A quantum computer would gain enormous processing power through this ability to be in multiple states at once, allowing it to solve some scientific and business problems millions of times faster than can be done today. IBM has made quantum computing available to the general public through IBM Cloud. Google's Alphabet and Lockheed Martin currently use quantum platforms (Follow, 2016).

Virtualization

Virtualization is the process of presenting a set of computing resources (such as computing power or data storage) so that they can all be accessed in ways that are not restricted by physical configuration or geographic location. Virtualization enables a single physical resource (such as a server or a storage device) to appear to the user as multiple logical resources. For example, a server or mainframe can be configured to run many instances of an operating system (or different operating systems) so that it acts like many different machines. Each virtual server "looks" like a real physical server to software programs, and multiple virtual servers can run in parallel on a single machine. VMware is the leading virtualization software vendor for Windows and Linux servers.

Server virtualization is a common method of reducing technology costs by providing the ability to host multiple systems on a single physical machine. Most servers run at just 15 to 20 percent of capacity, and virtualization can boost server utilization rates to 70 percent or higher. Higher utilization rates translate into fewer computers required to process the same amount of work, reduced data center space to house machines, and lower energy usage. Virtualization also facilitates centralization and consolidation of hardware administration.

Virtualization also enables multiple physical resources (such as storage devices or servers) to appear as a single logical resource, as in **software-defined storage (SDS)**, which separates the software for managing data storage from storage hardware. Using software, firms can pool and arrange multiple storage infrastructure resources and efficiently allocate them to meet specific application needs. SDS enables firms to replace expensive storage hardware with lower-cost commodity hardware and cloud storage hardware. There is less under- or over-utilization of storage resources (Letschin, 2016).

Cloud Computing

It is now possible for companies and individuals to perform all of their computing work using a virtualized IT infrastructure in a remote location, as is the case with cloud computing. Cloud computing is a model of computing in which computer processing, storage, software, and other services are provided as a shared pool of virtualized resources over a network, primarily the Internet. These "clouds" of computing resources can be accessed on an as-needed basis from any connected device and location. Figure 5.9 illustrates the cloud computing concept.

The U.S. National Institute of Standards and Technology (NIST) defines cloud computing as having the following essential characteristics (Mell and Grance, 2009):

- **On-demand self-service:** Consumers can obtain computing capabilities such as server time or network storage as needed automatically on their own.
- **Ubiquitous network access:** Cloud resources can be accessed using standard network and Internet devices, including mobile platforms.
- **Location-independent resource pooling:** Computing resources are pooled to serve multiple users, with different virtual resources dynamically assigned according to user demand. The user generally does not know where the computing resources are located.

FIGURE 5.9   CLOUD COMPUTING PLATFORM

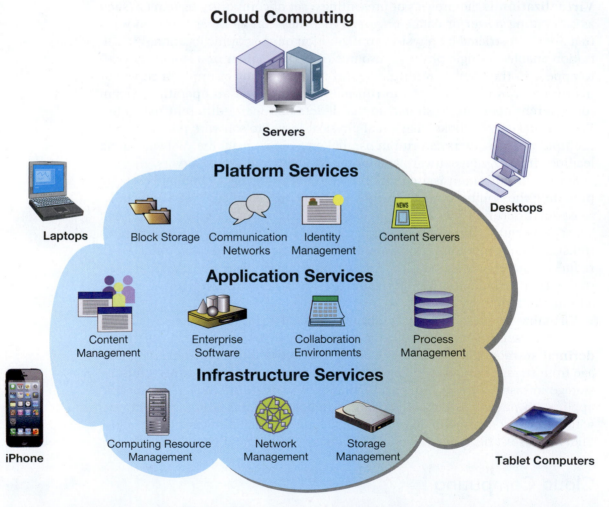

In cloud computing, hardware and software capabilities are a pool of virtualized resources provided over a network, often the Internet. Businesses and employees have access to applications and IT infrastructure anywhere, at any time, and on any device.

- **Rapid elasticity:** Computing resources can be rapidly provisioned, increased, or decreased to meet changing user demand.

- **Measured service:** Charges for cloud resources are based on amount of resources actually used.

Cloud computing consists of three different types of services:

- **Infrastructure as a service (IaaS):** Customers use processing, storage, networking, and other computing resources from cloud service providers to run their information systems. For example, Amazon uses the spare capacity of its IT infrastructure to provide a broadly based cloud environment selling IT infrastructure services. These include its Simple Storage Service (S3) for storing customers' data and its Elastic Compute Cloud (EC2) service for running their applications. Users pay only for the amount of computing and storage capacity they actually use. (See the Interactive Session on Organizations). Figure 5.10 shows the range of services Amazon Web Services offers.

- **Software as a service (SaaS):** Customers use software hosted by the vendor on the vendor's cloud infrastructure and delivered as a service over a network. Leading **software as a service (SaaS)** examples are Google Apps, which provides common business applications online, and Salesforce. com, which leases customer relationship management and related software services over the Internet. Both charge users an annual subscription fee, although Google Apps has a pared-down free version. Users access these applications from a web browser, and the data and software are maintained on the providers' remote servers.

- **Platform as a service (PaaS):** Customers use infrastructure and programming tools supported by the cloud service provider to develop their own applications. For example, IBM offers a Bluemix service for software development and testing on the IBM cloud. Another example is Salesforce.com's Force.com, which allows developers to build applications that are hosted on its servers as a service.

FIGURE 5.10 AMAZON WEB SERVICES

Amazon Web Services (AWS) is a collection of web services that Amazon provides to users of its cloud platform. AWS is the largest provider of cloud computing services In the United States.

INTERACTIVE SESSION: ORGANIZATIONS

Computing Takes Off in the Cloud

Cloud computing is now the fastest-growing form of computing. The biggest players in the cloud computing marketplace include Amazon Web Services (AWS), Microsoft, and Google. These companies have made cloud computing an affordable and sensible option for companies ranging from tiny Internet startups to established companies like Netflix and FedEx.

For example, AWS provides subscribing companies with flexible computing power and data storage as well as data management, messaging, payment, and other services that can be used together or individually as the business requires. Anyone with an Internet connection and a little bit of money can harness the same computing systems that Amazon itself uses to run its retail business. If customers provide specifications on the amount of server space, bandwidth, storage, and any other services they require, AWS can automatically allocate those resources. You don't pay a monthly or yearly fee to use Amazon's computing resources—instead, you pay for exactly what you use. Economies of scale keep costs astonishingly low, and AWS has been able to keep reducing prices. To remain competitive, other cloud computing vendors have had to follow suit.

Cloud computing also appeals to many businesses because the cloud services provider will handle all of the maintenance and upkeep of their IT infrastructures, allowing these businesses to spend more time on higher-value work. Startup companies and smaller companies are finding that they no longer need to build their own data center. With cloud infrastructures like Amazon's readily available, they have access to technical capability that was formerly available to only much larger businesses. Oscar Insurance is a New York–based health insurance company that relies heavily on information technology to help customers obtain better care and keep track of their health. The company built its HIPAA-compliant health insurance platform and analytics applications on AWS in just three months. By using AWS, Oscar can scale to support the traffic spikes during healthcare open enrollment season as well as support more than 125 production changes a day that continually improve customer experience.

Although cloud computing has been touted as a cheap and more flexible alternative to buying and owning information technology, it doesn't always deliver on its promise. For large companies, paying a public cloud provider a monthly service fee for 10,000 or more employees may actually be more expensive than having the company maintain its own IT infrastructure and staff. Companies also worry about unexpected "runaway costs" from using a pay-per-use model. Integrating cloud services with existing IT infrastructures, errors, mismanagement, or unusually high volumes of web traffic will run up the bill for cloud service users. The more data and systems that a company uses in the cloud, the bigger the job of changing cloud providers. When you buy cloud software, you may be stuck with it for a long time.

Gartner, Inc. technology consultants advise clients contemplating public cloud services to take into account the number of machines an organization will run, the number of hours per day or per week they'll run, and the amount of storage their data will require. Additional costs include licenses that need to be paid for on a recurring basis, the rate of change for the data, and how much new data the business is expected to generate. A very large company may find it cheaper to own and manage its own data center or private cloud. But as public clouds become more efficient and secure and the technology grows cheaper, large companies will start using more cloud resources.

A major barrier to widespread cloud adoption is concern about cloud reliability and security. Amazon Web Services experienced an outage on September 20, 2015, that affected Netflix, Reddit, IMDB, Product Hunt, Social Flow, and Amazon's own Alexa and Instant Video services for users across eastern North America. There were also significant Amazon cloud outages several times a year in the preceding five years. As cloud computing continues to mature and the major cloud infrastructure providers gain more experience, cloud service and reliability have steadily improved. Experts recommend that companies for whom an outage would be a major risk consider using another computing service as a backup.

In February 2016 Netflix completed a decade-long project to shut down its own data centers and use Amazon's cloud exclusively to run its business. Management liked not having to guess months beforehand what the firm's hardware, storage, and networking needs would be. AWS would provide whatever Netflix needed at the moment.

Netflix had experienced a major hardware failure in 2008 at its own data center and began moving its computing to AWS the following year. The first thing Netflix shifted was its jobs page, followed by functions such as its video player, iPhone-related technology, discovery and search, and accounts pages. Netflix shifted its big data platform to AWS in 2013 and billing and payments in 2014. Netflix is now fully reliant on AWS, using a variety of web-based software tools such as human resources software from Workday Inc. for its business applications.

Netflix also maintains a content-delivery network through Internet service providers and other third parties to speed up the delivery of movies and web traffic between Netflix and its customers. Netflix competes with Amazon in the video-streaming business, and it wanted to retain control of its own content delivery network.

About 12 percent of companies run IT operations entirely in the cloud, and nearly all of these companies are small or medium-sized businesses, according to a recent survey by BetterCloud, which makes management and security products. BetterCloud predicts that by 2022, slightly more than 20 percent of large enterprise companies will operate entirely in the cloud.

Glenn O'Donnell, vice president and research director at Forrester Research, believes that a 100 percent cloud operation will be extremely rare for large established companies. Many large companies are moving more of their computing to the cloud but are unable to migrate completely. Legacy systems are the most difficult to switch over.

Most midsized and large companies will gravitate toward a hybrid approach. The top cloud providers themselves—Amazon, Google, Microsoft, and IBM—use their own public cloud services for some purposes, but they continue to keep certain functions on private servers. Worries about reliability, security, and risks of change have made it difficult for them to move critical computing tasks to the public cloud.

Giant Eagle, one of the largest U.S. privately held multiformat food, fuel and pharmacy retailers, is adopting a hybrid cloud solution from IBM Cloud. The hybrid cloud will provide capablilties for consumption-based pricing, faster procurement, and customized deployment of applications along with integrated system management for greater visibility into enterprise data. Marriott is keeping its own data centers but updating them to use the latest cloud technology. It also uses IBM's cloud to host apps that it doesn't want to host itself. The hybrid cloud environment offers faster digital services to web-savvy guests and helps Marriott use analytics to uncover insights about traveler preferences for its more than 4,000 properties across the globe.

Sources: "AWS Case Study: Oscar Insurance," www.aws.amazon.com, accessed May 4, 2016; Robert McMillan," Cloud-Computing Kingpins Slow to Adapt to Own Movement," *Wall Street Journal*, August 4, 2015; Robert McMillan and Rachael King, "Netflix Is Ready to Pull Plug on Its Final Data Center," *Wall Street Journal*, August 14, 2015; Dan Berthiaume, "Giant Eagle Flies to the Cloud," *Chain Store Age*, December 4, 2015; Darryl K. Taft, "IBM Lands Cloud Deals with Marriott, Others," *eWeek*, February 2, 2015; Kelly Bit, "The $10 Hedge Fund Supercomputer That's Sweeping Wall Street," *Bloomberg Business Week*, May 20, 2015; David Streitfeld and Nick Wingfield, "With Amazon Atop the Cloud, Big Tech Rivals Are Giving Chase," *New York Times*, April 23, 2015.

CASE STUDY QUESTIONS

1. What business benefits do cloud computing services provide? What problems do they solve?

2. What are the disadvantages of cloud computing?

3. What kinds of businesses are most likely to benefit from using cloud computing? Why?

Chapter 2 discussed Google Docs, Google Apps, and related software services for desktop productivity and collaboration. These are among the most popular software services for consumers, although they are increasingly used in business. Salesforce.com is a leading software service for business. Salesforce provides customer relationship management (CRM) and other application software solutions as software services leased over the Internet. Its sales and service clouds offer applications for improving sales and customer service. A marketing cloud enables companies to engage in digital marketing interactions with customers through e-mail, mobile, social, web, and connected products. Salesforce.com also provides a community cloud platform for online collaboration and engagement and an analytics cloud platform to deploy sales, service, marketing, and custom analytics apps.

Salesforce.com is also a leading example of platform as a service (PaaS). Its Force.com is an application development platform where customers can develop their own applications for use within the broader Salesforce network. Force.com provides a set of development tools and IT services that enable users to customize their Salesforce.com customer relationship management applications or to build entirely new applications and run them in the cloud on Salesforce.com's data center infrastructure. Salesforce opened up Force.com to other independent software developers and listed their programs on its AppExchange, an online marketplace for third-party applications that run on the Force.com platform.

A cloud can be private or public. A **public cloud** is owned and maintained by a cloud service provider, such as Amazon Web Services, and made available to the general public or industry group. Public cloud services are often used for websites with public information and product descriptions, one-time large computing projects, developing and testing new applications, and consumer services such as online storage of data, music, and photos. Google Drive, Dropbox, and Apple iCloud are leading examples of these consumer public cloud services.

A **private cloud** is operated solely for an organization. It may be managed by the organization or a third party and may be hosted either internally or externally. Like public clouds, private clouds are able to allocate storage, computing power, or other resources seamlessly to provide computing resources on an as-needed basis. Companies that want flexible IT resources and a cloud service model while retaining control over their own IT infrastructure are gravitating toward these private clouds. (Review the chapter-opening case on EasyJet and the Interactive Session on Organizations).

Because organizations using public clouds do not own the infrastructure, they do not have to make large investments in their own hardware and software. Instead, they purchase their computing services from remote providers and pay only for the amount of computing power they actually use (utility computing) or are billed on a monthly or annual subscription basis. The term **on-demand computing** has also been used to describe such services.

Cloud computing has some drawbacks. Unless users make provisions for storing their data locally, the responsibility for data storage and control is in the hands of the provider. Some companies worry about the security risks related to entrusting their critical data and systems to an outside vendor that also works with other companies. Companies expect their systems to be available 24/7 and do not want to suffer any loss of business capability if cloud infrastructures malfunction. Nevertheless, the trend is for companies to shift more of their computer processing and storage to some form of cloud infrastructure. Startups and small companies with limited IT resources and budgets will find public cloud services especially helpful.

Large firms are most likely to adopt a **hybrid cloud** computing model where they use their own infrastructure for their most essential core activities and adopt public cloud computing for less-critical systems or for additional processing capacity during peak business periods. Table 5.2 compares the three cloud computing models. Cloud computing will gradually shift firms from having a fixed infrastructure capacity toward a more flexible infrastructure, some of it owned by the firm and some of it rented from giant computer centers owned by computer hardware vendors. You can find out more about cloud computing in the Learning Tracks for this chapter.

Green Computing

By curbing hardware proliferation and power consumption, virtualization has become one of the principal technologies for promoting green computing. **Green computing**, or **green IT**, refers to practices and technologies for designing, manufacturing, using, and disposing of computers, servers, and associated devices such as monitors, printers, storage devices, and networking and communications systems to minimize impact on the environment.

According to Green House Data, the world's data centers use as much energy as the output of 30 nuclear power plants, which amounts to 1.5 percent of all energy use in the world. Reducing computer power consumption has been a very high "green" priority. A corporate data center can easily consume over 100 times more power than a standard office building. All this additional power consumption has a negative impact on the environment and corporate operating costs. Data centers are now being designed with energy efficiency in mind, using state-of-the art air-cooling techniques, energy-efficient equipment, virtualization, and other energy-saving practices. Large companies like Microsoft, Google, Facebook, and Apple are starting to reduce their carbon footprint with clean energy–powered data centers with power-conserving equipment and extensive use of wind and hydropower.

TABLE 5.2 CLOUD COMPUTING MODELS COMPARED

TYPE OF CLOUD	DESCRIPTION	MANAGED BY	USES
Public cloud	Third-party service offering computing, storage, and software services to multiple customers and that is available to the public	Third-party service providers	Companies without major privacy concerns Companies seeking pay-as-you go IT services Companies lacking IT resources and expertise
Private cloud	Cloud infrastructure operated solely for a single organization and hosted either internally or externally.	In-house IT or private third-party host	Companies with stringent privacy and security requirements Companies that must have control over data sovereignty
Hybrid cloud	Combination of private and public cloud services that remain separate entities	In-house IT, private host, third-party providers	Companies requiring some in-house control of IT that are also willing to assign part of their IT infrastructures to a public cloud

High-Performance and Power-Saving Processors

Another way to reduce power requirements and hardware sprawl is to use more efficient and power-saving processors. Contemporary microprocessors now feature multiple processor cores (which perform the reading and execution of computer instructions) on a single chip. A **multicore processor** is an integrated circuit to which two or more processor cores have been attached for enhanced performance, reduced power consumption, and more efficient simultaneous processing of multiple tasks. This technology enables two or more processing engines with reduced power requirements and heat dissipation to perform tasks faster than a resource-hungry chip with a single processing core. Today you'll find PCs with dual-core, quad-core, six-core, and eight-core processors and servers with 16-core processors.

Intel and other chip manufacturers are working on microprocessors that minimize power consumption, which is essential for prolonging battery life in small mobile digital devices. Highly power-efficient microprocessors, such as the A9 and A10 processors used in Apple's iPhone and iPad and Intel's Atom processor, are used in lightweight smartphones and tablets, intelligent cars, and healthcare devices. The Apple processors have about one-fiftieth of the power consumption of a laptop dual-core processor. Intel introduced a line of ultrasmall, low-power microprocessors called Quark that can be used in wearable devices and skin patches or even swallowed to gather medical data.

5-4   What are the current computer software platforms and trends?

There are four major themes in contemporary software platform evolution:

- Linux and open source software
- Java, HTML, and HTML5
- Web services and service-oriented architecture
- Software outsourcing and cloud services

Linux and Open Source Software

Open source software is software produced by a community of several hundred thousand programmers around the world. According to the leading open source professional association, OpenSource.org, open source software is free and can be modified by users. Works derived from the original code must also be free, and the software can be redistributed by the user without additional licensing. Open source software is by definition not restricted to any specific operating system or hardware technology, although most open source software is currently based on a Linux or Unix operating system.

The open source movement has demonstrated that it can produce commercially acceptable, high-quality software. Popular open source software tools include the Linux operating system, the Apache HTTP web server, the Mozilla Firefox web browser, and the Apache OpenOffice desktop productivity suite. Google's Android mobile operating system and Chrome web browser are based on open source tools. You can find out more out more about the Open Source Definition from the Open Source Initiative and the history of open source software in the Learning Tracks for this chapter.

Linux

Perhaps the most well-known open source software is Linux, an operating system related to Unix. Linux was created by the Finnish programmer Linus Torvalds and first posted on the Internet in August 1991. Linux applications are embedded in cell phones, smartphones, tablet computers and consumer electronics. Linux is available in free versions downloadable from the Internet or in low-cost commercial versions that include tools and support from vendors such as Red Hat.

Although Linux is not used in many desktop systems, it is a leading operating system for servers, mainframe computers, and supercomputers. IBM, HP, Intel, Dell, and Oracle have made Linux a central part of their offerings to corporations. Linux has profound implications for corporate software platforms—cost reduction, reliability and resilience, and integration—because Linux works on all the major hardware platforms from mainframes to servers to clients.

Software for the Web: Java, HTML, and HTML5

Java is an operating system-independent, processor-independent, object-oriented programming language created by Sun Microsystems that has become the leading interactive programming environment for the web. The Java platform has migrated into mobile phones, smartphones, automobiles, music players, game machines, and set-top cable television systems serving interactive content and pay-per-view services. Java software is designed to run on any computer or computing device, regardless of the specific microprocessor or operating system the device uses. For each of the computing environments in which Java is used, a Java Virtual Machine interprets Java programming code for that machine. In this manner, the code is written once and can be used on any machine for which there exists a Java Virtual Machine.

Java developers can create small applet programs that can be embedded in webpages and downloaded to run on a web browser. A **web browser** is an easy-to-use software tool with a graphical user interface for displaying webpages and for accessing the web and other Internet resources. Microsoft's Internet Explorer, Mozilla Firefox, Google Chrome, and Apple Safari browsers are examples. At the enterprise level, Java is being used for more complex e-commerce and e-business applications that require communication with an organization's back-end transaction processing systems.

HTML and HTML5

Hypertext Markup Language (HTML) is a page description language for specifying how text, graphics, video, and sound are placed on a webpage and for creating dynamic links to other webpages and objects. Using these links, a user need only point at a highlighted keyword or graphic, click on it, and immediately be transported to another document.

HTML was originally designed to create and link static documents composed largely of text. Today, however, the web is much more social and interactive, and many webpages have multimedia elements—images, audio, and video. Third-party plug-in applications like Flash, Silverlight, and Java have been required to integrate these rich media with webpages. However, these add-ons require additional programming and put strains on computer processing. The next evolution of HTML, called **HTML5**, solves this problem by making it possible to embed images, audio, video, and other elements directly into a document without processor-intensive add-ons. HTML5 makes it easier for webpages to function across different display devices, including mobile devices as well as desktops, and it will support the storage of data offline for apps that run over the web. Other popular programming tools for web applications include Ruby and Python. Ruby is an object-oriented programming language known for speed and ease of use in building web applications, and Python (praised for its clarity) is being used for building cloud computing applications. Major websites such as Google, Facebook, Amazon, and Twitter use Python and Ruby as well as Java.

Web Services and Service-Oriented Architecture

Web services refer to a set of loosely coupled software components that exchange information with each other using universal web communication standards and languages. They can exchange information between two different systems regardless of the operating systems or programming languages on which the systems are based. They can be used to build open standard web-based applications linking systems of two different organizations, and they can also be used to create applications that link disparate systems within a single company. Different applications can use web services to communicate with each other in a standard way without time-consuming custom coding.

The foundation technology for web services is **XML**, which stands for **Extensible Markup Language**. This language was developed in 1996 by the World Wide Web Consortium (W3C, the international body that oversees the development of the web) as a more powerful and flexible markup language than hypertext markup language (HTML) for webpages. Whereas HTML is limited to describing how data should be presented in the form of webpages, XML can perform presentation, communication, and storage of data. In XML, a number is not simply a number; the XML tag specifies whether the number represents a price, a date, or a ZIP code. Table 5.3 illustrates some sample XML statements.

By tagging selected elements of the content of documents for their meanings, XML makes it possible for computers to manipulate and interpret their data automatically and perform operations on the data without human intervention. Web browsers and computer programs, such as order processing or enterprise resource planning (ERP) software, can follow programmed rules for applying and displaying the data. XML provides a standard format for data exchange, enabling web services to pass data from one process to another.

Web services communicate through XML messages over standard web protocols. Companies discover and locate web services through a directory. Using web protocols, a software application can connect freely to other applications without custom programming for each different application with which it wants to communicate. Everyone shares the same standards.

The collection of web services that are used to build a firm's software systems constitutes what is known as a service-oriented architecture. A **service-oriented architecture (SOA)** is set of self-contained services that

TABLE 5.3 EXAMPLES OF XML

PLAIN ENGLISH	XML
Subcompact	<AUTOMOBILETYPE="Subcompact">
4 passenger	<PASSENGERUNIT="PASS">4</PASSENGER>
$16,800	<PRICE CURRENCY="USD">$16,800</PRICE>

communicate with each other to create a working software application. Business tasks are accomplished by executing a series of these services. Software developers reuse these services in other combinations to assemble other applications as needed.

Virtually all major software vendors provide tools and entire platforms for building and integrating software applications using web services. IBM includes web service tools in its WebSphere e-business software platform, and Microsoft has incorporated web services tools in its Microsoft .NET platform.

Dollar Rent A Car's systems use web services for its online booking system with Southwest Airlines's website. Although both companies' systems are based on different technology platforms, a person booking a flight on Southwest.com can reserve a car from Dollar without leaving the airline's website. Instead of struggling to get Dollar's reservation system to share data with Southwest's information systems, Dollar used Microsoft .NET web services technology as an intermediary. Reservations from Southwest are translated into web services protocols, which are then translated into formats that can be understood by Dollar's computers.

Other car rental companies have linked their information systems to airline companies' websites before. But without web services, these connections had to be built one at a time. Web services provide a standard way for Dollar's computers to "talk" to other companies' information systems without having to build special links to each one. Dollar is now expanding its use of web services to link directly to the systems of a small tour operator and a large travel reservation system as well as a wireless website for cell phones and smartphones. It does not have to write new software code for each new partner's information systems or each new wireless device (see Figure 5.11).

FIGURE 5.11 HOW DOLLAR RENT A CAR USES WEB SERVICES

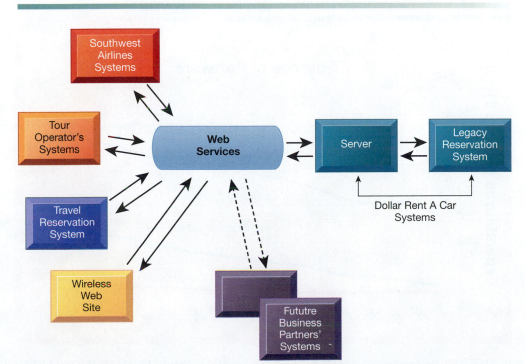

Dollar Rent A Car uses web services to provide a standard intermediate layer of software to "talk" to other companies' information systems. Dollar Rent A Car can use this set of web services to link to other companies' information systems without having to build a separate link to each firm's systems.

Software Outsourcing and Cloud Services

Today, many business firms continue to operate legacy systems that continue to meet a business need and that would be extremely costly to replace. But they will purchase or rent most of their new software applications from external sources. Figure 5.12 illustrates the rapid growth in external sources of software for U.S. firms.

There are three external sources for software: software packages from a commercial software vendor, outsourcing custom application development to an external vendor, (which may or may not be offshore), and cloud-based software services and tools.

Software Packages and Enterprise Software

We have already described software packages for enterprise applications as one of the major types of software components in contemporary IT infrastructures. A **software package** is a prewritten commercially available set of software programs that eliminates the need for a firm to write its own software programs for certain functions, such as payroll processing or order handling.

Enterprise application software vendors such as SAP and Oracle-PeopleSoft have developed powerful software packages that can support the primary business processes of a firm worldwide from warehousing, customer relationship management, and supply chain management to finance and human resources. These large-scale enterprise software systems provide a single, integrated, worldwide software system for firms at a cost much less than they would pay if they developed it themselves. Chapter 9 discusses enterprise systems in detail.

FIGURE 5.12 CHANGING SOURCES OF FIRM SOFTWARE

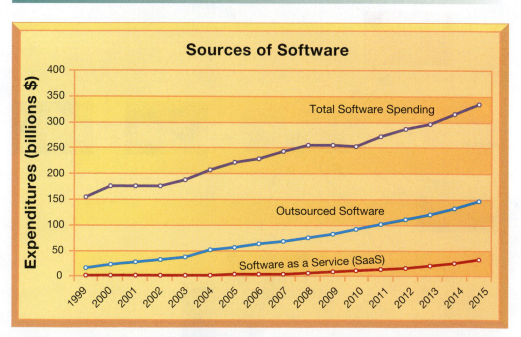

In 2015, U.S. firms spent and estimated $334 billion on software. About 44% of that originated outside the firm, provided by a variety of vendors. About 10% ($33 billion) was provided by SaaS vendors as an online cloud-based service.

Sources: BEA National Income and Product Accounts, 2016; authors' estimates.

Software Outsourcing

Software **outsourcing** enables a firm to contract custom software development or maintenance of existing legacy programs to outside firms, which often operate offshore in low-wage areas of the world. For example, UK communications regulator Ofcom recently signed a £23 million, six-year contract to outsource application and infrastructure management to NIIT Technologies. NIIT Technologies is an Indian firm specializing in application development and maintenance, infrastructure management, and business process management. NIIT provides Ofcom with a service desk, data center services, and application management and project management services (Flinders, 2016).

Offshore software outsourcing firms have primarily provided lower-level maintenance, data entry, and call center operations, although more sophisticated and experienced offshore firms, particularly in India, have been hired for new-program development. However, as wages offshore rise and the costs of managing offshore projects are factored in (see Chapter 13), some work that would have been sent offshore is returning to domestic companies.

Cloud-Based Software Services and Tools

In the past, software such as Microsoft Word or Adobe Illustrator came in a box and was designed to operate on a single machine. Today, you're more likely to download the software from the vendor's website or to use the software as a cloud service delivered over the Internet.

Cloud-based software and the data it uses are hosted on powerful servers in data centers and can be accessed with an Internet connection and standard web browser. In addition to free or low-cost tools for individuals and small businesses provided by Google or Yahoo, enterprise software and other complex business functions are available as services from the major commercial software vendors. Instead of buying and installing software programs, subscribing companies rent the same functions from these services, with users paying either on a subscription or per-transaction basis. A leading example is of software as a service (SaaS) is Salesforce.com, described earlier in this chapter, which provides on-demand software services for customer relationship management.

In order to manage their relationship with an outsourcer or technology service provider, firms need a contract that includes a **service level agreement (SLA)**. The SLA is a formal contract between customers and their service providers that defines the specific responsibilities of the service provider and the level of service expected by the customer. SLAs typically specify the nature and level of services provided, criteria for performance measurement, support options, provisions for security and disaster recovery, hardware and software ownership and upgrades, customer support, billing, and conditions for terminating the agreement. We provide a Learning Track on this topic.

Mashups and Apps

The software you use for both personal and business tasks today may be composed of interchangeable components that integrate freely with other applications on the Internet. Individual users and entire companies mix and match these software components to create their own customized applications and to share information with others. The resulting software applications are called **mashups**. The idea is to take different sources and produce a new work that is greater than the sum of its parts. You have performed a mashup if you've ever personalized your Facebook profile or your blog with a capability to display videos or slide shows.

Web mashups combine the capabilities of two or more online applications to create a kind of hybrid that provides more customer value than the original sources alone. For instance, ZipRealty uses Google Maps and data provided by online real estate database Zillow.com to display a complete list of multiple listing service (MLS) real estate listings for any ZIP code specified by the user.

Apps are small specialized software programs (application software) that are designed for mobile devices like smartphones and tablets. They are downloaded from app stores like Apple's App Store and Google Play. Google refers to its online services as apps, including the Google Apps suite of desktop productivity tools. Windows 10 refers to all of its desktop software programs as apps. But when we talk about apps today, most of the attention goes to the apps that have been developed for mobile devices like smartphones and tablets. It is these apps that turn smartphones and tablets into general-purpose computing tools. First appearing in 2008, in 2016 there are hundreds of millions of apps for the iOS and Android mobile operating systems. The use of apps now exceeds the use of mobile browsers, which are much slower and cumbersome for accessing mobile software.

Apps provide a streamlined non-browser pathway for users to perform a number of tasks, ranging from reading the newspaper to shopping, searching, personal health monitoring, playing games, and buying. They increasingly are used by managers as gateways to their firm's enterprise systems. Because so many people are now accessing the Internet from their mobile devices, some say that apps are "the new browsers." Apps are also starting to influence the design and function of traditional websites as consumers are attracted to the look and feel of apps and their speed of operation.

Many apps are free or purchased for a small charge, much less than conventional software, which further adds to their appeal. There are already more than 2 million apps for the Apple iPhone and iPad platform and a similar number that run on devices using Google's Android operating system. Apple reports that more than 100 billion apps have been downloaded by users. The success of these mobile platforms depends in large part on the quantity and the quality of the apps they provide. Apps tie the customer to a specific hardware platform: As the user adds more and more apps to his or her mobile phone, the cost of switching to a competing mobile platform rises.

At the moment, the most commonly downloaded apps are games, news and weather, maps/navigation, social networking, music, and video/movies. But there are also serious apps for business users that make it possible to create and edit documents, connect to corporate systems, schedule and participate in meetings, track shipments, and dictate voice messages (see the Chapter 1 Interactive Session on Management). Most large online retailers have apps for consumers for researching and buying goods and services online.

5-5 What are the challenges of managing IT infrastructure and management solutions?

Creating and managing a coherent IT infrastructure raises multiple challenges: dealing with platform and technology change (including cloud and mobile computing), management and governance, and making wise infrastructure investments.

Dealing with Platform and Infrastructure Change

As firms grow, they often quickly outgrow their infrastructure. As firms shrink, they can get stuck with excessive infrastructure purchased in better times. How can a firm remain flexible if investments in IT infrastructure are fixed-cost purchases and licenses? How well does the infrastructure scale? **Scalability** refers to the ability of a computer, product, or system to expand to serve a large number of users without breaking down. New applications, mergers and acquisitions, and changes in business volume all affect computer workload and must be considered when planning hardware capacity.

Firms using mobile computing and cloud computing platforms will require new policies and procedures for managing these platforms. They will need to inventory all of their mobile devices in business use and develop policies and tools for tracking, updating, and securing them and for controlling the data and applications that run on them. Firms using cloud computing and SaaS will need to fashion new contractual arrangements with remote vendors to make sure that the hardware and software for critical applications are always available when needed and that they meet corporate standards for information security. It is up to business management to determine acceptable levels of computer response time and availability for the firm's mission-critical systems to maintain the level of business performance that is expected.

Management and Governance

A long-standing issue among information system managers and CEOs has been the question of who will control and manage the firm's IT infrastructure. Chapter 2 introduced the concept of IT governance and described some issues it addresses. Other important questions about IT governance are: Should departments and divisions have the responsibility of making their own information technology decisions, or should IT infrastructure be centrally controlled and managed? What is the relationship between central information systems management and business unit information systems management? How will infrastructure costs be allocated among business units? Each organization will need to arrive at answers based on its own needs.

Making Wise Infrastructure Investments

IT infrastructure is a major investment for the firm. If too much is spent on infrastructure, it lies idle and constitutes a drag on the firm's financial performance. If too little is spent, important business services cannot be delivered and the firm's competitors (who spent the right amount) will outperform the under-investing firm. How much should the firm spend on infrastructure? This question is not easy to answer.

A related question is whether a firm should purchase and maintain its own IT infrastructure components or rent them from external suppliers, including those offering cloud services. The decision either to purchase your own IT assets or rent them from external providers is typically called the *rent-versus-buy* decision.

Cloud computing is a low-cost way to increase scalability and flexibility, but firms should evaluate this option carefully in light of security requirements and impact on business processes and workflows. In some instances, the cost of renting software adds up to more than purchasing and maintaining an application in-house. Yet there are many benefits to using cloud services including significant reductions in hardware, software, human resources, and maintenance costs. Moving to cloud computing allows firms to focus on their core businesses rather than technology issues. As the reliability of cloud computing has improved greatly in the last decade, in 2016 some Fortune 500 firms are planning to move the majority of their computing platforms to cloud services.

Total Cost of Ownership of Technology Assets

The actual cost of owning technology resources includes the original cost of acquiring and installing hardware and software as well as ongoing administration costs for hardware and software upgrades, maintenance, technical support, training, and even utility and real estate costs for running and housing the technology. The **total cost of ownership (TCO)** model can be used to analyze these direct and indirect costs to help firms determine the actual cost of specific technology implementations. Table 5.4 describes the most important TCO components to consider in a TCO analysis.

When all these cost components are considered, the TCO for a PC might run up to three times the original purchase price of the equipment. Gains in productivity and efficiency from equipping employees with mobile computing devices must be balanced against increased costs from integrating these devices into the firm's IT infrastructure and from providing technical support. Other cost components include fees for wireless airtime, end-user training, help desk support, and software for special applications. Costs are higher if the mobile devices run many different applications or need to be integrated into back-end systems such as enterprise applications.

Hardware and software acquisition costs account for only about 20 percent of TCO, so managers must pay close attention to administration costs to understand the full cost of the firm's hardware and software. It is possible to reduce some of these administration costs through better management. Many large firms are saddled with redundant, incompatible hardware and software because their departments and divisions have been allowed to make their own technology purchases.

In addition to switching to cloud services, these firms could reduce their TCO through greater centralization and standardization of their hardware and software resources. Companies could reduce the size of the information systems staff required to support their infrastructure if the firm minimizes the number of different computer models and pieces of software that employees are allowed to use. In a centralized infrastructure, systems can be administered from a central location and troubleshooting can be performed from that location.

TABLE 5.4 TOTAL COST OF OWNERSHIP (TCO) COST COMPONENTS

INFRASTRUCTURE COMPONENT	COST COMPONENTS
Hardware acquisition	Purchase price of computer hardware equipment, including computers, terminals, storage, and printers
Software acquisition	Purchase or license of software for each user
Installation	Cost to install computers and software
Training	Cost to provide training for information systems specialists and end users
Support	Cost to provide ongoing technical support, help desks, and so forth
Maintenance	Cost to upgrade the hardware and software
Infrastructure	Cost to acquire, maintain, and support related infrastructure, such as networks and specialized equipment (including storage backup units)
Downtime	Cost of lost productivity if hardware or software failures cause the system to be unavailable for processing and user tasks
Space and energy	Real estate and utility costs for housing and providing power for the technology

Competitive Forces Model for IT Infrastructure Investment

Figure 5.13 illustrates a competitive forces model you can use to address the question of how much your firm should spend on IT infrastructure.

Market demand for your firm's services. Make an inventory of the services you currently provide to customers, suppliers, and employees. Survey each group, or hold focus groups to find out if the services you currently offer are meeting the needs of each group. For example, are customers complaining of slow responses to their queries about price and availability? Are employees complaining about the difficulty of finding the right information for their jobs? Are suppliers complaining about the difficulties of discovering your production requirements?

Your firm's business strategy. Analyze your firm's five-year business strategy and try to assess what new services and capabilities will be required to achieve strategic goals.

Your firm's IT strategy, infrastructure, and cost. Examine your firm's information technology plans for the next five years and assess its alignment with the firm's business plans. Determine the total IT infrastructure costs. You will want to perform a TCO analysis. If your firm has no IT strategy, you will need to devise one that takes into account the firm's five-year strategic plan.

Information technology assessment. Is your firm behind the technology curve or at the bleeding edge of information technology? Both situations are to be avoided. It is usually not desirable to spend resources on advanced technologies that are still experimental, often expensive, and sometimes unreliable. You want to spend on technologies for which standards have been established and

FIGURE 5.13 COMPETITIVE FORCES MODEL FOR IT INFRASTRUCTURE

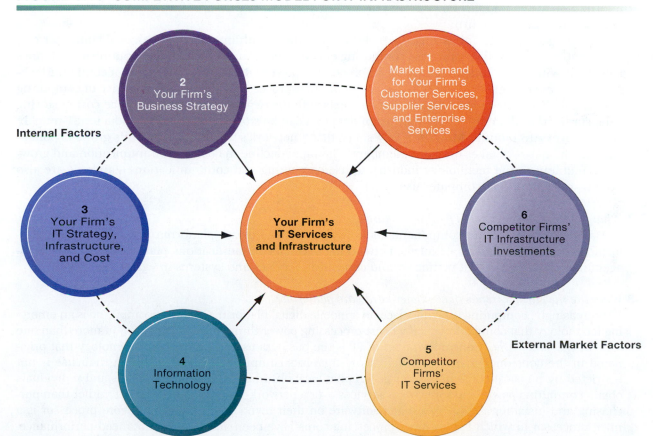

There are six factors you can use to answer the question "How much should our firm spend on IT infrastructure?"

IT vendors are competing on cost, not design, and where there are multiple suppliers. However, you do not want to put off investment in new technologies or allow competitors to develop new business models and capabilities based on the new technologies.

Competitor firm services. Try to assess what technology services competitors offer to customers, suppliers, and employees. Establish quantitative and qualitative measures to compare them to those of your firm. If your firm's service levels fall short, your company is at a competitive disadvantage. Look for ways your firm can excel at service levels.

Competitor firm IT infrastructure investments. Benchmark your expenditures for IT infrastructure against your competitors. Many companies are quite public about their innovative expenditures on IT. If competing firms try to keep IT expenditures secret, you may be able to find IT investment information in public companies' SEC Form 10-K annual reports to the federal government when those expenditures affect a firm's financial results.

Your firm does not necessarily need to spend as much as or more than your competitors. Perhaps it has discovered much less expensive ways of providing services, and this can lead to a cost advantage. Alternatively, your firm may be spending far less than competitors and experiencing commensurate poor performance and losing market share.

Review Summary

5-1 *What is IT infrastructure, and what are the stages and drivers of IT infrastructure evolution?*

IT infrastructure is the shared technology resources that provide the platform for the firm's specific information system applications. IT infrastructure includes hardware, software, and services that are shared across the entire firm.

The five stages of IT infrastructure evolution are: the mainframe era, the personal computer era, the client/server era, the enterprise computing era, and the cloud and mobile computing era. Moore's Law deals with the exponential increase in processing power and decline in the cost of computer technology, stating that every 18 months the power of microprocessors doubles and the price of computing falls in half. The Law of Mass Digital Storage deals with the exponential decrease in the cost of storing data, stating that the number of kilobytes of data that can be stored on magnetic media for $1 roughly doubles every 15 months. Metcalfe's Law states that a network's value to participants grows exponentially as the network takes on more members. The rapid decline in costs of communication and growing agreement in the technology industry to use computing and communications standards are also driving an explosion of computer use.

5-2 *What are the components of IT infrastructure?*

Major IT infrastructure components include computer hardware platforms, operating system platforms, enterprise software platforms, networking and telecommunications platforms, database management software, Internet platforms, and consulting services and systems integrators.

5-3 *What are the current trends in computer hardware platforms?*

Increasingly, computing is taking place on a mobile digital platform. Quantum computing is an emerging technology that could dramatically boost processing power through the ability to be in more than one state at the same time. Consumerization of IT is the business use of information technology that originated in the consumer market. Virtualization organizes computing resources so that their use is not restricted by physical configuration or geographic location. In cloud computing, firms and individuals obtain computing power and software as services over a network, including the Internet, rather than purchasing and installing the hardware and software on their own computers. A multicore processor is a microprocessor to which two or more processing cores have been attached for enhanced performance. Green computing includes practices and technologies for producing, using, and disposing of information technology hardware to minimize negative impact on the environment.

5-4 *What are the current computer software platforms and trends?*

Open source software is produced and maintained by a global community of programmers and is often downloadable for free. Linux is a powerful, resilient open source operating system that can run on multiple hardware platforms and is used widely to run web servers. Java is an operating system–and hardware-independent programming language that is the leading interactive programming environment for the web. HTML5 makes it possible to embed images, audio, and video directly into a web document without add-on programs. Web services are loosely coupled software components based on open web standards that work with any application software and operating system. They can be used as components of web-based applications linking the systems of two different organizations or to link disparate systems of a single company. Companies are purchasing their new software applications from outside sources, including software packages, by outsourcing custom application development to an external vendor (that may be offshore), or by renting online software services (SaaS). Mashups combine two different software services to create new software applications and services. Apps are software applications that run on mobile devices and are delivered over the Internet.

5-5 *What are the challenges of managing IT infrastructure and management solutions?*

Major challenges include dealing with platform and infrastructure change, infrastructure management and governance, and making wise infrastructure investments. Solution guidelines include using a competitive forces model to determine how much to spend on IT infrastructure and where to make strategic infrastructure investments, and establishing the total cost of ownership (TCO) of information technology assets. The total cost of owning technology resources includes not only the original cost of computer hardware and software but also costs for hardware and software upgrades, maintenance, technical support, and training. Many firms are turning to cloud computing in an effort to reduce their IT platform costs.

Key Terms

Android, 180
Application server, 171
Apps, 198
BYOD, 184
Chrome OS, 180
Clients, 171
Client/server computing, 171
Cloud computing, 172
Consumerization of IT, 184
Extensible Markup Language (XML), 194
Green computing (green IT), 191
HTML (Hypertext Markup Language), 193
HTML5, 193
Hybrid cloud, 191
Hypertext Markup Language (HTML), 193
iOS, 180
Java, 193
Legacy systems, 182
Linux, 180
Mainframe, 169
Mashup, 197
Minicomputers, 169
Moore's Law, 173
Multicore processor, 192
Multitiered (N-tier) client/server architecture, 171
Multitouch, 180
Nanotechnology, 175

On-demand computing, 180
Open source software, 192
Operating system, 180
Outsourcing, 197
Private cloud, 190
Public cloud, 190
Quantum computing, 185
Scalability, 199
Service level agreement (SLA), 197
Server, 171
Service-oriented architecture (SOA), 197
Software as a service (SaaS), 187
Software package, 196
Software-defined storage (SDS), 185
Tablet computers, 182
Technology standards, 176
Total cost of ownership (TCO), 200
Unix, 180
Virtualization, 185
Web browser, 193
Web hosting service, 181
Web server, 171
Web services, 194
Windows, 172
Windows 10, 180
Wintel PC, 170

MyMISLab

To complete the problems with the MyMISLab, go to EOC Discussion Questions in MyMISLab.

Review Questions

5-1 What is IT infrastructure, and what are the stages and drivers of IT infrastructure evolution?

- Define IT infrastructure from both a technology and a services perspective.
- List each of the eras in IT infrastructure evolution and describe its distinguishing characteristics.
- Define and describe the following: web server, application server, multitiered client/server architecture.
- Describe Moore's Law and the Law of Mass Digital Storage.
- Describe how network economics, declining communications costs, and technology standards affect IT infrastructure.

5-2 What are the components of IT infrastructure?

- List and describe the components of IT infrastructure that firms need to manage.

5-3 What are the current trends in computer hardware platforms?

- Describe the evolving mobile platform, consumerization of IT, and cloud computing.

- Explain how businesses can benefit from virtualization, green computing, and multicore processors.

5-4 What are the current computer software platforms and trends?

- Define and describe open source software and Linux and explain their business benefits.
- Define Java and HTML5 and explain why they are important.
- Define and describe web services and the role played by XML.
- Name and describe the three external sources for software.
- Define and describe software mashups and apps.

5-5 What are the challenges of managing IT infrastructure and management solutions?

- Name and describe the management challenges posed by IT infrastructure.
- Explain how using a competitive forces model and calculating the TCO of technology assets help firms make good infrastructure investments.

Discussion Questions

5-6 Why is selecting computer hardware and software for the organization an important management decision? What management, organization, and technology issues should be considered when selecting computer hardware and software?
MyMISLab

5-7 Should organizations use software service providers for all their software needs? Why or why not? What management, organization, and technology factors should be considered when making this decision?
MyMISLab

5-8 What are the advantages and disadvantages of cloud computing?
MyMISLab

Hands-On MIS Projects

The projects in this section give you hands-on experience in developing solutions for managing IT infrastructures and IT outsourcing, using spreadsheet software to evaluate alternative desktop systems, and using web research to budget for a sales conference. Visit MyMISLab's Multimedia Library to access this chapter's Hands-On MIS Projects.

Management Decision Problems

5-9 The University of Pittsburgh Medical Center (UPMC) relies on information systems to operate 19 hospitals, a network of other care sites, and international and commercial ventures. Demand for additional servers and storage technology was growing by 20 percent each year. UPMC was setting up a separate server for every application, and its servers and other computers were running a number of different operating systems, including several versions of Unix and Windows. UPMC had to manage technologies from many different vendors, including Hewlett-Packard (HP), Sun Microsystems, Microsoft, and IBM. Assess the impact of this situation on business performance. What factors and management decisions must be considered when developing a solution to this problem?

5-10 Qantas Airways, Australia's leading airline, faces cost pressures from high fuel prices and lower levels of global airline traffic. To remain competitive, the airline must find ways to keep costs low while providing a high level of customer service. Qantas had a 30-year-old data center. Management had to decide whether to replace its IT infrastructure with newer technology or outsource it. What factors should be considered by Qantas management when deciding whether to outsource? If Qantas decides to outsource, list and describe points that should be addressed in a service level agreement.

Improving Decision Making: Using a Spreadsheet to Evaluate Hardware and Software Options

Software skills: Spreadsheet formulas
Business skills: Technology pricing

5-11 In this exercise, you will use spreadsheet software to calculate the cost of desktop systems, printers, and software.

Use the Internet to obtain pricing information on hardware and software for an office of 30 people. You will need to price 30 PC desktop systems (monitors, computers, and keyboards) manufactured by Lenovo, Dell, and HP. (For the purposes of this exercise, ignore the fact that desktop systems usually come with preloaded software packages.) Also obtain pricing on 15 desktop printers manufactured by HP, Canon, and Dell. Each desktop system must satisfy the minimum specifications shown in tables that you can find in MyMISLab.

Also obtain pricing on 30 copies of the most recent versions of Microsoft Office and Apache OpenOffice (formerly Oracle Open Office) and on 30 copies of Microsoft Windows 10. Each desktop productivity package should contain programs for word processing, spreadsheets, database, and presentations. Prepare a spreadsheet showing your research results for the software and the desktop system, printer, and software combination offering the best performance and pricing per worker. Because every two workers share one printer (15 printers/30 systems), your calculations should assume only half a printer cost per worker.

Improving Decision Making: Using Web Research to Budget for a Sales Conference

Software skills: Internet-based software
Business skills: Researching transportation and lodging costs

5-12 The Foremost Composite Materials Company is planning a two-day sales conference for October 19–20, starting with a reception on the evening of October 18. The conference consists of all-day meetings that the entire sales force, numbering 120 sales representatives and their 16 managers, must attend. Each sales representative requires his or her own room, and the company needs two common meeting rooms, one large enough to hold the entire sales force plus a few visitors (200) and the other able to hold half the force. Management has set a budget of $175,000 for the representatives' room rentals. The company would like to hold the conference in either Miami or Marco Island, Florida, at a Hilton- or Marriott-owned hotel.

Use the Hilton and Marriott websites to select a hotel in whichever of these cities that would enable the company to hold its sales conference within its budget and meet its sales conference requirements. Then locate flights arriving the afternoon prior to the conference. Your attendees will be coming from Los Angeles (51), San Francisco (30), Seattle (22), Chicago (19), and Pittsburgh (14). Determine costs of each airline ticket from these cities. When you are finished, create a budget for the conference. The budget will include the cost of each airline ticket, the room cost, and $70 per attendee per day for food.

Collaboration and Teamwork Project

Evaluating Server and Mobile Operating Systems

5-13 Form a group with three or four of your classmates. Choose server or mobile operating systems to evaluate. You might research and compare the capabilities and costs of Linux versus UNIX or the most recent version of the Windows operating system for servers. Alternatively, you could compare the capabilities of the Android mobile operating system with iOS for the iPhone. If possible, use Google Docs and Google Drive or Google Sites to brainstorm, organize, and develop a presentation of your findings for the class.

BYOD: Business Opportunity or Big Headache?
CASE STUDY

Just about everyone who has a smartphone wants to be able to bring it to work and use it on the job. And why not? Employees using their own smartphones would allow companies to enjoy all the same benefits of a mobile workforce without spending their own money to purchase these devices. Smaller companies are able to go mobile without making large investments in devices and mobile services. According to Gartner, Inc., by 2017, 50 percent of employers will require employees to supply their own mobile devices for the workplace. BYOD is becoming the "new normal."

But … wait a minute. Half of all enterprises believe that BYOD represents a growing problem for their organizations, according to a number of studies. Although BYOD can improve employee job satisfaction and productivity, it also can cause a number of problems if not managed properly. Support for personally owned devices is more difficult than it is for company-supplied devices, the cost of managing mobile devices can increase, and protecting corporate data and networks becomes more difficult. Research conducted by the Aberdeen Group found that on average, an enterprise with 1,000 mobile devices spends an extra $170,000 per year when it allows BYOD. So it's not that simple.

BYOD requires a significant portion of corporate IT resources dedicated to managing and maintaining a large number of devices within the organization. In the past, companies tried to limit business smartphone use to a single platform. This made it easier to keep track of each mobile device and to roll out software upgrades or fixes because all employees were using the same devices or, at the very least, the same operating system. Today, the mobile digital landscape is much more complicated, with a variety of devices and operating systems on the market that do not have well-developed tools for administration and security. Android has 80 percent of the worldwide smartphone market, but it is more difficult to use for corporate work than Apple mobile devices using the iOS operating system. IOS is considered a closed system and runs only on a limited number of different Apple mobile devices. In contrast, Android's fragmentation makes it more difficult and costly for corporate IT to manage. There are about 25,000 different models of Android-based devices available around the world, according to a report by

OpenSignal, which researches wireless networks and devices. Android's huge consumer market share attracts many hackers. Android is also vulnerable because it has an open source architecture and comes in multiple versions.

If employees are allowed to work with more than one type of mobile device and operating system, companies need an effective way to keep track of all the devices employees are using. To access company information, the company's networks must be configured to receive connections from that device. When employees make changes to their personal phone, such as switching cellular carriers, changing their phone number, or buying a new mobile device altogether, companies will need to quickly and flexibly ensure that their employees are still able to remain productive. Firms need a system that keeps track of which devices employees are using, where the device is located, whether it is being used, and what software it is equipped with. For unprepared companies, keeping track of who gets access to what data could be a nightmare.

With the large variety of phones and operating systems available, providing adequate technical support for every employee could be difficult. When employees are not able to access critical data or encounter other problems with their mobile devices, they will need assistance from the information systems department. Companies that rely on desktop computers tend to have many of the same computers with the same specs and operating systems, making tech support that much easier. Mobility introduces a new layer of variety and complexity to tech support that companies need to be prepared to handle.

There are significant concerns with securing company information accessed with mobile devices. If a device is stolen or compromised, companies need ways to ensure that sensitive or confidential information isn't freely available to anyone. Mobility puts assets and data at greater risk than if they were only located within company walls and on company machines. Marble Security Labs analyzed 1.2 million Android and iOS apps and found that the consumer apps on mobile devices did not adequately protect business information. Companies often use technologies that allow them to wipe data from devices remotely or encrypt data so that if the device is stolen, it cannot be used. You'll find a detailed discussion of mobile security issues in Chapter 8.

Management at Michelin North America believes BYOD will make the business more flexible and productive. Initially, all 4,000 mobile devices used by the company were company-owned and obsolete, with a large number of traditional cell phones that could only be used for voice transmission and messaging. Only 90 employees were allowed access to e-mail on mobile devices, and fewer than 400 were allowed access to calendars on these devices. Service costs were high, and the business received little value from its mobility program. Management had identified significant business benefits from increasing mobility in sales, customer support, and operations.

In mid-2011, the company created a team composed of executives and representatives from the IT, human resources, finance, and legal departments as well as the business units to share in the development, rollout, and management of a new mobile strategy for corporate-owned and personal mobile devices. The team decided to transition the mobility business model from corporate-owned to personal-liable.

According to Gartner, Inc. consultants, about half of organizations with a formal BYOD program compensate their employees for the amount of time they use their personal devices on their jobs using stipends, reimbursements, or allowances. Handling employee reimbursement for using personal devices for corporate purposes has proved to be one of the most problematic aspects of BYOD mobile programs. Although most companies use expense reports or payroll stipends to reimburse employees for BYOD, these methods have drawbacks. Expense reports are an administrative burden for both the employee and the employer, and payroll stipends can have tax consequences for both as well.

For some companies, the best option is to make direct payments to wireless carriers to reimburse employees for the expense they incur when they use their own wireless devices for company business. The employer provides funds to the wireless carrier, which then applies a credit to the employee's account. When the employee's bill arrives, the employee pays the amount owed less the credit amount that was funded by the employer.

Michelin opted for a managed service from Cass Information Systems that enables the company to make payments directly to wireless carriers. Cass Information Systems is a leading provider of transportation, utility, waste, and telecom expense management and related business intelligence services. A single employee portal handles enrollment of corporate and BYOD devices and provides tracking and reporting of all ongoing mobile and related inventory and expenses. The portal can automatically register employees, verify user eligibility, ensure policy acknowledgment, and distribute credits directly to employees' wireless accounts for the amount of service they used for their jobs.

Since implementing its version of BYOD, Michelin North America increased the number of mobile-enabled employees to 7,000. Employee efficiency, productivity, and satisfaction have improved from updating the mobile technology and functionality available to employees and giving them choices in mobile devices and wireless carrier plans, The program is cost-neutral. Michelin has obtained new vendor discounts across all wireless vendors in the United States and Canada and has reduced the cost of deploying each mobile device by more than 30 percent.

Iftekhar Khan, IT director at Toronto's Chelsea Hotel, remains less sanguine. He believes BYOD might work for his company down the road but not in the immediate future. Khan notes that the hospitality industry and many others still want employees to use corporate-owned devices for any laptop, tablet, or smartphone requiring access to the corporate network. His business has sensitive information and needs that level of control. Although the hotel might possibly save money with BYOD, it's ultimately all about productivity.

Management at Rosendin Electric, a Silicon Valley electrical contractor, worried that BYOD would become a big headache. Rosendin has thousands of employees and deploys hundreds of smartphones, more than 400 iPads, and a few Microsoft Surface tablets. These mobile devices have greatly enhanced the company's productivity by enabling employees to order equipment and supplies on the spot at a job site or check on-site to see whether ordered items have arrived. However, CIO Sam Lamonica does not believe BYOD would work for this company. He worries employees would be too careless using apps, cloud, and technology devices. (An Aruba Networks study of 11,500 workers in 23 countries found that 60 percent share their work and personal devices with others regularly, nearly 20 percent don't have passwords on devices, and 31 percent have lost data due to misuse of a mobile device.)

Lamonica feels more confident about equipping employees with company-owned devices because they can be more easily managed and secured. Rosendin uses MobileIron mobile device management (MDM) software for its smartphones and tablets. If a device is lost or stolen, the MDM software is able to wipe the devices remotely. Because MobileIron allows Rosendin to separate and isolate business apps and data from personal apps and data, the company allows employees to use certain consumer apps and store personal photos on company-owned tablets. Rosendin has found that employees of companies that are able to personalize company-owned iPads are more likely to treat them as prized possessions, and this has helped lower the number of devices that become broken or lost. The company has the right to wipe the devices if they are lost.

Rosendin's mobile security is not iron-clad. An employee might be able to put company data in his or her personal Dropbox account instead of the company-authorized Box account. However, MobileIron is able to encrypt data before it gets into a Dropbox account, and this lowers the risk. With company-owned and managed devices, Rosendin still benefits from volume discounts from wireless carriers and does not have to do the extra work involved in reimbursing employees when they use their own devices for work.

Sources: Ryan Patrick, "Is a BYOD Strategy Best for Business?" IT World Canada, March 22, 2016; "5 BYOD Management Case Studies," Sunviewsoftware.com, accessed May 5, 2016; Aruba Networks, "Enterprise Security Threat Level Directly Linked to User Demographics, Industry and Geography," *Business Wire,* April 14, 2015; Alan F., "Open Signal: 24,093 Unique and Different Android-Powered Devices Are Available," Phonearena.com, August 5, 2015; Tom Kaneshige, "Why One CIO Is Saying 'No' to BYOD," *CIO,* June 24, 2014; "CIO Meets Mobile Challenges Head-On," *CIO,* July 7, 2014; and "Cass BYOD: How Michelin Became a Mobile-First Enterprise," Cass Information Systems Inc., 2014.

CASE STUDY QUESTIONS

5-14 What are the advantages and disadvantages of allowing employees to use their personal smartphones for work?

5-15 What management, organization, and technology factors should be addressed when deciding whether to allow employees to use their personal smartphones for work?

5-16 Compare the BYOD experiences of Michelin North America and Rosendin Electric. Why did BYOD at Michelin work so well?

5-17 Allowing employees to use their own smartphones for work will save the company money. Do you agree? Why or why not?

MyMISLab

Go to the Assignments section of MyMISLab to complete these writing exercises.

5-18 What are the distinguishing characteristics of cloud computing, and what are the three types of cloud services?

5-19 What is the total cost of ownership of technology assets, and what are its cost components?

Chapter 5 References

Andersson, Henrik, James Kaplan, and Brent Smolinski. "Capturing Value from IT Infrastructure Innovation." *McKinsey Quarterly* (October 2012).

Babcock, Charles. "Cloud's Thorniest Question: Does It Pay Off?" *Information Week* (June 4, 2012).

Benlian, Alexander, Marios Koufaris, and Thomas Hess. "Service Quality in Software-as-a-Service: Developing the SaaS-Qual Measure and Examining Its Role in Usage Continuance." *Journal of Management Information Systems* 28, No. 3 (Winter 2012).

Carr, Nicholas. *The Big Switch.* New York: Norton (2008).

Clark, Don. "Moore's Law Shows Its Age.." *Wall Street Journal* (April 17, 2015).

Choi, Jae, Derek L. Nazareth, and Hemant K. Jain. "Implementing Service-Oriented Architecture in Organizations." *Journal of Management Information Systems* 26, No. 4 (Spring 2010).

David, Julie Smith, David Schuff, and Robert St. Louis. "Managing Your IT Total Cost of Ownership." *Communications of the ACM* 45, No. 1 (January 2002).

Fitzgerald, Brian. "The Transformation of Open Source Software." *MIS Quarterly* 30, No. 3 (September 2006).

Flinders, Karl. "Ofcom Outsources IT Management to Indian Xervices Supplier NIIT." *Computer Weekly* (January 12, 2016).

Follow, Jaewon Kang. "IBM Bets on Next-Gen Technologies as It Tries to Stave Off Rivals." TheStreet.com (May 5, 2016).

Gantz, John and David Reinsal. "Extracting Value from Chaos." IDC (June 2011).

Gartner, Inc. "Gartner Says Worldwide IT Spending Is Forecast to Decline 0.5 Percent in 2016." *Business Wire* (April 7, 2016).

"How to Tap the Power of the Mainframe." ITBusinessEdge.com, accessed September 11, 2015.

International Data Corporation. "Worldwide Public Cloud Services Spending Forecast to Double by 2019, According to IDC." (January 21, 2016).

"Internet Users." Internetlivestats.com, accessed May 2, 2016.

Kauffman, Robert J. and Julianna Tsai. "The Unified Procurement Strategy for Enterprise Software: A Test of the 'Move to the Middle' Hypothesis." *Journal of Management Information Systems* 26, No. 2 (Fall 2009).

Letschin, Michael. "Six Trends that Will Change How You Think About Data Storage." *Information Management* (February 8, 2016).

Lyman, Peter and Hal R. Varian. "How Much Information 2003?" University of California at Berkeley School of Information Management and Systems (2003).

Markoff, John. "Moore's Law Running Out of Room, Tech Looks for a Successor," *New York Times* (May 4, 2016).

McCafferty, Dennis. "Eight Interesting Facts About Java." *CIO Insight* (June 16, 2014).

Mell, Peter and Tim Grance. "The NIST Definition of Cloud Computing" Version 15. NIST (October 17, 2009).

Moore, Gordon. "Cramming More Components Onto Integrated Circuits," *Electronics* 38, No. 8 (April 19, 1965).

Mueller, Benjamin, Goetz Viering, Christine Legner, and Gerold Riempp. "Understanding the Economic Potential of Service-Oriented Architecture." *Journal of Management Information Systems* 26, No. 4 (Spring 2010).

Netmarketshare. "Desktop Operating System Market Share April 2016." www.netmarketshare.com, accessed May 1, 2016.

Ray, Tierman. "Watch Out Intel, Here Comes Facebook." *Barrons* (October 31, 2015).

Schuff, David and Robert St. Louis. "Centralization vs. Decentralization of Application Software." *Communications of the ACM* 44, No. 6 (June 2001).

Stango, Victor. "The Economics of Standards Wars." *Review of Network Economics* 3, Issue 1 (March 2004).

Susarla, Anjana, Anitesh Barua, and Andrew B. Whinston. "A Transaction Cost Perspective of the 'Software as a Service' Business Model." *Journal of Management Information Systems* 26, No. 2 (Fall 2009).

Taft, Darryl K. "Application Development: Java Death Debunked: 10 Reasons Why It's Still Hot." *eWeek* (February 22, 2012).

Torode, Christine, Linda Tucci, and Karen Goulart. "Managing the Next-Generation Data Center." *Modern Infrastructure CIO Edition* (January 2013).

Weill, Peter and Marianne Broadbent. *Leveraging the New Infrastructure.* Cambridge, MA: Harvard Business School Press (1998).

Weitzel, Tim. *Economics of Standards in Information Networks.* Heidelberg, New York: Physica-Verlag (2004).

6 Foundations of Business Intelligence: Databases and Information Management

Learning Objectives

After reading this chapter, you will be able to answer the following questions:

6-1 What are the problems of managing data resources in a traditional file environment?

6-2 What are the major capabilities of database management systems (DBMS), and why is a relational DBMS so powerful?

6-3 What are the principal tools and technologies for accessing information from databases to improve business performance and decision making?

6-4 Why are information policy, data administration, and data quality assurance essential for managing the firm's data resources?

MyMISLab™

Visit **mymislab.com** for simulations, tutorials, and end-of-chapter problems.

CHAPTER CASES

VIDEO CASES

Better Data Management Helps the U.S. Postal Service Rebound

The U.S. Postal Service (USPS) delivers 154 billion pieces of mail per year. It is one of the oldest government agencies in the United States, but now its future is uncertain. With more people using e-mail, messaging systems, and social networking instead of "snail mail," the volume of first-class mail has plummeted. Private-sector rivals like UPS and FedEx have been luring customers away from the USPS's package delivery services, while tech giants such as Amazon and Google plan innovative new services such as 24/7 delivery lockers, weekend pickup points, and future drone deliveries. The USPS must compete using 20-year-old delivery vehicles and aging parcel- and letter-sorting systems.

It is no surprise, then, that the Postal Service handled nearly 1.4 billion fewer pieces of mail in 2015 than the year before and lost $5 billion. Despite aggressive cost-cutting measures like closing processing centers and slashing employee hours, 2015 marked the Postal Service's ninth consecutive year of losses. Can the ailing delivery service overcome its challenges?

James Cochrane, the USPS CIO, thinks it can, if it pays more attention to its data. The USPS collects a wealth of

© Anton Novik/Shutterstock

data as part of its daily operations. Cochrane wants to redesign the USPS mail tracking system to provide more useful information for operations and decision making. The USPS Intelligent Mail bar code (IMB) system uses Intelligent Mail scanning devices and more than 8,500 pieces of automated processing and sorting equipment to scan bar codes for data that are then transmitted to a central database. Bar codes for USPS letters and parcels contain as much data as possible, ranging from the type of mail being delivered to a parcel's final destination. The system is able to gather data from more than a billion tracking events each day. The IMB system provides more detailed and precise information about the mail stream, enabling the USPS to better manage cycle times, predict mail volume, and increase efficiencies at postal processing facilities and delivery routes.

By carefully tracking how mail moves around the country, from the moment a delivery vehicle arrives at a dock to the second a letter is delivered to its recipient, the Postal Service has built sophisticated computer models that map the most efficient and cost-effective mail delivery routes. The USPS is able to access and analyze its vast quantity of data very quickly because it uses in-memory computing tools that store the data in computer memory and the Apache Hadoop software framework to store and process large data sets in a distributed computing environment.

Another use for USPS big databases is to detect fraud in more than 528 million mail pieces each day. When a piece of mail is scanned at a post office facility, relevant data about the carrier, route, weight, and size are transmitted to the USPS supercomputing database in Eagan, Minnesota. The data from each mail piece are then compared to some 400 billion records in the database. Complex algorithms perform fraud detection and other tests on the data before transmission back to the delivery center. All of this happens in an average of 50 to 100 thousandths of a second. If something is not right, such as a package with insufficient, duplicated, or fraudulent postage, the problem is detected in near real time. Errors are tracked down, and fraud attempts are reported to the U.S. Postal Inspection Service for further investigation. With annual revenue of $65 billion, the USPS saves many millions per year by analyzing the data.

That's not all. Cochrane believes the USPS could use IMB data to help retailers and catalog companies drive more sales. For instance, the USPS could send a clothing retailer an e-mail or text message that a particular customer in Omaha, Nebraska, has just received the company's holiday catalog. Upon receiving this real-time alert, the retailer could immediately e-mail the customer a digital coupon or promotional offer. A great idea, but the USPS must adhere to privacy statutes binding U.S. government agencies. Although the service has data on every single piece of mail exchanged among hundreds of millions of Americans and the companies that sell to them, it is not supposed to use data for any purpose other than delivering the mail effectively. The USPS may or may not be able to use its data for other commercial purposes.

In November 2013, the USPS signed a deal with Amazon to deliver packages on Sundays in select cities, increasing its share of the profitable package-delivery market. USPS's package revenue increased 8 percent to $12.5 billion from 2012 to 2013. UPS and FedEx, watch out!

Sources: "Intelligent Mail" and "U.S. Postal Service 2015 Annual Report to Congress," www.usps.gov, accessed March 3, 2016; Derek Major, "USPS Plans for the Internet of Mailed Things," *Government Computer News*, June 15, 2015; Cindy Waxer, "Modernizing the Mail," *Computerworld*, December 2014; Federico Guerrini, "How Big Data and the Internet of Things Will Change the Postal Service," *Forbes*, July 3, 2014.

The experience of the U.S. Postal Service illustrates the importance of data management. Business performance depends on what an organization can or cannot do with its data. The U.S. Postal Service is a huge, sprawling government agency where insufficient data, along with antiquated equipment and business processes, affected both operational efficiency and management decision making. How businesses store, organize, and manage their data has an enormous impact on organizational effectiveness.

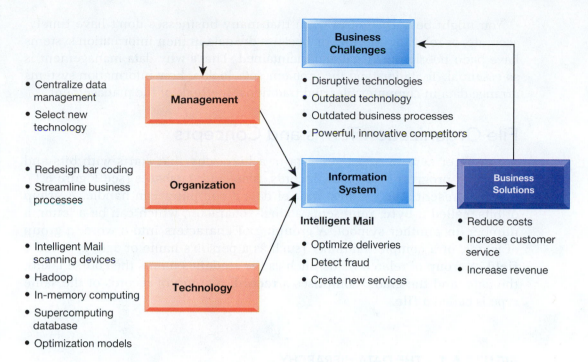

- Centralize data management
- Select new technology

Management

Business Challenges

- Disruptive technologies
- Outdated technology
- Outdated business processes
- Powerful, innovative competitors

- Redesign bar coding
- Streamline business processes

Organization

Information System

Business Solutions

Intelligent Mail

- Optimize deliveries
- Detect fraud
- Create new services

- Reduce costs
- Increase customer service
- Increase revenue

- Intelligent Mail scanning devices
- Hadoop
- In-memory computing
- Supercomputing database
- Optimization models

Technology

The chapter-opening diagram calls attention to important points raised by this case. The USPS is struggling to stay alive and relevant in the face of disruptive technologies such as e-mail and messaging and powerful, innovative competitors. USPS management believes the solution is to use better information to drive its operational activities and decisions. USPS now consolidates data collected from packages and letters scanned during the delivery process into a large central database where the data can be more easily accessed and analyzed to improve operations as well as management reporting and decision making. Technologies such as in-memory computing tools and Apache Hadoop for distributed processing and storage of large data sets made it much easier for the USPS to rapidly access and analyze its vast stores of data and turn the data into valuable information. In order to achieve more value from automated scanning and processing technologies as well as information from the database, the USPS had to redesign jobs, business processes, and workflows The solution increased efficiency, improved customer service, reduced costs, and enabled the USPS to offer new services such as Sunday package delivery for Amazon. However, other commercial possibilities for wringing even more value out of USPS data by sharing the data with retailers may be limited by privacy restrictions.

Here are some questions to think about: What was the business impact of not making maximum use of data at the USPS? How did better use of data collected by the USPS improve operational efficiency and management decision making? How much will analyzing the data it collects help the USPS survive?

6-1 What are the problems of managing data resources in a traditional file environment?

An effective information system provides users with accurate, timely, and relevant information. Accurate information is free of errors. Information is timely when it is available to decision makers when it is needed. Information is relevant when it is useful and appropriate for the types of work and decisions that require it.

You might be surprised to learn that many businesses don't have timely, accurate, or relevant information because the data in their information systems have been poorly organized and maintained. That's why data management is so essential. To understand the problem, let's look at how information systems arrange data in computer files and traditional methods of file management.

File Organization Terms and Concepts

A computer system organizes data in a hierarchy that starts with bits and bytes and progresses to fields, records, files, and databases (see Figure 6.1). A **bit** represents the smallest unit of data a computer can handle. A group of bits, called a **byte**, represents a single character, which can be a letter, a number, or another symbol. A grouping of characters into a word, a group of words, or a complete number (such as a person's name or age) is called a **field**. A group of related fields, such as the student's name, the course taken, the date, and the grade, comprises a **record**; a group of records of the same type is called a **file**.

FIGURE 6.1   THE DATA HIERARCHY

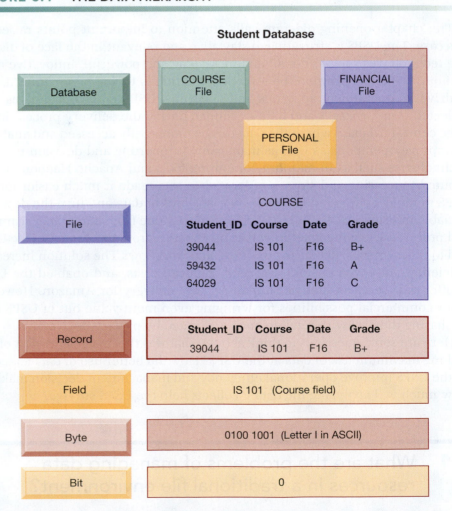

A computer system organizes data in a hierarchy that starts with the bit, which represents either a 0 or a 1. Bits can be grouped to form a byte to represent one character, number, or symbol. Bytes can be grouped to form a field, and related fields can be grouped to form a record. Related records can be collected to form a file, and related files can be organized into a database.

For example, the records in Figure 6.1 could constitute a student course file. A group of related files makes up a database. The student course file illustrated in Figure 6.1 could be grouped with files on students' personal histories and financial backgrounds to create a student database.

A record describes an entity. An **entity** is a person, place, thing, or event on which we store and maintain information. Each characteristic or quality describing a particular entity is called an **attribute**. For example, Student_ID, Course, Date, and Grade are attributes of the entity COURSE. The specific values that these attributes can have are found in the fields of the record describing the entity COURSE.

Problems with the Traditional File Environment

In most organizations, systems tended to grow independently without a companywide plan. Accounting, finance, manufacturing, human resources, and sales and marketing all developed their own systems and data files. Figure 6.2 illustrates the traditional approach to information processing.

Each application, of course, required its own files and its own computer program to operate. For example, the human resources functional area might have a personnel master file, a payroll file, a medical insurance file, a pension file, a mailing list file, and so forth, until tens, perhaps hundreds, of files and programs existed. In the company as a whole, this process led to multiple master files created, maintained, and operated by separate divisions or departments. As this process goes on for 5 or 10 years, the organization is saddled with hundreds of programs and applications that are very difficult to maintain

FIGURE 6.2   TRADITIONAL FILE PROCESSING

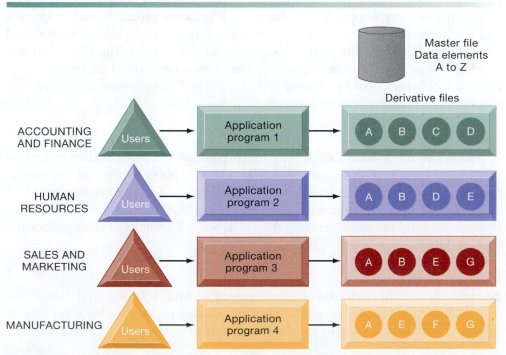

The use of a traditional approach to file processing encourages each functional area in a corporation to develop specialized applications. Each application requires a unique data file that is likely to be a subset of the master file. These subsets of the master file lead to data redundancy and inconsistency, processing inflexibility, and wasted storage resources.

and manage. The resulting problems are data redundancy and inconsistency, program-data dependence, inflexibility, poor data security, and an inability to share data among applications.

Data Redundancy and Inconsistency

Data redundancy is the presence of duplicate data in multiple data files so that the same data are stored in more than one place or location. Data redundancy occurs when different groups in an organization independently collect the same piece of data and store it independently of each other. Data redundancy wastes storage resources and also leads to **data inconsistency**, where the same attribute may have different values. For example, in instances of the entity COURSE illustrated in Figure 6.1, the Date may be updated in some systems but not in others. The same attribute, Student_ID, may also have different names in different systems throughout the organization. Some systems might use Student_ID and others might use ID, for example.

Additional confusion might result from using different coding systems to represent values for an attribute. For instance, the sales, inventory, and manufacturing systems of a clothing retailer might use different codes to represent clothing size. One system might represent clothing size as "extra large," whereas another might use the code "XL" for the same purpose. The resulting confusion would make it difficult for companies to create customer relationship management, supply chain management, or enterprise systems that integrate data from different sources.

Program-Data Dependence

Program-data dependence refers to the coupling of data stored in files and the specific programs required to update and maintain those files such that changes in programs require changes to the data. Every traditional computer program has to describe the location and nature of the data with which it works. In a traditional file environment, any change in a software program could require a change in the data accessed by that program. One program might be modified from a five-digit to a nine-digit ZIP code. If the original data file were changed from five-digit to nine-digit ZIP codes, then other programs that required the five-digit ZIP code would no longer work properly. Such changes could cost millions of dollars to implement properly.

Lack of Flexibility

A traditional file system can deliver routine scheduled reports after extensive programming efforts, but it cannot deliver ad hoc reports or respond to unanticipated information requirements in a timely fashion. The information required by ad hoc requests is somewhere in the system but may be too expensive to retrieve. Several programmers might have to work for weeks to put together the required data items in a new file.

Poor Security

Because there is little control or management of data, access to and dissemination of information may be out of control. Management may have no way of knowing who is accessing or even making changes to the organization's data.

Lack of Data Sharing and Availability

Because pieces of information in different files and different parts of the organization cannot be related to one another, it is virtually impossible for information to be shared or accessed in a timely manner. Information cannot flow freely across different functional areas or different parts of the organization. If users find different values of the same piece of information in two different systems, they may not want to use these systems because they cannot trust the accuracy of their data.

6-2 What are the major capabilities of database management systems (DBMS), and why is a relational DBMS so powerful?

Database technology cuts through many of the problems of traditional file organization. A more rigorous definition of a **database** is a collection of data organized to serve many applications efficiently by centralizing the data and controlling redundant data. Rather than storing data in separate files for each application, data appear to users as being stored in only one location. A single database services multiple applications. For example, instead of a corporation storing employee data in separate information systems and separate files for personnel, payroll, and benefits, the corporation could create a single common human resources database.

Database Management Systems

A **database management system (DBMS)** is software that permits an organization to centralize data, manage them efficiently, and provide access to the stored data by application programs. The DBMS acts as an interface between application programs and the physical data files. When the application program calls for a data item, such as gross pay, the DBMS finds this item in the database and presents it to the application program. Using traditional data files, the programmer would have to specify the size and format of each data element used in the program and then tell the computer where they were located.

The DBMS relieves the programmer or end user from the task of understanding where and how the data are actually stored by separating the logical and physical views of the data. The *logical view* presents data as they would be perceived by end users or business specialists, whereas the *physical view* shows how data are actually organized and structured on physical storage media.

The database management software makes the physical database available for different logical views required by users. For example, for the human resources database illustrated in Figure 6.3, a benefits specialist might require a view consisting of the employee's name, social security number, and health insurance coverage. A payroll department member might need data such as the employee's name, social security number, gross pay, and net pay. The data for all these views are stored in a single database, where they can be more easily managed by the organization.

How a DBMS Solves the Problems of the Traditional File Environment

A DBMS reduces data redundancy and inconsistency by minimizing isolated files in which the same data are repeated. The DBMS may not enable the organization to eliminate data redundancy entirely, but it can help control redundancy. Even if the organization maintains some redundant data, using a DBMS eliminates data inconsistency because the DBMS can help the organization ensure that every occurrence of redundant data has the same values. The DBMS

FIGURE 6.3   HUMAN RESOURCES DATABASE WITH MULTIPLE VIEWS

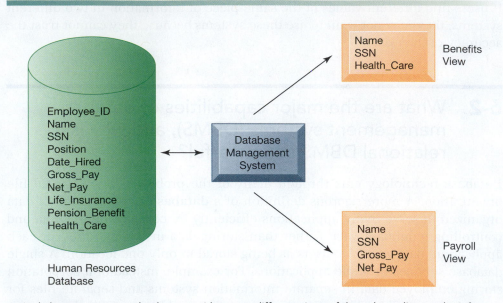

A single human resources database provides many different views of data, depending on the information requirements of the user. Illustrated here are two possible views, one of interest to a benefits specialist and one of interest to a member of the company's payroll department.

uncouples programs and data, enabling data to stand on their own. The description of the data used by the program does not have to be specified in detail each time a different program is written. Access and availability of information will be increased and program development and maintenance costs reduced because users and programmers can perform ad hoc queries of the database for many simple applications without having to write complicated programs. The DBMS enables the organization to centrally manage data, their use, and security. Data sharing throughout the organization is easier because the data are presented to users as being in a single location rather than fragmented in many different systems and files.

Relational DBMS

Contemporary DBMS use different database models to keep track of entities, attributes, and relationships. The most popular type of DBMS today for PCs as well as for larger computers and mainframes is the **relational DBMS**. Relational databases represent data as two-dimensional tables (called relations). Tables may be referred to as files. Each table contains data on an entity and its attributes. Microsoft Access is a relational DBMS for desktop systems, whereas DB2, Oracle Database, and Microsoft SQL Server are relational DBMS for large mainframes and midrange computers. MySQL is a popular open source DBMS.

Let's look at how a relational database organizes data about suppliers and parts (see Figure 6.4). The database has a separate table for the entity SUPPLIER and a table for the entity PART. Each table consists of a grid of columns and rows of data. Each individual element of data for each entity is stored as a separate field, and each field represents an attribute for that entity. Fields in a relational database are also called columns. For the entity SUPPLIER, the supplier identification number, name, street, city, state, and ZIP code are stored as separate fields within the SUPPLIER table and each field represents an attribute for the entity SUPPLIER.

FIGURE 6.4   RELATIONAL DATABASE TABLES

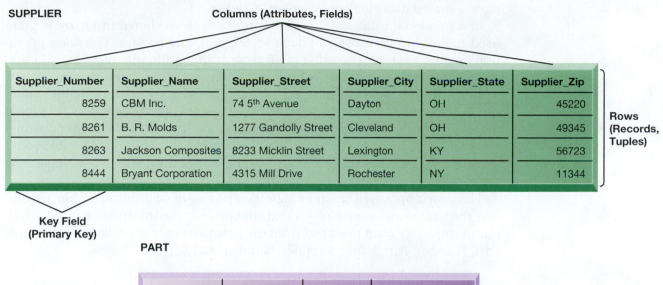

A relational database organizes data in the form of two-dimensional tables. Illustrated here are tables for the entities SUPPLIER and PART showing how they represent each entity and its attributes. Supplier_Number is a primary key for the SUPPLIER table and a foreign key for the PART table.

The actual information about a single supplier that resides in a table is called a row. Rows are commonly referred to as records, or in very technical terms, as **tuples**. Data for the entity PART have their own separate table.

The field for Supplier_Number in the SUPPLIER table uniquely identifies each record so that the record can be retrieved, updated, or sorted. It is called a **key field**. Each table in a relational database has one field that is designated as its **primary key**. This key field is the unique identifier for all the information in any row of the table and this primary key cannot be duplicated. Supplier_Number is the primary key for the SUPPLIER table and Part_Number is the primary key for the PART table. Note that Supplier_Number appears in both the SUPPLIER and PART tables. In the SUPPLIER table, Supplier_Number is the primary key. When the field Supplier_Number appears in the PART table, it is called a **foreign key** and is essentially a lookup field to look up data about the supplier of a specific part.

Operations of a Relational DBMS

Relational database tables can be combined easily to deliver data required by users, provided that any two tables share a common data element. Suppose we wanted to find in this database the names of suppliers who could provide us with part number 137 or part number 150. We would need information from two tables: the SUPPLIER table and the PART table. Note that these two files have a shared data element: Supplier_Number.

In a relational database, three basic operations, as shown in Figure 6.5, are used to develop useful sets of data: select, join, and project. The *select* operation creates a subset consisting of all records in the file that meet stated criteria. Select creates, in other words, a subset of rows that meet certain criteria. In our example, we want to select records (rows) from the PART table where the Part_Number equals 137 or 150. The *join* operation combines relational tables to provide the user with more information than is available in individual tables. In our example, we want to join the now-shortened PART table (only parts 137 or 150 will be presented) and the SUPPLIER table into a single new table.

The *project* operation creates a subset consisting of columns in a table, permitting the user to create new tables that contain only the information required. In our example, we want to extract from the new table only the following columns: Part_Number, Part_Name, Supplier_Number, and Supplier_Name.

Capabilities of Database Management Systems

A DBMS includes capabilities and tools for organizing, managing, and accessing the data in the database. The most important are its data definition language, data dictionary, and data manipulation language.

DBMS have a **data definition** capability to specify the structure of the content of the database. It would be used to create database tables and to define the characteristics of the fields in each table. This information about the database would be documented in a data dictionary. A **data dictionary** is an automated or manual file that stores definitions of data elements and their characteristics.

Microsoft Access has a rudimentary data dictionary capability that displays information about the name, description, size, type, format, and other properties of each field in a table (see Figure 6.6). Data dictionaries for large corporate databases may capture additional information, such as usage, ownership (who in the organization is responsible for maintaining the data), authorization, security, and the individuals, business functions, programs, and reports that use each data element.

Querying and Reporting

DBMS includes tools for accessing and manipulating information in databases. Most DBMS have a specialized language called a **data manipulation language** that is used to add, change, delete, and retrieve the data in the database. This language contains commands that permit end users and programming specialists to extract data from the database to satisfy information requests and develop applications. The most prominent data manipulation language today is **Structured Query Language**, or **SQL**. Figure 6.7 illustrates the SQL query that would produce the new resultant table in Figure 6.5. You can find out more about how to perform SQL queries in our Learning Tracks for this chapter.

Users of DBMS for large and midrange computers, such as DB2, Oracle, or SQL Server, would employ SQL to retrieve information they needed from the database. Microsoft Access also uses SQL, but it provides its own set of user-friendly tools for querying databases and for organizing data from databases into more polished reports.

FIGURE 6.5 THE THREE BASIC OPERATIONS OF A RELATIONAL DBMS

PART

Part_Number	Part_Name	Unit_Price	Supplier_Number
137	Door latch	22.00	8259
145	Side mirror	12.00	8444
150	Door molding	6.00	8263
152	Door lock	31.00	8259
155	Compressor	54.00	8261
178	Door handle	10.00	8259

Select Part_Number = 137 or 150

SUPPLIER

Supplier_Number	Supplier_Name	Supplier_Street	Supplier_City	Supplier_State	Supplier_Zip
8259	CBM Inc.	74 5th Avenue	Dayton	OH	45220
8261	B. R. Molds	1277 Gandolly Street	Cleveland	OH	49345
8263	Jackson Components	8233 Micklin Street	Lexington	KY	56723
8444	Bryant Corporation	4315 Mill Drive	Rochester	NY	11344

Join by Supplier_Number

Part_Number	Part_Name	Supplier_Number	Supplier_Name
137	Door latch	8259	CBM Inc.
150	Door molding	8263	Jackson Components

Project selected columns

The select, join, and project operations enable data from two different tables to be combined and only selected attributes to be displayed.

FIGURE 6.6   ACCESS DATA DICTIONARY FEATURES

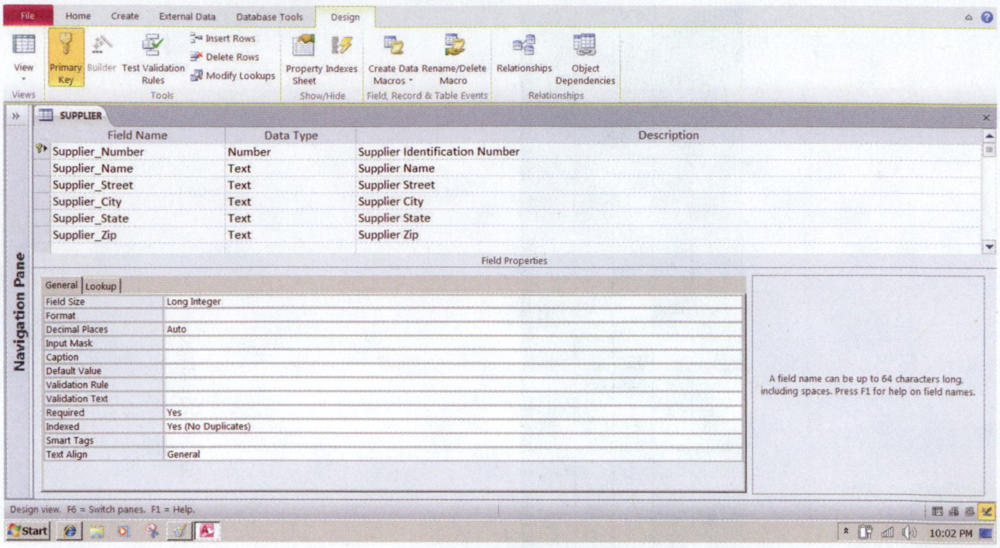

Microsoft Access has a rudimentary data dictionary capability that displays information about the size, format, and other characteristics of each field in a database. Displayed here is the information maintained in the SUPPLIER table. The small key icon to the left of Supplier_Number indicates that it is a key field.

In Microsoft Access, you will find features that enable users to create queries by identifying the tables and fields they want and the results and then selecting the rows from the database that meet particular criteria. These actions in turn are translated into SQL commands. Figure 6.8 illustrates how the same query as the SQL query to select parts and suppliers would be constructed using the Microsoft Access query-building tools.

Microsoft Access and other DBMS include capabilities for report generation so that the data of interest can be displayed in a more structured and polished format than would be possible just by querying. Crystal Reports is a popular report generator for large corporate DBMS, although it can also be used with Access. Access also has capabilities for developing desktop system applications. These include tools for creating data entry screens, reports, and developing the logic for processing transactions.

Designing Databases

To create a database, you must understand the relationships among the data, the type of data that will be maintained in the database, how the data will be used, and how the organization will need to change to manage data from a

FIGURE 6.7   EXAMPLE OF AN SQL QUERY

```
SELECT PART.Part_Number, PART.Part_Name, SUPPLIER.Supplier_Number,
SUPPLIER.Supplier_Name
FROM PART, SUPPLIER
WHERE PART.Supplier_Number = SUPPLIER.Supplier_Number AND
Part_Number = 137 OR Part_Number = 150;
```

Illustrated here are the SQL statements for a query to select suppliers for parts 137 or 150. They produce a list with the same results as Figure 6.5.

FIGURE 6.8   AN ACCESS QUERY

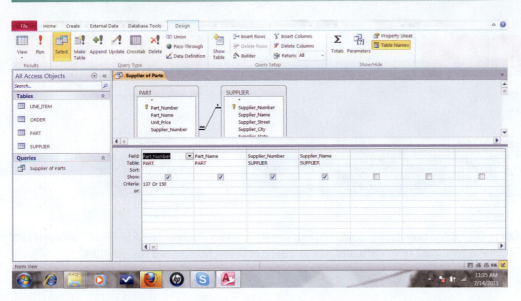

Illustrated here is how the query in Figure 6.7 would be constructed using Microsoft Access query-building tools. It shows the tables, fields, and selection criteria used for the query.

companywide perspective. The database requires both a conceptual design and a physical design. The conceptual, or logical, design of a database is an abstract model of the database from a business perspective, whereas the physical design shows how the database is actually arranged on direct-access storage devices.

Normalization and Entity-Relationship Diagrams

The conceptual database design describes how the data elements in the database are to be grouped. The design process identifies relationships among data elements and the most efficient way of grouping data elements together to meet business information requirements. The process also identifies redundant data elements and the groupings of data elements required for specific application programs. Groups of data are organized, refined, and streamlined until an overall logical view of the relationships among all the data in the database emerges.

To use a relational database model effectively, complex groupings of data must be streamlined to minimize redundant data elements and awkward many-to-many relationships. The process of creating small, stable, yet flexible and adaptive data structures from complex groups of data is called **normalization**. Figures 6.9 and 6.10 illustrate this process.

FIGURE 6.9   AN UNNORMALIZED RELATION FOR ORDER

ORDER (Before Normalization)

Order_Number	Order_Date	Part_Number	Part_Name	Unit_Price	Part_Quantity	Supplier_Number	Supplier_Name	Supplier_Street	Supplier_City	Supplier_State	Supplier_Zip

An unnormalized relation contains repeating groups. For example, there can be many parts and suppliers for each order. There is only a one-to-one correspondence between Order_Number and Order_Date.

FIGURE 6.10 NORMALIZED TABLES CREATED FROM ORDER

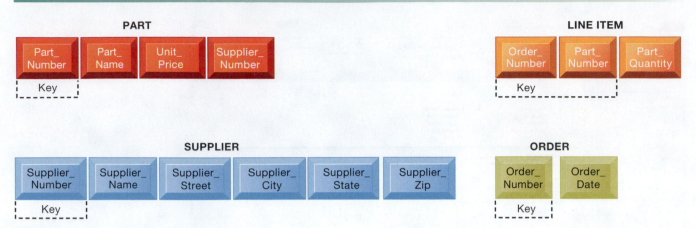

After normalization, the original relation ORDER has been broken down into four smaller relations. The relation ORDER is left with only two attributes, and the relation LINE_ITEM has a combined, or concatenated, key consisting of Order_Number and Part_Number.

In the particular business modeled here, an order can have more than one part, but each part is provided by only one supplier. If we build a relation called ORDER with all the fields included here, we would have to repeat the name and address of the supplier for every part on the order, even though the order is for parts from a single supplier. This relationship contains what are called repeating data groups because there can be many parts on a single order to a given supplier. A more efficient way to arrange the data is to break down ORDER into smaller relations, each of which describes a single entity. If we go step by step and normalize the relation ORDER, we emerge with the relations illustrated in Figure 6.10. You can find out more about normalization, entity-relationship diagramming, and database design in the Learning Tracks for this chapter.

Relational database systems try to enforce **referential integrity** rules to ensure that relationships between coupled tables remain consistent. When one table has a foreign key that points to another table, you may not add a record to the table with the foreign key unless there is a corresponding record in the linked table. In the database we examined earlier in this chapter, the foreign key Supplier_Number links the PART table to the SUPPLIER table. We may not add a new record to the PART table for a part with Supplier_Number 8266 unless there is a corresponding record in the SUPPLIER table for Supplier_Number 8266. We must also delete the corresponding record in the PART table if we delete the record in the SUPPLIER table for Supplier_Number 8266. In other words, we shouldn't have parts from nonexistent suppliers!

Database designers document their data model with an **entity-relationship diagram**, illustrated in Figure 6.11. This diagram illustrates the relationship between the entities SUPPLIER, PART, LINE_ITEM, and ORDER. The boxes represent entities. The lines connecting the boxes represent relationships. A line connecting two entities that ends in two short marks designates a one-to-one relationship. A line connecting two entities that ends with a crow's foot topped by a short mark indicates a one-to-many relationship. Figure 6.11 shows that one ORDER can contain many LINE_ITEMs. (A PART can be ordered many times and appear many times as a line item in a single order.) Each PART

FIGURE 6.11 AN ENTITY-RELATIONSHIP DIAGRAM

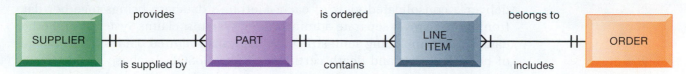

This diagram shows the relationships between the entities SUPPLIER, PART, LINE_ITEM, and ORDER that might be used to model the database in Figure 6.10.

can have only one SUPPLIER, but many PARTs can be provided by the same SUPPLIER.

It can't be emphasized enough: If the business doesn't get its data model right, the system won't be able to serve the business well. The company's systems will not be as effective as they could be because they'll have to work with data that may be inaccurate, incomplete, or difficult to retrieve. Understanding the organization's data and how they should be represented in a database is perhaps the most important lesson you can learn from this course.

For example, Famous Footwear, a shoe store chain with more than 800 locations in 49 states, could not achieve its goal of having "the right style of shoe in the right store for sale at the right price" because its database was not properly designed for rapidly adjusting store inventory. The company had an Oracle relational database running on a midrange computer, but the database was designed primarily for producing standard reports for management rather than for reacting to marketplace changes. Management could not obtain precise data on specific items in inventory in each of its stores. The company had to work around this problem by building a new database where the sales and inventory data could be better organized for analysis and inventory management.

Non-relational Databases and Databases in the Cloud

For more than 30 years, relational database technology has been the gold standard. Cloud computing, unprecedented data volumes, massive workloads for web services, and the need to store new types of data require database alternatives to the traditional relational model of organizing data in the form of tables, columns, and rows. Companies are turning to "NoSQL" non-relational database technologies for this purpose. **Non-relational database management systems** use a more flexible data model and are designed for managing large data sets across many distributed machines and for easily scaling up or down. They are useful for accelerating simple queries against large volumes of structured and unstructured data, including web, social media, graphics, and other forms of data that are difficult to analyze with traditional SQL-based tools.

There are several different kinds of NoSQL databases, each with its own technical features and behavior. Oracle NoSQL Database is one example, as is Amazon's SimpleDB, one of the Amazon Web Services that run in the cloud. SimpleDB provides a simple web services interface to create and store multiple data sets, query data easily, and return the results. There is no need to predefine a formal database structure or change that definition if new data are added later.

For example, MetLife used the MongoDB open source NoSQL database to quickly integrate disparate data on more than 100 million customers and deliver a consolidated view of each. MetLife's database brings together data from more than 70 separate administrative systems, claims systems, and other data sources, including semi-structured and unstructured data, such as images of health records and death certificates. The NoSQL database is able to use structured, semi-structured, and unstructured information without requiring tedious, expensive, and time-consuming database mapping.

Cloud Databases

Amazon and other cloud computing vendors provide relational database services as well. Amazon Relational Database Service (Amazon RDS) offers MySQL, SQL Server, Oracle Database, PostgreSQL, MariaDB, or Amazon Aurora DB (compatible with MySQL) as database engines. Pricing is based on usage. Oracle has its own Database Cloud Services using its relational Oracle Database, and Microsoft Windows SQL Azure Database is a cloud-based relational database service based on Microsoft's SQL Server DBMS. Cloud-based data management services have special appeal for web-focused start-ups or small to medium-sized businesses seeking database capabilities at a lower price than in-house database products.

In addition to public cloud-based data management services, companies now have the option of using databases in private clouds. For example, Sabre Holdings, the world's largest software as a service (SaaS) provider for the aviation industry, has a private database cloud that supports more than 100 projects and 700 users. A consolidated database spanning a pool of standardized servers running Oracle Database provides database services for multiple applications.

6-3 What are the principal tools and technologies for accessing information from databases to improve business performance and decision making?

Businesses use their databases to keep track of basic transactions, such as paying suppliers, processing orders, keeping track of customers, and paying employees. But they also need databases to provide information that will help the company run the business more efficiently and help managers and employees make better decisions. If a company wants to know which product is the most popular or who is its most profitable customer, the answer lies in the data.

The Challenge of Big Data

Most data collected by organizations used to be transaction data that could easily fit into rows and columns of relational database management systems. We are now witnessing an explosion of data from web traffic, e-mail messages, and social media content (tweets, status messages), as well as machine-generated data from sensors (used in smart meters, manufacturing sensors, and electrical meters) or from electronic trading systems. These data may be unstructured or semi-structured and thus not suitable for relational database products that organize data in the form of columns and rows. We now use the term **big data** to describe these data sets with volumes so huge that they are beyond the ability of typical DBMS to capture, store, and analyze.

Big data doesn't refer to any specific quantity but usually refers to data in the petabyte and exabyte range—in other words, billions to trillions of records, all from different sources. Big data are produced in much larger quantities and much more rapidly than traditional data. For example, a single jet engine is capable of generating 10 terabytes of data in just 30 minutes, and there are more than 25,000 airline flights each day. Even though "tweets" are limited to 140 characters each, Twitter generates more than 8 terabytes of data daily. According to the International Data Center (IDC) technology research firm, data are more than doubling every two years, so the amount of data available to organizations is skyrocketing.

Businesses are interested in big data because they can reveal more patterns and interesting relationships than smaller data sets, with the potential to provide new insights into customer behavior, weather patterns, financial market activity, or other phenomena. For example, Shutterstock, the global online image marketplace, stores 24 million images, adding 10,000 more each day. To find ways to optimize the buying experience, Shutterstock analyzes its big data to find out where its website visitors place their cursors and how long they hover over an image before making a purchase.

Big data is also finding many uses in the public sector. The chapter-opening case on the U.S. Postal Service is one example, as are city governments using big data to manage traffic flows and fight crime. The Interactive Session on Organizations describes how New York City is using big data to lower its crime rate.

However, to derive business value from these data, organizations need new technologies and tools capable of managing and analyzing nontraditional data along with their traditional enterprise data. They also need to know what questions to ask of the data and limitations of big data. Capturing, storing, and analyzing big data can be expensive, and information from big data may not necessarily help decision makers. It's important to have a clear understanding of the problem big data will solve for the business. The chapter-ending case explores these issues.

Business Intelligence Infrastructure

Suppose you wanted concise, reliable information about current operations, trends, and changes across the entire company. If you worked in a large company, the data you need might have to be pieced together from separate systems, such as sales, manufacturing, and accounting, and even from external sources, such as demographic or competitor data. Increasingly, you might need to use big data. A contemporary infrastructure for business intelligence has an array of tools for obtaining useful information from all the different types of data used by businesses today, including semi-structured and unstructured big data in vast quantities. These capabilities include data warehouses and data marts, Hadoop, in-memory computing, and analytical platforms. Some of these capabilities are available as cloud services.

Data Warehouses and Data Marts

The traditional tool for analyzing corporate data for the past two decades has been the data warehouse. A **data warehouse** is a database that stores current and historical data of potential interest to decision makers throughout the

New York City Moves To Data-Driven Crime Fighting

Nowhere have declining crime rates been as dramatic as in New York City. As reflected in the reported rates of the most serious types of crime, the city in 2015 was as safe as it had been since statistics have been kept. Crimes during the preceding few years have also been historically low.

Why is this happening? Experts point to a number of factors, including demographic trends, the proliferation of surveillance cameras, and increased incarceration rates. But New York City would also argue it is because of its proactive crime prevention program along with district attorney and police force willingness to aggressively deploy information technology.

Cyrus Vance Jr., New York County's district attorney, is vigorously trying to mine more crime-fighting information from the data collected by the city to drive crime rates even lower. He believes that New York could get crime rates to zero—if one looked harder at the data.

There has been a revolution in the use of big data for retailing and sports (think baseball and *Money-Ball*) as well as for police work. New York City has been at the forefront in intensively using data for crime fighting, and its CompStat crime-mapping program has been replicated by other cities.

CompStat features a comprehensive, citywide database that records all reported crimes or complaints, arrests, and summonses in each of the city's 76 precincts, including their time and location. The CompStat system analyzes the data and produces a weekly report on crime complaint and arrest activity at the precinct, patrol borough, and citywide levels. CompStat data can be displayed on maps showing crime and arrest locations, crime hot spots, and other relevant information to help precinct commanders and NYPD's senior leadership quickly identify patterns and trends and develop a targeted strategy for fighting crime, such as dispatching more foot patrols to high-crime neighborhoods.

Vance and his team think there is much more that can be done with data to reduce crime. Dealing with more than 105,000 cases per year in Manhattan, New York's assistant district attorneys did not have enough information to make fine-grained decisions about charges, bail, pleas, or sentences. They couldn't quickly separate minor delinquents from serious offenders.

In 2010 Vance's team created a Crime Strategies Unit (CSU) to identify and address crime issues and target priority offenders for aggressive prosecution. Rather than information being left on thousands of legal pads in the offices of hundreds of assistant district attorneys, CSU gathers and maps crime data for Manhattan's 22 precincts to visually depict criminal activity based on multiple identifiers such as gang affiliation and type of crime. Police commanders supply a list of each precinct's 25 worst offenders, which is added to a searchable database that now includes more than 9,000 chronic offenders. A large percentage are recidivists who have been repeatedly convicted of grand larceny, active gang members, and other priority targets. These are the people law enforcement wants to know about if they are arrested.

This database is used for an arrest alert system. When someone considered a priority defendant is picked up (even on a minor charge or parole violation) or arrested in another borough of the city, any interested prosecutor, parole officer, or police intelligence officer is automatically sent a detailed e-mail. The system can use the database to send arrest alerts for a particular defendant, a particular gang, or a particular neighborhood or housing project, and the database can be sorted to highlight patterns of crime ranging from bicycle theft to homicide.

The alert system helps assistant district attorneys ensure that charging decisions, bail applications, and sentencing recommendations address that defendant's impact on criminal activity in the community. The information gathered by CSU and disseminated through the arrest alert system differentiates among those for whom incarceration is an imperative from a community-safety standpoint and those defendants for whom alternatives to incarceration are appropriate and will not negatively affect overall community safety. If someone leaves a gang, goes to prison for a long time, moves out of the city or New York state, or dies, the data in the arrest alert system are edited accordingly.

In speeches praising intelligence-driven prosecution, Vance often cites the example of a 270-pound scam artist who for more than a decade made a living by bumping into pedestrians in the Times Square area and demanding money, claiming they had broken his glasses. He had been convicted

19 times but only for a misdemeanor charge and never served more than five months in jail. When flagged by CSU after his arrest in July 2010, he was convicted of felony robbery and sentenced to three and a half to seven years in prison.

Information developed by CSU helped Vance's Violent Criminal Enterprises Unit break up the most violent of Manhattan's 30 gangs. Since 2011, 17 gangs have been dismantled. According to New York's chief assistant district attorney Karen Friedman Agnifilo, murders dropped from 70 in 2010 to 29 in 2013 because the DA's office and police now had the information to identify the people driving crime in Manhattan and to take these people off the streets and put them behind bars.

There's another side to this, however. When prosecutors begin to compile databases for data-driven crime fighting, one needs to ask what people have been selected for inclusion in these databases, what are the selection criteria, and how harmful is this practice. Could the criminal justice databases include people who really shouldn't be there and nevertheless are targets for police scrutiny? According to

Steven Zeidman, director of the criminal-defense clinic at the City University of New York (CUNY) School of Law, the answer is yes. More than 1,000 people are arrested in New York City each day. An overwhelming and disproportionate number are people of color arrested for minor offenses like riding a bicycle on the sidewalk or jaywalking. Zeidman recalled a time when he was in court with a teenager arrested for jaywalking. The arresting officer said he had stopped the young man because he was wearing a red shirt that was known to be a gang color. The young man was not a gang member, but he's probably in the database. People with arrest and conviction records find it next to impossible to find legitimate work on release, and this result lasts for as long as the records are retained.

Sources: Pervaiz Shallwani and Mark Morales, "NYC Officials Tout New Low in Crime, but Homicide, Rape, Robbery Rose," *Wall Street Journal*, January 4, 2016; "Prosecution Gets Smart" and "Intelligence-Driven Prosecution/Crime Strategies Unit," www.manhattanda.org, accessed March 4, 2016; and Chip Brown, "The Data D.A.", *New York Times Magazine*, December 7, 2014.

CASE STUDY QUESTIONS

1. What are the benefits of intelligence-driven prosecution for crime fighters and the general public?

2. What problems does this approach to crime fighting pose?

3. What management, organization, and technology issues should be considered when setting up information systems for intelligence-driven prosecution?

company. The data originate in many core operational transaction systems, such as systems for sales, customer accounts, and manufacturing, and may include data from website transactions. The data warehouse extracts current and historical data from multiple operational systems inside the organization. These data are combined with data from external sources and transformed by correcting inaccurate and incomplete data and restructuring the data for management reporting and analysis before being loaded into the data warehouse.

The data warehouse makes the data available for anyone to access as needed, but the data cannot be altered. A data warehouse system also provides a range of ad hoc and standardized query tools, analytical tools, and graphical reporting facilities.

Companies often build enterprise-wide data warehouses, where a central data warehouse serves the entire organization, or they create smaller, decentralized warehouses called data marts. A **data mart** is a subset of a data warehouse in which a summarized or highly focused portion of the organization's data is placed in a separate database for a specific population of users. For example, a company might develop marketing and sales data marts to deal with customer information. Bookseller Barnes & Noble used to maintain a series of data marts—one for point-of-sale data in retail stores, another for college bookstore sales, and a third for online sales.

Hadoop

Relational DBMS and data warehouse products are not well suited for organizing and analyzing big data or data that do not easily fit into columns and rows used in their data models. For handling unstructured and semi-structured data in vast quantities, as well as structured data, organizations are using **Hadoop**. Hadoop is an open source software framework managed by the Apache Software Foundation that enables distributed parallel processing of huge amounts of data across inexpensive computers. It breaks a big data problem down into sub-problems, distributes them among up to thousands of inexpensive computer processing nodes, and then combines the result into a smaller data set that is easier to analyze. You've probably used Hadoop to find the best airfare on the Internet, get directions to a restaurant, do a search on Google, or connect with a friend on Facebook.

Hadoop consists of several key services, including the Hadoop Distributed File System (HDFS) for data storage and MapReduce for high-performance parallel data processing. HDFS links together the file systems on the numerous nodes in a Hadoop cluster to turn them into one big file system. Hadoop's MapReduce was inspired by Google's MapReduce system for breaking down processing of huge data sets and assigning work to the various nodes in a cluster. HBase, Hadoop's non-relational database, provides rapid access to the data stored on HDFS and a transactional platform for running high-scale real-time applications.

Hadoop can process large quantities of any kind of data, including structured transactional data, loosely structured data such as Facebook and Twitter feeds, complex data such as web server log files, and unstructured audio and video data. Hadoop runs on a cluster of inexpensive servers, and processors can be added or removed as needed. Companies use Hadoop for analyzing very large volumes of data as well as for a staging area for unstructured and semi-structured data before they are loaded into a data warehouse. Yahoo uses Hadoop to track users' behavior so it can modify its home page to fit their interests. Life sciences research firm NextBio uses Hadoop and HBase to process data for pharmaceutical companies conducting genomic research. Top database vendors such as IBM, Hewlett-Packard, Oracle, and Microsoft have their own Hadoop software distributions. Other vendors offer tools for moving data into and out of Hadoop or for analyzing data within Hadoop.

In-Memory Computing

Another way of facilitating big data analysis is to use **in-memory computing**, which relies primarily on a computer's main memory (RAM) for data storage. (Conventional DBMS use disk storage systems.) Users access data stored in system primary memory, thereby eliminating bottlenecks from retrieving and reading data in a traditional, disk-based database and dramatically shortening query response times. In-memory processing makes it possible for very large sets of data, amounting to the size of a data mart or small data warehouse, to reside entirely in memory. Complex business calculations that used to take hours or days are able to be completed within seconds, and this can even be accomplished using handheld devices.

The previous chapter describes some of the advances in contemporary computer hardware technology that make in-memory processing possible, such as powerful high-speed processors, multicore processing, and falling computer memory prices. These technologies help companies optimize the use of memory and accelerate processing performance while lowering costs.

Leading commercial products for in-memory computing include SAP HANA and Oracle Exalytics. Each provides a set of integrated software components, including in-memory database software and specialized analytics software, that run on hardware optimized for in-memory computing work.

Analytic Platforms

Commercial database vendors have developed specialized high-speed **analytic platforms** using both relational and non-relational technology that are optimized for analyzing large data sets. Analytic platforms such as IBM PureData System for Analytics, feature preconfigured hardware-software systems that are specifically designed for query processing and analytics. For example, IBM PureData System for Analytics features tightly integrated database, server, and storage components that handle complex analytic queries 10 to 100 times faster than traditional systems. Analytic platforms also include in-memory systems and NoSQL non-relational database management systems. Analytic platforms are now available as cloud services.

Figure 6.12 illustrates a contemporary business intelligence infrastructure using the technologies we have just described. Current and historical data are extracted from multiple operational systems along with web data, machine-generated data, unstructured audio/visual data, and data from external sources that have been restructured and reorganized for reporting and analysis. Hadoop clusters pre-process big data for use in the data warehouse, data marts, or an

FIGURE 6.12 CONTEMPORARY BUSINESS INTELLIGENCE INFRASTRUCTURE

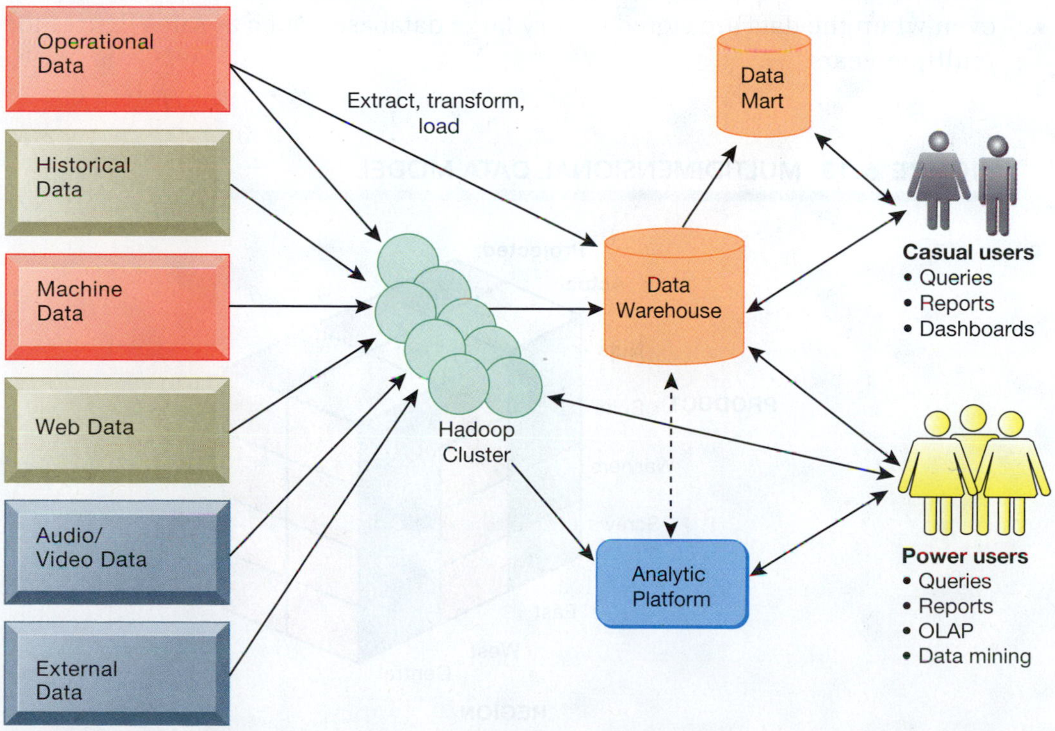

A contemporary business intelligence infrastructure features capabilities and tools to manage and analyze large quantities and different types of data from multiple sources. Easy-to-use query and reporting tools for casual business users and more sophisticated analytical toolsets for power users are included.

analytic platform or for direct querying by power users. Outputs include reports and dashboards as well as query results. Chapter 12 discusses the various types of BI users and BI reporting in greater detail.

Analytical Tools: Relationships, Patterns, Trends

Once data have been captured and organized using the business intelligence technologies we have just described, they are available for further analysis using software for database querying and reporting, multidimensional data analysis (OLAP), and data mining. This section will introduce you to these tools, with more detail about business intelligence analytics and applications in Chapter 12.

Online Analytical Processing (OLAP)

Suppose your company sells four different products—nuts, bolts, washers, and screws—in the East, West, and Central regions. If you wanted to ask a fairly straightforward question, such as how many washers sold during the past quarter, you could easily find the answer by querying your sales database. But what if you wanted to know how many washers sold in each of your sales regions and compare actual results with projected sales?

To obtain the answer, you would need **online analytical processing (OLAP)**. OLAP supports multidimensional data analysis, enabling users to view the same data in different ways using multiple dimensions. Each aspect of information—product, pricing, cost, region, or time period—represents a different dimension. So, a product manager could use a multidimensional data analysis tool to learn how many washers were sold in the East in June, how that compares with the previous month and the previous June, and how it compares with the sales forecast. OLAP enables users to obtain online answers to ad hoc questions such as these in a fairly rapid amount of time, even when the data are stored in very large databases, such as sales figures for multiple years.

FIGURE 6.13   MULTIDIMENSIONAL DATA MODEL

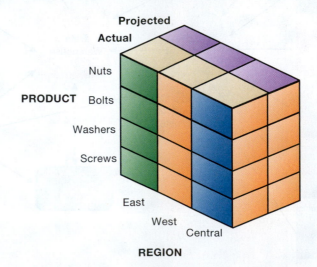

This view shows product versus region. If you rotate the cube 90 degrees, the face that will show is product versus actual and projected sales. If you rotate the cube 90 degrees again, you will see region versus actual and projected sales. Other views are possible.

Figure 6.13 shows a multidimensional model that could be created to represent products, regions, actual sales, and projected sales. A matrix of actual sales can be stacked on top of a matrix of projected sales to form a cube with six faces. If you rotate the cube 90 degrees one way, the face showing will be product versus actual and projected sales. If you rotate the cube 90 degrees again, you will see region versus actual and projected sales. If you rotate 180 degrees from the original view, you will see projected sales and product versus region. Cubes can be nested within cubes to build complex views of data. A company would use either a specialized multidimensional database or a tool that creates multidimensional views of data in relational databases.

Data Mining

Traditional database queries answer such questions as "How many units of product number 403 were shipped in February 2016?" OLAP, or multidimensional analysis, supports much more complex requests for information, such as "Compare sales of product 403 relative to plan by quarter and sales region for the past two years." With OLAP and query-oriented data analysis, users need to have a good idea about the information for which they are looking.

Data mining is more discovery-driven. Data mining provides insights into corporate data that cannot be obtained with OLAP by finding hidden patterns and relationships in large databases and inferring rules from them to predict future behavior. The patterns and rules are used to guide decision making and forecast the effect of those decisions. The types of information obtainable from data mining include associations, sequences, classifications, clusters, and forecasts.

- *Associations* are occurrences linked to a single event. For instance, a study of supermarket purchasing patterns might reveal that, when corn chips are purchased, a cola drink is purchased 65 percent of the time, but when there is a promotion, cola is purchased 85 percent of the time. This information helps managers make better decisions because they have learned the profitability of a promotion.

- In *sequences*, events are linked over time. We might find, for example, that if a house is purchased, a new refrigerator will be purchased within two weeks 65 percent of the time, and an oven will be bought within one month of the home purchase 45 percent of the time.

- *Classification* recognizes patterns that describe the group to which an item belongs by examining existing items that have been classified and by inferring a set of rules. For example, businesses such as credit card or telephone companies worry about the loss of steady customers. Classification helps discover the characteristics of customers who are likely to leave and can provide a model to help managers predict who those customers are so that the managers can devise special campaigns to retain such customers.

- *Clustering* works in a manner similar to classification when no groups have yet been defined. A data mining tool can discover different groupings within data, such as finding affinity groups for bank cards or partitioning a database into groups of customers based on demographics and types of personal investments.

- Although these applications involve predictions, *forecasting* uses predictions in a different way. It uses a series of existing values to forecast what other values will be. For example, forecasting might find patterns in data to help managers estimate the future value of continuous variables, such as sales figures.

These systems perform high-level analyses of patterns or trends, but they can also drill down to provide more detail when needed. There are data mining applications for all the functional areas of business and for government and scientific work. One popular use for data mining is to provide detailed analyses of patterns in customer data for one-to-one marketing campaigns or for identifying profitable customers.

Caesars Entertainment, formerly known as Harrah's Entertainment, is the largest gaming company in the world. It continually analyzes data about its customers gathered when people play its slot machines or use its casinos and hotels. The corporate marketing department uses this information to build a detailed gambling profile, based on a particular customer's ongoing value to the company. For instance, data mining lets Caesars know the favorite gaming experience of a regular customer at one of its riverboat casinos along with that person's preferences for room accommodations, restaurants, and entertainment. This information guides management decisions about how to cultivate the most profitable customers, encourage those customers to spend more, and attract more customers with high revenue-generating potential. Business intelligence improved Caesars's profits so much that it became the centerpiece of the firm's business strategy.

Text Mining and Web Mining

Unstructured data, most in the form of text files, is believed to account for more than 80 percent of useful organizational information and is one of the major sources of big data that firms want to analyze. E-mail, memos, call center transcripts, survey responses, legal cases, patent descriptions, and service reports are all valuable for finding patterns and trends that will help employees make better business decisions. **Text mining** tools are now available to help businesses analyze these data. These tools are able to extract key elements from unstructured big data sets, discover patterns and relationships, and summarize the information.

Businesses might turn to text mining to analyze transcripts of calls to customer service centers to identify major service and repair issues or to measure customer sentiment about their company. **Sentiment analysis** software is able to mine text comments in an e-mail message, blog, social media conversation, or survey form to detect favorable and unfavorable opinions about specific subjects.

For example, the discount broker Charles Schwab uses Attensity Analyze software to analyze hundreds of thousands of its customer interactions each month. The software analyzes Schwab's customer service notes, e-mails, survey responses, and online discussions to discover signs of dissatisfaction that might cause a customer to stop using the company's services. Attensity is able to automatically identify the various "voices" customers use to express their feedback (such as a positive, negative, or conditional voice) to pinpoint a person's intent to buy, intent to leave, or reaction to a specific product or marketing message. Schwab uses this information to take corrective actions such as stepping up direct broker communication with the customer and trying to quickly resolve the problems that are making the customer unhappy.

The web is another rich source of unstructured big data for revealing patterns, trends, and insights into customer behavior. The discovery and analysis of useful patterns and information from the World Wide Web are called **web mining**. Businesses might turn to web mining to help them understand customer behavior, evaluate the effectiveness of a particular website, or quantify the success of a marketing campaign. For instance, marketers use the Google Trends service, which tracks the popularity of various words and phrases used in Google search queries, to learn what people are interested in and what they are interested in buying.

Web mining looks for patterns in data through content mining, structure mining, and usage mining. Web content mining is the process of extracting knowledge from the content of webpages, which may include text, image, audio, and video data. Web structure mining examines data related to the structure of a particular website. For example, links pointing to a document indicate the popularity of the document, while links coming out of a document indicate the richness or perhaps the variety of topics covered in the document. Web usage mining examines user interaction data recorded by a web server whenever requests for a website's resources are received. The usage data records the user's behavior when the user browses or makes transactions on the website and collects the data in a server log. Analyzing such data can help companies determine the value of particular customers, cross-marketing strategies across products, and the effectiveness of promotional campaigns.

The chapter-ending case describes organizations' experiences as they use the analytical tools and business intelligence technologies we have described to grapple with "big data" challenges.

Databases and the Web

Have you ever tried to use the web to place an order or view a product catalog? If so, you were using a website linked to an internal corporate database. Many companies now use the web to make some of the information in their internal databases available to customers and business partners.

Suppose, for example, a customer with a web browser wants to search an online retailer's database for pricing information. Figure 6.14 illustrates how that customer might access the retailer's internal database over the web. The user accesses the retailer's website over the Internet using a web browser on his or her client PC or mobile device. The user's web browser software requests data from the organization's database, using HTML commands to communicate with the web server. Apps provide even faster access to corporate databases.

Because many back-end databases cannot interpret commands written in HTML, the web server passes these requests for data to software that translates HTML commands into SQL so the commands can be processed by the DBMS working with the database. In a client/server environment, the DBMS resides on a dedicated computer called a **database server**. The DBMS receives the

FIGURE 6.14 LINKING INTERNAL DATABASES TO THE WEB

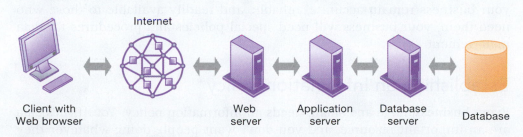

Users access an organization's internal database through the web using their desktop PC browsers or mobile apps.

SQL requests and provides the required data. Middleware transfers information from the organization's internal database back to the web server for delivery in the form of a web page to the user.

Figure 6.14 shows that the middleware working between the web server and the DBMS is an application server running on its own dedicated computer (see Chapter 5). The application server software handles all application operations, including transaction processing and data access, between browser-based computers and a company's back-end business applications or databases. The application server takes requests from the web server, runs the business logic to process transactions based on those requests, and provides connectivity to the organization's back-end systems or databases. Alternatively, the software for handling these operations could be a custom program or a CGI script. A CGI script is a compact program using the *Common Gateway Interface (CGI)* specification for processing data on a web server.

There are a number of advantages to using the web to access an organization's internal databases. First, web browser software is much easier to use than proprietary query tools. Second, the web interface requires few or no changes to the internal database. It costs much less to add a web interface in front of a legacy system than to redesign and rebuild the system to improve user access.

Accessing corporate databases through the web is creating new efficiencies, opportunities, and business models. ThomasNet.com provides an up-to-date online directory of more than 700,000 suppliers of industrial products, such as chemicals, metals, plastics, rubber, and automotive equipment. Formerly called Thomas Register, the company used to send out huge paper catalogs with this information. Now it provides this information to users online via its website and has become a smaller, leaner company.

Other companies have created entirely new businesses based on access to large databases through the web. One is the social networking service Facebook, which helps users stay connected with each other and meet new people. Facebook features "profiles" with information on 1.6 billion active users with information about themselves, including interests, friends, photos, and groups with which they are affiliated. Facebook maintains a very large database to house and manage all of this content. There are also many web-enabled databases in the public sector to help consumers and citizens access helpful information.

6-4 Why are information policy, data administration, and data quality assurance essential for managing the firm's data resources?

Setting up a database is only a start. In order to make sure that the data for your business remain accurate, reliable, and readily available to those who need them, your business will need special policies and procedures for data management.

Establishing an Information Policy

Every business, large and small, needs an information policy. Your firm's data are an important resource, and you don't want people doing whatever they want with them. You need to have rules on how the data are to be organized and maintained and who is allowed to view the data or change them.

An **information policy** specifies the organization's rules for sharing, disseminating, acquiring, standardizing, classifying, and inventorying information. Information policy lays out specific procedures and accountabilities, identifying which users and organizational units can share information, where information can be distributed, and who is responsible for updating and maintaining the information. For example, a typical information policy would specify that only selected members of the payroll and human resources department would have the right to change and view sensitive employee data, such as an employee's salary or social security number, and that these departments are responsible for making sure that such employee data are accurate.

If you are in a small business, the information policy would be established and implemented by the owners or managers. In a large organization, managing and planning for information as a corporate resource often require a formal data administration function. **Data administration** is responsible for the specific policies and procedures through which data can be managed as an organizational resource. These responsibilities include developing an information policy, planning for data, overseeing logical database design and data dictionary development, and monitoring how information systems specialists and end-user groups use data.

You may hear the term **data governance** used to describe many of these activities. Promoted by IBM, data governance deals with the policies and processes for managing the availability, usability, integrity, and security of the data employed in an enterprise with special emphasis on promoting privacy, security, data quality, and compliance with government regulations.

A large organization will also have a database design and management group within the corporate information systems division that is responsible for defining and organizing the structure and content of the database and maintaining the database. In close cooperation with users, the design group establishes the physical database, the logical relations among elements, and the access rules and security procedures. The functions it performs are called **database administration**.

Ensuring Data Quality

A well-designed database and information policy will go a long way toward ensuring that the business has the information it needs. However, additional steps must be taken to ensure that the data in organizational databases are accurate and remain reliable.

What would happen if a customer's telephone number or account balance were incorrect? What would be the impact if the database had the wrong price for the product you sold or your sales system and inventory system showed different prices for the same product? Data that are inaccurate, untimely, or inconsistent with other sources of information lead to incorrect decisions, product recalls, and financial losses. Gartner, Inc. reported that more than 25 percent of the critical data in large *Fortune* 1000 companies' databases is inaccurate or incomplete, including bad product codes and product descriptions, faulty inventory descriptions, erroneous financial data, incorrect supplier information, and incorrect employee data. Some of these data quality problems are caused by redundant and inconsistent data produced by multiple systems feeding a data warehouse. For example, the sales ordering system and the inventory management system might both maintain data on the organization's products. However, the sales ordering system might use the term

Item Number and the inventory system might call the same attribute *Product Number*. The sales, inventory, or manufacturing systems of a clothing retailer might use different codes to represent values for an attribute. One system might represent clothing size as "medium," whereas the other system might use the code "M" for the same purpose. During the design process for the warehouse database, data describing entities, such as a customer, product, or order, should be named and defined consistently for all business areas using the database.

Think of all the times you've received several pieces of the same direct mail advertising on the same day. This is very likely the result of having your name maintained multiple times in a database. Your name may have been misspelled or you used your middle initial on one occasion and not on another or the information was initially entered onto a paper form and not scanned properly into the system. Because of these inconsistencies, the database would treat you as different people! We often receive redundant mail addressed to Laudon, Lavdon, Lauden, or Landon.

If a database is properly designed and enterprise-wide data standards established, duplicate or inconsistent data elements should be minimal. Most data quality problems, however, such as misspelled names, transposed numbers, or incorrect or missing codes, stem from errors during data input. The incidence of such errors is rising as companies move their businesses to the web and allow customers and suppliers to enter data into their websites that directly update internal systems.

Before a new database is in place, organizations need to identify and correct their faulty data and establish better routines for editing data once their database is in operation. Analysis of data quality often begins with a **data quality audit**, which is a structured survey of the accuracy and level of completeness of the data in an information system. Data quality audits can be performed by surveying entire data files, surveying samples from data files, or surveying end users for their perceptions of data quality.

Data cleansing, also known as *data scrubbing*, consists of activities for detecting and correcting data in a database that are incorrect, incomplete, improperly formatted, or redundant. Data cleansing not only corrects errors but also enforces consistency among different sets of data that originated in separate information systems. Specialized data-cleansing software is available to automatically survey data files, correct errors in the data, and integrate the data in a consistent companywide format.

Data quality problems are not just business problems. They also pose serious problems for individuals, affecting their financial condition and even their jobs. For example, inaccurate or outdated data about consumers' credit histories maintained by credit bureaus can prevent creditworthy individuals from obtaining loans or lower their chances of finding or keeping a job.

A small minority of companies allow individual departments to be in charge of maintaining the quality of their own data. However, best data administration practices call for centralizing data governance, standardization of organizational data, data quality maintenance, and accessibility to data assets.

The Interactive Session on Management illustrates Keurig Green Mountain's experience with managing data as a resource. As you read this case, try to identify the policies, procedures, and technologies that were required to improve data management at this company.

INTERACTIVE SESSION: MANAGEMENT

Keurig Green Mountain Embraces Data Governance

More than 25 percent of all coffee consumed in the United States today comes from Keurig Green Mountain single-serve K-Cups. Keurig Green Mountain, headquartered in Waterbury, Vermont, has expanded so rapidly over the past decade that it has 80 brands and nearly 600 product varieties of hot and cold coffees (including Green Mountain), teas, cocoas, dairy-based beverages, cider, and fruit-based drinks. It also partners with other vendors such as Dunkin Donuts, Newman's Own, and Starbucks to package and sell their products in K-Cup pods. The company has more than 6,600 employees and generated nearly $4.4 billion in revenue in 2015. A business this large and complex must maintain a vast amount of data.

Keurig Green Mountain's meteoric growth called for a better approach to managing those data. The company had relied on what it called a "hero culture" for data governance. Different groups in charge of providing data would set up the data they were responsible for, such as customer records, vendor records, or material master data. The department receiving the data would correct any inaccuracies to make sure that the right products were produced, orders were placed, and items were shipped. The data providers were called "heroes" because their work was of such high value to the company. This way of working sufficed before Keurig's growth spurt. However, because the data corrections that were made downstream were not always conveyed to the data providers, the process was not repeatable and corrections might have to be made again the next time the data were used. This added to the time and cost to conduct business. Additionally, having different groups of "heroes" fix the data only for their specific business processes meant that managing data from a companywide standpoint was limited.

By 2013 Keurig Green Mountain had outgrown its legacy ERP system and switched to SAP ERP. This gave the entire company the opportunity to review how it was managing data and to take the necessary steps toward master data management, well-defined processes, standards for the maintenance of data across the organization, and comprehensive data cleansing. Master data management (MDM) is the organizational effort to create one single master reference source for all critical business data, leading to fewer errors and less redundancy in business processes. By providing one point of reference for critical information, MDM eliminates costly

redundancies that occur when organizations rely upon multiple conflicting sources of data.

Keurig Green Mountain enlisted DATUM LLC to help it establish a strong data governance framework. This was necessary to ensure that as the company's volume of data increased, it wouldn't return to disparate data management practices that would negate the efficiencies and benefits of the SAP ERP software. DATUM LLC is an information management solutions company based in Annapolis, Maryland, that provides data governance software and consulting services. Its Information Value Management SaaS (software as a service) translates business objectives into functional designs that improve quality and processing speed.

DATUM supplies expertise on defining data-centric processes, information value, and accountability. By incorporating best practices, Information Value Management provides a framework of data standards, governance rules, business metrics, and business processes that is useful for analytics, business intelligence, data governance, process improvement, performance management, ERP implementation, and managing big data.

Information Value Management (IVM) can be integrated with SAP Information Steward software, which provides a single environment to discover, assess, define, monitor, and improve the quality of enterprise data assets. Information Steward's functionality includes modules for discovering data characteristics and relationships, creating and running data validation rules, identifying bad data and improving data quality, cataloging data, defining business terms for data and organizing the terms into categories, and data cleansing tools. Information Steward helps ensure companywide reporting consistency so that the company's data stewards can easily monitor hanging data and make sure these changes are reflected in the organization's master data management. IVM can also be used with other SAP solutions for enterprise information management (EIM), including data quality assurance, master data management, content management, and information lifecycle management.

Keurig Green Mountain has used Information Steward to implement data quality reports. As data are collected, the tool alerts users to missing required fields. This capability lessens the need for a "hero culture," repeated errors, and repeated fixes to data downstream. Better data quality leads to more informed business decisions, and users of company data will have more trust in the data behind their business processes. Keurig believes its work building a fully automated data governance structure where the entire company is aligned to an enterprise-wide data strategy and standards won't be completed until 2020.

Sources: Ken Murphy, "Keurig Green Mountain Brews Up Data Governance," SAP Insider Profiles, January 2016; www.sap.com, accessed March 5, 2016; www.datumstrategy.com, accessed March 5, 2016; and Keurig Green Mountain Inc. Form 10-K, November 19, 2015.

CASE STUDY QUESTIONS

1. Discuss the role of data governance at Keurig Green Mountain.

2. What management, organization, and technology issues had to be addressed in order to establish enterprise-wide data governance?

3. What were the business benefits of data governance for Keurig Green Mountain?

4. How did data governance improve operations and management decision making?

Review Summary

6-1 *What are the problems of managing data resources in a traditional file environment?*

Traditional file management techniques make it difficult for organizations to keep track of all of the pieces of data they use in a systematic way and to organize these data so that they can be easily accessed. Different functional areas and groups were allowed to develop their own files independently. Over time, this traditional file management environment creates problems such as data redundancy and inconsistency, program-data dependence, inflexibility, poor security, and lack of data sharing and availability. A database management system (DBMS) solves these problems with software that permits centralization of data and data management so that businesses have a single consistent source for all their data needs. Using a DBMS minimizes redundant and inconsistent files.

6-2 *What are the major capabilities of DBMS, and why is a relational DBMS so powerful?*

The principal capabilities of a DBMS include a data definition capability, a data dictionary capability, and a data manipulation language. The data definition capability specifies the structure and content of the database. The data dictionary is an automated or manual file that stores information about the data in the database, including names, definitions, formats, and descriptions of data elements. The data manipulation language, such as SQL, is a specialized language for accessing and manipulating the data in the database.

The relational database has been the primary method for organizing and maintaining data in information systems because it is so flexible and accessible. It organizes data in two-dimensional tables called relations with rows and columns. Each table contains data about an entity and its attributes. Each row represents a record, and each column represents an attribute or field. Each table also contains a key field to uniquely identify each record for retrieval or manipulation. Relational database tables can be combined easily to deliver data required by users, provided that any two tables share a common data element. Non-relational databases are becoming popular for managing types of data that can't be handled easily by the relational data model. Both relational and non-relational database products are available as cloud computing services.

Designing a database requires both a logical design and a physical design. The logical design models the database from a business perspective. The organization's data model should reflect its key business processes and decision-making requirements. The process of creating small, stable, flexible, and adaptive data structures from complex groups of data when designing a relational database is termed normalization. A well-designed relational database will not have many-to-many relationships, and all attributes for a specific entity will only apply to that entity. It will try to enforce referential integrity rules to ensure that relationships between coupled tables remain consistent. An entity-relationship diagram graphically depicts the relationship between entities (tables) in a relational database.

6-3 *What are the principal tools and technologies for accessing information from databases to improve business performance and decision making?*

Contemporary data management technology has an array of tools for obtaining useful information from all the different types of data used by businesses today, including semi-structured and unstructured big data in vast quantities. These capabilities include data warehouses and data marts, Hadoop, in-memory computing, and analytical platforms. OLAP represents relationships among data as a multidimensional structure, which can be visualized as cubes of data and cubes within cubes of data, enabling more sophisticated data analysis. Data mining analyzes large pools of data, including the contents of data warehouses, to find patterns and rules that can be used to predict future behavior and guide decision making. Text mining tools help businesses analyze large unstructured data sets consisting of text. Web mining tools focus on analysis of useful patterns and information from the Web, examining the structure of websites and activities of website users as well as the contents of webpages. Conventional databases can be linked via middleware to the web or a web interface to facilitate user access to an organization's internal data.

6-4 *Why are information policy, data administration, and data quality assurance essential for managing the firm's data resources?*

Developing a database environment requires policies and procedures for managing organizational data as well as a good data model and database technology. A formal information policy governs the maintenance, distribution, and use of information in the organization. In large corporations, a formal data administration function is responsible for information policy as well as for data planning, data dictionary development, and monitoring data usage in the firm.

Data that are inaccurate, incomplete, or inconsistent create serious operational and financial problems for businesses because they may create inaccuracies in product pricing, customer accounts, and inventory data and lead to inaccurate decisions about the actions that should be taken by the firm. Firms must take special steps to make sure they have a high level of data quality. These include using enterprise-wide data standards, databases designed to minimize inconsistent and redundant data, data quality audits, and data cleansing software.

Key Terms

Analytic platform, 231
Attribute, 215
Big data, 227
Bit, 214
Byte, 214
Data administration, 237
Data cleansing, 238
Data definition, 220
Data dictionary, 220
Data governance, 237
Data inconsistency, 216
Data manipulation language, 220
Data mart, 229
Data mining, 233
Data quality audit, 238
Data redundancy, 216
Data warehouse, 227
Database, 217
Database administration, 237
Database management system (DBMS), 217
Database server, 235
Entity, 215

Entity-relationship diagram, 224
Field, 214
File, 214
Foreign key, 219
Hadoop, 230
In-memory computing, 230
Information policy, 237
Key field, 219
Non-relational database management systems, 225
Normalization, 223
Online analytical processing (OLAP), 232
Primary key, 219
Program-data dependence, 216
Record, 214
Referential integrity, 224
Relational DBMS, 218
Sentiment analysis, 234
Structured Query Language (SQL), 220
Text mining, 234
Tuple, 219
Web mining, 234

MyMISLab

To complete the problems marked with the MyMISLab, go to EOC Discussion Questions in MyMISLab.

Review Questions

6-1 What are the problems of managing data resources in a traditional file environment?

- List and describe each of the components in the data hierarchy.
- Define and explain the significance of entities, attributes, and key fields.
- List and describe the problems of the traditional file environment.

6-2 What are the major capabilities of database management systems (DBMS), and why is a relational DBMS so powerful?

- Define a database and a database management system.
- Name and briefly describe the capabilities of a DBMS.
- Define a relational DBMS and explain how it organizes data.
- List and describe the three operations of a relational DBMS.
- Explain why non-relational databases are useful.
- Define and describe normalization and referential integrity and explain how they contribute to a well-designed relational database.
- Define and describe an entity-relationship diagram and explain its role in database design.

6-3 What are the principal tools and technologies for accessing information from databases to improve business performance and decision making?

- Define big data and describe the technologies for managing and analyzing it.
- List and describe the components of a contemporary business intelligence infrastructure.
- Describe the capabilities of online analytical processing (OLAP).
- Define data mining, describing how it differs from OLAP and the types of information it provides.
- Explain how text mining and web mining differ from conventional data mining.
- Describe how users can access information from a company's internal databases through the web.

6-4 Why are information policy, data administration, and data quality assurance essential for managing the firm's data resources?

- Describe the roles of information policy and data administration in information management.
- Explain why data quality audits and data cleansing are essential.

Discussion Questions

6-5 It has been said there is no bad data, just bad management. Discuss the implications of this statement.
MyMISLab

6-6 To what extent should end users be involved in the selection of a database management system and database design?
MyMISLab

6-7 What are the consequences of an organization not having an information policy?
MyMISLab

Hands-On MIS Projects

The projects in this section give you hands-on experience in analyzing data quality problems, establishing companywide data standards, creating a database for inventory management, and using the web to search online databases for overseas business resources. Visit MyMISLab's Multimedia Library to access this chapter's Hands-On MIS Projects.

Management Decision Problems

6-8 Emerson Process Management, a global supplier of measurement, analytical, and monitoring instruments and services based in Austin, Texas, had a new data warehouse designed for analyzing customer activity to improve service and marketing. However, the data warehouse was full of inaccurate and redundant data. The data in the warehouse came from numerous transaction processing systems in Europe, Asia, and other locations around the world. The team that designed the warehouse had assumed that sales groups in all these areas would enter customer names and addresses the same way. In fact, companies in different countries were using multiple ways of entering quote, billing, shipping, and other data. Assess the potential business impact of these data quality problems. What decisions have to be made and steps taken to reach a solution?

6-9 Your industrial supply company wants to create a data warehouse where management can obtain a single corporate-wide view of critical sales information to identify bestselling products, key customers, and sales trends. Your sales and product information are stored in two different systems: a divisional sales system running on a Unix server and a corporate sales system running on an IBM mainframe. You would like to create a single standard format that consolidates these data from both systems. In MyMISLab, you can review the proposed format along with sample files from the two systems that would supply the data for the data warehouse. Then answer the following questions:

- What business problems are created by not having these data in a single standard format?
- How easy would it be to create a database with a single standard format that could store the data from both systems? Identify the problems that would have to be addressed.
- Should the problems be solved by database specialists or general business managers? Explain.
- Who should have the authority to finalize a single companywide format for this information in the data warehouse?

Achieving Operational Excellence: Building a Relational Database for Inventory Management

Software skills: Database design, querying, and reporting
Business skills: Inventory management

6-10 In this exercise, you will use database software to design a database for managing inventory for a small business. Sylvester's Bike Shop, located in San Francisco, California, sells road, mountain, hybrid, leisure, and children's bicycles. Currently, Sylvester's purchases bikes from three suppliers but plans to add new suppliers in the near future. Using the information found in the tables in MyMISLab, build a simple relational database to manage information about Sylvester's suppliers and products. Once you have built the database, perform the following activities.

- Prepare a report that identifies the five most expensive bicycles. The report should list the bicycles in descending order from most expensive to least expensive, the quantity on hand for each, and the markup percentage for each.
- Prepare a report that lists each supplier, its products, the quantities on hand, and associated reorder levels. The report should be sorted alphabetically by supplier. For each supplier, the products should be sorted alphabetically.
- Prepare a report listing only the bicycles that are low in stock and need to be reordered. The report should provide supplier information for the items identified.
- Write a brief description of how the database could be enhanced to further improve management of the business. What tables or fields should be added? What additional reports would be useful?

Improving Decision Making: Searching Online Databases for Overseas Business Resources

Software skills: Online databases
Business skills: Researching services for overseas operations

6-11 This project develops skills in searching web-enabled databases with information about products and services in faraway locations.

Your company is located in Greensboro, North Carolina, and manufactures office furniture of various types. You are considering opening a facility to manufacture and sell your products in Australia. You would like to contact organizations that offer many services necessary for you to open your Australian office and manufacturing facility, including lawyers, accountants, import-export experts, and telecommunications equipment and support firms. Access the following online databases to locate companies that you would like to meet with during your upcoming trip: Australian Business Directory Online, AustraliaTrade Now, and the Nationwide Business Directory of Australia. If necessary, use search engines such as Yahoo and Google.

- List the companies you would contact on your trip to determine whether they can help you with these and any other functions you think are vital to establishing your office.
- Rate the databases you used for accuracy of name, completeness, ease of use, and general helpfulness.

Collaboration and Teamwork Project

Identifying Entities and Attributes in an Online Database

6-12 With your team of three or four other students, select an online database to explore, such as AOL Music, iGo.com, or the Internet Movie Database. Explore one of these websites to see what information it provides. Then list the entities and attributes that the company running the website must keep track of in its databases. Diagram the relationship between the entities you have identified. If possible, use Google Docs and Google Drive or Google Sites to brainstorm, organize, and develop a presentation of your findings for the class.

Can We Trust Big Data?

CASE STUDY

Today's companies are dealing with an avalanche of data from social media, search, and sensors as well as from traditional sources. According to one estimate, 2.5 quintillion bytes of data per day are generated around the world. Making sense of "big data" to improve decision making and business performance has become one of the primary opportunities for organizations of all shapes and sizes, but it also represents big challenges.

Big data helps streaming music service Spotify create a service that feels personal to each of its 75 million global users. Spotify uses the big data it collects on user listening habits (more than 600 gigabytes daily) to design highly individualized products that captivate its users around a particular mood or moment in time rather than offering the same tired genres. Users can constantly enhance their listening experience with data-driven features such as the Discovery tool for new music, a Running tool that curates music timed to the beat of their workout, and Taste Rewind—which tells what they would have listened to in the past by analyzing what they listen to now. By constantly using big data to fine-tune its services, Spotify hopes to create the perfect user experience.

A number of services have emerged to analyze big data to help consumers. There are now online services to enable consumers to check thousands of different flight and hotel options and book their own reservations, tasks previously handled by travel agents. For instance, a mobile app from Skyscanner shows deals from all over the web in one list—sorted by price, duration, or airline—so travelers don't have

to scour multiple sites to book within their budget. Skyscanner uses information from more than 300 airlines, travel agents, and timetables and shapes the data into at-a-glance formats with algorithms to keep pricing current and make predictions about who will have the best deal for a given market.

Big data is also providing benefits in law enforcement (see this chapter's Interactive Session on Organizations), sports, education, science, and health care. A recent McKinsey Global Institute report estimated that the U.S. healthcare system could save $300 billion each year—$1,000 per American—through better integration and analysis of the data produced by everything from clinical trials to health insurance transactions to "smart" running shoes. Healthcare companies are currently analyzing big data to determine the most effective and economical treatments for chronic illnesses and common diseases and provide personalized care recommendations to patients.

There are limits to using big data. A number of companies have rushed to start big data projects without first establishing a business goal for this new information. Swimming in numbers and other data doesn't necessarily mean that the right information is being collected or that people will make smarter decisions.

Experts in big data analysis believe too many companies, seduced by the promise of big data, jump into big data projects with nothing to show for their efforts. They start amassing and analyzing mountains of data without no clear objective or understanding of exactly how analyzing big data will achieve their goal or what questions they are trying to answer. Darian Shirzai, founder of Radius Intelligence Inc., likens this to haystacks without needles. Companies don't know what they're looking for because they think big data alone will solve their problem.

According to Michael Walker of Rose Business Technologies, which helps companies build big data systems, a significant majority of big data projects aren't producing any valuable, actionable results. A recent report from Gartner, Inc. stated that through 2017, 60 percent of big data projects will fail to go beyond piloting and experimentation and will eventually be abandoned. This is especially true for very large-scale big data projects. Companies are often better off starting with smaller projects with narrower goals.

Hadoop has emerged as a major technology for handling big data because it allows distributed processing of large unstructured as well as structured data sets across clusters of inexpensive computers. However, Hadoop is not easy to use, requires a considerable learning curve, and does not always work well for all corporate big data tasks. For example, when Bank of New York Mellon used Hadoop to locate glitches in a trading system, Hadoop worked well on a small scale, but it slowed to a crawl when many employees tried to access it at once. Very few of the company's 13,000 IT specialists had the expertise to troubleshoot this problem. David Gleason, the bank's chief data officer at the time, said he liked Hadoop but felt it still wasn't ready for prime time. According to Gartner, Inc. research director for information management Neil Heudecker, technology originally built to index the web may not be sufficient for corporate big data tasks.

It often takes a lot of work for a company to combine data stored in legacy systems with data stored in Hadoop. Although Hadoop can be much faster than traditional databases for some tasks, it often isn't fast enough to respond to queries immediately or to process incoming data in real time (such as using smartphone location data to generate just-in-time offers).

Hadoop vendors are responding with improvements and enhancements. For example, Hortonworks produced a tool that lets other applications run on top of Hadoop. Other companies are offering tools as Hadoop substitutes. Databricks developed Spark open source software that is more adept than Hadoop at handling real-time data, and the Google spinoff Metanautix is trying to supplant Hadoop entirely.

It is difficult to find enough technical IT specialists with expertise in big data analytical tools, including Hive, Pig, Cassandra, MongoDB, or Hadoop. On top of that, many business managers lack numerical and statistical skills required for finding, manipulating, managing, and interpreting data.

Even with big data expertise, data analysts need some business knowledge of the problem they are trying to solve with big data. For example, if a pharmaceutical company monitoring point-of-sale data in real time sees a spike in aspirin sales in January, it might think that the flu season is intensifying. However, before pouring sales resources into a big campaign and increasing flu medication production, the company would do well to compare sales patterns to past years. People might also be buying aspirin to nurse their hangovers following New Year's Eve parties. In other words, analysts need to know the business and the right questions to ask of the data.

Just because something can be measured doesn't mean it should be measured. Suppose, for instance, that a large company wants to measure its website traffic in relation to the number of mentions on Twitter. It builds a digital dashboard to display the results continuously. In the past, the company had generated most of its sales leads and eventual sales from trade shows and conferences. Switching to Twitter mentions as the key metric to measure changes the sales department's focus. The department pours its energy and resources into monitoring website clicks and social media traffic, which produce many unqualified leads that never lead to sales.

Although big data is very good at detecting correlations, especially subtle correlations that an analysis of smaller data sets might miss, big data analysis doesn't necessarily show causation or which correlations are meaningful. For example, examining big data might show that from 2006 to 2011 the U.S. murder rate was highly correlated with the market share of Internet Explorer, since both declined sharply. But that doesn't necessarily mean there is any meaningful connection between the two phenomena.

Several years ago, Google developed what it thought was a leading-edge algorithm using data it collected from web searches to determine exactly how many people had influenza and how the disease was spreading. It tried to calculate the number of people with flu in the United States by relating people's location to flu-related search queries on Google. The service has consistently overestimated flu rates when compared to conventional data collected afterward by the U.S. Centers for Disease Control and Prevention (CDC). According to Google Flu Trends, nearly 11 percent of the U.S. population was supposed to have had influenza at the flu season's peak in mid-January 2013. However, an article in the science journal Nature stated that Google's results were nearly twice the actual amount estimated by the CDC, which had 6 percent of the population coming down with the disease. Why did this happen? Several scientists suggested that Google was "tricked" by widespread media coverage of that year's severe flu season in the United States, which was further amplified by social media coverage. Google's algorithm only looked at number of flu search requests, not the context of the searches.

Big data can also provide a distorted picture of the problem. Boston's Street Bump app uses a smartphone's accelerometer to detect potholes without the need for city workers to patrol the streets. Users of this mobile app collect road condition data while they drive and automatically provide city government with real-time information to fix problems and plan long-term investments. However, what Street Bump actually produces is a map of potholes that favors young, affluent areas where more people own smartphones. The capability to record every road bump or pothole from every enabled phone is not the same as recording every pothole. Data often contain systematic biases, and it takes careful thought to spot and correct for those biases.

And let's not forget that big data poses some challenges to information security and privacy. As Chapter 4 pointed out, companies are now aggressively collecting and mining massive data sets on people's shopping habits, incomes, hobbies, residences, and (via mobile devices) movements from place to place. They are using such big data to discover new facts about people, to classify them based on subtle patterns, to flag them as "risks" (for example, loan default risks or health risks), to predict their behavior, and to manipulate them for maximum profit.

When you combine someone's personal information with pieces of data from many different sources, you can infer new facts about that person (such as the fact that they are showing early signs of Parkinson's disease or are unconsciously drawn toward products that are colored blue or green). If asked, most people might not want to disclose such information, but they might not even know such information about them exists. Privacy experts worry that people will be tagged and suffer adverse consequences without due process, the ability to fight back, or even knowledge that they have been discriminated against or manipulated in the marketplace.

Sources: Nicole Laskowski and Niel Nikolaisen, "Seven Big Data Problems and How to Avoid Them," TechTarget Inc., 2016; "The Most Innovative Companies of 2016: Top Companies by Sector," www.fastcompany.com, accessed March 4. 2016; Ed Burns, "Big Data Analytics Not Just a Grab and Go Process," *Business Information,* February 2015; Elizabeth Dwoskin, "The Joys and Hype of Software Called Hadoop," *Wall Street Journal,* December 16, 2014; Tim Harford, "Big Data: Are We Making a Big Mistake?" *Financial Times Magazine,* March 28, 2014; Laura Kolodny, "How Consumers Can Use Big Data," *Wall Street Journal,* March 23, 2014; Joseph Stromberg, "Why Google Flu Trends Can't Track the Flu (Yet)," smithsonianmag.com, March 13, 2014; Gary Marcus and Ernest Davis, "Eight (No, Nine!) Problems with Big Data," *New York Times,* April 6, 2014; and Shira Ovide, "Big Data, Big Blunders," *Wall Street Journal,* March 11, 2013.

CASE STUDY QUESTIONS

6-13 What business benefits did the companies and services described in this case achieve by analyzing and using big data?

6-14 Identify two decisions at the organizations described in this case that were improved by using big data and two decisions that were not improved by using big data.

6-15 List and describe the limitations to using big data.

6-16 Should all organizations try to analyze big data? Why or why not? What people, organization, and technology issues should be addressed before a company decides to work with big data?

MyMISLab

Go to the Assignments section of MyMISLab to complete these writing exercises.

6-17 Identify the five problems of a traditional file environment and explain how a database management system solves them.

6-18 Discuss how the following facilitate the management of big data: Hadoop, in-memory computing, analytic platforms.

Chapter 6 References

Aiken, Peter, Mark Gillenson, Xihui Zhang, and David Rafner. "Data Management and Data Administration. Assessing 25 Years of Practice." *Journal of Database Management* (July-September 2011).

Barton, Dominic and David Court. "Making Advanced Analytics Work for You." *Harvard Business Review* (October 2012).

Beath, Cynthia, Irma Becerra-Fernandez, Jeanne Ross, and James Short. "Finding Value in the Information Explosion." *MIT Sloan Management Review* 53, No. 4 (Summer 2012).

Bughin, Jacques, John Livingston, and Sam Marwaha. "Seizing the Potential for Big Data." *McKinsey Quarterly* (October 2011).

Caserta, Joe and Elliott Cordo. "Data Warehousing in the Era of Big Data." *Big Data Quarterly* (January 19, 2016).

Clifford, James, Albert Croker, and Alex Tuzhilin. "On Data Representation and Use in a Temporal Relational DBMS." *Information Systems Research* 7, No. 3 (September 1996).

DataInformed. "The Database Decision: Key Considerations to Keep in Mind." Wellesley Information Services (2015).

Davenport, Thomas H. *Big Data at Work: Dispelling the Myths, Uncovering the Opportunities.* Boston, MA: Harvard Business School Press (2014).

Eckerson, Wayne W. "Analytics in the Era of Big Data: Exploring a Vast New Ecosystem." TechTarget (2012).

_____."Data Quality and the Bottom Line." The Data Warehousing Institute (2002).

Experian Information Solutions. "The 2016 Global Data Management Benchmark Report." (2016).

Henschen, Doug. "MetLife Uses NoSQL for Customer Service Breakthrough." *Information Week* (May 13, 2013).

Hoffer, Jeffrey A., Ramesh Venkataraman, and Heikki Toppi. *Modern Database Management* (12th ed.). Upper Saddle River, NJ: Prentice-Hall (2016).

Horst, Peter and Robert Dubroff. "Don't Let Big Data Bury Your Brand." *Harvard Business Review* (November 2015).

Jordan, John. "The Risks of Big Data for Companies." *Wall Street Journal* (October 20, 2013).

Kroenke, David M. and David Auer. *Database Processing: Fundamentals, Design, and Implementation* (14th ed.). Upper Saddle River, NJ: Prentice-Hall (2016).

Lee, Yang W. and Diane M. Strong. "Knowing-Why About Data Processes and Data Quality." *Journal of Management Information Systems* 20, No. 3 (Winter 2004).

Loveman, Gary. "Diamonds in the Datamine." *Harvard Business Review* (May 2003).

Marcus, Gary and Ernest Davis. "Eight (No, Nine!) Problems with Big Data." *New York Times* (April 6, 2014).

Martens, David and Foster Provost. "Explaining Data-Driven Document Classifications." *MIS Quarterly* 38, No. 1 (March 2014).

McAfee, Andrew and Erik Brynjolfsson. "Big Data: The Management Revolution." *Harvard Business Review* (October 2012).

McKinsey Global Institute. "Big Data: The Next Frontier for Innovation, Competition, and Productivity." McKinsey & Company (2011).

Morrow, Rich. "Apache Hadoop: The Swiss Army Knife of IT." Global Knowledge (2013).

Mulani, Narendra. "In-Memory Technology: Keeping Pace with Your Data." *Information Management* (February 27, 2013).

O'Keefe, Kate. "Real Prize in Caesars Fight: Data on Players." *Wall Street Journal* (March 19, 2015).

Redman, Thomas. *Data Driven: Profiting from Your Most Important Business Asset.* Boston: Harvard Business Press (2008).

Redman, Thomas C. "Data's Credibility Problem" *Harvard Business Review* (December 2013).

Ross, Jeanne W., Cynthia M. Beath, and Anne Quaadgras. "You May Not Need Big Data After All." *Harvard Business Review* (December 2013).

TechTarget Inc. "Identifying and Meeting the Challenges of Big Data." (2016).

Wallace, David J. "How Caesar's Entertainment Sustains a Data-Driven Culture." *DataInformed* (December 14, 2012).

Zoumpoulis, Spyros, Duncan Simester, and Theos Evgeniou, "Run Field Experiments to Make Sense of Your Big Data." *Harvard Business Review* (November 12, 2015).

7 Telecommunications, the Internet, and Wireless Technology

Learning Objectives

After reading this chapter, you will be able to answer the following questions:

7-1 What are the principal components of telecommunications networks and key networking technologies?

7-2 What are the different types of networks?

7-3 How do the Internet and Internet technology work, and how do they support communication and e-business?

7-4 What are the principal technologies and standards for wireless networking, communication, and Internet access?

MyMISLab™

Visit **mymislab.com** for simulations, tutorials, and end-of-chapter problems.

CHAPTER CASES

RFID Helps Macy's Pursue an Omnichannel Strategy
The Battle over Net Neutrality
Monitoring Employees on Networks: Unethical or Good Business?
Google, Apple, and Facebook Battle for Your Internet Experience

VIDEO CASES

Telepresence Moves out of the Boardroom and into the Field
Virtual Collaboration with IBM Sametime

RFID Helps Macy's Pursue an Omnichannel Strategy

Macy's is a major retail chain with 850 department stores (including Bloomingdale's) throughout the United States, Puerto Rico, Guam, and Dubai as well as e-commerce websites for online sales. The Macy's chain is known for its diversity of popular clothing, shoe, furniture, and housewares brands.

To remain competitive and relevant amid other powerful retail chains that also have an Internet presence, Macy's has adopted an omnichannel retail strategy. An omnichannel approach seeks to provide the customer with a seamless shopping experience, whether the customer is purchasing online from a desktop or mobile device, by telephone, or in a brick-and-mortar store. Macy's wants its customers to be able to shop anywhere, anytime, and any way they choose. Macy's sales staff are allowed to sell an item that may be out of stock locally by selecting merchandise from other store locations or from its online fulfillment centers. That means that Macy's brick-and-mortar retail stores are serving as potential fulfillment centers for orders coming in from all sources. If the customer sees online that a pair of boy's shorts is on the selling floor at the Southlake Mall Macy's in Indiana, those shorts need to be in stock at that location.

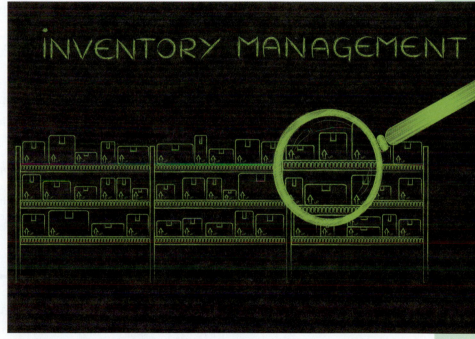

© Faithie/Shutterstock

This is not so easy. Retailers don't typically list the last remaining item of a specific product as being available for online purchasing because they don't have enough confidence in their inventory accuracy to ensure that the item is actually in stock. These last remaining units are usually marked down or not sold, and they account for 15 to 20 percent of inventory, significantly raising costs and lowering profits.

To solve this problem and maximize revenue from going omnichannel, Macy's implemented an item-level radio frequency identification (RFID) system called Pick to the Last Unit (P2LU) based on Tyco's TrueVUE RFID Inventory Visibility Platform. P2LU attempts to ensure that the last unit of an item in any store is able to be easily located and made available for sale. Macy's suppliers attach ultrahigh-frequency RFID tags to each item in frequently replenished products, such as men's dress shirts, underwear, and women's shoes, throughout all of its U.S. stores. Macy's sales staff use Zebra Technologies MC3190-Z handheld RFID readers to activate each RFID tag to broadcast data about the item to which it is attached. The RFID reader in turn transmits the RFID data to Macy's corporate inventory system. With an RFID reader Macy's staff can scan each pair of Levi's jeans stacked on shelves and determine what is in the backroom that should be on the sales floor. Data from the scan automatically update Macy's inventory system and are used to generate replenishment orders.

Before Macy's implemented this system, inventory was degrading at a rate of 2 to 3 percent per month due to theft or items checked out improperly at the register. By the beginning of retailers' peak selling season in November, inventory count at the floor levels was only 60 to 70 percent accurate. So much inaccuracy about inventory leads to very large numbers of lost sales.

Macy's now has enough confidence in its inventory accuracy so that if only one of an item is left in stock, it can leverage every unit in every store to fulfill orders. Deploying RFID has reduced costs by lowering interim inventory requirements by a third, eliminating $1 billion of inventory from Macy's stores. And, of course, having more items actually available when customers need them boosts sales.

In addition to expanding its use of passive EPC ultrahigh-frequency (UHF) RFID tags, Macy's Inc. is also deploying Shopkick Bluetooth Low Energy (BLE) beacons at multiple departments in all stores. If a customer has the Shopkick app, upon entering a store's handbag department, for instance, that shopper's mobile device would receive a promotional message such as a discount on a specific handbag.

Sources: Claire Swedberg, "Macy's Launches Pick to the Last Unit Program for Omnichannel Sales," *RFID Journal*, January 26, 2016; Tyco Retail Solutions, "Macy's Leverages the Power of RFID to Fuel Successful Omni-Channel Fulfillment Strategy," January 18, 2016; and "The Magic of Macy's: Leveraging RFID for 'Pick to the Last Unit' Omni-Channel Fulfillment,"Tyco Retail Solutions, 2016; www.sensormatic.com, accessed May 27, 2016; and Bob Trebilcock, "RFID: The Macy's Way," *Modern Materials Handling,* June 1, 2013.

The experience of Macy's illustrates some of the powerful capabilities and opportunities provided by contemporary networking technology. The Macy's chain uses wireless networking and radio frequency identification (RFID) technology to closely track inventory and to make on-the-spot sales pitches to customers on their mobile devices. Bluetooth wireless networking technology also helps Macy's increase sales by expanding its relationship with mobile device users.

The chapter-opening diagram calls attention to important points raised by this case and this chapter. Macy's has many competitors and feels it has to adopt an omnichannel strategy to remain competitive. It also wants to take advantage of new mobile networking technologies.

Improving inventory accuracy is absolutely critical for omnichannel fulfillment and a "buy anywhere, fulfill anywhere" model. Instead of tracking cases of goods or pallets, Macy's P2LU uses RFID to track individual items on store shelves. Thanks to its RFID inventory tracking system, Macy's has a complete view of inventory in stores, online, and across the supply chain.

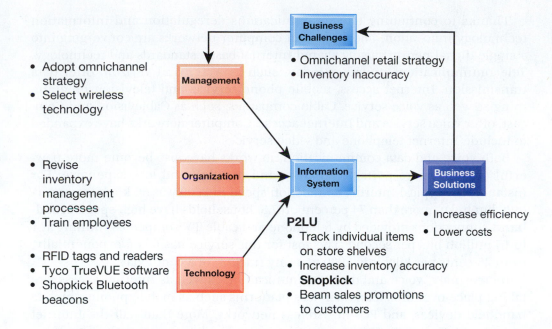

Now, Macy's is able to maximize revenue. Macy's is able to sell every single unit in inventory. There is no longer wasted inventory, and Macy's maximizes revenue from omnichannel programs and improves the overall customer experience.

Here are some questions to think about: Why has wireless technology played such a key role at Macy's? Describe how the RFID and Shopkick systems changed the sales and ordering processes at Macy's.

7-1 What are the principal components of telecommunications networks and key networking technologies?

If you run or work in a business, you can't do without networks. You need to communicate rapidly with your customers, suppliers, and employees. Until about 1990, businesses used the postal system or telephone system with voice or fax for communication. Today, however, you and your employees use computers, e-mail, text messaging, the Internet, mobile phones, and mobile computers connected to wireless networks for this purpose. Networking and the Internet are now nearly synonymous with doing business.

Networking and Communication Trends

Firms in the past used two fundamentally different types of networks: telephone networks and computer networks. Telephone networks historically handled voice communication, and computer networks handled data traffic. Telephone companies built telephone networks throughout the twentieth century by using voice transmission technologies (hardware and software), and these companies almost always operated as regulated monopolies throughout the world. Computer companies originally built computer networks to transmit data between computers in different locations.

Thanks to continuing telecommunications deregulation and information technology innovation, telephone and computer networks are converging into a single digital network using shared Internet-based standards and technology. Telecommunications providers today, such as AT&T and Verizon, offer data transmission, Internet access, mobile phone service, and television programming as well as voice service. Cable companies, such as Cablevision and Comcast, offer voice service and Internet access. Computer networks have expanded to include Internet telephone and video services.

Both voice and data communication networks have also become more powerful (faster), more portable (smaller and mobile), and less expensive. For instance, the typical Internet connection speed in 2000 was 56 kilobits per second, but today more than 74 percent of U.S. households have high-speed **broadband** connections provided by telephone and cable TV companies running at 1 to 15 million bits per second. The cost for this service has fallen exponentially, from 25 cents per kilobit in 2000 to a tiny fraction of a cent today.

Increasingly, voice and data communication, as well as Internet access, are taking place over broadband wireless platforms such as mobile phones, mobile handheld devices, and PCs in wireless networks. More than half the Internet users in the United States use smartphones and tablets to access the Internet.

What is a Computer Network?

If you had to connect the computers for two or more employees in the same office, you would need a computer network. In its simplest form, a network consists of two or more connected computers. Figure 7.1 illustrates the major hardware, software, and transmission components in a simple network: a client

FIGURE 7.1   COMPONENTS OF A SIMPLE COMPUTER NETWORK

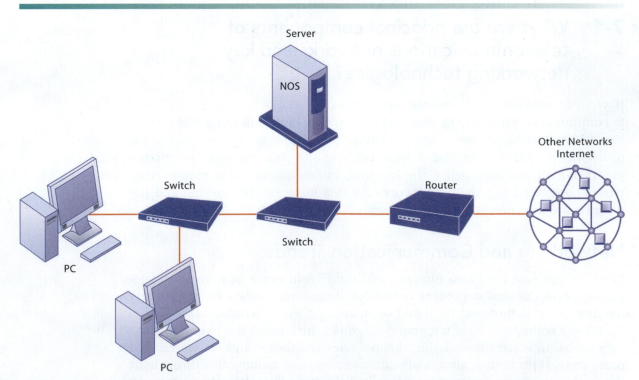

Illustrated here is a simple computer network consisting of computers, a network operating system (NOS) residing on a dedicated server computer, cable (wiring) connecting the devices, switches, and a router.

computer and a dedicated server computer, network interfaces, a connection medium, network operating system software, and either a hub or a switch.

Each computer on the network contains a network interface device to link the computer to the network. The connection medium for linking network components can be a telephone wire, coaxial cable, or radio signal in the case of cell phone and wireless local area networks (Wi-Fi networks).

The **network operating system (NOS)** routes and manages communications on the network and coordinates network resources. It can reside on every computer in the network or primarily on a dedicated server computer for all the applications on the network. A server is a computer on a network that performs important network functions for client computers, such as displaying web pages, storing data, and storing the network operating system (hence controlling the network). Microsoft Windows Server, Linux, and Novell Open Enterprise Server are the most widely used network operating systems.

Most networks also contain a switch or a hub acting as a connection point between the computers. **Hubs** are simple devices that connect network components, sending a packet of data to all other connected devices. A **switch** has more intelligence than a hub and can filter and forward data to a specified destination on the network.

What if you want to communicate with another network, such as the Internet? You would need a router. A **router** is a communications processor that routes packets of data through different networks, ensuring that the data sent get to the correct address.

Network switches and routers have proprietary software built into their hardware for directing the movement of data on the network. This can create network bottlenecks and makes the process of configuring a network more complicated and time-consuming. **Software-defined networking (SDN)** is a new networking approach in which many of these control functions are managed by one central program, which can run on inexpensive commodity servers that are separate from the network devices themselves. This is especially helpful in a cloud computing environment with many pieces of hardware because it allows a network administrator to manage traffic loads in a flexible and more efficient manner.

Networks in Large Companies

The network we've just described might be suitable for a small business, but what about large companies with many locations and thousands of employees? As a firm grows, its small networks can be tied together into a corporate-wide networking infrastructure. The network infrastructure for a large corporation consists of a large number of these small local area networks linked to other local area networks and to firmwide corporate networks. A number of powerful servers support a corporate website, a corporate intranet, and perhaps an extranet. Some of these servers link to other large computers supporting back-end systems.

Figure 7.2 provides an illustration of these more complex, larger scale corporate-wide networks. Here the corporate network infrastructure supports a mobile sales force using mobile phones and smartphones, mobile employees linking to the company website, and internal company networks using mobile wireless local area networks (Wi-Fi networks). In addition to these computer networks, the firm's infrastructure may include a separate telephone network that handles most voice data. Many firms are dispensing with their traditional telephone networks and using Internet telephones that run on their existing data networks (described later).

FIGURE 7.2   CORPORATE NETWORK INFRASTRUCTURE

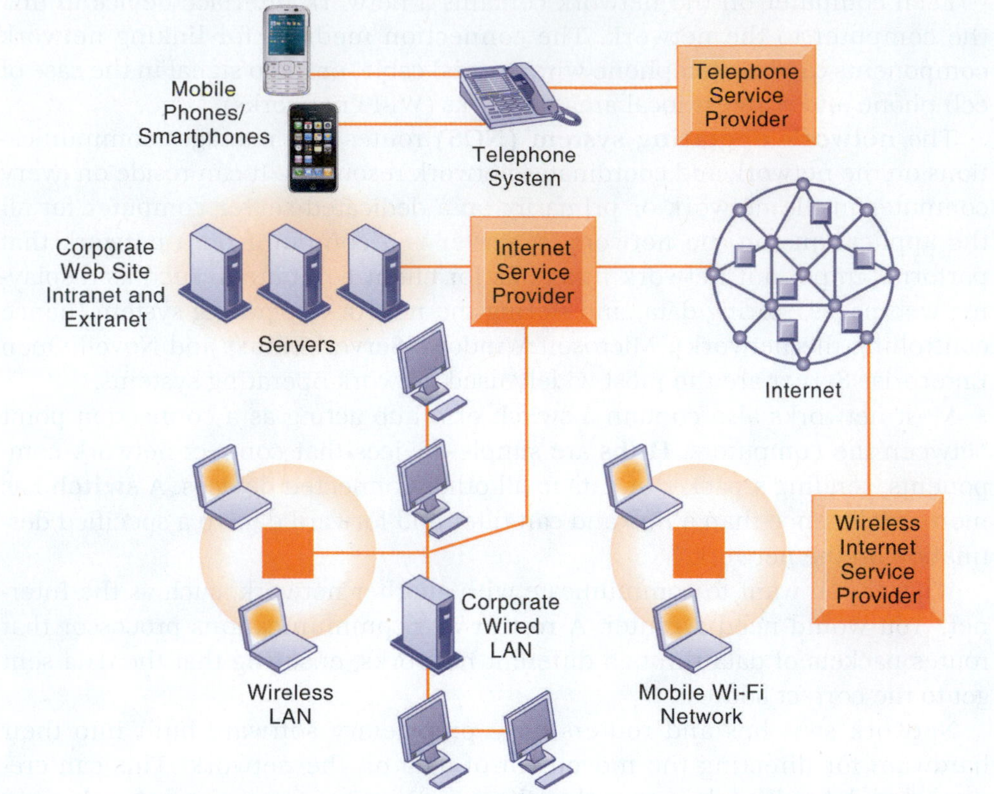

Today's corporate network infrastructure is a collection of many networks from the public switched telephone network, to the Internet, to corporate local area networks linking workgroups, departments, or office floors.

As you can see from this figure, a large corporate network infrastructure uses a wide variety of technologies—everything from ordinary telephone service and corporate data networks to Internet service, wireless Internet, and mobile phones. One of the major problems facing corporations today is how to integrate all the different communication networks and channels into a coherent system that enables information to flow from one part of the corporation to another and from one system to another.

Key Digital Networking Technologies

Contemporary digital networks and the Internet are based on three key technologies: client/server computing, the use of packet switching, and the development of widely used communications standards (the most important of which is Transmission Control Protocol/Internet Protocol, or TCP/IP) for linking disparate networks and computers.

Client/Server Computing

Client/server computing, introduced in Chapter 5, is a distributed computing model in which some of the processing power is located within small, inexpensive client computers and resides literally on desktops or laptops or in handheld devices. These powerful clients are linked to one another through a network that is controlled by a network server computer. The server sets the rules of communication for the network and provides every client with an address so others can find it on the network.

Client/server computing has largely replaced centralized mainframe computing in which nearly all the processing takes place on a central large mainframe computer. Client/server computing has extended computing to departments, workgroups, factory floors, and other parts of the business that could not be served by a centralized architecture. It also makes it possible for personal computing devices such as PCs, laptops, and mobile phones to be connected to networks such as the Internet. The Internet is the largest implementation of client/server computing.

Packet Switching

Packet switching is a method of slicing digital messages into parcels called packets, sending the packets along different communication paths as they become available and then reassembling the packets once they arrive at their destinations (see Figure 7.3). Prior to the development of packet switching, computer networks used leased, dedicated telephone circuits to communicate with other computers in remote locations. In circuit-switched networks, such as the telephone system, a complete point-to-point circuit is assembled, and then communication can proceed. These dedicated circuit-switching techniques were expensive and wasted available communications capacity—the circuit was maintained regardless of whether any data were being sent.

Packet switching makes much more efficient use of the communications capacity of a network. In packet-switched networks, messages are first broken down into small fixed bundles of data called packets. The packets include information for directing the packet to the right address and for checking transmission errors along with the data. The packets are transmitted over various communications channels by using routers, each packet traveling independently. Packets of data originating at one source will be routed through many paths and networks before being reassembled into the original message when they reach their destinations.

FIGURE 7.3   PACKET-SWITCHED NETWORKS AND PACKET COMMUNICATIONS

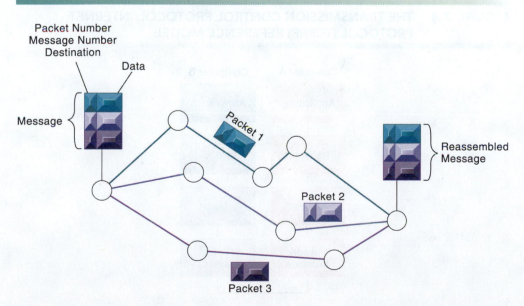

Data are grouped into small packets, which are transmitted independently over various communications channels and reassembled at their final destination.

TCP/IP and Connectivity

In a typical telecommunications network, diverse hardware and software components need to work together to transmit information. Different components in a network communicate with each other by adhering to a common set of rules called protocols. A **protocol** is a set of rules and procedures governing transmission of information between two points in a network.

In the past, diverse proprietary and incompatible protocols often forced business firms to purchase computing and communications equipment from a single vendor. However, today, corporate networks are increasingly using a single, common, worldwide standard called **Transmission Control Protocol/Internet Protocol (TCP/IP)**. TCP/IP was developed during the early 1970s to support U.S. Department of Defense Advanced Research Projects Agency (DARPA) efforts to help scientists transmit data among different types of computers over long distances.

TCP/IP uses a suite of protocols, the main ones being TCP and IP. TCP refers to the Transmission Control Protocol, which handles the movement of data between computers. TCP establishes a connection between the computers, sequences the transfer of packets, and acknowledges the packets sent. IP refers to the Internet Protocol (IP), which is responsible for the delivery of packets and includes the disassembling and reassembling of packets during transmission. Figure 7.4 illustrates the four-layered Department of Defense reference model for TCP/IP, and the layers are described as follows.

1. Application layer. The Application layer enables client application programs to access the other layers and defines the protocols that applications use to exchange data. One of these application protocols is the Hypertext Transfer Protocol (HTTP), which is used to transfer web page files.

2. Transport layer. The Transport layer is responsible for providing the Application layer with communication and packet services. This layer includes TCP and other protocols.

3. Internet layer. The Internet layer is responsible for addressing, routing, and packaging data packets called IP datagrams. The Internet Protocol is one of the protocols used in this layer.

FIGURE 7.4   **THE TRANSMISSION CONTROL PROTOCOL/INTERNET PROTOCOL (TCP/IP) REFERENCE MODEL**

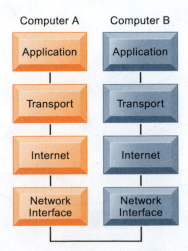

This figure illustrates the four layers of the TCP/IP reference model for communications.

4. Network Interface layer. At the bottom of the reference model, the Network Interface layer is responsible for placing packets on and receiving them from the network medium, which could be any networking technology.

Two computers using TCP/IP can communicate even if they are based on different hardware and software platforms. Data sent from one computer to the other passes downward through all four layers, starting with the sending computer's Application layer and passing through the Network Interface layer. After the data reach the recipient host computer, they travel up the layers and are reassembled into a format the receiving computer can use. If the receiving computer finds a damaged packet, it asks the sending computer to retransmit it. This process is reversed when the receiving computer responds.

7-2 What are the different types of networks?

Let's look more closely at alternative networking technologies available to businesses.

Signals: Digital Versus Analog

There are two ways to communicate a message in a network: an analog signal or a digital signal. An *analog signal* is represented by a continuous waveform that passes through a communications medium and has been used for voice communication. The most common analog devices are the telephone handset, the speaker on your computer, or your iPod earphone, all of which create analog waveforms that your ear can hear.

A *digital signal* is a discrete, binary waveform rather than a continuous waveform. Digital signals communicate information as strings of two discrete states: one bits and zero bits, which are represented as on-off electrical pulses. Computers use digital signals and require a modem to convert these digital signals into analog signals that can be sent over (or received from) telephone lines, cable lines, or wireless media that use analog signals (see Figure 7.5). **Modem** stands for modulator-demodulator. Cable modems connect your computer to the Internet by using a cable network. DSL modems connect your computer to the Internet using a telephone company's landline network. Wireless modems perform the same function as traditional modems, connecting your computer to a wireless network that could be a cell phone network or a Wi-Fi network.

Types of Networks

There are many kinds of networks and ways of classifying them. One way of looking at networks is in terms of their geographic scope (see Table 7.1).

FIGURE 7.5 FUNCTIONS OF THE MODEM

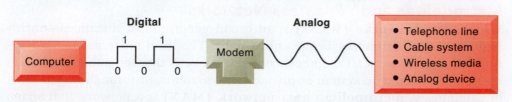

A modem is a device that translates digital signals into analog form (and vice versa) so that computers can transmit data over analog networks such as telephone and cable networks.

TABLE 7.1   TYPES OF NETWORKS

TYPE	AREA
Local area network (LAN)	Up to 500 meters (half a mile); an office or floor of a building
Campus area network (CAN)	Up to 1,000 meters (a mile); a college campus or corporate facility
Metropolitan area network (MAN)	A city or metropolitan area
Wide area network (WAN)	A regional, transcontinental, or global area

Local Area Networks

If you work in a business that uses networking, you are probably connecting to other employees and groups via a local area network. A **local area network (LAN)** is designed to connect personal computers and other digital devices within a half-mile or 500-meter radius. LANs typically connect a few computers in a small office, all the computers in one building, or all the computers in several buildings in close proximity. LANs also are used to link to long-distance wide area networks (WANs, described later in this section) and other networks around the world, using the Internet.

Review Figure 7.1, which could serve as a model for a small LAN that might be used in an office. One computer is a dedicated network, providing users with access to shared computing resources in the network, including software programs and data files.

The server determines who gets access to what and in which sequence. The router connects the LAN to other networks, which could be the Internet, or another corporate network, so that the LAN can exchange information with networks external to it. The most common LAN operating systems are Windows, Linux, and Novell.

Ethernet is the dominant LAN standard at the physical network level, specifying the physical medium to carry signals between computers, access control rules, and a standardized set of bits that carry data over the system. Originally, Ethernet supported a data transfer rate of 10 megabits per second (Mbps). Newer versions, such as Gigabit Ethernet, support a data transfer rate of 1 gigabit per second (Gbps).

The LAN illustrated in Figure 7.1 uses a client/server architecture by which the network operating system resides primarily on a single server, and the server provides much of the control and resources for the network. Alternatively, LANs may use a **peer-to-peer** architecture. A peer-to-peer network treats all processors equally and is used primarily in small networks with 10 or fewer users. The various computers on the network can exchange data by direct access and can share peripheral devices without going through a separate server.

Larger LANs have many clients and multiple servers, with separate servers for specific services such as storing and managing files and databases (file servers or database servers), managing printers (print servers), storing and managing e-mail (mail servers), or storing and managing web pages (web servers).

Metropolitan and Wide Area Networks

Wide area networks (WANs) span broad geographical distances—entire regions, states, continents, or the entire globe. The most universal and powerful WAN is the Internet. Computers connect to a WAN through public networks, such as the telephone system or private cable systems, or through leased lines or satellites. A **metropolitan area network (MAN)** is a network that spans a metropolitan area, usually a city and its major suburbs. Its geographic scope falls between a WAN and a LAN.

TABLE 7.2 PHYSICAL TRANSMISSION MEDIA

TRANSMISSION MEDIUM	DESCRIPTION	SPEED
Twisted pair wire (CAT 5)	Strands of copper wire twisted in pairs for voice and data communications. CAT 5 is the most common 10 Mbps LAN cable. Maximum recommended run of 100 meters.	10–100+ Mbps
Coaxial cable	Thickly insulated copper wire, which is capable of high-speed data transmission and less subject to interference than twisted wire. Currently used for cable TV and for networks with longer runs (more than 100 meters).	Up to 1 Gbps
Fiber-optic cable	Strands of clear glass fiber, transmitting data as pulses of light generated by lasers. Useful for high-speed transmission of large quantities of data. More expensive than other physical transmission media and harder to install; often used for network backbone.	15 Mbps to 6+ Tbps
Wireless transmission media	Based on radio signals of various frequencies and includes both terrestrial and satellite microwave systems and cellular networks. Used for long-distance, wireless communication and Internet access.	Up to 600+ Mbps

Transmission Media and Transmission Speed

Networks use different kinds of physical transmission media, including twisted pair wire, coaxial cable, fiber-optic cable, and media for wireless transmission. Each has advantages and limitations. A wide range of speeds is possible for any given medium, depending on the software and hardware configuration. Table 7.2 compares these media.

Bandwidth: Transmission Speed

The total amount of digital information that can be transmitted through any telecommunications medium is measured in bits per second (bps). One signal change, or cycle, is required to transmit one or several bits; therefore, the transmission capacity of each type of telecommunications medium is a function of its frequency. The number of cycles per second that can be sent through that medium is measured in **hertz**—one hertz is equal to one cycle of the medium.

The range of frequencies that can be accommodated on a particular telecommunications channel is called its **bandwidth**. The bandwidth is the difference between the highest and lowest frequencies that can be accommodated on a single channel. The greater the range of frequencies, the greater the bandwidth and the greater the channel's transmission capacity.

7-3 How do the Internet and Internet technology work, and how do they support communication and e-business?

The Internet has become an indispensable personal and business tool—but what exactly is the Internet? How does it work, and what does Internet technology have to offer for business? Let's look at the most important Internet features.

What is the Internet?

The Internet is the world's most extensive public communication system. It's also the world's largest implementation of client/server computing and Internetworking, linking millions of individual networks all over the world. This global network of networks began in the early 1970s as a U.S. Department of Defense network to link scientists and university professors around the world.

Most homes and small businesses connect to the Internet by subscribing to an Internet service provider. An **Internet service provider (ISP)** is a commercial organization with a permanent connection to the Internet that sells temporary connections to retail subscribers. EarthLink, NetZero, AT&T, and Time Warner are ISPs. Individuals also connect to the Internet through their business firms, universities, or research centers that have designated Internet domains.

There is a variety of services for ISP Internet connections. Connecting via a traditional telephone line and modem, at a speed of 56.6 kilobits per second (Kbps), used to be the most common form of connection worldwide, but broadband connections have largely replaced it. Digital subscriber line, cable, satellite Internet connections, and T lines provide these broadband services.

Digital subscriber line (DSL) technologies operate over existing telephone lines to carry voice, data, and video at transmission rates ranging from 385 Kbps all the way up to 40 Mbps, depending on usage patterns and distance. **Cable Internet connections** provided by cable television vendors use digital cable coaxial lines to deliver high-speed Internet access to homes and businesses. They can provide high-speed access to the Internet of up to 50 Mbps, although most providers offer service ranging from 1 Mbps to 6 Mbps. Where DSL and cable services are unavailable, it is possible to access the Internet via satellite, although some satellite Internet connections have slower upload speeds than other broadband services.

T1 and T3 are international telephone standards for digital communication. They are leased, dedicated lines suitable for businesses or government agencies requiring high-speed guaranteed service levels. **T1 lines** offer guaranteed delivery at 1.54 Mbps, and T3 lines offer delivery at 45 Mbps. The Internet does not provide similar guaranteed service levels but, simply, best effort.

Internet Addressing and Architecture

The Internet is based on the TCP/IP networking protocol suite described earlier in this chapter. Every computer on the Internet is assigned a unique **Internet Protocol (IP) address**, which currently is a 32-bit number represented by four strings of numbers ranging from 0 to 255 separated by periods. For instance, the IP address of www.microsoft.com is 207.46.250.119.

When a user sends a message to another user on the Internet, the message is first decomposed into packets using the TCP protocol. Each packet contains its destination address. The packets are then sent from the client to the network server and from there on to as many other servers as necessary to arrive at a specific computer with a known address. At the destination address, the packets are reassembled into the original message.

The Domain Name System

Because it would be incredibly difficult for Internet users to remember strings of 12 numbers, the **Domain Name System (DNS)** converts domain names to IP addresses. The **domain name** is the English-like name that corresponds to the unique 32-bit numeric IP address for each computer connected to the Internet. DNS servers maintain a database containing IP addresses mapped to their corresponding domain names. To access a computer on the Internet, users need only specify its domain name.

DNS has a hierarchical structure (see Figure 7.6). At the top of the DNS hierarchy is the root domain. The child domain of the root is called a top-level domain, and the child domain of a top-level domain is called a second-level domain. Top-level domains are two- and three-character names you are familiar with from surfing the web, for example, .com, .edu, .gov, and the various country codes such as .ca for Canada or .it for Italy. Second-level domains have two parts, designating a top-level name and a second-level name—such as buy.com, nyu.edu, or amazon.ca. A host name at the bottom of the hierarchy designates a specific computer on either the Internet or a private network.

The following list shows the most common domain extensions currently available and officially approved. Countries also have domain names such as .uk, .au, and .fr (United Kingdom, Australia, and France, respectively), and there is a new class of internationalized top-level domains that use non-English characters. In the future, this list will expand to include many more types of organizations and industries.

.com   Commercial organizations/businesses
.edu   Educational institutions
.gov   U.S. government agencies
.mil   U.S. military
.net   Network computers
.org   Any type of organization
.biz   Business firms
.info   Information providers

FIGURE 7.6   THE DOMAIN NAME SYSTEM

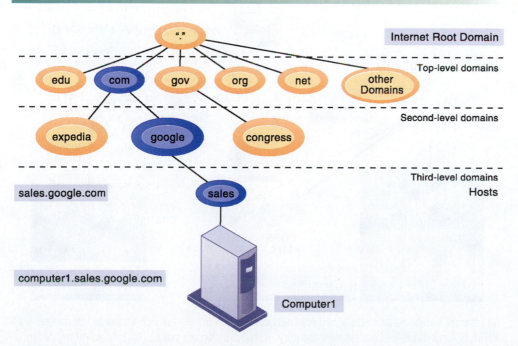

Domain Name System is a hierarchical system with a root domain, top-level domains, second-level domains, and host computers at the third level.

Internet Architecture and Governance

Internet data traffic is carried over transcontinental high-speed backbone networks that generally operate in the range of 155 Mbps to 2.5 Gbps (see Figure 7.7). These trunk lines are typically owned by long-distance telephone companies (called *network service providers*) or by national governments. Local connection lines are owned by regional telephone and cable television companies in the United States and in other countries that connect retail users in homes and businesses to the Internet. The regional networks lease access to ISPs, private companies, and government institutions.

Each organization pays for its own networks and its own local Internet connection services, a part of which is paid to the long-distance trunk line owners. Individual Internet users pay ISPs for using their service, and they generally pay a flat subscription fee, no matter how much or how little they use the Internet. A debate is now raging on whether this arrangement should continue or whether heavy Internet users who download large video and music files should pay more for the bandwidth they consume. The Interactive Session on Organizations explores this topic by examining the pros and cons of net neutrality.

No one owns the Internet, and it has no formal management. However, worldwide Internet policies are established by a number of professional organizations and government bodies, including the Internet Architecture Board (IAB), which helps define the overall structure of the Internet; the Internet Corporation for Assigned Names and Numbers (ICANN), which manages the domain name system; and the World Wide Web Consortium (W3C), which sets Hypertext Markup Language and other programming standards for the web.

FIGURE 7.7   INTERNET NETWORK ARCHITECTURE

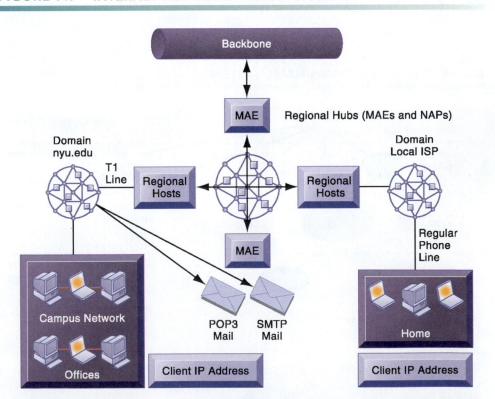

The Internet backbone connects to regional networks, which in turn provide access to Internet service providers, large firms, and government institutions. Network access points (NAPs) and metropolitan area exchanges (MAEs) are hubs where the backbone intersects regional and local networks and where backbone owners connect with one another.

INTERACTIVE SESSION: ORGANIZATIONS

The Battle Over Net Neutrality

What kind of Internet user are you? Do you primarily use the Net to do a little e-mail and online banking? Or are you online all day, watching YouTube videos, downloading music files, or playing online games? Do you use your iPhone to stream TV shows and movies on a regular basis? If you're a power Internet or smartphone user, you are consuming a great deal of bandwidth. Could hundreds of millions of people like you start to slow the Internet down?

Video streaming on Netflix has accounted for 32 percent of all bandwidth use in the United States and Google's YouTube for 19 percent of web traffic at peak hours. If user demand overwhelms network capacity, the Internet might not come to a screeching halt, but users could face sluggish download speeds and video transmission. Heavy use of iPhones in urban areas such as New York and San Francisco has degraded service on the AT&T wireless network. AT&T had reported that 3 percent of its subscriber base accounted for 40 percent of its data traffic.

Internet service providers (ISPs) assert that network congestion is a serious problem and that expanding their networks would require passing on burdensome costs to consumers. These companies believe differential pricing methods, which include data caps and metered use—charging based on the amount of bandwidth consumed—are the fairest way to finance necessary investments in their network infrastructures. However, metering Internet use is not widely accepted because of an ongoing debate about net neutrality.

Net neutrality is the idea that Internet service providers must allow customers equal access to content and applications, regardless of the source or nature of the content. Presently, the Internet is neutral; all Internet traffic is treated equally on a first-come, first-served basis by Internet backbone owners. However, this arrangement prevents telecommunications and cable companies from charging differentiated prices based on the amount of bandwidth consumed by the content being delivered over the Internet.

The strange alliance of net neutrality advocates includes MoveOn.org; the Electronic Frontier Foundation; the Christian Coalition; the American Library Association; data-intensive web businesses such as Netflix, Amazon, and Google; major consumer groups; and a host of bloggers and small businesses. Net neutrality advocates argue that differentiated

pricing would impose heavy costs on heavy bandwidth users such as YouTube, Skype, and other innovative services, preventing high-bandwidth start-up companies from gaining traction. Net neutrality supporters also argue that without net neutrality, ISPs that are also cable companies, such as Comcast, might block online streaming video from Netflix or Hulu to force customers to use the cable company's on-demand movie rental services.

Network owners believe regulation to enforce net neutrality will impede U.S. competitiveness by discouraging capital expenditure for new networks and curbing their networks' ability to cope with the exploding demand for Internet and wireless traffic. U.S. Internet service lags behind many other nations in overall speed, cost, and quality of service, adding credibility to this argument. Moreover, with enough options for Internet access, dissatisfied consumers could simply switch to providers who enforce net neutrality and allow unlimited Internet use.

On January 14, 2014, the U.S. Court of Appeals for the District of Columbia struck down the Federal Communication Commission (FCC) Open Internet rules that required equal treatment of Internet traffic and prevented broadband providers from blocking traffic favoring certain sites or charging special fees to companies that account for the most traffic. The court said the FCC saddled broadband providers with the same sorts of obligations as traditional common carrier telecommunications services, such as landline phone systems, even though the commission had explicitly decided not to classify broadband as a telecommunications service.

President Barack Obama has favored net neutrality and an open Internet and urged the FCC to implement the strongest possible rules to protect it. On February 26, 2015, FCC chairman Tom Wheeler announced a decision to regulate broadband as a public utility. The agency's order reclassifies high-speed Internet as a telecommunications service rather than an information service, subjecting providers to regulation under Title II of the Communications Act of 1934. On March 12, 2015, the FCC released extensive details about these regulations.

The new rules, approved 3 to 2 along Democratic–Republican party lines, are intended to ensure that no content is blocked and that the Internet cannot be divided into pay-to-play fast lanes for Internet and media companies that can afford them and slow lanes for everyone else. Outright blocking of content, slowing of transmissions, and the creation of so-called fast lanes were prohibited. The FCC stated that it favors a light touch rather than the heavy-handed regulations to which the old regulated telephone companies were subjected. One provision requiring "just and reasonable" conduct allows the FCC to decide what is acceptable on a case-by-case basis. The new rules apply to mobile data service for smartphones and tablets in addition to wired lines. The order also includes provisions to protect consumer privacy and ensure that Internet service is available to people with disabilities and in remote areas.

On April 13, 2015, United States Telecom Association, an industry trade group, filed a lawsuit to overturn the government's net neutrality rules. AT&T, the National Cable & Telecommunications Association, and CTIA, which represents wireless carriers, filed similar legal challenges. Pro-net neutrality

forces have asked the FCC to look at "zero-rating" practices, in which certain services, like Spotify and Netflix, are exempt from data caps in a customer's data plan. Digital rights activists believe this gives certain types of data priority over others, violating net neutrality principles.

On June 14, 2016 the U.S. Court of Appeals for the District of Columbia Circuit upheld the FCC's new rules on net neutrality. Industry appeals to the U.S. Supreme Court are likely. The battle over net neutrality is not yet over.

Sources: John D. McKinnon and Brett Kendall, "FCC's Net- Neutrality Rules Uheld by Appeals Court,"Wall Street Journal, June 14, 2016; Darren Orf, "The Next Battle for Net Neutrality Is Getting Bloody," *Gizmodo*, May 25, 2016; Stephanie Milot, "GOP Moves to Gut Net Neutrality, FCC Budget," PC Magazine, February 26, 2016; Rebecca Ruiz, "FCC Sets Net Neutrality Rules," *New York Times*, March 12, 2015; Rebecca Ruiz and Steve Lohr, "F.C.C. Approves Net Neutrality Rules, Classifying Broadband Internet Service as a Utility," *New York Times*, February. 26, 2015; Robert M. McDowell, "The Turning Point for Internet Freedom," *Wall Street Journal*, January 19, 2015; Ryan Knutson, "AT&T Sues to Overturn FCC's Net Neutrality Rules," *Wall Street Journal*, April 14, 2015.

CASE STUDY QUESTIONS

1. What is net neutrality? Why has the Internet operated under net neutrality up to this point?

2. Who's in favor of net neutrality? Who's opposed? Why?

3. What would be the impact on individual users, businesses, and government if Internet providers switched to a tiered service model for transmission over landlines as well as wireless?

4. It has been said that net neutrality is the most important issue facing the Internet since the advent of the Internet. Discuss the implications of this statement.

5. Are you in favor of legislation enforcing network neutrality? Why or why not?

These organizations influence government agencies, network owners, ISPs, and software developers with the goal of keeping the Internet operating as efficiently as possible. The Internet must also conform to the laws of the sovereign nation-states in which it operates as well as to the technical infrastructures that exist within the nation-states. Although in the early years of the Internet and the web there was very little legislative or executive interference, this situation is changing as the Internet plays a growing role in the distribution of information and knowledge, including content that some find objectionable.

The Future Internet: IPV6 and Internet2

The Internet was not originally designed to handle the transmission of massive quantities of data and billions of users. Because of sheer Internet population growth, the world is about to run out of available IP addresses using the old addressing convention. The old addressing system is being replaced by a new version of the IP addressing schema called **IPv6** (Internet Protocol version 6), which contains 128-bit addresses (2 to the power of 128), or more than a quadrillion possible unique addresses. IPv6 is compatible with most modems and routers sold today, and IPv6 will fall back to the old addressing system if IPv6 is not available on local networks. The transition to IPv6 will take several years as systems replace older equipment.

Internet2 is an advanced networking consortium representing more than 500 U.S. universities, private businesses, and government agencies working with 66,000 institutions across the United States and international networking partners from more than 100 countries. To connect these communities, Internet2 developed a high-capacity, 100 Gbps network that serves as a test bed for leading-edge technologies that may eventually migrate to the public Internet, including large-scale network performance measurement and management tools, secure identity and access management tools, and capabilities such as scheduling high-bandwidth, high-performance circuits.

Internet Services and Communication Tools

The Internet is based on client/server technology. Individuals using the Internet control what they do through client applications on their computers, such as web browser software. The data, including e-mail messages and web pages, are stored on servers. A client uses the Internet to request information from a particular web server on a distant computer, and the server sends the requested information back to the client over the Internet. Client platforms today include not only PCs and other computers but also smartphones and tablets.

Internet Services

A client computer connecting to the Internet has access to a variety of services. These services include e-mail, chatting and instant messaging, electronic discussion groups, **Telnet**, **File Transfer Protocol (FTP)**, and the web. Table 7.3 provides a brief description of these services.

Each Internet service is implemented by one or more software programs. All the services may run on a single server computer, or different services may be allocated to different machines. Figure 7.8 illustrates one way these services can be arranged in a multitiered client/server architecture.

E-mail enables messages to be exchanged from computer to computer, with capabilities for routing messages to multiple recipients, forwarding messages, and attaching text documents or multimedia files to messages. Most e-mail today is sent through the Internet. The cost of e-mail is far lower than equivalent voice, postal, or overnight delivery costs, and e-mail messages arrive anywhere in the world in a matter of seconds.

TABLE 7.3 MAJOR INTERNET SERVICES

CAPABILITY	FUNCTIONS SUPPORTED
E-mail	Person-to-person messaging; document sharing
Chatting and instant messaging	Interactive conversations
Newsgroups	Discussion groups on electronic bulletin boards
Telnet	Logging on to one computer system and doing work on another
File Transfer Protocol (FTP)	Transferring files from computer to computer
World Wide Web	Retrieving, formatting, and displaying information (including text, audio, graphics, and video) by using hypertext links

FIGURE 7.8   **CLIENT/SERVER COMPUTING ON THE INTERNET**

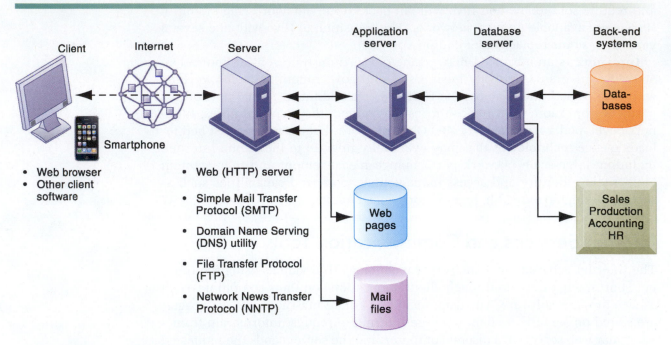

Client computers running web browsers and other software can access an array of services on servers over the Internet. These services may all run on a single server or on multiple specialized servers.

Chatting enables two or more people who are simultaneously connected to the Internet to hold live, interactive conversations. **Chat** systems now support voice and video chat as well as written conversations. Many online retail businesses offer chat services on their websites to attract visitors, to encourage repeat purchases, and to improve customer service.

Instant messaging is a type of chat service that enables participants to create their own private chat channels. The instant messaging system alerts the user whenever someone on his or her private list is online so that the user can initiate a chat session with other individuals. Instant messaging systems for consumers include Yahoo! Messenger, Google Hangouts, AOL Instant Messenger, and Facebook Chat. Companies concerned with security use proprietary communications and messaging systems such as IBM Sametime.

Newsgroups are worldwide discussion groups posted on Internet electronic bulletin boards on which people share information and ideas on a defined topic such as radiology or rock bands. Anyone can post messages on these bulletin boards for others to read.

Employee use of e-mail, instant messaging, and the Internet is supposed to increase worker productivity, but the accompanying Interactive Session on Management shows that this may not always be the case. Many company managers now believe they need to monitor and even regulate their employees' online activity, but is this ethical? Although there are some strong business reasons companies may need to monitor their employees' e-mail and web activities, what does this mean for employee privacy?

Voice over IP

The Internet has also become a popular platform for voice transmission and corporate networking. **Voice over IP (VoIP)** technology delivers voice information in digital form using packet switching, avoiding the tolls charged by

FIGURE 7.9   HOW VOICE OVER IP WORKS

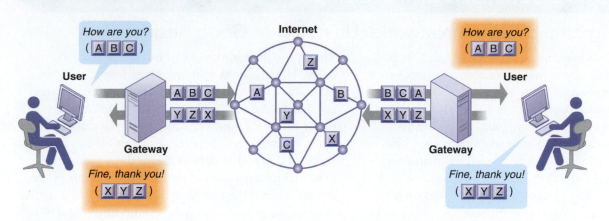

A VoIP phone call digitizes and breaks up a voice message into data packets that may travel along different routes before being reassembled at the final destination. A processor nearest the call's destination, called a gateway, arranges the packets in the proper order and directs them to the telephone number of the receiver or the IP address of the receiving computer.

local and long-distance telephone networks (see Figure 7.9). Calls that would ordinarily be transmitted over public telephone networks travel over the corporate network based on the Internet protocol, or the public Internet. Voice calls can be made and received with a computer equipped with a microphone and speakers or with a VoIP-enabled telephone.

Cable firms such as Time Warner and Cablevision provide VoIP service bundled with their high-speed Internet and cable offerings. Skype offers free VoIP worldwide using a peer-to-peer network, and Google has its own free VoIP service.

Although up-front investments are required for an IP phone system, VoIP can reduce communication and network management costs by 20 to 30 percent. For example, VoIP saves Virgin Entertainment Group $700,000 per year in long-distance bills. In addition to lowering long-distance costs and eliminating monthly fees for private lines, an IP network provides a single voice-data infrastructure for both telecommunications and computing services. Companies no longer have to maintain separate networks or provide support services and personnel for each type of network.

Unified Communications

In the past, each of the firm's networks for wired and wireless data, voice communications, and videoconferencing operated independently of each other and had to be managed separately by the information systems department. Now, however, firms can merge disparate communications modes into a single universally accessible service using unified communications technology. **Unified communications** integrates disparate channels for voice communications, data communications, instant messaging, e-mail, and electronic conferencing into a single experience by which users can seamlessly switch back and forth between different communication modes. Presence technology shows whether a person is available to receive a call.

CenterPoint Properties, a major Chicago area industrial real estate company, used unified communications technology to create collaborative websites for each of its real estate deals. Each website provides a single point for accessing

INTERACTIVE SESSION: MANAGEMENT

Monitoring Employees on Networks: Unethical or Good Business?

The Internet has become an extremely valuable business tool, but it's also a huge distraction for workers on the job. Employees are wasting valuable company time by surfing inappropriate websites (Facebook, shopping, sports, etc.), sending and receiving personal e-mail, talking to friends via online chat, and downloading videos and music. A series of studies have found that employees spend between one and three hours per day at work surfing the web on personal business. A company with 1,000 workers using the Internet could lose up to $35 million in productivity annually from just an hour of daily web surfing by workers.

Many companies have begun monitoring employee use of e-mail and the Internet, sometimes without their knowledge. Many tools are now available for this purpose, including Spector CNE Investigator, OsMonitor, IMonitor, Work Examiner, Mobistealth, and Spytech. These products enable companies to record online searches, monitor file downloads and uploads, record keystrokes, keep tabs on e-mails, create transcripts of chats, or take certain screenshots of images displayed on computer screens. Instant messaging, text messaging, and social media monitoring are also increasing. Although U.S. companies have the legal right to monitor employee Internet and e-mail activity while they are at work, is such monitoring unethical, or is it simply good business?

Managers worry about the loss of time and employee productivity when employees are focusing on personal rather than company business. Too much time on personal business translates into lost revenue. Some employees may even be billing time they spend pursuing personal interests online to clients, thus overcharging them.

If personal traffic on company networks is too high, it can also clog the company's network so that legitimate business work cannot be performed. GMI Insurance Services, which serves the U.S. transportation industry, found that employees were downloading a great deal of music and streaming video and storing them on company servers. GMI's server backup space was being eaten up.

When employees use e-mail or the web (including social networks) at employer facilities or with employer equipment, anything they do, including anything illegal, carries the company's name.

Therefore, the employer can be traced and held liable. Management in many firms fear that racist, sexually explicit, or other potentially offensive material accessed or traded by their employees could result in adverse publicity and even lawsuits for the firm. An estimated 27 percent of *Fortune* 500 organizations have had to defend themselves against claims of sexual harassment stemming from inappropriate e-mail. Even if the company is found not to be liable, responding to lawsuits could run up huge legal bills. Companies also fear leakage of confidential information and trade secrets through e-mail or social networks. Another survey conducted by the American Management Association and the ePolicy Institute found that 14 percent of the employees polled admitted they had sent confidential or potentially embarrassing company e-mails to outsiders.

U.S. companies have the legal right to monitor what employees are doing with company equipment during business hours. The question is whether electronic surveillance is an appropriate tool for maintaining an efficient and positive workplace. Some companies try to ban all personal activities on corporate networks—zero tolerance. Others block employee access to specific websites or social sites, closely monitor e-mail messages, or limit personal time on the web.

GMI Insurance implemented Veriato Investigator and Veriato 360 software to record and analyze the Internet and computer activities of each GMI employee. The Veriato software is able to identify which websites employees visit frequently, how much time employees spend at these sites, whether employees are printing out or copying confidential documents to take home on a portable USB storage device, and whether there are any inappropriate communication conversations taking place. GMI and its sister company, CCS, had an acceptable use policy (AUP) in place prior to monitoring, providing rules about what employees are allowed and not allowed to do with the organization's computing resources. However, GMI's AUP was nearly impossible to enforce until implementation of the Veriato employee monitoring software. To deal with music and video downloads, GMI additionally developed a "software download policy," which must be reviewed and signed by employees. Management at both GMI and CCS believe employee productivity increased by

15 to 20 percent as a result of using the Veriato monitoring software.

A number of firms have fired employees who have stepped out of bounds. A Proofpoint survey found that one in five large U.S. companies had fired an employee for violating e-mail policies. Among managers who fired employees for Internet misuse, the majority did so because the employees' e-mail contained sensitive, confidential, or embarrassing information.

No solution is problem-free, but many consultants believe companies should write corporate policies on employee e-mail, social media, and web use. The policies should include explicit ground rules that state, by position or level, under what circumstances employees can use company facilities for e-mail, blogging, or web surfing. The policies should also inform employees whether these activities are monitored and explain why.

IBM now has "social computing guidelines" that cover employee activity on sites such as Facebook and Twitter. The guidelines urge employees not to conceal their identities, to remember that they are personally responsible for what they publish, and to refrain from discussing controversial topics that are not related to their IBM role.

The rules should be tailored to specific business needs and organizational cultures. For example, investment firms will need to allow many of their employees access to other investment sites. A company dependent on widespread information sharing, innovation, and independence could very well find that monitoring creates more problems than it solves.

Sources: Susan M. Heathfield, "Surfing the Web at Work," About.com, May 27, 2016; Veriato, "Veriato 'Golden' for GMI Insurance Services," 2016; "Office Slacker Stats," www.staffmonitoring.com, accessed May 28, 2016; "How Do Employers Monitor Internet Usage at Work?" wisegeek.org, accessed April 15, 2016; "Could HR Be Snooping on Your Emails and Web Browsing? What Every Worker Should Know," Philly.com, March 30, 2015; "How Do Employers Monitor Internet Usage at Work?" wisegeek.org, accessed April 15, 2015; Dune Lawrence, "Companies Are Tracking Employees to Nab Traitors," *Bloomberg*, March 23, 2015; and "Should Companies Monitor Their Employees' Social Media?" *Wall Street Journal*, May 11, 2014.

CASE STUDY QUESTIONS

1. Should managers monitor employee e-mail and Internet usage? Why or why not?

2. Describe an effective e-mail and web use policy for a company.

3. Should managers inform employees that their web behavior is being monitored? Or should managers monitor secretly? Why or why not?

structured and unstructured data. Integrated presence technology lets team members e-mail, instant message, call, or videoconference with one click.

Virtual Private Networks

What if you had a marketing group charged with developing new products and services for your firm with members spread across the United States? You would want them to be able to e-mail each other and communicate with the home office without any chance that outsiders could intercept the communications. In the past, one answer to this problem was to work with large private networking firms that offered secure, private, dedicated networks to customers, but this was an expensive solution. A much less expensive solution is to create a virtual private network within the public Internet.

A **virtual private network (VPN)** is a secure, encrypted, private network that has been configured within a public network to take advantage of the economies of scale and management facilities of large networks, such as the Internet (see Figure 7.10). A VPN provides your firm with secure, encrypted communications at a much lower cost than the same capabilities offered by traditional non-Internet providers that use their private networks to secure communications. VPNs also provide a network infrastructure for combining voice and data networks.

FIGURE 7.10 A VIRTUAL PRIVATE NETWORK USING THE INTERNET

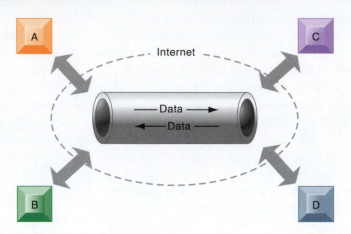

This VPN is a private network of computers linked using a secure tunnel connection over the Internet. It protects data transmitted over the public Internet by encoding the data and wrapping them within the Internet protocol. By adding a wrapper around a network message to hide its content, organizations can create a private connection that travels through the public Internet.

Several competing protocols are used to protect data transmitted over the public Internet, including Point-to-Point Tunneling Protocol (PPTP). In a process called *tunneling*, packets of data are encrypted and wrapped inside IP packets. By adding this wrapper around a network message to hide its content, business firms create a private connection that travels through the public Internet.

The Web

The web is the most popular Internet service. It's a system with universally accepted standards for storing, retrieving, formatting, and displaying information by using a client/server architecture. Web pages are formatted using hypertext with embedded links that connect documents to one another and that also link pages to other objects, such as sound, video, or animation files. When you click a graphic and a video clip plays, you have clicked a hyperlink. A typical **website** is a collection of web pages linked to a home page.

Hypertext

Web pages are based on a standard Hypertext Markup Language (HTML), which formats documents and incorporates dynamic links to other documents and pictures stored in the same or remote computers (see Chapter 5). Web pages are accessible through the Internet because web browser software operating your computer can request web pages stored on an Internet host server by using the **Hypertext Transfer Protocol (HTTP)**. HTTP is the communications standard that transfers pages on the web. For example, when you type a web address in your browser, such as http://www.sec.gov, your browser sends an HTTP request to the sec.gov server requesting the home page of sec.gov.

HTTP is the first set of letters at the start of every web address, followed by the domain name, which specifies the organization's server computer that is storing the document. Most companies have a domain name that is the same as or closely related to their official corporate name. The directory path and document name are two more pieces of information within the web address that help the browser track down the requested page. Together, the address is called a **uniform resource locator (URL)**. When typed into a browser, a URL tells the browser software exactly where to look for the information. For example, in the URL http://www.megacorp.com/content/features/082610. html, *http* names the protocol that displays web pages, www.megacorp.com is the domain name, content/features is the directory path that identifies where on the domain web server the page is stored, and 082610.html is the document name and the name of the format it is in. (It is an HTML page.)

Web Servers

A web server is software for locating and managing stored web pages. It locates the web pages a user requests on the computer where they are stored and delivers the web pages to the user's computer. Server applications usually run on dedicated computers, although they can all reside on a single computer in small organizations.

The most common web server in use today is Apache HTTP Server, followed by Microsoft Internet Information Services (IIS). Apache is an open source product that is free of charge and can be downloaded from the web.

Searching for Information on the Web

No one knows for sure how many web pages there really are. The surface web is the part of the web that search engines visit and about which information is recorded. For instance, Google indexed an estimated 60 trillion pages in 2016, and this reflects a large portion of the publicly accessible web page population. But there is a deep web that contains an estimated 1 trillion additional pages, many of them proprietary (such as the pages of *Wall Street Journal Online*, which cannot be visited without a subscription or access code) or that are stored in protected corporate databases. Searching for information on Facebook is another matter. With more than 1.6 billion members, each with pages of text, photos, and media, the population of web pages is larger than many estimates. However, Facebook is a closed web, and its pages are not completely searchable by Google or other search engines.

Search Engines Obviously, with so many web pages, finding specific ones that can help you or your business, nearly instantly, is an important problem. The question is, how can you find the one or two pages you really want and need out of billions of indexed web pages? **Search engines** attempt to solve the problem of finding useful information on the web nearly instantly and, arguably, they are the killer app of the Internet era. Today's search engines can sift through HTML files; files of Microsoft Office applications; PDF files; and audio, video, and image files. There are hundreds of search engines in the world, but the vast majority of search results come from Google, Yahoo, and Microsoft's Bing (see Figure 7.11). While we typically think of Amazon as an online store, it is also a powerful product search engine.

Web search engines started out in the early 1990s as relatively simple software programs that roamed the nascent web, visiting pages and gathering information about the content of each page. The first search engines were simple keyword indexes of all the pages they visited, leaving users with lists of pages that may not have been truly relevant to their search.

In 1994, Stanford University computer science students David Filo and Jerry Yang created a hand-selected list of their favorite web pages and called it "Yet Another Hierarchical Officious Oracle," or Yahoo. Yahoo was not initially a search engine but rather an edited selection of websites organized by categories

FIGURE 7.11 TOP WEB SEARCH ENGINES IN THE UNITED STATES

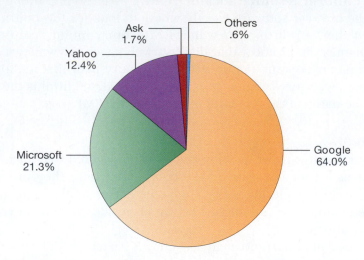

Google is the most popular search engine, handling about 64 percent of web searches in the United States and about 90 percent in Europe. Sources: Based on data from comScore Inc., February 2016.

the editors found useful. Currently, Yahoo relies on Microsoft's Bing for search results.

In 1998, Larry Page and Sergey Brin, two other Stanford computer science students, released their first version of Google. This search engine was different. Not only did it index each web page's words but it also ranked search results based on the relevance of each page. Page patented the idea of a page ranking system (called *PageRank System*), which essentially measures the popularity of a web page by calculating the number of sites that link to that page as well as the number of pages to which it links. The premise is that popular web pages are more relevant to users. Brin contributed a unique web crawler program that indexed not only keywords on a page but also combinations of words (such as authors and the titles of their articles). These two ideas became the foundation for the Google search engine. Figure 7.12 illustrates how Google works.

Mobile Search With the growth of mobile smartphones and tablet computers, and with about 210 million Americans accessing the Internet via mobile devices, the nature of e-commerce and search is changing. Mobile search from smartphones and tablets made up more than 50 percent of all searches in 2016 and will expand rapidly in the next few years. Google, Amazon, and Yahoo have developed new search interfaces to make searching and shopping from smartphones more convenient. Google revised its search algorithm to favor sites that look good on smartphone screens. Although smartphones are widely used to shop, actual purchases typically take place on laptops or desktops, followed by tablets.

Semantic Search Another way for search engines to become more discriminating and helpful is to make search engines capable of understanding what we are really looking for. Called **semantic search**, the goal is to build a search engine that could really understand human language and behavior. Google and other search engine firms are attempting to refine search engine algorithms to capture more of what the user intended and the meaning of a search. In September 2013, Google introduced its Hummingbird search algorithm. Rather than evaluate each word separately in a search, Google's semantically informed

FIGURE 7.12 HOW GOOGLE WORKS

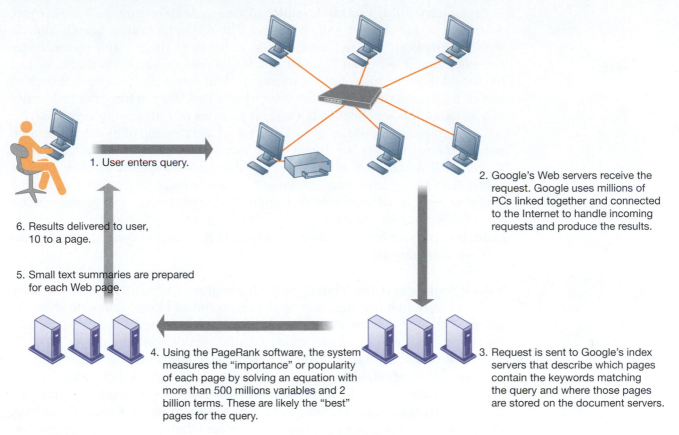

1. User enters query.

2. Google's Web servers receive the request. Google uses millions of PCs linked together and connected to the Internet to handle incoming requests and produce the results.

6. Results delivered to user, 10 to a page.

5. Small text summaries are prepared for each Web page.

4. Using the PageRank software, the system measures the "importance" or popularity of each page by solving an equation with more than 500 millions variables and 2 billion terms. These are likely the "best" pages for the query.

3. Request is sent to Google's index servers that describe which pages contain the keywords matching the query and where those pages are stored on the document servers.

The Google search engine is continuously crawling the web, indexing the content of each page, calculating its popularity, and storing the pages so that it can respond quickly to user requests to see a page. The entire process takes about half a second.

Hummingbird tries to evaluate an entire sentence, focusing on the meaning behind the words. For instance, if your search is a long sentence like "Google annual report selected financial data 2015," Hummingbird should be able to figure out that you really want Google's SEC Form 10K report filed with the Securities and Exchange Commission on March 31, 2016.

Google searches also take advantage of Knowledge Graph, an effort of the search algorithm to anticipate what you might want to know more about as you search on a topic. Results of the knowledge graph appear on the right of the screen and contain more information about the topic or person you are searching on. For example, if you search "Lake Tahoe," the search engine will return basic facts about Tahoe (altitude, average temperature, and local fish), a map, and hotel accommodations. Google has made **predictive search** part of most search results. This part of the search algorithm guesses what you are looking for and suggests search terms as you type your search words.

Social Search One problem with Google and mechanical search engines is that they are so thorough. Enter a search for "ultra computers" and, in 0.2 seconds, you will receive over 300 million responses! Search engines are not very discriminating. **Social search** is an effort to provide fewer, more relevant, and trustworthy search results based on a person's network of social contacts. In contrast to the top search engines that use a mathematical algorithm to find pages that satisfy your query, a social search website would review your friends' recommendations (and their friends'), their past web visits, and their use of Like buttons.

In January 2013, Facebook launched Graph Search (now called *Facebook Search*), a social network search engine that responds to user search queries with information from the user's social network of friends and connections. Facebook Search relies on the huge amount of data on Facebook that is, or can be, linked to individuals and organizations. You might use Facebook Search to search for Boston restaurants that your friends like, alumni from the University of South Carolina who like Lady Gaga, or pictures of your friends before 2012.

Google has developed Google +1 as a social layer on top of its existing search engine. Users can place a +1 next to the websites they found helpful, and their friends will be notified automatically. Subsequent searches by their friends would list the +1 sites recommended by friends higher up on the page. One problem with social search is that your close friends may not have intimate knowledge of topics you are exploring, or they may have tastes you don't appreciate. It's also possible your close friends don't have any knowledge about what you are searching for.

Visual Search and the Visual Web Although search engines were originally designed to search text documents, the explosion of photos and videos on the Internet created a demand for searching and classifying these visual objects. Facial recognition software can create a digital version of a human face. In 2012, Facebook introduced facial recognition software combined with tagging to create a new feature called *Tag Suggest*. The software creates a digital facial print, similar to a fingerprint. Users can put their own tagged photo on their timeline and their friends' timelines. Once a person's photo is tagged, Facebook can pick that person out of a group photo and identify for others who is in the photo. You can also search for people on Facebook by using their digital image to find and identify them. Facebook is now using artificial intelligence technology to make its facial recognition capabilities more accurate.

Searching photos, images, and video has become increasingly important as the web becomes more visual. The **visual web** refers to websites such as Pinterest, where pictures replace text documents, where users search pictures, and where pictures of products replace display ads for products. Pinterest is a social networking site that provides users (as well as brands) with an online board to which they can pin interesting pictures. One of the fastest-growing websites in history, Pinterest had 270 million monthly visitors worldwide in 2016. Instagram is another example of the visual web. Instagram is a photo and video sharing site that allows users to take pictures, enhance them, and share them with friends on other social sites such as Facebook, Twitter, and Google +. In 2016, Instagram had 400 million monthly active users.

Intelligent Agent Shopping Bots Chapter 11 describes the capabilities of software agents with built-in intelligence that can gather or filter information and perform other tasks to assist users. **Shopping bots** use intelligent agent software for searching the Internet for shopping information. Shopping bots such as MySimon or PriceGrabber can help people interested in making a purchase filter and retrieve information about products of interest, evaluate competing products according to criteria the users have established, and negotiate with vendors for price and delivery terms. Many of these shopping agents search the web for pricing and availability of products specified by the user and return a list of sites that sell the item along with pricing information and a purchase link.

Search Engine Marketing Search engines have become major advertising platforms and shopping tools by offering what is now called **search engine marketing**. Searching for information is one of the web's most popular activities; 70 percent of American adult Internet users will use a search engine at least once a day in 2016, generating about 20 billion queries a month. In addition, 180 million smartphone users will generate another 12 billion monthly searches. With this huge audience, search engines are the foundation for the most lucrative form of online marketing and advertising, search engine marketing. When users enter a search term on Google, Bing, Yahoo, or any of the other sites serviced by these search engines, they receive two types of listings: sponsored links, for which advertisers have paid to be listed (usually at the top of the search results page), and unsponsored, organic search results. In addition, advertisers can purchase small text boxes on the side of search results pages. The paid, sponsored advertisements are the fastest growing form of Internet advertising and are powerful new marketing tools that precisely match consumer interests with advertising messages at the right moment. Search engine marketing monetizes the value of the search process. In 2016, search engine marketing is expected to generate $28 billion in revenue, nearly half of all online advertising ($67 billion). About 90 percent of Google's revenue of $74 billion in 2015 came from online advertising, and 90 percent of that ad revenue came from search engine marketing (Google, 2016).

Because search engine marketing is so effective (it has the highest click-through rate and the highest return on ad investment), companies seek to optimize their websites for search engine recognition. The better optimized the page is, the higher a ranking it will achieve in search engine result listings. **Search engine optimization (SEO)** is the process of improving the quality and volume of web traffic to a website by employing a series of techniques that help a website achieve a higher ranking with the major search engines when certain keywords and phrases are put into the search field. One technique is to make sure that the keywords used in the website description match the keywords likely to be used as search terms by prospective customers. For example, your website is more likely to be among the first ranked by search engines if it uses the keyword *lighting* rather than *lamps* if most prospective customers are searching for *lighting*. It is also advantageous to link your website to as many other websites as possible because search engines evaluate such links to determine the popularity of a web page and how it is linked to other content on the web.

Search engines can be gamed by scammers who create thousands of phony website pages and link them or link them to a single retailer's site in an attempt to fool Google's search engine. Firms can also pay so-called link farms to link to their site. Google changed its search algorithm in 2012 to deal with this problem. Code named *Penguin*, the revised algorithm examines the quality of links more carefully with the intent of down-ranking sites that have a suspicious pattern of sites linking to them. Penguin is updated annually.

In general, search engines have been very helpful to small businesses that cannot afford large marketing campaigns. Because shoppers are looking for a specific product or service when they use search engines, they are what marketers call hot prospects—people who are looking for information and often intending to buy. Moreover, search engines charge only for click-throughs to a site. Merchants do not have to pay for ads that don't work, only for ads that receive a click. Consumers benefit from search engine marketing because ads for merchants appear only when consumers are looking for a specific product. Thus, search engine marketing saves consumers cognitive energy and reduces search costs (including the cost of transportation needed to search for products physically). One study estimated the global value of search to both merchants and consumers to be more than $800 billion, with about 65 percent of the benefit going to consumers in the form of lower search costs and lower prices (McKinsey & Company, 2011).

Web 2.0

Today's websites don't just contain static content—they enable people to collaborate, share information, and create new services and content online. These second-generation interactive Internet-based services are referred to as **Web 2.0**. If you have pinned a photo on Pinterest, posted a video to YouTube, created a blog, or added an app to your Facebook page, you've used some of these Web 2.0 services.

Web 2.0 has four defining features: interactivity, real-time user control, social participation (sharing), and user-generated content. The technologies and services behind these features include cloud computing, software mashups and apps, blogs, RSS, wikis, and social networks. We have already describd cloud computing, mashups, and apps in Chapter 5 and introduced social networks in Chapter 2.

A **blog**, the popular term for a weblog, is a personal website that typically contains a series of chronological entries (newest to oldest) by its author and links to related web pages. The blog may include a *blogroll* (a collection of links to other blogs) and *trackbacks* (a list of entries in other blogs that refer to a post on the first blog). Most blogs allow readers to post comments on the blog entries as well. The act of creating a blog is often referred to as blogging. Blogs can be hosted by a third-party service such as Blogger.com, TypePad.com, and Xanga.com, and blogging features have been incorporated into social networks such as Facebook and collaboration platforms such as IBM Notes. WordPress is a leading open source blogging tool and content management system. **Microblogging**, used in Twitter, is a type of blogging that features short posts of 140 characters or fewer.

Blog pages are usually variations on templates provided by the blogging service or software. Therefore, millions of people without HTML skills of any kind can post their own web pages and share content with others. The totality of blog-related websites is often referred to as the **blogosphere**. Although blogs have become popular personal publishing tools, they also have business uses (see Chapters 2 and 10).

If you're an avid blog reader, you might use RSS to keep up with your favorite blogs without constantly checking them for updates. **RSS**, which stands for Really Simple Syndication or Rich Site Summary, pulls specified content from websites and feeds it automatically to users' computers. RSS reader software gathers material from the websites or blogs that you tell it to scan and brings new information from those sites to you. RSS readers are available through websites such as Google and Yahoo, and they have been incorporated into the major web browsers and e-mail programs.

Blogs allow visitors to add comments to the original content, but they do not allow visitors to change the original posted material. **Wikis**, in contrast, are collaborative websites on which visitors can add, delete, or modify content, including the work of previous authors. Wiki comes from the Hawaiian word for *quick*.

Wiki software typically provides a template that defines layout and elements common to all pages, displays user-editable software program code, and then renders the content into an HTML-based page for display in a web browser. Some wiki software allows only basic text formatting, whereas other tools allow the use of tables, images, or even interactive elements, such as polls or games.

Most wikis provide capabilities for monitoring the work of other users and correcting mistakes.

Because wikis make information sharing so easy, they have many business uses. The U.S. Department of Homeland Security's National Cyber Security Center (NCSC) deployed a wiki to facilitate information sharing with other federal agencies on threats, attacks, and responses and as a repository for technical and standards information. Pixar Wiki is a collaborative community wiki for publicizing the work of Pixar Animation Studios. The wiki format allows anyone to create or edit an article about a Pixar film.

Social networking sites enable users to build communities of friends and professional colleagues. Members typically create a profile—a web page for posting photos, videos, audio files, and text—and then share these profiles with others on the service identified as their friends or contacts. Social networking sites are highly interactive, offer real-time user control, rely on user-generated content, and are broadly based on social participation and sharing of content and opinions. Leading social networking sites include Facebook, Twitter (with more than 1.6 billion and 310 million monthly active users, respectively, in 2016), and LinkedIn (for professional contacts).

For many, social networking sites are the defining Web 2.0 application and one that has radically changed how people spend their time online; how people communicate and with whom; how business people stay in touch with customers, suppliers, and employees; how providers of goods and services learn about their customers; and how advertisers reach potential customers. The large social networking sites are also application development platforms where members can create and sell software applications to other members of the community. Facebook alone has more than 1 million external developers who created more than 9 million applications for gaming, video sharing, and communicating with friends and family. In 2016 Facebook supported 3.5 billion app installations. We talk more about business applications of social networking in Chapters 2 and 10, and you can find social networking discussions in many other chapters of this book. You can also find a more detailed discussion of Web 2.0 in our Learning Tracks.

Web 3.0 and the Future Web

The future of the Internet, so-called Web 3.0, is already visible. The key features of **Web 3.0** are more tools for individuals to make sense out of the trillions of pages on the Internet, or the millions of apps available for smartphones and a visual, even three-dimensional (3D) Web where you can walk through pages in a 3D environment. (Review the discussion of semantic search and visual search earlier in this chapter.)

Even closer in time is a pervasive web that controls everything from a city's traffic lights and water usage, to the lights in your living room, to your car's rear view mirror, not to mention managing your calendar and appointments. This is referred to as the **Internet of Things** and is based on billions of Internet-connected sensors throughout our physical world. Objects, animals, or people are provided with unique identifiers and the ability to transfer data over a network without requiring human-to-human or human-to-computer interaction. Firms such as General electric, IBM, HP, and Oracle, and hundreds of smaller start-ups, are exploring how to build smart machines, factories, and cities through extensive use of remote sensors and fast cloud computing. A related Web 3.0 development is the emerging Internet of People (IoP) based on sensors attached to clothing and personal effects that monitor physical states and locations of individuals. We provide more detail on this topic in the following section.

The App Internet is another element in the future web. The growth of apps within the mobile platform is astounding. More than 80 percent of mobile minutes in the United States are generated through apps, only 20 percent using browsers. Apps give users direct access to content and are much faster than loading a browser and searching for content.

Other complementary trends leading toward a future Web 3.0 include more widespread use of cloud computing and software as a service (SaaS) business models, ubiquitous connectivity among mobile platforms and Internet access devices, and the transformation of the web from a network of separate siloed applications and content into a more seamless and interoperable whole. These more modest visions of the future Web 3.0 are more likely to be realized in the near term.

7-4   What are the principal technologies and standards for wireless networking, communication, and Internet access?

Welcome to the wireless revolution! Cell phones, smartphones, tablets, and wireless-enabled personal computers have morphed into portable media and computing platforms that let you perform many of the computing tasks you used to do at your desk, and a whole lot more. We introduced smartphones in our discussions of the mobile digital platform in Chapters 1 and 5. **Smartphones** such as the iPhone, Android phones, and BlackBerry combine the functionality of a cell phone with that of a mobile laptop computer with Wi-Fi capability. This makes it possible to combine music, video, Internet access, and telephone service in one device. A large part of the Internet is becoming a mobile, access-anywhere, broadband service for the delivery of video, music, and web search.

Cellular Systems

In 2015, more than 1.5 billion cell phones were sold worldwide. In the United States, there are 351 million cell phone subscriptions, and 190 million people have smartphones. About 193 million people access the web by using their phone (eMarketer, 2015). Smartphones, not the desktop PC, are now responsible for more than half of all Internet searches.

Digital cellular service uses several competing standards. In Europe and much of the rest of the world outside the United Sates, the standard is Global System for Mobile Communications (GSM). GSM's strength is its international roaming capability. There are GSM cell phone systems in the United States, including T-Mobile and AT&T.

A competing standard in the United States is Code Division Multiple Access (CDMA), which is the system Verizon and Sprint use. CDMA was developed by the military during World War II. It transmits over several frequencies, occupies the entire spectrum, and randomly assigns users to a range of frequencies over time, making it more efficient than GSM.

Earlier generations of cellular systems were designed primarily for voice and limited data transmission in the form of short text messages. Today wireless carriers offer 3G and 4G networks. **3G networks**, with transmission speeds ranging from 144 Kbps for mobile users in, say, a car, to more than 2 Mbps for stationary users, offer fair transmission speeds for e-mail, browsing the web, and online shopping but are too slow for videos. **4G networks** have much higher speeds: 100 megabits/second download and 50 megabits upload speed, with more than enough capacity for watching high-definition video on your smartphone. Long Term Evolution (LTE) and mobile Worldwide Interoperability for Microwave Access (WiMax—see the following section) are the current 4G standards.

Wireless Computer Networks and Internet Access

An array of technologies provides high-speed wireless access to the Internet for PCs and mobile devices. These new high-speed services have extended Internet access to numerous locations that could not be covered by traditional wired Internet services and have made ubiquitous computing, anywhere, anytime, a reality.

Bluetooth

Bluetooth is the popular name for the 802.15 wireless networking standard, which is useful for creating small **personal area networks (PANs)**. It links up to eight devices within a 10-meter area using low-power, radio-based communication and can transmit up to 722 Kbps in the 2.4-GHz band.

Wireless phones, pagers, computers, printers, and computing devices using Bluetooth communicate with each other and even operate each other without direct user intervention (see Figure 7.13). For example, a person could direct a notebook computer to send a document file wirelessly to a printer. Bluetooth connects wireless keyboards and mice to PCs or cell phones to earpieces without wires. Bluetooth has low power requirements, making it appropriate for battery-powered handheld computers or cell phones.

Although Bluetooth lends itself to personal networking, it has uses in large corporations. For example, FedEx drivers use Bluetooth to transmit the delivery data captured by their handheld computers to cellular transmitters, which forward the data to corporate computers. Drivers no longer need to spend time

FIGURE 7.13 A BLUETOOTH NETWORK (PAN)

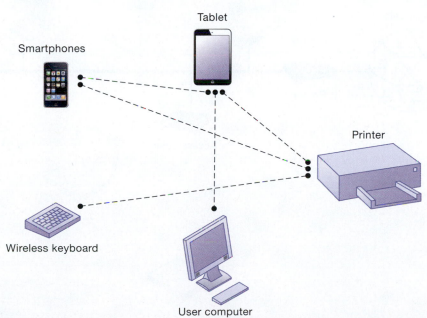

Bluetooth enables a variety of devices, including cell phones, smartphones, wireless keyboards and mice, PCs, and printers, to interact wirelessly with each other within a small, 30-foot (10-meter) area. In addition to the links shown, Bluetooth can be used to network similar devices to send data from one PC to another, for example.

docking their handheld units physically in the transmitters, and Bluetooth has saved FedEx $20 million per year.

Wi-Fi and Wireless Internet Access

The 802.11 set of standards for wireless LANs and wireless Internet access is also known as **Wi-Fi**. The first of these standards to be widely adopted was 802.11b, which can transmit up to 11 Mbps in the unlicensed 2.4-GHz band and has an effective distance of 30 to 50 meters. The 802.11g standard can transmit up to 54 Mbps in the 2.4-GHz range. 802.11n is capable of transmitting over 100 Mbps. Today's PCs and netbooks have built-in support for Wi-Fi, as do the iPhone, iPad, and other smartphones.

In most Wi-Fi communication, wireless devices communicate with a wired LAN using access points. An access point is a box consisting of a radio receiver/transmitter and antennas that links to a wired network, router, or hub.

Figure 7.14 illustrates an 802.11 wireless LAN that connects a small number of mobile devices to a larger wired LAN and to the Internet. Most wireless devices are client machines. The servers that the mobile client stations need to use are on the wired LAN. The access point controls the wireless stations and acts as a bridge between the main wired LAN and the wireless LAN. The access point also controls the wireless stations.

The most popular use for Wi-Fi today is for high-speed wireless Internet service. In this instance, the access point plugs into an Internet connection, which

FIGURE 7.14 AN 802.11 WIRELESS LAN

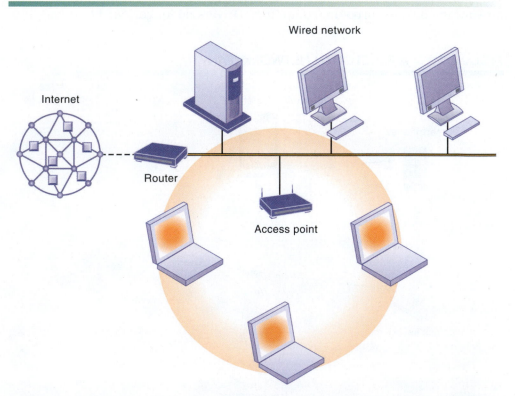

Mobile laptop computers equipped with network interface cards link to the wired LAN by communicating with the access point. The access point uses radio waves to transmit network signals from the wired network to the client adapters, which convert them to data that the mobile device can understand. The client adapter then transmits the data from the mobile device back to the access point, which forwards the data to the wired network.

could come from a cable service or DSL telephone service. Computers within range of the access point use it to link wirelessly to the Internet.

Hotspots are locations with one or more access points providing wireless Internet access and are often in public places. Some hotspots are free or do not require any additional software to use; others may require activation and the establishment of a user account by providing a credit card number over the web.

Businesses of all sizes are using Wi-Fi networks to provide low-cost wireless LANs and Internet access. Wi-Fi hotspots can be found in hotels, airport lounges, libraries, cafes, and college campuses to provide mobile access to the Internet. Dartmouth College is one of many campuses where students now use Wi-Fi for research, course work, and entertainment.

Wi-Fi technology poses several challenges, however. One is Wi-Fi's security features, which make these wireless networks vulnerable to intruders. We provide more detail about Wi-Fi security issues in Chapter 8.

Another drawback of Wi-Fi networks is susceptibility to interference from nearby systems operating in the same spectrum, such as wireless phones, microwave ovens, or other wireless LANs. However, wireless networks based on the 802.11n standard solve this problem by using multiple wireless antennas in tandem to transmit and receive data and technology called MIMO (multiple input multiple output) to coordinate multiple simultaneous radio signals.

WiMax

A surprisingly large number of areas in the United States and throughout the world do not have access to Wi-Fi or fixed broadband connectivity. The range of Wi-Fi systems is no more than 300 feet from the base station, making it difficult for rural groups that don't have cable or DSL service to find wireless access to the Internet.

The Institute of Electrical and Electronics Engineers (IEEE) developed a new family of standards known as WiMax to deal with these problems. **WiMax**, which stands for Worldwide Interoperability for Microwave Access, is the popular term for IEEE Standard 802.16. It has a wireless access range of up to 31 miles and transmission speed of up to 75 Mbps.

WiMax antennas are powerful enough to beam high-speed Internet connections to rooftop antennas of homes and businesses that are miles away. Cellular handsets and laptops with WiMax capabilities are appearing in the marketplace. Mobile WiMax is one of the 4G network technologies we discussed earlier in this chapter.

RFID and Wireless Sensor Networks

Mobile technologies are creating new efficiencies and ways of working throughout the enterprise. In addition to the wireless systems we have just described, radio frequency identification systems and wireless sensor networks are having a major impact.

Radio Frequency Identification (RFID) and Near Field Communication (NFC)

Radio frequency identification (RFID) systems provide a powerful technology for tracking the movement of goods throughout the supply chain. RFID systems use tiny tags with embedded microchips containing data about an item and its location to transmit radio signals over a short distance to RFID readers. The RFID readers then pass the data over a network to a computer for processing. Unlike bar codes, RFID tags do not need line-of-sight contact to be read.

The RFID tag is electronically programmed with information that can uniquely identify an item plus other information about the item such as its location, where and when it was made, or its status during production. The reader emits radio waves in ranges anywhere from 1 inch to 100 feet. When an RFID tag comes within the range of the reader, the tag is activated and starts sending data. The reader captures these data, decodes them, and sends them back over a wired or wireless network to a host computer for further processing (see Figure 7.15). Both RFID tags and antennas come in a variety of shapes and sizes.

In inventory control and supply chain management, RFID systems capture and manage more detailed information about items in warehouses or in production than bar coding systems. If a large number of items are shipped together, RFID systems track each pallet, lot, or even unit item in the shipment. This technology may help companies such as Walmart improve receiving and storage operations by improving their ability to see exactly what stock is stored in warehouses or on retail store shelves. Macy's, described in the chapter-opening case, uses RFID technology to track individual items for sale on store shelves.

Walmart has installed RFID readers at store receiving docks to record the arrival of pallets and cases of goods shipped with RFID tags. The RFID reader reads the tags a second time just as the cases are brought onto the sales floor from backroom storage areas. Software combines sales data from Walmart's point-of-sale systems and the RFID data regarding the number of cases brought out to the sales floor. The program determines which items will soon be depleted and automatically generates a list of items to pick in the warehouse to replenish store shelves before they run out. This information helps Walmart reduce out-of-stock items, increase sales, and further shrink its costs.

The cost of RFID tags used to be too high for widespread use, but now it starts at around 7 cents per tag in the United States. As the price decreases, RFID is starting to become cost-effective for many applications.

In addition to installing RFID readers and tagging systems, companies may need to upgrade their hardware and software to process the massive amounts of data produced by RFID systems—transactions that could add up to tens or hundreds of terabytes.

Software is used to filter, aggregate, and prevent RFID data from overloading business networks and system applications. Applications often need to be redesigned to accept large volumes of frequently generated RFID data and to share

FIGURE 7.15 HOW RFID WORKS

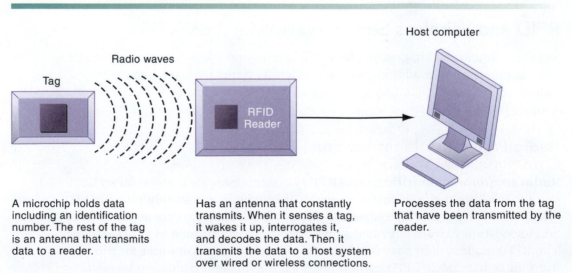

A microchip holds data including an identification number. The rest of the tag is an antenna that transmits data to a reader.

Has an antenna that constantly transmits. When it senses a tag, it wakes it up, interrogates it, and decodes the data. Then it transmits the data to a host system over wired or wireless connections.

Processes the data from the tag that have been transmitted by the reader.

RFID uses low-powered radio transmitters to read data stored in a tag at distances ranging from 1 inch to 100 feet. The reader captures the data from the tag and sends them over a network to a host computer for processing.

those data with other applications. Major enterprise software vendors now offer RFID-ready versions of their supply chain management applications.

Tap-and-go services like Apple Pay or Google Wallet use an RFID-related technology called **near field communication (NFC)**. NFC is a short-range wireless connectivity standard that uses electromagnetic radio fields to enable two compatible devices to exchange data when brought within a few centimeters of each other. A smartphone or other NFC-compatible device sends out radio frequency signals that interact with an NFC tag found in compatible card readers or smart posters. The signals create a current that flows through the NFC tag, allowing the device and the tag to communicate with one another. In most cases the tag is passive and only sends out information while the other device (such as a smartphone) is active and can both send and receive information. (There are NFC systems where both components are active.)

NFC is used in wireless payment services, to retrieve information, and even to exchange videos or information with friends on the go. You could share a website link by passing your phone over a friend's phone, while waving the phone in front of a poster or display containing an NFC tag could show information about what you're viewing at a museum or exhibit.

Wireless Sensor Networks

If your company wanted state-of-the art technology to monitor building security or detect hazardous substances in the air, it might deploy a wireless sensor network. **Wireless sensor networks (WSNs)** are networks of interconnected wireless devices that are embedded in the physical environment to provide measurements of many points over large spaces. These devices have built-in processing, storage, and radio frequency sensors and antennas. They are linked into an interconnected network that routes the data they capture to a computer for analysis.

These networks range from hundreds to thousands of nodes. Because wireless sensor devices are placed in the field for years at a time without any maintenance or human intervention, they must have very low power requirements and batteries capable of lasting for years.

Figure 7.16 illustrates one type of wireless sensor network, with data from individual nodes flowing across the network to a server with greater processing power. The server acts as a gateway to a network based on Internet technology.

Wireless sensor networks are valuable for uses such as monitoring environmental changes; monitoring traffic or military activity; protecting property; efficiently operating and managing machinery and vehicles; establishing security perimeters; monitoring supply chain management; or detecting chemical, biological, or radiological material.

Output from RFID systems and wireless networks is fueling the Internet of Things (IoT), introduced earlier in this chapter, in which machines such as jet engines, power plant turbines, or agricultural sensors constantly gather data and send the data over the Internet for analysis. The data might signal the need to take action such as replacing a part that's close to wearing out, restocking a product on a store shelf, starting the watering system for a soybean field, or slowing down a turbine. Over time, more and more everyday physical objects will be connected to the Internet and will be able to identify themselves to other devices, creating networks that can sense and respond as data changes. Macy's Pick to the Last Unit system, described in the chapter opening case, is an example of an IoT application. According to the McKinsey Global Institute, up to 50 billion devices connected to the Internet could add $3.9 trillion to $11.1 trillion a year of new economic value to business and society by 2025 (Manyika et al., 2015). You'll find more examples of the Internet of Things in Chapters 2 and 12.

FIGURE 7.16 A WIRELESS SENSOR NETWORK

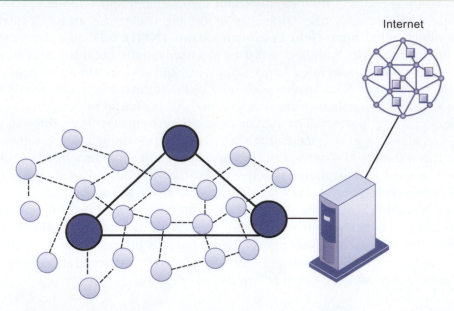

The small circles represent lower-level nodes, and the larger circles represent high-end nodes. Lower-level nodes forward data to each other or to higher-level nodes, which transmit data more rapidly and speed up network performance.

Review Summary

7-1 *What are the principal components of telecommunications networks and key networking technologies?*

A simple network consists of two or more connected computers. Basic network components include computers, network interfaces, a connection medium, network operating system software, and either a hub or a switch. The networking infrastructure for a large company includes the traditional telephone system, mobile cellular communication, wireless local area networks, videoconferencing systems, a corporate website, intranets, extranets, and an array of local and wide area networks, including the Internet.

Contemporary networks have been shaped by the rise of client/server computing, the use of packet switching, and the adoption of Transmission Control Protocol/ Internet Protocol (TCP/IP) as a universal communications standard for linking disparate networks and computers, including the Internet. Protocols provide a common set of rules that enable communication among diverse components in a telecommunications network.

7-2 *What are the different types of networks?*

The principal physical transmission media are twisted copper telephone wire, coaxial copper cable, fiber-optic cable, and wireless transmission.

Local area networks (LANs) connect PCs and other digital devices within a 500-meter radius and are used today for many corporate computing tasks. Wide area networks (WANs) span broad geographical distances, ranging from several miles to continents and are often private networks that are independently managed. Metropolitan area networks (MANs) span a single urban area.

Digital subscriber line (DSL) technologies, cable Internet connections, and T1 lines are often used for high-capacity Internet connections.

7-3 *How do the Internet and Internet technology work, and how do they support communication and e-business?*

The Internet is a worldwide network of networks that uses the client/server model of computing and the TCP/IP network reference model. Every computer on the Internet is assigned a unique numeric IP address. The Domain Name System (DNS) converts IP addresses to more user-friendly domain names. Worldwide Internet policies are established by organizations and government bodies such as the Internet Architecture Board (IAB) and the World Wide Web Consortium (W3C).

Major Internet services include e-mail, newsgroups, chatting, instant messaging, Telnet, FTP, and the web. Web pages are based on Hypertext Markup Language (HTML) and can display text, graphics, video, and audio. Website directories, search engines, and RSS technology help users locate the information they need on the web. RSS, blogs, social networking, and wikis are features of Web 2.0. The future Web 3.0 will feature more semantic search, visual search, prevalence of apps, and interconnectedness of many different devices (Internet of Things).

Firms are also starting to realize economies by using VoIP technology for voice transmission and virtual private networks (VPNs) as low-cost alternatives to private WANs.

7-4 *What are the principal technologies and standards for wireless networking, communication, and Internet access?*

Cellular networks are evolving toward high-speed, high-bandwidth, digital packet–switched transmission. Broadband 3G networks are capable of transmitting data at speeds ranging from 144 Kbps to more than 2 Mbps. 4G networks capable of transmission speeds of 100 Mbps are starting to be rolled out.

Major cellular standards include Code Division Multiple Access (CDMA), which is used primarily in the United States, and Global System for Mobile Communications (GSM), which is the standard in Europe and much of the rest of the world.

Standards for wireless computer networks include Bluetooth (802.15) for small personal area networks (PANs), Wi-Fi (802.11) for local area networks (LANs), and WiMax (802.16) for metropolitan area networks (MANs).

Radio frequency identification (RFID) systems provide a powerful technology for tracking the movement of goods by using tiny tags with embedded data about an item and its location. RFID readers read the radio signals transmitted by these tags and pass the data over a network to a computer for processing. Wireless sensor networks (WSNs) are networks of interconnected wireless sensing and transmitting devices that are embedded in the physical environment to provide measurements of many points over large spaces.

Key Terms

3G networks, 278
4G networks, 278
Bandwidth, 259
Blog, 276
Blogosphere, 276
Bluetooth, 279
Broadband, 252
Cable Internet connections, 260
Chat, 266
Digital subscriber line (DSL), 260
Domain name, 260
Domain Name System (DNS), 260
E-mail, 265
File Transfer Protocol (FTP), 265
Hertz, 259
Hotspots, 281
Hubs, 253
Hypertext Transfer Protocol (HTTP), 270
Instant messaging, 266
Internet of Things, 277
Internet Protocol (IP) address, 260
Internet service provider (ISP), 260
Internet2, 265
IPv6, 264
Local area network (LAN), 258

Metropolitan area network (MAN), 258
Microblogging, 276
Modem, 257
Near field communication (NFC), 283
Network operating system (NOS), 253
Packet switching, 255
Peer-to-peer, 258
Personal area networks (PANs), 279
Predictive search, 272
Protocol, 256
Radio frequency identification (RFID), 281
Router, 253
RSS, 276
Search engine marketing, 275
Search engine optimization (SEO), 275
Search engines, 271
Semantic search, 272
Shopping bots, 274
Smartphones, 278
Social networking, 277
Social search, 272
Software-defined networking (SDN), 253
Switch, 253
T1 lines, 260

MyMISLab

To complete the problems with the MyMISLab, go to the EOC Discussion Questions in MyMISLab.

Review Questions

7-1 What are the principal components of telecommunications networks and key networking technologies?

- Describe the features of a simple network and the network infrastructure for a large company.

- Name and describe the principal technologies and trends that have shaped contemporary telecommunications systems.

7-2 What are the different types of networks?

- Define an analog and a digital signal.

- Distinguish between a LAN, MAN, and WAN.

7-3 How do the Internet and Internet technology work, and how do they support communication and e-business?

- Define the Internet, describe how it works, and explain how it provides business value.

- Explain how the Domain Name System (DNS) and IP addressing system work.

- List and describe the principal Internet services.

- Define and describe VoIP and virtual private networks and explain how they provide value to businesses.

- List and describe alternative ways of locating information on the web.

- Describe how online search technologies are used for marketing.

7-4 What are the principal technologies and standards for wireless networking, communications, and Internet access?

- Define Bluetooth, Wi-Fi, WiMax, and 3G and 4G networks.

- Describe the capabilities of each and for which types of applications each is best suited.

- Define RFID, explain how it works, and describe how it provides value to businesses.

- Define WSNs, explain how they work, and describe the kinds of applications that use them.

Discussion Questions

7-5 It has been said that within the next few years, smartphones will become the single-most important digital device we own. Discuss the implications of this statement.

7-6 Should all major retailing and manufacturing companies switch to RFID? Why or why not?

7-7 What are some of the issues to consider in determining whether the Internet would provide your business with a competitive advantage?

Hands-On MIS Projects

The projects in this section give you hands-on experience evaluating and selecting communications technology, using spreadsheet software to improve selection of telecommunications services, and using web search engines for business research. Visit MyMISLab's Multimedia Library to access this chapter's Hands-On MIS Projects.

Management Decision Problems

7-8 Your company supplies ceramic floor tiles to Home Depot, Lowe's, and other home improvement stores. You have been asked to start using radio frequency identification tags on each case of tiles you ship to help your customers improve the management of your products and those of other suppliers in their warehouses. Use the web to identify the cost of hardware, software, and networking components for an RFID system for your company. What factors should be considered? What are the key decisions that have to be made in determining whether your firm should adopt this technology?

7-9 BestMed Medical Supplies Corporation sells medical and surgical products and equipment from more than 700 manufacturers to hospitals, health clinics, and medical offices. The company employs 500 people at seven locations in western and midwestern states, including account managers, customer service and support representatives, and warehouse staff. Employees communicate by traditional telephone voice services, e-mail, instant messaging, and cell phones. Management is inquiring about whether the company should adopt a system for unified communications. What factors should be considered? What are the key decisions that must be made in determining whether to adopt this technology? Use the web, if necessary, to find out more about unified communications and its costs.

Improving Decision Making: Using Spreadsheet Software to Evaluate Wireless Services

Software skills: Spreadsheet formulas, formatting
Business skills: Analyzing telecommunications services and costs

7-10 In this project, you'll use the web to research alternative wireless services and use spreadsheet software to calculate wireless service costs for a sales force.

You would like to equip your sales force of 35, based in St. Louis, Missouri, with mobile phones that have capabilities for voice transmission, text messaging, Internet access, and taking and sending photos. Use the web to select two wireless providers that offer nationwide voice and data service as well as good service in your home area. Examine the features of the mobile handsets and wireless plans offered by each of these vendors. Assume that each of the 35 salespeople will need to spend three hours per weekday between 8 a.m. and 6 p.m. on mobile voice communication, send 30 text messages per weekday, use 1 gigabyte of data per month, and send five photos per week. Use your spreadsheet software to determine the wireless service and handset that will offer the best pricing per user over a two-year period. For the purposes of this exercise, you do not need to consider corporate discounts.

Achieving Operational Excellence: Using Web Search Engines for Business Research

Software skills: Web search tools
Business skills: Researching new technologies

7-11 This project will help develop your Internet skills in using web search engines for business research.

Use Google and Bing to obtain information about ethanol as an alternative fuel for motor vehicles. If you wish, try some other search engines as well. Compare the volume and quality of information you find with each search tool. Which tool is the easiest to use? Which produced the best results for your research? Why?

Collaboration and Teamwork Project

Evaluating Smartphones

7-12 Form a group with three or four of your classmates. Compare the capabilities of Apple's iPhone with a smartphone from another vendor with similar features. Your analysis should consider the purchase cost of each device, the wireless networks where each device can operate, plan and handset costs, and the services available for each device. You should also consider other capabilities of each device, including available software, security features, and the ability to integrate with existing corporate or PC applications. Which device would you select? On what criteria would you base your selection? If possible, use Google Docs and Google Drive or Google Sites to brainstorm, organize, and develop a presentation of your findings for the class.

Google, Apple, and Facebook Battle for Your Internet Experience
CASE STUDY

Three Internet titans—Google, Apple, and Facebook—are in an epic struggle to dominate your Internet experience, and caught in the crossfire are search, music, video, and other media along with the devices you use for all of these things, cloud computing, and a host of other issues that are likely central to your life. Mobile devices with advanced functionality and ubiquitous Internet access are rapidly overtaking traditional desktop machines as the most popular form of computing. Today, people spend more than half their time online using mobile devices that take advantage of a growing cloud of computing capacity. It's no surprise, then, that today's tech titans are aggressively battling for control of this brave new mobile world.

Apple, which started as a personal computer company, quickly expanded into software and consumer electronics. Since upending the music industry with its MP3 player, the iPod, and the iTunes digital music service, Apple took mobile computing by storm with the iPhone, iPod Touch, and iPad. Now Apple wants to be the computing platform of choice for the Internet.

Apple is the leader in mobile software applications, thanks to the popularity of the App Store, with more than 2 million apps for mobile and tablet devices. Applications greatly enrich the experience of using a mobile device, and whoever creates the most appealing set of devices and applications will derive a significant competitive advantage over rival companies. Apps are the new equivalent of the traditional browser.

Apple thrives on its legacy of innovation. In 2011, it unveiled the potentially market-disrupting Siri (Speech Interpretation and Recognition Interface), a combination search/navigation tool and personal assistant. Siri promises personalized recommendations that improve as it gains user familiarity—all from a verbal command. Google countered by quickly releasing its own AI tool, Google Now.

Apple faces strong competition for its phones and tablets both in the United States and in developing markets like China from inexpensive Chinese smartphones and from Samsung Android phones that have larger screens and lower prices. iPhone sales have started to slow, but Apple is not counting on hardware devices alone for future growth. Services have always played a large part in the Apple ecosystem, and they have emerged as a major revenue source. Apple has more than 1 billion active devices in circulation, creating a huge installed base of users willing to purchase services and a source of new revenue streams. Apple Pay, now available in more than 10 million locations around the world, has been adding 1 million new users per week. Four months after the Apple Music service started collecting revenue, it had more than 10 million subscribers, adding $1.2 billion to Apple's annual bottom line. Revenue from the App Store is skyrocketing. In the two weeks ending January 3, 2016, customers spent more than $1.1 billion on apps and in-app purchases. According to CEO Tim Cook, Apple has become one of the largest service businesses in the world.

This service-driven strategy is not without worry. Both Google and Facebook offer stiff competition in the services area. Apple's Siri may be good for setting an alarm or making a phone call, but she can't carry on a conversation or execute complex tasks across many apps and services the way her rivals can. Within Facebook Messenger, you can send money to a friend, order an Uber ride, or obtain customer service from airlines like United and Delta. Google's Allo messaging app for iOS and Android will enable users to chat with an assistant to have it perform tasks such as getting the news, finding out travel times —just about anything you could search for on the web. It can even suggest responses or web searches while you're in conversations with other humans.

Google continues to be the world's leading search engine, accounting for three-quarters of the world's web searches. About 90 percent of Google's revenue comes from ads, most of that on its search engine. Google dominates online advertising. However, Google is slipping in its position as the gateway to the Internet. New search start-ups focus on actions and apps instead of the web. Apple has also become a mobile search competitor. Its iOS mobile operating system software gives iPhone and iPad users the ability use Apple's own search engine for searches of music, apps and local services, bypassing Google.

In 2005, Google had purchased the Android open source mobile operating system to compete in mobile computing. Google provides Android at no cost to smartphone manufacturers, generating revenue indirectly through app purchases and advertising. Many different manufacturers have adopted Android as a standard. In contrast, Apple allows only its own devices to use its proprietary operating system, and all the apps it sells can run only on Apple products. Android is deployed on 76 percent of smartphones worldwide, is the most common operating system for tablets, and runs on watches, car dashboards and TVs—more than 4,000 distinct devices. Google wants to extend Android to as many devices as possible.

Google's Android mobile operating system is expected to gain even more market share in the coming years, which could be problematic for Apple as it tries to maintain customer loyalty and keep software developers focused on the iOS platform. Whoever has the dominant smartphone operating system will have control over the apps where smartphone users spend most of their time and built-in channels for serving ads to mobile devices.

Although Google search technology can't easily navigate the mobile apps where users are spending most of their time, Google is starting to index the content inside mobile apps and provide links pointing to that content featured in Google's search results on smartphones. Since about half of Google searches are for mobile devices, the company revised its search algorithms to add "mobile friendliness" to the 200 or so factors it uses to rank websites on its search engine. This favors sites that look good on smartphone screens. The cost-per-click paid for mobile ads has trailed desktop ads. Google instituted a design change to merge PC ads and mobile ads and present a cleaner mobile search page.

Much of Google's efforts to make its search and related services more powerful and user-friendly in the years ahead are based on the company's investments in artificial intelligence and machine learning. These technologies already have been implemented in applications such as voice search, Google Translate, and spam filtering. The goal is to evolve search into more of a smart assistance capability, where users will be able to get help from Google based on context, situation, and needs. Allo is a smart messaging app that can learn your texting patterns over time to make conversations more expressive and productive. It suggests automatic replies to incoming messages, and you can get suggestions and even book a restaurant reservation without leaving the chat. Google Assistant is meant to provide a continuing, conversational dialogue between users and the search engine.

Google is always looking for new ways to connect more people to the Internet, including fleets of little satellites, solar-powered drones that would fly around the world, and balloons that float high into the stratosphere, beaming the Internet to those below. Such devices in the sky will help Google spread the Internet to the roughly 4 billion people in undeveloped areas who currently lack Internet access. The more people who are connected directly to Google, the more ads it can show them.

Facebook is the world's largest social networking service, with 1.65 billion monthly active users. People use Facebook to stay connected with their friends and family and to express what matters most to them. Facebook Platform enables developers to build applications and websites that integrate with Facebook to reach its global network of users and to build personalized and social products.

Facebook has persistently worked on ways to convert its popularity and trove of user data into advertising dollars, with the expectation that these dollars will increasingly come from mobile smartphones and tablets. On an average day, about 989 million people around the world log on to Facebook using mobile devices. Facebook ads allow companies to target its users based on their real identities and expressed interests rather than educated guesses derived from web-browsing habits and other online behavior.

Mobile advertising accounts for about 75 percent of Facebook's revenue, with many of those ads highly targeted by age, gender, and other demographics. Facebook is now a serious competitor to Google in the mobile ad market and is even trying to compete with emerging mobile platforms, having purchased Oculus VR Inc., a maker of virtual reality goggles, for $2 billion.

In March 2013, Facebook overhauled its home page to increase the size of both photos and links and allow users to create topical streams. This move gives advertisers more opportunities and more information with which to target markets. A "personalized newspaper" with, for example, an op-ed feed featuring followed commentary pages, a sports section tailored to preferred events and teams, and a hometown news feed will swell Facebook's database with useful tidbits. Facebook also introduced a mobile application suite to replace the typical smartphone home screen. Facebook Home is an interface running on top of the Android operating system that replaces the smartphone's typical cover screen with Facebook content, such as photos, messages, and status updates. Home still provides access to apps on the phone, but the experience is centered around Facebook.

About the same time, Facebook launched a new search tool to challenge Google's dominance of search. Facebook Search (formerly Graph Search) mines Facebook's vast repository of user data and delivers results based on social signals, such as Facebook "likes," and friend recommendations. It's a more "social" way of searching than Google. Although Facebook search is not in the same league as Google, it offers more precise data on its users, such as gender, age, marital status, and interests. Facebook's share of worldwide digital advertising revenue has been growing.

Facebook CEO Mark Zuckerberg is convinced that social networking is the ideal way to use the web and to consume all of the other content people might desire, including news and video. That makes it an ideal marketing platform for companies. But he also knows that Facebook can't achieve long-term growth and prosperity based on social networking alone. During the past few years Facebook has moved into virtual reality, messaging, video, and more. Facebook is challenging YouTube as the premier destination for personal videos, and it is making its messages "smarter" by deploying chatbots. Chatbots are stripped-down software agents that understand what you type or say and respond by answering questions or executing tasks, and they run in the background of Facebook's Messenger service.

Zuckerberg has said that he intends to help bring the next billion people online by attracting users in developing countries with affordable web connectivity. Facebook has launched several services in emerging markets, such as the Free Basics Internet service designed to get people online so they can explore web applications including its social network. Facebook wants to beam the Internet to underserved areas through the use of drones and satellites along with other technologies. Zuckerberg thinks that Facebook could eventually be an Internet service provider to underserved areas. If Facebook

can match Google on this front and succeed in making itself synonymous with mobile access, the company could very well compete for global advertising dominance.

Sources: Don Reisinger, "How Mark Zuckerberg Is Shaping the Future of Facebook, Social Media," *eWeek,* May 16, 2016; Robert McMillan, "Facebook Hopes Chatbots Can Solve App Overload," *Wall Street Journal,* April 17, 2016; Nathan Olivarez-Giles, "Google Takes on Apple, Facebook with Allo and Duo Chat Apps," *Wall Street Journal,* May 18, 2016; Eric Emin Wood, "Is a Shift to Being a Service Provider in Apple's Future?" IT World Canada, May 5, 2016; Joanna Stern, "Dear Apple, Please Make the iPhone Smarter," *Wall Street Journal,* May 31, 2016; Yoni Heisler, "Apple's Growth Strategy Is Hiding in Plain Sight," BGR.com, January 28, 2016; Rolfe Winkler, "Mobile Alters Landscape Where Google Operates," *Wall Street Journal,* March 26, 2015; Farhad Manjoo, "Google Mighty Now, but Not Forever," *New York Times,* February 11, 2015; Alistair Barr, "Mobile Devices Upend Google Search," *Wall Street Journal,* February 25, 2016, and " How Google Aims to Delve Deeper into Users' Lives," *Wall Street Journal,* May 28, 2015; and Connor Dougherty, "Google Hopes to Take the Web Directly to Billions Lacking Access," *New York Times,* January 21, 2015, and "Reinventing Google for a Mobile World," *New York Times,* July 9, 2015.

CASE STUDY QUESTIONS

7-13 Compare the business models and core competencies of Google, Apple, and Facebook.

7-14 Why is mobile computing so important to these three firms? Evaluate the mobile strategies of each firm.

7-15 What is the significance of search to the success or failure of mobile computing? How have Apple and Facebook attempted to compete with Google? Will their strategies succeed?

7-16 Which company and business model do you think is most likely to dominate the Internet, and why?

7-17 What difference would it make to a business or to an individual consumer if Apple, Google, or Facebook dominated the Internet experience? Explain your answer.

MyMISLab

Go to the Assignments section of MyMISLab to complete these writing exercises.

7-18 Compare Web 2.0 and Web 3.0.

7-19 How do social search, semantic search, and mobile search differ from searching for information on the web by using conventional search engines?

Chapter 7 References

Barr, Alistair. "Mobile Devices Upend Google Search." *Wall Street Journal* (February 25, 2016).

Chiang, I. Robert and Jhih-Hua Jhang-Li. "Delivery Consolidation and Service Competition Among Internet Service Providers." *Journal of Management Information Systems* 34 No. 3 (Winter 2014).

Deichmann, Johannes, Matthias Roggendorf, and Dominik Wee. "Preparing IT Systems and Organizations for the Internet of Things." McKinsey & Company (2015).

eMarketer, "It's 2015. What Does Mobile Mean Now?" (February 18, 2015).

Google, Inc. "SEC Form 10k for the Fiscal Year Ending December 31, 2015" (February 11, 2016).

IBM Global Technology Services. "Software-Defined Networking in the New Business Frontier." (July 2015).

Iyer, Bala. "To Project the Trajectory of the Internet of Things, Look to the Software Industry." *Harvard Business Review* (February 25, 2016).

Manjoo, Farhad. "Google Mighty Now, but Not Forever." *New York Times* (February 11, 2015).

Manyika, James, Michael Chui, Peter Bisson, Jonathan Woetzel, Richard Dobbs, Jacques Bughin, and Dan Aharon. "Unlocking the Potential of the Internet of Things." McKinsey Global Institute (2015).

McKinsey & Company. "The Impact of Internet Technologies: Search." (July 2011).

National Telecommunications and Information Agency. "NTIA Announces Intent to Transition Key Internet Domain Name Functions." (March 14, 2014).

Panko, Raymond R. and Julia Panko. *Business Data Networks and Security* 10e. Upper Saddle River, NJ: Prentice-Hall (2015).

Reisinger, Don. "How Mark Zuckerberg Is Shaping the Future of Facebook, Social Media." *eWeek* (May 16, 2016).

Winkler, Rolfe. "Getting More Than Just Words in a Google Search Result." *Wall Street Journal* (Aug. 18, 2014).

Wittman, Art. "Here Comes the Internet of Things" *Information Week* (July 22, 2013).

Wyatt, Edward. "U.S. to Cede Its Oversight of Addresses on Internet." *New York Times* (March 14, 2014).

8

Securing Information Systems

Learning Objectives

After reading this chapter, you will be able to answer the following questions:

8-1 Why are information systems vulnerable to destruction, error, and abuse?

8-2 What is the business value of security and control?

8-3 What are the components of an organizational framework for security and control?

8-4 What are the most important tools and technologies for safeguarding information resources?

MyMISLab™

Visit **mymislab.com** for simulations, tutorials, and end-of-chapter problems.

CHAPTER CASES

Hackers Attack the SWIFT Global Banking Network
The Flash Crash: A New Culprit
BYOD: A Security Nightmare?
U.S. Office of Personnel Management Data Breach: No Routine Hack

VIDEO CASES

Stuxnet and Cyberwarfare
Cyberespionage: The Chinese Threat
Instructional Videos:
Sony PlayStation Hacked; Data Stolen from 77 Million Users
Meet the Hackers: Anonymous Statement on Hacking Sony

Hackers Attack the SWIFT Global Banking Network

SWIFT, which stands for Society for Worldwide Interbank Financial Telecommunication, is considered the Rolls-Royce of payment networks. It is a system used by more than 11,000 financial institutions worldwide to authorize payments from one account to another. SWIFT's secure messaging system sends about 25 million messages on a typical day, including orders and confirmations for payments, securities settlements, and currency exchanges. Obviously, this is a very important system for global finance. If you receive a message from SWIFT, you can be sure it's legitimate and move the money as expected.

SWIFT is a highly secure system, but apparently not secure enough. In early 2016 revelations surfaced about multiple attempts to use SWIFT messaging to rob financial institutions. Bangladesh's central bank disclosed that in February 2016 it had lost $81 million to hackers who breached its security, accessed SWIFT, and tricked the Federal Reserve Bank of New York into sending funds it held for the bank to hacker-controlled accounts in the Philippines.

Each bank in the SWIFT network is identified by a set of codes. Hackers

© Brian Jackson/123RF

somehow managed to steal the Bangladesh bank's credentials to transmit the messages and used malware targeting a PDF reader for checking statements. SWIFT's core messaging system was not compromised. Security breaches occurred in the computers of individual institutions that interact with the system, and these computers remain the responsibility of individual SWIFT members. The hackers had access only to the compromised banks' funds but not to the funds of the thousands of other institutions that use SWIFT. However, investigators have identified breaches at 12 other banks, including Vietnam's Tien Phong Commercial Joint Stock Bank and Ecuador's Banco del Austro.

How could this have happened? SWIFT isn't regulated like a bank because it doesn't hold funds or manage accounts. It's overseen by the National Bank of Belgium and representatives from the U.S. Federal Reserve, the Bank of England, the European Central Bank, the Bank of Japan, and other major banks. Experts point out that the SWIFT system is based on flexibility and trust. A bank can choose to let employees open SWIFT's main interface right from their desktop browser. That same feature that makes SWIFT easy to use also makes the system susceptible to hacking. Hackers apparently were able to obtain the banks' SWIFT access codes, send authenticated but fraudulent requests to transfer funds, and cover their tracks with malware surreptitiously placed onto bank computer systems. These attacks showed a deep and sophisticated knowledge of specific controls at the targeted banks, which may have been acquired from insiders, cyberattacks, or both.

Most banks in the United States take special precautions with their SWIFT-linked computers, including multiple firewalls to isolate SWIFT from the bank's other networks and even operating the machines in separate locked rooms. Unfortunately some banks in other countries take fewer precautions. The Bangladesh bank may have been especially vulnerable, using $10 routers and no firewalls, according to experts.

Security firms and intelligence agencies are still trying to learn who is behind the attacks. Symantec Corp, a leading security company, says the attacks resemble earlier hacking efforts attributed to North Korea.

SWIFT plans to toughen software requirements, expand the use of two-factor authentication (which provides additional identity checking), monitor compliance more rigorously, and provide more information about fraud detection. Ultimately, however, SWIFT can only do so much. The real solution must come from the participating banks themselves. And according to SWIFT CEO Gottfried Leibbrandt, fully armoring the network's defenses is likely to take years.

Sources: Michael Corkery, "Hackers' $81 Million Sneak Attack on World Banking," *New York Times*, April 30, 2016; Katy Burne, Robin Sidel, and Syed Zain Al-Mahmood, "Swift Banking Network Struggles with Wave of Cyberattacks," *Wall Street Journal*, May 20, 2016; "What a Bank Heist Reveals About Global Security," *Bloomberg View*, May 31, 2016; John Detrixhe, Gavin Finch, and John Follain, "Swift CEO Expects More Hacking Surprises as Fix Is Years Away," *Bloomberg Business Week*, June 2, 2016.

The problems created by the $81 million theft resulting from break-ins to the SWIFT global banking network illustrate some of the reasons businesses need to pay special attention to information system security. The SWIFT system is a critical tool for global business. But from a security standpoint, as this case illustrates, the system was vulnerable to hackers who were able to access supposedly protected user authentication data.

The chapter-opening diagram calls attention to important points raised by this case and this chapter. The SWIFT system is flexible and easy to use and does not require the same high level of security among its participating institutions. Although major banks in the United States using the SWIFT network have strong information system security in place, the security used by other SWIFT network members for protecting global banking transactions was weak. Despite the strong security safeguards of the SWIFT network itself, criminals were able to break into the systems of SWIFT member banks and send false

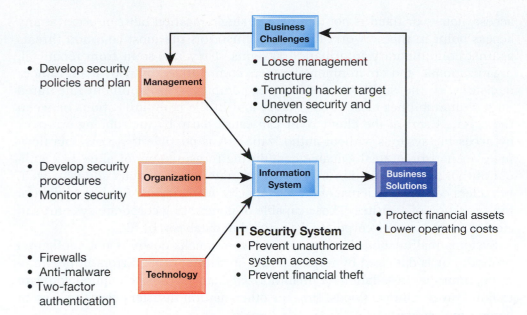

instructions over the SWIFT system to illicitly transfer funds to their accounts. SWIFT is now working with member institutions to upgrade their security, but it will take years before all participants in the network are fully protected.

Here are some questions to think about: What security vulnerabilities were exploited by the hackers? What management, organizational, and technological factors contributed to these security weaknesses? What was the business impact of these problems?

8-1 Why are information systems vulnerable to destruction, error, and abuse?

Can you imagine what would happen if you tried to link to the Internet without a firewall or antivirus software? Your computer would be disabled in a few seconds, and it might take you many days to recover. If you used the computer to run your business, you might not be able to sell to your customers or place orders with your suppliers while it was down. And you might find that your computer system had been penetrated by outsiders, who perhaps stole or destroyed valuable data, including confidential payment data from your customers. If too much data were destroyed or divulged, your business might never be able to recover!

In short, if you operate a business today, you need to make security and control a top priority. **Security** refers to the policies, procedures, and technical measures used to prevent unauthorized access, alteration, theft, or physical damage to information systems. **Controls** are methods, policies, and organizational procedures that ensure the safety of the organization's assets, the accuracy and reliability of its records, and operational adherence to management standards.

Why Systems are Vulnerable

When large amounts of data are stored in electronic form, they are vulnerable to many kinds of threats. Through communications networks, information systems in different locations are interconnected. The potential for unauthorized access, abuse, or fraud is not limited to a single location but can occur at any access point in the network. Figure 8.1 illustrates the most common threats against contemporary information systems. They can stem from technical, organizational, and environmental factors compounded by poor management decisions. In the multitier client/server computing environment illustrated here, vulnerabilities exist at each layer and in the communications between the layers. Users at the client layer can cause harm by introducing errors or by accessing systems without authorization. It is possible to access data flowing over networks, steal valuable data during transmission, or alter data without authorization. Radiation may disrupt a network at various points as well. Intruders can launch denial-of-service attacks or malicious software to disrupt the operation of websites. Those capable of penetrating corporate systems can steal, destroy, or alter corporate data stored in databases or files.

Systems malfunction if computer hardware breaks down, is not configured properly, or is damaged by improper use or criminal acts. Errors in programming, improper installation, or unauthorized changes cause computer software to fail. Power failures, floods, fires, or other natural disasters can also disrupt computer systems.

Domestic or offshore partnering with another company contributes to system vulnerability if valuable information resides on networks and computers outside the organization's control. Without strong safeguards, valuable data could be lost, destroyed, or fall into the wrong hands, revealing important trade secrets or information that violates personal privacy.

The popularity of handheld mobile devices for business computing adds to these woes. Portability makes cell phones, smartphones, and tablet computers easy to lose or steal. Smartphones share the same security weaknesses as other Internet devices and are vulnerable to malicious software and penetration from outsiders. Smartphones that corporate employees use often contain sensitive data such as sales figures, customer names, phone numbers, and e-mail addresses. Intruders may also be able to access internal corporate systems through these devices.

FIGURE 8.1   CONTEMPORARY SECURITY CHALLENGES AND VULNERABILITIES

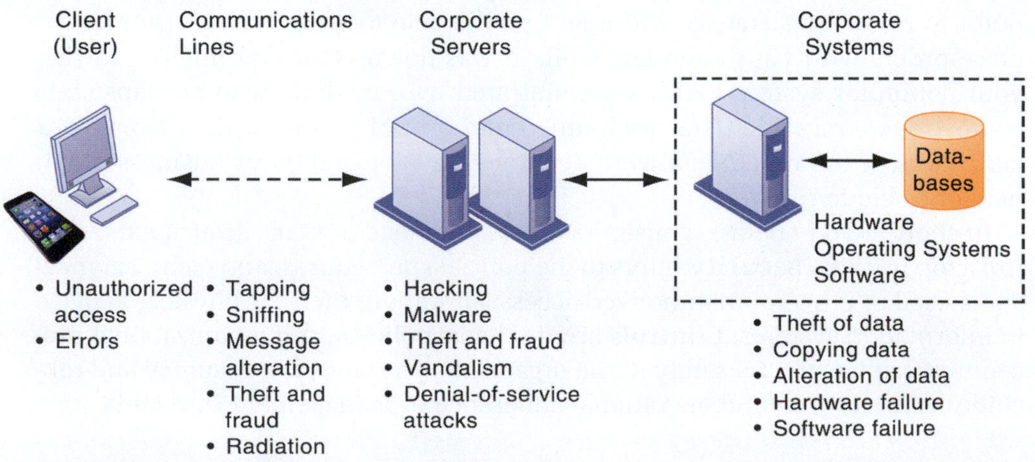

The architecture of a web-based application typically includes a web client, a server, and corporate information systems linked to databases. Each of these components presents security challenges and vulnerabilities. Floods, fires, power failures, and other electrical problems can cause disruptions at any point in the network.

Internet Vulnerabilities

Large public networks, such as the Internet, are more vulnerable than internal networks because they are virtually open to anyone. The Internet is so huge that when abuses do occur, they can have an enormously widespread impact. When the Internet becomes part of the corporate network, the organization's information systems are even more vulnerable to actions from outsiders.

Telephone service based on Internet technology (see Chapter 7) is more vulnerable than the switched voice network if it does not run over a secure private network. Most Voice over IP (VoIP) traffic over the Internet is not encrypted. Hackers can intercept conversations or shut down voice service by flooding servers supporting VoIP with bogus traffic.

Vulnerability has also increased from widespread use of e-mail, instant messaging (IM), and peer-to-peer (P2P) file-sharing programs. E-mail may contain attachments that serve as springboards for malicious software or unauthorized access to internal corporate systems. Employees may use e-mail messages to transmit valuable trade secrets, financial data, or confidential customer information to unauthorized recipients. Popular IM applications for consumers do not use a secure layer for text messages, so they can be intercepted and read by outsiders during transmission over the Internet. Instant messaging activity over the Internet can in some cases be used as a back door to an otherwise secure network. Sharing files over P2P networks, such as those for illegal music sharing, may also transmit malicious software or expose information on either individual or corporate computers to outsiders.

Wireless Security Challenges

Is it safe to log on to a wireless network at an airport, library, or other public location? It depends on how vigilant you are. Even the wireless network in your home is vulnerable because radio frequency bands are easy to scan. Both Bluetooth and Wi-Fi networks are susceptible to hacking by eavesdroppers. Local area networks (LANs) using the 802.11 standard can be easily penetrated by outsiders armed with laptops, wireless cards, external antennae, and hacking software. Hackers use these tools to detect unprotected networks, monitor network traffic, and, in some cases, gain access to the Internet or to corporate networks.

Wi-Fi transmission technology was designed to make it easy for stations to find and hear one another. The service set identifiers (SSIDs) that identify the access points in a Wi-Fi network are broadcast multiple times and can be picked up fairly easily by intruders' sniffer programs (see Figure 8.2). Wireless networks in many locations do not have basic protections against **war driving**, in which eavesdroppers drive by buildings or park outside and try to intercept wireless network traffic.

An intruder who has associated with an access point by using the correct SSID is capable of accessing other resources on the network. For example, the intruder could use the Windows operating system to determine which other users are connected to the network, access their computer hard drives, and open or copy their files.

Intruders also use the information they have gleaned to set up rogue access points on a different radio channel in physical locations close to users to force a user's radio network interface controller (NIC) to associate with the rogue access point. Once this association occurs, hackers using the rogue access point can capture the names and passwords of unsuspecting users.

FIGURE 8.2 WI-FI SECURITY CHALLENGES

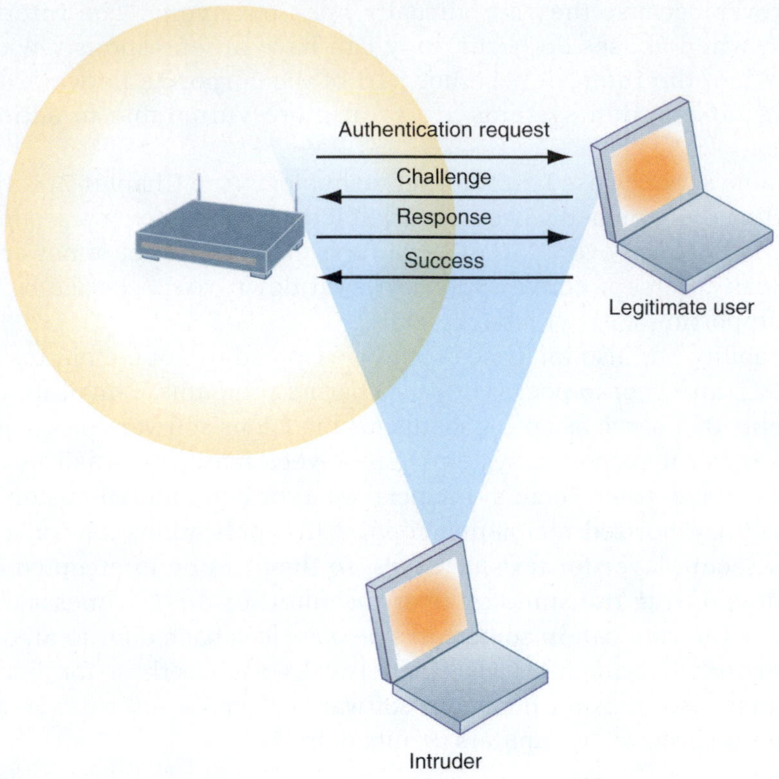

Many Wi-Fi networks can be penetrated easily by intruders using sniffer programs to obtain an address to access the resources of a network without authorization.

Malicious Software: Viruses, Worms, Trojan Horses, and Spyware

Malicious software programs are referred to as **malware** and include a variety of threats such as computer viruses, worms, and Trojan horses. (See Table 8.1.) A **computer virus** is a rogue software program that attaches itself to other software programs or data files to be executed, usually without user knowledge or permission. Most computer viruses deliver a payload. The payload may be relatively benign, such as instructions to display a message or image, or it may be highly destructive—destroying programs or data, clogging computer memory, reformatting a computer's hard drive, or causing programs to run improperly. Viruses typically spread from computer to computer when humans take an action, such as sending an e-mail attachment or copying an infected file.

Most recent attacks have come from **worms**, which are independent computer programs that copy themselves from one computer to other computers over a network. Unlike viruses, worms can operate on their own without attaching to other computer program files and rely less on human behavior to spread from computer to computer. This explains why computer worms spread much more rapidly than computer viruses. Worms destroy data and programs as well as disrupt or even halt the operation of computer networks.

Worms and viruses are often spread over the Internet from files of downloaded software; from files attached to e-mail transmissions; or from compromised e-mail messages, online ads, or instant messaging. Viruses have also invaded computerized information systems from infected disks or infected

TABLE 8.1 EXAMPLES OF MALICIOUS CODE

NAME	TYPE	DESCRIPTION
Cryptolocker	Ransomware/Trojan	Hijacks users' photos, videos, and text documents; encrypts them with virtually unbreakable asymmetric encryption; and demands ransom payment for them
Conficker	Worm	First detected in November 2008 and still a problem. Uses flaws in Windows software to take over machines and link them into a virtual computer that can be commanded remotely. Had more than 5 million computers worldwide under its control. Difficult to eradicate.
Sasser.ftp	Worm	First appeared in May 2004. Spread over the Internet by attacking random IP addresses. Causes computers to continually crash and reboot and infected computers to search for more victims. Affected millions of computers worldwide and caused an estimated $14.8 billion to $18.6 billion in damages.
ILOVEYOU	Virus	First detected on May 3, 2000. Script virus written in Visual Basic script and transmitted as an attachment to e-mail with the subject line ILOVEYOU. Overwrites music, image, and other files with a copy of itself and did an estimated $10 billion to $15 billion in damage.

machines. Especially prevalent today are **drive-by downloads**, consisting of malware that comes with a downloaded file that a user intentionally or unintentionally requests.

Hackers can do to a smartphone just about anything they can do to any Internet device: request malicious files without user intervention, delete files, transmit files, install programs running in the background to monitor user actions, and potentially convert the smartphone to a robot in a botnet to send e-mail and text messages to anyone. With smartphones outselling PCs and increasingly used as payment devices, they are becoming a major avenue for malware.

According to IT security experts, mobile devices now pose the greatest security risks, outpacing those from larger computers. By the end of 2015, McAfee Labs had collected more than 6 million samples of mobile malware (Snell, 2016). Android, which is the world's leading mobile operating system, is the platform targeted by most hackers. Mobile device viruses pose serious threats to enterprise computing because so many wireless devices are now linked to corporate information systems (see the Interactive Session on Technology in Section 8-4).

Blogs, wikis, and social networking sites such as Facebook, Twitter, and LinkedIn have emerged as new conduits for malware. Members are more likely to trust messages they receive from friends, even if this communication is not legitimate. One malware scam in spring 2015 appeared to be a video link from a friend saying something like, "This is awesome." If the recipient clicked the link, a pop-up window appeared and prompted that person to click an Adobe Flash Player update to continue. Instead of downloading the player, the malware took over the user's computer, looking for bank account numbers, medical records, and other personal data (Thompson, 2015).

Security risks are bound to increase from the mushrooming number of Internet-linked devices within companies and across the Internet. The Internet of Things (IoT) introduces a wide range of new security challenges to

IoT devices themselves, their platforms and operating systems, their communications, and even the systems to which they're connected. Additional security tools will be required to protect IoT devices and platforms from both information attacks and physical tampering, to encrypt their communications, and to address new challenges such as attacks that drain batteries. Many IoT devices such as sensors have simple processors and operating systems that may not support sophisticated security approaches.

Panda Security reported that it had identified and neutralized more than 84 million new malware samples throughout 2015 and that it had detected 230,000 new malware samples each day. More than 27 percent of all malware samples ever recorded were created in that one year alone (Panda Security, 2016).

More than 51 percent of the infections Panda found were Trojan horses. A **Trojan horse** is a software program that appears to be benign but then does something other than expected. The Trojan horse is not itself a virus because it does not replicate, but it is often a way for viruses or other malicious code to be introduced into a computer system. The term *Trojan horse* is based on the huge wooden horse the Greeks used to trick the Trojans into opening the gates to their fortified city during the Trojan War. Once inside the city walls, Greek soldiers hidden in the horse revealed themselves and captured the city.

An example of a modern-day Trojan horse is the Zeus Trojan. It is often used to steal login credentials for banking by surreptitiously capturing people's keystrokes as they use their computers. Zeus is spread mainly through drive-by downloads and phishing, and recent variants are hard for anti-malware tools to detect.

SQL injection attacks have become a major malware threat. SQL injection attacks take advantage of vulnerabilities in poorly coded web application software to introduce malicious program code into a company's systems and networks. These vulnerabilities occur when a web application fails to validate properly or filter data a user enters on a web page, which might occur when ordering something online. An attacker uses this input validation error to send a rogue SQL query to the underlying database to access the database, plant malicious code, or access other systems on the network. Large web applications have hundreds of places for inputting user data, each of which creates an opportunity for an SQL injection attack.

Malware known as **ransomware** is proliferating on both desktop and mobile devices. Ransomware tries to extort money from users by taking control of their computers or displaying annoying pop-up messages. One nasty example, CryptoLocker, encrypts an infected computer's files, forcing users to pay hundreds of dollars to regain access. You can get ransomware from downloading an infected attachment, clicking a link inside an e-mail, or visiting the wrong website.

Some types of **spyware** also act as malicious software. These small programs install themselves surreptitiously on computers to monitor user web-surfing activity and serve up advertising. Thousands of forms of spyware have been documented.

Many users find such spyware annoying, and some critics worry about its infringement on computer users' privacy. Some forms of spyware are especially nefarious. **Keyloggers** record every keystroke made on a computer to steal serial numbers for software, to launch Internet attacks, to gain access to e-mail accounts, to obtain passwords to protected computer systems, or to pick up personal information such as credit card or bank account numbers. The Zeus Trojan described earlier uses keylogging. Other spyware programs reset web browser home pages, redirect search requests, or slow performance by taking up too much memory.

Hackers and Computer Crime

A **hacker** is an individual who intends to gain unauthorized access to a computer system. Within the hacking community, the term *cracker* is typically used to denote a hacker with criminal intent, although in the public press, the terms *hacker* and *cracker* are used interchangeably. Hackers gain unauthorized access by finding weaknesses in the security protections websites and computer systems employ, often taking advantage of various features of the Internet that make it an open system and easy to use. Hacker activities have broadened beyond mere system intrusion to include theft of goods and information as well as system damage and **cybervandalism**, the intentional disruption, defacement, or even destruction of a website or corporate information system.

Spoofing and Sniffing

Hackers attempting to hide their true identities often spoof, or misrepresent, themselves by using fake e-mail addresses or masquerading as someone else. **Spoofing** may also involve redirecting a web link to an address different from the intended one, with the site masquerading as the intended destination. For example, if hackers redirect customers to a fake website that looks almost exactly like the true site, they can then collect and process orders, effectively stealing business as well as sensitive customer information from the true site. We will provide more detail about other forms of spoofing in our discussion of computer crime.

A **sniffer** is a type of eavesdropping program that monitors information traveling over a network. When used legitimately, sniffers help identify potential network trouble spots or criminal activity on networks, but when used for criminal purposes, they can be damaging and very difficult to detect. Sniffers enable hackers to steal proprietary information from anywhere on a network, including e-mail messages, company files, and confidential reports.

Denial-of-Service Attacks

In a **denial-of-service (DoS) attack**, hackers flood a network server or web server with many thousands of false communications or requests for services to crash the network. The network receives so many queries that it cannot keep up with them and is thus unavailable to service legitimate requests. A **distributed denial-of-service (DDoS)** attack uses numerous computers to inundate and overwhelm the network from numerous launch points.

Although DoS attacks do not destroy information or access restricted areas of a company's information systems, they often cause a website to shut down, making it impossible for legitimate users to access the site. For example, on April 27, 2015, the state of Hawaii and the Thirty Meter Telescope (TMT) were hit with a DoS attack believed to have been launched by a group called Operation Green Rights. (The TMT organization is constructing one of the biggest telescopes in the world in Hawaii.) Both organizations' websites were flooded with so much illicit traffic that they were not available until the following day (Wakida, 2015).

For busy e-commerce sites, these attacks are costly; while the site is shut down, customers cannot make purchases. Especially vulnerable are small and midsize businesses whose networks tend to be less protected than those of large corporations.

Perpetrators of DDoS attacks often use thousands of zombie PCs infected with malicious software without their owners' knowledge and organized into a **botnet**. Hackers create these botnets by infecting other people's computers with bot malware that opens a back door through which an attacker can give instructions. The infected computer then becomes a slave, or zombie, serving a master computer belonging to someone else. When hackers infect enough computers, they can use the amassed resources of the botnet to launch DDoS attacks, phishing campaigns, or unsolicited spam e-mail.

Ninety percent of the world's spam and 80 percent of the world's malware are delivered by botnets. For example, a new version of the Pushdo spamming botnet was detected in spring 2015. Computers in more than 50 countries were infected. Pushdo has existed since 2007 despite numerous attempts to shut it down. The latest version has been pushing malware that steals login credentials and accesses online banking systems. At one time, Pushdo-infected computers sent as many as 7.7 billion spam messages per day (Kirk, 2015).

Computer Crime

Most hacker activities are criminal offenses, and the vulnerabilities of systems we have just described make them targets for other types of **computer crime** as well. Computer crime is defined by the U.S. Department of Justice as "any violations of criminal law that involve a knowledge of computer technology for their perpetration, investigation, or prosecution." Table 8.2 provides examples of the computer as both a target and an instrument of crime. The chapter-opening case describes one of the largest financial computer crime cases reported to date.

No one knows the magnitude of the computer crime problem—how many systems are invaded, how many people engage in the practice, or the total economic damage. According to the Ponemon Institute's 2015 Annual Cost of Cyber Crime Study, the average annualized cost of cybercrime for U.S. companies benchmarked was $15 million per year (Ponemon Institute, 2015). Many

TABLE 8.2 EXAMPLES OF COMPUTER CRIME

COMPUTERS AS TARGETS OF CRIME
Breaching the confidentiality of protected computerized data
Accessing a computer system without authority
Knowingly accessing a protected computer to commit fraud
Intentionally accessing a protected computer and causing damage negligently or deliberately
Knowingly transmitting a program, program code, or command that intentionally causes damage to a protected computer
Threatening to cause damage to a protected computer

COMPUTERS AS INSTRUMENTS OF CRIME
Theft of trade secrets
Unauthorized copying of software or copyrighted intellectual property, such as articles, books, music, and video
Schemes to defraud
Using e-mail or messaging for threats or harassment
Intentionally attempting to intercept electronic communication
Illegally accessing stored electronic communications, including e-mail and voice mail
Transmitting or possessing child pornography by using a computer

companies are reluctant to report computer crimes because the crimes may involve employees, or the company fears that publicizing its vulnerability will hurt its reputation. The most economically damaging kinds of computer crime are DoS attacks, activities of malicious insiders, and web-based attacks.

Identity Theft

With the growth of the Internet and electronic commerce, identity theft has become especially troubling. **Identity theft** is a crime in which an imposter obtains key pieces of personal information, such as social security numbers, driver's license numbers, or credit card numbers, to impersonate someone else. The information may be used to obtain credit, merchandise, or services in the name of the victim or to provide the thief with false credentials.

Identity theft has flourished on the Internet, with credit card files a major target of website hackers. According to the 2016 Identity Fraud Study by Javelin Strategy & Research, 13.1 million consumers lost $15 billion to identity fraud in 2015 (Javelin, 2016). E-commerce sites are wonderful sources of customer personal information—name, address, and phone number. Armed with this information, criminals can assume new identities and establish new credit for their own purposes.

One increasingly popular tactic is a form of spoofing called **phishing**. Phishing involves setting up fake websites or sending e-mail messages that look like those of legitimate businesses to ask users for confidential personal data. The e-mail message instructs recipients to update or confirm records by providing social security numbers, bank and credit card information, and other confidential data either by responding to the e-mail message, by entering the information at a bogus website, or by calling a telephone number. eBay, PayPal, Amazon.com, Walmart, and a variety of banks have been among the top spoofed companies. In a more targeted form of phishing called *spear phishing*, messages appear to come from a trusted source, such as an individual within the recipient's own company or a friend.

Phishing techniques called evil twins and pharming are harder to detect. **Evil twins** are wireless networks that pretend to offer trustworthy Wi-Fi connections to the Internet, such as those in airport lounges, hotels, or coffee shops. The bogus network looks identical to a legitimate public network. Fraudsters try to capture passwords or credit card numbers of unwitting users who log on to the network.

Pharming redirects users to a bogus web page, even when the individual types the correct web page address into his or her browser. This is possible if pharming perpetrators gain access to the Internet address information Internet service providers (ISPs) store to speed up web browsing and the ISP companies have flawed software on their servers that allows the fraudsters to hack in and change those addresses.

According to the Ponemon Institute's 2015 Cost of a Data Breach Study, the average cost of a breach to a company was $3.5 million (Ponemon, 2015). Moreover, brand damage can be significant, albeit hard to quantify. In addition to the data breaches described in the opening and ending case studies for this chapter, Table 8.3 describes other major data breaches.

The U.S. Congress addressed the threat of computer crime in 1986 with the Computer Fraud and Abuse Act, which makes it illegal to access a computer system without authorization. Most states have similar laws, and nations in Europe have comparable legislation. Congress passed the National Information Infrastructure Protection Act in 1996 to make malware distribution and hacker attacks to disable websites federal crimes.

TABLE 8.3 MAJOR DATA BREACHES

DATA BREACH	DESCRIPTION
Anthem Health Insurance	In February 2015 hackers stole the personal information on more than 80 million customers of the giant health insurer, including names, birthdays, medical IDs, social security numbers, and income data. No medical or credit information was stolen. This was the largest healthcare breach ever recorded
Sony	In November 2014 hackers stole more than 100 terabytes of corporate data, including trade secrets, e-mail, personnel records, and copies of films for future release. Malware erased data from Sony's corporate systems, leading to hundreds of millions of dollars in losses as well as a tarnished brand image. Sony was hacked earlier in April 2011 when intruders obtained personal information, including credit, debit, and bank account numbers, from more than 100 million PlayStation Network users and Sony Online Entertainment users.
Home Depot	Hacked in 2014 with a malicious software program that plundered store registers while disguising itself as antivirus software. Fifty-six million credit card accounts were compromised, and 53 million customer e-mail addresses were stolen.
Target	Malware surreptitiously installed on security and payment systems in late 2013 stole credit card numbers and identifying data for 40 million Target customers and e-mail addresses of 70 million customers.
eBay	Cyberattack on eBay servers during February and March 2014 compromised database containing customer names, encrypted passwords, e-mail addresses, physical addresses, phone numbers, and birthdates; 145 million people were affected.

U.S. legislation, such as the Wiretap Act, Wire Fraud Act, Economic Espionage Act, Electronic Communications Privacy Act, CAN-SPAM Act, and Protect Act of 2003 (prohibiting child pornograpy), covers computer crimes involving intercepting electronic communication, using electronic communication to defraud, stealing trade secrets, illegally accessing stored electronic communications, using e-mail for threats or harassment, and transmitting or possessing child pornography. A proposed federal Data Security and Breach Notification Act would mandate organizations that possess personal information to put in place "reasonable" security procedures to keep the data secure and notify anyone affected by a data breach, but it has not been enacted.

Click Fraud

When you click an ad displayed by a search engine, the advertiser typically pays a fee for each click, which is supposed to direct potential buyers to its products. **Click fraud** occurs when an individual or computer program fraudulently clicks an online ad without any intention of learning more about the advertiser or making a purchase. Click fraud has become a serious problem at Google and other websites that feature pay-per-click online advertising.

Some companies hire third parties (typically from low-wage countries) to click a competitor's ads fraudulently to weaken them by driving up their marketing costs. Click fraud can also be perpetrated with software programs doing the clicking, and botnets are often used for this purpose. Search engines such as Google attempt to monitor click fraud and have made some changes to curb it.

Global Threats: Cyberterrorism and Cyberwarfare

The cyber criminal activities we have described—launching malware, DoS attacks, and phishing probes—are borderless. Attack servers for malware are now hosted in more than 200 countries and territories. The most popular sources of malware attacks include the United States, India, Germany, South Korea, China, Netherlands, United Kingdom, and Russia. The global nature of the Internet makes it possible for cybercriminals to operate—and to do harm—anywhere in the world.

Internet vulnerabilities have also turned individuals and even entire nation-states into easy targets for politically motivated hacking to conduct sabotage and espionage. **Cyberwarfare** is a state-sponsored activity designed to cripple and defeat another state or nation by penetrating its computers or networks to cause damage and disruption. Cyberwarfare also includes defending against these types of attacks.

Cyberwarfare is more complex than conventional warfare. Although many potential targets are military, a country's power grids, financial systems, and communications networks can also be crippled. Non-state actors such as terrorists or criminal groups can mount attacks, and it is often difficult to tell who is responsible. Nations must constantly be on the alert for new malware and other technologies that could be used against them, and some of these technologies developed by skilled hacker groups are openly for sale to interested governments.

Preparations for cyberwarfare attacks have become much more widespread, sophisticated, and potentially devastating. Between 2011 and 2015, foreign hackers stole source code and blueprints to the oil and water pipelines and power grid of the United States and infiltrated the Department of Energy's networks 150 times (Perlroth, 2015). Over the years, hackers have stolen plans for missile tracking systems, satellite navigation devices, surveillance drones, and leading-edge jet fighters.

A 2015 report documented 29 countries with formal military and intelligence units dedicated to offensive cyberwarfare. Their cyberarsenals include collections of malware for penetrating industrial, military, and critical civilian infrastructure controllers, e-mail lists and text for phishing attacks on important targets, and algorithms for DoS attacks. U.S. cyberwarfare efforts are concentrated in the United States Cyber Command, which coordinates and directs the operations and defense of Department of Defense information networks and prepares for military cyberspace operations. Cyberwarfare poses a serious threat to the infrastructure of modern societies, since their major financial, health, government, and industrial institutions rely on the Internet for daily operations.

Internal Threats: Employees

We tend to think the security threats to a business originate outside the organization. In fact, company insiders pose serious security problems. Employees have access to privileged information, and in the presence of sloppy internal security procedures, they are often able to roam throughout an organization's systems without leaving a trace.

Studies have found that user lack of knowledge is the single greatest cause of network security breaches. Many employees forget their passwords to access computer systems or allow coworkers to use them, which compromises the system. Malicious intruders seeking system access sometimes trick employees into revealing their passwords by pretending to be legitimate members of the company in need of information. This practice is called **social engineering**.

Both end users and information systems specialists are also a major source of errors introduced into information systems. End users introduce errors by entering faulty data or by not following the proper instructions for processing data and using computer equipment. Information systems specialists may create software errors as they design and develop new software or maintain existing programs.

Software Vulnerability

Software errors pose a constant threat to information systems, causing untold losses in productivity and sometimes endangering people who use or depend on systems. Growing complexity and size of software programs, coupled with demands for timely delivery to markets, have contributed to an increase in software flaws or vulnerabilities. On April 29, 2015, American Airlines had to delay 40 flights due to faulty software on iPads pilots use to look at airport maps and navigational documents. The problem was fixed by having the pilots delete the malfunctioning app and reinstall it (Bajaj, 2015).

A major problem with software is the presence of hidden **bugs** or program code defects. Studies have shown that it is virtually impossible to eliminate all bugs from large programs. The main source of bugs is the complexity of decision-making code. A relatively small program of several hundred lines will contain tens of decisions leading to hundreds or even thousands of paths. Important programs within most corporations are usually much larger, containing tens of thousands or even millions of lines of code, each with many times the choices and paths of the smaller programs.

Zero defects cannot be achieved in larger programs. Complete testing simply is not possible. Fully testing programs that contain thousands of choices and millions of paths would require thousands of years. Even with rigorous testing, you would not know for sure that a piece of software was dependable until the product proved itself after much operational use.

Flaws in commercial software not only impede performance but also create security vulnerabilities that open networks to intruders. Each year security firms identify thousands of software vulnerabilities in Internet and PC software. A recent example is the Heartbleed bug, which is a flaw in OpenSSL, an open-source encryption technology that an estimated two-thirds of web servers use. Hackers could exploit the bug to access visitors' personal data as well as a site's encryption keys, which can be used to collect even more protected data.

Especially troublesome are **zero-day vulnerabilities**, which are holes in the software unknown to its creator. Hackers then exploit this security hole before the vendor becomes aware of the problem and hurries to fix it. This type of vulnerability is called zero day because the author of the software has zero days after learning about it to patch the code before it can be exploited in an attack. Sometimes security researchers spot the software holes but, more often, they remain undetected until an attack has occurred.

To correct software flaws once they are identified, the software vendor creates small pieces of software called **patches** to repair the flaws without disturbing the proper operation of the software. It is up to users of the software to track these vulnerabilities, test, and apply all patches. This process is called *patch management*.

Because a company's IT infrastructure is typically laden with multiple business applications, operating system installations, and other system services, maintaining patches on all devices and services a company uses is often time-consuming and costly. Malware is being created so rapidly that companies have very little time to respond between the time a vulnerability and a patch are announced and the time malicious software appears to exploit the vulnerability.

8-2 What is the business value of security and control?

Companies have very valuable information assets to protect. Systems often house confidential information about individuals' taxes, financial assets, medical records, and job performance reviews. They also can contain information on corporate operations, including trade secrets, new product development plans, and marketing strategies. Government systems may store information on weapons systems, intelligence operations, and military targets. These information assets have tremendous value, and the repercussions can be devastating if they are lost, destroyed, or placed in the wrong hands. Systems that are unable to function because of security breaches, disasters, or malfunctioning technology can have permanent impacts on a company's financial health. Some experts believe that 40 percent of all businesses will not recover from application or data losses that are not repaired within three days.

Inadequate security and control may result in serious legal liability. Businesses must protect not only their own information assets but also those of customers, employees, and business partners. Failure to do so may open the firm to costly litigation for data exposure or theft. An organization can be held liable for needless risk and harm created if the organization fails to take appropriate protective action to prevent loss of confidential information, data corruption, or breach of privacy. For example, Target had to pay $39 million to several U.S. banks servicing Mastercard that were forced to reimburse Target customers millions of dollars when those customers lost money due to a massive 2013 hack of Target's payment systems affecting 40 million people. Target also paid $67 million to Visa for the data hack and $10 million to settle a class-action lawsuit brought by Target customers. A sound security and control framework that protects business information assets can thus produce a high return on investment. Strong security and control also increase employee productivity and lower operational costs.

Legal and Regulatory Requirements for Electronic Records Management

U.S. government regulations are forcing companies to take security and control more seriously by mandating the protection of data from abuse, exposure, and unauthorized access. Firms face new legal obligations for the retention and storage of electronic records as well as for privacy protection.

If you work in the healthcare industry, your firm will need to comply with the Health Insurance Portability and Accountability Act (HIPAA) of 1996. **HIPAA** outlines medical security and privacy rules and procedures for simplifying the administration of healthcare billing and automating the transfer of healthcare data between healthcare providers, payers, and plans. It requires members of the healthcare industry to retain patient information for six years and ensure the confidentiality of those records. It specifies privacy, security, and electronic transaction standards for healthcare providers handling patient information, providing penalties for breaches of medical privacy, disclosure of patient records by e-mail, or unauthorized network access.

If you work in a firm providing financial services, your firm will need to comply with the Financial Services Modernization Act of 1999, better known as the **Gramm-Leach-Bliley Act** after its congressional sponsors. This act requires financial institutions to ensure the security and confidentiality of customer data. Data must be stored on a secure medium, and special security measures must be enforced to protect such data on storage media and during transmittal.

If you work in a publicly traded company, your company will need to comply with the Public Company Accounting Reform and Investor Protection Act of 2002, better known as the **Sarbanes-Oxley Act** after its sponsors Senator Paul Sarbanes of Maryland and Representative Michael Oxley of Ohio. This act was designed to protect investors after the financial scandals at Enron, WorldCom, and other public companies. It imposes responsibility on companies and their management to safeguard the accuracy and integrity of financial information that is used internally and released externally. One of the Learning Tracks for this chapter discusses Sarbanes-Oxley in detail.

Sarbanes-Oxley is fundamentally about ensuring that internal controls are in place to govern the creation and documentation of information in financial statements. Because information systems are used to generate, store, and transport such data, the legislation requires firms to consider information systems security and other controls required to ensure the integrity, confidentiality, and accuracy of their data. Each system application that deals with critical financial reporting data requires controls to make sure the data are accurate. Controls to secure the corporate network, prevent unauthorized access to systems and data, and ensure data integrity and availability in the event of disaster or other disruption of service are essential as well.

Electronic Evidence and Computer Forensics

Security, control, and electronic records management have become essential for responding to legal actions. Much of the evidence today for stock fraud, embezzlement, theft of company trade secrets, computer crime, and many civil cases is in digital form. In addition to information from printed or typewritten pages, legal cases today increasingly rely on evidence represented as digital data stored on portable storage devices, CDs, and computer hard disk drives as well as in e-mail, instant messages, and e-commerce transactions over the Internet. E-mail is currently the most common type of electronic evidence.

In a legal action, a firm is obligated to respond to a discovery request for access to information that may be used as evidence, and the company is required by law to produce those data. The cost of responding to a discovery request can be enormous if the company has trouble assembling the required data or the data have been corrupted or destroyed. Courts now impose severe financial and even criminal penalties for improper destruction of electronic documents.

An effective electronic document retention policy ensures that electronic documents, e-mail, and other records are well organized, accessible, and neither retained too long nor discarded too soon. It also reflects an awareness of how to preserve potential evidence for computer forensics. **Computer forensics** is the scientific collection, examination, authentication, preservation, and analysis of data held on or retrieved from computer storage media in such a way that the information can be used as evidence in a court of law. It deals with the following problems.

- Recovering data from computers while preserving evidential integrity
- Securely storing and handling recovered electronic data

- Finding significant information in a large volume of electronic data
- Presenting the information to a court of law

Electronic evidence may reside on computer storage media in the form of computer files and as *ambient data*, which are not visible to the average user. An example might be a file that has been deleted on a PC hard drive. Data that a computer user may have deleted on computer storage media can often be recovered through various techniques. Computer forensics experts try to recover such hidden data for presentation as evidence.

An awareness of computer forensics should be incorporated into a firm's contingency planning process. The CIO, security specialists, information systems staff, and corporate legal counsel should all work together to have a plan in place that can be executed if a legal need arises. You can find out more about computer forensics in the Learning Tracks for this chapter.

8-3 What are the components of an organizational framework for security and control?

Even with the best security tools, your information systems won't be reliable and secure unless you know how and where to deploy them. You'll need to know where your company is at risk and what controls you must have in place to protect your information systems. You'll also need to develop a security policy and plans for keeping your business running if your information systems aren't operational.

Information Systems Controls

Information systems controls are both manual and automated and consist of general and application controls. **General controls** govern the design, security, and use of computer programs and the security of data files in general throughout the organization's information technology infrastructure. On the whole, general controls apply to all computerized applications and consist of a combination of hardware, software, and manual procedures that create an overall control environment.

General controls include software controls, physical hardware controls, computer operations controls, data security controls, controls over the systems development process, and administrative controls. Table 8.4 describes the functions of each of these controls.

Application controls are specific controls unique to each computerized application, such as payroll or order processing. They include both automated and manual procedures that ensure that only authorized data are completely and accurately processed by that application. Application controls can be classified as (1) input controls, (2) processing controls, and (3) output controls.

Input controls check data for accuracy and completeness when they enter the system. There are specific input controls for input authorization, data conversion, data editing, and error handling. *Processing controls* establish that data are complete and accurate during updating. *Output controls ensure* that the results of computer processing are accurate, complete, and properly distributed. You can find more detail about application and general controls in our Learning Tracks.

TABLE 8.4 GENERAL CONTROLS

TYPE OF GENERAL CONTROL	DESCRIPTION
Software controls	Monitor the use of system software and prevent unauthorized access and use of software programs, system software, and computer programs.
Hardware controls	Ensure that computer hardware is physically secure and check for equipment malfunction. Organizations that are critically dependent on their computers also must make provisions for backup or continued operation to maintain constant service.
Computer operations controls	Oversee the work of the computer department to ensure that programmed procedures are consistently and correctly applied to the storage and processing of data. They include controls over the setup of computer processing jobs and backup and recovery procedures for processing that ends abnormally.
Data security controls	Ensure that valuable business data files maintained internally or by an external hosting service are not subject to unauthorized access, change, or destruction while they are in use or in storage.
Implementation controls	Audit the systems development process at various points to ensure that the process is properly controlled and managed.
Administrative controls	Formalize standards, rules, procedures, and control disciplines to ensure that the organization's general and application controls are properly executed and enforced.

Information systems controls should not be an afterthought. They need to be incorporated into the design of a system and should consider not only how the system will perform under all possible conditions but also the behavior of organizations and people using the system. The Interactive Session on Organizations describes control weaknesses in systems that many organizations and people use for electronic trading and the role they played in the 2010 flash crash.

Risk Assessment

Before your company commits resources to security and information systems controls, it must know which assets require protection and the extent to which these assets are vulnerable. A risk assessment helps answer these questions and determine the most cost-effective set of controls for protecting assets.

A **risk assessment** determines the level of risk to the firm if a specific activity or process is not properly controlled. Not all risks can be anticipated and measured, but most businesses will be able to acquire some understanding of the risks they face. Business managers working with information systems specialists should try to determine the value of information assets, points of vulnerability, the likely frequency of a problem, and the potential for damage. For example, if an event is likely to occur no more than once a year, with a maximum of a $1000 loss to the organization, it is not wise to spend $20,000 on the design and maintenance of a control to protect against that event. However, if that same event could occur at least once a day, with a potential loss of more than $300,000 a year, $100,000 spent on a control might be entirely appropriate.

INTERACTIVE SESSION: ORGANIZATIONS

The Flash Crash: A New Culprit

At 2:42 p.m. on May 6, 2010, U.S. stock markets suffered a trillion-dollar stock market crash lasting 26 minutes. During that brief period, the Dow Jones Industrial Average, which represents 30 of the largest American companies, plummeted more than 600 points in less than five minutes. Shares of some prominent companies such as Procter & Gamble and Accenture traded down as low as a penny or as high as $100,000. By 3:07 p.m., the market had regained nearly all the points it had lost that afternoon. Nevertheless, some were left with huge losses and others with enormous profits from this flash crash, and the confidence of the American public in the stock market was severely shaken.

How could this have happened? Several financial companies, such as Universa Investments and Waddell & Reed, had placed very large trades betting that the S&P 500 index would drop. After these trades, the market began spiraling downward as other investors rapidly followed suit, selling or making bets of their own to reduce their risk. The market was overwhelmed by sell orders with no legitimate buyers to meet those orders.

Experts initially attributed the crash to structural and organizational features of the electronic trading systems that execute the majority of trades on the Dow and the rest of the world's major stock exchanges. The huge wave of flash crash sell orders intensified because of high-speed computerized trading programs. High-frequency traders (HFTs) have taken over many of the responsibilities once filled by stock exchange specialists and market makers whose job was to provide the majority of stock market liquidity. But many electronic systems, such as those HFTs use, are automated, using algorithms to place their nearly instant trades. In situations like the flash crash, when an algorithm is insufficient to handle the complexity of the event in progress, electronic trading systems have the potential to make a bad situation much worse.

Five years later, another explanation emerged. A single trader who operated out of his West London home was largely responsible for the event. On April 21, 2015, the United States Justice Department had British authorities arrest 36-year-old Navinder Sarao, charging him with profiting from the flash crash by boldly manipulating markets and using illegal trading strategies between 2009 and 2014. Sarao was accused of having placed and withdrawn thousands of orders worth tens of millions of dollars each on hundreds of trading days to push down the price of futures contracts tied to the value of the Standard & Poor's 500 stock index. (A futures contract is an agreement to buy or sell a particular commodity or financial instrument at a predetermined price in the future.) When the price fell, Sarao would buy the contract and realize profits.

On the day of the flash crash, Sarao repeatedly placed large orders representing $170 million to more than $200 million and then canceled them just before they were executed, making the market even more vulnerable to big moves when several other investors made a big trade that day. The falling price of the futures contracts that Sarao was trading spread to related markets, triggering a cascade of trades and contributing to the Dow Jones industrial average 600-point free fall.

This technique is called *spoofing* or *layering*, and it is illegal. A trader enters large orders to buy or sell a contract to trick other traders into thinking the price is rising or falling. That trader then quickly cancels the original order and places other orders that take advantage of the price movements. The illegal strategy can be executed in fractions of a second, which makes surveillance difficult.

Authorities said Sarao had pocketed $40 million in profits from 2010 to 2014 through such manipulations, including $879,000 on the day of the flash crash. They allege that Sarao tinkered with commercially available software to create an automated trading algorithm that allowed him to place and cancel orders instantaneously. Sarao claims that he is an "old school point-and-click" trader with unusually good reflexes and intuition and that he had canceled large volumes of orders manually without the help of an automated trading program. He also noted that he had complained more than 100 times to the Chicago Mercantile Exchange, where he had traded futures contracts, about the manipulative trading practices of other HFTs.

Long before the flash crash, the exchange had questioned Sarao about his trading activity, but the exchange did not take any action against him, and Sarao continued his trading activities until April 2015. Finally, a whistleblower brought new information to the Commodity Futures Trading Commission

(CFTC), which oversees the futures markets. This whistleblower, who declined to be identified, had spent hundreds of hours analyzing data. A new team of investigators from the U.S. Justice Department and the CFTC worked over two years to construct a case against Sarao for manipulating the market and contributing to the flash crash.

The CFTC did not blame the crash solely on Sarao, but according to the Commission's director of enforcement, Aitan Goelman, Sarao's conduct was significantly responsible for the order imbalance that led to the crash. Sarao's lawyers argued that the crash was caused by other factors and market participants. If convicted of all charges, Sarao could face a prison sentence of more than 300 years.

It is now believed that investigators overlooked evidence available hours after the flash crash that could have led them to Sarao. At that time, investigators had access to the full set of data from the day of the flash crash but focused only on the data related to actual trades. If they had included all bids and offers entered, they would have more likely noticed the pattern of Sarao's market manipulation.

After the flash crash, several reforms were implemented, including a system to slow trading in stocks if they became too volatile and a requirement for trading firms sending orders into the market to tighten their risk controls. The financial industry is also working on a consolidated audit trail, or CAT, that would enable regulators to monitor stock and options orders in real time and quickly pinpoint manipulators. CAT has yet to be completed.

Sources: Aruna Chad Bray, "Judge Orders Extradition to U.S. in 'Flash Crash' Case," *New York Times,* March 23, 2016; Aruna Viswanatha, Bradley Hope, and Chiara Albanese, "Accused Trader Accused His Rivals," *Wall Street Journal,* May 14, 2015; Aruna Viswatnatha, Bradley Hope, and Jennny Strasburg, " ' Flash Crash' Charges Filed," *Wall Street Journal,* April 21, 2015; Bradley Hope and Andrew Ackerman, "'Flash Crash' Overhaul Is Snarled in Red Tape," *Wall Street Journal,* May 5, 2015; Nathaniel Popper and Jenny Anderson, "Trader Arrested in Manipulation That Contributed to 2010 'Flash Crash,'" *New York Times,* April 21, 2015; Bradley Hope and Andrew Ackerman, "'Flash Crash' Investigators Likely Missed Clues," *Wall Street Journal,* April 26, 2015.

CASE STUDY QUESTIONS

1. Identify the problem and the control weaknesses described in this case.

2. What management, organization, and technology factors contributed to this problem? To what extent was it a technology problem? To what extent was it a management and organizational problem?

3. To what extent was Sarao responsible? Explain your answer.

4. Is there an effective solution to this problem? Can another flash crash be prevented? Explain your answer.

Table 8.5 illustrates sample results of a risk assessment for an online order processing system that processes 30,000 orders per day. The likelihood of each exposure occurring over a one-year period is expressed as a percentage. The next column shows the highest and lowest possible loss that could be expected each time the exposure occurred and an average loss calculated by adding the highest and lowest figures and dividing by two. The expected annual loss for each exposure can be determined by multiplying the average loss by its probability of occurrence.

This risk assessment shows that the probability of a power failure occurring in a one-year period is 30 percent. Loss of order transactions while power is down could range from $5000 to $200,000 (averaging $102,500) for each occurrence, depending on how long processing is halted. The probability of embezzlement occurring over a yearly period is about 5 percent, with potential losses ranging from $1000 to $50,000 (and averaging $25,500) for each occurrence. User errors have a 98 percent chance of occurring over a yearly period, with losses ranging from $200 to $40,000 (and averaging $20,100) for each occurrence.

TABLE 8.5 ONLINE ORDER PROCESSING RISK ASSESSMENT

EXPOSURE	PROBABILITY OF OCCURRENCE (%)	LOSS RANGE/ AVERAGE ($)	EXPECTED ANNUAL LOSS ($)
Power failure	30%	$5000–$200,000 ($102,500)	$30,750
Embezzlement	5%	$1000–$50,000 ($25,500)	$1275
User error	98%	$200–$40,000 ($20,100)	$19,698

After the risks have been assessed, system builders will concentrate on the control points with the greatest vulnerability and potential for loss. In this case, controls should focus on ways to minimize the risk of power failures and user errors because anticipated annual losses are highest for these areas.

Security Policy

After you've identified the main risks to your systems, your company will need to develop a security policy for protecting the company's assets. A **security policy** consists of statements ranking information risks, identifying acceptable security goals, and identifying the mechanisms for achieving these goals. What are the firm's most important information assets? Who generates and controls this information in the firm? What existing security policies are in place to protect the information? What level of risk is management willing to accept for each of these assets? Is it willing, for instance, to lose customer credit data once every 10 years? Or will it build a security system for credit card data that can withstand the once-in-a-hundred-year disaster? Management must estimate how much it will cost to achieve this level of acceptable risk.

The security policy drives other policies determining acceptable use of the firm's information resources and which members of the company have access to its information assets. An **acceptable use policy (AUP)** defines acceptable uses of the firm's information resources and computing equipment, including desktop and laptop computers, wireless devices, telephones, and the Internet. A good AUP defines unacceptable and acceptable actions for every user and specifies consequences for noncompliance.

Security policy also includes provisions for identity management. **Identity management** consists of business processes and software tools for identifying the valid users of a system and controlling their access to system resources. It includes policies for identifying and authorizing different categories of system users, specifying what systems or portions of systems each user is allowed to access, and the processes and technologies for authenticating users and protecting their identities.

Figure 8.3 is one example of how an identity management system might capture the access rules for different levels of users in the human resources function. It specifies what portions of a human resource database each user is permitted to access, based on the information required to perform that person's job. The database contains sensitive personal information such as employees' salaries, benefits, and medical histories.

The access rules illustrated here are for two sets of users. One set of users consists of all employees who perform clerical functions, such as inputting employee data into the system. All individuals with this type of profile can update the system but can neither read nor update sensitive fields, such as

FIGURE 8.3   ACCESS RULES FOR A PERSONNEL SYSTEM

SECURITY PROFILE 1	
User: Personnel Dept. Clerk	
Location: Division 1	
Employee Identification Codes with This Profile:	00753, 27834, 37665, 44116
Data Field Restrictions	**Type of Access**
All employee data for Division 1 only	Read and Update
• Medical history data	None
• Salary	None
• Pensionable earnings	None

SECURITY PROFILE 2	
User: Divisional Personnel Manager	
Location: Division 1	
Employee Identification Codes with This Profile: 27321	
Data Field Restrictions	**Type of Access**
All employee data for Division 1 only	Read Only

These two examples represent two security profiles or data security patterns that might be found in a personnel system. Depending on the security profile, a user would have certain restrictions on access to various systems, locations, or data in an organization.

salary, medical history, or earnings data. Another profile applies to a divisional manager, who cannot update the system but who can read all employee data fields for his or her division, including medical history and salary. We provide more detail about the technologies for user authentication later on in this chapter.

Disaster Recovery Planning and Business Continuity Planning

If you run a business, you need to plan for events, such as power outages, floods, earthquakes, or terrorist attacks, that will prevent your information systems and your business from operating. **Disaster recovery planning** devises plans for the restoration of disrupted computing and communications services. Disaster recovery plans focus primarily on the technical issues involved in keeping systems up and running, such as which files to back up and the maintenance of backup computer systems or disaster recovery services.

For example, MasterCard maintains a duplicate computer center in Kansas City, Missouri, to serve as an emergency backup to its primary computer center in St. Louis. Rather than build their own backup facilities, many firms contract with disaster recovery firms such as SunGard Availability Services and Acronis. These disaster recovery firms provide hot sites housing spare computers at locations around the country where subscribing firms can run their critical applications in an emergency. For example, Champion Technologies, which supplies chemicals used in oil and gas operations, can switch its enterprise systems from Houston to a SunGard data center in Scottsdale, Arizona, in two hours.

Business continuity planning focuses on how the company can restore business operations after a disaster strikes. The business continuity plan identifies critical business processes and determines action plans for handling mission-critical functions if systems go down. For example, Deutsche Bank, which provides investment banking and asset management services in 74 countries, has a well-developed business continuity plan that it continually updates and refines. It maintains full-time teams in Singapore, Hong Kong, Japan, India, and Australia to coordinate plans addressing loss of facilities, personnel, or critical systems so that the company can continue to operate when a catastrophic event occurs. Deutsche Bank's plan distinguishes between processes critical for business survival and those critical to crisis support and is coordinated with the company's disaster recovery planning for its computer centers.

Business managers and information technology specialists need to work together on both types of plans to determine which systems and business processes are most critical to the company. They must conduct a business impact analysis to identify the firm's most critical systems and the impact a systems outage would have on the business. Management must determine the maximum amount of time the business can survive with its systems down and which parts of the business must be restored first.

The Role of Auditing

How does management know that information systems security and controls are effective? To answer this question, organizations must conduct comprehensive and systematic audits. An **information systems audit** examines the firm's overall security environment as well as controls governing individual information systems. The auditor should trace the flow of sample transactions through the system and perform tests, using, if appropriate, automated audit software. The information systems audit may also examine data quality.

Security audits review technologies, procedures, documentation, training, and personnel. A thorough audit will even simulate an attack or disaster to test the response of the technology, information systems staff, and business employees.

The audit lists and ranks all control weaknesses and estimates the probability of their occurrence. It then assesses the financial and organizational impact of each threat. Figure 8.4 is a sample auditor's listing of control weaknesses for a loan system. It includes a section for notifying management of such weaknesses and for management's response. Management is expected to devise a plan for countering significant weaknesses in controls.

8-4 What are the most important tools and technologies for safeguarding information resources?

Businesses have an array of technologies for protecting their information resources. They include tools for managing user identities, preventing unauthorized access to systems and data, ensuring system availability, and ensuring software quality.

FIGURE 8.4   SAMPLE AUDITOR'S LIST OF CONTROL WEAKNESSES

Function: Loans Location: Peoria, IL	Prepared by: J. Ericson Date: June 16, 2016		Received by: T. Benson Review date: June 28, 2016	
Nature of Weakness and Impact	**Chance for Error/Abuse**		**Notification to Management**	
	Yes/No	Justification	Report date	Management response
User accounts with missing passwords	Yes	Leaves system open to unauthorized outsiders or attackers	5/10/16	Eliminate accounts without passwords
Network configured to allow some sharing of system files	Yes	Exposes critical system files to hostile parties connected to the network	5/10/16	Ensure only required directories are shared and that they are protected with strong passwords
Software patches can update production programs without final approval from Standards and Controls group	No	All production programs require management approval; Standards and Controls group assigns such cases to a temporary production status		

This chart is a sample page from a list of control weaknesses that an auditor might find in a loan system in a local commercial bank. This form helps auditors record and evaluate control weaknesses and shows the results of discussing those weaknesses with management as well as any corrective actions management takes.

Identity Management and Authentication

Midsize and large companies have complex IT infrastructures and many systems, each with its own set of users. Identity management software automates the process of keeping track of all these users and their system privileges, assigning each user a unique digital identity for accessing each system. It also includes tools for authenticating users, protecting user identities, and controlling access to system resources.

To gain access to a system, a user must be authorized and authenticated. **Authentication** refers to the ability to know that a person is who he or she claims to be. Authentication is often established by using **passwords** known only to authorized users. An end user uses a password to log on to a computer system and may also use passwords for accessing specific systems and files. However, users often forget passwords, share them, or choose poor passwords that are easy to guess, which compromises security. Password systems that are too rigorous hinder employee productivity. When employees must change complex passwords frequently, they often take shortcuts, such as choosing passwords that are easy to guess or keeping their passwords at their workstations in plain view. Passwords can also be sniffed if transmitted over a network or stolen through social engineering.

New authentication technologies, such as tokens, smart cards, and biometric authentication, overcome some of these problems. A **token** is a physical device, similar to an identification card, that is designed to prove the identity of a single user. Tokens are small gadgets that typically fit on key rings and display passcodes that change frequently. A **smart card** is a device about the size of a credit card that contains a chip formatted with access permission and other data. (Smart cards are also used in electronic payment systems.) A reader device interprets the data on the smart card and allows or denies access.

Biometric authentication uses systems that read and interpret individual human traits, such as fingerprints, irises, and voices to grant or deny access. Biometric authentication is based on the measurement of a physical or behavioral trait that makes each individual unique. It compares a person's unique characteristics, such as the fingerprints, face, or retinal image, against a stored profile of these characteristics to determine any differences between these characteristics and the stored profile. If the two profiles match, access is granted. Fingerprint and facial recognition technologies are just beginning to be used for security applications, with many PC laptops (and some smartphones) equipped with fingerprint identification devices and several models with built-in webcams and face recognition software.

The steady stream of incidents in which hackers have been able to access traditional passwords highlights the need for more secure means of authentication. **Two-factor authentication** increases security by validating users through a multistep process. To be authenticated, a user must provide two means of identification, one of which is typically a physical token, such as a smartcard or chip-enabled bank card, and the other of which is typically data, such as a password or personal identification number (PIN). Biometric data, such as fingerprints, iris prints, or voice prints, can also be used as one of the authenticating mechanisms. A common example of two-factor authentication is a bank card; the card itself is the physical item, and the PIN is the data that go with it.

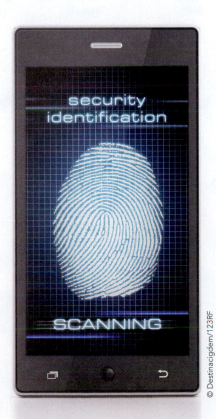

© Destinacigdem/123RF

This smartphone has a biometric fingerprint reader for fast yet secure access to files and networks. New models of PCs and smartphones are starting to use biometric identification to authenticate users.

Firewalls, Intrusion Detection Systems, and Antivirus Software

Without protection against malware and intruders, connecting to the Internet would be very dangerous. Firewalls, intrusion detection systems, and antivirus software have become essential business tools.

Firewalls

Firewalls prevent unauthorized users from accessing private networks. A firewall is a combination of hardware and software that controls the flow of incoming and outgoing network traffic. It is generally placed between the organization's private internal networks and distrusted external networks, such as the Internet, although firewalls can also be used to protect one part of a company's network from the rest of the network (see Figure 8.5).

The firewall acts like a gatekeeper that examines each user's credentials before it grants access to a network. The firewall identifies names, IP addresses, applications, and other characteristics of incoming traffic. It checks this information against the access rules that the network administrator has programmed into the system. The firewall prevents unauthorized communication into and out of the network.

In large organizations, the firewall often resides on a specially designated computer separate from the rest of the network, so no incoming request directly accesses private network resources. There are a number of firewall screening technologies, including static packet filtering, stateful inspection, Network

FIGURE 8.5   **A CORPORATE FIREWALL**

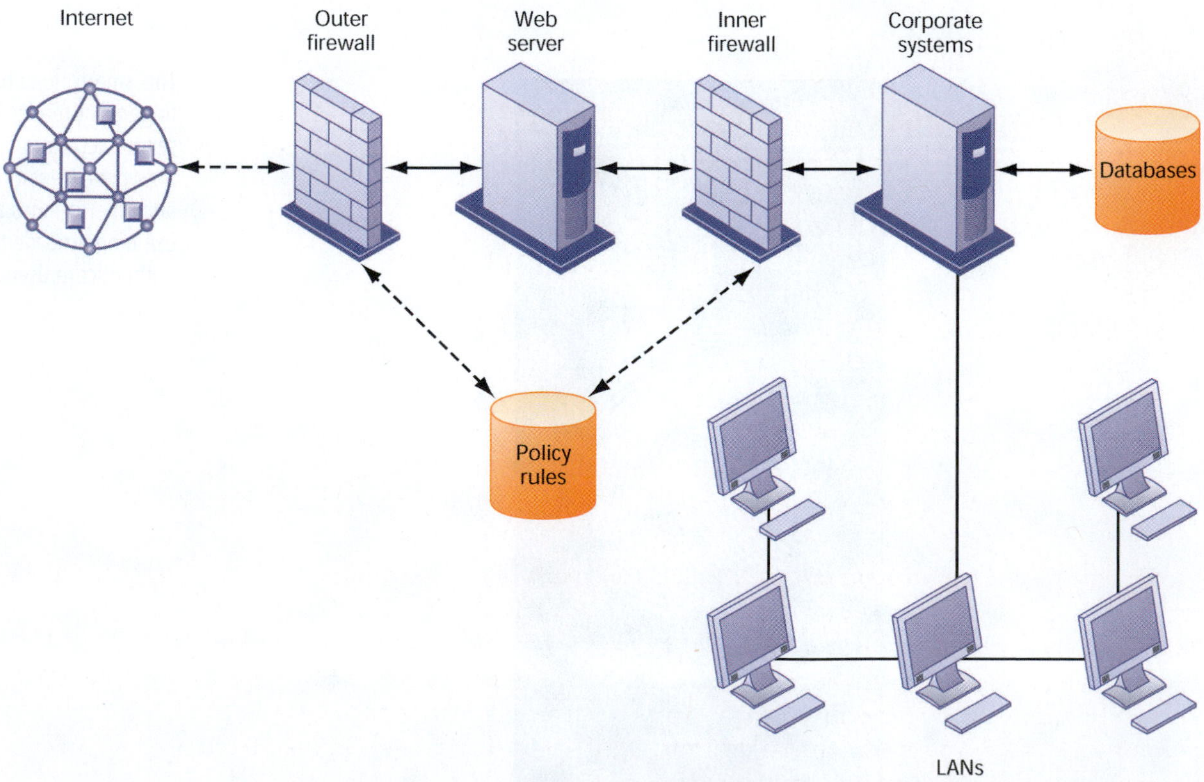

The firewall is placed between the firm's private network and the public Internet or another distrusted network to protect against unauthorized traffic.

Address Translation, and application proxy filtering. They are frequently used in combination to provide firewall protection.

Packet filtering examines selected fields in the headers of data packets flowing back and forth between the trusted network and the Internet, examining individual packets in isolation. This filtering technology can miss many types of attacks.

Stateful inspection provides additional security by determining whether packets are part of an ongoing dialogue between a sender and a receiver. It sets up state tables to track information over multiple packets. Packets are accepted or rejected based on whether they are part of an approved conversation or attempting to establish a legitimate connection.

Network Address Translation (NAT) can provide another layer of protection when static packet filtering and stateful inspection are employed. NAT conceals the IP addresses of the organization's internal host computer(s) to prevent sniffer programs outside the firewall from ascertaining them and using that information to penetrate internal systems.

Application proxy filtering examines the application content of packets. A proxy server stops data packets originating outside the organization, inspects them, and passes a proxy to the other side of the firewall. If a user outside the company wants to communicate with a user inside the organization, the outside user first communicates with the proxy application, and the proxy application communicates with the firm's internal computer. Likewise, a computer user inside the organization goes through the proxy to talk with computers on the outside.

To create a good firewall, an administrator must maintain detailed internal rules identifying the people, applications, or addresses that are allowed or rejected. Firewalls can deter, but not completely prevent, network penetration by outsiders and should be viewed as one element in an overall security plan.

Intrusion Detection Systems

In addition to firewalls, commercial security vendors now provide intrusion detection tools and services to protect against suspicious network traffic and attempts to access files and databases. **Intrusion detection systems** feature full-time monitoring tools placed at the most vulnerable points or hot spots of corporate networks to detect and deter intruders continually. The system generates an alarm if it finds a suspicious or anomalous event. Scanning software looks for patterns indicative of known methods of computer attacks such as bad passwords, checks to see whether important files have been removed or modified, and sends warnings of vandalism or system administration errors. The intrusion detection tool can also be customized to shut down a particularly sensitive part of a network if it receives unauthorized traffic.

Antivirus and Antispyware Software

Defensive technology plans for both individuals and businesses must include anti-malware protection for every computer. **Antivirus software** prevents, detects, and removes malware, including computer viruses, computer worms, Trojan horses, spyware, and adware. However, most antivirus software is effective only against malware already known when the software was written. To remain effective, the antivirus software must be continually updated. Even then it is not always effective because some malware can evade antivirus detection. Organizations need to use additional malware detection tools for better protection.

Unified Threat Management Systems

To help businesses reduce costs and improve manageability, security vendors have combined into a single appliance various security tools, including firewalls, virtual private networks, intrusion detection systems, and web content filtering and anti-spam software. These comprehensive security management products are called **unified threat management (UTM)** systems. UTM products are available for all sizes of networks. Leading UTM vendors include Fortinent, Sophos, and Check Point, and networking vendors such as Cisco Systems and Juniper Networks provide some UTM capabilities in their products.

Securing Wireless Networks

The initial security standard developed for Wi-Fi, called Wired Equivalent Privacy (WEP), is not very effective because its encryption keys are relatively easy to crack. WEP provides some margin of security, however, if users remember to enable it. Corporations can further improve Wi-Fi security by using it in conjunction with virtual private network (VPN) technology when accessing internal corporate data.

In June 2004, the Wi-Fi Alliance industry trade group finalized the 802.11i specification (also referred to as Wi-Fi Protected Access 2 or WPA2) that replaces WEP with stronger security standards. Instead of the static encryption keys used in WEP, the new standard uses much longer keys that continually change, making them harder to crack.

Encryption and Public Key Infrastructure

Many businesses use encryption to protect digital information that they store, physically transfer, or send over the Internet. **Encryption** is the process of transforming plain text or data into cipher text that cannot be read by anyone other than the sender and the intended receiver. Data are encrypted by using a secret numerical code, called an encryption key, that transforms plain data into cipher text. The message must be decrypted by the receiver.

Two methods for encrypting network traffic on the web are SSL and S-HTTP. **Secure Sockets Layer (SSL)** and its successor, Transport Layer Security (TLS), enable client and server computers to manage encryption and decryption activities as they communicate with each other during a secure web session. **Secure Hypertext Transfer Protocol (S-HTTP)** is another protocol used for encrypting data flowing over the Internet, but it is limited to individual messages, whereas SSL and TLS are designed to establish a secure connection between two computers.

The capability to generate secure sessions is built into Internet client browser software and servers. The client and the server negotiate what key and what level of security to use. Once a secure session is established between the client and the server, all messages in that session are encrypted.

Two methods of encryption are symmetric key encryption and public key encryption. In symmetric key encryption, the sender and receiver establish a secure Internet session by creating a single encryption key and sending it to the receiver so both the sender and receiver share the same key. The strength of the encryption key is measured by its bit length. Today, a typical key will be 56 to 256 bits long (a string of from 56 to 256 binary digits) depending on the level of security desired. The longer the key, the more difficult it is to break the key. The downside is that the longer the key, the more computing power it takes for legitimate users to process the information.

FIGURE 8.6   PUBLIC KEY ENCRYPTION

A public key encryption system can be viewed as a series of public and private keys that lock data when they are transmitted and unlock the data when they are received. The sender locates the recipient's public key in a directory and uses it to encrypt a message. The message is sent in encrypted form over the Internet or a private network. When the encrypted message arrives, the recipient uses his or her private key to decrypt the data and read the message.

The problem with all symmetric encryption schemes is that the key itself must be shared somehow among the senders and receivers, which exposes the key to outsiders who might just be able to intercept and decrypt the key. A more secure form of encryption called **public key encryption** uses two keys: one shared (or public) and one totally private as shown in Figure 8.6. The keys are mathematically related so that data encrypted with one key can be decrypted using only the other key. To send and receive messages, communicators first create separate pairs of private and public keys. The public key is kept in a directory, and the private key must be kept secret. The sender encrypts a message with the recipient's public key. On receiving the message, the recipient uses his or her private key to decrypt it.

Digital certificates are data files used to establish the identity of users and electronic assets for protection of online transactions (see Figure 8.7). A digital

FIGURE 8.7   DIGITAL CERTIFICATES

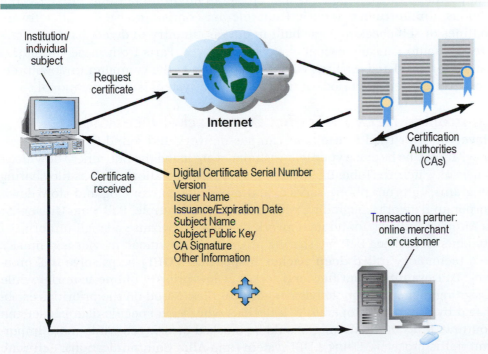

Digital certificates help establish the identity of people or electronic assets. They protect online transactions by providing secure, encrypted, online communication.

certificate system uses a trusted third party, known as a certificate authority (CA), to validate a user's identity. There are many CAs in the United States and around the world, including Symantec, GoDaddy, and Comodo.

The CA verifies a digital certificate user's identity offline. This information is put into a CA server, which generates an encrypted digital certificate containing owner identification information and a copy of the owner's public key. The certificate authenticates that the public key belongs to the designated owner. The CA makes its own public key available either in print or perhaps on the Internet. The recipient of an encrypted message uses the CA's public key to decode the digital certificate attached to the message, verifies it was issued by the CA, and then obtains the sender's public key and identification information contained in the certificate. By using this information, the recipient can send an encrypted reply. The digital certificate system would enable, for example, a credit card user and a merchant to validate that their digital certificates were issued by an authorized and trusted third party before they exchange data. **Public key infrastructure (PKI)**, the use of public key cryptography working with a CA, is now widely used in e-commerce.

Ensuring System Availability

As companies increasingly rely on digital networks for revenue and operations, they need to take additional steps to ensure that their systems and applications are always available. Firms such as those in the airline and financial services industries with critical applications requiring online transaction processing have traditionally used fault-tolerant computer systems for many years to ensure 100 percent availability. In **online transaction processing**, transactions entered online are immediately processed by the computer. Multitudinous changes to databases, reporting, and requests for information occur each instant.

Fault-tolerant computer systems contain redundant hardware, software, and power supply components that create an environment that provides continuous, uninterrupted service. Fault-tolerant computers use special software routines or self-checking logic built into their circuitry to detect hardware failures and automatically switch to a backup device. Parts from these computers can be removed and repaired without disruption to the computer or downtime. **Downtime** refers to periods of time in which a system is not operational.

Controlling Network Traffic: Deep Packet Inspection

Have you ever tried to use your campus network and found that it was very slow? It may be because your fellow students are using the network to download music or watch YouTube. Bandwith-consuming applications such as file-sharing programs, Internet phone service, and online video can clog and slow down corporate networks, degrading performance. For example, Ball State University in Muncie, Indiana, found its network had slowed because a small minority of students were using P2P file-sharing programs to download movies and music.

A technology called **deep packet inspection (DPI)** helps solve this problem. DPI examines data files and sorts out low-priority online material while assigning higher priority to business-critical files. Based on the priorities established by a network's operators, it decides whether a specific data packet can continue to its destination or should be blocked or delayed while more important traffic proceeds. Using a DPI system from Allot Communications, Ball State was able to cap the amount of file-sharing traffic and assign it a much lower priority. Ball State's preferred network traffic sped up.

Security Outsourcing

Many companies, especially small businesses, lack the resources or expertise to provide a secure high-availability computing environment on their own. They can outsource many security functions to **managed security service providers (MSSPs)** that monitor network activity and perform vulnerability testing and intrusion detection. SecureWorks, AT&T, Verizon, IBM, Perimeter eSecurity, and Symantec are leading providers of MSSP services.

Security Issues for Cloud Computing and the Mobile Digital Platform

Although cloud computing and the emerging mobile digital platform have the potential to deliver powerful benefits, they pose new challenges to system security and reliability. We now describe some of these challenges and how they should be addressed.

Security in the Cloud

When processing takes place in the cloud, accountability and responsibility for protection of sensitive data still reside with the company owning that data. Understanding how the cloud computing provider organizes its services and manages the data is critical.

Cloud computing is highly distributed. Cloud applications reside in large remote data centers and server farms that supply business services and data management for multiple corporate clients. To save money and keep costs low, cloud computing providers often distribute work to data centers around the globe where work can be accomplished most efficiently. When you use the cloud, you may not know precisely where your data are being hosted.

The dispersed nature of cloud computing makes it difficult to track unauthorized activity. Virtually all cloud providers use encryption, such as SSL, to secure the data they handle while the data are being transmitted. However, if the data are stored on devices that also store other companies' data, it's important to ensure that these stored data are encrypted as well. According to research from Alert Logic, there has been a 45 percent year-over-year increase in attacks on the cloud. DDoS attacks are especially harmful because they render cloud services unavailable to legitimate customers.

Companies expect their systems to be running 24/7. Cloud providers still experience occasional outages, but their reliability has increased to the point where a number of large companies are using cloud services for part of their IT infrastructures. Most keep their critical systems in-house.

Cloud users need to confirm that regardless of where their data are stored, they are protected at a level that meets their corporate requirements. They should stipulate that the cloud provider store and process data in specific jurisdictions according to the privacy rules of those jurisdictions. Cloud clients should find how the cloud provider segregates their corporate data from those of other companies and ask for proof that encryption mechanisms are sound. It's also important to know how the cloud provider will respond if a disaster strikes, whether the provider will be able to restore your data completely, and how long this should take. Cloud users should also ask whether cloud providers will submit to external audits and security certifications. These kinds of controls can be written into the service level agreement (SLA) before signing with a cloud provider. The Cloud Security Alliance (CSA) has created industrywide standards for cloud security, specifying best practices to secure cloud computing.

Securing Mobile Platforms

If mobile devices are performing many of the functions of computers, they need to be secured like desktops and laptops against malware, theft, accidental loss, unauthorized access, and hacking attempts. The Interactive Session on Technology describes these mobile vulnerabilities in greater detail and their implications for both individuals and businesses.

Mobile devices accessing corporate systems and data require special protection. Companies should make sure that their corporate security policy includes mobile devices, with additional details on how mobile devices should be supported, protected, and used. They will need mobile device management tools to authorize all devices in use; to maintain accurate inventory records on all mobile devices, users, and applications; to control updates to applications; and to lock down or erase lost or stolen devices so they can't be compromised. Data loss prevention technology can identify where critical data are saved, who is accessing the data, how data are leaving the company, and where the data are going. Firms should develop guidelines stipulating approved mobile platforms and software applications as well as the required software and procedures for remote access of corporate systems. The organization's mobile security policy should forbid employees from using unsecured, consumer-based applications for transferring and storing corporate documents and files or sending such documents and files to oneself by e-mail without encryption.

Companies should encrypt communication whenever possible. All mobile device users should be required to use the password feature found in every smartphone. Mobile security products are available from Kaspersky, Symantec, Trend Micro, and McAfee.

Ensuring Software Quality

In addition to implementing effective security and controls, organizations can improve system quality and reliability by employing software metrics and rigorous software testing. Software metrics are objective assessments of the system in the form of quantified measurements. Ongoing use of metrics allows the information systems department and end users to measure the performance of the system jointly and identify problems as they occur. Examples of software metrics include the number of transactions that can be processed in a specified unit of time, online response time, the number of payroll checks printed per hour, and the number of known bugs per hundred lines of program code. For metrics to be successful, they must be carefully designed, formal, objective, and used consistently.

Early, regular, and thorough testing will contribute significantly to system quality. Many view testing as a way to prove the correctness of work they have done. In fact, we know that all sizable software is riddled with errors, and we must test to uncover these errors.

Good testing begins before a software program is even written, by using a *walkthrough*—a review of a specification or design document by a small group of people carefully selected based on the skills needed for the particular objectives being tested. When developers start writing software programs, coding walkthroughs can also be used to review program code. However, code must be tested by computer runs. When errors are discovered, the source is found and eliminated through a process called *debugging*. You can find out more about the various stages of testing required to put an information system into operation in Chapter 13. Our Learning Tracks also contain descriptions of methodologies for developing software programs that contribute to software quality.

INTERACTIVE SESSION: TECHNOLOGY

BYOD: A Security Nightmare?

Bring your own device has become a huge trend, with half of employees with mobile computing tools at workplaces worldwide using their own devices. This figure is expected to increase even more in the years to come. But while use of the iPhone, iPad, and other mobile computing devices in the workplace is growing, so are security problems. Quite a few security experts believe that smartphones and other mobile devices now pose one of the most serious security threats for organizations today.

Whether mobile devices are company-assigned or employee-owned, they are opening up new avenues for accessing corporate data that need to be closely monitored and protected. Sensitive data on mobile devices travel, both physically and electronically, from the office to home and possibly other off-site locations. According to a February 2016 Ponemon Institute study of 588 U.S. IT and security professionals, 67 percent of those surveyed reported that it was certain or likely that an employee's mobile access to confidential corporate data had resulted in a data breach. Unfortunately, only 41 percent of respondents said their companies had policies for accessing corporate data from mobile devices.

More than half of security breaches occur when devices are lost or stolen. That puts all of the personal and corporate data stored on the device, as well as access to corporate data on remote servers, at risk. Physical access to mobile devices may be a greater threat than hacking into a network because less effort is required to gain entry. Experienced attackers can easily circumvent passwords or locks on mobile devices or access encrypted data. Moreover, many smartphone users leave their phones totally unprotected to begin with or fail to keep the security features of their devices up-to-date. In the Websense and the Ponemon Institute's Global Study on Mobility Risks, 59 percent of respondents reported that employees circumvented or disabled security features such as passwords and key locks.

Another worry today is large-scale data leakage caused by use of cloud computing services. Employees are increasingly using public cloud services such as Google Drive or Dropbox for file sharing and collaboration. Valiant Entertainment, Cenoric Projects, Vita Coco, and BCBGMAXAZRIAGROUP are among the companies allowing employees and freelance contractors to use Dropbox for Business to post and share files. There are also many instances where employees are using Dropbox to store and exchange files without their employers' approval. In early 2015 Dropbox had to patch a security flaw that allowed cyberattackers to steal new information uploaded to accounts through compromised third-party apps that work with Dropbox services on Android devices. There's very little a company can do to prevent employees who are allowed to use their smartphones from downloading corporate data so they can work on those data remotely.

Text messaging and other mobile messaging technologies are being used to deliver all kinds of scam campaigns, such as adult content and rogue pharmacy, phishing, and banking scams, and text messages have been a propagation medium for Trojan horses and worms. A malicious source is now able to send a text message that will open in a mobile browser by default, which can be readily utilized to exploit the recipient.

To date, deliberate hacker attacks on mobile devices have been limited in scope and impact, but this situation is worsening. Android is now the world's most popular operating system for mobile devices with 81 percent of the global market, and most mobile malware is targeted at the Android platform. When corporate and personal data are stored on the same device, mobile malware unknowingly installed by the user could find its way onto the corporate network.

Apple uses a closed "walled garden" model for managing its apps and reviews each one before releasing it on its App Store. Android application security has been weaker than that for Apple devices, but it is improving. Android application security uses sandboxing, which confines apps, minimizing their ability to affect one another or manipulate device features without user permission. Google removes any apps that break its rules against malicious activity from Google Play, its digital distribution platform that serves as the official app store for the Android operating system. Google also vets the backgrounds of developers. Recent Android security enhancements include assigning varying levels of trust to each app, dictating what kind of data an app can access inside its confined domain, and providing a more robust way to store cryptographic credentials used to access sensitive information and resources.

Google Play now provides security scanning of all applications before they are available to download, ongoing security checks for as long as the application is available, and a Verify Apps service for mobile device protection for apps installed outside of Google Play. However, these Android improvements are largely only for people who use a phone or tablet running a newer version of Android and restrict their app downloads to Google's own Play store.

Companies need to develop mobile security strategies that strike the right balance between improving worker productivity and effective information security. Aetna's Chief Security Officer (CSO) Jim Routh says there is a certain minimum level of mobile security he requires regardless of whether a device is company- or personally owned. Aetna has about 6,000 users equipped with mobile devices that are either personally owned or issued by the company. Each device has mandatory protection that provides an encrypted channel to use in unsecured Wi-Fi networks and alerts the user and the company if a malicious app is about to be installed on the device.

Colin Minihan, director of security and best practices at VMWare AirWatch, believes that understanding users and their needs helps a mobile security strategy progress further. VmAirWatch categorizes similar groups of users and devises a specific plan of action for each group, choosing the right tools for the job.

According to Patrick Hevesi, Nordstrom's former director of security, if users need access to critical corporate data that must be protected, the firm should probably allow only fully managed, fully controlled, approved types of devices. Users who only want mobile tools for e-mail and contacts can more easily bring their own devices. The key questions to ask are called the "three Ws": Who needs access? What do they need to access? What is the security posture of the device?

Sources: Michael Heller, "Mobile Security Strategy Matures with BYOD," and Kathleen Richards, "CISOs Battle to Control Mobile Risk in the Workplace," *Information Security Magazine*, June 1, 2016; Nathan Olivarez-Giles, "Android's Security Improves—for the Few," *Wall Street Journal*, April 21, 2016; Ponemon Institute, "The Economic Risk of Confidential Data on Mobile Devices in the Workplace," February, 2016; McAfee Inc., "Mobile Threat Report: What's on the Horizon for 2016," 2016; Charlie Osborne, "Dropbox Patches Android Security Flaw," *Zero Day*, March 11, 2015; Edel Creely, "5 BYOD Security Implications and How to Overcome Them," Trilogy Technologies, May 26, 2015; Tony Kontzer, "Most of Your Mobile Apps Have Been Hacked," *Baseline*, January 16, 2015; and Ponemon Institute, Global Study on Mobility Risks (February 2012).

CASE STUDY QUESTIONS

1. It has been said that a smartphone is a computer in your hand. Discuss the security implications of this statement.

2. What kinds of security problems do mobile computing devices pose?

3. What management, organizational, and technology issues must be addressed by smartphone security?

4. What steps can individuals and businesses take to make their smartphones more secure?

Review Summary

8-1 *Why are information systems vulnerable to destruction, error, and abuse?*

Digital data are vulnerable to destruction, misuse, error, fraud, and hardware or software failures. The Internet is designed to be an open system and makes internal corporate systems more vulnerable to actions from outsiders. Hackers can unleash denial-of-service (DoS) attacks or penetrate corporate networks, causing serious system disruptions. Wi-Fi networks can easily be penetrated by intruders using sniffer programs to obtain an address to access the resources of the network. Computer viruses and worms can disable systems and websites. The dispersed nature of cloud computing makes it difficult to track unauthorized activity or to apply controls from afar. Software presents problems because software bugs may be impossible to eliminate and because software vulnerabilities can be exploited by hackers and malicious software. End users often introduce errors.

8-2 *What is the business value of security and control?*

Lack of sound security and control can cause firms relying on computer systems for their core business functions to lose sales and productivity. Information assets, such as confidential employee records, trade secrets, or business plans, lose much of their value if they are revealed to outsiders or if they expose the firm to legal liability. Laws, such as HIPAA, the Sarbanes-Oxley Act, and the Gramm-Leach-Bliley Act, require companies to practice stringent electronic records management and adhere to strict standards for security, privacy, and control. Legal actions requiring electronic evidence and computer forensics also require firms to pay more attention to security and electronic records management.

8-3 *What are the components of an organizational framework for security and control?*

Firms need to establish a good set of both general and application controls for their information systems. A risk assessment evaluates information assets, identifies control points and control weaknesses, and determines the most cost-effective set of controls. Firms must also develop a coherent corporate security policy and plans for continuing business operations in the event of disaster or disruption. The security policy includes policies for acceptable use and identity management. Comprehensive and systematic information systems auditing helps organizations determine the effectiveness of security and controls for their information systems.

8-4 *What are the most important tools and technologies for safeguarding information resources?*

Firewalls prevent unauthorized users from accessing a private network when it is linked to the Internet. Intrusion detection systems monitor private networks for suspicious network traffic and attempts to access corporate systems. Passwords, tokens, smart cards, and biometric authentication are used to authenticate system users. Antivirus software checks computer systems for infections by viruses and worms and often eliminates the malicious software; antispyware software combats intrusive and harmful spyware programs. Encryption, the coding and scrambling of messages, is a widely used technology for securing electronic transmissions over unprotected networks. Digital certificates combined with public key encryption provide further protection of electronic transactions by authenticating a user's identity. Companies can use fault-tolerant computer systems to make sure that their information systems are always available. Use of software metrics and rigorous software testing help improve software quality and reliability.

Key Terms

Acceptable use policy (AUP), 313
Antivirus software, 319
Application controls, 309
Authentication, 316
Biometric authentication, 317
Botnet, 301
Bugs, 306
Business continuity planning, 315
Click fraud, 304
Computer crime, 302
Computer forensics, 308
Computer virus, 298
Controls, 295
Cybervandalism, 301
Cyberwarfare, 305
Deep packet inspection (DPI), 322
Denial-of-service (DoS) attack, 301
Digital certificates, 321
Disaster recovery planning, 314
Distributed denial-of-service (DDoS) attack, 301
Downtime, 322
Drive-by download, 299

Encryption, 320
Evil twin, 303
Fault-tolerant computer systems, 322
Firewall, 318
General controls, 309
Gramm-Leach-Bliley Act, 308
Hacker, 301
HIPAA, 307
Identity management, 313
Identity theft, 303
Information systems audit, 315
Intrusion detection systems, 319
Keyloggers, 300
Malware, 298
Managed security service providers (MSSPs), 323
Online transaction processing, 322
Password, 316
Patches, 306
Pharming, 303
Phishing, 303
Public key encryption, 320
Public key infrastructure (PKI), 322

MyMISLab

To complete the problems with the MyMISLab, go to EOC Discussion Questions in the MyMISLab.

Review Questions

8-1 Why are information systems vulnerable to destruction, error, and abuse?

- List and describe the most common threats against contemporary information systems.
- Define malware and distinguish among a virus, a worm, and a Trojan horse.
- Define a hacker and explain how hackers create security problems and damage systems.
- Define computer crime. Provide two examples of crime in which computers are targets and two examples in which computers are used as instruments of crime.
- Define identity theft and phishing and explain why identity theft is such a big problem today.
- Describe the security and system reliability problems employees create.
- Explain how software defects affect system reliability and security.

8-2 What is the business value of security and control?

- Explain how security and control provide value for businesses.
- Describe the relationship between security and control and recent U.S. government regulatory requirements and computer forensics.

8-3 What are the components of an organizational framework for security and control?

- Define general controls and describe each type of general control.

- Define application controls and describe each type of application control.
- Describe the function of risk assessment and explain how it is conducted for information systems.
- Define and describe the following: security policy, acceptable use policy, and identity management.
- Explain how information systems auditing promotes security and control.

8-4 What are the most important tools and technologies for safeguarding information resources?

- Name and describe three authentication methods.
- Describe the roles of firewalls, intrusion detection systems, and antivirus software in promoting security.
- Explain how encryption protects information.
- Describe the role of encryption and digital certificates in a public key infrastructure.
- Distinguish between disaster recovery planning and business continuity planning.
- Identify and describe the security problems cloud computing poses.
- Describe measures for improving software quality and reliability.

Discussion Questions

8-5 Security isn't simply a technology issue, it's a business issue. Discuss.

8-6 If you were developing a business continuity plan for your company, where would you start? What aspects of the business would the plan address?

8-7 Suppose your business had an e-commerce website where it sold goods and accepted credit card payments. Discuss the major security threats to this website and their potential impact. What can be done to minimize these threats?

Hands-On MIS Projects

The projects in this section give you hands-on experience analyzing security vulnerabilities, using spreadsheet software for risk analysis, and using web tools to research security outsourcing services. Visit MyMISLab's Multimedia Library to access this chapter's Hands-On MIS Projects.

Management Decision Problems

8-8 Reloaded Games is an online games platform that powers leading massively multiplayer online games. The Reloaded platform serves more than 30 million users. The games can accommodate millions of players at once and are played simultaneously by people all over the world. Prepare a security analysis for this Internet-based business. What kinds of threats should it anticipate? What would be their impact on the business? What steps can it take to prevent damage to its websites and continuing operations?

8-9 A survey of your firm's IT infastructure has identified a number of security vulnerabilities. Review the data about these vulnerabilities, which can be found in a table in MyMISLab. Use the table to answer the following questions:

- Calculate the total number of vulnerabilities for each platform. What is the potential impact of the security problems for each computing platform on the organization?
- If you only have one information systems specialist in charge of security, which platforms should you address first in trying to eliminate these vulnerabilities? Second? Third? Last? Why?
- Identify the types of control problems these vulnerabilities illustrate and explain the measures that should be taken to solve them.
- What does your firm risk by ignoring the security vulnerabilities identified?

Improving Decision Making: Using Spreadsheet Software to Perform a Security Risk Assessment

Software skills: Spreadsheet formulas and charts
Business skills: Risk assessment

8-10 This project uses spreadsheet software to calculate anticipated annual losses from various security threats identified for a small company.

Mercer Paints is a paint manufacturing company located in Alabama that uses a network to link its business operations. A security risk assessment that management requested identified a number of potential exposures. These exposures, their associated probabilities, and average losses are summarized in a table, which can be found in MyMISLab. Use the table to answer the following questions:

- In addition to the potential exposures listed, identify at least three other potential threats to Mercer Paints, assign probabilities, and estimate a loss range.
- Use spreadsheet software and the risk assessment data to calculate the expected annual loss for each exposure.
- Present your findings in the form of a chart. Which control points have the greatest vulnerability? What recommendations would you make to Mercer Paints? Prepare a written report that summarizes your findings and recommendations.

Improving Decision Making: Evaluating Security Outsourcing Services

Software skills: Web browser and presentation software
Business skills: Evaluating business outsourcing services

8-11 This project will help develop your Internet skills in using the web to research and evaluate security outsourcing services.

You have been asked to help your company's management decide whether to outsource security or keep the security function within the firm. Search the web to find information to help you decide whether to outsource security and to locate security outsourcing services.

- Present a brief summary of the arguments for and against outsourcing computer security for your company.
- Select two firms that offer computer security outsourcing services and compare them and their services.
- Prepare an electronic presentation for management, summarizing your findings. Your presentation should make the case of whether your company should outsource computer security. If you believe your company should outsource, the presentation should identify which security outsourcing service you selected and justify your decision.

Collaboration and Teamwork Project

Evaluating Security Software Tools

8-12 With a group of three or four students, use the web to research and evaluate security products from two competing vendors, such as for antivirus software, firewalls, or antispyware software. For each product, describe its capabilities, for what types of businesses it is best suited, and its cost to purchase and install. Which is the best product? Why? If possible, use Google Docs and Google Drive or Google Sites to brainstorm, organize, and develop a presentation of your findings for the class.

U.S. Office of Personnel Management Data Breach: No Routine Hack

CASE STUDY

The U.S. Office of Personnel Management (OPM) is responsible for recruiting and retaining a world-class workforce to serve the American people and is also responsible for background investigations on prospective employees and security clearances. In June 2015, the OPM announced that it had been the target of a data breach targeting the records of as many as 4 million people. In the following months, the number of stolen records was upped to 21.5 million. This was no routine hack. Federal officials believe this data breach is among the largest breaches of government data in U.S. history

Information targeted in the breach included personally identifiable information such as social security numbers as well as names, dates and places of birth, and addresses. Also stolen was detailed security clearance–related background information. This included records of people who had undergone background checks but who were not necessarily current or former government employees.

The data breach is believed to have begun in March 2014 and perhaps earlier, but it was not noticed by the OPM until April 2015, and it is unclear how it was actually discovered. The intrusion occurred before OPM had finished implementing new security procedures that restricted remote access for network administrators and reviewed all Internet connections to the outside world.

U.S. government officials suspect that the breach was the work of Chinese hackers, although there is no proof that it was actually sponsored by the Chinese government. Chinese officials have denied involvement. The attackers had stolen user credentials from contractor KeyPoint Government Solutions to access OPM networks, most likely through social engineering. The hackers then planted malware, which installed itself within OPM's network and established a backdoor for plundering data. From there, attackers escalated their privileges to gain access to a wide range of OPM systems.

The hackers' biggest prize was probably more than 20 years of background check data on the highly sensitive 127-page Standard Forms SF-86 Questionnaire for National Security Positions. SF-86 forms contain information about family members, college roommates, foreign contacts, and psychological information. OPM systems containing information related to the background investigations of current, former, and prospective federal government employees, including U.S. military personnel, and those for whom a federal background investigation was conducted, may have been extracted. Government officials say that the exposure of security clearance information could pose a problem for years.

The Central Intelligence Agency (CIA) does not use the OPM system, and its records were protected during the breach. However, intelligence and congressional officials worried that the hackers or Chinese intelligence operatives could still use the detailed OPM information they did obtain to identify U.S. spies by process of elimination. If they combined the stolen data with other information gathered over time, they could use big data analytics to identify operatives.

The potential exposure of U.S. intelligence officers could prevent many of them from ever being posted abroad again. Adm. Michael S. Rogers, director of the National Security Agency, suggested that the personnel data could also be used to develop "spear phishing" attacks on government officials. In such attacks, victims are duped into clicking on what appear to be e-mails from people they know, allowing malware into their computer networks.

The stolen data also included 5.6 million sets of fingerprints. According to biometrics expert Ramesh Kesanupalli, this could compromise secret agents because they could be identified by their fingerprints even if their names had been changed.

The OPM had been warned multiple times of security vulnerabilities and failings. A March 2015 OPM Office of the Inspector General semiannual report to Congress mentioned persistent deficiencies in OPM's information system security program, including incomplete security authorization packages, weaknesses in testing information security controls, and inaccurate plans of action and milestones.

Security experts have stated that the biggest problem with the breach was not OPM's failure to prevent remote break-ins but the absence of mechanisms to detect outside intrusion and inadequate encryption of sensitive data. Assistant Secretary for Cybersecurity and Communications Andy Ozment pointed out that if someone has the credentials of a user on the network, then he or she can access data even if they are encrypted, so encryption in this instance would not have protected the OPM data.

OPM was saddled with outdated technology and weak management. A DHS Federal Information Security Management Act (FISMA) Audit for fiscal year 2014 and audit of the Office of the Inspector General found serious flaws in OPM's network and the way it was managed. OPM did not maintain an inventory of systems and baseline configurations, with 11 servers operating without valid authorization. The auditors could not independently verify OPM's monthly automated vulnerability scanning program for all servers. There was no senior information security specialist or chief information security officer (CISO) responsible for network security. OPM lacked an effective multifactor authentication strategy and had poor management of user rights, inadequate monitoring of multiple systems, many unpatched computers, and a decentralized and ineffective cybersecurity function. Sensitive data were unencrypted and stored in old database systems that were vulnerable. What's more, OPM used contractors in China to manage some of its databases. These deficiencies had been pointed out to OPM over and over again since a FISMA audit in 2007. OPM had the vulnerabilities, no security-oriented leadership, and a skillful and motivated adversary.

Some security experts see OPM's vulnerabilities as a sign of the times, a reflection of large volumes of data, contemporary network complexity, weak organizational and cultural practices, and a legacy of outdated and poorly written software. As Thomas Bayer, CIO at Standard & Poor's Ratings, explained, until you have a serious data breach like the OPM hack, everyone invests in other things. It's only when a massive data breach occurs that organizations focus on their infrastructure. The expertise and technology for halting or slowing down cyberattacks such as that on OPM are not a mystery, and many companies and some government organizations are effectively defending themselves against most of the risks they face.

OPM lacked leadership and accountability. The prevailing mentality was for everyone to sit and bide their time. The CEO, CIO, and CISO in a private organization would be held accountable by the board of directors.

OPM is a top-heavy organization, with a large management layer of senior advisers to the director. For example, CIO Donna Seymour has 28 staff members under her and four direct reporting organizations, none of which is security-focused. There is no listed CISO function. OPM's director has 62 senior leaders in four groups. Many OPM managers are politically appointed and lack the expertise to make informed decisions about cybersecurity. It's only when managers in an organization understand and appreciate information security risks that they will authorize their IT department to develop an effective set of controls.

Most directors in the U.S. government do not have people in their organizations with the expertise and power to make changes, and many staff members are just not right for the job. OPM director Katherine Archuleta had formerly been the National Political Director for Barak Obama's 2012 presidential reelection campaign. CIO Donna Seymour, who was supposed to advise Archuleta on how to manage risk in IT systems, was a career government employee for more than 34 years. She had some IT and management roles at the Department of Defense and other agencies and has a degree in computer science but no specific expertise in cybersecurity. It is also difficult to bring in experienced managers from the business world because federal government pay scales are so low. A chief information officer (CIO) or chief information security officer (CISO) in the federal government would probably be paid about $168,000 annually, whereas an equivalent position in the private sector would probably have annual compensation of $400,000.

Since the OPM break-in, there has been a massive effort to rectify years of poor IT management. OPM is moving toward more centralized management of security. Information system security officers (ISSOs) report directly to a CISO. These positions are filled by individuals with professional security backgrounds. OPM hired a cybersecurity advisor, Clifton Triplett, and increased its IT modernization budget from $31 million to $87 million, with another $21 million scheduled for 2016.

OPM told current and former federal employees they could have free credit monitoring for 18 months to make sure their identities had not been stolen, but it has been slapped with numerous lawsuits from victims. Seymour faces a lawsuit for her role in failing to protect millions of personal employee data files, and Archuleta had to resign.

The FBI and Department of Homeland Security released a "cyber alert" memo describing lessons learned from the OPM hack. The memo lists generally recommended security practices for OPM to adopt, including encrypting data, activating a personal firewall at agency workstations, monitoring users' online habits, and blocking potentially malicious sites. The Obama administration ordered a 30-day Cybersecurity Sprint across all agencies to try to fix the big problems. Without a strong foundation, this investment could prove futile in the long run. OPM and the federal government as a whole need to invest more in managers with IT security expertise and give those individuals real authority to act.

The Obama administration is trying to determine whether other federal agencies storing sensitive information have weak protection. An audit issued before the Chinese attacks pointed to lax security at the Internal Revenue Service, the Nuclear Regulatory Commission, the Energy Department, the Securities and Exchange Commission, and even the Department of Homeland Security, which is responsible for securing the nation's critical networks and infrastructure. Computer security failure remains across agencies even though the government has spent at least $65 billion on security since 2006.

Sources: Sean Lyngaas, "What DHS and the FBI Learned from the OPM Breach," *FCW*, January 11, 2016; Adam Rice, "Warnings, Neglect and a Massive OPM Breach," SearchSecurity.com, accessed June 15, 2016; Steve Rosenbush, "The Morning Download: Outdated Tech Infrastructure Led to Massive OPM Breach," *Wall Street Journal*, July 10, 2015; Mark Mazzette and David E. Sanger, "U.S. Fears Data Stolen by Chinese Hacker Could Identify Spies," *New York Times,* July 24, 2015; Damian Paletta and Danny Yadron, "OPM Ratches Up Estimate of Hack's Scope" *Wall Street Journal*, July 9, 2015; David E. Sanger, Nicole Perlroth, and Michael D. Shear, "Attack Gave Chinese Hackers Privileged Access to U.S. Systems," *New York Times*, June 20, 2015; and David E. Sanger and Julie Hirschfield, "Hacking Linked to China Exposes Millions of U.S. Workers," *New York Times*, June 4, 2015.

CASE STUDY QUESTIONS

8-13 List and describe the security and control weaknesses at OPM that are discussed in this case.

8-14 What management, organization, and technology factors contributed to these problems? How much was management responsible?

8-15 What was the impact of the OPM hack?

8-16 Is there a solution to this problem? Explain your answer.

MyMISLab

Go to the Assignments section of MyMISLab to complete these writing exercises.

8-17 Describe three spoofing tactics employed in identity theft by using information systems.

8-18 Describe four reasons mobile devices used in business are difficult to secure.

Chapter 8 References

Bajaj, Vikas. "The Perils of Automated Flight." *New York Times* (April 30, 2015).

Boss, Scott R., Dennis F. Galletta, Paul Benjamin Lowry, Gregory D. Moody, and Peter Polak. "What Do Systems Users Have to Fear? Using Fear Appeals to Engender Threats and Fear that Motivate Protective Security Behaviors. MIS Quarterly 39, No. 4 (December 2015).

Boyle, Randall J. and Raymond R. Panko. *Corporate Computer Security* (4th ed.). Upper Saddle River, NJ: Prentice-Hall (2015).

Chen, Yan and Fatemeh Mariam Zahedi. "Individuals' Internet Security Perceptions and Behaviors: Polycontextual Contrasts Between the United States and China" *MIS Quarterly* 40, No. 1 (March 2016).

Chen, Yan, K. Ram Ramamurthy, and Kuang-Wei Wen. "Organizations' Information Security Policy Compliance: Stick or Carrot Approach?" *Journal of Management Information Systems* 29, No. 3 (Winter 2013).

CSA Top Threats Working Group. "The Treacherous Twelve: CSA's Cloud Computing Top Threats in 2016." Cloud Security Alliance (February 2016).

FireEye. "Out of Pocket: A Comprehensive Mobile Threat Assessment of 7 Million iOS and Android Apps." (February 2015).

Focus Research. "Devastating Downtime: The Surprising Cost of Human Error and Unforeseen Events." (October 2010).

Galbreth, Michael R. and Mikhael Shor. "The Impact of Malicious Agents on the Enterprise Software Industry." *MIS Quarterly* 34, No. 3 (September 2010).

Hui, Kai Lung, Wendy Hui and Wei T. Yue. "Information Security Outsourcing with System Interdependency and Mandatory Security Requirement." *Journal of Management Information Systems* 29, No. 3 (Winter 2013).

Javelin Strategy & Research. "2016 Identity Fraud Study." (February 2, 2016).

Kaplan, James, Chris Rezek, and Kara Sprague. "Protecting Information in the Cloud." *McKinsey Quarterly* (January 2013).

Karlovsky, Brian. "FireEye Names Malware's Favorite Targets, Sources." *Australian Reseller News* (March 2, 2014).

Kirk, Jeremy. "Pushdo Spamming Botnet Gains Strength Again." IDG News Service (April 20, 2015).

Osterman Research. "The Risks of Social Media and What Can Be Done to Manage Them." Commvault (June 2011).

Paletta, Damian, Danny Yadron, and Jennifer Valentino-Devries. "Cyberwar Ignites a New Arms Race." *Wall Street Journal* (October 11, 2015).

Panda Security. "PandaLabs 2015 Annual Report." (January 28, 2016).

Panko, Raymond R. and Julie L. Panko. *Business Data Networks and Security.* Upper Saddle River, NJ: Pearson (2015).

Perlroth, Nicole. "Online Attacks on Infrastructure Are Increasing at a Worrying Pace," *New York Times* (October 1, 2015).

Ponemon Institute. "2015 Cost of Cybercrime Study: United States" (October 9, 2015).

_____. "2015 Cost of Data Breach Study: United States" (2015).

_____. "The Cost of Malware Containment" (January 2015).

Poremba, Sue Marquette. "Hackers Targeting the Cloud at Higher Rates Than Ever." *IT Business Edge* (October 15, 2015).

Posey, Clay, Tom L. Roberts, and Paul Benjamin Lowry. "The Impact of Organizational Commitment on Insiders' Motivation to Protect Organizational Information Assets." *Journal of Management Information Systems* 32 No. 4 (2015).

Reisinger, Don. "Android Security Remains a Glaring Problem: 10 Reasons Why." *eWeek* (March 2, 2014).

Ribeiro, John. "Hacker Group Targets Skype Social Media Accounts," *Computer World* (January 2, 2014).

Sadeh, Norman M. "Phish Isn't Spam." *Information Week* (June 25, 2012).

Samuel, Alexandra. "Online Security as Herd Immunity." *Harvard Business Review* (March 13, 2014).

Scharr, Jill. "Fake Instagram 'Image Viewers' Are Latest Malware Fad." *Tom's Guide* (May 8, 2014).

Schwartz, Matthew J. "Android Trojan Looks, Acts Like Windows Malware." *Information Week* (June 7, 2013).

Sen, Ravi and Sharad Borle. "Estimating the Contextual Risk of Data Breach: An Empirical Approach." *Journal of Management Information Systems* 32, No. 2 (2015).

Sengupta, Somini. "Machines That Know You Without Using a Password." *New York Times* (September 10, 2013).

Snell, Bruce. "Mobile Threat Report." McAfee Inc. (2016).

Solutionary. "Solutionary Security Engineering Research Team Unveils Annual Global Threat Intelligence Report." (March 12, 2013).

Spears, Janine L. and Henri Barki. "User Participation in Information Systems Security Risk Management." *MIS Quarterly* 34, No. 3 (September 2010).

Temizkan, Orcun, Ram L. Kumar, Sungjune Park, and Chandrasekar Subramaniam. "Patch Release Behaviors of Software Vendors in Response to Vulnerabilities: An Empirical Analysis. " *Journal of Management Information Systems* 28, No. 4 (Spring 2012).

Thompson, Jadiann. "Scam Alert: Two Clicks on Facebook Could Leak All Your Personal Info to an International Scammer." Kshb.com (April 30, 2015).

Vance, Anthony, Paul Benjamin Lowry, and Dennis Eggett. "Using Accountability to Reduce Access Policy Violations in Information Systems." *Journal of Management Information Systems* 29, No. 4 (Spring 2013).

Verizon. "2016 Data Breach Investigations Report." (2016).

Wakida, Clayton. "Anonymous Accused of Hacking TMT Web Site." KMTV.com (April 27, 2015).

Wang, Jingguo, Manish Gupta, and H. Raghav Rao. "Insider Threats in a Financial Institution: Analysis of Attack-Proneness of Information Systems Applications." *MIS Quarterly* 39, No. 1 (March 2015).

Young, Carl S. "The Enemies of Data Security: Convenience and Collaboration." *Harvard Business Review* (February 11, 2015).

Zhao, Xia, Ling Xue, and Andrew B. Whinston. "Managing Interdependent Information Security Risks: Cyberinsurance, Managed Security Services, and Risk Pooling Arrangements." *Journal of Management Information Systems* 30, No. 1 (Summer 2013).

Key System Applications for the Digital Age

PART THREE examines the core information system applications businesses are using today to improve operational excellence and decision making. These applications include enterprise systems; systems for supply chain management, customer relationship management, and knowledge management; e-commerce applications; and business intelligence systems. This part answers questions such as: How can enterprise applications improve business performance? How do firms use e-commerce to extend the reach of their businesses? How can systems improve decision making and help companies make better use of their knowledge assets?

9
Achieving Operational Excellence and Customer Intimacy: Enterprise Applications

Learning Objectives

After reading this chapter, you will be able to answer the following questions:

9-1 How do enterprise systems help businesses achieve operational excellence?

9-2 How do supply chain management systems coordinate planning, production, and logistics with suppliers?

9-3 How do customer relationship management systems help firms achieve customer intimacy?

9-4 What are the challenges that enterprise applications pose, and how are enterprise applications taking advantage of new technologies?

MyMISLab™

Visit **mymislab.com** for simulations, tutorials, and end-of-chapter problems.

CHAPTER CASES

Skullcandy Rocks with ERP in the Cloud
Logistics and Transportation Management at LG Electronics
Customer Relationship Management Helps Celcom Become Number One
How Supply Chain Management Problems Killed Target Canada

VIDEO CASES

Life Time Fitness Gets in Shape with Salesforce CRM
Evolution Homecare Manages Patients with Microsoft Dynamics CRM
Instructional Video:
GSMS Protects Patients by Serializing Every Bottle of Drugs

Skullcandy Rocks with ERP in the Cloud

Those colorful edgy earbuds for your mobile phone might very well come from Skullcandy, a leading maker of audio and gaming headphones, earbuds, speakers, and other accessories. Skullcandy was born in 2003 on a chairlift, when founder Rick Alden came up with the idea for a device that could control both a mobile phone and a MP3 music player with a hassle-free one-touch button built into a set of earbuds. Skullcandy's bold colors and designs as well as products that could be integrated directly into helmets and backpacks made the brand a favorite of skiers, surfers, skaters, and other action sports enthusiasts. Skullcandy became wildly popular worldwide, growing 200 percent each year, and now has annual revenue of $250 million.

With such explosive growth, the company quickly outgrew its distribution model, which consisted of Alden delivering products personally from his basement to ski and skate shops in the Park City, Utah, area (the site of Skullcandy corporate headquarters). Skullcandy's business processes were primarily manual, with individual spreadsheets serving as the system of record for its business transactions. In order to grow to a company that could ship a million items each year, Skullcandy needed to automate its processes and use a new set of information systems to support them.

© Rh2010/Fotolia

In 2008, the company started to replace its spreadsheets and manual processes with SAP Business ByDesign cloud-based software providing a single enterprise resource planning (ERP) system supporting finance, planning, purchasing, inventory management, and order management. Business ByDesign is an enterprise resource planning and business management software product designed for small and medium-sized enterprises. The software is designed to track end-to-end business processes for financial management, project management, supply chain management, supplier relationship management, human resources management, customer relationship management, executive management support, and compliance management. The applications are integrated, and the system is the backbone for tracking all the transactions of the company. As Skullcandy continued to grow, it implemented additional Business ByDesign capabilities for managing third-party logistics (3PL) providers, omnichannel sales, and additional financial processes. (Omnichannel sales seek to provide the customer with a seamless shopping experience whether the customer is shopping online from a desktop or mobile device, by telephone, or in a brick-and-mortar store.) Skullcandy uses the Business ByDesign software running in SAP cloud computing centers. It doesn't need a computer center of its own to run these systems or more than a few people in its IT department.

How have the new ERP applications worked out? Very well, according to Skullcandy's management. The new system functionality has been credited with helping the business pursue a strategic acquisition, expand internationally, and significantly increase its customer base. In 2011, Skullcandy acquired Astro Gaming, a premium gaming headset company based in San Francisco. The Business ByDesign system was able to absorb this acquisition and run its transactions as a new and separate legal entity. The system also supports Sarbanes-Oxley (SOX) compliance, which is one of the requirements for filing as a public company, smoothing the way for Skullcandy to issue an IPO (initial public offering).

Shortly after going public, Skullcandy set up operations in Zurich, Switzerland, which became its European headquarters. The company also has locations in Canada, Mexico, Japan, and China. Business ByDesign already incorporated the regulations and laws of each country where Skullcandy operated. Skullcandy did not have to implement another system to transact in euros or deal with value-added taxes. This functionality was already included in the Business ByDesign software, so Skullcandy could easily set up operations in other countries with their own laws, regulations, languages, and currencies.

Skullcandy's distribution channels continued to expand. Best Buy, Target, and Walmart began selling its products. Today nearly 80 percent of Skullcandy's transactions are fully automated from point-of-sale through delivery. Everything is so interconnected and automated that from the time a customer clicks "buy," it takes less than a half hour for the transaction to move through Skullcandy's systems with a credit check, a check for fraud, interfacing with SAP Business ByDesign, checking availability, and warehouse fulfillment. Skullcandy can better manage its inventory, accounts, and information as it grows.

Sources: Ken Murphy, "Skullcandy Rocks the Cloud," *SAP Insider Profiles* 7, No. 1 (January 2016); "Every Revolution Needs a Soundtrack" and "Case Study: Skullcandy Inc.," www.sap.com, accessed February 27, 2016; and www.Skullcandy.com, accessed February 27, 2016.

Skullcandy's problems with its legacy systems and its need to find integrated systems to support its new distribution model and global growth strategy illustrate why companies need enterprise applications. Enterprise resource planning (ERP) systems as well as those for supply chain management and customer relationship management can dramatically improve operational effectiveness and decision making by integrating different business functions and providing consistent information throughout the company.

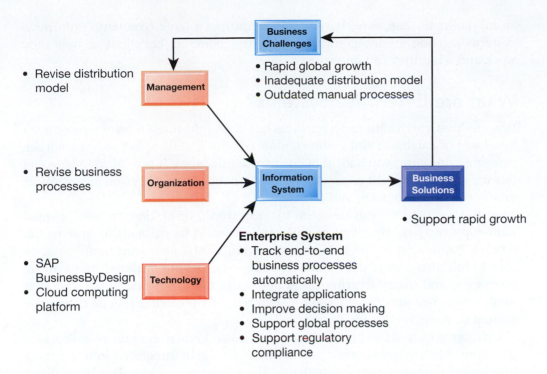

- Revise distribution model

Management

Business Challenges
- Rapid global growth
- Inadequate distribution model
- Outdated manual processes

- Revise business processes

Organization

Information System

Business Solutions
- Support rapid growth

- SAP BusinessByDesign
- Cloud computing platform

Technology

Enterprise System
- Track end-to-end business processes automatically
- Integrate applications
- Improve decision making
- Support global processes
- Support regulatory compliance

The chapter-opening case calls attention to important points raised by this case and this chapter. Skullcandy's business performance and ability to expand to new markets domestically and overseas suffered because it was saddled with outdated systems designed primarily for its old distribution model as a small company selling to local ski and skate shops. Its spreadsheet-based systems and manual processes made it difficult for different parts of the company to work together and respond to new market opportunities. They left the company operating too inefficiently and unable to pursue its new business goals. By implementing SAP's Business ByDesign enterprise applications, Skullcandy was able to transition to more efficient business processes and coordinate for its new business model, including forecasting, planning, profitability analysis, and new-product development, and it could support its strategic growth plan based on new acquisitions.

Skullcandy's new systems made it possible to run its business more efficiently and effectively and also had the functionality to support global expansion. However, in order to obtain these benefits from the enterprise software, Skullcandy had change some of its outdated business processes as well as its old legacy systems.

Here are some questions to think about: What problems did Skullcandy solve by implementing Business ByDesign? How did the new system change the way Skullcandy ran its business? What were the benefits of using cloud-based software for Skullcandy's solution?

9-1 How do enterprise systems help businesses achieve operational excellence?

Around the globe, companies are increasingly becoming more connected, both internally and with other companies. If you run a business, you'll want to be able to react instantaneously when a customer places a large order or when a shipment from a supplier is delayed. You may also want to know the impact of these events on every part of the business and how the business is performing at any point in time, especially if you're running a large company. Enterprise systems provide the integration to make this possible. Let's look at how they work and what they can do for the firm.

What are Enterprise Systems?

Imagine that you had to run a business based on information from tens or even hundreds of databases and systems, none of which could speak to one another. Imagine your company had 10 major product lines, each produced in separate factories and each with separate and incompatible sets of systems controlling production, warehousing, and distribution.

At the very least, your decision making would often be based on manual hard-copy reports, often out of date, and it would be difficult to understand what is happening in the business as a whole. Sales personnel might not be able to tell at the time they place an order whether the ordered items are in inventory, and manufacturing could not easily use sales data to plan for new production. You now have a good idea of why firms need a special enterprise system to integrate information.

Chapter 2 introduced enterprise systems, also known as enterprise resource planning (ERP) systems, which are based on a suite of integrated software modules and a common central database. The database collects data from many divisions and departments in a firm and from a large number of key business processes in manufacturing and production, finance and accounting, sales and marketing, and human resources, making the data available for applications that support nearly all an organization's internal business activities. When new information is entered by one process, the information is made immediately available to other business processes (see Figure 9.1).

FIGURE 9.1 HOW ENTERPRISE SYSTEMS WORK

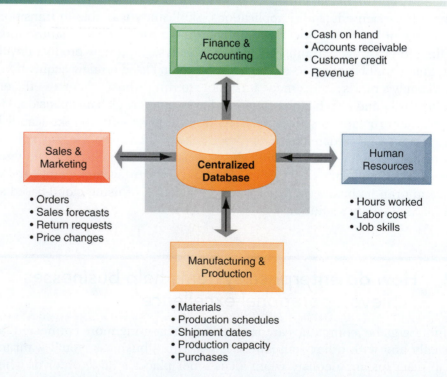

Enterprise systems feature a set of integrated software modules and a central database by which business processes and functional areas throughout the enterprise can share data.

If a sales representative places an order for tire rims, for example, the system verifies the customer's credit limit, schedules the shipment, identifies the best shipping route, and reserves the necessary items from inventory. If inventory stock is insufficient to fill the order, the system schedules the manufacture of more rims, ordering the needed materials and components from suppliers. Sales and production forecasts are immediately updated. General ledger and corporate cash levels are automatically updated with the revenue and cost information from the order. Users can tap into the system and find out where that particular order is at any minute. Management can obtain information at any point in time about how the business was operating. The system can also generate enterprise-wide data for management analyses of product cost and profitability.

Enterprise Software

Enterprise software is built around thousands of predefined business processes that reflect best practices. Table 9.1 describes some of the major business processes that enterprise software supports.

Companies implementing this software first have to select the functions of the system they wish to use and then map their business processes to the predefined business processes in the software. (One of our Learning Tracks shows how SAP enterprise software handles the procurement process for a new piece of equipment.) Configuration tables provided by the software manufacturer enable the firm to tailor a particular aspect of the system to the way it does business. For example, the firm could use these tables to select whether it wants to track revenue by product line, geographical unit, or distribution channel.

If the enterprise software does not support the way the organization does business, companies can rewrite some of the software to support the way their business processes work. However, enterprise software is unusually complex, and extensive customization may degrade system performance, compromising the information and process integration that are the main benefits of the system. If companies want to reap the maximum benefits from enterprise software, they must change the way they work to conform to the business processes defined by the software.

To implement a new enterprise system, Tasty Baking Company identified its existing business processes and then translated them into the business processes built into the SAP ERP software it had selected. To ensure that it obtained the maximum benefits from the enterprise software, Tasty Baking Company deliberately planned for customizing less than 5 percent

TABLE 9.1 BUSINESS PROCESSES SUPPORTED BY ENTERPRISE SYSTEMS

Financial and accounting processes, including general ledger, accounts payable, accounts receivable, fixed assets, cash management and forecasting, product-cost accounting, cost-center accounting, asset accounting, tax accounting, credit management, and financial reporting
Human resources processes, including personnel administration, time accounting, payroll, personnel planning and development, benefits accounting, applicant tracking, time management, compensation, workforce planning, performance management, and travel expense reporting
Manufacturing and production processes, including procurement, inventory management, purchasing, shipping, production planning, production scheduling, material requirements planning, quality control, distribution, transportation execution, and plant and equipment maintenance
Sales and marketing processes, including order processing, quotations, contracts, product configuration, pricing, billing, credit checking, incentive and commission management, and sales planning

of the system and made very few changes to the SAP software itself. It used as many tools and features that were already built into the SAP software as it could. SAP has more than 3,000 configuration tables for its enterprise software.

Leading enterprise software vendors include SAP, Oracle, IBM, Infor Global Solutions, and Microsoft. Versions of enterprise software packages are designed for small and medium-sized businesses and on-demand software services running in the cloud (see the chapter-opening case and Section 9-4).

Business Value of Enterprise Systems

Enterprise systems provide value by both increasing operational efficiency and providing firmwide information to help managers make better decisions. Large companies with many operating units in different locations have used enterprise systems to enforce standard practices and data so that everyone does business the same way worldwide.

Coca-Cola, for instance, implemented a SAP enterprise system to standardize and coordinate important business processes in 200 countries. Lack of standard, companywide business processes prevented the company from using its worldwide buying power to obtain lower prices for raw materials and from reacting rapidly to market changes. Crocs used ERP for similar purposes, as described in the Chapter 15 ending case study.

Enterprise systems help firms respond rapidly to customer requests for information or products. Because the system integrates order, manufacturing, and delivery data, manufacturing is better informed about producing only what customers have ordered, procuring exactly the right number of components or raw materials to fill actual orders, staging production, and minimizing the time that components or finished products are in inventory.

Alcoa, the world's leading producer of aluminum and aluminum products with operations spanning 31 countries and more than 200 locations, had initially been organized around lines of business, each of which had its own set of information systems. Many of these systems were redundant and inefficient. Alcoa's costs for executing requisition-to-pay and financial processes were much higher, and its cycle times were longer than those of other companies in its industry. (Cycle time refers to the total elapsed time from the beginning to the end of a process.) The company could not operate as a single worldwide entity.

After implementing enterprise software from Oracle, Alcoa eliminated many redundant processes and systems. The enterprise system helped Alcoa reduce requisition-to-pay cycle time by verifying receipt of goods and automatically generating receipts for payment. Alcoa's accounts payable transaction processing dropped 89 percent. Alcoa was able to centralize financial and procurement activities, which helped the company reduce nearly 20 percent of its worldwide costs.

Enterprise systems provide much valuable information for improving management decision making. Corporate headquarters has access to up-to-the-minute data on sales, inventory, and production and uses this information to create more accurate sales and production forecasts. Enterprise software includes analytical tools to use data the system captures to evaluate overall organizational performance. Enterprise system data have common standardized definitions and formats that are accepted by the entire organization. Performance figures mean the same thing across the company. Enterprise systems allow senior management to find out easily at any moment how a particular organizational unit is performing, determine which products are most or least profitable, and calculate costs for the company as a whole.

For example, Alcoa's enterprise system includes functionality for global human resources management that shows correlations between investment in employee training and quality, measures the companywide costs of delivering services to employees, and measures the effectiveness of employee recruitment, compensation, and training.

9-2 How do supply chain management systems coordinate planning, production, and logistics with suppliers?

If you manage a small firm that makes a few products or sells a few services, chances are you will have a small number of suppliers. You could coordinate your supplier orders and deliveries by using just a telephone and fax machine. But if you manage a firm that produces more complex products and services, you will have hundreds of suppliers, and each of your suppliers will have its own set of suppliers. Suddenly, you will need to coordinate the activities of hundreds or even thousands of other firms to produce your products and services. Supply chain management (SCM) systems, which we introduced in Chapter 2, are an answer to the problems of supply chain complexity and scale.

The Supply Chain

A firm's **supply chain** is a network of organizations and business processes for procuring raw materials, transforming these materials into intermediate and finished products, and distributing the finished products to customers. It links suppliers, manufacturing plants, distribution centers, retail outlets, and customers to supply goods and services from source through consumption. Materials, information, and payments flow through the supply chain in both directions.

Goods start out as raw materials and, as they move through the supply chain, are transformed into intermediate products (also referred to as components or parts) and, finally, into finished products. The finished products are shipped to distribution centers and from there to retailers and customers. Returned items flow in the reverse direction from the buyer back to the seller.

Let's look at the supply chain for Nike sneakers as an example. Nike designs, markets, and sells sneakers, socks, athletic clothing, and accessories throughout the world. Its primary suppliers are contract manufacturers with factories in China, Thailand, Indonesia, Brazil, and other countries. These companies fashion Nike's finished products.

Nike's contract suppliers do not manufacture sneakers from scratch. They obtain components for the sneakers—the laces, eyelets, uppers, and soles— from other suppliers and then assemble them into finished sneakers. These suppliers in turn have their own suppliers. For example, the suppliers of soles have suppliers for synthetic rubber, suppliers for chemicals used to melt the rubber for molding, and suppliers for the molds into which to pour the rubber. Suppliers of laces have suppliers for their thread, for dyes, and for the plastic lace tips.

Figure 9.2 provides a simplified illustration of Nike's supply chain for sneakers; it shows the flow of information and materials among suppliers, Nike, Nike's

FIGURE 9.2 NIKE'S SUPPLY CHAIN

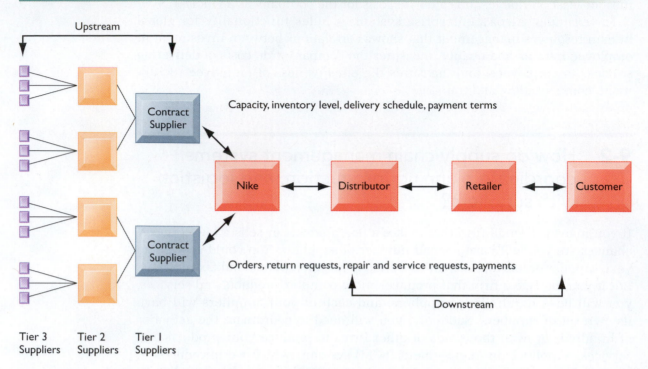

This figure illustrates the major entities in Nike's supply chain and the flow of information upstream and downstream to coordinate the activities involved in buying, making, and moving a product. Shown here is a simplified supply chain, with the upstream portion focusing only on the suppliers for sneakers and sneaker soles.

distributors, retailers, and customers. Nike's contract manufacturers are its primary suppliers. The suppliers of soles, eyelets, uppers, and laces are the secondary (Tier 2) suppliers. Suppliers to these suppliers are the tertiary (Tier 3) suppliers.

The *upstream* portion of the supply chain includes the company's suppliers, the suppliers' suppliers, and the processes for managing relationships with them. The *downstream* portion consists of the organizations and processes for distributing and delivering products to the final customers. Companies that manufacture, such as Nike's contract suppliers of sneakers, also manage their own *internal supply chain processes* for transforming materials, components, and services their suppliers furnish into finished products or intermediate products (components or parts) for their customers and for managing materials and inventory.

The supply chain illustrated in Figure 9.2 has been simplified. It only shows two contract manufacturers for sneakers and only the upstream supply chain for sneaker soles. Nike has hundreds of contract manufacturers turning out finished sneakers, socks, and athletic clothing, each with its own set of suppliers. The upstream portion of Nike's supply chain actually comprises thousands of entities. Nike also has numerous distributors and many thousands of retail stores where its shoes are sold, so the downstream portion of its supply chain is also large and complex.

Information Systems and Supply Chain Management

Inefficiencies in the supply chain, such as parts shortages, underused plant capacity, excessive finished goods inventory, or high transportation costs, are caused by inaccurate or untimely information. For example, manufacturers may keep too many parts in inventory because they do not know exactly when they will receive their next shipments from their suppliers. Suppliers may order too few raw materials because they do not have precise information on demand. These supply chain inefficiencies waste as much as 25 percent of a company's operating costs.

If a manufacturer had perfect information about exactly how many units of product customers wanted, when they wanted them, and when they could be produced, it would be possible to implement a highly efficient **just-in-time strategy**. Components would arrive exactly at the moment they were needed, and finished goods would be shipped as they left the assembly line.

In a supply chain, however, uncertainties arise because many events cannot be foreseen—uncertain product demand, late shipments from suppliers, defective parts or raw materials, or production process breakdowns. To satisfy customers, manufacturers often deal with such uncertainties and unforeseen events by keeping more material or products in inventory than they think they may actually need. The *safety stock* acts as a buffer for the lack of flexibility in the supply chain. Although excess inventory is expensive, low fill rates are also costly because business may be lost from canceled orders.

One recurring problem in supply chain management is the **bullwhip effect**, in which information about the demand for a product gets distorted as it passes from one entity to the next across the supply chain. A slight rise in demand for an item might cause different members in the supply chain—distributors, manufacturers, suppliers, secondary suppliers (suppliers' suppliers), and tertiary suppliers (suppliers' suppliers' suppliers)—to stockpile inventory so each has enough just in case. These changes ripple throughout the supply chain, magnifying what started out as a small change from planned orders and creating excess inventory, production, warehousing, and shipping costs (see Figure 9.3).

For example, Procter & Gamble (P&G) found it had excessively high inventories of its Pampers disposable diapers at various points along its supply chain because of such distorted information. Although customer purchases in stores were fairly stable, orders from distributors spiked when P&G offered aggressive price promotions. Pampers and Pampers' components accumulated in warehouses along the supply chain to meet demand that did not actually exist. To eliminate this problem, P&G revised its marketing, sales, and supply chain processes and used more accurate demand forecasting.

The bullwhip effect is tamed by reducing uncertainties about demand and supply when all members of the supply chain have accurate and up-to-date information. If all supply chain members share dynamic information about inventory levels, schedules, forecasts, and shipments, they have more precise knowledge about how to adjust their sourcing, manufacturing, and distribution plans. Supply chain management systems provide the kind of information that helps members of the supply chain make better purchasing and scheduling decisions.

Supply Chain Management Software

Supply chain software is classified as either software to help businesses plan their supply chains (supply chain planning) or software to help them execute the supply chain steps (supply chain execution). **Supply chain planning systems** enable the firm to model its existing supply chain, generate demand forecasts for products, and develop optimal sourcing and manufacturing plans. Such systems help companies make better decisions such as determining how much of a specific product to manufacture in a given time period; establishing

FIGURE 9.3   THE BULLWHIP EFFECT

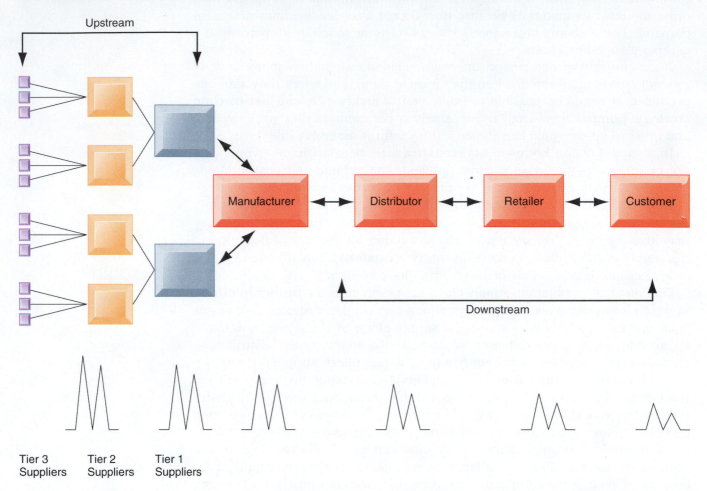

Inaccurate information can cause minor fluctuations in demand for a product to be amplified as one moves further back in the supply chain. Minor fluctuations in retail sales for a product can create excess inventory for distributors, manufacturers, and suppliers.

inventory levels for raw materials, intermediate products, and finished goods; determining where to store finished goods; and identifying the transportation mode to use for product delivery.

For example, if a large customer places a larger order than usual or changes that order on short notice, it can have a widespread impact throughout the supply chain. Additional raw materials or a different mix of raw materials may need to be ordered from suppliers. Manufacturing may have to change job scheduling. A transportation carrier may have to reschedule deliveries. Supply chain planning software makes the necessary adjustments to production and distribution plans. Information about changes is shared among the relevant supply chain members so that their work can be coordinated. One of the most important—and complex—supply chain planning functions is **demand planning**, which determines how much product a business needs to make to satisfy all its customers' demands. JDA Software, SAP, and Oracle all offer supply chain management solutions.

Supply chain execution systems manage the flow of products through distribution centers and warehouses to ensure that products are delivered to the right locations in the most efficient manner. They track the physical status of goods, the management of materials, warehouse and transportation operations, and financial information involving all parties. An example is the Warehouse

Management System (WMS) that Haworth Incorporated uses. Haworth is a world-leading manufacturer and designer of office furniture, with distribution centers in four states. The WMS tracks and controls the flow of finished goods from Haworth's distribution centers to its customers. Acting on shipping plans for customer orders, the WMS directs the movement of goods based on immediate conditions for space, equipment, inventory, and personnel.

Global Supply Chains and the Internet

Before the Internet, supply chain coordination was hampered by the difficulties of making information flow smoothly among disparate internal supply chain systems for purchasing, materials management, manufacturing, and distribution. It was also difficult to share information with external supply chain partners because the systems of suppliers, distributors, or logistics providers were based on incompatible technology platforms and standards. Enterprise and supply chain management systems enhanced with Internet technology supply some of this integration.

A manager uses a web interface to tap into suppliers' systems to determine whether inventory and production capabilities match demand for the firm's products. Business partners use web-based supply chain management tools to collaborate online on forecasts. Sales representatives access suppliers' production schedules and logistics information to monitor customers' order status.

Global Supply Chain Issues

More and more companies are entering international markets, outsourcing manufacturing operations, and obtaining supplies from other countries as well as selling abroad. Their supply chains extend across multiple countries and regions. There are additional complexities and challenges to managing a global supply chain.

Global supply chains typically span greater geographic distances and time differences than domestic supply chains and have participants from a number of countries. Performance standards may vary from region to region or from nation to nation. Supply chain management may need to reflect foreign government regulations and cultural differences.

The Internet helps companies manage many aspects of their global supply chains, including sourcing, transportation, communications, and international finance. Today's apparel industry, for example, relies heavily on outsourcing to contract manufacturers in China and other low-wage countries. Apparel companies are starting to use the web to manage their global supply chain and production issues. (Review the discussion of Li & Fung in Chapter 3.)

In addition to contract manufacturing, globalization has encouraged outsourcing warehouse management, transportation management, and related operations to third-party logistics providers, such as UPS Supply Chain Solutions and Schneider National. These logistics services offer web-based software to give their customers a better view of their global supply chains. Customers can check a secure website to monitor inventory and shipments, helping them run their global supply chains more efficiently.

Demand-Driven Supply Chains: From Push to Pull Manufacturing and Efficient Customer Response

In addition to reducing costs, supply chain management systems facilitate efficient customer response, enabling the workings of the business to be driven more by customer demand. (We introduced efficient customer response systems in Chapter 3.)

Earlier supply chain management systems were driven by a push-based model (also known as build-to-stock). In a **push-based model**, production master schedules are based on forecasts or best guesses of demand for products, and products are pushed to customers. With new flows of information made possible by web-based tools, supply chain management more easily follows a pull-based model. In a **pull-based model**, also known as a demand-driven or build-to-order model, actual customer orders or purchases trigger events in the supply chain. Transactions to produce and deliver only what customers have ordered move up the supply chain from retailers to distributors to manufacturers and eventually to suppliers. Only products to fulfill these orders move back down the supply chain to the retailer. Manufacturers use only actual order demand information to drive their production schedules and the procurement of components or raw materials, as illustrated in Figure 9.4. Walmart's continuous replenishment system described in Chapter 3 is an example of the pull-based model.

The Internet and Internet technology make it possible to move from sequential supply chains, where information and materials flow sequentially from company to company, to concurrent supply chains, where information flows in many directions simultaneously among members of a supply chain network. Complex supply networks of manufacturers, logistics suppliers, outsourced manufacturers, retailers, and distributors can adjust immediately to changes in schedules or orders. Ultimately, the Internet will enable a digital logistics nervous system for supply chains (see Figure 9.5).

Business Value of Supply Chain Management Systems

You have just seen how supply chain management systems enable firms to streamline both their internal and external supply chain processes and provide management with more accurate information about what to produce, store, and move. By implementing a networked and integrated supply chain management system, companies match supply to demand, reduce inventory levels, improve delivery service, speed product time to market, and use assets more effectively (see the Interactive Session on Management).

FIGURE 9.4   PUSH- VERSUS PULL-BASED SUPPLY CHAIN MODELS

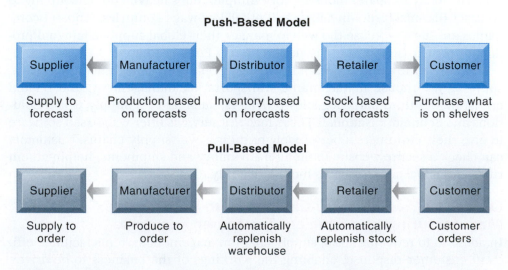

The difference between push- and pull-based models is summarized by the slogan "Make what we sell, not sell what we make."

FIGURE 9.5   THE EMERGING INTERNET-DRIVEN SUPPLY CHAIN

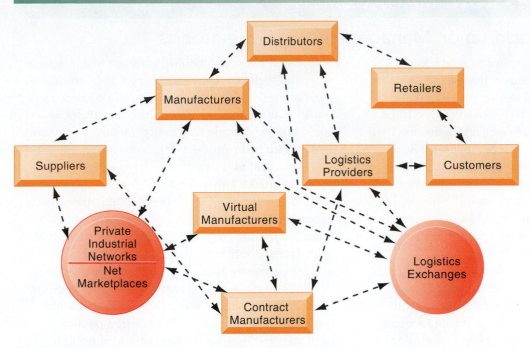

The emerging Internet-driven supply chain operates like a digital logistics nervous system. It provides multidirectional communication among firms, networks of firms, and e-marketplaces so that entire networks of supply chain partners can immediately adjust inventories, orders, and capacities.

Total supply chain costs represent the majority of operating expenses for many businesses and in some industries approach 75 percent of the total operating budget. Reducing supply chain costs has a major impact on firm profitability.

In addition to reducing costs, supply chain management systems help increase sales. If a product is not available when a customer wants it, customers often try to purchase it from someone else. More precise control of the supply chain enhances the firm's ability to have the right product available for customer purchases at the right time.

9-3   How do customer relationship management systems help firms achieve customer intimacy?

You've probably heard phrases such as "the customer is always right" or "the customer comes first." Today these words ring truer than ever. Because competitive advantage based on an innovative new product or service is often very short lived, companies are realizing that their most enduring competitive strength may be their relationships with their customers. Some say that the basis of competition has switched from who sells the most products and services to who "owns" the customer and that customer relationships represent a firm's most valuable asset.

What is Customer Relationship Management?

What kinds of information would you need to build and nurture strong, long-lasting relationships with customers? You'd want to know exactly who your customers are, how to contact them, whether they are costly to service and sell to,

INTERACTIVE SESSION: MANAGEMENT

Logistics and Transportation Management at LG Electronics

From its origins as the progenitor of South Korea's electronics industry and then its first global exporter, LG Electronics has evolved to a respected global brand with manufacturing facilities in China, India, Mexico, Brazil, Poland, and Russia and a presence in 49 countries. Headquartered in Seoul, South Korea, the company has 84,000 employees in 112 locations around the world, including 81 subsidiaries. Perhaps best known today for its quality mobile phones, LG Electronics is also one of the world's top manufacturers of flat-screen televisions, air conditioners, washing machines, and refrigerators.

Led primarily by exploding demand for flat-screen televisions and mobile phones in the past 15 years, LG Electronics' European operations grew exponentially. By 2015, its logistics network was inadequate and severely overtaxed. Most of its transportation needs were outsourced to third-party logistics (3PL) providers. Internal knowledge and expertise were nonexistent. LG Electronics Europe wanted to change this equation. By creating a collaborative effort with its partners, LG believed that it could better control coordination of its transportation networks and realize aggregate cost savings.

Management was clamoring for increased logistics visibility so that it could preempt bottlenecks rather than fashioning reflexive, and often imprudent, remedies. Dependent on their 3PL providers, managers had little to no control over transportation planning. Fixed routing in outsourced systems hamstrung management's ability to optimize carriers, loads, and overall capacity. In order to control performance and costs, LG Electronics Europe knew it had to take control of its logistics system and adopt robust performance evaluation tools so that it could continually adapt and revise transportation decisions.

LG Electronics already had a relationship with JDA Software, a leading vendor of supply chain management systems, employing many of its products in localities across the globe. Impressed with JDA's global presence and armed with positive reports about its partnerships with other divisions, LG Electronics Europe chose JDA Software's Intelligent Fulfillment solutions— Transportation Modeler, Transportation Manager, and Transportation Planner. The ease of use and exceptional data-sharing capabilities of this unified supply chain planning, optimization, and business analytics platform immediately drew favorable reviews.

Once all managers could log in to a single source where all logistics data were shared, they could collaborate to find the most efficient and cost-effective transportation options. Transportation strategies could now be flexible and easily adapted to respond to fluctuations in product demand, shipping rates, fuel costs, and other factors.

LG used JDA Transportation Modeler to model an ideal logistics system that consolidated orders, established transportation hubs, and selected carriers in a flexible manner based on costs and service levels. With Transportation Modeler, LG Electronics Europe can assess the abilities of alternative transportation hubs and associated carriers to optimize order consolidation. What-if scenarios examine various requirements and objectives to design possible networks and outline the best way to run them.

Once a logistics system model has been settled upon, it is run through Transportation Manager to generate a new network. Transportation orders can then be dynamically managed. What's more, cross-company workflows now connect LG Electronics Europe to its supplier network. Rather than ceding control to its 3PL providers, LG works in partnership with them. Freight audits reveal comprehensive statistical insight into logistics spending. Truck-loading efficiency ratios are used to optimize the vehicle-miles needed to transport like tonnages of freight. Consolidation ratios show how to combine two or more shipments to yield maximum cost savings.

Transportation Planner then weighs product availability, customer delivery commitments, and facility, inventory, and transportation network constraints to create benchmarks. By focusing managerial attention only on activities that fall outside of these accepted norms, labor productivity is maximized. This built-in exception-based management functionality minimizes the need for human intervention and review.

Three-dimensional load building automatically uses order line data to optimally configure pallets, taking into account weights, dimensions, stacking protocols, and other factors. A web-enabled interface displays this customizable 3-D view, and a Gantt bar chart illustrates the project schedule for dock and vehicle utilization. All transportation plans are archived so that they can be used in historical analysis and future what-if scenario construction, and previous asset allocations and carrier assignments are considered as new transportation plans are created. Multiple users can access and edit any active plan.

As LG Electronics Europe's users became comfortable with the system, they progressed beyond basic tasks such as loading trucks and scheduling deliveries to more complex issues including managing tariffs and checking for invoice duplication. Workload efficiency was bolstered by the ability to access real-time information, the exception-based management tools, and the ability to tailor logistics to local environments. Managers quickly gained confidence in their logistics decision making.

Investing in JDA Services—Consulting, Education, Performance Engineering, and Support Services—provided valuable support with system implementation. Although change was introduced systematically with a comprehensive training regimen, LG Electronics Europe's transportation manager, Menno Cleton, was thankful to have JDA consultants during the final three steps of the seven-step JDA Enterprise Methodology (JEM): Deploy, Transition, and Evolve. These experts walked users through equipment use, interface details, tool usage minutiae, and other miscellaneous issues. In addition, LG participated in a JDA Special Interest Group (SIG), which organized and supervised group meetings with other JDA customers to share experiences and offer peer-to-peer support.

A true supply chain transportation knowledge base and increased visibility into LG's transportation network quickly produced significant cost savings, yielding a generous profit. Dedicated performance analysis using the built-in business intelligence (BI) tools resulted in improvements in all transportation metrics. Managers can now see a load plan's optimized cost compared with its implemented cost or how shipment costs are calculated from loads along with 60 other key metrics by selecting a report or dashboard directly within their current transportation workflow. Improved service (in-stock) levels, faster order cycle times, reduced time to implementation, and improvements in the freight audit process have all been achieved.

LG Electronics Europe can now also assess the performance of its carriers and allocate loads accordingly. Improved service levels have yielded increased customer satisfaction. Consolidation ratios in all implementations saw a 10 percent improvement, and optimized load configurations improved truck-loading efficiency ratios. In partnership with its 3PL providers, LG Electronics Europe is poised for continuing improvement in its service levels and adoption of additional JDA solutions.

Sources: "JDA Intelligent Fulfillment: Transportation & Logistics Management," JDA Software Group Inc., June 4, 2015; "LG Life's Good: Taking Control: LG Electronics Optimizes Its European Logistics with JDA Transportation Solutions," JDA Software Group Inc., July 8. 2015; "JDA Transportation Modeler," www.jda.com, accessed February 28, 2016; "LG History," www.lg.com, accessed March 4, 2016.

CASE STUDY QUESTIONS

1. Identify the supply chain management problems LG Electronics faced. What was the business impact of its inability to manage its supply chain well?

2. What management, organization, and technology factors contributed to LG's supply chain problems?

3. How did implementing JDA Software solutions change the way LG ran its business?

4. How did LG's new logistics and transportation management system improve management decision making? Describe two decisions that the new system solution improved.

what kinds of products and services they are interested in, and how much money they spend on your company. If you could, you'd want to make sure you knew each of your customers well, as if you were running a small-town store. And you'd want to make your good customers feel special.

In a small business operating in a neighborhood, it is possible for business owners and managers to know their customers well on a personal, face-to-face basis, but in a large business operating on a metropolitan, regional, national, or even global basis, it is impossible to know your customer in this intimate way. In these kinds of businesses, there are too many customers and too many ways that customers interact with the firm (over the web, the phone, e-mail, blogs, and in person). It becomes especially difficult to integrate information from all these sources and deal with the large number of customers.

A large business's processes for sales, service, and marketing tend to be highly compartmentalized, and these departments do not share much essential customer information. Some information on a specific customer might be stored and organized in terms of that person's account with the company. Other pieces of information about the same customer might be organized by products that were purchased. In this traditional business environment, there is no convenient way to consolidate all this information to provide a unified view of a customer across the company.

This is where customer relationship management systems help. Customer relationship management (CRM) systems, which we introduced in Chapter 2, capture and integrate customer data from all over the organization, consolidate the data, analyze the data, and then distribute the results to various systems and customer touch points across the enterprise. A **touch point** (also known as a contact point) is a method of interaction with the customer, such as telephone, e-mail, customer service desk, conventional mail, Facebook, Twitter, website, wireless device, or retail store. Well-designed CRM systems provide a single enterprise view of customers that is useful for improving both sales and customer service (see Figure 9.6.)

Good CRM systems provide data and analytical tools for answering questions such as these: What is the value of a particular customer to the firm over his or her lifetime? Who are our most loyal customers? Who are our most profitable customers? What do these profitable customers want to buy? Firms use the answers to these questions to acquire new customers, provide better service and support to existing customers, customize their offerings more precisely to customer preferences, and provide ongoing value to retain profitable customers.

FIGURE 9.6   CUSTOMER RELATIONSHIP MANAGEMENT (CRM)

CRM systems examine customers from a multifaceted perspective. These systems use a set of integrated applications to address all aspects of the customer relationship, including customer service, sales, and marketing.

Customer Relationship Management Software

Commercial CRM software packages range from niche tools that perform limited functions, such as personalizing websites for specific customers, to large-scale enterprise applications that capture myriad interactions with customers, analyze them with sophisticated reporting tools, and link to other major enterprise applications, such as supply chain management and enterprise systems. The more comprehensive CRM packages contain modules for **partner relationship management (PRM)** and **employee relationship management (ERM)**.

PRM uses many of the same data, tools, and systems as customer relationship management to enhance collaboration between a company and its selling partners. If a company does not sell directly to customers but rather works through distributors or retailers, PRM helps these channels sell to customers directly. It provides a company and its selling partners with the ability to trade information and distribute leads and data about customers, integrating lead generation, pricing, promotions, order configurations, and availability. It also provides a firm with tools to assess its partners' performances so it can make sure its best partners receive the support they need to close more business.

ERM software deals with employee issues that are closely related to CRM, such as setting objectives, employee performance management, performance-based compensation, and employee training. Major CRM application software vendors include Oracle, SAP, Salesforce.com, and Microsoft Dynamics CRM.

Customer relationship management systems typically provide software and online tools for sales, customer service, and marketing. We briefly describe some of these capabilities.

Sales Force Automation

Sales force automation (SFA) modules in CRM systems help sales staff increase productivity by focusing sales efforts on the most profitable customers, those who are good candidates for sales and services. SFA modules provide sales prospect and contact information, product information, product configuration capabilities, and sales quote generation capabilities. Such software can assemble information about a particular customer's past purchases to help the salesperson make personalized recommendations. SFA modules enable sales, marketing, and shipping departments to share customer and prospect information easily. SFA increases each salesperson's efficiency by reducing the cost per sale as well as the cost of acquiring new customers and retaining old ones. SFA modules also provide capabilities for sales forecasting, territory management, and team selling.

Customer Service

Customer service modules in CRM systems provide information and tools to increase the efficiency of call centers, help desks, and customer support staff. They have capabilities for assigning and managing customer service requests.

One such capability is an appointment or advice telephone line. When a customer calls a standard phone number, the system routes the call to the correct service person, who inputs information about that customer into the system only once. When the customer's data are in the system, any service representative can handle the customer relationship. Improved access to consistent and accurate customer information helps call centers handle more calls per day and decrease the duration of each call. Thus, call centers and customer service groups achieve greater productivity, reduced transaction time, and higher quality of service at lower cost. The customer is happier because he or she spends less time on the phone restating his or her problem to customer service representatives.

CRM systems may also include web-based self-service capabilities: The company website can be set up to provide inquiring customers personalized support information as well as the option to contact customer service staff by phone for additional assistance.

Marketing

CRM systems support direct-marketing campaigns by providing capabilities for capturing prospect and customer data, for providing product and service information, for qualifying leads for targeted marketing, and for scheduling and tracking direct-marketing mailings or e-mail (see Figure 9.7). Marketing modules also include tools for analyzing marketing and customer data, identifying profitable and unprofitable customers, designing products and services to satisfy specific customer needs and interests, and identifying opportunities for cross-selling.

Cross-selling is the marketing of complementary products to customers. (For example, in financial services, a customer with a checking account might be sold a money market account or a home improvement loan.) CRM tools also help firms manage and execute marketing campaigns at all stages, from planning to determining the rate of success for each campaign.

Figure 9.8 illustrates the most important capabilities for sales, service, and marketing processes found in major CRM software products. Like enterprise software, this software is business-process driven, incorporating hundreds of business processes thought to represent best practices in each of these areas. To achieve maximum benefit, companies need to revise and model their business processes to conform to the best-practice business processes in the CRM software.

FIGURE 9.7   HOW CRM SYSTEMS SUPPORT MARKETING

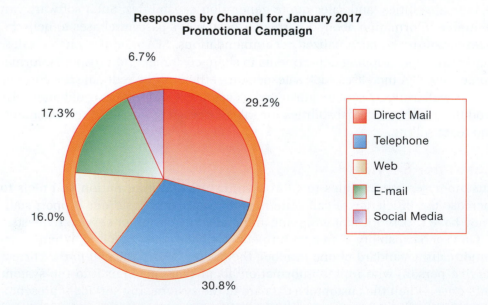

Responses by Channel for January 2017 Promotional Campaign

- Direct Mail
- Telephone
- Web
- E-mail
- Social Media

Customer relationship management software provides a single point for users to manage and evaluate marketing campaigns across multiple channels, including e-mail, direct mail, telephone, the web, and social media.

FIGURE 9.8   CRM SOFTWARE CAPABILITIES

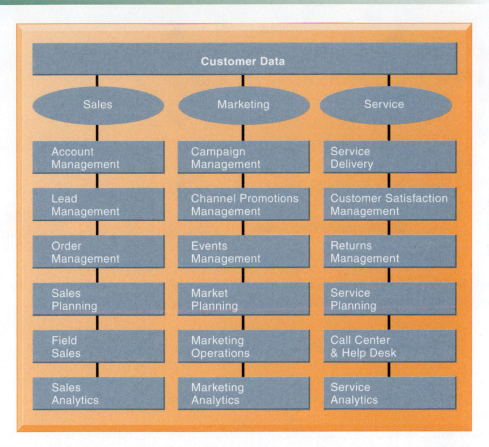

The major CRM software products support business processes in sales, service, and marketing, integrating customer information from many sources. Included is support for both the operational and analytical aspects of CRM.

Figure 9.9 illustrates how a best practice for increasing customer loyalty through customer service might be modeled by CRM software. Directly servicing customers provides firms with opportunities to increase customer retention by singling out profitable long-term customers for preferential treatment. CRM software can assign each customer a score based on that person's value and loyalty to the company and provide that information to help call centers route each customer's service request to agents who can best handle that customer's needs. The system would automatically provide the service agent with a detailed profile of that customer that includes his or her score for value and loyalty. The service agent would use this information to present special offers or additional service to the customer to encourage the customer to keep transacting business with the company. You will find more information on other best-practice business processes in CRM systems in our Learning Tracks.

Operational and Analytical CRM

All of the applications we have just described support either the operational or analytical aspects of customer relationship management. **Operational CRM** includes customer-facing applications, such as tools for sales force automation, call center and customer service support, and marketing automation. **Analytical CRM** includes applications that analyze customer data generated by operational CRM applications to provide information for improving business performance.

FIGURE 9.9 CUSTOMER LOYALTY MANAGEMENT PROCESS MAP

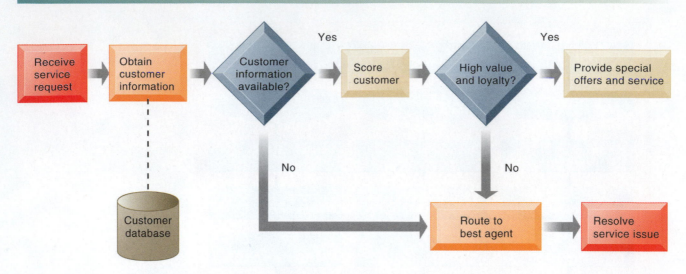

This process map shows how a best practice for promoting customer loyalty through customer service would be modeled by customer relationship management software. The CRM software helps firms identify high-value customers for preferential treatment.

Analytical CRM applications are based on data from operational CRM systems, customer touch points, and other sources that have been organized in data warehouses or analytic platforms for use in online analytical processing (OLAP), data mining, and other data analysis techniques (see Chapter 6). Customer data collected by the organization might be combined with data from other sources, such as customer lists for direct-marketing campaigns purchased from other companies or demographic data. Such data are analyzed to identify buying patterns, to create segments for targeted marketing, and to pinpoint profitable and unprofitable customers (see Figure 9.10).

FIGURE 9.10 ANALYTICAL CRM

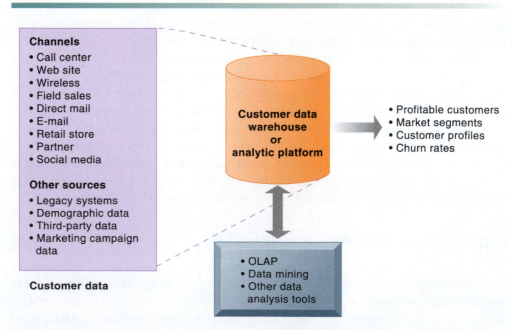

Analytical CRM uses a customer data warehouse or analytic platform and tools to analyze customer data collected from the firm's customer touch points and from other sources.

Customer Relationship Management Helps Celcom Become Number One

Celcom Axiata Berhad (Celcom) is the oldest mobile telecommunications company in Malaysia and also its largest, with an unrivaled reputation for quality and reliability. Nevertheless, maintaining its competitive edge has been a struggle. In 2006 Celcom dropped to third place among Malaysian cellular providers. Since then, management has worked feverishly to turn the company around, and Celcom has regained the top spot in its market. This turnaround required new technology and business processes for managing the customer experience.

To become number one in the Malaysian market again, Celcom's senior management knew that the company had to build better networks and market more aggressively. But the real key to success lay in improving the customer experience. According to Suresh Sidhu, Celcom's chief corporate and operations officer, there will always be a competitor who can beat you on price or even out-innovate you. But it's much harder for a competitor to disrupt a strong, positive relationship with customers. Celcom believes it's the market's best differentiator.

The Malaysia telecommunications market is quite mature, with few opportunities to acquire new customers. Customer retention is essential, as is luring customers away from competitors. Malaysia's customer base of 14 million is large and diverse, which requires multiple approaches to interacting with them. Older customers prefer in-person service from Celcom dealers or retail outlets, while sophisticated young urban users prefer to do business online. All want reliable mobile service.

Celcom was saddled with a siloed information technology architecture and business processes that could not provide a complete view of customers. For instance, customer data from one system such as billing were not easily available to other systems such as inventory. This is a common problem for mobile providers because carriers have traditionally counted customers by looking at SIM (subscriber identity modules in mobile phones) IDs. However many customers have multiple devices and SIMs for personal and work uses. Celcom needed systems that could identify and serve each customer rather than that person's SIMs. Otherwise, Celcom service representatives would waste valuable company and customer time making sense of a customer's

multiple SIM IDs scattered among various records in the system. The company wanted to be able to see a customer as a specific person, not a SIM or a number.

Celcom's solution involved changes to the company's technology, processes, and people. At the core is an Oracle-based business support system (BSS) that consolidated customer records, centralized inventory management, and sped up business processes. This system consolidates customer information into a single view of the customer to improve customer service across online, call center, and retail channels. The Oracle implementation included new customer portal sites and retail stores as well as an Oracle Siebel call center system and Oracle inventory management and Communications Order and Service Management applications.

The BSS project team asked approximately 700 Celcom employees in customer service, retail, marketing, and other divisions to list the top 10 experiences that users and dealers wanted, such as fast activation, less paperwork, and always having the most popular phones in stock. The BSS transformation team then developed technical and business process requirements based on these top 10 lists and compared offerings from several vendors.

Celcom chose Oracle as the primary technology provider for the new customer experience management system. The company wanted the most complete suite of customer relationship management (CRM) tools that would support multichannel and cross-channel marketing efforts. Oracle seemed the best fit and had the most functionality built in without requiring additional modifications.

Celcom's transformation plan entailed retaining some of Celcom's existing systems, and the Celcom team liked Oracle Communications' modularity and interoperability as well as its cross-channel capabilities. Oracle Communications is a cross-channel product suite that provides a variety of services, including broadband data, wireless data, and mobile voice services. It helps communications services provider such as Celcom manage and integrate customer interactions across multiple channels to improve customer support, reduce problem resolution time, customize marketing to narrow market segments, and expedite time-to-market for new products and services. Celcom understood the importance of cross-channel customer experiences and wanted to make this differentiate the company among its competitors. Celcom's systems solution enables customer interactions to seamlessly traverse its retail shop, online shop, call center, and partner/dealer channels.

The BSS provides a single customer record, regardless of how many services (mobile, landline, and data) and devices a customer purchases, that is populated with data from various touchpoints. By consolidating customer data into a unified customer record, Celcom can offer tailored promotions offers in real time that fit a customer's individual history. Celcom's holistic view of a customer includes family relationships, which has special significance when marketing in Asia. The company is able to see every aspect of service each customer uses, which makes cross-marketing and up-selling more efficient.

Celcom completed the BSS implementation in just 18 months, replacing 17 separate systems with one seven-module Oracle system.

Celcom officials explicitly tried to get employees invested in the new system to ensure it aligned with the business. The company enlisted project directors from both business and IT departments. Representatives from sales and marketing chaired the technology selection committees to ensure that people outside of IT were making the case for the project. Top management, including sales and marketing department heads and Celcom's CEO, are part of a steering committee for customer experience management that meets every two weeks.

Celcom's integrated systems make it possible for call center representatives to respond much more rapidly to customer queries. In the past, customer agents needed to toggle between two to five screens to do their work. Now they work with just a single screen, which increases efficiency. Using fewer screens cuts average call-handling time by 15 to 20 percent. BSS includes a new tablet-based app for Celcom dealers that makes signing a customer up for a new mobile phone completely paperless. New phone activation time has been cut from two hours to two minutes. Fewer activations require manual follow-up. Celcom dealers and customers are happier.

Inventory of mobile handsets at Celcom facilities and dealer stores is now centralized and managed using BSS. Dealers can see what Celcom has in stock, and Celcom inventory managers can monitor the stock on dealer shelves. More detailed inventory control helps Celcom move more products because it can ship fast-selling units to dealers before shortages occur or have marketers target promotions in regions where the company want to move specific products. This would have been impossible before. Salespeople are beginning to use big data collected in BSS to better manage sales by region.

Celcom is now much closer to achieving its brand vision: pleasing its customers and exceeding their expectations.

Sources: Jessica Sirkin, "Oracle Implementation at Celcom Brings IT, Business Together," searchoracle.techtarget.com, accessed January 17, 2016; www.celcom.com, accessed January 18, 2016; Fred Sandsmark, "Customers First," *Profit Magazine*, May 2014; and Oracle Corporation, "Celcom Transforms Its Customer Experience with Industry Leading Oracle Communications Suite," March 31, 2014.

CASE STUDY QUESTIONS

1. What was the problem at Celcom described in this case? What management, organization, and technology factors contributed to this problem?

2. What was Celcom's business strategy, and what was the role of customer relationship management in that strategy?

3. Describe Celcom's solution to its problem. What management, organization, and technology issues had to be addressed by the solution?

4. How effective was this solution? How did it affect the way Celcom ran its business and its business performance?

Another important output of analytical CRM is the customer's lifetime value to the firm. **Customer lifetime value (CLTV)** is based on the relationship between the revenue produced by a specific customer, the expenses incurred in acquiring and servicing that customer, and the expected life of the relationship between the customer and the company.

Business Value of Customer Relationship Management Systems

Companies with effective customer relationship management systems realize many benefits, including increased customer satisfaction, reduced direct-marketing costs, more effective marketing, and lower costs for customer acquisition and retention. Information from CRM systems increases sales revenue by identifying the most profitable customers and segments for focused marketing and cross-selling (see the Interactive Session on Organizations).

Customer churn is reduced as sales, service, and marketing respond better to customer needs. The **churn rate** measures the number of customers who stop using or purchasing products or services from a company. It is an important indicator of the growth or decline of a firm's customer base.

9-4 What are the challenges that enterprise applications pose, and how are enterprise applications taking advantage of new technologies?

Many firms have implemented enterprise systems and systems for supply chain and customer relationship management because they are such powerful instruments for achieving operational excellence and enhancing decision making. But precisely because they are so powerful in changing the way the organization works, they are challenging to implement. Let's briefly examine some of these challenges as well as new ways of obtaining value from these systems.

Enterprise Application Challenges

Promises of dramatic reductions in inventory costs, order-to-delivery time, more efficient customer response, and higher product and customer profitability make enterprise systems and systems for SCM and CRM very alluring. But to obtain this value, you must clearly understand how your business has to change to use these systems effectively.

Enterprise applications involve complex pieces of software that are very expensive to purchase and implement. It might take a large Fortune 500 company several years to complete a large-scale implementation of an enterprise system or a system for SCM or CRM. According to a 2015 survey of 562 companies conducted by Panorama Consulting Solutions, the average cost of an ERP project was $6.1 million. Projects took an average of 15.7 months to complete, and 53 percent of the projects delivered 50 percent or less of the expected benefits. Approximately 58 percent of these projects exceeded their planned budgets, and 65 percent experienced schedule overruns (Panorama Consulting Solutions, 2015). Changes in project scope and additional customization work add to implementation delays and costs.

Enterprise applications require not only deep-seated technological changes but also fundamental changes in the way the business operates. Companies must make sweeping changes to their business processes to work with the software. Employees must accept new job functions and responsibilities. They must learn how to perform a new set of work activities and understand how the information they enter into the system can affect other parts of the company.

This requires new organizational learning and should also be factored into ERP implementation costs.

SCM systems require multiple organizations to share information and business processes. Each participant in the system may have to change some of its processes and the way it uses information to create a system that best serves the supply chain as a whole.

Some firms experienced enormous operating problems and losses when they first implemented enterprise applications because they didn't understand how much organizational change was required. For example, Kmart had trouble getting products to store shelves when it first implemented i2 Technologies (now JDA Software) SCM software. The i2 software did not work well with Kmart's promotion-driven business model, which created sharp spikes in demand for products. Overstock.com's order tracking system went down for a full week when the company replaced a homegrown system with an Oracle enterprise system. The company rushed to implement the software and did not properly synchronize the Oracle software's process for recording customer refunds with its accounts receivable system. The chapter-ending case shows how rushed implementation of enterprise applications contributed to Target Canada's business failure.

Enterprise applications also introduce switching costs. When you adopt an enterprise application from a single vendor, such as SAP, Oracle, or others, it is very costly to switch vendors, and your firm becomes dependent on the vendor to upgrade its product and maintain your installation.

Enterprise applications are based on organization-wide definitions of data. You'll need to understand exactly how your business uses its data and how the data would be organized in a CRM, SCM, or ERP system. CRM systems typically require some data cleansing work.

Enterprise software vendors are addressing these problems by offering pared-down versions of their software and fast-start programs for small and medium-sized businesses and best-practice guidelines for larger companies. Companies are also achieving more flexibility by using cloud applications for functions not addressed by the basic enterprise software so that they are not constrained by a single do-it-all type of system.

Companies adopting enterprise applications can also save time and money by keeping customizations to a minimum. For example, Kennametal, a $2 billion metal-cutting tools company in Pennsylvania, had spent $10 million over 13 years maintaining an ERP system with more than 6400 customizations. The company replaced it with a plain-vanilla, uncustomized version of SAP enterprise software and changed its business processes to conform to the software.

Next-Generation Enterprise Applications

Today, enterprise application vendors are delivering more value by becoming more flexible, web-enabled, mobile, and capable of integration with other systems. Stand-alone enterprise systems, customer relationship management systems, and SCM systems are becoming a thing of the past. The major enterprise software vendors have created what they call *enterprise solutions, enterprise suites,* or e-business suites to make their CRM, SCM, and ERP systems work closely with each other and link to systems of customers and suppliers. SAP Business Suite, Oracle E-Business Suite, and Microsoft Dynamics Suite (aimed at midsized companies) are examples, and they now use web services and service-oriented architecture (SOA) (see Chapter 5).

SAP's next-generation enterprise applications incorporate SOA standards and can link SAP's own applications and web services developed by independent software vendors. Oracle also has included SOA and business process management capabilities in its Fusion middleware products. Businesses can use these tools to create platforms for new or improved business processes that integrate information from multiple applications.

Next-generation enterprise applications also include open source and cloud solutions as well as more functionality available on mobile platforms. Open source products such as Compiere, Apache Open for Business (OFBiz), and Openbravo do not offer as many capabilities as large commercial enterprise software but are attractive to companies such as small manufacturers because of their low cost.

For small- and medium-sized businesses, SAP offers cloud-based versions of its Business One and Business ByDesign enterprise software solutions (see the chapter-opening case study). Cloud-based enterprise systems are also offered by smaller vendors such as NetSuite and Plex Systems, but they are not as popular as cloud-based CRM products. The undisputed global market leader in cloud-based CRM systems is Salesforce.com, with more than 100,000 customers. Salesforce.com delivers its service through Internet-connected computers or mobile devices, and it is widely used by small, medium, and large enterprises. As cloud-based products mature, more companies will be choosing to run all or part of their enterprise applications in the cloud on an as-needed basis. Several Fortune 500 firms are planning to move most of their enterprise software to cloud based platforms in the next five years where they will not incur the costs of maintaining their own hardware, and the software will be charged on a metered basis.

Social CRM and Business Intelligence

CRM software vendors are enhancing their products to take advantage of social networking technologies. These social enhancements help firms identify new ideas more rapidly, improve team productivity, and deepen interactions with customers (see Chapter 10). Using **social CRM** tools, businesses can better engage with their customers by, for example, analyzing their sentiments about their products and services.

Social CRM tools enable a business to connect customer conversations and relationships from social networking sites to CRM processes. The leading CRM vendors now offer such tools to link data from social networks into their CRM software. SAP, Salesforce.com and Oracle CRM products now feature technology to monitor, track, and analyze social media activity in Facebook, LinkedIn, Twitter, YouTube, and other sites. Business intelligence and analytics software vendors such as SAS also have capabilities for social media analytics (with several measures of customer engagement across a variety of social networks) along with campaign management tools for testing and optimizing both social and traditional web-based campaigns.

Salesforce.com connected its system for tracking leads in the sales process with social-listening and social-media marketing tools, enabling users to tailor their social-marketing dollars to core customers and observe the resulting comments. If an ad agency wants to run a targeted Facebook or Twitter ad, these capabilities make it possible to aim the ad specifically at people in the client's lead pipeline who are already being tracked in the CRM system. Users will be able to view tweets as they take place in real time and perhaps uncover new leads. They can also manage multiple campaigns and compare them all to figure out which ones generate the highest click-through rates and cost per click.

Business Intelligence in Enterprise Applications

Enterprise application vendors have added business intelligence features to help managers obtain more meaningful information from the massive amounts of data these systems generate. SAP now makes it possible for its enterprise applications to use HANA in-memory computing technology so that they are capable of much more rapid and complex data analysis. Included are tools for flexible reporting, ad hoc analysis, interactive dashboards, what-if scenario analysis, and data visualization. Rather than requiring users to leave an application and launch separate reporting and analytics tools, the vendors are starting to embed analytics within the context of the application itself. They are also offering complementary analytics products such as SAP BusinessObjects and Oracle Business Intelligence Enterprise Edition.

The major enterprise application vendors offer portions of their products that work on mobile handhelds. You can find out more about this topic in our Learning Track on Wireless Applications for Customer Relationship Management, Supply Chain Management, and Healthcare.

Review Summary

9-1 *How do enterprise systems help businesses achieve operational excellence?*

Enterprise software is based on a suite of integrated software modules and a common central database. The database collects data from and feeds the data into numerous applications that can support nearly all of an organization's internal business activities. When one process enters new information, the information is made available immediately to other business processes.

Enterprise systems support organizational centralization by enforcing uniform data standards and business processes throughout the company and a single unified technology platform. The firmwide data that enterprise systems generate help managers evaluate organizational performance.

9-2 *How do supply chain management systems coordinate planning, production, and logistics with suppliers?*

Supply chain management (SCM) systems automate the flow of information among members of the supply chain so they can use it to make better decisions about when and how much to purchase, produce, or ship. More accurate information from supply chain management systems reduces uncertainty and the impact of the bullwhip effect.

Supply chain management software includes software for supply chain planning and for supply chain execution. Internet technology facilitates the management of global supply chains by providing the connectivity for organizations in different countries to share supply chain information. Improved communication among supply chain members also facilitates efficient customer response and movement toward a demand-driven model.

9-3 *How do customer relationship management systems help firms achieve customer intimacy?*

Customer relationship management (CRM) systems integrate and automate customer-facing processes in sales, marketing, and customer service, providing an enterprise-wide view of customers. Companies can use this customer knowledge when they interact with customers to provide them with better service or sell new products and services. These systems also identify profitable or unprofitable customers or opportunities to reduce the churn rate.

The major customer relationship management software packages provide capabilities for both operational CRM and analytical CRM. They often include modules for managing relationships with selling partners (partner relationship management) and for employee relationship management.

9-4 *What are the challenges that enterprise applications pose, and how are enterprise applications taking advantage of new technologies?*

Enterprise applications are difficult to implement. They require extensive organizational change, large new software investments, and careful assessment of how these systems will enhance organizational performance. Enterprise applications cannot provide value if they are implemented atop flawed processes or if firms do not know how to use these systems to measure performance improvements. Employees require training to prepare for new procedures and roles. Attention to data management is essential.

Enterprise applications are now more flexible, web-enabled, and capable of integration with other systems, using web services and service-oriented architecture (SOA). They also have open source and on-demand versions and can run in cloud infrastructures or on mobile platforms. CRM software has added social networking capabilities to enhance internal collaboration, deepen interactions with customers, and use data from social networking sites. Open source, mobile, and cloud versions of some of these products are becoming available.

Key Terms

Analytical CRM, 355
Bullwhip effect, 345
Churn rate, 359
Cross-selling, 354
Customer lifetime value (CLTV), 358
Demand planning, 346
Employee relationship management (ERM), 353
Enterprise software, 341
Just-in-time strategy, 345
Operational CRM, 355

Partner relationship management (PRM), 353
Pull-based model, 348
Push-based model, 348
Sales force automation (SFA), 353
Social CRM, 361
Supply chain, 343
Supply chain execution systems, 346
Supply chain planning systems, 345
Touch point, 352

MyMISLab

To complete the problems with the MyMISLab, go to the EOC Discussion Questions in MyMISLab.

Review Questions

9-1 How do enterprise systems help businesses achieve operational excellence?

- Define an enterprise system and explain how enterprise software works.
- Describe how enterprise systems provide value for a business.

9-2 How do supply chain management systems coordinate planning, production, and logistics with suppliers?

- Define a supply chain and identify each of its components.
- Explain how supply chain management systems help reduce the bullwhip effect and how they provide value for a business.
- Define and compare supply chain planning systems and supply chain execution systems.

- Describe the challenges of global supply chains and how Internet technology can help companies manage them better.
- Distinguish between a push-based and a pull-based model of supply chain management and explain how contemporary supply chain management systems facilitate a pull-based model.

9-3 How do customer relationship management systems help firms achieve customer intimacy?

- Define customer relationship management and explain why customer relationships are so important today.
- Describe how partner relationship management (PRM) and employee relationship management (ERM) are related to customer relationship management (CRM).

- Describe the tools and capabilities of customer relationship management software for sales, marketing, and customer service.
- Distinguish between operational and analytical CRM.

9-4 What are the challenges that enterprise applications pose, and how are enterprise applications taking advantage of new technologies?

- List and describe the challenges enterprise applications pose.

- Explain how these challenges can be addressed.
- Describe how enterprise applications are taking advantage of SOA, cloud computing, and open source software.
- Define social CRM and explain how customer relationship management systems are using social networking.

Discussion Questions

9-5 Supply chain management is less about managing the physical movement of goods and more about managing information. Discuss the implications of this statement.

9-6 If a company wants to implement an enterprise application, it had better do its homework. Discuss the implications of this statement.

9-7 Which enterprise application should a business install first: ERP, SCM, or CRM? Explain your answer.

Hands-On MIS Projects

The projects in this section give you hands-on experience analyzing business process integration, suggesting supply chain management and customer relationship management applications, using database software to manage customer service requests, and evaluating supply chain management business services. Visit MyMISLab's Multimedia Library to access this chapter's Hands-On MIS Projects,

Management Decision Problems

9-8 Toronto-based Mercedes-Benz Canada, with a network of 55 dealers, did not know enough about its customers. Dealers provided customer data to the company on an ad hoc basis. Mercedes did not force dealers to report this information. There was no real incentive for dealers to share information with the company. How could CRM and PRM systems help solve this problem?

9-9 Office Depot sells a wide range of office supply products and services in the United States and internationally. The company tries to offer a wider range of office supplies at lower cost than other retailers by using just-in-time replenishment and tight inventory control systems. It uses information from a demand forecasting system and point-of-sale data to replenish its inventory in its 1,600 retail stores. Explain how these systems help Office Depot minimize costs and any other benefits they provide. Identify and describe other supply chain management applications that would be especially helpful to Office Depot.

Improving Decision Making: Using Database Software to Manage Customer Service Requests

Software skills: Database design; querying and reporting
Business skills: Customer service analysis

9-10 In this exercise, you'll use database software to develop an application that tracks customer service requests and analyzes customer data to identify customers meriting priority treatment.

Prime Service is a large service company that provides maintenance and repair services for close to 1,200 commercial businesses in New York, New Jersey, and Connecticut. Its customers include businesses of all sizes. Customers with service needs call into its customer service department with requests for repairing heating ducts, broken windows, leaky roofs, broken water pipes, and other problems. The company assigns each request a number and writes down the service request number, the identification number of the customer account, the date of the request, the type of equipment requiring repair, and a brief description of the problem. The service requests are handled on a first-come-first-served basis. After the service work has been completed, Prime calculates the cost of the work, enters the price on the service request form, and bills the client. This arrangement treats the most important and profitable clients—those with accounts of more than $70,000—no differently from its clients with small accounts. Management would like to find a way to provide its best customers with better service. It would also like to know which types of service problems occur most frequently so that it can make sure it has adequate resources to address them.

Prime Service has a small database with client account information, which can be found in MyMIS-Lab. Use database software to design a solution that would enable Prime's customer service representatives to identify the most important customers so that they could receive priority service. Your solution will require more than one table. Populate your database with at least 10 service requests. Create several reports that would be of interest to management, such as a list of the highest—and lowest—priority accounts and a report showing the most frequently occurring service problems. Create a report listing service calls that customer service representatives should respond to first on a specific date.

Achieving Operational Excellence: Evaluating Supply Chain Management Services

Software skills: Web browser and presentation software
Business skills: Evaluating supply chain management services

9-11 In addition to carrying goods from one place to another, some trucking companies provide supply chain management services and help their customers manage their information. In this project, you'll use the web to research and evaluate two of these business services. Investigate the websites of two companies, UPS Logistics and Schneider Logistics, to see how these companies' services can be used for supply chain management. Then respond to the following questions:

- What supply chain processes can each of these companies support for its clients?
- How can customers use the websites of each company to help them with supply chain management?
- Compare the supply chain management services these companies provide. Which company would you select to help your firm manage its supply chain? Why?

Collaboration and Teamwork Project

Analyzing Enterprise Application Vendors

9-12 With a group of three or four other students, use the web to research and evaluate the products of two vendors of enterprise application software. You could compare, for example, the SAP and Oracle enterprise systems, the supply chain management systems from JDA Software and SAP, or the customer relationship management systems of Oracle and Salesforce.com. Use what you have learned from these companies' websites to compare the software products you have selected in terms of business functions supported, technology platforms, cost, and ease of use. Which vendor would you select? Why? Would you select the same vendor for a small business (50–300 employees) as well as for a large one? If possible, use Google Docs and Google Drive or Google Sites to brainstorm, organize, and develop a presentation of your findings for the class.

How Supply Chain Management Problems Killed Target Canada
CASE STUDY

Target is one of the world's most successful general merchandise retailers, with 1,801 retail store locations and a powerful brand image as a fashion-forward discounter. It is not as big or far-flung as Walmart, with $74 billion in annual revenue compared with $482 billion for Walmart, and all of its stores are located in the United States. (Walmart has 11,600 all over the world.) Target is very good at what it does and, ideally, would to like to grow like Walmart. In 2011 it decided to make its first foray into global expansion by opening up retail stores in Canada. That year Target acquired the leaseholds of 189 locations operated by Hudson's Bay Company's Zellers discount chain for $1.8 billion, hoping to open Target stores in 124 of these sites by the end of 2013. This was a very ambitious—and possibly unrealistic—timetable.

Target opened its first Canadian stores in March 2013. Target's expansion into Canada was highly anticipated by consumers and feared by rivals, but it failed miserably. On January 15, 2015, Target Canada filed for bankruptcy protection, announcing that it would close all of its 133 Canadian stores, and began liquidating their inventory. All Target Canada stores were closed by April 12, 2015. Some experts consider Target Canada a case study in what retailers should not do when they enter a new market.

Target quickly moved to build three new gigantic distribution centers in Canada. (A distribution center is where all the products from thousands of vendors are sorted and prepared for shipment to individual stores.) Unfortunately, Target Canada was unable to keep track of its products or make sure that the right amounts of products were being ordered, stored, and shipped. At first too few products were arriving at the distribution centers, leaving store shelves bare and Canadian customers empty-handed. Later the distribution centers became overwhelmed with too much product. Target's information systems could not properly compute shelving locations. Target had the stock, but it was stuck in the distribution centers and store shelves still remained empty. Making matters worse, the retail store checkout system was unreliable and didn't process transactions properly. And Target Canada also had higher product prices and less product selection than U.S. Target stores. Canadian sales never took off, and Target had to end its business in Canada.

How could this have happened? First, Target's business was geared to operating domestically in the United States. To operate in Canada, its information systems would have to be able to calculate prices in Canadian currency, which is worth about 72 percent of a U.S. dollar, with the conversion rate constantly fluctuating. Canada also uses the metric system, so the system would have to convert inches and feet into centimeters and meters as well. Knowing the size of an item and the size of packaging is essential for stocking shelves and inventory management. Target's supply chain management and pricing software would have to be modified to handle multiple measurement systems and currencies. Adding to the complexity, products for Target's Canadian market might have different dimensions from those for the United States. A box of shower curtain hooks for the U.S. market might be 12 inches long but only 11 ½ inches for Canada, expressed in centimeters. In other words, internationalizing systems takes a great deal of work and planning.

Target's U.S. operations used custom-built systems for ordering products from vendors, moving goods through warehouses, and stocking store shelves. These systems worked very well, and Target's IT staff and business end users were highly experienced in using them. Target's management had to decide whether to customize these domestic systems so they could work abroad or move to completely new systems for Canada. Because it would require considerable time and effort to internationalize these systems, Target's management opted for a new ready-made software package solution, thinking that it could be implemented faster, even if the company had little experience actually using the new system.

SAP was selected because of its functionality in enterprise resource planning (ERP) and supply chain management as well as capabilities for supporting different languages and currencies. Data on the products in Target's Canadian stores would be fed from the SAP system to other systems to forecast demand for products, manage its distribution centers, and replenish stock in the stores. Target hoped that eventually it could replace its custom homegrown systems with SAP so that the entire company would have the same set of systems worldwide. However, SAP implementations in large companies typically take a long time—often three to five years—and many millions of dollars. Target wanted to go live with SAP in only two years. This was exceedingly, if not unrealistically, ambitious, but management thought using consultants from Accenture who were highly experienced in SAP implementations would speed things up.

In 2012, once Target began ordering items for its pending Canadian launch, items sourced overseas with long lead times were stalled. Products weren't fitting into shipping containers as expected, and tariff codes were missing or incomplete. Other items weren't able to fit properly onto store shelves. The data used by Target's supply chain software was full of flaws, and the system required correct data to function properly and ensure products moved as anticipated Product dimensions were in inches, not centimeters, or entered in the wrong order. Sometimes the wrong currency was used. Important information was missing, and there were numerous typos.

Target's rush to launch pressured suppliers to enter data quickly into SAP for roughly 75,000 different products. The data had to either be imported from other systems or entered from scratch. A record for a single item might have dozens of fields to fill out, such as fields for the manufacturer, the model, the dimensions, the weight, and how many units can fit into a shipping case. Much of the data were entered incorrectly. Widths were entered instead of lengths, and prices and item descriptions were entered incorrectly as well. Young merchandising assistants in charge of obtaining the details from suppliers were often not experienced enough to challenge vendors on the accuracy of the product information they provided. Information in Target's system was estimated to be only 30 percent accurate, compared with an accuracy rate of 98 to 99 percent for similar data in U.S. firms.

It also turned out that Manhattan, the company's software for running its warehouses, did not communicate well with SAP. For example, an employee at headquarters might have ordered 1,000 toothbrushes but mistakenly entered into SAP data that the shipment would be packaged as 10 boxes of 100 toothbrushes each. But the shipment might actually be configured differently as four large packages containing 250 toothbrushes each. Target's distribution system would treat this shipment as if it didn't exist and couldn't process the information. It would identify the shipment as a "problem area." These kinds of problems crop up at any warehouse, but at Target Canada, they occurred way too often.

Target had purchased a sophisticated and highly regarded system from JDA Software for supply chain forecasting and replenishment. However, this software typically requires years of historical data before it can provide accurate sales forecasts. Lacking such data to feed the system, Target's buying team instead used wildly optimistic projections, which assumed Canadian store sales from the start would be as high as operational stores in the United States even though Target Canada was not yet that well established.

Adding to Target Canada's system woes, the point-of-sale (POS) system was not working properly. Terminals for cash payments took too long to boot up and sometimes froze, items wouldn't scan, the self-checkout stations gave incorrect change, or the POS system would not provide the correct price. Target Canada had purchased POS software from an Israeli company called Retalix. Unlike SAP, Retalix is not an industry standard. It is believed that Target chose this software package because of touted capabilities for processing payments on mobile devices. Target Canada didn't have time to replace this software and kept going with all these bugs.

By fall of 2013, Target's three distribution centers were overflowing with goods. Target had to rent additional storage facilities to accommodate the inventory overflow, making it even more difficult to track down items. Target stores might end up with too much of some products and too little of others. The auto-replenishment system, which kept track of what a store had in stock, wasn't functioning properly, either. Target Canada's system required data about the exact dimensions of every product and every shelf in order to calculate whether employees needed to fill an empty rack. Much of the data were still incorrect, so the system couldn't make accurate calculations. The auto-replenishment system performed so badly that Target shut off the system at its three test stores and had employees replenish shelves manually. Auto-replenishment wasn't reinstated until months later.

There was another reason for the discrepancies between what items appeared to be in stock at headquarters and were actually missing from stores. Target Canada's replenishment system had a feature to notify distribution centers to ship more product when a store ran out. Some of the business analysts responsible for this function, however, were purposely turning it off. These business analysts were judged based on the percentage of their products that were in stock at any given time. When the auto-replenishment switch was turned off, the system wouldn't report an item as out of stock, so the analyst's numbers would look good on paper. To prevent further gaming the system, Target's IT team built a tool that reported when the system was turned on or off and determined whether there was a legitimate reason for it to be turned off (for example, if an item was seasonal.) The analysts were denied access to these controls.

In 2014 Target's IT staff was finally able to install an automatic verification tool to catch bad data before they could enter SAP. The system wouldn't allow a purchase order to proceed until an employee entered product code data that were correct. The problem was that the verification tool was deployed too late. On January 15, 2015, Target Canada announced it was filing for bankruptcy protection. The company had already spent $7 billion on expanding into Canada and was not projected to show a profit until 2021 at the earliest. All of Target Canada's 133 stores were closed, and 17,600 employees lost their jobs.

Sources: David Gewirtz, "Billion Dollar Mistake: How Inferior IT Killed Target Canada," *ZDNet,* February 11, 2016; Joe Castaldo, "The Last Days of Target," www.canadianbusiness.com, accessed February 12, 2016; www.target.com, accessed March 1, 2016; and Marc Wulfraat, "The Aftermath of Target Canada's Collapse," Canadian Grocer, March 10, 2015.

CASE STUDY QUESTIONS

9-13 How important was supply chain management for Target Canada? How did it relate to its business model? Explain your answer.

9-14 Identify all the problems Target Canada encountered that prevented it from becoming a successful retailer. What were the management, organization, and technology factors that contributed to these problems?

9-15 How much of Target Canada's problems were technology based? Explain your answer.

9-16 How responsible was management for Target Canada's problems? Explain your answer.

9-17 What things should Target Canada have done differently to be successful?

MyMISLab

Go to the Assignments section of your MyMISLab to complete these writing exercises.

9-18 What are three reasons a company would want to implement an enterprise resource planning (ERP) system and two reasons it might not want to do so?

9-19 What are the sources of data for analytical CRM systems? Provide three examples of outputs from analytical CRM systems.

Chapter 9 References

Bozarth, Cecil, and Robert B. Handfield. *Introduction to Operations and Supply Chain Management* (4th ed.). (Upper Saddle River, NJ: Prentice-Hall, 2016.)

Cole, Brenda. "Cloud ERP Users Say Up, Up and Away." *Business Information* (February 2014).

D'Avanzo, Robert, Hans von Lewinski, and Luk N. Van Wassenhove. "The Link Between Supply Chain and Financial Performance." *Supply Chain Management Review* (November 1, 2003).

Davenport, Thomas H. *Mission Critical: Realizing the Promise of Enterprise Systems.* (Boston: Harvard Business School Press, 2000.)

Davenport, Thomas H., Leandro Dalle Mule, and John Lucke. "Know What Your Customers Want Before They Do." *Harvard Business Review* (December 2011).

Essex, David. "Tomorrow's ERP Raises New Hopes, Fears." *Business Information* (February 2014).

Hitt, Lorin, D. J. Wu, and Xiaoge Zhou. "Investment in Enterprise Resource Planning: Business Impact and Productivity Measures." *Journal of Management Information Systems* 19, No. 1 (Summer 2002).

Hu, Michael and Sean T. Monahan. "Sharing Supply Chain Data in the Digital Era." *MIT Sloan Management Review* (Fall 2015).

Kanaracus, Chris. "ERP Software Project Woes Continue to Mount, Survey Says." *IT World* (February 20, 2013).

Kimberling, Eric. "5 Lessons from Successful CRM Implementations." Panorama-consulting.com (January 28, 2015).

Klein, Richard, and Arun Rai. "Interfirm Strategic Information Flows in Logistics Supply Chain Relationships." *MIS Quarterly* 33, No. 4 (December 2009).

Laudon, Kenneth C. "The Promise and Potential of Enterprise Systems and Industrial Networks." Working paper, The Concours Group. Copyright Kenneth C. Laudon (1999).

Lee, Hau, L., V. Padmanabhan, and Seugin Whang. "The Bullwhip Effect in Supply Chains." *Sloan Management Review* (Spring 1997).

Liang, Huigang, Nilesh Sharaf, Quing Hu, and Yajiong Xue. "Assimilation of Enterprise Systems: The Effect of Institutional Pressures and the Mediating Role of Top Management." *MIS Quarterly* 31, No. 1 (March 2007).

Liang, Huigang, Zeyu Peng, Yajiong Xue, Xitong Guo, and Nengmin Wang. "Employees' Exploration of Complex Systems: An Integrative View." *Journal of Management Information Systems* 32, No. 1 (2015).

Maklan, Stan, Simon Knox, and Joe Peppard. "When CRM Fails." *MIT Sloan Management Review* 52, No. 4 (Summer 2011).

Malik, Yogesh, Alex Niemeyer, and Brian Ruwadi. "Building the Supply Chain of the Future." *McKinsey Quarterly* (January 2011).

Mehta, Krishna. "Best Practices for Developing a Customer Lifetime Value Program." *Information Management* (July 28, 2011).

Morrison, Tod. "Custom ERP No Longer in Vogue." *Business Information* (February 2014).

Maurno, Dann Anthony. "The New Word on ERP." *CFO Magazine* (July 25, 2014).

Oracle Corporation. "Alcoa Implements Oracle Solution 20% Below Projected Cost, Eliminates 43 Legacy Systems." www.oracle.com, accessed August 21, 2005.

Panorama Consulting Solutions. "2015 ERP Report." (2015).

Rai, Arun, Paul A. Pavlou, Ghiyoung Im, and Steve Du. "Interfirm IT Capability Profiles and Communications for Cocreating Relational Value: Evidence from the Logistics Industry." *MIS Quarterly* 36, No. 1 (March 2012).

Rai, Arun, Ravi Patnayakuni, and Nainika Seth. "Firm Performance Impacts of Digitally Enabled Supply Chain Integration Capabilities." *MIS Quarterly* 30, No. 2 (June 2006).

Ranganathan, C., and Carol V. Brown. "ERP Investments and the Market Value of Firms: Toward an Understanding of Influential ERP Project Variables." *Information Systems Research* 17, No. 2 (June 2006).

Sarker, Supreteek, Saonee Sarker, Arvin Sahaym, and Bjørn-Andersen. "Exploring Value Cocreation in Relationships Between an ERP Vendor and its Partners: A Revelatory Case Study." *MIS Quarterly* 36, No. 1 (March 2012).

Seldon, Peter B., Cheryl Calvert, and Song Yang. "A Multi-Project Model of Key Factors Affecting Organizational Benefits from Enterprise Systems." *MIS Quarterly* 34, No. 2 (June 2010).

Strong, Diane M., and Olga Volkoff. "Understanding Organization-Enterprise System Fit: A Path to Theorizing the Information Technology Artifact." *MIS Quarterly* 34, No. 4 (December 2010).

SupplyChainBrain. "Trends in Enterprise Resource Planning Cloud Technology." (February 25, 2015).

Sussin, Jenny. "Top Use Cases and Benefits of Social for CRM in 2015." Gartner, Inc. (February 12, 2015).

Sykes, Tracy Ann, Viswanath Venkatesh, and Jonathan L. Johnson. "Enterprise System Implementation and Employee Job Performance: Understanding the Role of Advice Networks." *MIS Quarterly* 38, No. 1 (March 2014).

Tate, Wendy L., Diane Mollenkopf, Theodore Stank, and Andrea Lago da Silva. "Integrating Supply and Demand." *MIT Sloan Management Review* (Summer 2015).

Tian, Feng, and Sean Xin Xu. "How Do Enterprise Resource Planning Systems Affect Firm Risk? Post-Implementation Impact." *MIS Quarterly* 39, No. 1 (March 2015).

"Top 5 Reasons ERP Implementations Fail and What You Can Do About It." Ziff Davis (2013).

"Trends in Enterprise Resource Planning Cloud Technology." *SupplyChainBrain* (February 25, 2015).

Van Caeneghem, Alexander and Jean-Marie Becquevort. "Turning on ERP Systems Can Turn Off People." *CFO* (February 5, 2016).

Wong, Christina W.Y., Lai, Kee-Hung, and Cheng, T.C.E. "Value of Information Integration to Supply Chain Management: Roles of Internal and External Contingencies." *Journal of Management Information Systems* 28, No. 3 (Winter 2012).

10

E-commerce: Digital Markets, Digital Goods

Learning Objectives

After reading this chapter, you will be able to answer the following questions:

10-1 What are the unique features of e-commerce, digital markets, and digital goods?

10-2 What are the principal e-commerce business and revenue models?

10-3 How has e-commerce transformed marketing?

10-4 How has e-commerce affected business-to-business transactions?

10-5 What is the role of m-commerce in business, and what are the most important m-commerce applications?

10-6 What issues must be addressed when building an e-commerce presence?

MyMISLab™

Visit **mymislab.com** for simulations, tutorials, and end-of-chapter problems.

CHAPTER CASES

Uber Digitally Disrupts the Taxi Industry

Getting Social with Customers

Can Instacart Deliver?

Walmart and Amazon Duke It Out for E-commerce Supremacy

VIDEO CASES

Walmart Takes on Amazon: A Battle of IT and Management Systems

Groupon: Deals Galore

Etsy: A Marketplace and Community

Instructional Videos:

Walmart's E-commerce Fulfillment Center Network

Behind the Scenes of an Amazon Warehouse

Uber Digitally Disrupts the Taxi Industry

You're in New York, Paris, Chicago, or another major city and need a ride. Instead of trying to hail a cab, you pull out your smartphone and tap the Uber app. A Google map pops up displaying your nearby surroundings. You select a spot on the screen designating an available driver, and the app secures the ride, showing how long it will take for the ride to arrive and how much it will cost. Once you reach your destination, the fare is automatically charged to your credit card. No fumbling for money.

Rates take into account the typical factors of time and distance but also demand. Uber's software predicts areas where rides are likely to be in high demand at different times of the day. This information appears on a driver's smartphone so that the driver knows where to linger and, ideally, pick up customers within minutes of a request for a ride. Uber also offers a higher-priced town car service for business executives and a ride-sharing service.

Uber runs much leaner than a traditional taxi company does. Uber does not own taxis and has no maintenance and financing costs. It does not have employees, so it claims, but instead calls the drivers independent contractors, who receive a cut of each fare. Uber is not encumbered with employee costs such as workers' compensation, minimum wage requirements, background checks on drivers, driver training, health insurance, or commercial licensing costs. Uber has shifted the costs of running a taxi service entirely to the drivers and to the customers using their cell phones. What Uber does is provide a smartphone-based platform that enables people who want a service—like a taxi—to find a provider who can meet that need.

© FocusTechnology/Alamy Stock Photo

Uber relies on user reviews of drivers and the ride experience to identify problematic drivers and driver reviews of customers to identify problematic passengers. It also sets standards for cleanliness. It uses the reviews to discipline drivers. Uber does not publicly report how many poorly rated drivers or passengers there are in its system. Uber also uses software that monitors sensors in drivers' smartphones to monitor their driving behavior.

Uber is headquartered in San Francisco and was founded in 2009 by Travis Kalanick and Garrett Camp. By 2016, it had more than 400,000 drivers working in 400 cities and 60 countries generating estimated revenue of $10 billion and gross earnings (after paying its drivers but not including marketing and other operating expenses) of $2 billion. Once these other expenses are accounted for, Uber is losing $1 billion annually. More than 8 million people use Uber on a regular basis. However, Uber's over-the-top success has created its own set of challenges.

By digitally disrupting a traditional and highly regulated industry, Uber has ignited a firestorm of opposition from existing taxi services in the United States and around the world. Who can compete with an upstart firm offering a 40 percent price reduction when demand for taxis is low? (When demand is high, Uber prices surge.) What city or state wants to give up regulatory control over passenger safety, protection from criminals, driver training, and a healthy revenue stream generated by charging taxi firms for a taxi license?

If Uber is the poster child for the new on-demand economy, it's also an iconic example of the social costs and conflict associated with this new kind of business model. Uber has been accused of denying its drivers the benefits of employee status by classifying them as contractors; violating public transportation laws and regulations throughout the United States and the world; abusing the personal information it has collected on ordinary people; and failing to protect public safety by refusing to perform criminal, medical, and financial background checks on its drivers.

Critics fear that Uber and other on-demand firms have the potential for creating a society of part-time, low-paid, temp work, displacing traditionally full-time, secure jobs—the so-called Uberization of work. Uber responds to this fear by saying it is lowering the cost of transportation, expanding the demand for ride services, and expanding opportunities for car drivers, whose pay is about the same as other taxi drivers.

Does Uber have a sustainable business model? If the company continues to triple revenue every year, the answer is yes, but Uber has competitors, including Lyft in the United States and local firms in Asia and Europe. New, smaller competing firms offering app-based cab-hailing services are cropping up, including Sidecar, Via, Tipda, and Shuddl. Established taxi firms in New York and other cities are launching their own hailing apps and trumpeting their fixed-rate prices. Uber is pressing on, with a new service for same-day deliveries, and continuing to disrupt established industries.

Sources: Rob Berger, "Uber Settlement Takes Customers for a Ride," *Forbes,* April 22, 2016; Mike Isaac and Noam Scheiber, "Uber Settles Cases with Concessions, but Drivers Stay Freelancers," *New York Times,* April 21, 2016; Brian Solomon, "Leaked: Uber's Financials Show Huge Growth, Even Bigger Losses," *Forbes,* January 12, 2016; Douglas MacMillan, "Uber's App Will Soon Begin Tracking Driving Behavior," *Wall Street Journal,* June 29, 2016; Christopher Mims, "How Everyone Misjudges the Sharing Economy," *Wall Street Journal*, May 26, 2015; Douglas Macmillan, "Icahn Puts Big Wager on Uber Rival Lyft," *Wall Street Journal*, May 16, 2015; and Douglas MacMillan, "The $50 Billion Question: Can Uber Deliver?" *Wall Street Journal*, June 15, 2015.

Uber exemplifies two major trends in e-commerce today. This e-commerce business is powered by the near-ubiquitous use of mobile smartphones, and it is one of so-called on-demand companies such as Lyft (Uber's primary competitor), Airbnb (rooms for rent), Handy and Homejoy (both part-time household helpers), Instacart (grocery shoppers), and Washio (clothes washing). These on-demand firms don't sell goods; instead, they have built a platform by which people who want a service—such as a taxi—can find a

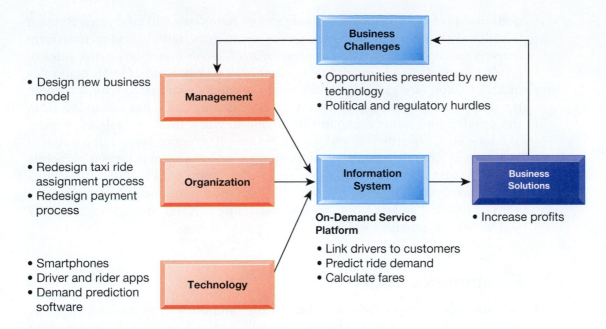

- Design new business model

Management

- Opportunities presented by new technology
- Political and regulatory hurdles

- Redesign taxi ride assignment process
- Redesign payment process

Organization

Information System

Business Solutions

On-Demand Service Platform

- Increase profits

- Smartphones
- Driver and rider apps
- Demand prediction software

Technology

- Link drivers to customers
- Predict ride demand
- Calculate fares

provider to fill the demand. On-demand firms are currently considered the hottest business model in e-commerce, and they are disrupting major industries.

The chapter-opening diagram calls attention to important points this case and this chapter raise. The business challenge facing Uber is how to create a profitable company based on a new, on-demand business model. Uber's management decided to base its business on the use of wireless smartphones and apps that link buyers and sellers of taxi transportation services. The business earns revenue by charging users' credit cards for fares and giving a percentage of each fare to the driver, and it can charge prices that vary dynamically with demand. Uber has a lower cost structure than traditional cab companies because it does not have to pay employee wages or benefits, auto insurance, fuel, and licensing fees. Participating drivers pay for their own cars, fuel, and insurance. Under certain conditions, if demand is high, Uber can be more expensive than taxis, but it has disrupted the taxi industry because it offers a reliable, fast, convenient alternative to traditional taxi companies that book rides using the telephone, a central dispatcher using antiquated radio communications, or potential customers standing on street corners trying to hail a cab. Uber's growth is skyrocketing, but the company has to contend with many competitors and political and regulatory opposition from workers and the industries it is disrupting. It is still too early to tell whether Uber and other on-demand businesses will succeed.

Here are some questions to think about: Do you think Uber's business model is viable? Why or why not? How do you feel about using Uber compared with a regulated taxi?

10-1 What are the unique features of e-commerce, digital markets, and digital goods?

In 2017, purchasing goods and services online by using smartphones, tablets, and desktop computers will be ubiquitous. In 2017, an estimated 217 million Americans will shop online, and 185 million will purchase something online, as did millions of others worldwide. Although most purchases still take place through traditional channels, e-commerce continues to grow rapidly and to transform the way many companies do business. In 2017, e-commerce consumer sales of goods, services, travel, and online content, about 12 percent of total retail sales of $5.6 trillion, are growing at 15 percent annually (compared with 3 percent for traditional retailers) (eMarketer, 2016a). E-commerce has expanded from the desktop and home computer to mobile devices, from an isolated activity to a new social commerce, and from a *Fortune* 1000 commerce with a national audience to local merchants and consumers whose location is known to mobile devices. At the top 100 e-commerce retail sites, more than half of online shoppers arrive from their smartphones, although most continue to purchase using a PC or tablet. The key words for understanding this new e-commerce in 2017 will be "social, mobile, local."

E-commerce Today

E-commerce refers to the use of the Internet and the web to transact business. More formally, e-commerce is about digitally enabled commercial transactions between and among organizations and individuals. For the most part, this refers to transactions that occur over the Internet and the web. Commercial transactions involve the exchange of value (e.g., money) across organizational or individual boundaries in return for products and services.

E-commerce began in 1995 when one of the first Internet portals, Netscape. com, accepted the first ads from major corporations and popularized the idea that the web could be used as a new medium for advertising and sales. No one envisioned at the time what would turn out to be an exponential growth curve for e-commerce retail sales, which doubled and tripled in the early years. E-commerce grew at double-digit rates until the recession of 2008–2009, when growth slowed to a crawl, and revenues flattened (see Figure 10.1), not bad considering that traditional retail sales were shrinking by 5 percent annually. Since then, offline retail sales have increased only a few percentage points a year, whereas online e-commerce has been a stellar success.

FIGURE 10.1 THE GROWTH OF E-COMMERCE

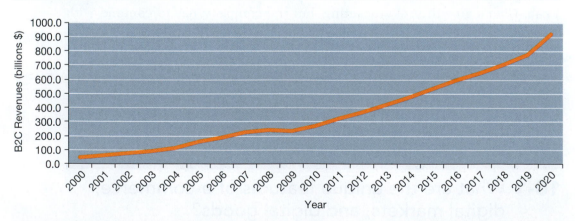

Retail e-commerce revenues grew 15–25 percent per year until the recession of 2008–2009, when they slowed measurably. In 2016, e-commerce revenues grew at an estimated 15 percent annually.

Sources: Based on data from eMarketer, "US Retail Ecommerce Sales, 2014–2020," 2016; eMarketer, "US Digital Travel Sales, 2014–2020," 2016; and eMarketer chart, "US Mobile Downloads and In-App Revenues, 2013–2016," 2016.

The very rapid growth in e-commerce in the early years created a market bubble in e-commerce stocks. Like all bubbles, the dot-com bubble burst (in March 2001). A large number of e-commerce companies failed during this process. Yet for many others, such as Amazon, eBay, Expedia, and Google, the results have been more positive: soaring revenues, fine-tuned business models that produce profits and rising stock prices. By 2006, e-commerce revenues returned to solid growth, and have continued to be the fastest-growing form of retail trade in the United States, Europe, and Asia.

- Online consumer sales will grow to an estimated $669 billion in 2017, an increase of more than 15 percent over 2016 (including travel services and digital downloads), with 185 million people purchasing online and an additional 217 million shopping and gathering information but not purchasing (eMarketer, 2016a). The Internet influences more than $1.3 trillion in retail commerce that takes places in physical stores.

- The number of individuals of all ages online in the United States is expected to grow to 270 million in 2017, up from 147 million in 2004. In the world, more than 3.3 billion people are now connected to the Internet. Growth in the overall Internet population has spurred growth in e-commerce (Internet World Stats, 2016).

- Approximately 96 million households will have broadband access to the Internet in 2017, representing about 78 percent of all households.

- About 223 million Americans will access the Internet by using a smartphone. Mobile e-commerce has begun a rapid growth based on apps, ringtones, downloaded entertainment, and location-based services. Mobile e-commerce will account for about $170 billion in 2017, 25 percent of all e-commerce, and about 50 percent of all retail e-commerce. In a few years, mobile phones and tablets will be the most common Internet access device. Currently, more than 80 percent of all mobile phone users access the Internet by using their phones (eMarketer, 2016b).

- B2B e-commerce (use of the Internet for business-to-business commerce and collaboration among business partners) expanded to more than $7 trillion. Table 10.1 highlights these new e-commerce developments.

The New E-commerce: Social, Mobile, Local

One of the biggest changes is the extent to which e-commerce has become more social, mobile, and local. Online marketing once consisted largely of creating a corporate website, buying display ads on Yahoo, purchasing ad words on Google, and sending e-mail messages. The workhorse of online marketing was the display ad. It still is, but it's increasingly being replaced by video ads, which are far more effective. Display ads from the very beginning of the Internet were based on television ads, where brand messages were flashed before millions of users who were not expected to respond immediately, ask questions, or make observations. If the ads did not work, the solution was often to repeat the ad. The primary measure of success was how many eyeballs (unique visitors) a website produced and how many impressions a marketing campaign generated. (An impression was one ad shown to one person.) Both of these measures were carryovers from the world of television, which measures marketing in terms of audience size and ad views.

From Eyeballs to Conversations: Conversational Commerce

After 2007, all this changed with the rapid growth of Facebook and other social sites, the explosive growth of smartphones beginning with Apple iPhone, and the growing interest in local marketing. What's different about the new

TABLE 10.1 THE GROWTH OF E-COMMERCE

BUSINESS TRANSFORMATION

E-commerce remains the fastest-growing form of commerce when compared to physical retail stores, services, and entertainment. Social, mobile, and local commerce have become the fastest-growing forms of e-commerce.

The breadth of e-commerce offerings grows, especially in the services economy of social networking, travel, entertainment, retail apparel, jewelry, appliances, and home furnishings.

The online demographics of shoppers broaden to match that of ordinary shoppers.

Pure e-commerce business models are refined further to achieve higher levels of profitability, whereas traditional retail brands, such as Walmart, Sears, JCPenney, L.L.Bean, and Macy's, use e-commerce to retain their dominant retail positions. Walmart, the world's largest retailer, has decided to get serious about e-commerce and take on Amazon with a more than $1 billion investment in its e-commerce efforts (see the chapter-ending case study).

Small businesses and entrepreneurs continue to flood the e-commerce marketplace, often riding on the infrastructures created by industry giants, such as Amazon, Apple, and Google, and increasingly taking advantage of cloud-based computing resources.

Mobile e-commerce has taken off in the United States with location-based services and entertainment downloads, including e-books, movies, music, and television shows. Mobile e-commerce will generate more than $170 billion in 2017.

TECHNOLOGY FOUNDATIONS

Wireless Internet connections (Wi-Fi, WiMax, and 4G smartphones) grow rapidly.

Powerful smartphones and tablet computers provide access to music, web surfing, and entertainment as well as voice communication. Podcasting and streaming take off as media for distribution of video, radio, and user-generated content.

Mobile devices expand to include wearable computers such as Apple Watch and Fitbit trackers.

The Internet broadband foundation becomes stronger in households and businesses as transmission prices fall.

Social networking apps and sites such as Facebook, Twitter, LinkedIn, Instagram, and others seek to become a major new platform for e-commerce, marketing, and advertising. Facebook has 1.65 billion users worldwide and 222 million in the United States (Facebook, 2016). One hundred ninety million Americans use social networks, about 70 percent of the Internet user population.

Internet-based models of computing, such as smartphone apps, cloud computing, software as a service (SaaS), and database software greatly reduce the cost of e-commerce websites.

NEW BUSINESS MODELS EMERGE

More than 70 percent of the Internet population has joined an online social network, created blogs, and shared photos and music. Together, these sites create an online audience as large as that of television that is attractive to marketers. In 2017, social networking will account for an estimated 28 percent of online time. Social sites have become the primary gateway to the Internet in news, music, and, increasingly, products.

The traditional advertising industry is disrupted as online advertising grows twice as fast as TV and print advertising; Google, Yahoo, and Facebook display nearly 1 trillion ads a year.

On-demand service e-commerce sites such as Uber and Airbnb extend the market creator business model to new areas of economy.

Newspapers and other traditional media adopt online, interactive models but are losing advertising revenues to the online players despite gaining online readers. The *New York Times* adopts a paywall for its online edition and succeeds in capturing over 1 million subscribers, growing at 15 percent annually. Book publishing thrives because of the growth in e-books and the continuing appeal of traditional books.

Online entertainment business models offering television, movies, music, and games grow with cooperation among the major copyright owners in Hollywood and New York and with Internet distributors such as Apple, Amazon, Google, YouTube, and Facebook. Increasingly, the online distributors are moving into movie and TV production.

world of social-mobile-local e-commerce are the dual and related concepts of conversations and engagement. In the popular literature, this is often referred to as conversational commerce. Marketing in this new period is based on firms engaging in multiple online conversations with their customers, potential customers, and even critics. Your brand is being talked about on the web and social media (that's the conversation part), and marketing your firm, building, and restoring your brands requires you to locate, identify, and participate in these conversations. Social marketing means all things social: listening, discussing, interacting, empathizing, and engaging. The emphasis in online marketing has shifted from a focus on eyeballs to a focus on participating in customer-oriented conversations. In this sense, social marketing is not simply a new ad channel but a collection of technology-based tools for communicating with shoppers. The leading social commerce platforms are Facebook, Instagram, and Pinterest.

In the past, firms could tightly control their brand messaging and lead consumers down a funnel of cues that ended in a purchase. That is not true of social marketing. Consumer purchase decisions are increasingly driven by the conversations, choices, tastes, and opinions of their social network. Social marketing is all about firms participating in and shaping this social process.

From the Desktop to the Smartphone

Traditional online marketing (browser-based, search, display ads, video ads, e-mail, and games) still constitutes the majority (63 percent) of all online marketing ($77 billion), but it's growing much more slowly than social-mobile-local marketing. The marketing dollars are following customers and shoppers from the PC to mobile devices.

Social, mobile, and local e-commerce are connected. As mobile devices become more powerful, they are more useful for accessing Facebook and other social sites. As mobile devices become more widely adopted, customers can use them to find local merchants, and merchants can use them to alert customers in their neighborhood of special offers.

Why E-commerce is Different

Why has e-commerce grown so rapidly? The answer lies in the unique nature of the Internet and the web. Simply put, the Internet and e-commerce technologies are much richer and more powerful than previous technology revolutions such as radio, television, and the telephone. Table 10.2 describes the unique features of the Internet and web as a commercial medium. Let's explore each of these unique features in more detail.

Ubiquity

In traditional commerce, a marketplace is a physical place, such as a retail store, that you visit to transact business. E-commerce is ubiquitous, meaning that it is available just about everywhere all the time. It makes it possible to shop from your desktop, at home, at work, or even from your car, using smartphones. The result is called a **marketspace**—a marketplace extended beyond traditional boundaries and removed from a temporal and geographic location.

From a consumer point of view, ubiquity reduces **transaction costs**—the costs of participating in a market. To transact business, it is no longer necessary for you to spend time or money traveling to a market, and much less mental effort is required to make a purchase.

TABLE 10.2 EIGHT UNIQUE FEATURES OF E-COMMERCE TECHNOLOGY

E-COMMERCE TECHNOLOGY DIMENSION	BUSINESS SIGNIFICANCE
Ubiquity. Internet/web technology is available everywhere: at work, at home, and elsewhere by desktop and mobile devices. Mobile devices extend service to local areas and merchants.	The marketplace is extended beyond traditional boundaries and is removed from a temporal and geographic location. Marketspace is created; shopping can take place anytime, anywhere. Customer convenience is enhanced, and shopping costs are reduced.
Global Reach. The technology reaches across national boundaries, around the earth.	Commerce is enabled across cultural and national boundaries seamlessly and without modification. The marketspace includes, potentially, billions of consumers and millions of businesses worldwide.
Universal Standards. There is one set of technology standards, namely Internet standards.	With one set of technical standards across the globe, disparate computer systems can easily communicate with each other.
Richness. Video, audio, and text messages are possible.	Video, audio, and text marketing messages are integrated into a single marketing message and consumer experience.
Interactivity. The technology works through interaction with the user.	Consumers are engaged in a dialogue that dynamically adjusts the experience to the individual and makes the consumer a participant in the process of delivering goods to the market.
Information Density. The technology reduces information costs and raises quality.	Information processing, storage, and communication costs drop dramatically, whereas currency, accuracy, and timeliness improve greatly. Information becomes plentiful, cheap, and more accurate.
Personalization/Customization. The technology allows personalized messages to be delivered to individuals as well as to groups.	Personalization of marketing messages and customization of products and services are based on individual characteristics.
Social Technology. The technology supports content generation and social networking.	New Internet social and business models enable user content creation and distribution and support social networks.

Global Reach

E-commerce technology permits commercial transactions to cross cultural and national boundaries far more conveniently and cost effectively than is true in traditional commerce. As a result, the potential market size for e-commerce merchants is roughly equal to the size of the world's online population (estimated to be more than 3 billion).

In contrast, most traditional commerce is local or regional—it involves local merchants or national merchants with local outlets. Television, radio stations, and newspapers, for instance, are primarily local and regional institutions with limited, but powerful, national networks that can attract a national audience but not easily cross national boundaries to a global audience.

Universal Standards

One strikingly unusual feature of e-commerce technologies is that the technical standards of the Internet and, therefore, the technical standards for conducting e-commerce are universal standards. All nations around the world share them and enable any computer to link with any other computer regardless of the technology platform each is using. In contrast, most traditional commerce technologies differ from one nation to the next. For instance, television and radio standards differ around the world, as does cellular telephone technology.

The universal technical standards of the Internet and e-commerce greatly lower **market entry costs**—the cost merchants must pay simply to bring their goods to market. At the same time, for consumers, universal standards reduce **search costs**—the effort required to find suitable products.

Richness

Information **richness** refers to the complexity and content of a message. Traditional markets, national sales forces, and small retail stores have great richness; they can provide personal, face-to-face service, using aural and visual cues when making a sale. The richness of traditional markets makes them powerful selling or commercial environments. Prior to the development of the web, there was a trade-off between richness and reach; the larger the audience reached, the less rich the message. The web makes it possible to deliver rich messages with text, audio, and video simultaneously to large numbers of people.

Interactivity

Unlike any of the commercial technologies of the twentieth century, with the possible exception of the telephone, e-commerce technologies are interactive, meaning they allow for two-way communication between merchant and consumer and peer-to-peer communication among friends. Television, for instance, cannot ask viewers any questions or enter conversations with them, and it cannot request customer information to be entered on a form. In contrast, all these activities are possible on an e-commerce website or mobile app. Interactivity allows an online merchant to engage a consumer in ways similar to a face-to-face experience but on a massive, global scale.

Information Density

The Internet and the web vastly increase **information density**—the total amount and quality of information available to all market participants, consumers, and merchants alike. E-commerce technologies reduce information collection, storage, processing, and communication costs while greatly increasing the currency, accuracy, and timeliness of information.

Information density in e-commerce markets make prices and costs more transparent. **Price transparency** refers to the ease with which consumers can find out the variety of prices in a market; **cost transparency** refers to the ability of consumers to discover the actual costs merchants pay for products.

There are advantages for merchants as well. Online merchants can discover much more about consumers than in the past. This allows merchants to segment the market into groups that are willing to pay different prices and permits the merchants to engage in **price discrimination**—selling the same goods, or nearly the same goods, to different targeted groups at different prices. For instance, an online merchant can discover a consumer's avid interest in expensive, exotic vacations and then pitch high-end vacation plans to that consumer at a premium price, knowing this person is willing to pay extra for such a vacation. At the same time, the online merchant can pitch the same vacation plan at a lower price to a more price-sensitive consumer. Information density also helps merchants differentiate their products in terms of cost, brand, and quality.

Personalization/Customization

E-commerce technologies permit **personalization**. Merchants can target their marketing messages to specific individuals by adjusting the message to a person's clickstream behavior, name, interests, and past purchases. The technology also permits **customization**—changing the delivered product or service based on a user's preferences or prior behavior. Given the interactive nature of e-commerce technology, much information about the consumer can be gathered in the marketplace at the moment of purchase. With the increase in information density, a great deal of information about the consumer's past purchases and behavior can be stored and used by online merchants.

The result is a level of personalization and customization unthinkable with traditional commerce technologies. For instance, you may be able to shape what you see on television by selecting a channel, but you cannot change the content of the channel you have chosen. In contrast, online news outlets such as the *Wall Street Journal Online* allow you to select the type of news stories you want to see first and gives you the opportunity to be alerted when certain events happen.

Social Technology: User Content Generation and Social Networking

In contrast to previous technologies, the Internet and e-commerce technologies have evolved to be much more social by allowing users to create and share with their friends (and a larger worldwide community) content in the form of text, videos, music, or photos. By using these forms of communication, users can create new social networks and strengthen existing ones.

All previous mass media in modern history, including the printing press, use a broadcast model (one-to-many) in which content is created in a central location by experts (professional writers, editors, directors, and producers), and audiences are concentrated in huge numbers to consume a standardized product. The new Internet and e-commerce empower users to create and distribute content on a large scale and permit users to program their own content consumption. The Internet provides a unique many-to-many model of mass communications.

Key Concepts in E-commerce: Digital Markets and Digital Goods in a Global Marketplace

The location, timing, and revenue models of business are based in some part on the cost and distribution of information. The Internet has created a digital marketplace where millions of people all over the world can exchange massive amounts of information directly, instantly, and free. As a result, the Internet has changed the way companies conduct business and increased their global reach.

The Internet reduces information asymmetry. An **information asymmetry** exists when one party in a transaction has more information that is important for the transaction than the other party. That information helps determine their relative bargaining power. In digital markets, consumers and suppliers can see the prices being charged for goods, and in that sense, digital markets are said to be more transparent than traditional markets.

For example, before automobile retailing sites appeared on the web, there was significant information asymmetry between auto dealers and customers. Only the auto dealers knew the manufacturers' prices, and it was difficult for consumers to shop around for the best price. Auto dealers' profit margins depended on this asymmetry of information. Today's consumers have access to a legion of websites providing competitive pricing information, and three-fourths of U.S. auto buyers use the Internet to shop around for the best deal. Thus, the web has reduced the information asymmetry surrounding an auto purchase. The Internet has also helped businesses seeking to purchase from other businesses reduce information asymmetries and locate better prices and terms.

Digital markets are very flexible and efficient because they operate with reduced search and transaction costs, lower **menu costs** (merchants' costs of changing prices), greater price discrimination, and the ability to change prices dynamically based on market conditions. In **dynamic pricing**, the price of a product varies depending on the demand characteristics of the customer or the supply situation of the seller. For instance, online retailers from Amazon to Walmart change prices on many products based on time of day, demand for the product, and users' prior visits to their sites. Using big data analytics, some online firms can adjust prices at the individual level based on behavioral targeting parameters such as whether the consumer is a price haggler (who will receive a lower price offer) versus a person who accepts offered prices and does not search for lower prices. Prices can also vary by ZIP code, with higher prices set for poor sections of a community. Uber, along with other ride services, uses surge pricing to adjust prices of a ride based on demand (which always rises during storms and major conventions).

These new digital markets can either reduce or increase switching costs, depending on the nature of the product or service being sold, and they might cause some extra delay in gratification due to shipping times. Unlike a physical market, you can't immediately consume a product such as clothing purchased over the web (although immediate consumption is possible with digital music downloads and other digital products).

Digital markets provide many opportunities to sell directly to the consumer, bypassing intermediaries such as distributors or retail outlets. Eliminating intermediaries in the distribution channel can significantly lower purchase transaction costs. To pay for all the steps in a traditional distribution channel, a product may have to be priced as high as 135 percent of its original cost to manufacture.

Figure 10.2 illustrates how much savings result from eliminating each of these layers in the distribution process. By selling directly to consumers or reducing the number of intermediaries, companies can raise profits while charging lower prices. The removal of organizations or business process layers responsible for intermediary steps in a value chain is called **disintermediation**. E-commerce has also given rise to a completely new set of new intermediaries such as Amazon, eBay, PayPal, and Blue Nile. Therefore, disintermediation differs from one industry to another.

FIGURE 10.2 THE BENEFITS OF DISINTERMEDIATION TO THE CONSUMER

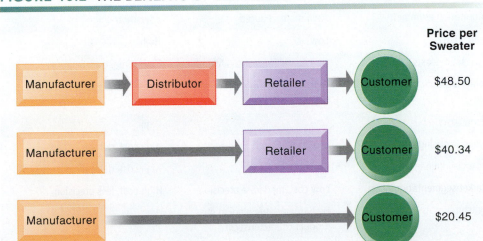

The typical distribution channel has several intermediary layers, each of which adds to the final cost of a product, such as a sweater. Removing layers lowers the final cost to the customer.

Disintermediation is affecting the market for services. Airlines and hotels operating their own reservation sites online earn more per ticket because they have eliminated travel agents as intermediaries. Table 10.3 summarizes the differences between digital markets and traditional markets.

Digital Goods

The Internet digital marketplace has greatly expanded sales of **digital goods**—goods that can be delivered over a digital network. Music tracks, video, Hollywood movies, software, newspapers, magazines, and books can all be expressed, stored, delivered, and sold as purely digital products. For the most part, digital goods are intellectual property, which is defined as "works of the mind." Intellectual property is protected from misappropriation by copyright, patent, trademark, and trade secret laws (see Chapter 4). Today, all these products are delivered as digital streams or downloads while their physical counterparts decline in sales.

In general, for digital goods, the marginal cost of producing another unit is about zero (it costs nothing to make a copy of a music file). However, the cost of producing the original first unit is relatively high—in fact, it is nearly the total cost of the product because there are few other costs of inventory and distribution. Costs of delivery over the Internet are very low, marketing costs often remain the same, and pricing can be highly variable. On the Internet, the merchant can change prices as often as desired because of low menu costs.

The impact of the Internet on the market for these kinds of digital goods is nothing short of revolutionary, and we see the results around us every day. Businesses dependent on physical products for sales—such as bookstores, music stores, book publishers, music labels, and film studios—face the possibility of declining sales and even destruction of their businesses. Newspapers and magazines subscriptions to hard copies are declining, while online readership and subscriptions are expanding.

Total record label industry revenues have fallen 50 percent from $14 billion in 1999 to about $6.9 billion in 2016, due almost entirely to the rapid decline in CD album sales and the growth of digital music services (both legal and

TABLE 10.3 DIGITAL MARKETS COMPARED WITH TRADITIONAL MARKETS

	DIGITAL MARKETS	TRADITIONAL MARKETS
Information asymmetry	Asymmetry reduced	Asymmetry high
Search costs	Low	High
Transaction costs	Low (sometimes virtually nothing)	High (time, travel)
Delayed gratification	High (or lower in the case of a digital good)	Lower: purchase now
Menu costs	Low	High
Dynamic pricing	Low cost, instant	High cost, delayed
Price discrimination	Low cost, instant	High cost, delayed
Market segmentation	Low cost, moderate precision	High cost, less precision
Switching costs	Higher/lower (depending on product characteristics)	High
Network effects	Strong	Weaker
Disintermediation	More possible/likely	Less possible/unlikely

illegal music piracy). On the plus side, the Apple iTunes Store has sold more than 35 billion songs for 99 cents each since opening in 2003, providing the industry with a digital distribution model that has restored some of the revenues lost to digital music channels. Since iTunes, illegal downloading has been cut in half, and legitimate online music sales (both downloads and streaming) are estimated to be approximately $4.5 billion in 2016. As cloud streaming services expand, illegal downloading will decline further. Digital music sales account for more than 70 percent of all music revenues. Yet the music labels make only about 32 cents from a single track download and only 0.5 cents for a streamed track (with the hope that sales of downloaded tracks or CDs will result). Although the record labels make revenue from ownership of the song (both words and music), the artists who perform the music make virtually nothing from streamed music.

Hollywood has not been similarly disrupted by digital distribution platforms, in part because it is more difficult to download high-quality, pirated copies of full-length movies and because of the availability of low-cost, high-quality legal movies. To avoid the fate of the music industry, Hollywood has struck lucrative distribution deals with Netflix, Google, Hulu, Amazon, and Apple, making it convenient to download and pay for high-quality movies and television series. These arrangements are not enough to compensate entirely for the loss in DVD sales, which fell 50 percent from 2006 to 2015, although this is changing rapidly as online distributors such as Netflix pay millions for high-quality Hollywood content. In 2017, for the first time, consumers will view more and pay more for web-based movie downloads, rentals, and streams than for DVDs or related physical products. As with television series, the demand for feature-length Hollywood movies appears to be expanding in part because of the growth of smartphones and tablets, making it easier to watch movies in more locations. In addition, the surprising resurgence of music videos, led by the VEVO website, is attracting millions of younger viewers on smartphones and tablets.

Online movies began a growth spurt in 2010 as broadband services spread throughout the country. In 2017, about 126 million Internet users are expected to view movies, about one-half of the adult Internet audience. Although this rapid growth will not continue forever, there is little doubt that the Internet is becoming a movie distribution and television channel that rivals cable television, and someday may replace cable television entirely. Table 10.4 describes digital goods and how they differ from traditional physical goods.

TABLE 10.4 HOW THE INTERNET CHANGES THE MARKETS FOR DIGITAL GOODS

	DIGITAL GOODS	TRADITIONAL GOODS
Marginal cost/unit	Zero	Greater than zero, high
Cost of production	High (most of the cost)	Variable
Copying cost	Approximately zero	Greater than zero, high
Distributed delivery cost	Low	High
Inventory cost	Low	High
Marketing cost	Variable	Variable
Pricing	More variable (bundling, random pricing games)	Fixed, based on unit costs

10-2 What are the principal e-commerce business and revenue models?

E-commerce has grown from a few advertisements on early web portals in 1995 to more than 12 percent of all retail sales in 2017 (an estimated $669 billion), surpassing the mail-order catalog business. E-commerce is a fascinating combination of business models and new information technologies. Let's start with a basic understanding of the types of e-commerce and then describe e-commerce business and revenue models.

Types of E-commerce

There are many ways to classify electronic commerce transactions—one is by looking at the nature of the participants. The three major electronic commerce categories are business-to-consumer (B2C) e-commerce, business-to-business (B2B) e-commerce, and consumer-to-consumer (C2C) e-commerce.

- **Business-to-consumer (B2C)** electronic commerce involves retailing products and services to individual shoppers. Amazon, Walmart, and iTunes are examples of B2C commerce. BarnesandNoble.com, which sells books, software, and music to individual consumers, is an example of B2C e-commerce.
- **Business-to-business (B2B)** electronic commerce involves sales of goods and services among businesses. Elemica's website for buying and selling chemicals and energy is an example of B2B e-commerce.
- **Consumer-to-consumer (C2C)** electronic commerce involves consumers selling directly to consumers. For example, eBay, the giant web auction site, enables people to sell their goods to other consumers by auctioning their merchandise off to the highest bidder or for a fixed price. eBay acts as a middleman by creating a digital platform for peer-to-peer commerce. Craigslist is the most widely used platform consumers use to buy from and sell directly to others.

Another way of classifying electronic commerce transactions is in terms of the platforms participants use in a transaction. Until recently, most e-commerce transactions took place using a desktop PC connected to the Internet over a wired network. Several wireless mobile alternatives have such as smartphones and tablet computers. The use of handheld wireless devices for purchasing goods and services from any location is termed **mobile commerce** or **m-commerce**. All three types of e-commerce transactions can take place using m-commerce technology, which we discuss in detail in Section 10.3.

E-commerce Business Models

Changes in the economics of information described earlier have created the conditions for entirely new business models to appear, while destroying older business models. Table 10.5 describes some of the most important Internet business models that have emerged. All, in one way or another, use the Internet (including apps on mobile devices) to add extra value to existing products and services or to provide the foundation for new products and services.

Portal

Portals are gateways to the web and are often defined as those sites that users set as their home page. Some definitions of a portal include search engines such as Google and Bing even if few make these sites their home page. Portals

TABLE 10.5 INTERNET BUSINESS MODELS

CATEGORY	DESCRIPTION	EXAMPLES
E-tailer	Sells physical products directly to consumers or to individual businesses.	Amazon Blue Nile
Transaction broker	Saves users money and time by processing online sales transactions and generating a fee each time a transaction occurs.	ETrade.com Expedia
Market creator	Provides a digital environment where buyers and sellers can meet, search for products, display products, and establish prices for those products; can serve consumers or B2B e-commerce, generating revenue from transaction fees.	eBay Priceline.com Exostar Elemica
Content provider	Creates revenue by providing digital content, such as news, music, photos, or video, over the web. The customer may pay to access the content, or revenue may be generated by selling advertising space.	WSJ.com GettyImages.com iTunes.com Games.com
Community provider	Provides an online meeting place where people with similar interests can communicate and find useful information.	Facebook Google+ Twitter
Portal	Provides initial point of entry to the web along with specialized content and other services.	Yahoo Bing Google
Service provider	Provides applications such as photo sharing, video sharing, and user-generated content as services; provides other services such as online data storage and backup.	Google Apps Photobucket.com Dropbox

such as Yahoo, Facebook, MSN, and AOL offer powerful web search tools as well as an integrated package of content and services such as news, e-mail, instant messaging, maps, calendars, shopping, music downloads, video streaming, and more all in one place. The portal business model now provides a destination site where users start their web searching and linger to read news, find entertainment, meet other people, and, of course, be exposed to advertising, which provides the revenues to support the portal. Facebook is a very different kind of portal based on social networking. Portals generate revenue primarily by attracting very large audiences, charging advertisers for display ad placement (similar to traditional newspapers), collecting referral fees for steering customers to other sites, and charging for premium services. In 2017, portals (not including Google or Bing) will generate an estimated $37 billion in display ad revenues. Although there are hundreds of portal/search engine sites, the top four portals (Yahoo, Facebook, MSN, and AOL) gather more than 95 percent of the Internet portal traffic because of their superior brand recognition.

E-tailer

Online retail stores, often called **e-tailers**, come in all sizes, from giant Amazon with 2015 revenues of more than $107 billion, to tiny local stores that have websites. An e-tailer is similar to the typical bricks-and-mortar storefront, except that customers only need to connect to the Internet to check their inventory and place an order. Altogether, online retail (the sale of physical goods online) will generate about $457 billion in revenues in 2017. The value proposition of e-tailers is to provide convenient, low-cost shopping 24/7; large selections; and consumer choice. Some e-tailers, such as Walmart.com or Staples.com, referred to as bricks-and-clicks, are subsidiaries or divisions of existing physical stores and carry the same products. Others, however, operate only in the virtual world, without any ties to physical locations. Amazon, BlueNile.com, and Drugstore.com are examples of this type of e-tailer. Several other variations of e-tailers—such as online versions of direct-mail catalogs, online malls, and manufacturer-direct online sales—also exist.

Content Provider

Although e-commerce began as a retail product channel, it has increasingly become a global content channel. *Content* is defined broadly to include all forms of intellectual property. **Intellectual property** refers to tangible and intangible products of the mind for which the creator claims a property right. Content providers distribute information content—such as digital video, music, photos, text, and artwork—over the web. The value proposition of online content providers is that consumers can conveniently find a wide range of content online and purchase this content inexpensively to be played or viewed on multiple computer devices or smartphones.

Providers do not have to be the creators of the content (although sometimes they are, like Disney.com) and are more likely to be Internet-based distributors of content produced and created by others. For example, Apple sells music tracks at its iTunes Store, but it does not create or commission new music.

The phenomenal popularity of the iTunes Store, and Apple's Internet-connected devices such as the iPhone, iPod, and iPad, have enabled new forms of digital content delivery from podcasting to mobile streaming. **Podcasting** is a method of publishing audio or video broadcasts through the Internet, allowing subscribing users to download audio or video files onto their personal computers, smartphones, tablets, or portable music players. **Streaming** is a publishing method for music and video files that flows a continuous stream of content to a user's device without being stored locally on the device.

Estimates vary, but total online content will generate about around $24 billion in 2017, one of the fastest-growing e-commerce segments, growing at an estimated 18 percent annual rate.

Transaction Broker

Sites that process transactions for consumers normally handled in person, by phone, or by mail are transaction brokers. The largest industries using this model are financial services and travel services. The online transaction broker's primary value propositions are savings of money and time and providing an extraordinary inventory of financial products and travel packages in a single location. Online stock brokers and travel booking services charge fees that are considerably less than traditional versions of these services. Fidelity Financial Services and Expedia are the largest online financial and travel service firms based on a transaction broker model.

Market Creator

Market creators build a digital environment in which buyers and sellers can meet, display products, search for products, and establish prices. The value proposition of online market creators is that they provide a platform where sellers can easily display their wares and purchasers can buy directly from sellers. Online auction markets such as eBay and Priceline are good examples of the market creator business model. Another example is Amazon's Merchants platform (and similar programs at eBay), where merchants are allowed to set up stores on Amazon's website and sell goods at fixed prices to consumers. The so-called on-demand economy (mistakenly referred to often as the sharing economy), exemplified by Uber (described in the chapter-opening case) and Airbnb, is based on the idea of a market creator building a digital platform where supply meets demand; for instance, spare auto or room rental capacity finds individuals who want transportation or lodging. Crowdsource funding markets such as Kickstarter.com and Mosaic Inc. bring together private equity investors and entrepreneurs in a funding marketplace. Both are examples of B2B financial market places.

Service Provider

Whereas e-tailers sell products online, service providers offer services online. Photo sharing and online sites for data backup and storage all use a service provider business model. Software is no longer a physical product with a CD in a box but, increasingly, software as a service (SaaS) that you subscribe to online rather than purchase from a retailer, such as Office 365. Google has led the way in developing online software service applications such as Google Apps, Google Sites, Gmail, and online data storage services. Salesforce.com is a major provider of cloud-based software for customer management (see Chapter 5).

Community Provider (Social Networks)

Community providers are sites that create a digital online environment where people with similar interests can transact (buy and sell goods); share interests, photos, videos; communicate with like-minded people; receive interest-related information; and even play out fantasies by adopting online personalities called *avatars*. Social networking sites Facebook, Google +, Tumblr, Instagram, LinkedIn, and Twitter and hundreds of other smaller, niche sites such as Sportsvite all offer users community-building tools and services. Social networking sites have been the fastest-growing websites in recent years, often doubling their audience size in a year.

E-commerce Revenue Models

A firm's **revenue model** describes how the firm will earn revenue, generate profits, and produce a superior return on investment. Although many e-commerce revenue models have been developed, most companies rely on one, or some combination, of the following six revenue models: advertising, sales, subscription, free/freemium, transaction fee, and affiliate.

Advertising Revenue Model

In the **advertising revenue model**, a website generates revenue by attracting a large audience of visitors who can then be exposed to advertisements. The advertising model is the most widely used revenue model in e-commerce, and arguably, without advertising revenues, the web would be a vastly different experience from what it is now because people would be asked to pay for access to content. Content on the web—everything from news to videos and opinions—is free to visitors because advertisers pay the production and distribution costs in return for the right to expose visitors to ads. Companies will spend an estimated $77.3 billion on online advertising in 2017 (in the form of a paid message on a website, paid search listing, video, app, game, or other online medium, such as instant messaging). About $53 billion of this will be for mobile ads. Mobile ads will account for 68 percent of all digital advertising. In the past five years, advertisers have increased online spending and cut outlays on traditional channels such as radio and newspapers. In 2017, online advertising will grow at 15 percent and constitute about 38 percent of all advertising in the United States (eMarketer, 2016d).

Websites with the largest viewership or that attract a highly specialized, differentiated viewership and are able to retain user attention (stickiness) can charge higher advertising rates. Yahoo, for instance, derives nearly all its revenue from display ads (banner ads), video ads, and, to less extent, search engine text ads. Ninety-five percent of Google's revenue derives from advertising, including selling keywords (AdWord), selling ad spaces (AdSense), and selling display ad spaces to advertisers (DoubleClick). Facebook displayed one-third of the trillion display ads shown on all sites in 2016. Facebook's users spend an average of over 6 hours a week on the site, far longer than any of the other portal sites. In contrast, Americans spend an average of five hours watching television each day (eMarketer, 2016e).

Sales Revenue Model

In the **sales revenue model**, companies derive revenue by selling goods, information, or services to customers. Companies such as Amazon (which sells books, music, and other products), LLBean.com, and Gap.com all have sales revenue models. Content providers make money by charging for downloads of entire files such as music tracks (iTunes Store) or books or for downloading music and/or video streams (Hulu.com TV shows). Apple has pioneered and strengthened the acceptance of micropayments. **Micropayment systems** provide content providers with a cost-effective method for processing high volumes of very small monetary transactions (anywhere from 25 cents to $5.00 per transaction). The largest micropayment system on the web is Apple's iTunes Store, which has more than 800 million customers worldwide who purchase individual music tracks for 99 cents and feature length movies for various prices. A Learning Track is available with more detail on micropayment and other e-commerce payment systems, including Bitcoin.

Subscription Revenue Model

In the **subscription revenue model**, a website offering content or services charges a subscription fee for access to some or all of its offerings on an ongoing basis. Content providers often use this revenue model. For instance, the online version of *Consumer Reports* provides access to premium content, such as detailed ratings, reviews, and recommendations, only to subscribers, who have a choice of paying a $7.99 to 12.99 monthly subscription fee or a $30.00 annual fee. Netflix is one of the most successful subscriber sites with more that 75 million customers worldwide in 2016. The *New York Times* had about 1.3 million online paid subscribers, and the *Wall Street Journal* about 1 million in 2016. To be successful, the subscription model requires the content to be perceived as differentiated, having high added value, and not readily available elsewhere or easily replicated. Companies successfully offering content or services online on a subscription basis include Match.com and eHarmony (dating services), Ancestry.com and Genealogy.com (genealogy research), and Microsoft Xbox Live.

Free/Freemium Revenue Model

In the **free/freemium revenue model**, firms offer basic services or content for free and charge a premium for advanced or special features. For example, Google offers free applications but charges for premium services. Pandora, the subscription radio service, offers a free service with limited play time and advertising and a premium service with unlimited play. Spotify music service also uses a freemium business model. The idea is to attract very large audiences with free services and then convert some of this audience to pay a subscription for premium services. One problem with this model is converting people from being free loaders into paying customers. "Free" can be a powerful model for losing money. None of the freemium music streaming sites have earned a profit to date. Nevertheless, they are finding that free service with ad revenue is more profitable than the paid subscriber part of their business.

Transaction Fee Revenue Model

In the **transaction fee revenue model**, a company receives a fee for enabling or executing a transaction. For example, eBay provides an online auction marketplace and receives a small transaction fee from a seller if the seller is successful in selling an item. E*Trade, an online stockbroker, receives transaction fees each time it executes a stock transaction on behalf of a customer. The transaction revenue model enjoys wide acceptance in part because the true cost of using the platform is not immediately apparent to the user.

Affiliate Revenue Model

In the **affiliate revenue model**, websites (called *affiliate websites*) send visitors to other websites in return for a referral fee or percentage of the revenue from any resulting sales. Referral fees are also referred to as lead generation fees. For example, MyPoints makes money by connecting companies to potential customers by offering special deals to its members. When members take advantage of an offer and make a purchase, they earn points they can redeem for free products and services, and MyPoints receives a referral fee. Community feedback sites such as Epinions and Yelp receive much of their revenue from steering potential customers to websites where they make a purchase. Amazon uses affiliates that steer business to the Amazon website by placing the Amazon logo on their blogs. Personal blogs often contain display ads as part of affiliate programs. Some bloggers are paid directly by manufacturers, or receive free products, for speaking highly of products and providing links to sales channels.

10-3 How has e-commerce transformed marketing?

Although e-commerce and the Internet have changed entire industries and enabled new business models, no industry has been more affected than marketing and marketing communications.

The Internet provides marketers with new ways of identifying and communicating with millions of potential customers at costs far lower than traditional media, including search engine marketing, data mining, recommender systems, and targeted e-mail. The Internet enables **long tail marketing**. Before the Internet, reaching a large audience was very expensive, and marketers had to focus on attracting the largest number of consumers with popular hit products, whether music, Hollywood movies, books, or cars. In contrast, the Internet allows marketers to find potential customers inexpensively for products where demand is very low. For instance, the Internet makes it possible to sell independent music profitably to very small audiences. There's always some demand for almost any product. Put a string of such long tail sales together and you have a profitable business.

The Internet also provides new ways—often instantaneous and spontaneous—to gather information from customers, adjust product offerings, and increase customer value. Table 10.6 describes the leading marketing and advertising formats used in e-commerce.

Behavioral Targeting

Many e-commerce marketing firms use **behavioral targeting** techniques to increase the effectiveness of banners, rich media, and video ads. Behavioral targeting refers to tracking the clickstreams (history of clicking behavior) of individuals on thousands of websites to understand their interests and intentions and expose them to advertisements that are uniquely suited to their online behavior. Marketers and most researchers believe this more precise understanding of the customer leads to more efficient marketing (the firm pays for ads only to those shoppers who are most interested in their products) and larger sales and revenues. Unfortunately, behavioral targeting of millions of web users also leads to the invasion of personal privacy without user consent. When consumers lose trust in their web experience, they tend not to purchase anything. Backlash is growing against the aggressive uses of personal information as consumers seek out safer havens for purchasing and messaging. Snapchat offers disappearing messages, and even Facebook has retreated by making its default for new posts "for friends only."

Popular websites have hundreds of beacon programs on their home pages, which collect data about visitors' behavior and report that behavior to their databases. There the information is often sold to data brokers, firms that collect billions of data elements on every U.S. consumer and household, frequently combining online with offline purchase information. The data brokers in turn

TABLE 10.6 ONLINE MARKETING AND ADVERTISING FORMATS (BILLIONS)

MARKETING FORMAT	2015 REVENUE	DESCRIPTION
Search engine	$30	Text ads targeted at precisely what the customer is looking for at the moment of shopping and purchasing. Sales oriented.
Display ads	$33	Banner ads (pop-ups and leave-behinds) with interactive features; increasingly behaviorally targeted to individual web activity. Brand development and sales. Includes social media and blog display ads.
Video	$9.8	Fastest-growing format, engaging and entertaining; behaviorally targeted, interactive. Branding and sales.
Classified	$3.1	Job, real estate, and services ads; interactive, rich media, and personalized to user searches. Sales and branding.
Rich media	$7.6	Animations, games, and puzzles. Interactive, targeted, and entertaining. Branding orientation.
Lead generation	$2.1	Marketing firms that gather sales and marketing leads online and then sell them to online marketers for a variety of campaign types. Sales or branding orientation.
Sponsorships	$1.8	Online games, puzzles, contests, and coupon sites sponsored by firms to promote products. Sales orientation.
E-mail	$.3	Effective, targeted marketing tool with interactive and rich media potential. Sales oriented.

sell this information to advertisers who want to place ads on web pages. A recent Federal Trade Commission report about nine data brokers found that one data broker's database had information on 1.4 billion consumer transactions and more than 700 billion aggregated data elements. Another data broker had 3,000 data measures for nearly every consumer in the United States (FTC, 2014).

Behavioral targeting takes place at two levels: at individual websites or from within apps and on various advertising networks that track users across thousands of websites. All websites collect data on visitor browser activity and store it in a database. They have tools to record the site that users visited prior to coming to the website, where these users go when they leave that site, the type of operating system they use, browser information, and even some location data. They also record the specific pages visited on the particular site, the time spent on each page of the site, the types of pages visited, and what the visitors purchased (see Figure 10.3). Firms analyze this information about customer interests and behavior to develop precise profiles of existing and potential customers. In addition, most major websites have hundreds of tracking programs on their home pages, which track your clickstream behavior across the web by following you from site to site and re-target ads to you by showing you the same ads on different sites. The leading online advertising networks are Google's DoubleClick, Yahoo's RightMedia, and AOL's Ad Network. Ad networks represent publishers who have space to sell and advertisers who want to market online. The lubricant of this trade is information about millions of web shoppers, which helps advertisers target their ads to precisely the groups and individuals they desire.

This information enables firms to understand how well their website is working, create unique personalized web pages that display content or ads

FIGURE 10.3 WEBSITE VISITOR TRACKING

The shopper clicks on the home page. The store can tell that the shopper arrived from the Yahoo! portal at 2:30 PM (which might help determine staffing for customer service centers) and how long she lingered on the home page (which might indicate trouble navigating the site). Tracking beacons load cookies on the shopper's browser to follow her across the web.

The shopper clicks on blouses, clicks to select a woman's white blouse, then clicks to view the same item in pink. The shopper clicks to select this item in a size 10 in pink and clicks to place it in her shopping cart. This information can help the store determine which sizes and colors are most popular. If the visitor moves to a different site, ads for pink blouses will appear from the same or different vendor.

From the shopping cart page, the shopper clicks to close the browser to leave the Website without purchasing the blouse. This action could indicate the shopper changed her mind or that she had a problem with the website's checkout and payment process. Such behavior might signal that the website was not well designed.

E-commerce websites and advertising platforms like Google's DoubleClick have tools to track a shopper's every step through an online store and then across the web as shoppers move from site to site. Close examination of customer behavior at a website selling women's clothing shows what the store might learn at each step and what actions it could take to increase sales.

for products or services of special interest to each user, improve the customer's experience, and create additional value through a better understanding of the shopper (see Figure 10.4). By using personalization technology to modify the web pages presented to each customer, marketers achieve some of the benefits of using individual salespeople at dramatically lower costs. For instance, General Motors will show a Chevrolet banner ad to women emphasizing safety and utility, whereas men will receive ads emphasizing power and ruggedness.

It's a short step from ad networks to programmatic ad buying. Ad networks create real-time bidding platforms (RTB) where marketers bid in an automated environment for highly targeted slots available from web publishers. Here, ad platforms can predict how many targeted individuals will view the ads, and ad buyers can estimate how much this exposure is worth to them.

What if you are a large national advertising company with many clients trying to reach millions of consumers? What if you were a large global manufacturer trying to reach potential consumers for your products? With millions of websites, working with each one would be impractical. Advertising networks solve this problem by creating a network of several thousand of the most popular websites millions of people visit, tracking the behavior of these users across the entire network, building profiles of each user, and then selling these profiles to advertisers in a real-time bidding environment. Popular websites download dozens of web tracking cookies, bugs, and beacons, which report user online behavior to remote servers without the users' knowledge. Looking for young, single consumers with college degrees, living in the Northeast,

FIGURE 10.4 WEBSITE PERSONALIZATION

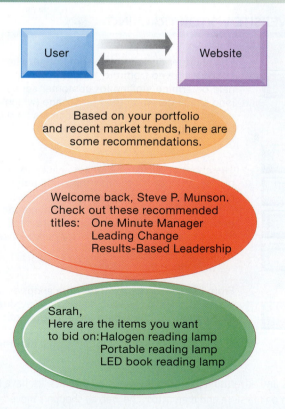

Firms can create unique personalized web pages that display content or ads for products or services of special interest to individual users, improving the customer experience and creating additional value.

in the 18- to 34-age range who are interested in purchasing a European car? Not a problem. Advertising networks can identify and deliver thousands of people who fit this profile and expose them to ads for European cars as they move from one website to another. Estimates vary, but behaviorally targeted ads are generally 10 times more likely to produce a consumer response than a randomly chosen banner or video ad (see Figure 10.5). So-called advertising exchanges use this same technology to auction access to people with very specific profiles to advertisers in a few milliseconds. In 2016, about 50 percent of online display ads are targeted ads developed by programmatic ad buys, and the rest depend on the context of the pages shoppers visit—the estimated demographics of visitors, or so-called blast-and-scatter advertising—which is placed randomly on any available page with minimal targeting, such as time of day or season.

It's another short step to **native advertising**. Native advertising involves placing ads in social network newsfeeds or within traditional editorial content, such as a newspaper article. This is also referred to as organic advertising, where content and advertising are in very close proximity or integrated together.

Two-thirds (68 percent) of Internet users disapprove of search engines and websites tracking their online behavior to aim targeted ads at them. Twenty-eight percent of those surveyed approve of behavioral targeting because they believe it produces more relevant ads and information. A majority of Americans want a Do Not Track option in browsers that will stop websites from collecting information about their online behavior. More than 50 percent are very concerned about the wealth of personal data online; 86 percent have taken steps to mask their online behavior; 25 percent of web users use ad-blocking software. Next to hackers, Americans try to avoid advertisers pursuing them while online, and 64 percent block cookies to make tracking more difficult (Rainie and Duggan, 2016).

FIGURE 10.5 HOW AN ADVERTISING NETWORK SUCH AS DOUBLECLICK WORKS

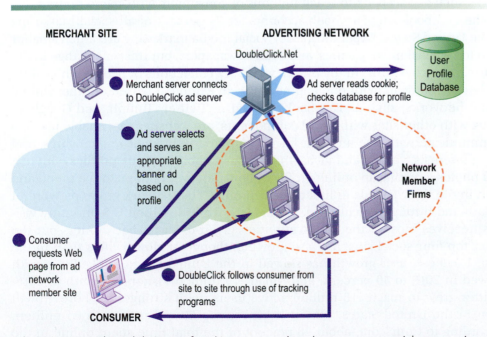

Advertising networks and their use of tracking programs have become controversial among privacy advocates because of their ability to track individual consumers across the Internet.

Social E-Commerce and Social Network Marketing

Social e-commerce is commerce based on the idea of the digital **social graph**, a mapping of all significant online social relationships. The social graph is synonymous with the idea of a social network used to describe offline relationships. You can map your own social graph (network) by drawing lines from yourself to the 10 closest people you know. If they know one another, draw lines between these people. If you are ambitious, ask these 10 friends to list and draw in the names of the 10 people closest to them. What emerges from this exercise is a preliminary map of your social network. Now imagine if everyone on the Internet did the same and posted the results to a very large database with a website. Ultimately, you would end up with Facebook or a site like it. The collection of all these personal social networks is called the *social graph*.

According to small world theory, you are only six links away from any other person on earth. If you entered your personal address book, which has, say, 100 names in it, in a list and sent it to your friends, and they in turn entered 50 new names of their friends, and so on, five times, the social network created would encompass 31 billion people! The social graph is therefore a collection of millions of personal social graphs (and all the people in them). So, it's a small world indeed, and we are all more closely linked than we ever thought.

If you understand the interconnectedness of people, you will see just how important this concept is to e-commerce: The products and services you buy will influence the decisions of your friends, and their decisions will in turn influence you. If you are a marketer trying to build and strengthen a brand, the implication is clear: Take advantage of the fact that people are enmeshed in social networks, share interests and values, and communicate and influence one another. As a marketer, your target audience is not a million isolated people watching a TV show but the social network of people who watch the show and the viewers' personal networks. Table 10.7 describes the features of social commerce that are driving its growth.

In 2017, one of the fastest-growing media for branding and marketing is social media. Companies will spend an estimated $16.5 billion in 2017 using social networks such as Facebook to reach millions of consumers who spend hours a day on the Facebook site. Facebook accounts for 74 percent of all social marketing in the United States. Expenditures for social media marketing are much smaller than for television, magazines, and even newspapers, but this will change in the future. Social networks in the offline world are collections of people who voluntarily communicate with one another over an extended period of time. Online social networks, such as Facebook, LinkedIn, Twitter, Tumblr, and Google+, along with other sites with social components, are websites that enable users to communicate with one another, form group and individual relationships, and share interests, values, and ideas. Individuals establish online profiles with text and photos, creating an online profile of how they want others to see them, and then invite their friends to link to their profile. The network grows by word of mouth and through e-mail links. Facebook, with 258 million U.S. monthly visitors, receives most of the public attention given to social networking, but the other top four social sites are also growing, though at slower rates than in the past. Facebook user growth has slowed in the United States. LinkedIn growth slowed in 2015 to 40 percent, and it had 119 million visitors a month in 2016. Twitter grew to reach 118 million active users, with stronger offshore growth than in the United States. Pinterest hit the top 50 websites with 63 million. According to ComScore, about 28 percent of the total time spent online in the United States was spent on social network sites, and it is the most common

TABLE 10.7 FEATURES OF SOCIAL COMMERCE

SOCIAL COMMERCE FEATURE	DESCRIPTION
Newsfeed	A stream of notifications from friends and advertisers that social users find on their home pages.
Timelines	A stream of photos and events in the past that create a personal history for users, one that can be shared with friends.
Social sign-on	Websites allow users to sign into their sites through their social network pages on Facebook or another social site. This allows websites to receive valuable social profile information from Facebook and use it in their own marketing efforts.
Collaborative shopping	An environment where consumers can share their shopping experiences with one another by viewing products, chatting, or texting. Friends can chat online about brands, products, and services.
Network notification	An environment where consumers can share their approval (or disapproval) of products, services, or content or share their geolocation, perhaps a restaurant or club, with friends. Facebook's ubiquitous Like button is an example, as are Twitter's tweets and followers.
Social search (recommendations)	An environment where consumers can ask their friends for advice on purchases of products, services, and content. Although Google can help you find things, social search can help you evaluate the quality of things by listening to the evaluations of your friends or their friends. For instance, Amazon's social recommender system can use your Facebook social profile to recommend products.

online activity (ComScore, 2016). The fastest-growing smartphone applications are social network apps; nearly half of smartphone users visit social sites daily. More than 60 percent of all visits to Facebook in 2016 came from smartphones.

At **social shopping** sites such as Pinterest and Kaboodle, you can swap shopping ideas with friends. Facebook offers the Like button and Google the +1 button to let your friends know you admire a product, service, or content and, in some cases, purchase something online. Facebook processes around 4.5 billion Likes a day. Online communities are also ideal venues to employ viral marketing techniques. Online viral marketing is like traditional word-of-mouth marketing except that the word can spread across an online community at the speed of light and go much further geographically than a small network of friends.

The Wisdom of Crowds

Creating sites where thousands, even millions, of people can interact offers business firms new ways to market and advertise and to discover who likes (or hates) their products. In a phenomenon called the **wisdom of crowds**, some argue that large numbers of people can make better decisions about a wide range of topics or products than a single person or even a small committee of experts.

Obviously, this is not always the case, but it can happen in interesting ways. In marketing, the wisdom of crowds concept suggests that firms should consult with thousands of their customers first as a way of establishing a relationship with them and, second, to understand better how their products and services are used and appreciated (or rejected). Actively soliciting the comments of your customers builds trust and sends the message to your customers that you care what they are thinking and that you need their advice.

INTERACTIVE SESSION: TECHNOLOGY

Getting Social with Customers

Businesses of all sizes are finding Facebook, Twitter, and other social media to be powerful tools for engaging customers, amplifying product messages, discovering trends and influencers, building brand awareness, and taking action on customer requests and recommendations. Half of all Twitter users recommend products in their tweets.

About 1.6 billion people use Facebook, and more than 30 million businesses have active brand pages, enabling users to interact with the brand through blogs, comment pages, contests, and offerings on the brand page. The "like" button gives users a chance to share with their social network their feelings about content and other objects they are viewing and websites they are visiting. With like buttons on millions of websites, Facebook can track user behavior on other sites and then sell this information to marketers. Facebook also sells display ads to firms that show up in the right column of users' home pages and most other pages in the Facebook interface such as photos and apps.

Twitter has developed many new offerings to interest advertisers, like "promoted tweets" and "promoted trends." These features give advertisers the ability to have their tweets displayed more prominently when Twitter users search for certain keywords. Many big advertisers are using Twitter's Vine service, which allows users to share short, repeating videos with a mobile-phone app or post them on other platforms such as Facebook.

Lowe's is using Facebook mobile video and Snapchat image messaging to help first-time millennial home buyers learn home improvement skills. The home improvement retailer launched a new series of social videos in April 2016 to showcase spring cleaning and do-it-yourself projects. Lowe's believes this is a more immediate and interactive way to reach younger consumers who are increasingly spending time on visual-driven social media platforms.

Lowe's "FlipSide" videos are short, two-sided live action videos that show simultaneously what can happen if a homeowner doesn't clean the gutters and air filters or prune overgrown shrubs compared with the results of proper spring cleaning. These videos take advantage of the flip video application in Facebook's mobile feed that enables users to change the orientation of the video, and the videos link back to the Lowes.com website.

Lowe's "In-a-Snap" Snapchat series tries to inspire young homeowners and renters to undertake simple home improvement projects such as installing shelves to build a study nook. During the Lowe's Snapchat story, users can tap on the screen to put a nail in a wall or chisel off an old tile. Lowe's is working on another series of video tutorials on Facebook and Instagram called "Home School" that uses drawings from chalk artists to animate maintenance projects.

Lowe's social media activities have helped increase brand engagement. Although the company's social campaigns are designed to teach first-time homeowners or young renters about home improvement, the company is also hoping they will encourage consumers to think differently about the brand beyond its products and services. Management believes millennials who are becoming first-time homeowners want to know the deeper meaning of what a company is trying to stand for, not just the products and services it offers.

An estimated 90 percent of customers are influenced by online reviews, and nearly half of U.S. social media users actively seek customer service through social media. As a result, marketing is now placing much more emphasis on customer satisfaction and customer service. Social media monitoring helps marketers and business owners understand more about likes, dislikes, and complaints concerning products, additional products or product modifications customers want, and how people are talking about a brand (positive or negative sentiment).

General Motors (GM) has 26 full-time social media customer care advisers for North America alone, covering more than 150 company social channels from GM, Chevrolet, Buick, GMC, and Cadillac, and approximately 85 sites such as automotive enthusiast forums. These advisers are available to assist customers seven days a week, 16 operational hours per day. GM believes that the processes for identifying and resolving quality concerns are very important.

GM recognized early on that there was a wealth of information in online vehicle owner forums that should be utilized in product development. GM social media advisers actively monitor vehicle owner forums and other social media platforms to identify potential issues and provide real-time customer feedback to the company's brand quality and engineering leaders. In some cases, GM social media advisers were able to identify issues much earlier than traditional surveying or dealer feedback.

For example, GM's social media team identified a faulty climate-control part when a customer posted the issue on a product-owner blog. The complaint received dozens of replies and thousands of views, prompting GM that it needed to investigate further. Once GM specialists determined the root cause of the issue, the company released a technical service bulletin to all dealerships to replace the affected HVAC control modules on vehicles already built. GM fixed the original customer's vehicle within 10 days and adjusted production to ensure no additional customers would be affected.

Still, the results of a social presence can be unpredictable and not always beneficial, as a number of companies have learned. In October 2014, Microsoft CEO Satya Nadella triggered negative reaction on Twitter after he spoke about women not needing to ask for pay raises at work and how they should trust the employment system. Nadella later tweeted an apology. Social media provided a platform for angry backlash against Starbucks in March 2015 for its "Race Together" campaign. Starbucks has taken on sensitive social issues before, and it launched the campaign to encourage conversation with its customers about race relations. Critics hammered Starbucks on social media for trying to capitalize on racial tensions in the United States.

Companies everywhere have rushed to create Facebook pages and Twitter accounts, but many still don't understand how to make effective use of these social media tools. While large companies have learned how to stand out on social networks and get lots of help from sites like Facebook and Twitter, most local business owners remain stumped by social marketing. This is true in the auto industry. Car manufacturers including Hyundai and Ford Motor have embraced social media and spend tens of millions of dollars on sophisticated marketing campaigns. Yet many of their local dealers barely maintain a Facebook page, and those that do report little or no gains in sales from going social.

Traditional marketing is all about creating and delivering a message using communication that is primarily one-way. Social media marketing is all about two-way communication and interaction. It enables businesses to receive an immediate response to a message—and to react and change the message, if necessary. Many companies still don't understand that difference.

Sources: Claudia Kubowicz Malhotra, and Arvind Malhotra, "How CEOs Can Leverage Twitter," *MIT Sloan Management Review*, Winter 2016; Daniel Matthews, "Social Customer Service Metrics: 3 Case Studies," Ducttapemarketing.com, accessed July 1, 2016; Nathalie Tadena, "Lowe's Enlists Snapchat, Facebook Mobile Video in New Push to Reach Millennials," *Wall Street Journal*, April 25, 2016; Vindu Goel, "The Gap Between Auto Dealers and Social Media," *New York Times*, April 9, 2015; and Ben DiPetro, "The Morning Risk Report: Takeaways from Starbucks' Race Relations Gambit," *Wall Street Journal*, March 24, 2015.

CASE STUDY QUESTIONS

1. Assess the management, organization, and technology issues for using social media technology to engage with customers.

2. What are the advantages and disadvantages of using social media for advertising, brand building, market research, and customer service?

3. Give an example of a business decision in this case study that was facilitated by using social media to interact with customers.

4. Should all companies use social media technology for customer service and marketing? Why or why not? What kinds of companies are best suited to use these platforms?

Beyond merely soliciting advice, firms can be actively helped in solving some business problems by using **crowdsourcing**. For instance, BMW launched a crowdsourcing project to enlist the aid of customers in designing an urban vehicle for 2025. Kickstarter.com is arguably one of the most famous e-commerce crowdfunding sites where visitors invest in start-up companies. Other examples include Caterpillar working with customers to design better machinery, IKEA for designing furniture, and Pepsico using Super Bowl viewers to build an online video.

Marketing through social media is still in its early stages, and companies are experimenting in hopes of finding a winning formula. Social interactions and customer sentiment are not always easy to manage, presenting new challenges for companies eager to protect their brands. The Interactive Session on Technology provides specific examples of companies' social marketing efforts using Facebook and Twitter.

10-4 How has e-commerce affected business-to-business transactions?

The trade between business firms (business-to-business commerce, or B2B) represents a huge marketplace. The total amount of B2B trade in the United States in 2015 was estimated to be about $14.6 trillion, with B2B e-commerce (online B2B) contributing about $6.2 trillion of that amount (U.S. Bureau of the Census, 2015; authors' estimates). By 2019, B2B e-commerce is expected to grow to about $8.6 trillion in the United States. The process of conducting trade among business firms is complex and requires significant human intervention; therefore, it consumes significant resources. Some firms estimate that each corporate purchase order for support products costs them, on average, at least $100 in administrative overhead. Administrative overhead includes processing paper, approving purchase decisions, spending time using the telephone and fax machines to search for products and arrange for purchases, arranging for shipping, and receiving the goods. Across the economy, this adds up to trillions of dollars annually spent for procurement processes that could be automated. If even just a portion of inter-firm trade were automated, and parts of the entire procurement process were assisted by the Internet, literally trillions of dollars might be released for more productive uses, consumer prices potentially would fall, productivity would increase, and the economic wealth of the nation would expand. This is the promise of B2B e-commerce. The challenge of B2B e-commerce is changing existing patterns and systems of procurement and designing and implementing new Internet-based B2B solutions.

Electronic Data Interchange (EDI)

B2B e-commerce refers to the commercial transactions that occur among business firms. Increasingly, these transactions are flowing through a variety of Internet-enabled mechanisms. About 80 percent of online B2B e-commerce is still based on proprietary systems for **Electronic Data Interchange (EDI)**. EDI enables the computer-to-computer exchange between two organizations of standard transactions such as invoices, bills of lading, shipment schedules, or purchase orders. Transactions are automatically transmitted from one information system to another through a network, eliminating the printing and handling of paper at one end and the inputting of data at the other. Each major industry in the United States and much of the rest of the world has EDI standards that define the structure and information fields of electronic documents for that industry.

EDI originally automated the exchange of documents such as purchase orders, invoices, and shipping notices. Although many companies still use EDI for document automation, firms engaged in just-in-time inventory replenishment and continuous production use EDI as a system for continuous replenishment. Suppliers have online access to selected parts of the purchasing firm's production and delivery schedules and automatically ship materials and goods to meet prespecified targets without intervention by firm purchasing agents (see Figure 10.6).

FIGURE 10.6 ELECTRONIC DATA INTERCHANGE (EDI)

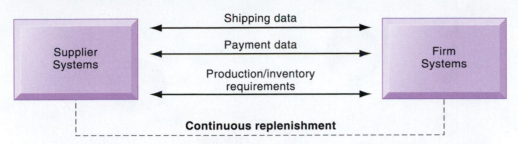

Companies use EDI to automate transactions for B2B e-commerce and continuous inventory replenishment. Suppliers can automatically send data about shipments to purchasing firms. The purchasing firms can use EDI to provide production and inventory requirements and payment data to suppliers.

Although many organizations still use private networks for EDI, they are increasingly web-enabled because Internet technology provides a much more flexible and low-cost platform for linking to other firms. Businesses can extend digital technology to a wider range of activities and broaden their circle of trading partners.

Procurement, for example, involves not only purchasing goods and materials but also sourcing, negotiating with suppliers, paying for goods, and making delivery arrangements. Businesses can now use the Internet to locate the lowest-cost supplier, search online catalogs of supplier products, negotiate with suppliers, place orders, make payments, and arrange transportation. They are not limited to partners linked by traditional EDI networks.

New Ways of B2B Buying and Selling

The Internet and web technology enable businesses to create electronic storefronts for selling to other businesses using the same techniques as used for B2C commerce. Alternatively, businesses can use Internet technology to create extranets or electronic marketplaces for linking to other businesses for purchase and sale transactions.

Private industrial networks typically consist of a large firm using a secure website to link to its suppliers and other key business partners (see Figure 10.7). The buyer owns the network, and it permits the firm and designated suppliers, distributors, and other business partners to share product design and development, marketing, production scheduling, inventory management, and unstructured communication, including graphics and e-mail. Another term for a private industrial network is a **private exchange**.

An example is VW Group Supply, which links the Volkswagen Group and its suppliers. VW Group Supply handles 90 percent of all global purchasing for Volkswagen, including all automotive and parts components.

Net marketplaces, which are sometimes called e-hubs, provide a single, digital marketplace based on Internet technology for many buyers and sellers (see Figure 10.8). They are industry-owned or operate as independent intermediaries between buyers and sellers. Net marketplaces generate revenue from purchase and sale transactions and other services provided to clients. Participants in Net marketplaces can establish prices through online negotiations, auctions, or requests for quotations, or they can use fixed prices.

There are many types of Net marketplaces and ways of classifying them. Some sell direct goods and some sell indirect goods. **Direct goods** are goods

FIGURE 10.7 A PRIVATE INDUSTRIAL NETWORK

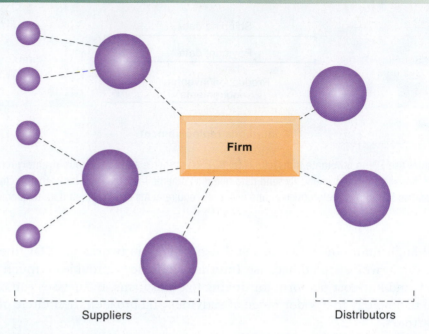

Suppliers   Distributors

A private industrial network, also known as a private exchange, links a firm to its suppliers, distributors, and other key business partners for efficient supply chain management and other collaborative commerce activities.

used in a production process, such as sheet steel for auto body production. **Indirect goods** are all other goods not directly involved in the production process, such as office supplies or products for maintenance and repair. Some Net marketplaces support contractual purchasing based on long-term relationships with designated suppliers, and others support short-term spot purchasing, where goods are purchased based on immediate needs, often from many suppliers.

FIGURE 10.8 A NET MARKETPLACE

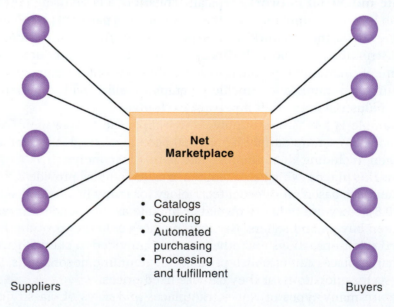

Suppliers   Buyers

Net marketplaces are online marketplaces where multiple buyers can purchase from multiple sellers.

Some Net marketplaces serve vertical markets for specific industries, such as automobiles, telecommunications, or machine tools, whereas others serve horizontal markets for goods and services that can be found in many industries, such as office equipment or transportation.

Exostar is an example of an industry-owned Net marketplace, focusing on long-term contract purchasing relationships and on providing common networks and computing platforms for reducing supply chain inefficiencies. This aerospace and defense industry-sponsored Net marketplace was founded jointly by BAE Systems, Boeing, Lockheed Martin, Raytheon, and Rolls-Royce plc to connect these companies to their suppliers and facilitate collaboration. More than 100,000 trading partners in the commercial, military, and government sectors use Exostar's sourcing, e-procurement, and collaboration tools for both direct and indirect goods.

Exchanges are independently owned third-party Net marketplaces that connect thousands of suppliers and buyers for spot purchasing. Many exchanges provide vertical markets for a single industry, such as food, electronics, or industrial equipment, and they primarily deal with direct inputs. For example, Go2Paper enables a spot market for paper, board, and craft among buyers and sellers in the paper industries from more than 75 countries.

Exchanges proliferated during the early years of e-commerce, but many have failed. Suppliers were reluctant to participate because the exchanges encouraged competitive bidding that drove prices down and did not offer any long-term relationships with buyers or services to make lowering prices worthwhile. Many essential direct purchases are not conducted on a spot basis because they require contracts and consideration of issues such as delivery timing, customization, and quality of products.

10-5 What is the role of m-commerce in business, and what are the most important m-commerce applications?

Walk down the street in any major metropolitan area and count how many people are pecking away at their iPhones, Samsungs, or BlackBerrys. Ride the trains or fly the planes, and you'll see your fellow travelers reading an online newspaper, watching a video on their phone, or reading a novel on their Kindle. In five years, the majority of Internet users in the United States will rely on mobile devices as their primary device for accessing the Internet. As the mobile audience expands in leaps and bounds, mobile advertising and m-commerce have taken off.

In 2017, m-commerce constituted about 37 percent of all e-commerce, with about $170 billion in annual revenues generated by retail goods and services, apps, advertising, music, videos, ring tones, movies, television, and location-based services such as local restaurant locators and traffic updates. However, m-commerce is the fastest-growing form of e-commerce, expanding at a rate of 50 percent or more per year, and is estimated to grow to $300 billion by 2020 (see Figure 10.9) (eMarketer, 2016c)

The main areas of growth in mobile e-commerce are mass market retailing such as Amazon ($16.8 billion) and Apple (about $14 billion); sales of digital content such as music, TV shows, movies, and e-books (about $6 billion); and in-app sales to mobile devices (about $7 billion) (eMarketer, 2016d). These estimates do not include mobile advertising or location-based services. On-demand

FIGURE 10.9 MOBILE RETAIL COMMERCE REVENUES

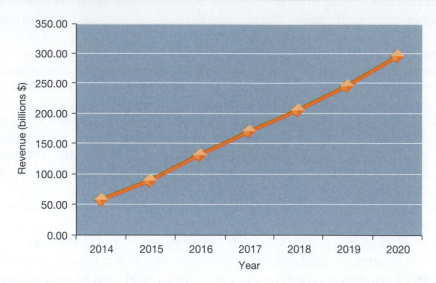

Mobile e-commerce is the fastest-growing type of B2C e-commerce and represented about 33 percent of all e-commerce in 2016.

Sources: Data from e-Marketer chart, "US Retail Mcommerce Sales, 2013-2019," May 2015.

firms such as Uber (described in the chapter-opening case) and Airbnb are location-based services, but they are certainly examples of mobile commerce as well.

Location-Based Services and Applications

Location-based services include geosocial, geoadvertising, and geoinformation services. Seventy-four percent of smartphone owners use location-based services. What ties these activities together and is the foundation for mobile commerce is the global positioning system (GPS)–enabled map services available on smartphones. A **geosocial service** can tell you where your friends are meeting. **Geoadvertising services** can tell you where to find the nearest Italian restaurant, and **geoinformation services** can tell you the price of a house you are looking at or about special exhibits at a museum you are passing. In 2017, the fastest-growing and most popular location-based services are on-demand economy firms such as Uber, Lyft, Airbnb, Instacart (see the Interactive Session on Organizations), and hundreds more that provide services to users in local areas and are based on the user's location (or, in the case of Airbnb, the user's intended travel location).

Waze is an example of a popular, social geoinformation service. Waze is a GPS-based map and navigational app for smartphones, now owned by Google. Waze locates the user's car on a digital map using GPS and, like other navigation programs, collects information on the user's speed and direction continuously. What makes Waze different is that it collects traffic information from users who submit accident reports, speed traps, landmarks, street fairs, protests, and even addresses. Waze uses this information to come up with suggested alternative routes, travel times, and warnings and can even make recommendations for gas stations along the way. The Waze app is used extensively by Uber and Lyft drivers and more than 25 million other drivers in the United States.

Foursquare and new offerings by Facebook and Google are examples of geosocial services. Geosocial services help you find friends, or your friends to

INTERACTIVE SESSION: ORGANIZATIONS

Can Instacart Deliver?

The online grocery store Webvan was perhaps the most well-known flop of the dot-com boom. Its 2001 failure led many pundits and investors to conclude that the online grocery business model was untenable.

However, Webvan's downfall was due mainly to pursuing a first-mover advantage strategy. It paid more than $1 billion to build huge distribution warehouses, bought fleets of delivery trucks, and invested heavily in marketing. Then it offered free deliveries on any size order, at virtually any hour, at prices that trumped its brick-and-mortar competitors. This was not a formula for generating profits.

In recent years other companies are testing the waters again for online grocery sales. FreshDirect in New York City has succeeded by combining fresh local produce, organic and kosher items, and custom-prepared meals with standard grocery store fare. Established brick-and-mortar firms including Albertson's, Safeway and Peapod.com (the online entity for both Stop & Shop and Giant) took over as pure play online firms perished.

The newest entrant, Instacart bypasses the expenses of warehousing and transportation altogether by using a legion of independent contractors and local food retailers. These personal shoppers receive orders via the Instacart smartphone app, fill them from grocery store aisles, and use their own vehicles to deliver them to customers' doors. Like fellow "sharing economy" firm Uber, Instacart minimizes labor costs by requiring its personal shoppers to pay for their own auto and health insurance and Social Security contributions. Purportedly paid between $15 and $20 an hour, depending on how quickly they can fill and deliver an order, most Instacart shoppers work part-time on flexible schedules.

Instacart co-founder and CEO Apoorva Mehta believes Instacart's competitive advantage is two-fold. First, customers are not limited to a single vendor and can combine items from multiple stores on one order, so product selection is truly customized. (Instacart uses special software that can track inventory across multiple supermarkets.) And since personal shoppers are on call around the clock, customers have to neither order many hours in advance of delivery nor wait for a delivery window. In fact, customers can have their grocery list filled and delivered in less than an hour!

Instacart's app provides a detailed map of each local establishment including store aisle contents. The customer's grocery list, compiled using extensive drop-down menus either on the website or in the app, is organized by merchant and aisle to provide maximum order fulfillment efficiency. Inventory is tracked for all of Instacart-affiliated merchants. As a personal shopper skims an aisle, bedecked in a bright green T-shirt flaunting the Instacart logo, items can be selected for different orders placed at different times. The software can also plan delivery routes and predict future customer orders.

iPhone users can connect to the Instacart app from Yummly, the largest recipe search engine in the world, and have the ingredients delivered in time for dinner. Visitors to Food Network websites, with more than half a million recipes, can browse recipes online and then click a button to add ingredients they need to their Instacart shopping cart. The Instacart app is integrated with Google Now cards so that Android users can place orders for either delivery or pickup using a token generated within the app.

Instacart's core competencies thus dictate its target market: the price-insensitive, convenience shopper. At first, item prices were marked up (20 percent in one sampling) and a $3.99 delivery fee charged. An Amazon Prime–like service called Instacart Express requires a certain volume of business and a $99 yearly fee in exchange for free delivery. One of Webvan's big mistakes was pursuing a mass-market strategy. It was never going to be able to turn a profit by providing quality and selection at rock-bottom prices—with free delivery to boot. Instacart is instead catering to shoppers who are willing to pay a premium to have both quality and selection.

By mid-2015 Instacart had 200 employees and 4,000 personal shoppers in New York, Los Angeles, San Francisco, San Jose, Washington, DC, Chicago, Boston, Austin, Seattle, Philadelphia, Atlanta, Boulder, Denver, Houston, and Portland, Oregon. It continues to grow. Grocery purveyors, from large chains such as Costco, BJ's Wholesale Club, Safeway, Kroger, Super Fresh, Trader Joe's, and Whole Foods to local specialty shops such as Erewhon Organic Grocer & Café in LA, Marczyk Fine Foods in Denver, and Green Zebra in Portland are now welcoming Instacart as a way to expand their customer bases ahead of the full national rollout of Amazon subsidiary Amazon Fresh.

While many analysts predict that matching the bargain basement prices of Amazon and Walmart is unavoidable, Instacart is instead modifying its business model. Partnerships with Petco and Tomlinson's Pet Supplies in Austin, Texas, hint of additional product areas on the horizon, while Mehta speculates that expansion into general logistics is conceivable.

Many of Instacart's grocery store partners now set their own prices, paying Instacart a cut of each order. This has freed Instacart of the burden of markups, protected it from the vagaries of variable food prices, and provided a more stable profit structure. Retailers have been willing to pay Instacart in the hope of gaining more business because Instacart enables a single store to serve people across a larger geographic area. Affiliated retailers are reporting gains, although the numbers are small. Nilam Ganenthiran, head of Business Development and Strategy, maintains that different types of agreements have been reached, declining to specify whether partners are outsourcing their e-commerce to Instacart for a monthly fee or are charged per item purchased, per order placed, or per customer serviced.

With national chains achieving just 1 to 2 percent margins on grocery delivery, the Instacart model of layering labor on top of the existing grocery infrastructure is still unproven. According to a *Wall Street Journal* analysis, an order of 15 common items such as frozen peas, milk, cereal, and fresh fruit costing about $68 from a San Francisco Safeway store would produce a profit of only $1.50 for Instacart. If the order were smaller by one 28-ounce jar of peanut butter, Instacart would break even, and a smaller order could push it into the red. Without price concessions from participating merchants, can Instacart attract enough customers? *And* maintain a pay scale that ensures the topnotch customer service demanded by its target market? *And* still make a profit? And can retailers' sales gains from Instacart be sustained? Instacart may be a great idea, but it's a very big bet.

Sources: Sarah Perez, "Instacart Becomes the Default Ingredients-Buying App for Food Network's Websites," TechCrunch.com, June 2, 2016; Megan Rose Dickey, "Instacart Cutting Wages for Shoppers Starting March 14," TechCrunch.com, March 11, 2016; Brad Stone, "Instacart Rings Up $220 Million More for its Grocery Delivery Service," *Bloomberg Business*, January 13, 2015; Carmel DeAmicis, "On the Way to $220M in Funding, Instacart Quietly Changed Its Business Model,"gigaom.com, January 14, 2015; Farhad Manjoo, "Instacart's Bet on Online Grocery Shopping, *New York Times*, April 29, 2015 and "Grocery Deliveries in the Sharing Economy," *New York Times*, May 21, 2014.

CASE STUDY QUESTIONS

1. Analyze Instacart using the value chain and competitive forces models. What competitive forces does the company have to deal with? What is its value proposition?

2. Explain how Instacart's business model works. How does the company generate revenue?

3. What is the role of information technology in Instacart's business model?

4. Is Instacart's model for selling online groceries viable? Why or why not?

find you, by checking in to the service, announcing your presence in a restaurant or other place. Your friends are instantly notified. About 20 percent of smartphone owners use geosocial services.

Foursquare provides a location-based social networking service to 60 million registered individual users, who may connect with friends, update their location, and provide reviews and tips for enjoying a location. Points are awarded for checking in at designated venues. Users choose to post their check-ins on their accounts on Twitter, Facebook, or both. Users also earn badges by checking in at locations with certain tags, for check-in frequency, or for the time of check-in. More than 500,000 local merchants worldwide use the merchant platform for marketing.

Connecting people to local merchants in the form of geoadvertising is the economic foundation for mobile commerce. Geoadvertising sends ads to users based on their GPS locations. Smartphones report their locations back to Google and Apple. Merchants buy access to these consumers when they come within range of a merchant. For instance, Kiehl Stores, a cosmetics retailer, sent special offers and announcements to customers who came within 100 yards of their store.

Other Mobile Commerce Services

Banks and credit card companies have developed services that let customers manage their accounts from their mobile devices. JPMorgan Chase and Bank of America customers can use their cell phones to check account balances, transfer funds, and pay bills. Apple Pay for the iPhone 6 and Apple Watch, along with other Android and Windows smartphone models, allows users to charge items to their credit card accounts with a swipe of their phone. (See our Learning Track on mobile payment systems.)

The mobile advertising market is the fastest-growing online ad platform, racking up $52 billion in ad revenue in 2017 and growing at 21 percent annually. Ads eventually move to where the eyeballs are, and increasingly that means mobile phones and, to less extent, tablets. Google is the largest mobile advertising market, posting about $10 billion in mobile ads, with Facebook number two with $4.9 billion. Yahoo displays ads on its mobile home page for companies such as Pepsico, Procter & Gamble, Hilton, Nissan, and Intel. Google is displaying ads linked to cell phone searches by users of the mobile version of its search engine; Microsoft offers banner and text advertising on its MSN Mobile portal in the United States. Ads are embedded in games, videos, and other mobile applications.

Shopkick is a mobile application that enables retailers such as Best Buy, Sports Authority, and Macy's to offer coupons to people when they walk into their stores. The Shopkick app automatically recognizes when the user has entered a partner retail store and offers a new virtual currency called kick-bucks, which can be redeemed for Facebook credits, iTunes gift cards, travel vouchers, DVDs, or immediate cashback rewards at any of the partner stores.

Fifty-five percent of online retailers now have m-commerce websites—simplified versions of their websites that enable shoppers to use cell phones to shop and place orders. Clothing retailers Lilly Pulitzer and Armani Exchange, Home Depot, Amazon, Walmart, and 1-800-Flowers are among those companies with apps for m-commerce sales. In 2016, more than half of m-commerce sales occurred within apps rather than mobile web browsers.

10-6 What issues must be addressed when building an e-commerce presence?

Building a successful e-commerce presence requires a keen understanding of business, technology, and social issues as well as a systematic approach. Today, an e-commerce presence is not just a corporate website but also includes a social network site on Facebook, a Twitter feed, and smartphone apps where customers can access your services. Developing and coordinating all these customer venues can be difficult. A complete treatment of the topic is beyond the scope of this text, and students should consult books devoted to just this topic (Laudon and Traver, 2016). The two most important management challenges in building a successful e-commerce presence are (1) developing a clear understanding of your business objectives and (2) knowing how to choose the right technology to achieve those objectives.

Develop an E-Commerce Presence Map

E-commerce has moved from being a PC-centric activity on the web to a mobile and tablet-based activity. Currently, a majority of Internet users in the United States use smartphones and tablets to shop for goods and services, look up prices, enjoy entertainment, and access social sites, less so to make purchases. Your potential customers use these various devices at different times during the day and involve themselves in different conversations, depending what they are doing—touching base with friends, tweeting, or reading a blog. Each of these is a touch point where you can meet the customer, and you have to think about how you develop a presence in these different virtual places. Figure 10.10 provides a roadmap to the platforms and related activities you will need to think about when developing your e-commerce presence.

Figure 10.10 illustrates four kinds of e-commerce presence: websites, e-mail, social media, and offline media. You must address different platforms for each of these types. For instance, in the case of website presence, there are three platforms: traditional desktop, tablets, and smartphones, each with different capabilities. Moreover, for each type of e-commerce presence, there are related activities you will need to consider. For instance, in the case of websites, you will want to engage in search engine marketing, display ads, affiliate programs, and sponsorships. Offline media, the fourth type of e-commerce presence, is included here because many firms use multiplatform or integrated marketing by which print ads refer customers to websites.

FIGURE 10.10 E-COMMERCE PRESENCE MAP

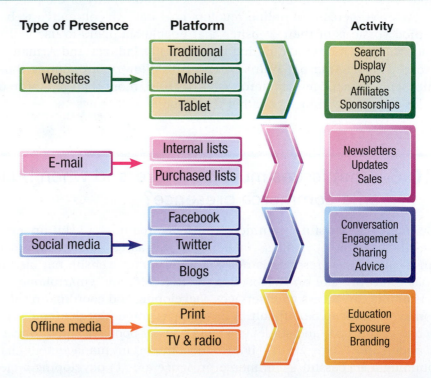

An e-commerce presence requires firms to consider the four types of presence, with specific platforms and activities associated with each.

TABLE 10.8 E-COMMERCE PRESENCE TIMELINE

PHASE	ACTIVITY	MILESTONE
Phase 1: Planning	Envision web presence; determine personnel.	Web mission statement
Phase 2: Website development	Acquire content; develop a site design; arrange for hosting the site.	Website plan
Phase 3: Web Implementation	Develop keywords and metatags; focus on search engine optimization; identify potential sponsors.	A functional website
Phase 4: Social media plan	Identify appropriate social platforms and content for your products and services.	A social media plan
Phase 5: Social media implementation	Develop Facebook, Twitter, and Pinterest presence.	Functioning social media presence
Phase 6: Mobile plan	Develop a mobile plan; consider options for porting your website to smartphones.	A mobile media plan

Develop a Timeline: Milestones

Where would you like to be a year from now? It's very helpful for you to have a rough idea of the time frame for developing your e-commerce presence when you begin. You should break your project down into a small number of phases that could be completed within a specified time. Table 10.8 illustrates a one-year timeline for the development of an e-commerce presence for a start-up company devoted to fashions for teenagers. You can also find more detail about developing an e-commerce website in the Learning Tracks for this chapter.

Review Summary

10-1 *What are the unique features of e-commerce, digital markets, and digital goods?*

E-commerce involves digitally enabled commercial transactions between and among organizations and individuals. Unique features of e-commerce technology include ubiquity, global reach, universal technology standards, richness, interactivity, information density, capabilities for personalization and customization, and social technology. E-commerce is becoming increasingly social, mobile, and local.

Digital markets are said to be more transparent than traditional markets, with reduced information asymmetry, search costs, transaction costs, and menu costs along with the ability to change prices dynamically based on market conditions. Digital goods, such as music, video, software, and books, can be delivered over a digital network. Once a digital product has been produced, the cost of delivering that product digitally is extremely low.

10-2 *What are the principal e-commerce business and revenue models?*

E-commerce business models are e-tailers, transaction brokers, market creators, content providers, community providers, service providers, and portals. The principal e-commerce revenue models are advertising, sales, subscription, free/freemium, transaction fee, and affiliate.

10-3 *How has e-commerce transformed marketing?*

The Internet provides marketers with new ways of identifying and communicating with millions of potential customers at costs far lower than traditional media. Crowdsourcing using the wisdom of crowds helps companies learn from customers to improve product offerings and increase customer value. Behavioral targeting techniques increase the effectiveness of banner, rich media, and video ads. Social commerce uses social networks and social network sites to improve targeting of products and services.

10-4 *How has e-commerce affected business-to-business transactions?*

B2B e-commerce generates efficiencies by enabling companies to locate suppliers, solicit bids, place orders, and track shipments in transit electronically. Net marketplaces provide a single, digital marketplace for many buyers and sellers. Private industrial networks link a firm with its suppliers and other strategic business partners to develop highly efficient and responsive supply chains.

10-5 *What is the role of m-commerce in business, and what are the most important m-commerce applications?*

M-commerce is especially well suited for location-based applications such as finding local hotels and restaurants, monitoring local traffic and weather, and providing personalized location-based marketing. Mobile phones and handhelds are being used for mobile bill payment, banking, securities trading, transportation schedule updates, and downloads of digital content such as music, games, and video clips. M-commerce requires wireless portals and special digital payment systems that can handle micropayments. The GPS capabilities of smartphones make geoadvertising, geosocial, and geoinformation services possible.

10-6 *What issues must be addressed when building an e-commerce presence?*

Building a successful e-commerce presence requires a clear understanding of the business objectives to be achieved and selection of the right platforms, activities, and timeline to achieve those objectives. An e-commerce presence includes not only a corporate website but also a presence on Facebook, Twitter, and other social networking sites and smartphone apps.

Key Terms

Advertising revenue model, 387
Affiliate revenue model, 389
Behavioral targeting, 390
Business-to-business (B2B), 384
Business-to-consumer (B2C), 384
Community providers, 387
Consumer-to-consumer (C2C), 384
Cost transparency, 379
Crowdsourcing, 397
Customization, 379
Digital goods, 382
Direct goods, 399
Disintermediation, 381
Dynamic pricing, 381
Electronic Data Interchange (EDI), 398
E-tailer, 385
Exchanges, 401
Free/freemium revenue model, 388
Geoadvertising services, 402
Geoinformation services, 402
Geosocial services, 402
Indirect goods, 400
Information asymmetry, 380
Information density, 379
Intellectual property, 386
Location-based services, 402

Long tail marketing, 389
Market creator, 386
Market entry costs, 379
Marketspace, 377
Menu costs, 381
Micropayment systems, 388
Mobile commerce (m-commerce), 384
Native advertising, 393
Net marketplaces, 399
Personalization, 379
Podcasting, 386
Price discrimination, 379
Price transparency, 379
Private exchange, 399
Private industrial networks, 399
Revenue model, 387
Richness, 379
Sales revenue model, 388
Search costs, 379
Social graph, 394
Social shopping, 395
Streaming, 386
Subscription revenue model, 388
Transaction costs, 377
Transaction fee revenue model, 389
Wisdom of crowds, 395

MyMISLab

To complete the problems with the MyMISLab, go to the EOC Discussion Questions in the MyMISLab.

Review Questions

10-1 What are the unique features of e-commerce, digital markets, and digital goods?

- Name and describe four business trends and three technology trends shaping e-commerce today.
- List and describe the eight unique features of e-commerce.
- Define a digital market and digital goods and describe their distinguishing features.

10-2 What are the principal e-commerce business and revenue models?

- Name and describe the principal e-commerce business models.
- Name and describe the e-commerce revenue models.

10-3 How has e-commerce transformed marketing?

- Explain how social networking and the wisdom of crowds help companies improve their marketing.
- Define behavioral targeting and explain how it works at individual websites and on advertising networks.

- Define the social graph and explain how it is used in e-commerce marketing.

10-4 How has e-commerce affected business-to-business transactions?

- Explain how Internet technology supports business-to-business electronic commerce.
- Define and describe Net marketplaces and explain how they differ from private industrial networks (private exchanges).

10-5 What is the role of m-commerce in business, and what are the most important m-commerce applications?

- List and describe important types of m-commerce services and applications.

10-6 What issues must be addressed when building an e-commerce presence?

- List and describe the four types of e-commerce presence.

Discussion Questions

10-7 How does the Internet change consumer and
MyMISLab supplier relationships?

10-8 The Internet may not make corporations
MyMISLab obsolete, but the corporations will have to change their business models. Do you agree? Why or why not?

10-9 How have social technologies changed e-com-
MyMISLab merce?

Hands-On MIS Projects

The projects in this section give you hands-on experience developing e-commerce strategies for businesses, using spreadsheet software to research the profitability of an e-commerce company, and using web tools to research and evaluate e-commerce hosting services. Visit MyMISLab's Multimedia Library to access this chapter's Hands-On MIS Projects.

Management Decision Problems

10-10 Columbiana is a small, independent island in the Caribbean that has many historical buildings, forts, and other sites along with rain forests and striking mountains. A few first-class hotels and several dozen less expensive accommodations lie along its beautiful white-sand beaches. The major airlines have regular flights to Columbiana, as do several small airlines. Columbiana's government wants to increase tourism and develop new markets for the country's tropical agricultural products. How can a web presence help? What Internet business model would be appropriate? What functions should the web presence perform?

10-11 Explore the websites of the following companies: Blue Nile, Swatch, Lowe's, and Priceline. Determine which of these websites would benefit most from adding a company-sponsored blog to the website. List the business benefits of the blog. Specify the intended audience for the blog. Decide who in the company should author the blog and select some topics for the blog.

Improving Decision Making: Using Spreadsheet Software to Analyze a Dot-Com Business

Software skills: Spreadsheet downloading, formatting, and formulas
Business skills: Financial statement analysis

10-12 Pick one e-commerce company on the Internet—for example, Ashford, Yahoo, or Priceline. Study the web pages that describe the company and explain its purpose and structure. Use the web to find articles that comment on the company. Then visit the Securities and Exchange Commission's website at www.sec.gov to access the company's 10-K (annual report) form showing income statements and balance sheets. Select only the sections of the 10-K form containing the desired portions of financial statements that you need to examine and download them into your spreadsheet. (MyMISLab provides more detailed instructions on how to download this 10-K data into a spreadsheet.) Create simplified spreadsheets of the company's balance sheets and income statements for the past three years.

- Is the company a dot-com success, borderline business, or failure? What information provides the basis of your decision? Why? When answering these questions, pay special attention to the company's three-year trends in revenues, costs of sales, gross margins, operating expenses, and net margins.

- Prepare an overhead presentation (with a minimum of five slides), including appropriate spreadsheets or charts, and present your work to your professor and classmates.

Achieving Operational Excellence: Evaluating E-Commerce Hosting Services

Software skills: Web browser software
Business skills: Evaluating e-commerce hosting services

10-13 This project will help develop your Internet skills in evaluating commercial services for hosting an e-commerce site for a small start-up company.

You would like to set up a website to sell towels, linens, pottery, and tableware from Portugal and are examining services for hosting small business Internet storefronts. Your website should be able to take secure credit card payments and calculate shipping costs and taxes. Initially, you would like to display photos and descriptions of 40 products. Visit eHost.com, GoDaddy, and iPage and compare the range of e-commerce hosting services they offer to small businesses, their capabilities, and their costs. Examine the tools they provide for creating an e-commerce site. Compare these services and decide which you would use if you were actually establishing a web store. Write a brief report indicating your choice and explaining the strengths and weaknesses of each service.

Collaboration and Teamwork Project

Performing a Competitive Analysis of E-commerce Sites

10-14 Form a group with three or four of your classmates. Select two businesses that are competitors in the same industry and that use their websites for electronic commerce. Visit these websites. You might compare, for example, the websites for Pandora and Spotify, Amazon and BarnesandNoble.com, or E*Trade and Scottrade. Prepare an evaluation of each business's website in terms of its functions, user friendliness, and ability to support the company's business strategy. Which website does a better job? Why? Can you make some recommendations to improve these websites? If possible, use Google Docs and Google Drive or Google Sites to brainstorm, organize, and develop a presentation of your findings for the class.

Walmart and Amazon Duke It Out for E-commerce Supremacy
CASE STUDY

Walmart is the world's largest and most successful retailer, with $483 billion in 2015 sales and more than 11,500 stores worldwide, including more than 4,600 in the United States. Walmart has 2.3 million employees and ranks number one on the *Fortune* 500 list of companies. Walmart had such a large and powerful selling machine that it really didn't have any serious competitors—until now.

Today Walmart's greatest threat is Amazon.com, often called the "Walmart of the Web." Amazon sells not only books but just about everything else people want to buy—DVDs, video and music streaming downloads, software, video games, electronics, apparel, furniture, food, toys, and jewelry. The company also produces consumer electronics—notably the Amazon Kindle e-book reader, Kindle Fire tablet, Echo and Tap speakers, and Fire TV set-top box. No other online retailer can match Amazon's breadth of selection, low prices, and fast, reliable shipping. For many years, Amazon has been the world's largest e-commerce retailer with the world's largest and most powerful online selling machine. Moreover, Amazon has changed the habits and expectations of consumers in ways to which Walmart and other retailers must adapt. Instead of a "push" model, where merchandisers have a large degree of control of what items they stock and sell, retailers must adapt to a "pull" model, where shoppers are more empowered than ever. According to Brian Yarbrough, a retail analyst at Edward Jones in St. Louis, Amazon and online retailing is probably the biggest disrupter of retail since Walmart itself.

Walmart was founded as a traditional, offline, physical store in 1962, and that's still what it does best. But it is being forced to compete in e-commerce as well. Seven years ago, only one-fourth of all Walmart customers shopped at Amazon.com, according to data from researcher Kantar Retail. Today, however, half of Walmart customers say they've shopped at both retailers. Online competition and the profits to be reaped from e-commerce have become too important to ignore.

Walmart's traditional customers—who are primarily bargain hunters making less than $50,000 per year—are becoming more comfortable using technology. More affluent customers who started shopping at Walmart during the recession are returning to Amazon as their finances improve. Amazon has started stocking merchandise categories that Walmart traditionally sold, such as vacuum bags, diapers, and apparel, and its revenue is growing much faster than Walmart's. In 2015, Amazon had sales of more than $113 billion.

If more people want to do even some of their shopping online, Amazon has some clear-cut advantages. Amazon has created a recognizable and highly successful brand in online retailing. The company has developed extensive warehousing facilities and an extremely efficient distribution network specifically designed for web shopping. Its premium shipping service, Amazon Prime, provides fast "free" two-day shipping at an affordable fixed annual subscription price ($99 per year), often considered to be a weak point for online retailers. According to the *Wall Street Journal*, Amazon's shipping costs are lower than Walmart's, ranging from $3 to $4 per package, while Walmart's online shipping can run $5 to $7 per parcel. Walmart's massive supply chain needs to support more than 11,000 physical stores worldwide, which Amazon doesn't have to worry about. Shipping costs can make a big difference for a store like Walmart where popular purchases tend to be low-cost items like $10 packs of underwear. It makes no sense for Walmart to create a duplicate supply chain for e-commerce.

However, Walmart is no pushover. It is an even larger and more recognizable brand than Amazon. Consumers associate Walmart with the lowest price, which Walmart has the flexibility to offer on any given item because of its size. The company can lose money selling a hot product at extremely low margins and expect to make money on the strength of the large quantities of other items it sells. Walmart also has a significant physical presence, and its stores provide the instant gratification of shopping, buying an item, and taking it home immediately as opposed to waiting when ordering from Amazon. Seventy percent of the U.S. population is within five miles of a Walmart store, according to company management.

Walmart has steadily increased its investment in its online business, spending between $1.2 billion and $1.5 billion annually in 2015 and the next few years on e-commerce, including fulfillment centers and technology. Walmart has constructed one of the world's largest private cloud computing centers, which provides the computing horsepower for Walmart to increase the number of items available for sale on Walmart.com from 1 million three years ago to 10 million today. In the spring of 2015 the company opened four new fulfillment centers around the country, each of which is more than 1 million square feet. To further counter Amazon, Walmart introduced its own "free" two-day shipping program called Shipping Pass, similar to Amazon Prime but costing only $49 per year.

New technology will also give Walmart more expertise in improving the product recommendations for web visitors to Walmart.com, using smartphones as a marketing channel, and personalizing the shopping experience. Walmart has been steadily adding new applications to its mobile and online shopping channels and is expanding its integration with social networks such as Pinterest.

A Pay With Cash program enables the 25 percent of Walmart customers who don't have credit cards or bank accounts to order their products online and then pay for them in cash at their nearest Walmart store. Walmart's online and digital development division @WalmartLabs acquired the recipe technology start-up Yumprint in order to expand its online grocery delivery services. Management hopes that Yumprint will help Walmart customers more easily make shopping lists from recipes they find in Yumprint before they shop.

Walmart is also trying to improve links between its store inventory, website, and mobile phone apps so that more customers can order online and pick up their purchases at stores. Shoppers can order items online and pick them up from lockers in local stores without waiting in line. Walmart's lockers are similar to Amazon's recent deal with Staples and 7-Eleven to do the same. The idea is to be able to offer Walmart products anywhere a consumer prefers to shop, whether that's online, in stores, or on the phone.

The company is rethinking its in-store experience to draw more people into its stores. More than half of Walmart customers own smartphones. Walmart has designed its mobile app to maximize Walmart's advantage over Amazon: its physical locations. About 140 million people visit a Walmart store each week. The company started testing the app's in-store mode, which detects when a customer is in a physical store. When the mode is activated, customers can check their wish lists, locate items of interest in the store, and see local promotions. The app's "Scan & Go" feature lets customers scan items as they shop so they can move quickly through self-checkout. Shoppers can add items to their lists using voice or by scanning bar codes.

The Walmart website uses software to monitor prices at competing retailers in real time and lower its online prices if necessary. The company is also doubling inventory sold from third-party retailers in its online marketplace and tracking patterns in search and social media data to help it select more trendy products. This strikes directly at Amazon's third-party marketplace, which accounts for a significant revenue stream for Amazon. Additionally, Walmart is expanding its online offerings to include upscale items like $146 Nike sunglasses and wine refrigerators costing more than $2,500 to attract customers who never set foot in a Walmart store. A new Product Content Collection System will facilitate vendors sending their product catalogs to Walmart, and the product information will then be available online

Walmart's commitment to e-commerce is not designed to replicate Amazon's business model. Instead, CEO Doug McMillon is crafting a strategy that gives consumers the best of both worlds—what is called an omnichannel approach to retailing. Walmart's management believes the company's advantage is that it is not a pure-play e-commerce retailer and that customers want some real interaction with physical stores as well as digital. Walmart will sell vigorously through the web and also in its physical stores, retaining its hallmark everyday low prices and wide product assortment in both channels and using its large network of stores as distribution points. Walmart will closely integrate online shopping and fulfillment with its physical stores so that customers can shop however they want, whether it's ordering on their mobile phones for home delivery, through in-store pickup, or by wandering down the aisles of a Walmart superstore. Walmart is aiming to be the world's biggest omnichannel retailer.

Amazon is working on expanding its selection of goods to be as exhaustive as Walmart's. Amazon has allowed third-party sellers to sell goods through its website for a number of years, and it has dramatically expanded product selection via acquisitions such as its 2009 purchase of online shoe shopping site Zappos.com to give the company an edge in footwear. Amazon has been building its grocery offerings, with Amazon Prime, Prime Now, Prime Pantry, and Amazon Fresh offering delivery times as short as an hour in some cases. Amazon has opened a retail bookstore in Seattle and plans more in other U.S. locations. Customers will be able to use Amazon's Alexa voice-controlled digital assistant (built into the Echo and Tap speakers and Fire TV) to order tens of millions of products from Amazon's online store.

Amazon continues to build more fulfillment centers closer to urban centers and expand its same-day delivery services, and it has a supply chain optimized for online commerce that Walmart just can't match. It now has more than 100 warehouses from which to package and ship goods. Warehouses speed up Amazon's shipping, encouraging users to shop more at Amazon, and the cost of these centers as a portion of Amazon's operations is decreasing. Both Amazon and Walmart are experimenting with drones to accelerate fulfilment and delivery. But Walmart has thousands of stores, one in almost every neighborhood, which Amazon won't ever be able to replicate. The winner of this epic struggle will be which company leverages its advantage better. Walmart's technology initiative looks promising, but it still has work to do before its local stores are anything more than local stores. Can Walmart successfully move to an omnichannel strategy?

Sources: Julie Verhage, "One Wall Street Firm Says Amazon Is About to 'Feast' on the Food and Beverage Market," *Bloomberg Business*, March 17, 2016; Rachel Abrams, "Walmart Outperforms Estimates, but Online Retail Lags," *New York Times*, May 19,2016; Sarah Nassauer and Loretta Chao, "Wal-Mart Expands Free Two-Day Shipping," *Wall Street Journal*, June 29, 2016; Nathan Olivarez-Giles, "Amazon's Alexa Now Lets You Order Tens of Millions of Products with Your Voice," *Wall Street Journal*, July 1, 2016; Farhad Manjoo, "How Amazon's Long Game Yielded a Retail Juggernaut," *New York Times*, November 19, 2015; Brian O'Keefe, "The Man Who's Reinventing Walmart," *Fortune*, June 4, 2015; Nathan Layne, "Wal-Mart Eyes Amazon in Potentially Costly E-commerce Battle," *Reuters*, May 20, 2015; Anna Rose Welch, "Walmart, Sam's Club Amp Up Online Shopping Experiences," Integrated Solutions for Retailers, February 28, 2014; Donna Tam, "Walmart: Amazon Image Recognition a 'Shiny Object,'" CNET, February 6, 2014; and Claire Cain Miller and Stephanie Clifford, "To Catch Up, Walmart Moves to Amazon Turf," *New York Times*, October 19, 2013.

CASE STUDY QUESTIONS

10-15 Analyze Walmart and Amazon.com using the competitive forces and value chain models.

10-16 Compare Walmart and Amazon's business models and business strategies.

10-17 What role does information technology play in each of these businesses? How is it helping them refine their business strategies?

10-18 Will Walmart be successful against Amazon.com? Explain your answer.

MyMISLab

Go to the Assignments section of MyMISLab to complete these writing exercises.

10-19 Describe the six features of social commerce. Provide an example for each feature, describing how a business could use that feature for selling to consumers online.

10-20 List and describe the main activities involved in building an e-commerce presence.

Chapter 10 References

Adomavicius, Gediminas, Jesse Bockstedt, and Shawn P. Curley. "Bundling Effects on Variety Seeking for Digital Information Goods." *Journal of Management Information Systems* 31, No. 4 (Spring 2015).

Brynjolfsson, Erik, Yu Hu, and Michael D. Smith. "Consumer Surplus in the Digital Economy: Estimating the Value of Increased Product Variety at Online Booksellers." *Management Science* 49, No. 11 (November 2003).

Brynjolfsson, Erik, Yu Jeffrey Hu, and Mohammad S. Rahman. "Competing in the Age of Multichannel Retailing." *MIT Sloan Management Review* (May 2013).

Butler, Brian S., Patrick J. Bateman, Peter H. Gray, and E. Ilana Diamant. "An Attraction-Selection-Attrition Theory of Online Community Size and Resilience." *MIS Quarterly* 38, No. 3 (September 2014).

Chandlee, Blake and Gerald C. (Jerry) Kane. "How Facebook Is Delivering Personalization on a Whole New Scale." *MIT Sloan Management Review* 55, No. 4 (August 5, 2014).

Chen, Jianquing and Jan Stallaert. "An Economic Analysis of Online Advertising Using Behavioral Targeting." *MIS Quarterly* 38, No. 2 (June 2014).

comScore Inc. "ComScore 2013 US Digital Future in Focus." [Nick Mulligan] (April 2, 2014).

Doyle, Cathy. "US Mobile StatPack."eMarketer (March 2016).

eMarketer. "E-Commerce Sales, 2014–2020," Chart (June 2016b).

eMarketer. "US Retail Sales to Near $5 Trillion in 2016," Report (December 2016e).

eMarketer. "US Mobile Commerce Update 2016," Report, eMarketer (May 2016d).

eMarketer. "Digital Ad Spending United States," 2014–2018, Chart (2016a).

eMarketer. "US Ad Spending: Estimates for 2016," Report, eMarketer (March 2016c).

Federal Trade Commission. "Data Brokers: A Call for Transparency and Accountability," Federal Trade Commission (May 2014).

Fang, Yulin, Israr Qureshi, Heshan Sun, Patrick McCole, Elaine Ramsey, and Kai H. Lim. "Trust, Satisfaction, and Online Repurchase Intention: The Moderating Role of Perceived Effectiveness of E-Commerce Institutional Mechanisms." *MIS Quarterly* 38, No. 2 (June 2014).

Gast, Arne and Michele Zanini. "The Social Side of Strategy." *McKinsey Quarterly* (May 2012).

Ghoshal, Abhijeet, Subodha Kumar, and Vijay Mookerjee. "Impact of Recommender System on Competition Between Personalizing and Non-Personalizing Firms." *Journal of Management Information Systems* 31, No. 4 (Spring 2015).

Gupta, Sunil. "For Mobile Devices, Think Apps, Not Ads." *Harvard Business Review* (March 2013).

Hinz, Oliver, Il-Horn Hann, and Martin Spann. "Price Discrimination in E-Commerce? An Examination of Dynamic Pricing in Name-Your-Own Price Markets." *MIS Quarterly* 35, No. 1 (March 2011).

Holt, Douglas. "Branding in the Age of Social Media." *Harvard Business Review* (March 2016).

Hoofnagle, Chris Jay, Jennifer M. Urban, and Su Li. "Privacy and Modern Advertising: Most US Internet Users Want 'Do Not Track' to Stop Collection of Data About Their Online Activities." Berkeley Consumer Privacy Survey. BCLT Research Paper (October 8, 2012).

Im, Il, Jongkun Jun, Wonseok Oh, and Seok-Oh Jeong. "Deal-Seeking Versus Brand-Seeking: Search Behaviors and Purchase Propensities in Sponsored Search Platforms." *MIS Quarterly* 40, No. 1 (March 2016).

Internet Retailer. "Mobile Commerce Top 400 2015." (2015).

Internet World Stats. "Internet Users in the World." Internetworldstats.com (2016).

Kumar, V. and Rohan Mirchandan "Increasing the ROI of Social Media Marketing." *MIT Sloan Management Review* 54, No. 1 (Fall 2012).

Laudon, Kenneth C. and Carol Guercio Traver. *E-commerce: Business, Technology, Society*, 12th ed. Upper Saddle River, NJ: Prentice-Hall (2016).

Li, Xitong. "Could Deal Promotion Improve Merchants' Online Reputations? The Moderating Role of Prior Reviews." *Journal of Management Information Systems* 33, No.1 (2016).

Liu, Charles Zhechao, Yoris A Au., and Hoon Seok Choi. "Effects of Freemium Strategy in the Mobile App Market: An Empirical Study of Google Play." *Journal of Management Information Systems* 31, No. 3 (Winter 2014).

Oestreicher-Singer, Gal and Arun Sundararajan. "Recommendation Networks and the Long Tail of Electronic Commerce." *MIS Quarterly* 36, No. 1 (March 2012).

Oh, Hyelim, Animesh Animesh, and Alain Pinsonneault. "Free Versus For-a-Fee: The Impact of a Paywall on the Pattern and Effectiveness of Word-of-Mouth via Social Media." *MIS Quarterly* 40, No. 1 (March 2016).

Orlikowski, Wanda and Susan V. Scott. "The Algorithm and the Crowd: Considering the Materiality of Service Innovation." *MIS Quarterly* 39, No.1 (March 2015).

Pew Internet and American Life Project. "Americans' Attitudes About Privacy, Security, and Surveillance." (May 20, 2015a).

Pew Internet and American Life Project. "Americans' Privacy Strategies Post-Snowden." (March 16, 2015b).

Rainie, Lee and Maeve Duggan. "Privacy and Information Sharing." Pew Research Center (January, 2016).

Reynolds, Tracy. "NRF Forecasts Retail Sales to Grow 3.1 Percent in 2016." National Retail Federation (February 10, 2016).

Rigby, Darrell K. "Digital Physical Mashups." *Harvard Business Review* (September 2014).

Schulze, Christian, Lisa Schöler, and Bernd Skier. "Customizing Social Media Marketing." *MIT Sloan Management Review* (Winter 2015).

Shuk, Ying Ho and David Bodoff. "The Effects of Web Personalization on User Attitude and Behavior: An Integration of the Elaboration Likelihood Model and Consumer Search Theory." *MIS Quarterly* 38, No. 2 (June 2014).

Susarla, Anjana, Jeong-Ha Oh, and Young Tan. "Influentials, Imitables, or Susceptibles? Virality and Word-of-Mouth Conversations in Online Social Networks." *Journal of Management Information Systems* 33, No.1 (2016).

Urban, Glen L. and Fareena Sultan. "The Case for 'Benevolent' Mobile Apps." *MIT Sloan Management Review* (Winter 2015).

U.S. Bureau of the Census. "E-Stats. 2014." http://www.census. gov/econ/index.html (May 22, 2014).

Xiaojuan Ou, Carol, Paul A. Pavlou, and Robert M. Davison. "Swift Guanxi in Online Marketplaces: The Role of Computer-Mediated Communication Technologies." *MIS Quarterly* 38, No. 1 (March 2014).

Yin, Dezhi, Samuel D. Bond, and Han Zhang. "Anxious or Angry? Effects of Discrete Emotions on the Perceived Helpfulness of Online Reviews." *MIS Quarterly* 38, No. 2 (June 2014).

Zhang, Zan, Guofang Nan, Minqiang Li, and Yong Tan. "Duopoly Pricing Strategy for Information Products with Premium Service: Free Product or Bundling?" *Journal of Management Information Systems* 33, No. 1 (2016).

Zhou, Wenqi and Wenjing Duan. "Do Professional Reviews Affect Online User Choices Through User Reviews? An Empirical Study." *Journal of Management Information Systems* 33, No. 1 (2016).

11

Managing Knowledge

Learning Objectives

After reading this chapter, you will be able to answer the following questions:

11-1 What is the role of knowledge management systems in business?

11-2 What types of systems are used for enterprise-wide knowledge management, and how do they provide value for businesses?

11-3 What are the major types of knowledge work systems, and how do they provide value for firms?

11-4 What are the business benefits of using intelligent techniques for knowledge management?

MyMISLab™

Visit **mymislab.com** for simulations, tutorials, and end-of-chapter problems.

CHAPTER CASES

Cadillac Creates Virtual Dealerships
ECM in the Cloud Empowers New Zealand Department of Conservation
Will Robots Replace People in Manufacturing?
Does IBM's Watson Have a Future in Business?

VIDEO CASES

How IBM's Watson Became a Jeopardy Champion
Alfresco: Open Source Document Management and Collaboration

Cadillac Creates Virtual Dealerships

Suppose you are interested in buying a car and want to check out a similar car on the dealer's lot. Well, you might see a few examples of the car you are interested in, but they might not be exactly what you were looking for. They might not have the color or combination of options you want, for instance. But what if you could look at every possible variant of the car without that car actually being on the premises? Today that's possible thanks to virtual reality. Virtual reality (VR) is a computer-simulated environment that appears to the user as a real environment with which the user can interact.

Audi has pioneered using VR in its "dealership in a briefcase" program. By donning an Oculus Rift virtual reality headset, prospective buyers can feel they are sitting behind the wheel of a car or opening up the trunk. A camera tracks viewer's head movements and adjusts the image on the goggles accordingly. The VR headset displays in 3-D exactly what you'd see if you were looking over a real-life Audi. Bang & Olufsen headphones simulate the sounds of doors slamming shut and music from the stereo system of the cars being browsed. This VR experience is available for the entire Audi model range and customization options, including colors, upholstery, and infotainment systems.

© Syda Productions/Fotolia

Now Cadillac is embracing VR. This luxury division of General Motors has a problem: It has too many dealers—about three times as many U.S. dealerships as German luxury automakers or Toyota's Lexus—but sells only half as many cars as they do. That means that there's a lot of excess inventory in car lots waiting too long to be sold. The inventory must be financed by the dealership, which must also pay for insurance and sales staff. Some of these charges, called "dealer's prep," show up in the final price of a new car, and these can amount to $500 or more. Using VR may help Cadillac reduce its unsold inventory and help dealers become more price-competitive.

Cadillac plans to remove new-vehicle inventory from a portion of its 925 U.S. dealerships and use virtual reality headsets to display cars that previously would have been on dealer lots. Outside of urban areas, many Cadillacs are sold by dealers who also sell Chevrolet or Buick GMC cars. These combined dealerships sell very few Cadillacs—about 30 per year. The dealers would retain their service, financing, and used-car operations. Salespeople would be equipped with touchscreen configurators and virtual reality devices and visit prospective buyers at their workplaces and homes. Dealers would have a few tester cars on site, but Cadillacs purchased would be obtained from regional inventory centers instead of dealer lots. This move to VR is part of a new retail strategy called Project Pinnacle launched by Cadillac's president Johan de Nysschen.

Not all Cadillac dealers are enthusiastic, especially those whose sales depend on rock-bottom pricing. Project Pinnacle wants dealer compensation to shift from being based only on the number of vehicles sold to services and perks such as free roadside assistance offered by luxury car competitors. Another worry is that if Cadillac can sell via virtual showrooms, the company might be able to bypass dealers altogether. And some dealers believe that with today's customers wanting immediate gratification, it might be impossible to compete without having real cars on the sales lot. These dealers argue that there's nothing like the feel and smell of leather in luxury cars and the touch of the controls and nothing like the real thing when it comes to sales.

Sources: Eric Bank, "Cadillac Swapping Dealerships for Virtual Reality," Get.com, June 7, 2016; Sean Szymkowski, "Johan de Nysschen Pitches Virtual Stores for Low-Volume Cadillac Dealerships," GM Authority, February 22, 2016; Christina Rogers, John D. Stoll, and Gautham Nagesh, "Cadillac Bets on Virtual Dealerships," *Wall Street Journal*, June 5, 2016; "Audi Reveals Virtual Reality 'Dealership in a Briefcase,'" AutoBlog, January 19, 2015; and Bob Sorokanich, "Audi Crams an Entire Dealership with Infinite Inventory into a Virtual Reality Headset," *Car and Driver*, January 15, 2015.

Cadillac's plan to use virtual reality technology to replace some dealer showrooms shows how business performance can benefit by using technology to facilitate the acquisition and application of knowledge. Facilitating access to knowledge, using knowledge tools to create and visualize products, improving the quality and currency of knowledge, and using that knowledge to improve business processes are vital to success and survival in all areas of business.

The chapter-opening diagram calls attention to important points raised by this case and this chapter. Cadillac has been saddled with too many dealerships selling too few cars. The company would like to eliminate physical cars on lots of dealers that do not sell many Cadillacs and replace them with virtual reality headsets that simulate the experience of seeing, touching, and listening to a Cadillac car that can be configured digitally with any options desired by the prospective customer. Using knowledge technology would reduce costs by eliminating excess physical inventory on the lots of dealers who don't sell many Cadillacs, and it could potentially increase sales by providing customers with the ability to experience the car model and options of their choice right on the spot. Thanks to better systems for visualizing and creating knowledge, Cadillac believes it has a much more cost-effective process for selling cars. However, the Cadillac dealers themselves are not so sure.

Here are some questions to think about: How does using VR change the auto sales process? Is virtual reality an appropriate tool for auto sales? Why or why not?

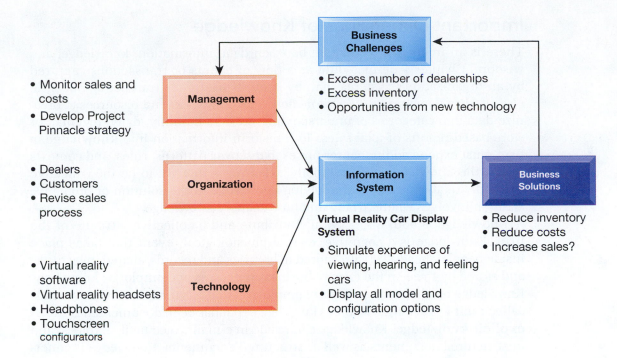

11-1 What is the role of knowledge management systems in business?

Knowledge management and collaboration systems are among the fastest-growing areas of corporate and government software investment. The past decade has shown an explosive growth in research on knowledge and knowledge management in the economics, management, and information systems fields.

Knowledge management and collaboration are closely related. Knowledge that cannot be communicated and shared with others is nearly useless. Knowledge becomes useful and actionable when shared throughout the firm. We have already described the major tools for collaboration and social business in Chapter 2. In this chapter, we will focus on knowledge management systems and be mindful that communicating and sharing knowledge are becoming increasingly important.

We live in an information economy in which the major source of wealth and prosperity is the production and distribution of information and knowledge. An estimated 37 percent of the U.S. labor force consists of knowledge and information workers, the largest single segment of the labor force. About 55 percent of the gross domestic product (GDP) of the United States is generated by the knowledge and information sectors (U.S. Department of Labor, 2016).

Knowledge management has become an important theme at many large business firms as managers realize that much of their firm's value depends on the firm's ability to create and manage knowledge. Studies have found that a substantial part of a firm's stock market value is related to its intangible assets, of which knowledge is one important component, along with brands, reputations, and unique business processes. Well-executed knowledge-based projects have been known to produce extraordinary returns on investment, although the impacts of knowledge-based investments are difficult to measure (Gu and Lev, 2001).

Important Dimensions of Knowledge

There is an important distinction between data, information, knowledge, and wisdom. Chapter 1 defines **data** as a flow of events or transactions captured by an organization's systems that, by itself, is useful for transacting but little else. To turn data into useful *information*, a firm must expend resources to organize data into categories of understanding, such as monthly, daily, regional, or store-based reports of total sales. To transform information into **knowledge**, a firm must expend additional resources to discover patterns, rules, and contexts where the knowledge works. Finally, **wisdom** is thought to be the collective and individual experience of applying knowledge to the solution of problems. Wisdom involves where, when, and how to apply knowledge.

Knowledge is both an individual attribute and a collective attribute of the firm. Knowledge is a cognitive, even a physiological, event that takes place inside people's heads. It is also stored in libraries and records, shared in lectures, and stored by firms in the form of business processes and employee know-how. Knowledge residing in the minds of employees that has not been documented is called **tacit knowledge**, whereas knowledge that has been documented is called **explicit knowledge**. Knowledge can reside in e-mail, voice mail, graphics, and unstructured documents as well as structured documents. Knowledge is generally believed to have a location, either in the minds of humans or in specific business processes. Knowledge is "sticky" and not universally applicable or easily moved. Finally, knowledge is thought to be situational and contextual. For example, you must know when to perform a procedure as well as how to perform it. Table 11.1 reviews these dimensions of knowledge.

TABLE 11.1 IMPORTANT DIMENSIONS OF KNOWLEDGE

KNOWLEDGE IS A FIRM ASSET

Knowledge is an intangible asset.

The transformation of data into useful information and knowledge requires organizational resources.

Knowledge is not subject to the law of diminishing returns as are physical assets but instead experiences network effects as its value increases as more people share it.

KNOWLEDGE HAS DIFFERENT FORMS

Knowledge can be either tacit or explicit (codified).

Knowledge involves know-how, craft, and skill.

Knowledge involves knowing how to follow procedures.

Knowledge involves knowing why, not simply when, things happen (causality).

KNOWLEDGE HAS A LOCATION

Knowledge is a cognitive event involving mental models and maps of individuals.

There is both a social and an individual basis of knowledge.

Knowledge is "sticky" (hard to move), situated (enmeshed in a firm's culture), and contextual (works only in certain situations).

KNOWLEDGE IS SITUATIONAL

Knowledge is conditional; knowing when to apply a procedure is just as important as knowing the procedure (conditional).

Knowledge is related to context; you must know how to use a certain tool and under what circumstances.

We can see that knowledge is a different kind of firm asset from, say, buildings and financial assets; that knowledge is a complex phenomenon; and that there are many aspects to the process of managing knowledge. We can also recognize that knowledge-based core competencies of firms—the two or three things that an organization does best—are key organizational assets. Knowing how to do things effectively and efficiently in ways that other organizations cannot duplicate is a primary source of profit and competitive advantage that cannot be purchased easily by competitors in the marketplace.

For instance, having a unique build-to-order production system constitutes a form of knowledge and perhaps a unique asset that other firms cannot copy easily. With knowledge, firms become more efficient and effective in their use of scarce resources. Without knowledge, firms become less efficient and less effective in their use of resources and ultimately fail.

Organizational Learning and Knowledge Management

Like humans, organizations create and gather knowledge using a variety of organizational learning mechanisms. Through collection of data, careful measurement of planned activities, trial and error (experiment), and feedback from customers and the environment in general, organizations gain experience. Organizations that learn adjust their behavior to reflect that learning by creating new business processes and by changing patterns of management decision making. This process of change is called **organizational learning**. Arguably, organizations that can sense and respond to their environments rapidly will survive longer than organizations that have poor learning mechanisms.

The Knowledge Management Value Chain

Knowledge management refers to the set of business processes developed in an organization to create, store, transfer, and apply knowledge. Knowledge management increases the ability of the organization to learn from its environment and to incorporate knowledge into its business processes. Figure 11.1 illustrates the four value-adding steps in the knowledge management value chain. Each stage in the value chain adds value to raw data and information as they are transformed into usable knowledge.

In Figure 11.1, information systems activities are separated from related management and organizational activities, with information systems activities on the top of the graphic and organizational and management activities below. One apt slogan of the knowledge management field is "Effective knowledge management is 80 percent managerial and organizational and 20 percent technology."

In Chapter 1, we define *organizational and management capital* as the set of business processes, culture, and behavior required to obtain value from investments in information systems. In the case of knowledge management, as with other information systems investments, supportive values, structures, and behavior patterns must be built to maximize the return on investment in knowledge management projects. In Figure 11.1, the management and organizational activities in the lower half of the diagram represent the investment in organizational capital required to obtain substantial returns on the information technology (IT) investments and systems shown in the top half of the diagram.

FIGURE 11.1 THE KNOWLEDGE MANAGEMENT VALUE CHAIN

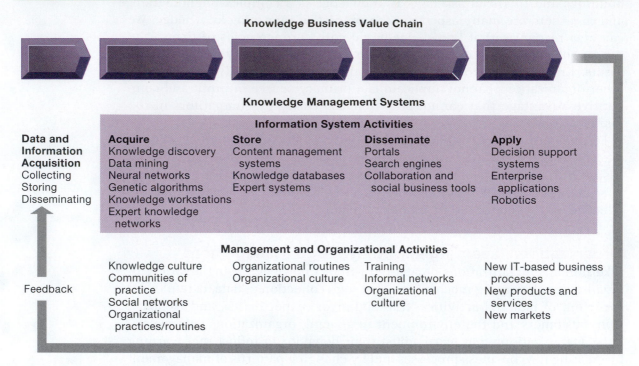

Knowledge management today involves both information systems activities and a host of enabling management and organizational activities.

Knowledge Acquisition

Organizations acquire knowledge in a number of ways, depending on the type of knowledge they seek. The first knowledge management systems sought to build corporate repositories of documents, reports, presentations, and best practices. These efforts have been extended to include unstructured documents (such as e-mail). In other cases, organizations acquire knowledge by developing online expert networks so that employees can "find the expert" in the company who is personally knowledgeable.

In still other cases, firms must create new knowledge by discovering patterns in corporate data or by using knowledge workstations where engineers can discover new knowledge. These various efforts are described throughout this chapter. A coherent and organized knowledge system also requires systematic data from the firm's transaction processing systems that track sales, payments, inventory, customers, and other vital data as well as data from external sources such as news feeds, industry reports, legal opinions, scientific research, and government statistics.

Knowledge Storage

Once they are discovered, documents, patterns, and expert rules must be stored so they can be retrieved and used by employees. Knowledge storage generally involves the creation of a database. Document management systems that digitize, index, and tag documents according to a coherent framework are large databases adept at storing collections of documents. Expert systems also help corporations preserve the knowledge that is acquired by incorporating that knowledge into organizational processes and culture. Each of these is discussed later in this chapter and in the following chapter.

Management must support the development of planned knowledge storage systems, encourage the development of corporate-wide schemas for indexing documents, and reward employees for taking the time to update and store documents properly. For instance, it would reward the sales force for submitting names of prospects to a shared corporate database of prospects where all sales personnel can identify each prospect and review the stored knowledge.

Knowledge Dissemination

Portals, e-mail, instant messaging, wikis, social business tools, and search engine technology have added to an existing array of collaboration tools for sharing calendars, documents, data, and graphics (see Chapter 2). Contemporary technology seems to have created a deluge of information and knowledge. How can managers and employees discover, in a sea of information and knowledge, that which is really important for their decisions and their work? Here, training programs, informal networks, and shared management experience communicated through a supportive culture help managers focus their attention on the important knowledge and information.

Knowledge Application

Regardless of what type of knowledge management system is involved, knowledge that is not shared and applied to the practical problems facing firms and managers does not add business value. To provide a return on investment, organizational knowledge must become a systematic part of management decision making and become situated in systems for decision support (described in Chapter 12). Ultimately, new knowledge must be built into a firm's business processes and key application systems, including enterprise applications for managing key internal business processes and relationships with customers and suppliers. Management supports this process by creating—based on new knowledge—new business practices, new products and services, and new markets for the firm.

Building Organizational and Management Capital: Collaboration, Communities of Practice, and Office Environments

In addition to the activities we have just described, managers can help by developing new organizational roles and responsibilities for the acquisition of knowledge, including the creation of chief knowledge officer executive positions, dedicated staff positions (knowledge managers), and communities of practice. **Communities of practice (COPs)** are informal social networks of professionals and employees within and outside the firm who have similar work-related activities and interests. The activities of these communities include self-education and group education, conferences, online newsletters, and day-to-day sharing of experiences and techniques to solve specific work problems. Many organizations, such as IBM, the U.S. Federal Highway Administration, and the World Bank, have encouraged the development of thousands of online communities of practice. These communities of practice depend greatly on software environments that enable collaboration and communication.

COPs can make it easier for people to reuse knowledge by pointing community members to useful documents, creating document repositories, and filtering information for newcomers. COPs members act as facilitators, encouraging contributions and discussion. COPs can also reduce the learning curve for new employees by providing contacts with subject matter experts and access to a community's established methods and tools. Finally, COPs can act as a spawning ground for new ideas, techniques, and decision-making behavior.

Types of Knowledge Management Systems

There are essentially three major types of knowledge management systems: enterprise-wide knowledge management systems, knowledge work systems, and intelligent techniques. Figure 11.2 shows the knowledge management system applications for each of these major categories.

Enterprise-wide knowledge management systems are general-purpose firmwide efforts to collect, store, distribute, and apply digital content and knowledge. These systems include capabilities for searching for information, storing both structured and unstructured data, and locating employee expertise within the firm. They also include supporting technologies such as portals, search engines, collaboration and social business tools, and learning management systems.

The development of powerful networked workstations and software for assisting engineers and scientists in the discovery of new knowledge has led to the creation of knowledge work systems such as computer-aided design (CAD), visualization, simulation, and virtual reality systems. **Knowledge work systems (KWS)** are specialized systems built for engineers, scientists, and other knowledge workers charged with discovering and creating new knowledge for a company. We discuss knowledge work applications in detail in Section 11.3.

Knowledge management also includes a diverse group of **intelligent techniques**, such as data mining, expert systems, neural networks, fuzzy logic, genetic algorithms, and intelligent agents. These techniques have different objectives, from a focus on discovering knowledge (data mining and neural networks) to distilling knowledge in the form of rules for a computer program (expert systems and fuzzy logic) to discovering optimal solutions for problems (genetic algorithms). Section 11.4 provides more detail about these intelligent techniques.

FIGURE 11.2 MAJOR TYPES OF KNOWLEDGE MANAGEMENT SYSTEMS

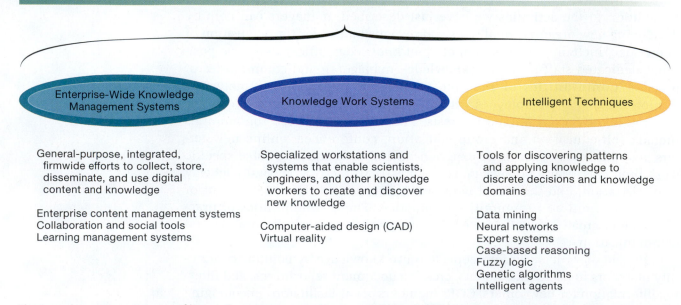

There are three major categories of knowledge management systems, and each can be broken down further into more specialized types of knowledge management systems.

11-2 What types of systems are used for enterprise-wide knowledge management, and how do they provide value for businesses?

Firms must deal with at least three kinds of knowledge. Some knowledge exists within the firm in the form of structured text documents (reports and presentations). Decision makers also need knowledge that is semistructured, such as e-mail, voice mail, chat room exchanges, videos, digital pictures, brochures, or bulletin board postings. In still other cases, there is no formal or digital information of any kind, and the knowledge resides in the heads of employees. Much of this knowledge is tacit knowledge that is rarely written down. Enterprise-wide knowledge management systems deal with all three types of knowledge.

Enterprise Content Management Systems

Businesses today need to organize and manage both structured and semistructured knowledge assets. **Structured knowledge** is explicit knowledge that exists in formal documents as well as in formal rules that organizations derive by observing experts and their decision-making behaviors. But, according to experts, at least 80 percent of an organization's business content is semistructured or unstructured—information in folders, messages, memos, proposals, e-mails, graphics, electronic slide presentations, and even videos created in different formats and stored in many locations.

Enterprise content management (ECM) systems help organizations manage both types of information. They have capabilities for knowledge capture, storage, retrieval, distribution, and preservation to help firms improve their business processes and decisions. Such systems include corporate repositories of documents, reports, presentations, and best practices, as well as capabilities for collecting and organizing semistructured knowledge such as e-mail (see Figure 11.3). Major enterprise content management systems also

FIGURE 11.3 AN ENTERPRISE CONTENT MANAGEMENT SYSTEM

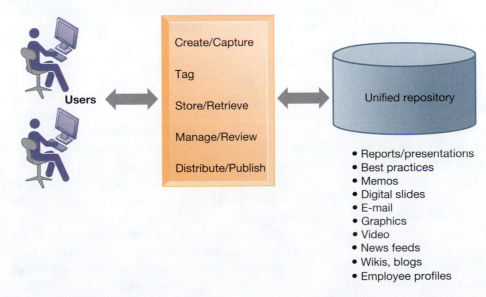

An enterprise content management system has capabilities for classifying, organizing, and managing structured and semistructured knowledge and making it available throughout the enterprise.

ECM in the Cloud Empowers New Zealand Department of Conservation

The New Zealand Department of Conservation (DOC) is charged with overseeing the national parks, protecting endangered wildlife and ecosystems, and safeguarding one of the world's largest marine sanctuaries. Its mission includes preserving natural habitats over more than a third of New Zealand's land mass and protecting numerous offshore havens harboring 44 marine reserves and six marine mammal sanctuaries. Educational programs for both public-land users (hikers, hunters, campers, fishermen, boaters, mountain bikers, cavers, etc.) and the general public expand knowledge about protecting endangered wildlife and fragile ecosystems across nearly 20 million acres of territory. Specific tasks include flood warnings, managing threats to native species from invasive plants, animals, pests, and diseases, wetlands restoration, and conservation of historic sites.

Because personnel and government funding are inadequate to cover all vital services and research, the DOC depends upon private conservation groups, universities, scientists, and other constituencies to perform field work, compile data, run statistical analysis, and document findings. Fourteen regional conservation boards and six regional conservation partnerships engage local business, community groups, and volunteers. In order for all stakeholders to effectively coordinate activities and share outcomes, research findings and data analysis must be accessible to all parties. In the past DOC couldn't produce documents quickly on demand because it had 2.3 million of them stored in folders with poor searching ability.

As collaborative efforts increased between 2010 and 2015, the DOC recognized that a state-of-the-art enterprise content management (ECM) system was required. A cloud content as a service called ContentWorX was created specifically for the government by TEAM Asparona, a joint venture of two Oracle implementation partners, TEAM Informatics and Deloitte Asparona. The service allows participating government agencies to deploy web content, manage digital assets, and systematize document, records, and library management, all on a common platform with a content-centric workflow.

The two primary components of ContentWorX are Oracle WebCenter Content and Oracle WebCenter Portal. The New Zealand government wanted to maintain its government data center and connected wide area network (WAN), so TEAM Asparona developed ContentWorX as a private cloud behind the government's firewall. Government agencies can purchase ContentWorX from a catalog of business application services. DOC CIO Mike Edginton felt the department was not yet ready to fully transition to a public cloud platform but wanted the benefits of cloud architecture concept and cloud pricing. A subscription model charges customers users per-month fees that decrease as user numbers rise.

The private cloud can link to public cloud services in the future as data sharing needs and departmental readiness warrant. The groundwork has been laid for an authentication system that will allow external stakeholders to access documents based on device used, departmental policies, and content classification.

Oracle Database and Oracle WebCenter Content technologies are embedded in an ECM system that can now store 2.3 million documents including research materials, meeting minutes, policy files, scientific reports, heritage and historical articles, and population inventories. Eighty percent of these documents are now accessible and searchable, a dramatic rise from the 7.4 percent previously available. DOC upgraded its wide area network (WAN) so that its 137 agency offices, spread across an island nation 990 miles long and a number of far-flung outlying islands, have the network capacity to search and retrieve even lengthy documents and handle the new system's encrypted traffic.

Automated document tagging and classification using Smartlogic's Semaphore software enabled the DOC to jettison its traditional hierarchical folder structure. A directory of 95,000 commonly used key terms forms the basis of a relational classification system. The relationships between terms are the key to document analysis that will ultimately flag sensitive documents and guide the management of the content life cycle, identifying documents for deletion or retention based on departmental and governmental policies.

As a record is saved to the ContentWorX repository, a metadata tag is added to classify its function, for example, population survey, conservation policy, or vendor contract. Another metadata tag identifies the record's DOC-specific contents, for example, the group generating it, project it is associated with, or project location. Ease of use when users were no longer required to manually add metadata helped drive a 95 percent adoption rate among DOC staff.

WebCenter Content also audits document creation, access, and editing. Each document interaction identifies the user, date, and time. Users manage version control themselves, reverting to earlier document versions with no system administrator intervention required. This has reduced the time DOC staff has to invest in document auditing processes. It has also simplified compliance with national archiving requirements set forth in New Zealand's Public Records Act of 2005. Since implementation of the law, every document must be open to the public absent a compelling reason for sealing it, a reversal of previous policy in which all information was closed unless an agency decided to make it publicly available.

Document retrieval time has been cut to seconds as opposed to the up to four minutes previously required for users to navigate the folder hierarchy. Even scientists on remote islands or in isolated forests can quickly access reports. Knowledge and learning are easily transferred to regional offices, supporting enhanced conservation efforts and cooperation with partners.

If documents classified as public information could be replicated to a public cloud service, more useful DOC information would be available to outside organizations. ContentWorX can be synchronized to a public cloud file and to document-sharing services via Oracle Documents Cloud or another content collaboration solution. But to expand public access, DOC must develop an identity management infrastructure for authenticating external users. Presently, partners outside of government must be granted an account on the government network just like an employee. Since this represents a security risk, it is only done for key university researchers.

Sources: David F. Carr, "Collaboration in the Cloud," *Profit Magazine*, February 2016; David F. Carr, "Better Search Replaces Folders," *Profit Magazine*, February 2016; New Zealand Department of Conservation website, www.doc.govt.nz, accessed April 27, 2016; Team Asparona Cloud New Zealand, http://contentworx.co.nz/contentworx-cloud/, accessed April 27, 2016; "Department of Conservation, New Zealand Gains Ability to Rapidly Search and Share 2.2 Million Documents Anytime Anywhere, and Enhances Collaboration," www.oracle.com, accessed April 27, 2016.

CASE STUDY QUESTIONS

1. Describe the knowledge management problem discussed in this case study.
2. What management, organization, and technology factors contributed to the problem?
3. How did implementing enterprise content management solve the problem? How did the new ECM system change the way the DOC worked?
4. How successful was this solution? Explain.

enable users to access external sources of information, such as news feeds and research, and to communicate via e-mail, chat/instant messaging, discussion groups, and videoconferencing. They are starting to incorporate blogs, wikis, and other enterprise social networking tools. Open Text Corporation, EMC (Documentum), IBM, and Oracle Corporation are leading vendors of enterprise content management software. The Interactive Session on Organizations describes how the New Zealand Department of Conservation benefited from ECM technology.

A key problem in managing knowledge is the creation of an appropriate classification scheme, or **taxonomy**, to organize information into meaningful categories so that it can be easily accessed. Once the categories for classifying knowledge have been created, each knowledge object needs to be "tagged," or classified, so that it can be easily retrieved. Enterprise content management systems have capabilities for tagging, interfacing with corporate databases and content repositories, and creating enterprise knowledge portals that provide a single point of access to information resources.

Firms in publishing, advertising, broadcasting, and entertainment have special needs for storing and managing unstructured digital data such as photographs, graphic images, video, and audio content. For example, Coca-Cola must keep track of all the images of the Coca-Cola brand that have been created in the past at all of the company's worldwide offices to prevent both redundant work and variation from a standard brand image. **Digital asset management systems** help companies classify, store, and distribute these digital objects.

Locating and Sharing Expertise

Some of the knowledge businesses need is not in the form of a digital document but instead resides in the memory of individual experts in the firm. Contemporary enterprise content management systems, along with the systems for collaboration and social business introduced in Chapter 2, have capabilities for locating experts and tapping their knowledge. These include online directories of corporate experts and their profiles with details about their job experience, projects, publications, and educational degrees, and repositories of expert-generated content. Specialized search tools make it easier for employees to find the appropriate expert in a company. For knowledge resources outside the firm, social networking and social business tools enable users to bookmark web pages of interest, tag these bookmarks with keywords, and share the tags and web page links with other people.

Learning Management Systems

Companies need ways to keep track of and manage employee learning and to integrate it more fully into their knowledge management and other corporate systems. A **learning management system (LMS)** provides tools for the management, delivery, tracking, and assessment of various types of employee learning and training.

Contemporary LMS support multiple modes of learning, including CD-ROM, downloadable videos, web-based classes, live instruction in classes or online, and group learning in online forums and chat sessions. The LMS consolidates mixed-media training, automates the selection and administration of courses, assembles and delivers learning content, and measures learning effectiveness.

CVM Solutions, LLC (CVM) uses Digitec's Knowledge Direct learning management system to provide training about how to manage suppliers for clients such as Procter & Gamble, Colgate-Palmolive, and Delta Airlines. Knowledge Direct provides a portal for accessing course content online along with hands-free administration features such as student registration and assessment tools, built-in help and contact support, automatic e-mail triggers to remind users of courses or deadlines, automatic e-mail acknowledgement of course completions, and web-based reporting for courses accessed.

Businesses run their own learning management systems, but they are also turning to publicly available **massive open online courses (MOOCs)** to educate their employees. A MOOC is an online course made available via the web to very large numbers of participants. Companies view MOOCs as a new way to design and deliver online learning where learners can collaborate with each other, watch short videos, and participate in threaded discussion groups. Firms such as Microsoft, AT&T, and Tenaris have developed their own MOOCs, while others such as Bank of America and Qualcomm are adapting publicly available MOOCs aligned with their core competencies (Meister, 2015).

11-3 What are the major types of knowledge work systems, and how do they provide value for firms?

The enterprise-wide knowledge systems we have just described provide a wide range of capabilities that can be used by many if not all the workers and groups in an organization. Firms also have specialized systems for knowledge workers to help them create new knowledge and to ensure that this knowledge is properly integrated into the business.

Knowledge Workers and Knowledge Work

Knowledge workers, which we introduced in Chapter 1, include researchers, designers, architects, scientists, and engineers who primarily create knowledge and information for the organization. Knowledge workers usually have high levels of education and memberships in professional organizations and are often asked to exercise independent judgment as a routine aspect of their work. For example, knowledge workers create new products or find ways of improving existing ones. Knowledge workers perform three key roles that are critical to the organization and to the managers who work within the organization:

- Keeping the organization current in knowledge as it develops in the external world—in technology, science, social thought, and the arts
- Serving as internal consultants regarding the areas of their knowledge, the changes taking place, and opportunities
- Acting as change agents, evaluating, initiating, and promoting change projects

Requirements of Knowledge Work Systems

Most knowledge workers rely on office systems, such as word processors, voice mail, e-mail, videoconferencing, and scheduling systems, which are designed to increase worker productivity in the office. However, knowledge workers also require highly specialized knowledge work systems with powerful graphics, analytical tools, and communications and document management capabilities.

These systems require sufficient computing power to handle the sophisticated graphics or complex calculations necessary for such knowledge workers as scientific researchers, product designers, and financial analysts. Because knowledge workers are so focused on knowledge in the external world, these systems also must give the worker quick and easy access to external databases. They typically feature user-friendly interfaces that enable users to perform needed tasks without having to spend a great deal of time learning how to use the system. Knowledge workers are highly paid—wasting a knowledge worker's time is simply too expensive. Figure 11.4 summarizes the requirements of knowledge work systems.

Knowledge workstations often are designed and optimized for the specific tasks to be performed; for example, a design engineer requires a different workstation setup than a financial analyst. Design engineers need graphics with enough power to handle three-dimensional (3-D) CAD systems. However, financial analysts are more interested in access to a myriad number of external databases and large databases for efficiently storing and accessing massive amounts of financial data.

FIGURE 11.4 REQUIREMENTS OF KNOWLEDGE WORK SYSTEMS

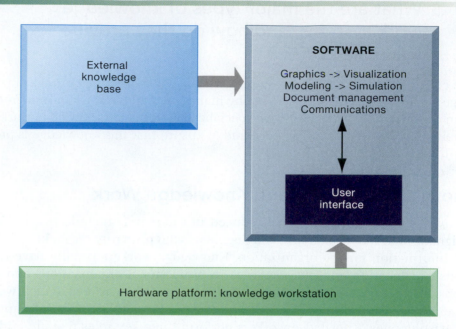

Knowledge work systems require strong links to external knowledge bases in addition to specialized hardware and software.

Examples of Knowledge Work Systems

Major knowledge work applications include CAD systems and virtual reality systems for simulation and modeling. **Computer-aided design (CAD)** automates the creation and revision of designs, using computers and sophisticated graphics software. Using a more traditional physical design methodology, each design modification requires a mold to be made and a prototype to be tested physically. That process must be repeated many times, which is a very expensive and time-consuming process. Using a CAD workstation, the designer need only make a physical prototype toward the end of the design process because the design can be easily tested and changed on the computer. The ability of CAD software to provide design specifications for the tooling and manufacturing processes also saves a great deal of time and money while producing a manufacturing process with far fewer problems.

For example, Ford Motor Company used a computer simulation to create an engine cylinder that came up with the most efficient design possible. Engineers altered that design to account for manufacturing constraints and tested the revised design virtually in models that used decades of data on material properties and engine performance. Ford then created the mold to make a real part that could be bolted onto an engine for further testing. The entire process took days instead of months and cost thousands of dollars instead of millions.

CAD systems are able to supply data for **3-D printing**, also known as additive manufacturing, which uses machines to make solid objects, layer by layer, from specifications in a digital file. Unlike traditional techniques, by which objects are cut or drilled from molds, resulting in wasted materials, 3-D printing lets workers model an object on a computer and print it out with plastic, metal, or composite materials. 3-D printing is currently used for prototyping, custom manufacturing, and fashioning items with small production runs. Today's 3-D printers can handle materials including plastic, titanium, and human cartilage and produce fully functional components including batteries, transistors, prosthetic devices, LEDs, and other complex mechanisms, and there are now 3-D printing services that run over the cloud, such as that offered by Staples.

Virtual reality (VR) systems have visualization, rendering, and simulation capabilities that go far beyond those of conventional CAD systems. They use interactive graphics software to create computer-generated simulations that are so close to reality that users almost believe they are participating in a real-world situation. In many virtual reality systems, the user dons special clothing, headgear, and equipment, depending on the application. The clothing contains sensors that record the user's movements and immediately transmit that information back to the computer. For instance, to walk through a virtual reality simulation of a house, you would need garb that monitors the movement of your feet, hands, and head. You also would need goggles containing video screens and sometimes audio attachments and feeling gloves so that you can be immersed in the computer feedback. In the chapter-opening case, users of Cadillac's VR dealer system wear special VR headsets and headphones that make them feel they are seeing and listening to a real-world car.

At NYU Langone Medical Center in New York City, students wearing 3-D glasses are able to "dissect" a virtual cadaver projected on a screen. With the help of a computer, they can move through the virtual body, scrutinizing layers of muscles or watching a close-up of a pumping heart along with bright red arteries and deep blue veins. The virtual human body was created by BioDigital Systems, a New York City medical visualization firm. NYU medical school has no current plans to phase out dissection, but the 3-D virtual cadaver is a valuable complementary teaching tool.

Augmented reality (AR) is a related technology for enhancing visualization. AR provides a live direct or indirect view of a physical real-world environment whose elements are augmented by virtual computer-generated imagery. The user is grounded in the real physical world, and the virtual images are merged with the real view to create the augmented display. The digital technology provides additional information to enhance the perception of reality, making the surrounding real world of the user more interactive and meaningful. The yellow first-down markers shown on televised football games are examples of augmented reality as are medical procedures like image-guided surgery, where data acquired from computerized tomography (CT) and magnetic resonance imaging (MRI) scans or from ultrasound imaging are superimposed on the patient in the operating room. Other industries where AR has caught on include military training, engineering design, robotics, and consumer design.

Virtual reality applications developed for the web use a standard called **Virtual Reality Modeling Language (VRML)**. VRML is a set of specifications for interactive, 3-D modeling on the web that can organize multiple media types, including animation, images, and audio to put users in a simulated real-world environment. VRML is platform independent, operates over a desktop computer, and requires little bandwidth.

DuPont, the Wilmington, Delaware, chemical company, created a VRML application called HyperPlant, which enables users to access 3-D data over the Internet using web browser software. Engineers can go through 3-D models as if they were physically walking through a plant, viewing objects at eye level. This level of detail reduces the number of mistakes they make during construction of oil rigs, oil plants, and other structures.

11-4 What are the business benefits of using intelligent techniques for knowledge management?

Artificial intelligence and database technology provide a number of intelligent techniques that organizations can use to capture individual and collective knowledge and to extend their knowledge base. Expert systems, case-based reasoning, and fuzzy logic are used for capturing tacit knowledge. Neural networks and data mining are used for **knowledge discovery**. They can discover underlying patterns, categories, and behaviors in large data sets that could not be discovered by managers alone or simply through experience. Genetic algorithms are used for generating solutions to problems that are too large and complex for human beings to analyze on their own. Intelligent agents can automate routine tasks to help firms search for and filter information for use in electronic commerce, supply chain management, and other activities.

Data mining, which we introduced in Chapter 6, helps organizations capture undiscovered knowledge residing in large databases, providing managers with new insight for improving business performance. It has become an important tool for management decision making, and we provide a detailed discussion of data mining for management decision support in Chapter 12.

The intelligent techniques discussed in this chapter are based on **artificial intelligence (AI)** technology, which consists of computer-based systems (both hardware and software) that attempt to emulate human behavior. Such systems would be able to learn languages, accomplish physical tasks (robotics), use a perceptual apparatus that informs physical behavior and language, and emulate human expertise and decision making.

AI applications play an important role in contemporary knowledge management, but they do not exhibit the breadth, complexity, originality, and generality of human intelligence. Existing AI systems do not come up with new and novel solutions to problems. AI systems extend the powers of humans but in no way substitute for them or capture much of their intelligence. Briefly, existing systems lack the common sense and generality of naturally intelligent human beings. Human intelligence is vastly more complex than the most sophisticated computer programs and covers a much broader range of activities than is currently possible with so-called artificially intelligent devices. The Interactive Session on Technology on robots in manufacturing discusses some of these issues as does the chapter-ending case study on IBM's Watson.

Capturing Knowledge: Expert Systems

Expert systems are an intelligent technique for capturing tacit knowledge in a very specific and limited domain of human expertise. These systems capture the knowledge of skilled employees in the form of a set of rules in a software system that can be used by others in the organization. The set of rules in the expert system adds to the memory, or stored learning, of the firm.

Expert systems lack the breadth of knowledge and the understanding of fundamental principles of a human expert. They typically perform very limited tasks that can be performed by professionals in a few minutes or hours, such as diagnosing a malfunctioning machine or determining whether to grant credit for a loan. Problems that cannot be solved by human experts in the same short period of time are far too difficult for an expert system. However, by capturing human expertise in limited areas, expert systems can provide benefits, helping

INTERACTIVE SESSION: TECHNOLOGY

Will Robots Replace People in Manufacturing?

For the past four decades, robots have been incorporated into manufacturing assembly lines in Europe, Japan, and the United States. These industrial robots—with mechanical arms that can be programmed to weld, paint, and pick up and place objects with predictable regularity—have not taken over many tasks performed by humans. The biggest users of robotic technology have been automobile manufacturing plants, where robots do heavy lifting, welding, applying glue, and painting. People still do most of the final assembly of cars, especially when installing small parts or wiring that needs to be guided into place.

For most manufacturing work, it has been less expensive to use manual labor than it is to own, operate, and maintain a robotics system, given the tasks that robots can perform. But this is changing. Robots have become smaller, more mobile, more collaborative and more adaptable, and their uses are widening. New robot models can work alongside humans without endangering them and help assemble all types of objects, as large as aircraft engines and as small and delicate as smartphones. They can also sense whether parts are being assembled correctly.

Robots are becoming easier to operate. Companies no longer need a software engineer to write program code to get a robot to perform a task. With some of today's robots, you can simply push a button, turn the robot's arm, and move it through the operation you want it to perform. The robot learns by doing.

A Renault SA plant in Cleon, France, now uses robots made by Universal Robots AS of Denmark to drive screws into engines, especially those that go into places people find hard to access. The robots have reach of more than 50 inches and six rotating joints to do the work. They also verify that parts are properly fastened and check to make sure the correct part is being used. The Renault robots weigh only about 64 pounds each so they can easily be moved around to different locations as needed. They are also "collaborative," designed to work in proximity to people. Using sonar, cameras, or other technologies, these robots can sense where people are and slow down or stop to avoid hurting them.

These new-style robots are moving into other industries as well. ABB Ltd of Switzerland and others have recently introduced robots to help assemble consumer-electronics items. The robots were designed to work close to people and handle small parts. JCB Laboratories is using robots at its Wichita, Kansas, plant to pick up syringes, fill them with medications, and snap on caps. The robots work five to six times faster than people.

This new generation of robots promises to bring major changes to the factory floor and perhaps the global competitive landscape. The Boston Consulting Group predicts that by 2025 the share of tasks performed by robots will rise from a global average of about 10 percent across all manufacturing industries to about 25 percent. In some industries, more than 40 percent of manufacturing tasks will be performed by robots. There will be dramatic productivity gains in many industries around the world (potentially boosting output per worker by 30 percent) and shifts in competitiveness among manufacturing countries.

Does this mean that robots will take over the production line? Unlikely. They still lack the flexibility, delicacy, and insight provided by humans. For example, today's collaborative robots often have to slow down or stop whenever people veer into their paths, disrupting production. Sales have been disappointing for Baxter, a two-armed collaborative robot from Rethink, which is used primarily for simple tasks such as moving materials, picking up parts, and packing or unpacking boxes. The robot's speed is restricted by safety considerations. For all their recent advances, robots still can't duplicate a human being's fine motor skills in manipulating materials and small parts. Robots still have trouble dealing with soft or floppy material, such as cloth or bundles of electrical wire.

Although robots are good at reliably and repeatedly performing defined tasks, they're not good at adapting. Mercedes-Benz had to cut back on its use of robots on the production line because the level of customization demanded by its customers requires a level of flexibility and dexterity that only humans can provide. Today's Mercedes customer wants to configure his or her own car, choosing among customization options such as carbon-fiber trim, four types of tire valve caps, and heated and cooled cup holders for 30 different models. Robots can't deal with the amount of variation in options that Mercedes cars have today.

Mercedes has found that if manufacturing focuses around a skilled crew of workers, it can shift a production line in a weekend. It would take weeks to reprogram robots and shift assembly patterns, and during that downtime, production would be at a standstill. Going forward, robots won't completely disappear from the Mercedes factory floor, but they'll be smaller and more flexible, operating alongside human workers. BMW AG and Volkswagen AG's Audi are also testing lightweight, sensor-equipped robots safe enough to work alongside people. Auto manufacturers are under continuing pressure to upgrade their models more frequently than the traditional seven-year cycle.

As robots become more widespread, manufacturing tasks performed by humans will become higher-level and more complex. Workers will be expected to supervise and perhaps even program robots, and there will be fewer low-level manufacturing jobs. Workers will need more sophisticated skills to succeed in tomorrow's manufacturing plants.

Sources: Bloomberg, "Why Mercedes Is Halting Robots' Reign on the Production Line," *Industry Week*, February 25, 2016; Harold L. Sirkin, Michael Zinser, and Justin Rose, "The Robotics Revolution: The Next Great Leap in Manufacturing," *BCG Perspectives*, September 23, 2015; "Industries and Economies Leading the Robotics Revolution," *BCG Perspectives*, September 23, 2015; and James R. Hagerty, "Meet the New Generation of Robots for Manufacturing," *Wall Street Journal*, June 2, 2015.

CASE STUDY QUESTIONS

1. Why have robots caught on in manufacturing? What knowledge to they require?

2. Can robots replace human workers in manufacturing? Explain your answer.

3. If you were considering introducing robots in your manufacturing plant, what management, organization, and technology issues would you need to address?

organizations make high-quality decisions with fewer people. Today, expert systems are used in business in discrete, highly structured decision-making situations.

How Expert Systems Work

Human knowledge must be modeled or represented in a way that a computer can process. Expert systems model human knowledge as a set of rules that collectively are called the **knowledge base**. The rules are obtained by carefully interviewing one or several "experts" who have a thorough command of the knowledge base for the system or by documenting business rules found in manuals, books, or reports. Expert systems have from 200 to many thousands of these rules, depending on the complexity of the problem. These rules are much more interconnected and nested than in a traditional software program (see Figure 11.5).

The strategy used to search through the knowledge base is called the **inference engine**. Two strategies are commonly used: forward chaining and backward chaining (see Figure 11.6).

In **forward chaining**, the inference engine begins with the information entered by the user and searches the rule base to arrive at a conclusion. The strategy is to fire, or carry out, the action of the rule when a condition is true. In Figure 11.6, beginning on the left, if the user enters a client's name with income greater than $100,000, the engine will fire all rules in sequence from left to right. If the user then enters information indicating that the same client owns real estate, another pass of the rule base will occur and more rules will fire. Processing continues until no more rules can be fired.

In **backward chaining**, the strategy for searching the rule base starts with a hypothesis and proceeds by asking the user questions about selected facts

FIGURE 11.5 RULES IN AN EXPERT SYSTEM

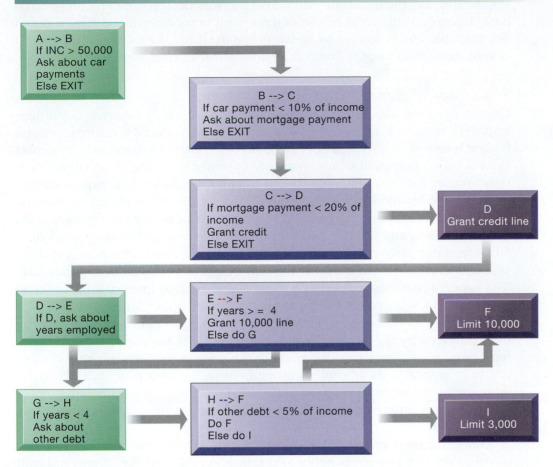

An expert system contains a number of rules to be followed. The rules are interconnected, the number of outcomes is known in advance and is limited, there are multiple paths to the same outcome, and the system can consider multiple rules at a single time. The rules illustrated are for simple credit-granting expert systems.

FIGURE 11.6 INFERENCE ENGINES IN EXPERT SYSTEMS

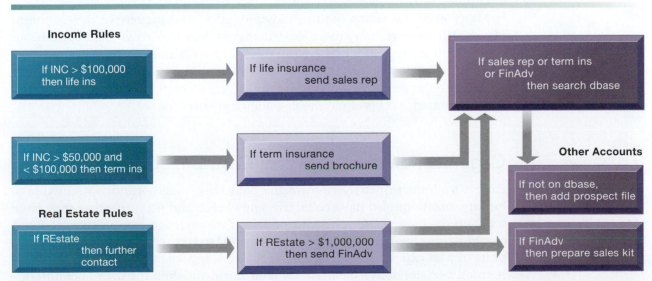

An inference engine works by searching through the rules and "firing" those rules that are triggered by facts gathered and entered by the user. Basically, a collection of rules is similar to a series of nested IF statements in a traditional software program; however, the magnitude of the statements and degree of nesting are much greater in an expert system.

until the hypothesis is either confirmed or disproved. In our example, in Figure 11.6, ask the question "Should we add this person to the prospect database?" Begin on the right of the diagram and work toward the left. You can see that the person should be added to the database if a sales representative is sent, term insurance is granted, or a financial adviser visits the client.

Examples of Successful Expert Systems

Expert systems provide businesses with an array of benefits including improved decisions, reduced errors, reduced costs, reduced training time, and higher levels of quality and service. Con-Way Transportation built an expert system called Line-haul to automate and optimize planning of overnight shipment routes for its nationwide freight-trucking business. The expert system captures the business rules that dispatchers follow when assigning drivers, trucks, and trailers to transport 50,000 shipments of heavy freight each night across 25 states and Canada and then plots their routes. Line-haul runs on a Sun computer platform and uses data on daily customer shipment requests, available drivers, trucks, trailer space, and weight stored in an Oracle database. The expert system uses thousands of rules and 100,000 lines of program code written in C + + to crunch the numbers and create optimum routing plans for 95 percent of daily freight shipments. Con-Way dispatchers tweak the routing plan provided by the expert system and relay final routing specifications to field personnel responsible for packing the trailers for their nighttime runs. Con-Way recouped its $3 million investment in the system within two years by reducing the number of drivers, packing more freight per trailer, and reducing damage from rehandling. The system also reduces dispatchers' arduous nightly tasks.

Although expert systems lack the robust and general intelligence of human beings, they can provide benefits to organizations if their limitations are well understood. Only certain classes of problems can be solved using expert systems. Virtually all successful expert systems deal with problems of classification in limited domains of knowledge where there are relatively few alternative outcomes and these possible outcomes are all known in advance. Expert systems are much less useful for dealing with unstructured problems typically encountered by managers.

Many expert systems require large, lengthy, and expensive development efforts. Hiring or training more experts may be less expensive than building an expert system. Typically, the environment in which an expert system operates is continually changing so that the expert system must also continually change. Some expert systems, especially large ones, are so complex that in a few years the maintenance costs equal the development costs.

Organizational Intelligence: Case-Based Reasoning

Expert systems primarily capture the tacit knowledge of individual experts, but organizations also have collective knowledge and expertise that they have built up over the years. This organizational knowledge can be captured and stored using case-based reasoning. In **case-based reasoning (CBR)**, descriptions of past experiences of human specialists, represented as cases, are documented and stored in a database for later retrieval when the user encounters a new case with similar parameters. The system searches for stored cases with problem characteristics similar to the new one, finds the closest fit, and applies the solutions of the old case to the new case. Successful solutions are tagged to the new case and both are stored together with the other cases in the knowledge base. Unsuccessful solutions also are appended to the case database along with explanations as to why the solutions did not work (see Figure 11.7).

Expert systems work by applying a set of IF-THEN-ELSE rules extracted from human experts. Case-based reasoning, in contrast, represents knowledge as a series of cases, and this knowledge base is continuously expanded and refined by users. You'll find case-based reasoning in diagnostic systems in medicine or customer support where users can retrieve past cases whose characteristics are similar to the new case. The system suggests a solution or diagnosis based on the best-matching retrieved case.

Fuzzy Logic Systems

Most people do not think in terms of traditional IF-THEN rules or precise numbers. Humans tend to categorize things imprecisely using rules for making decisions that may have many shades of meaning. For example, a man or a woman can be *strong* or *intelligent*. A company can be *large*, *medium*, or *small* in size. Temperature can be *hot*, *cold*, *cool*, or *warm*. These categories represent a range of values.

FIGURE 11.7 HOW CASE-BASED REASONING WORKS

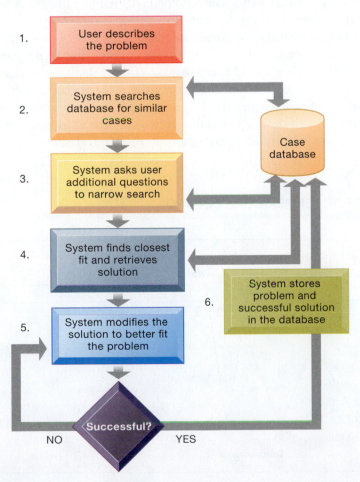

Case-based reasoning represents knowledge as a database of past cases and their solutions.
The system uses a six-step process to generate solutions to new problems encountered by the user.

Fuzzy logic is a rule-based technology that can represent such imprecision by creating rules that use approximate or subjective values. It can describe a particular phenomenon or process linguistically and then represent that description in a small number of flexible rules. Organizations can use fuzzy logic to create software systems that capture tacit knowledge where there is linguistic ambiguity.

Let's look at the way fuzzy logic would represent various temperatures in a computer application to control room temperature automatically. The terms (known as *membership functions*) are imprecisely defined so that, for example, in Figure 11.8, cool is between 45 degrees and 70 degrees, although the temperature is most clearly cool between about 60 degrees and 67 degrees. Note that *cool* is overlapped by *cold* or *norm*. To control the room environment using this logic, the programmer would develop similarly imprecise definitions for humidity and other factors, such as outdoor wind and temperature. The rules might include one that says: "If the temperature is *cool* or *cold* and the humidity is low while the outdoor wind is high and the outdoor temperature is low, raise the heat and humidity in the room." The computer would combine the membership function readings in a weighted manner and, using all the rules, raise and lower the temperature and humidity.

Fuzzy logic provides solutions to problems requiring expertise that is difficult to represent in the form of crisp IF-THEN rules. In Japan, Sendai's subway system uses fuzzy logic controls to accelerate so smoothly that standing passengers need not hold on. Mitsubishi Heavy Industries in Tokyo has been able to reduce the power consumption of its air conditioners by 20 percent by implementing control programs in fuzzy logic. The autofocus device in cameras is only possible because of fuzzy logic. In these instances, fuzzy logic allows incremental changes in inputs to produce smooth changes in outputs instead of discontinuous ones, making it useful for consumer electronics and engineering applications.

Management also has found fuzzy logic useful for decision making and organizational control. A Wall Street firm created a system that selects companies for potential acquisition using the language stock traders understand. A fuzzy logic system has been developed to detect possible fraud in medical claims submitted by health care providers anywhere in the United States.

FIGURE 11.8 FUZZY LOGIC FOR TEMPERATURE CONTROL

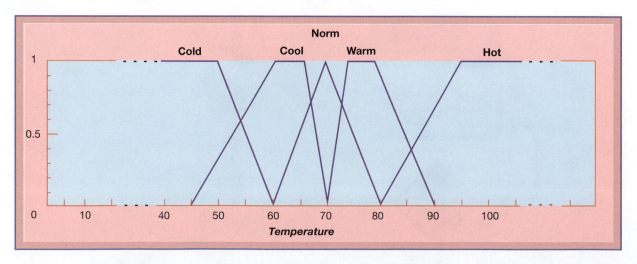

The membership functions for the input called temperature are in the logic of the thermostat to control the room temperature. Membership functions help translate linguistic expressions such as warm into numbers that the computer can manipulate.

Machine Learning

Machine learning is the study of how computer programs can improve their performance without explicit programming. Why does this constitute learning? A machine that learns is a machine that, like a human being, can recognize patterns in data, and change its behavior based on its recognition of patterns, experience, or prior learnings (a database). For instance, a car-driving robot should be able to recognize the presence of other cars and objects (people), and change its behavior accordingly (stop, go, slow down, speed up, or turn). The idea of a self-taught, self-correcting, computer program is not new, and has been a part of the artificial intelligence field at least since the 1970s. Up until the 1990s, however, machine learning was not very capable of producing useful devices or solving interesting business problems.

Machine learning has expanded greatly in the past 10 years because of the growth in computing power available to scientists and firms and its falling cost along with advances in the design of algorithms, databases, and robots (see the chapter-ending case on IBM's Watson). The Internet and the big data (see Chapter 6) made available on the Internet have proved to be very useful testing and proving grounds for machine learning.

We use machine learning every day but don't recognize it. Every Google search is resolved using algorithms that rank the billions of web pages based on your query and change the results based on any changes you make in your search, all in a few milliseconds. Search results also vary according to your prior searches and the items you clicked on. Every time you buy something on Amazon, its recommender engine will suggest other items you might be interested in based on patterns in your prior consumption, behavior on other websites, and the purchases of others who are "similar" to you. Every time you visit Netflix, a recommender system will come up with movies you might be interested in based on a similar set of factors.

Neural Networks

Neural networks are used for solving complex, poorly understood problems for which large amounts of data have been collected. They find patterns and relationships in massive amounts of data that would be too complicated and difficult for a human being to analyze. Neural networks discover this knowledge by using hardware and software that parallel the processing patterns of the biological or human brain. Neural networks "learn" patterns from large quantities of data by sifting through data, searching for relationships, building models, and correcting over and over again the model's own mistakes.

A neural network has a large number of sensing and processing nodes that continuously interact with each other. Figure 11.9 represents one type of neural network comprising an input layer, an output layer, and a hidden processing layer. Humans "train" the network by feeding it a set of training data for which the inputs produce a known set of outputs or conclusions. This helps the computer learn the correct solution by example. As the computer is fed more data, each case is compared with the known outcome. If it differs, a correction is calculated and applied to the nodes in the hidden processing layer. These steps are repeated until a condition, such as corrections being less than a certain amount, is reached. The neural network in Figure 11.9 has learned how to identify a fraudulent credit card purchase. Also, self-organizing neural networks can be trained by exposing them to large amounts of data and allowing them to discover the patterns and relationships in the data.

FIGURE 11.9 **HOW A NEURAL NETWORK WORKS**

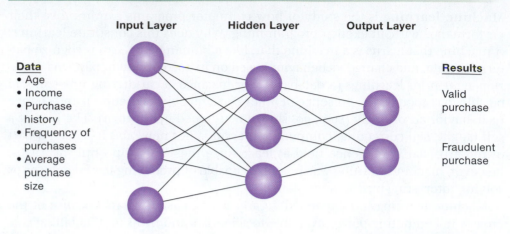

A neural network uses rules it "learns" from patterns in data to construct a hidden layer of logic. The hidden layer then processes inputs, classifying them based on the experience of the model. In this example, the neural network has been trained to distinguish between valid and fraudulent credit card purchases.

A Google research team headed by Stanford University computer scientist Andrew Y. Ng and Google fellow Jeff Dean recently created a neural network with more than a billion connections that could identify cats. The network used an array of 16,000 processors and was fed random thumbnails of images, each extracted from a collection of 10 million YouTube videos. The neural network taught itself to recognize cats without human help in identifying specific features during the learning process. Google believes this neural network has promising applications in image search, speech recognition, and machine language translation. IBM has developed an energy-efficient processor chip that relies on a dense web of transistors similar to the brain's neural network. It is still in experimental mode, with great promise for pattern recognition (Markoff, 2012, 2013).

Whereas expert systems seek to emulate or model a human expert's way of solving problems, neural network builders claim that they do not program solutions and do not aim to solve specific problems. Instead, neural network designers seek to put intelligence into the hardware in the form of a generalized capability to learn. In contrast, the expert system is highly specific to a given problem and cannot be retrained easily.

Neural network applications in medicine, science, and business address problems in pattern classification, prediction, financial analysis, and control and optimization. In medicine, neural network applications are used for screening patients for coronary artery disease, for diagnosing patients with epilepsy and Alzheimer's disease, and for performing pattern recognition of pathology images. The financial industry uses neural networks to discern patterns in large pools of data that might help predict the performance of equities, corporate bond ratings, or corporate bankruptcies. Visa International uses a neural network to help detect credit card fraud by monitoring all Visa transactions for sudden changes in the buying patterns of cardholders.

There are many puzzling aspects of neural networks. Unlike expert systems, which typically provide explanations for their solutions, neural networks cannot always explain why they arrived at a particular solution. Moreover, they cannot always guarantee a completely certain solution, arrive at the same solution again with the same input data, or guarantee the best solution. They are very sensitive and may not perform well if their training covers too little or too much data. In most current applications, neural networks are best used as aids to human decision makers instead of substitutes for them.

Genetic Algorithms

Genetic algorithms are useful for finding the optimal solution for a specific problem by examining a very large number of possible solutions for that problem. They are based on techniques inspired by evolutionary biology, such as inheritance, mutation, selection, and crossover (recombination).

A genetic algorithm works by representing information as a string of 0s and 1s. The genetic algorithm searches a population of randomly generated strings of binary digits to identify the right string representing the best possible solution for the problem. As solutions alter and combine, the worst ones are discarded and the better ones survive to go on to produce even better solutions.

In Figure 11.10, each string corresponds to one of the variables in the problem. One applies a test for fitness, ranking the strings in the population according to their level of desirability as possible solutions. After the initial population is evaluated for fitness, the algorithm then produces the next generation of strings, consisting of strings that survived the fitness test plus offspring strings produced from mating pairs of strings, and tests their fitness. The process continues until a solution is reached.

Genetic algorithms are used to solve problems that are very dynamic and complex, involving hundreds or thousands of variables or formulas. The problem must be one where the range of possible solutions can be represented genetically and criteria can be established for evaluating fitness. Genetic algorithms expedite the solution because they are able to evaluate many solution alternatives quickly to find the best one. For example, General Electric engineers used genetic algorithms to help optimize the design for jet turbine aircraft engines, where each design change required changes in up to 100 variables.

FIGURE 11.10 THE COMPONENTS OF A GENETIC ALGORITHM

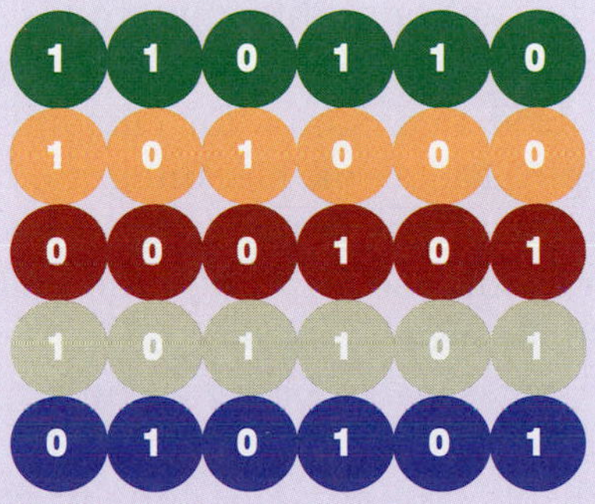

		Length	Width	Weight	Fitness
110110	1	Long	Wide	Light	55
101000	2	Short	Narrow	Heavy	49
000101	3	Long	Narrow	Heavy	36
101101	4	Short	Medium	Light	61
010101	5	Long	Medium	Very light	74

A population of chromosomes — Decoding of chromosomes — Evaluation of chromosomes

This example illustrates an initial population of "chromosomes," each representing a different solution. The genetic algorithm uses an iterative process to refine the initial solutions so that the better ones, those with the higher fitness, are more likely to emerge as the best solution.

The supply chain management software from JDA Software uses genetic algorithms to optimize production-scheduling models incorporating hundreds of thousands of details about customer orders, material and resource availability, manufacturing and distribution capability, and delivery dates.

Intelligent Agents

Intelligent agent technology helps businesses navigate through large amounts of data to locate and act on information that is considered important. **Intelligent agents** are software programs that work without direct human intervention to carry out specific tasks for an individual user, business process, or software application. The agent uses a built-in or learned knowledge base to accomplish tasks or make decisions on the user's behalf, such as deleting junk e-mail, scheduling appointments, or traveling over interconnected networks to find the cheapest airfare to California.

There are many intelligent agent applications today in operating systems, application software, e-mail systems, mobile computing software, and network tools. For example, the wizards found in Microsoft Office software tools have built-in capabilities to show users how to accomplish various tasks, such as formatting documents or creating graphs, and to anticipate when users need assistance. Chapter 7 describes how intelligent agent shopping bots can help consumers find products they want and assist them in comparing prices and other features.

Although some intelligent agents are programmed to follow a simple set of rules, others are capable of learning from experience and adjusting their behavior. Siri, an application on Apple's iOS operating system for the iPhone and iPad, is an example. Siri is an intelligent personal assistant that uses voice recognition technology to answer questions, make recommendations, and perform actions. The software adapts to the user's individual preferences over time and personalizes results, performing tasks such as finding nearby restaurants, purchasing movie tickets, getting directions, scheduling appointments, and sending messages. Siri understands natural speech, and it asks the user questions if it needs more information to complete a task. Google Now, Microsoft's Cortana, and Amazon's Echo are other intelligent agent tools for consumers with similar capabilities.

Chatbots (chatterbots) are software agents designed to simulate a conversation with one or more human users via textual or auditory methods. They try to understand what you type or say and respond by answering questions or executing tasks. Chatbots are typically used in systems for customer service or information acquisition. For example, Facebook has integrated chatbots into its Messenger messaging app so that an outside company with a Facebook brand page can interact with Facebook users through the chat program. A Facebook user could, for example, browse for a pair of lightweight running shoes on Messenger by texting a message to begin a conversation with Spring, a mobile shopping app. Spring would ask the user for his or her preferred price range for the shoes and display small selections of what it thinks the user might like.

Many complex phenomena can be modeled as systems of autonomous agents that follow relatively simple rules for interaction. **Agent-based modeling** applications have been developed to model the behavior of consumers, stock markets, and supply chains and to predict the spread of epidemics.

Procter & Gamble (P&G) used agent-based modeling to improve coordination among different members of its supply chain in response to changing business conditions (see Figure 11.11). It modeled a complex supply chain as a group of semiautonomous "agents" representing individual supply chain components, such as trucks, production facilities, distributors, and retail stores. The behavior of each agent is programmed to follow rules that mimic actual behavior, such as "order an item when it is out of stock." Simulations using the agents enable the company to perform what-if analyses on inventory levels, in-store stockouts, and transportation costs.

Using intelligent agent models, P&G discovered that trucks should often be dispatched before being fully loaded. Although transportation costs would be higher using partially loaded trucks, the simulation showed that retail store stockouts would occur less often, thus reducing the amount of lost sales, which would more than make up for the higher distribution costs. Agent-based modeling has saved P&G $300 million annually on an investment of less than 1 percent of that amount.

Hybrid AI Systems

Genetic algorithms, fuzzy logic, neural networks, and expert systems can be integrated into a single application to take advantage of the best features of these technologies. Such systems are called **hybrid AI systems**. Hybrid applications in business are growing. In Japan, Hitachi, Mitsubishi, Ricoh, Sanyo, and others are starting to incorporate hybrid AI in products such as home appliances, factory machinery, and office equipment. Matsushita has developed a "neurofuzzy" washing machine that combines fuzzy logic with neural networks.

FIGURE 11.11 INTELLIGENT AGENTS IN P&G'S SUPPLY CHAIN NETWORK

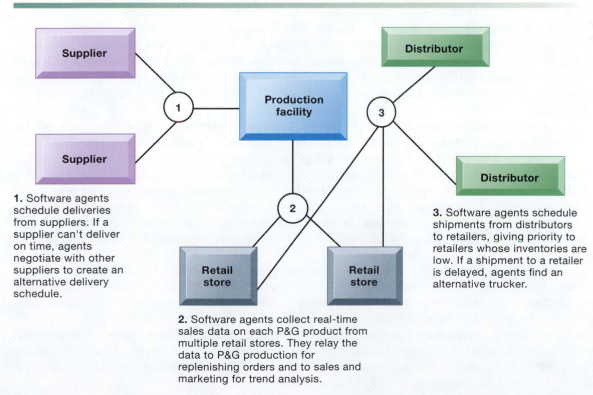

1. Software agents schedule deliveries from suppliers. If a supplier can't deliver on time, agents negotiate with other suppliers to create an alternative delivery schedule.

2. Software agents collect real-time sales data on each P&G product from multiple retail stores. They relay the data to P&G production for replenishing orders and to sales and marketing for trend analysis.

3. Software agents schedule shipments from distributors to retailers, giving priority to retailers whose inventories are low. If a shipment to a retailer is delayed, agents find an alternative trucker.

Intelligent agents are helping P&G shorten the replenishment cycles for products such as a box of Tide.

Review Summary

11-1 *What is the role of knowledge management systems in business?*

Knowledge management is a set of processes to create, store, transfer, and apply knowledge in the organization. Much of a firm's value depends on its ability to create and manage knowledge. Knowledge management promotes organizational learning by increasing the ability of the organization to learn from its environment and to incorporate knowledge into its business processes. There are three major types of knowledge management systems: enterprise-wide knowledge management systems, knowledge work systems, and intelligent techniques.

11-2 *What types of systems are used for enterprise-wide knowledge management, and how do they provide value for businesses?*

Enterprise-wide knowledge management systems are firmwide efforts to collect, store, distribute, and apply digital content and knowledge. Enterprise content management systems provide databases and tools for organizing and storing structured documents and tools for organizing and storing semistructured knowledge, such as e-mail or rich media. Often these systems include group collaboration tools (including wikis and social bookmarking), portals to simplify information access, search tools, tools for locating experts, and tools for classifying information based on a taxonomy that is appropriate for the organization. Learning management systems provide tools for the management, delivery, tracking, and assessment of various types of employee learning and training.

11-3 *What are the major types of knowledge work systems, and how do they provide value for firms?*

Knowledge work systems (KWS) support the creation of new knowledge and its integration into the organization. KWS require easy access to an external knowledge base; powerful computer hardware that can support software with intensive graphics, analysis, document management, and communications capabilities; and a user-friendly interface. Computer-aided design (CAD) systems, augmented reality applications, and virtual reality systems, which create interactive simulations that behave like the real world, require graphics and powerful modeling capabilities.

11-4 *What are the business benefits of using intelligent techniques for knowledge management?*

Artificial intelligence lacks the flexibility, breadth, and generality of human intelligence, but it can be used to capture, codify, and extend organizational knowledge. Expert systems capture tacit knowledge from a limited domain of human expertise and express that knowledge in the form of rules. Expert systems are most useful for problems of classification or diagnosis. Case-based reasoning represents organizational knowledge as a database of cases that can be continually expanded and refined.

Fuzzy logic is a software technology for expressing knowledge in the form of rules that use approximate or subjective values. Fuzzy logic has been used for controlling physical devices and is starting to be used for limited decision-making applications.

Machine learning refers to the ability of computer programs to automatically learn and improve with experience. Neural networks consist of hardware and software that attempt to mimic the thought processes of the human brain. Neural networks are notable for their ability to learn without programming and to recognize patterns that cannot be easily described by humans. They are being used in science, medicine, and business to discriminate patterns in massive amounts of data.

Genetic algorithms develop solutions to particular problems using genetically based processes such as fitness, crossover, and mutation. Genetic algorithms are beginning to be applied to problems involving optimization, product design, and monitoring industrial systems where many alternatives or variables must be evaluated to generate an optimal solution.

Intelligent agents are software programs with built-in or learned knowledge bases that carry out specific tasks for an individual user, business process, or software application. Intelligent agents can be programmed to navigate through large amounts of data to locate useful information and in some cases act on that information on behalf of the user.

Key Terms

3-D printing, 430
Agent-based modeling, 442
Artificial intelligence (AI), 432
Augmented reality (AR), 431
Backward chaining, 434
Case-based reasoning (CBR), 436
Chatbot, 442
Communities of practice (COPs), 423
Computer-aided design (CAD), 430
Data, 420
Digital asset management systems, 428
Enterprise content management (ECM), 425
Enterprise-wide knowledge management systems, 424
Expert systems, 432
Explicit knowledge, 420
Forward chaining, 434
Fuzzy logic, 438
Genetic algorithms, 441
Hybrid AI systems, 443

Inference engine, 434
Intelligent agents, 442
Intelligent techniques, 424
Knowledge, 420
Knowledge base, 434
Knowledge discovery, 432
Knowledge management, 421
Knowledge work systems (KWS), 424
Learning management system (LMS), 428
Machine learning, 439
Massive open online course (MOOC), 428
Neural networks, 439
Organizational learning, 421
Structured knowledge, 425
Tacit knowledge, 420
Taxonomy, 427
Virtual Reality Modeling Language (VRML), 431
Virtual reality (VR), 431
Wisdom, 420

MyMISLab

To complete the problems with the MyMISLab, go to the EOC Discussion Questions in MyMISLab.

Review Questions

11-1 What is the role of knowledge management systems in business?

- Define knowledge management and explain its value to businesses.
- Describe the important dimensions of knowledge.
- Distinguish between data, knowledge, and wisdom and between tacit knowledge and explicit knowledge.
- Describe the stages in the knowledge management value chain.

11-2 What types of systems are used for enterprise-wide knowledge management, and how do they provide value for businesses?

- Define and describe the various types of enterprise-wide knowledge management systems and explain how they provide value for businesses.
- Describe the role of the following in facilitating knowledge management: taxonomies, MOOCs, and learning management systems.

11-3 What are the major types of knowledge work systems, and how do they provide value for firms?

- Define knowledge work systems and describe the generic requirements of knowledge work systems.
- Describe how the following systems support knowledge work: CAD, virtual reality, and augmented reality.

11-4 What are the business benefits of using intelligent techniques for knowledge management?

- Define an expert system, describe how it works, and explain its value to business.
- Define case-based reasoning and explain how it differs from an expert system.
- Define machine learning and give some examples.
- Define a neural network and describe how it works and how it benefits businesses.
- Define and describe fuzzy logic, genetic algorithms, and intelligent agents. Explain how each works and the kinds of problems for which each is suited.

Discussion Questions

11-5 Knowledge management is a business
MyMISLab process, not a technology. Discuss.

11-6 Describe various ways that knowledge manage-
MyMISLab ment systems could help firms with sales and
marketing or with manufacturing and production.

11-7 Your company wants to do more with knowl-
MyMISLab edge management. Describe the steps it
should take to develop a knowledge management program and select knowledge management applications.

Hands-On MIS Projects

The projects in this section give you hands-on experience designing a knowledge portal, identifying opportunities for knowledge management, creating a simple expert system, and using intelligent agents to research products for sale on the web. Visit MyMISLab's Multimedia Library to access this chapter's Hands-On MIS Projects.

Management Decision Problems

11-8 U.S. Pharma Corporation is headquartered in New Jersey but has research sites in Germany, France, the
United Kingdom, Switzerland, and Australia. Research and development of new pharmaceuticals is key to
ongoing profits, and U.S. Pharma researches and tests thousands of possible drugs. The company's
researchers need to share information with others within and outside the company, including the U.S.
Food and Drug Administration, the World Health Organization, and the International Federation of Pharmaceutical Manufacturers & Associations. Also critical is access to health information sites, such as the
U.S. National Library of Medicine, and to industry conferences and professional journals. Design a knowledge portal for U.S. Pharma's researchers. Include in your design specifications relevant internal systems
and databases, external sources of information, and internal and external communication and collaboration tools. Design a home page for your portal.

11-9 Canadian Tire is one of Canada's largest companies, with 50,000 employees and 1,100 stores and gas bars
(gas stations) across Canada selling sports, leisure, home products, apparel, and financial services as well
as automotive and petroleum products. The retail outlets are independently owned and operated. Canadian Tire has been using daily mailings and thick product catalogs to inform its dealers about new products, merchandise setups, best practices, product ordering, and problem resolution, and it is looking for a
better way to provide employees with human resources and administrative documents. Describe the problems created by this way of doing business and how knowledge management systems might help.

Improving Decision Making: Building a Simple Expert System for Retirement Planning

Software skills: Spreadsheet formulas and IF function or expert system tool
Business skills: Benefits eligibility determination

11-10 Expert systems typically use a large number of rules. This project has been simplified to reduce the number of rules, but it will give you experience working with a series of rules to develop an application.

When employees at your company retire, they are given cash bonuses. These cash bonuses are
based on the length of employment and the retiree's age. To receive a bonus, an employee must be at least
50 years of age and have worked for the company for more than five years. The following table summarizes
the criteria for determining bonuses.

LENGTH OF EMPLOYMENT	BONUS
<5 years	No bonus
5–10 years	20 percent of current annual salary
11–15 years	30 percent of current annual salary
16–20 years	40 percent of current annual salary
21–25 years	50 percent of current annual salary
26 or more years	100 percent of current annual salary

Using the information provided, build a simple expert system. Find a demonstration copy of an expert system software tool on the web that you can download. Alternatively, use your spreadsheet software to build the expert system. (If you are using spreadsheet software, we suggest using the IF function so you can see how rules are created.)

Improving Decision Making: Using Intelligent Agents for Comparison Shopping

Software skills: Web browser and shopping bot software
Business skills: Product evaluation and selection

11-11 This project will give you experience using shopping bots to search online for products, find product information, and find the best prices and vendors. Select a digital camera you might want to purchase, such as the Canon PowerShot SX530 or the Olympus Tough TG-4. Visit MySimon (www.mysimon.com), BizRate.com (www.bizrate.com), and Google Shopping to do price comparisons for you. Evaluate these shopping sites in terms of their ease of use, number of offerings, speed in obtaining information, thoroughness of information offered about the product and seller, and price selection. Which site or sites would you use, and why? Which camera would you select, and why? How helpful were these sites for making your decision?

Collaboration and Teamwork Project

Rating Enterprise Content Management Systems

11-12 With a group of classmates, select two enterprise content management (ECM) products, such as those from Oracle, Open Text, IBM, or EMC Documentum. Compare their features and capabilities. To prepare your analysis, use articles from computer magazines and the websites of the ECM software vendors. If possible, use Google Docs and Google Drive or Google Sites to brainstorm, organize, and develop a presentation of your findings for the class.

Does IBM's Watson Have a Future in Business?

CASE STUDY

In February 2011, an IBM computer named Watson made history by handily defeating the two most decorated champions of the game show *Jeopardy!*, Ken Jennings and Brad Rutter. Watson was named after IBM's founder, Thomas J. Watson, and its achievement marked a milestone in the ability of computers to process and interpret human language.

The Watson version used in Jeopardy took 20 IBM engineers three years to build at an $18 million labor cost and an estimated $1 million in equipment. The project's goal was to develop a more effective set of techniques that computers can use to process *natural language*—language that human beings instinctively use, not language specially formatted to be understood by computers. Watson had to be able to register the intent of a question, search through millions of

lines of text and data, pick up nuances of meaning and context, and rank potential responses for a user to select, all in less than three seconds.

The hardware for Watson used in *Jeopardy!* consisted of 10 racks of IBM POWER 750 servers running Linux with 15 terabytes of RAM and 2,880 processor cores (equivalent to 6,000 top-end home computers) and operated at 80 teraflops. Watson needed this amount of power to quickly scan its enormous database of information, including information from the Internet. To prepare for *Jeopardy!*, the IBM researchers downloaded more than 10 million documents, including encyclopedias and Wikipedia, the Internet Movie Database (IMDB), and the entire archive of *The New York Times*. All of the data sat in Watson's primary memory, as opposed to a much slower hard drive, so that Watson could find the data it needed within three seconds.

Watson is able to learn from its mistakes as well as its successes. To solve a typical problem, Watson tries many of the thousands of algorithms that the team has programmed it to use. The algorithms evaluate the language used in each clue, gather information about the important people and places mentioned in the clue, and generate hundreds of solutions. Human beings don't need to take such a formal approach to generate the solutions that fit a question best, but Watson compensates for this with superior computing power and speed. If a certain algorithm works to solve a problem, Watson remembers what type of question it was and the algorithm it used to get the right answer. In this way, Watson improves at answering questions over time. Watson also learns another way—the team gave Watson thousands of old *Jeopardy!* questions to process. Watson analyzed both questions and answers to determine patterns or similarities between clues, and using these patterns, it assigns varying degrees of confidence to the answers it gives.

Although Watson was only able to correctly answer a small fraction of the questions it was initially given, machine learning allowed the system to continue to improve until it reached *Jeopardy!* champion level. IBM terms Watson's ability to interpret speech and text, rapidly mine large volumes of data, answer questions, draw conclusions, and learn from its mistakes *cognitive computing*.

IBM sees its investment in Watson as a stepping stone to broader commercial uses of its AI technology, including applications for health care, financial services, or any industry where sifting through large amounts of data (including unstructured data) to answer questions is important. Watson is expected to become more useful and powerful by learning from new sets of experts in new fields of knowledge. In January 2014, the company created a new division, the Watson Business Group, with 2,000 employees. IBM has invested more than $1 billion in this group and has allocated one-third of its overall research efforts to Watson.

IBM is developing new cloud-based products based on Watson's cognitive intelligence and capabilities. IBM Watson Discovery Advisor is aimed at the pharmaceutical, publishing, and education industries and will wade through search results to deliver data faster and help researchers formulate conclusions. IBM Watson Analytics is a cloud-based service that provides insights, including visual representations,

based on raw big data enterprises send to Watson. IBM Watson Explorer is a cloud service that will provide a unified view of a user's information, facilitating the revelation and sharing of data-driven insights. Watson Health is a cloud-based service that will make it easier for healthcare companies to analyze large stores of patient data.

Some of the earliest applications for Watson have been in health care, where medical information doubles every three years and in 2020 will be doubling every 73 days. Physicians won't be able to keep abreast of that volume of information, but IBM believes Watson can. Watson is able to read and understand all this information in context and become an assistant to medical professionals.

In September 2011, WellPoint Inc., the largest U.S. healthcare provider, with 34.2 million members, enlisted Watson for an Interactive Care Reviewer application designed to determine if physicians' requested treatment meets the guidelines of the company and a patient's insurance policy. The application combines data from electronic patient records maintained by a physician or hospital, the insurance company's history of medicines and treatments, and Watson's huge library of textbooks and medical journals. According to WellPoint vice president Elizabeth Bingham, Watson initially took too long to "learn" WellPoint's policies, but IBM was able to improve the system by revising the Watson training routine for WellPoint, and the Interactive Care Reviewer has been rolled out to 1,600 healthcare providers.

In 2012, Memorial Sloan Kettering Cancer Center began work on a Watson for Oncology application to recommend personalized cancer treatments, using data from Sloan Kettering's clinical database of more than a million patients, 500 medical journals and textbooks, and 12 million pages of medical literature. Currently, the system offers recommendations for lung, breast, and colorectal cancers and is expanding to gastric-related cancers. Once Watson for Oncology has a patient's information, it can instantly search through medical literature from all over the world to identify the literature that is most relevant to that patient's specific cancer and prioritize potential treatment options (color-coded for risk and confidence) based on the evidence and the patient's health record. The system understands context. If Watson reads in notes that a breast cancer patient's sister had a mastectomy, the system knows that's an indication of family history even though the word *family* may not appear. Watson is able to present an analysis in about 15 minutes that would typically take humans months to develop.

Using Watson for Oncology turned out to be more complex than originally envisioned. For instance, Sloan Kettering oncologist Dr. Mark Kris displayed a screen from Watson that listed three potential treatments, but Watson was less than 32 percent confident that any of them were correct. But progress is genuine, and Watson for Oncology is now used at a number of hospitals worldwide, including Bumrungrad International Hospital in Bangkok and Manipal Hospitals in seven cities in India as well as Memorial Sloan Kettering in New York. Additional Watson oncology-related solutions are being used at MD Anderson Cancer Center and the Cleveland Clinic.

In November 2013, IBM announced it would make Watson technology available via the Internet as a cloud service that could be used by many different industries. IBM opened parts of the system to outside developers to create businesses and mobile applications based on cognitive computing. A Watson Developer Cloud provides tools and methodologies for developers to work with a Watson system, a content store supplying both free and fee-based data for new applications, and about 500 subject matter experts from IBM and third parties. IBM has also made Watson easier and less expensive to use.

The Watson Health Cloud launched in 2015 is a secure platform where corporations and researchers can build systems and exchange data. Initial industry partners are Johnson & Johnson, Medtronic, and Apple. Johnson & Johnson will use Watson to personalize patient care before and after knee and hip replacements. Medical equipment maker Medtronic wants to use Watson to spot diabetes patients trending toward trouble, automatically adjust insulin doses from its devices, and send alerts to care providers and the patients. Apple and Under Armour are using Watson analytics to decipher the deluge of data from connected watches and fitness bands.

Other industries are starting to use Watson as well. The U.S. Air Force is developing an intelligent system to help government procurement officials manage the Federal Acquisition Regulation, consisting of 1,897 pages of documents. The number and complexity of the documents make it virtually impossible for an individual to understand in order to answer a specific question. Businesses will be able to query the system to find programs they might be eligible to bid on or to determine the requirements for competing for a contract. Genesys, which provides customer experience and call center technology solutions, is building a platform that allows clients to call into a bank and interact with Watson. The software understands and uses natural language to offer assistance and even recommends products based on the conversation.

IBM has aggressively been moving away from hardware and focusing on cloud-based analytic and artificially intelligent software. Although Watson is one key to IBM's future, analysts believe it's not growing fast enough to offset the weakness in its legacy computer and consulting businesses. CEO Virginia Rometty is hoping Watson will bring in $1 billion in revenue annually by 2018 but states that it is too early to break out financial results for the Watson unit because the company is still growing the product.

In order to effectively commercialize the technology, IBM will need to expand Watson's knowledge domains, and this is its greatest challenge. Turning Watson into a useful business tool requires an enormous amount of work. Watson has to learn the terminology and master the domains of expertise in many different areas, including health care and scientific research, understand the context of how that language is used, and learn how to correlate questions with the correct answers. Watson can't come up yet with its own ideas.

IBM will have to be careful not to oversell what Watson can do so that Watson does not end up like other artificial intelligence systems where expectations were way overblown. Making machines that beat humans at chess or a TV game is much easier than solving problems in the real world. According to Curt Monash, president of Monash Research, Watson hasn't yet overcome the hurdle that derailed AI in the 1980s, when it was only able to capture very small pieces of a limited knowledge domain for a single-purpose use. Watson is having more trouble solving real-life problems than *Jeopardy!* questions. Watson's basic learning process requiring IBM engineers to master the technicalities of a customer's business and translate those requirements into usable software has been very arduous. It remains to be seen whether the complexity of establishing a body of knowledge and training an intelligent system is repeatable and scalable for other types of work and whether it creates opportunities for differentiation and competitive advantage. Watson is very much a work in progress.

Sources: Christian Davenport, " IBM's Watson Supercomputer May Have Met Its Match: The Federal Procurement Mess," *Los Angeles Times*, March 26, 2016; International Business Machines Corporation, "Form 10-K Annual Report," February 23, 2016; Greg Bensinger, "IBM CEO: Too Soon to Break Out Watson Revenue," *Wall Street Journal*, June 1, 2016; Virginia Lau, "How Watson for Oncology Is Advancing Cancer Care," *Medical Marketing & Media*, April 19, 2016; John Markman, "IBM Makes Its Big Data Play," *Forbes*, July 11, 2016; Greg Slabodkin, "CVS Taps IBM Watson for Predictive Analytics," *Information Management*, August 3, 2015; Steve Lohr, "IBM Creates Watson Health to Analyze Medical Data," *New York Times*, April 13, 2015; Mohana Ravindranath, "How IBM Is Trying to Commercialize Watson," *Washington Post*, May 11, 2014; Spencer E. Ante, "IBM Struggles to Turn Watson Computer into Big Business," *Wall Street Journal*, January 7, 2014; Michael Goldberg, "Five Things to Know About IBM Watson, Where It Is, and Where It's Going," *DataInformed*, January 14, 2014; and Larry Dignan, "IBM Forms Watson Business Group: Will Commercialization Follow?" *ZDNet*, January 9, 2014.

CASE STUDY QUESTIONS

11-13 How powerful is Watson? Describe its technology. Why does it require so much powerful hardware?

11-14 How "intelligent" is Watson? What can it do? What can't it do?

11-15 What kinds of problems is Watson able to solve? How useful a tool is it for knowledge management and decision making?

11-16 Do you think Watson will be as useful in other industries and disciplines as IBM hopes? Will it be beneficial to everyone? Explain your answer.

MyMISLab

Go to the Assignments section of MyMISLab to complete these writing exercises.

11-17 How do each of the following types of systems acquire and represent knowledge: expert system, case-based reasoning, neural network?

11-18 How do enterprise content management systems help organizations manage structured and semistructured knowledge? What are two examples of each type of knowledge handled by these systems?

Chapter 11 References

Alavi, Maryam and Dorothy Leidner. "Knowledge Management and Knowledge Management Systems: Conceptual Foundations and Research Issues," *MIS Quarterly* 25, No. 1(March 2001).

Althuizen, Niek and Berend Wierenga. "Supporting Creative Problem Solving with a Case-Based Reasoning System." *Journal of Management Information Systems* 31. No. 1 (Summer 2014).

Althuizen, Niek and Astrid Reichel. "The Effects of IT-Enabled Cognitive Stimulation Tools on Creative Problem Solving: A Dual Pathway to Creativity." *Journal of Management Information Systems* 33, No. 1 (2016).

Burtka, Michael. "Generic Algorithms." *The Stern Information Systems Review* 1, No. 1 (Spring 1993).

Clark, Don. "IBM Unveils Chip Simulating Brain Functions." *Wall Street Journal* (August 7, 2014).

Davenport, Thomas H. and Julia Kirby. "Just How Smart Are Smart Machines?" *MIT Sloan Management Review* 57, No. 3 (Spring 2016).

Davenport, Thomas H., and Lawrence Prusak. *Working Knowledge: How Organizations Manage What They Know*. Boston, MA: Harvard Business School Press (1997).

Davenport, Thomas H., Laurence Prusak, and Bruce Strong. "Putting Ideas to Work." *Wall Street Journal* (March 10, 2008).

Davenport, Thomas H., Robert J. Thomas, and Susan Cantrell. "The Mysterious Art and Science of Knowledge-Worker Performance." *MIT Sloan Management Review* 44, No. 1 (Fall 2002).

Dhar, Vasant and Roger Stein. *Intelligent Decision Support Methods: The Science of Knowledge Work*. Upper Saddle River, NJ: Prentice Hall (1997).

El Najdawi, M. K., and Anthony C. Stylianou. "Expert Support Systems: Integrating AI Technologies." *Communications of the ACM* 36, No. 12 (December 1993).

Gelernter, David. "Machines That Will Think and Feel." *Wall Street Journal* (March 18, 2016).

Gu, Feng and Baruch Lev. "Intangible Assets. Measurements, Drivers, Usefulness." (2001). http://pages.stern.nyu.edu/~blev/.

Holland, John H. "Genetic Algorithms." *Scientific American* (July 1992).

Housel, Tom and Arthur A. Bell. *Measuring and Managing Knowledge*. New York: McGraw-Hill (2001).

"How Machines Learn and You Win." *Harvard Business Review* (November 2015).

Iyengar, Kishen, Jeffrey R. Sweeney, and Ramiro Montealegre. "Information Technology Use as a Learning Mechanism: The Impact of IT Use on Knowledge Transfer Effectiveness, Absorptive Capacity, and Franchisee Performance." *MIS Quarterly* 39, No. 3 (September 2015).

Kim, Seung Hyun, Tridas Mukhopadhyay, and Robert E. Kraut. "When Does Repository KMS Use Lift Performance? The Role of Alternative Knowledge Sources and Task Environments?" *MIS Quarterly* 40, No. 1 (March 2016).

Leonard-Barton, Dorothy and Walter Swap. "Deep Smarts." *Harvard Business Review* (September 1, 2004).

Leonardi, Paul M. "Ambient Awareness and Knowledge Acquisition: Using Social Media to Learn 'Who Knows What' and 'Who Knows Whom'." *MIS Quarterly* 39, No. 4 (December 2015).

Lev, Baruch. "Sharpening the Intangibles Edge." *Harvard Business Review* (June 1, 2004).

Lim, Shi Ying, Sirkka L. Jarvenpaa, and Holly J Lanham. "Barriers to Interorganizational Knowledge Transfer in Post-Hospital Care Transitions: Review and Directions for Information Systems Research." *Journal of Management Information Systems* 32, No. 3 (2015).

Lohr, Steve. "The Promise of Artificial Intelligence Unfolds in Small Steps." New York Times, February 28, 2016.

Malone, Thomas W., Robert Laubacher, and Chrysanthos Dellarocas. "The Collective Intelligence Genome." *MIT Sloan Management Review* 51, No. 3 (Spring 2010).

Markoff, John. "Brainlike Computers, Learning from Experience." *New York Times* (December 28, 2013).

Markoff, John. "How Many Computers to Identify a Cat? 16,000." *New York Times* (June 26, 2012).

Markus, M. Lynne, Ann Majchrzak, and Less Gasser. "A Design Theory for Systems That Support Emergent Knowledge Processes." *MIS Quarterly* 26, No. 3 (September 2002).

McCarthy, John. "Generality in Artificial Intelligence." *Communications of the ACM* (December 1987).

Mehra, Amit, Nishtha Langer, Ravi Bapna, and Ram Gopal. "Estimating Returns to Training in the Knowledge Economy: A Firm-Level Analysis of Small and Medium Enterprises." *MIS Quarterly* 38, No. 3 (September 2014).

Meister, Jeanne. "MOOCs Emerge as Disruptors to Corporate Learning." *Forbes* (June 10, 2015).

Nurmohamed, Zafred, Nabeel Gillani, and Michael Lenox. "New Use for MOOCs: Real-World Problem-Solving." *Harvard Business Review* (July 2013).

Orlikowski, Wanda J. "Knowing in Practice: Enacting a Collective Capability in Distributed Organizing." *Organization Science* 13, No. 3 (May–June 2002).

Pyle, Dorian and Cristina San Jose. "An Executive's Guide to Machine Learning." *McKinsey Quarterly* (June 2015).

Sadeh, Norman, David W. Hildum, and Dag Kjenstad. "Agent-Based E-supply Chain Decision Support." *Journal of Organizational Computing and Electronic Commerce* 13, No. 3 & 4 (2003).

Singer, Natasha. "The Virtual Anatomy, Ready for Dissection." *New York Times* (January 7, 2012).

"Smarter, Smaller, Safer Robots." *Harvard Business Review* (November 2015).

U.S. Department of Labor, Occupational Employment Statistics. "May 2015 National Occupational Employment and Wage Estimates." Bureau of Labor Statisics (2016).

Weill, Peter, Thomas Malone, and Thomas G. Apel. "The Business Models Investors Prefer." *MIT Sloan Management Review* 52, No. 4 (Summer 2011).

Zadeh, Lotfi A. "Fuzzy Logic, Neural Networks, and Soft Computing." *Communications of the ACM* 37, No. 3 (March 1994).

Zadeh, Lotfi A. "The Calculus of Fuzzy If/Then Rules." *AI Expert* (March 1992).

Zeying Wan, Deborah Compeau, and Nicole Haggerty. "The Effects of Self- Regulated Learning Processes on E-Learning Outcomes in Organizational Settings." *Journal of Management Information Systems* 29, No. 1 (Summer 2012).

Zhao, Li, Brian Detlor, and Catherine E. Connelly. "Sharing Knowledge in Social Q&A Sites: The Unintended Consequences of Extrinsic Motivation." *Journal of Management Information Systems* 33, No. 1 (2016).

12

Enhancing Decision Making

Learning Objectives

After reading this chapter, you will be able to answer the following questions:

12-1 What are the different types of decisions, and how does the decision-making process work?

12-2 How do information systems support the activities of managers and management decision making?

12-3 How do business intelligence and business analytics support decision making?

12-4 How do different decision-making constituencies in an organization use business intelligence, and what is the role of information systems in helping people working in a group make decisions more efficiently?

MyMISLab™

Visit **mymislab.com** for simulations, tutorials, and end-of-chapter problems.

CHAPTER CASES

Can Big Data Analytics Help People Find Love?

The Tension Between Technology and Human Decision Makers

Data Drive Starbucks Location Decisions

GE Bets on the Internet of Things and Big Data Analytics

VIDEO CASES

PSEG Leverages Big Data and Business Analytics Using GE's PREDIX Platform

FreshDirect Uses Business Intelligence to Manage Its Online Grocery

Business Intelligence Helps the Cincinnati Zoo Work Smarter

Can Big Data Analytics Help People Find Love?

Can computers help people find love? Online dating website eHarmony, with more than 20 million registered users, thinks so. eHarmony is the first online dating service to use a "scientific" approach to matching highly compatible singles. The company employs a 29 Dimensions® model to match couples based on features of compatibility found in thousands of successful relationships, processing more than 3.5 million matches daily using 30 gigabytes of data and the MongoDB non-relational database management system.

Users joining eHarmony are required to fill out a questionnaire containing 200 questions that cover everything from characteristics to values. The information is then run through an eHarmony-patented algorithm, where matches are found for users. This may not be the most romantic way to find a spouse, but according to a survey conducted by Harris Interactive, 438 people on average get married every day in the United States after meeting through the eHarmony website. That's nearly 4 percent of new U.S. marriages!

eHarmony also mines terabytes of data on its users, collected mainly from their activities on its website. This helps predict how users will behave. For example, people using eHarmony have different communication levels. From data such as how many times users log on to the website, how many photos they post, and the number of words they use to describe themselves on their eHarmony profiles, eHarmony can tell who is more introverted or who is likely to be an initiator. The data also helps eHarmony determine whether users would be more likely to communicate with their matches at certain times of the day. The matching process is highly automated, allowing eHarmony to generate matches for users in a matter of minutes most of the time.

eHarmony's couple-matching algorithm varies from country to country and is regularly refined based on user behavior and new relationship research from educational institutions. Big data analysis is also helpful for marketing, indicating when is a good time for eHarmony to send out promotions to individual users.

Drawing on its success in matching couples, eHarmony is applying its expertise to matching people with the right job. On April 1, 2016, the company launched Elevated Careers, a new service to match job seekers with potential employers based on 24 value, culture, and personality factors. Sixteen of those factors deal with culture and how well employee values match with the target company. The goal is to make employees happier while reducing churn and improving company business performance.

Just as eHarmony works by finding out what predicts happy and unhappy marriages, Elevated Careers works by identifying people who are full-time employed, having them describe themselves and their companies, and then applying those models to people interested in working at those companies.

eHarmony collected information for its database from resumes and profiles of users, company profiles submitted by current employees, and job listings. Elevated Careers' team arranged with employment website Simply Hired to have all the job listings of companies that Simply Hired is working with in the Elevated Careers database. Elevated Careers is hosted on the Amazon Web Services (AWS) public cloud computing platform. For companies that do not have a profile, Elevated Careers makes recommendations based on geospatial data. By knowing a specific company's industry and locale, Elevated Careers can make predictions, based on that information, of the company's culture or values.

Sources: Conner Forrest, "eHarmony's Elevated Careers Uses Big Data to Match You with the Perfect Job," *Tech Republic*, April 1, 2016; www.eharmony.com, accessed May 12, 2016; "eHarmony Inc.," www.ibm.com, accessed May 12, 2016; and "Big Dating at eHarmony," www.mongodb.com, accessed March 28, 2016.

eHarmony is a powerful illustration of how information systems improve decision making. This is a relatively new company that uses big data and sophisticated models to analyze the data to carve out a new web-based service and business model. There are many other online dating sites that use personal data to help people find dating or marital prospects. However, eHarmony claims to have the competitive edge because it has powerful and unique analytic tools to analyze large quantities of detailed data, generate accurate predictions of couples that will be most compatible, and recommend potential partners to customers. Other online dating sites lack the range of data and analytic tools to predict compatibility as does eHarmony.

The chapter-opening diagram calls attention to important points raised by this case and this chapter. eHarmony is an Internet business with many competitors, it is an online matchmaking service, and its business strategy is based on skillful analysis of detailed data. eHarmony was able to take advantage of new opportunities offered by big data and business intelligence technology. eHarmony collects vast quantities of detailed personal and behavioral data about its customers and uses the data along with relationship research findings to analyze these data along 29 dimensions to predict a couple's potential compatibility. eHarmony also uses big data to fine-tune its marketing decisions, and it is using its business intelligence expertise to launch a new business matching companies and job seekers. Big data and data analytics have made it possible for eHarmony to make more accurate and insightful decisions and to offer the results of those decisions as a service. Better decision making using business intelligence has clearly made eHarmony more profitable and competitive.

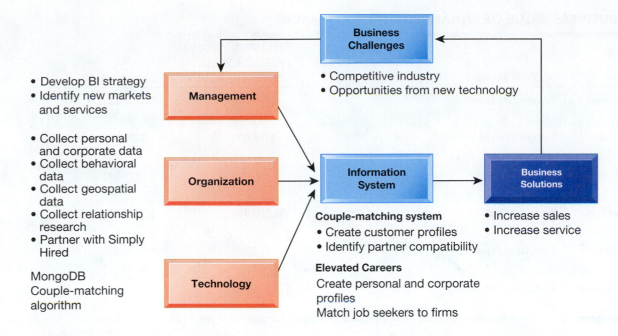

Management
- Develop BI strategy
- Identify new markets and services

Organization
- Collect personal and corporate data
- Collect behavioral data
- Collect geospatial data
- Collect relationship research
- Partner with Simply Hired

Technology
MongoDB
Couple-matching algorithm

Business Challenges
- Competitive industry
- Opportunities from new technology

Information System

Couple-matching system
- Create customer profiles
- Identify partner compatibility

Elevated Careers
Create personal and corporate profiles
Match job seekers to firms

Business Solutions
- Increase sales
- Increase service

12-1 What are the different types of decisions, and how does the decision-making process work?

Decision making in businesses used to be limited to management. Today, lower-level employees are responsible for some of these decisions, as information systems make information available to lower levels of the business. But what do we mean by better decision making? How does decision making take place in businesses and other organizations? Let's take a closer look.

Business Value of Improved Decision Making

What does it mean to the business to make better decisions? What is the monetary value of improved decision making? Table 12.1 attempts to measure the monetary value of improved decision making for a small U.S. manufacturing firm with $280 million in annual revenue and 140 employees. The firm has identified a number of key decisions where new system investments might improve the quality of decision making. The table provides selected estimates of annual value (in the form of cost savings or increased revenue) from improved decision making in selected areas of the business.

We can see from Table 12.1 that decisions are made at all levels of the firm and that some of these decisions are common, routine, and numerous. Although the value of improving any single decision may be small, improving hundreds of thousands of "small" decisions adds up to a large annual value for the business.

Types of Decisions

Chapters 1 and 2 showed that there are different levels in an organization. Each of these levels has different information requirements for decision support and responsibility for different types of decisions (see Figure 12.1). Decisions are classified as structured, semi-structured, and unstructured.

TABLE 12.1 BUSINESS VALUE OF ENHANCED DECISION MAKING

EXAMPLE DECISION	DECISION MAKER	NUMBER OF ANNUAL DECISIONS	ESTIMATED VALUE TO FIRM OF A SINGLE IMPROVED DECISION	ANNUAL VALUE
Allocate support to most valuable customers	Accounts manager	12	$100,000	$1,200,000
Predict call center daily demand	Call center management	4	$150,000	$600,000
Decide parts inventory levels daily	Inventory manager	365	$5,000	$1,825,000
Identify competitive bids from major suppliers	Senior management	1	$2,000,000	$2,000,000
Schedule production to fill orders	Manufacturing manager	150	$10,000	$1,500,000
Allocate labor to complete a job	Production floor manager	100	$4,000	$400,000

Unstructured decisions are those in which the decision maker must provide judgment, evaluation, and insight to solve the problem. Each of these decisions is novel, important, and nonroutine, and there is no well-understood or agreed-on procedure for making them.

Structured decisions, by contrast, are repetitive and routine, and they involve a definite procedure for handling them so that they do not have to be treated each time as if they were new. Many decisions have elements of both types of decisions and are **semi-structured**, where only part of the problem has

FIGURE 12.1 INFORMATION REQUIREMENTS OF KEY DECISION-MAKING GROUPS IN A FIRM

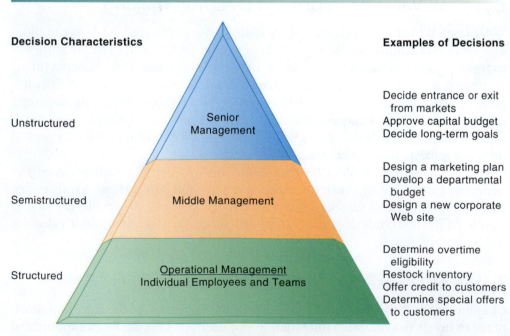

Senior managers, middle managers, operational managers, and employees have different types of decisions and information requirements.

a clear-cut answer provided by an accepted procedure. In general, structured decisions are more prevalent at lower organizational levels, whereas unstructured problems are more common at higher levels of the firm.

Senior executives face many unstructured decision situations, such as establishing the firm's 5- or 10-year goals or deciding new markets to enter. Answering the question "Should we enter a new market?" would require access to news, government reports, and industry views as well as high-level summaries of firm performance. However, the answer would also require senior managers to use their own best judgment and poll other managers for their opinions.

Middle managers face more structured decision scenarios, but their decisions may include unstructured components. A typical middle-level management decision might be "Why is the reported order fulfillment report showing a decline over the past six months at a distribution center in Minneapolis?" This middle manager will obtain a report from the firm's enterprise system or distribution management system on order activity and operational efficiency at the Minneapolis distribution center. This is the structured part of the decision. But before arriving at an answer, this middle manager will have to interview employees and gather more unstructured information from external sources about local economic conditions or sales trends.

Operational management and rank-and-file employees tend to make more structured decisions. For example, a supervisor on an assembly line has to decide whether an hourly paid worker is entitled to overtime pay. If the employee worked more than eight hours on a particular day, the supervisor would routinely grant overtime pay for any time beyond eight hours that was clocked on that day.

A sales account representative often has to make decisions about extending credit to customers by consulting the firm's customer database that contains credit information. If the customer met the firm's prespecified criteria for granting credit, the account representative would grant that customer credit to make a purchase. In both instances, the decisions are highly structured and are routinely made thousands of times each day in most large firms. The answer has been preprogrammed into the firm's payroll and accounts receivable systems.

The Decision-Making Process

Making a decision is a multistep process. Simon (1960) described four different stages in decision making: intelligence, design, choice, and implementation (see Figure 12.2).

Intelligence consists of discovering, identifying, and understanding the problems occurring in the organization—why a problem exists, where, and what effects it is having on the firm.

Design involves identifying and exploring various solutions to the problem.

Choice consists of choosing among solution alternatives.

Implementation involves making the chosen alternative work and continuing to monitor how well the solution is working.

What happens if the solution you have chosen doesn't work? Figure 12.2 shows that you can return to an earlier stage in the decision-making process and repeat it if necessary. For instance, in the face of declining sales, a sales management team may decide to pay the sales force a higher commission for making more sales to spur on the sales effort. If this does not produce sales increases, managers would need to investigate whether the problem stems from

FIGURE 12.2 STAGES IN DECISION MAKING

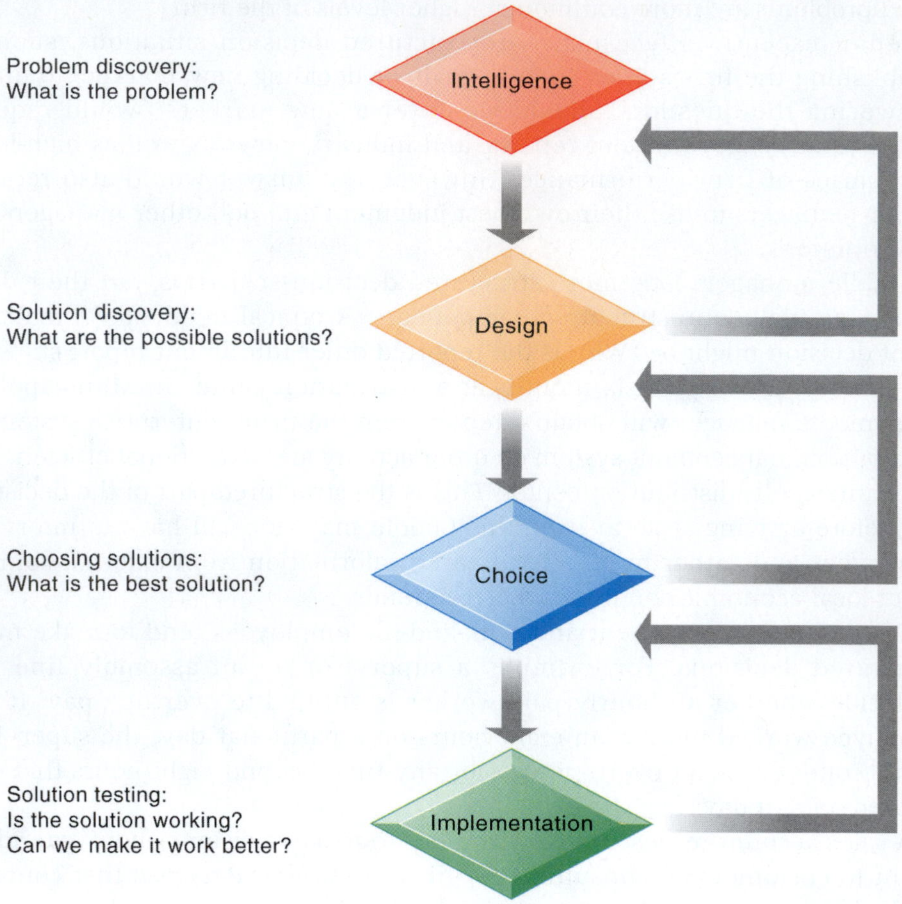

Problem discovery:
What is the problem?

Intelligence

Solution discovery:
What are the possible solutions?

Design

Choosing solutions:
What is the best solution?

Choice

Solution testing:
Is the solution working?
Can we make it work better?

Implementation

The decision-making process is broken down into four stages.

poor product design, inadequate customer support, or a host of other causes that call for a different solution.

12-2 How do information systems support the activities of managers and management decision making?

The premise of this book and this chapter is that systems to support decision making produce better decision making by managers and employees, above-average returns on investment for the firm, and ultimately higher profitability. However, information systems cannot improve every decision taking place in an organization. Let's examine the role of managers and decision making in organizations to see why this is so.

Managerial Roles

Managers play key roles in organizations. Their responsibilities range from making decisions, to writing reports, to attending meetings, to arranging birthday parties. We are able to better understand managerial functions and roles by examining classical and contemporary models of managerial behavior.

The **classical model of management**, which describes what managers do, was largely unquestioned for the more than 70 years since the 1920s. Henri Fayol and other early writers first described the five classical functions of managers as planning, organizing, coordinating, deciding, and controlling. This description of management activities dominated management thought for a long time, and it is still popular today.

The classical model describes formal managerial functions but does not address exactly what managers do when they plan, decide things, and control the work of others. For this, we must turn to the work of contemporary behavioral scientists who have studied managers in daily action. **Behavioral models** argue that the actual behavior of managers appears to be less systematic, more informal, less reflective, more reactive, and less well organized than the classical model would have us believe.

Observers find that managerial behavior actually has five attributes that differ greatly from the classical description. First, managers perform a great deal of work at an unrelenting pace—studies have found that managers engage in more than 600 different activities each day, with no break in their pace. Second, managerial activities are fragmented; most activities last for less than nine minutes, and only 10 percent of the activities exceed one hour in duration. Third, managers prefer current, specific, and ad hoc information (printed information often will be too old). Fourth, they prefer oral forms of communication to written forms because oral media provide greater flexibility, require less effort, and bring a faster response. Fifth, managers give high priority to maintaining a diverse and complex web of contacts that acts as an informal information system and helps them execute their personal agendas and short- and long-term goals.

Analyzing managers' day-to-day behavior, Henry Mintzberg found that it could be classified into 10 managerial roles. **Managerial roles** are expectations of the activities that managers should perform in an organization. Mintzberg found that these managerial roles fell into three categories: interpersonal, informational, and decisional.

Interpersonal Roles

Managers act as figureheads for the organization when they represent their companies to the outside world and perform symbolic duties, such as giving out employee awards, in their **interpersonal role**. Managers act as leaders, attempting to motivate, counsel, and support subordinates. Managers also act as liaisons between various organizational levels; within each of these levels, they serve as liaisons among the members of the management team. Managers provide time and favors, which they expect to be returned.

Informational Roles

In their **informational role**, managers act as the nerve centers of their organizations, receiving the most concrete, up-to-date information and redistributing it to those who need to be aware of it. Managers are therefore information disseminators and spokespersons for their organizations.

Decisional Roles

Managers make decisions. In their **decisional role**, they act as entrepreneurs by initiating new kinds of activities, they handle disturbances arising in the organization, they allocate resources to staff members who need them, and they negotiate conflicts and mediate between conflicting groups.

Table 12.2, based on Mintzberg's role classifications, is one look at where systems can and cannot help managers. The table shows that information systems are now capable of supporting most, but not all, areas of managerial life.

Real-World Decision Making

We now see that information systems are not helpful for all managerial roles. And in those managerial roles where information systems might improve decisions, investments in information technology do not always produce positive results. There are three main reasons: information quality, management filters, and organizational culture (see Chapter 3).

Information Quality

High-quality decisions require high-quality information. Table 12.3 describes information quality dimensions that affect the quality of decisions.

If the output of information systems does not meet these quality criteria, decision making will suffer. Chapter 6 describes how corporate databases and files have varying levels of inaccuracy and incompleteness, which in turn will degrade the quality of decision making.

Management Filters

Even with timely, accurate information, managers often make bad decisions. Managers (like all human beings) absorb information through a series of filters to make sense of the world around them. Cognitive scientists, behavioral economists, and recently neuro-economists have found that managers, like other humans, are poor at assessing risk, are risk averse, perceive patterns where none exist, and make decisions based on intuition, feelings, and the framing of the problem as opposed to empirical data (Kahneman, 2011; Tversky and Kahneman, 1986).

TABLE 12.2 MANAGERIAL ROLES AND SUPPORTING INFORMATION SYSTEMS

ROLE	BEHAVIOR	SUPPORT SYSTEMS
INTERPERSONAL ROLES		
Figurehead		Telepresence systems
Leader	Interpersonal	Telepresence, social networks, Twitter
Liaison		Smartphones, social networks
INFORMATIONAL ROLES		
Nerve center		Management information systems, executive support system
Disseminator	Information	Texting, e-mail, social networks
Spokesperson	processing	Webinars, telepresence
DECISIONAL ROLES		
Entrepreneur	Decision	None exist
Disturbance handler	making	None exist
Resource allocator		Business intelligence, decision-support system
Negotiator		None exist

Sources: Authors and Mintzberg, 1971.

TABLE 12.3 INFORMATION QUALITY DIMENSIONS

QUALITY DIMENSION	DESCRIPTION
Accuracy	Do the data represent reality?
Integrity	Are the structure of data and relationships among the entities and attributes consistent?
Consistency	Are data elements consistently defined?
Completeness	Are all the necessary data present?
Validity	Do data values fall within defined ranges?
Timeliness	Are data available when needed?
Accessibility	Are the data accessible, comprehensible, and usable?

For instance, Wall Street firms such as Bear Stearns and Lehman Brothers imploded in 2008 because they underestimated the risk of their investments in complex mortgage securities, many of which were based on subprime loans that were more likely to default. The computer models they and other financial institutions used to manage risk were based on overly optimistic assumptions and overly simplistic data about what might go wrong. Management wanted to make sure that their firms' capital was not all tied up as a cushion against defaults from risky investments, preventing them from investing it to generate profits. So the designers of these risk management systems were encouraged to measure risks in a way that minimized their risk. Some trading desks also over-simplified the information maintained about the mortgage securities to make them appear as simple bonds with higher ratings than were warranted by their underlying components. The rating firms went along with their clients' wishes and provided high quality ratings to low quality bonds.

Organizational Inertia and Politics
Organizations are bureaucracies with limited capabilities and competencies for acting decisively. When environments change and businesses need to adopt new business models to survive, strong forces within organizations resist making decisions calling for major change. Decisions taken by a firm often represent a balancing of the firm's various interest groups rather than the best solution to the problem.

Studies of business restructuring find that firms tend to ignore poor performance until threatened by outside takeovers, and they systematically blame poor performance on external forces beyond their control—such as economic conditions (the economy), foreign competition, and rising prices—rather than blaming senior or middle management for poor business judgment. When the external business environment is positive and firm performance improves, managers typically credit themselves for the improved performance rather than the positive environment.

High-Velocity Automated Decision Making

Today, many decisions made by organizations are not made by managers—or any humans. For instance, when you enter a query into Google's search engine, Google has to decide which URLs to display in about half a second on average (500 milliseconds). High-frequency traders at electronic stock exchanges execute their trades in under 30 milliseconds.

The class of decisions that are highly structured and automated is growing rapidly. What makes this kind of automated high-speed decision making possible are computer algorithms that precisely define the steps to be followed to produce a decision, very large databases, very high-speed processors, and software optimized to the task. In these situations, humans (including managers) are eliminated from the decision chain because they are too slow.

This also means organizations in these areas are making decisions faster than what managers can monitor or control. The past few years have seen a series of breakdowns in computerized trading systems, including one on August 1, 2012, when a software error caused Knight Capital to enter millions of faulty trades in less than an hour. The trading glitch created wild surges and plunges in nearly 150 stocks and left Knight with $440 million in losses. In high-velocity decision environments, the intelligence, design, choice, and implementation parts of the decision-making process are captured by the software's algorithms. The humans who wrote the software have already identified the problem, designed a method for finding a solution, defined a range of acceptable solutions, and implemented the solution. Obviously, with humans out of the loop, great care needs to be taken to ensure the proper operation of these systems to prevent significant harm.

12-3 How do business intelligence and business analytics support decision making?

Chapter 2 introduced you to the different types of systems used for supporting management decision making. At the foundation of all of these decision support systems are a business intelligence and business analytics infrastructure that supplies the data and the analytic tools for supporting decision making.

What is Business Intelligence?

Business intelligence (BI) is a term used by hardware and software vendors and information technology consultants to describe the infrastructure for warehousing, integrating, reporting, and analyzing data that come from the business environment, including big data. The foundation infrastructure collects, stores, cleans, and makes relevant information available to managers. Think databases, data warehouses, data marts, Hadoop, and analytic platforms, which we described in Chapter 6. *Business analytics (BA)* is also a vendor-defined term that focuses more on tools and techniques for analyzing and understanding data. Think online analytical processing (OLAP), statistics, models, and data mining, which we also introduced in Chapter 6.

Business intelligence and analytics are essentially about integrating all the information streams produced by a firm into a single, coherent enterprise-wide set of data and then using modeling, statistical analysis tools and data mining tools to make sense out of all these data so managers can make better decisions and plans. eHarmony, described in the chapter-opening case, is using business intelligence and analytics to make some very fine-grained decisions about matching potential couples based on personality traits.

It is important to remember that business intelligence and analytics are products defined by technology vendors and consulting firms. Leading providers of these products include Oracle, SAP, IBM, Microsoft, and SAS. A number of BI and BA products now have cloud and mobile versions.

The Business Intelligence Environment

Figure 12.3 gives an overview of a business intelligence environment, highlighting the kinds of hardware, software, and management capabilities that the major vendors offer and that firms develop over time. There are six elements in this business intelligence environment:

- **Data from the business environment:** Businesses must deal with both structured and unstructured data from many different sources, including big data. The data need to be integrated and organized so that they can be analyzed and used by human decision makers.

- **Business intelligence infrastructure:** The underlying foundation of business intelligence is a powerful database system that captures all the relevant data to operate the business. The data may be stored in transactional databases or combined and integrated into an enterprise-data warehouse or series of interrelated data marts.

- **Business analytics toolset:** A set of software tools are used to analyze data and produce reports, respond to questions posed by managers, and track the progress of the business using key indicators of performance.

- **Managerial users and methods:** Business intelligence hardware and software are only as intelligent as the human beings who use them. Managers impose order on the analysis of data using a variety of managerial methods that define strategic business goals and specify how progress will be measured. These include business performance management and balanced scorecard approaches focusing on key performance indicators and industry strategic analyses focusing on changes in the general business environment, with special attention to competitors. Without strong senior management oversight, business analytics can produce a great deal of information, reports, and online screens that focus on the wrong matters and divert attention from the real issues.

FIGURE 12.3 BUSINESS INTELLIGENCE AND ANALYTICS FOR DECISION SUPPORT

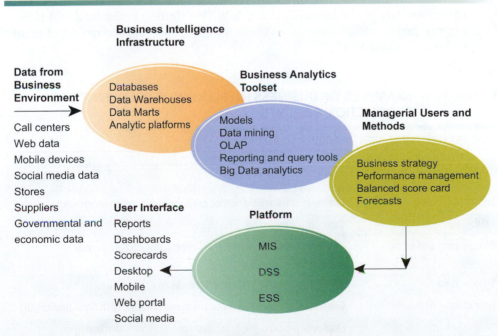

Business intelligence and analytics require a strong database foundation, a set of analytic tools, and an involved management team that can ask intelligent questions and analyze data.

- **Delivery platform—MIS, DSS, ESS:** The results from business intelligence and analytics are delivered to managers and employees in a variety of ways, depending on what they need to know to perform their jobs. MIS, DSS, and ESS, which we introduced in Chapter 2, deliver information and knowledge to different people and levels in the firm—operational employees, middle managers, and senior executives. In the past, these systems could not share data and operated as independent systems. Today, one suite of hardware and software tools in the form of a business intelligence and analytics package is able to integrate all this information and bring it to managers' desktop or mobile platforms.
- **User interface:** Businesspeople are no longer tied to their desks and desktops. They often learn quicker from a visual representation of data than from a dry report with columns and rows of information. Today's business analytics software suites feature **data visualization** tools, such as rich graphs, charts, dashboards, and maps. They also are able to deliver reports on iPhones, iPads, and other mobile handhelds as well as on the firm's web portal. BA software is adding capabilities to post information on Twitter, Facebook, or internal social media to support decision making in an online group setting rather than in a face-to-face meeting.

Business Intelligence and Analytics Capabilities

Business intelligence and analytics promise to deliver correct, nearly real-time information to decision makers, and the analytic tools help them quickly understand the information and take action. There are six analytic functionalities that BI systems deliver to achieve these ends:

- **Production reports:** These are predefined reports based on industry-specific requirements (see Table 12.4).
- **Parameterized reports:** Users enter several parameters as in a pivot table to filter data and isolate impacts of parameters. For instance, you might want to enter region and time of day to understand how sales of a product vary by region and time. If you were Starbucks, you might find that customers in the East buy most of their coffee in the morning, whereas in the Northwest customers buy coffee throughout the day. This finding might lead to different marketing and ad campaigns in each region. (See the discussion of pivot tables in Section 12.4.)

TABLE 12.4 EXAMPLES OF BUSINESS INTELLIGENCE PREDEFINED PRODUCTION REPORTS

BUSINESS FUNCTIONAL AREA	PRODUCTION REPORTS
Sales	Forecast sales; sales team performance; cross-selling; sales cycle times
Service/call center	Customer satisfaction; service cost; resolution rates; churn rates
Marketing	Campaign effectiveness; loyalty and attrition; market basket analysis
Procurement and support	Direct and indirect spending; off-contract purchases; supplier performance
Supply chain	Backlog; fulfillment status; order cycle time; bill of materials analysis
Financials	General ledger; accounts receivable and payable; cash flow; profitability
Human resources	Employee productivity; compensation; workforce demographics; retention

- **Dashboards/scorecards:** These are visual tools for presenting performance data defined by users.
- **Ad hoc query/search/report creation:** These allow users to create their own reports based on queries and searches.
- **Drill down:** This is the ability to move from a high-level summary to a more detailed view.
- **Forecasts, scenarios, models:** These include the ability to perform linear forecasting and what-if scenario analysis and analyze data using standard statistical tools.

Predictive Analytics

An important capability of business intelligence analytics is the ability to model future events and behaviors, such as the probability that a customer will respond to an offer to purchase a product. **Predictive analytics** use statistical analysis, data mining techniques, historical data, and assumptions about future conditions to predict future trends and behavior patterns. Variables that can be measured to predict future behavior are identified. For example, an insurance company might use variables such as age, gender, and driving record as predictors of driving safety when issuing auto insurance policies. A collection of such predictors is combined into a predictive model for forecasting future probabilities with an acceptable level of reliability.

FedEx has been using predictive analytics to develop models that predict how customers will respond to price changes and new services, which customers are most at risk of switching to competitors, and how much revenue will be generated by new storefront or drop-box locations. The accuracy rate of FedEx's predictive analytics system ranges from 65 to 90 percent.

Predictive analytics are being incorporated into numerous business intelligence applications for sales, marketing, finance, fraud detection, and health care. One of the most well-known applications is credit scoring, which is used throughout the financial services industry. When you apply for a new credit card, scoring models process your credit history, loan application, and purchase data to determine your likelihood of making future credit payments on time. Healthcare insurers have been analyzing data for years to identify which patients are most likely to generate high costs.

Many companies employ predictive analytics to predict response to direct marketing campaigns. By identifying customers less likely to respond, companies are able to lower their marketing and sales costs by bypassing this group and focusing their resources on customers who have been identified as more promising. For instance, the U.S. division of The Body Shop PLC used predictive analytics and its database of catalog, web, and retail store customers to identify customers who were more likely to make catalog purchases. That information helped the company build a more precise and targeted mailing list for its catalogs, improving the response rate for catalog mailings and catalog revenues.

Big Data Analytics

Predictive analytics are starting to use big data from both private and public sectors, including data from social media, customer transactions, and output from sensors and machines. In e-commerce, many online retailers have capabilities for making personalized online product recommendations to their website visitors to help stimulate purchases and guide their decisions about what merchandise to stock. However, most of these product recommendations have been based on the behaviors of similar groups of customers, such as those with incomes under $50,000 or whose ages are between 18 and 25 years. Now some retailers are starting to analyze the tremendous quantities of online and in-store customer data they collect along with social media data to make these recommendations more individualized. These efforts are translating into higher customer spending and customer retention rates. Table 12.5 provides examples of companies using big data analytics.

In the public sector, big data analytics have been driving the movement toward "smart cities," which make intensive use of digital technology to make better decisions about running cities and serving their residents. Public recordkeeping has produced warehouses full of property transfers, tax records, corporate filings, environmental compliance audits, restaurant inspections, building maintenance reports, mass transit appraisals, crime data, health department stats, public education records, utility reviews, and more. Municipalities are adding more data captured through sensors, location data from mobile phones, and targeted smartphone apps. Predictive modeling programs now inform public policy decisions on utility management, transportation operation, healthcare delivery, and public safety. What's more, the ability to evaluate how changes in one service affect the operation and delivery of other services enables holistic problem solving that could only be dreamed of a generation ago.

Operational Intelligence and Analytics

Many decisions deal with how to run the business of these cities on a day-to-day basis. These are largely operational decisions, and this type of business activity monitoring is called **operational intelligence**. An example of operational intelligence is the use of data generated by sensors on trucks, trailers, and intermodal containers owned by Schneider National, one of North America's largest truckload, logistics, and intermodal services providers. The sensors monitor location, driving behaviors, fuel levels, and whether a trailer or container is

TABLE 12.5 WHAT BIG DATA ANALYTICS CAN DO

Bank of America	Able to analyze all of its 50 million customers at once to understand each customer across all channels and interactions and present consistent, finely customized offers. Can determine which of its customers has a credit card or a mortgage loan that could benefit from refinancing at a competitor. When the customer visits BofA online, calls a call center, or visits a branch, that information is available for the online app or sales associate to present BofA's competing offer.
Vestas Wind Systems	Improves wind turbine placement for optimal energy output using IBM BigInsights software and an IBM "Firestorm" supercomputer to analyze 2.8 petabytes of structured and unstructured data such as weather reports, tidal phases, geospatial and sensor data, satellite images, deforestation maps, and weather modeling research. The analysis, which used to take weeks, can now be completed in less than one hour.
Hunch.com	Analyzes massive database with data from customer purchases, social networks, and signals from around the web to produce a "taste graph" that maps users with their predicted affinity to products, services, and websites. The taste graph includes predictions about 500 million people, 200 million objects (videos, gadgets, books), and 30 billion connections between people and objects. Helps eBay develop more finely customized recommendations on items to offer.
Actian	Provides Fidelity National Information Services and other financial companies with platform to run fraud analytics against 440,000 ATMs, supporting 95 million cards and more than 2 million point-of-sale locations.

INTERACTIVE SESSION: TECHNOLOGY

The Tension Between Technology and Human Decision Makers

Big data and analytics have swept the business world, and the professional sports industry is no exception. Baseball, football, soccer, hockey, tennis, and even sailboat racing are finding ways to analyze data about players and competing teams in order to improve performance. Baseball has its own statistical analysis discipline called sabermetrics, first popularized in the popular book and film *Moneyball*.

Given the huge disparities in Major League Baseball (MLB) team budgets, wealthier teams typically have the advantage in recruiting the best players. *Moneyball* describes how Oakland Athletics manager Billy Beane was able to turn the underdog A's into a winning team by using advanced analytics to guide decisions about which players to recruit and cultivate. Rigorous statistical analysis had demonstrated that on-base percentage and slugging percentage were better indicators of offensive success (and cheaper to obtain on the open market) than more historically valued qualities such as speed and contact. These observations often flew in the face of conventional baseball wisdom and the beliefs of many baseball talent scouts and coaches. Beane rebuilt the A's based on these findings, producing a consistently winning team for a number of years by using advanced analytics to gain insights into each player's value and contribution to team success that wealthier teams had overlooked.

Beane and his data-driven approach to baseball had a seismic impact on the game. After observing the A's phenomenal success in 2002, the Boston Red Sox adopted Beane's strategy, only with more money. Two years later, they won the World Series. To varying degrees, every Major League Baseball team today uses data and deep analytics to support decisions about many aspects of the game.

Nevertheless, some teams are not fully committed to using sabermetrics to drive their decisions. Many baseball experts continue to believe that traditional methods of player evaluation, along with gut instinct, money, and luck, are still key ingredients for winning teams. Take the San Francisco Giants, for example, who have won more games and have more outstanding players in the Baseball Hall of Fame than any team in U.S. baseball history. The Giants use statistics but also base their player recruitment decisions on the opinions of scouts and coaches.

According to Giants bench coach Ron Wotus, numbers really can't tell the whole story about the quality of the player. So the Giants integrate statistical data with scouting, coaching, and player experience, especially when dealing with opponents outside the National League the Giants do not see regularly. Being able to exploit an individual player's strengths comes more from knowing the player and his ability as opposed to the statistics, Wotus believes. Shortstops with good arms can play farther from home plate than normal at times, while fast runners can play closer to home plate than usual. There are nuances to defending the opposition that are not statistically related, but statistics help when you don't know players well enough to know what to expect from them. The instinct of the player and what the player is seeing on the field often override the statistical information.

Another example of the tension between human- and data-driven decisions comes from the 34th America's Cup race pitting Oracle Team USA against Emirates Team New Zealand in October 2013. This was the most high-tech sailboat race in history. Decisions about how to sail the boats were based on a continual stream of data from the boats, which were 72-foot twin-hull catamarans capable of speeds exceeding 50 miles per hour. Controlling these wickedly sleek sailing machines required a lightning-fast collection of massive amounts of data, powerful data management, rapid real-time data analysis, quick decision making, and immediate measurement of the results. For Team USA, this meant using 250 sensors on the wing, hull, and rudder to gather real-time data on pressure, angles, loads, and strains to monitor the effectiveness of each adjustment. The sensors tracked 4,000 variables, 10 times a second, producing 90 million data points an hour, which were transmitted on a wireless network to crew member wrist displays. The data were wirelessly transferred to a tender ship running Oracle 11g database management software for nearly real-time analysis using velocity prediction formulas geared to understanding what makes the boat go fast and also to Oracle's Austin data center for more in-depth analysis. Each USA crew member wore a small mobile handheld computer on his wrist to display data on the key performance variables customized for that person's responsibilities. The captain and tactician had data displayed on their sunglasses. In this way, each crew member instantly received the data he needed to perform his job. The crew was trained to sail like pilots looking at instruments rather than sailors looking at the boat and sea for clues.

Despite all the advanced technology and detailed data to guide decision making, Team USA lost seven races in a row. The sailors and engineers disagreed about what to do. The engineers called for boat modifications, while the sailors called for more attention to be paid to sailing and less attention to monitoring their wrist computers. The engineers' software program had instructed Team USA to sail as close as possible to wind on the upwind legs (about 45 degrees to the wind), but the sailors' observations of the actual races suggested New Zealand was winning because it sailed five degrees off the wind at about 50 degrees, sailing a longer but faster upwind course. The difference was seconds per mile, which, all other things

being equal, adds up to victory in a 12-mile race. The sailors claimed the engineers' software was just wrong. Team USA pursued both solutions: multiple small changes were made in the boat hull and underwater foils, and on the race course Captain James Spithill and his team stopped looking so much at their wrist computer screens and started to act like sailors. Team USA won every upwind leg of the last eight races. Competitive sailboat racing is still not ready to rely totally on computers.

Sources: Dennis McCafferty, "8 Ways Technology Has Changed Sports," *Baseline*, May 23, 2016; Christina Kahrl, "How the Giants Use Metrics on D," ESPN.com, March 11, 2015; Allen St. John, "'Moneyball' Makes a Quiet Comeback as Data-Driven Baseball Teams Dominate the MLB Playoffs," *Forbes*, October 15, 2015; Stu Wood, "Against the Wind, One of the Greatest Comebacks in Sports History," *Wall Street Journal*, February 28, 2014; and "America's Cup: Resolving the Tension Between Man and Technology," *Wall Street Journal*, March 3, 2014.

CASE STUDY QUESTIONS

1. How did information technology change the game of baseball and America's Cup sailboat racing? Explain.

2. How did information technology affect decision making at Team USA and the Oakland Athletics? What kinds of decisions changed as the result of using computers?

3. How much was technology responsible for Team USA's America's Cup victory?

4. How much does baseball rely on sabermetrics? Explain your answer.

loaded or empty. Data from fuel tank sensors help Schneider identify the optimal location at which a driver should stop for fuel based on how much is left in the tank, the truck's destination, and fuel prices en route. The chapter-ending case describes how General Electric (GE) is using operational intelligence to monitor and analyze the performance of generators, jet engines, locomotives, and oil-refining gear and to connect these devices to the cloud.

The Internet of Things is creating huge streams of data from web activities, smartphones, sensors, gauges, and monitoring devices that can be used for operational intelligence about activities inside and outside the organization. Software for operational intelligence and analytics enables organizations to analyze these streams of big data as they are generated in real time. Companies can set trigger alerts on events or have them fed into live dashboards to help managers with their decisions. For example, Schneider's sensors capture hard braking in a moving truck and relay the data to corporate headquarters, where the data are tracked in dashboards monitoring safety metrics. The event initiates a conversation between the driver and that person's supervisor.

Another example of operational intelligence is the use of real-time data in the 34th America's Cup race as described in the Interactive Session on Technology. This case also looks at the use of big data analytics in baseball. As you read this case, try to determine the extent to which information technology was able to replace human decision makers.

Location Analytics and Geographic Information Systems

Data and decisions are also based on location data. BI analytics include **location analytics**, the ability to gain business insight from the location (geographic) component of data, including location data from mobile phones, output from sensors or scanning devices, and data from maps. For example, location analytics might help a marketer determine which people to target with mobile ads about nearby restaurants and stores or quantify the impact of mobile ads on in-store visits. Location analytics would help a utility company view and measure outages and their associated costs as related to customer location to help prioritize marketing, system upgrades, and customer service efforts. UPS's package tracking and delivery-routing systems described in Chapter 1 use location analytics, as does an application used by Starbucks to determine where to open new stores described in the Interactive Session on Management.

The Starbucks application is an example of a **geographic information system (GIS)**. GIS provide tools to help decision makers visualize problems that benefit from mapping. GIS software ties location data about the distribution of people or other resources to points, lines, and areas on a map. Some GIS have modeling capabilities for changing the data and automatically revising business scenarios.

GIS might be used to help state and local governments calculate response times to natural disasters and other emergencies, to help banks identify the best location for new branches or ATM terminals, or to help police forces pinpoint locations with the highest incidence of crime.

Management Strategies for Developing BI and BA Capabilities

There are two different strategies for adopting BI and BA capabilities for the organization: one-stop integrated solutions versus multiple best-of-breed vendor solutions. The hardware firms (IBM, HP, and now Oracle, which owns

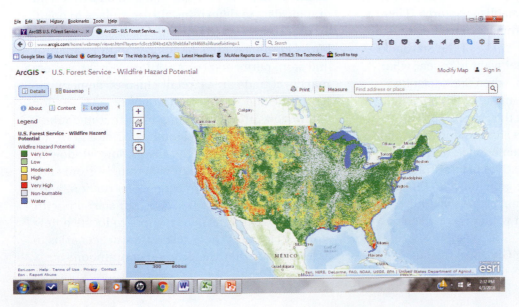

The U.S. Forest Service and Fire Modeling Institute created this map of Wildfire Hazard Potential (WHP) to assess wildfire risk and for prioritization of fuels management needs across large landscapes.

INTERACTIVE SESSION: MANAGEMENT

Data Drive Starbucks Location Decisions

One of the keys to success for national restaurant and beverage chains is identifying the right location for new stores and franchises. Where merchants place their stores plays an outsized role in determining whether their chains fly or flop. Proximity to customers and large-enough numbers of customers are key. Retailers need to know where their potential customers are and where they will be over the 10- to 25-year lifetime of the investment they make in a new physical space. Let us look at how information technology helped Starbucks deal with this problem.

Geographic information systems (GIS) play an important role at Starbucks for both site selection and product placement. Starbucks is America's most recognizable coffee company and the largest coffeehouse company in the world, operating 23,921 cafes today. For years, Starbucks has continued to grow throughout the United States and internationally, opening franchises at an extremely rapid rate—as many as 800 per year. The company had tripled the number of stores it operated worldwide, from 5,886 in 2002 to 15,011 in 2007. It was forced to close 600 stores during the 2008 economic downturn but began adding many new locations as business improved.

The challenge for this company lies not so much in penetrating new overseas markets as it is in delivering solid growth in more saturated markets. And saturated markets don't come more laden with Starbucks stores than the United States. There are risks: improperly situated, new stores could easily cannibalize sales of more established stores. There's also the possibility that Starbucks stores become too commonplace and consumers tire of the Starbucks brand. Management does not want to repeat what happened in 2007 and 2008, when Starbucks had to close hundreds of stores, many of which should never have been opened in the first place. The majority of Starbucks stores shuttered in 2007 and 2008 were ones that had been opened in the previous 18 months. At that time Starbucks's strategy focused on accelerating the growth of its U.S. business. It appeared to be opening stores just for the sake of opening them, even where there wasn't a profitable opportunity.

Starbucks has been using GIS since the late 1990s. The company was using GIS technology to support its 2007–2008 decision to open so many stores that were subsequently closed. Starbucks decision makers were inundated with data, especially the decision makers working with real estate. At that time Starbucks staff had access to massive amounts of data but lacked sufficient expertise and tools to analyze the data properly.

So many store closings helped convince Starbucks senior management of the need for a data-driven, disciplined approach to store-opening decisions. When Starbucks tried again to open a series of new stores in 2011 and 2012, the results were very different. The stores opened during that time produced some of the best unit economics in the history of the company, with a sales-to-investment ratio of 2:1, very strong compound growth, and average per-store volumes at record levels. New U.S. stores were delivering first-year sales of $1,052,000 compared with a target of $900,000, and the stores cost on average $494,000 to build (the 2:1 sales-to-investment result). Starbucks is continuing to grow its U.S. business, with plans to open at least 1,500 new stores by 2017 in the United States alone. With more experienced and sophisticated use of GIS, management strongly believes the new additions to the Starbucks chain will produce returns that mirror those of 2011 and 2012.

Starbucks now uses a market planning and store development application called Atlas powered by software from ESRI, a leading vendor of GIS and location analytics systems. The software analyzes massive amounts of location-based data and demographic data to determine the best place to open Starbucks stores without hurting sales at other Starbucks locations. Atlas handles workflow, analysis, and store performance. An Atlas user can see on a map local trade areas, retail clusters, demographics, traffic and transportation nodes, and locations where new offices are being built that might be important sources of customers. After adding a new target area, Atlas provides a workflow window to help the user move the new Starbucks store site through approval, permitting, construction, and opening. Starbucks real estate staff start out with certain assumptions about where to locate a new store; Atlas helps them test different scenarios to ascertain whether the original assumptions are correct.

Starbucks also uses GIS to analyze where its customers spend more money than average on coffee purchases to support decisions on where to install its high-end Clover Brewing System, which brews one cup of coffee at a time at a precise temperature and length of time to create exceptionally flavorful coffee.

Starbucks staff members can access GIS information from desktops, the Internet, and mobile devices. The company's focus now is on the profitability of individual stores, and it is pinpointing stores, including smaller stores and drive-throughs, in locations that are more convenient for customers. Management doesn't want Starbucks growing for the sake of growing and looks much more carefully at the individual profitability prospects of each newly opened

store. It no longer assumes that just because stores are Starbucks, they can succeed anywhere.

According to Rob Sopkin, Starbucks vice president of Store Development–East, every decision about opening a store represents about a $1 million investment for Starbucks. Although one would think that a few underperforming stores wouldn't matter that much, one poor decision will negate five good decisions.

Sources: Carla Wheeler, "Going Big with GIS," www.esri.com, accessed May 14, 2016; "Starbucks: 1 Store = $1 Million Investment and GIS Helps Get It Right," *Directions Magazine*, www.directions-mag.com, accessed May 14, 2016; www.sonicdrivein.com, accessed May 14, 2016; Samuel Greengard, "Sonic Chain Gets a Taste of Geospatial Analytics," *Baseline*, November 20, 2015; and Barbara Thau, "How Big Data Helps Chains Like Starbucks Pick Store Locations—An (Unsung) Key to Retail Success," *Forbes*, April 24, 2014.

CASE STUDY QUESTIONS

1. How important is location data to Starbucks's business strategy? Explain your answer.
2. How do location analytics help Starbucks managers make better decisions? Give examples of two decisions that the Atlas system helps support.
3. Compare Starbucks decisions about store location in 2007–2008 and 2012. What made the later

decisions more successful? What management, organization, and technology factors were involved?
4. What is the value to Starbucks of a good decision about where to open a Starbucks store? Explain your answer.

Sun Microsystems) want to sell your firm integrated hardware/software solutions that tend to run only on their hardware (the totally integrated solution). It's called "one-stop shopping." The software firms (SAP, SAS, and Microsoft) encourage firms to adopt the "best-of-breed" software that runs on any machine they want. In this strategy, you adopt the best database and data warehouse solution, and select the business intelligence and analytics package from whatever vendor you believe is best.

The first solution carries the risk that a single vendor provides your firm's total hardware and software solution, making your firm dependent on its pricing power. However, it offers the advantage of dealing with a single vendor who can deliver on a global scale. The second solution offers greater flexibility and independence, but with the risk of potential difficulties integrating the software to the hardware platform, as well as to other software. Vendors always claim their software is "compatible" with other software, but the reality is that it can be very difficult to integrate software from different vendors.

Regardless of which strategy your firm adopts, all BI and BA systems lock the firm into a set of vendors and switching is very costly. Once you train thousands of employees across the world on using a particular set of tools, it is extremely difficult to switch. When you adopt these systems, you are in essence taking in a new partner.

12-4 How do different decision-making constituencies in an organization use business intelligence, and what is the role of information systems in helping people working in a group make decisions more efficiently?

Earlier in this text and in this chapter, we described the different information constituencies in business firms—from senior managers to middle managers, analysts, and operational employees. This also holds true for BI and BA systems (see Figure 12.4). More than 80 percent of the audience for BI consists of casual users who rely largely on production reports. Senior executives tend to use BI to monitor firm activities using visual interfaces like dashboards and scorecards. Middle managers and analysts are much more likely to be immersed in the data and software, entering queries and slicing and dicing the data along different dimensions. Operational employees will, along with customers and suppliers, be looking mostly at prepackaged reports.

Decision Support for Operational And Middle Management

Operational and middle management are generally charged with monitoring the performance of key aspects of the business, ranging from the downtime of machines on a factory floor to the daily or even hourly sales at franchise food stores to the daily traffic at a company's website. Most of the decisions these managers make are fairly structured. Management information systems (MIS), which we introduced in Chapter 2, are typically used by middle managers to support this type of decision making. Increasingly, middle managers receive these reports online and are able to interactively query the data to find out why events are happening. Managers at this level often turn to exception reports, which highlight only exceptional conditions, such as when the sales quotas for

FIGURE 12.4 BUSINESS INTELLIGENCE USERS

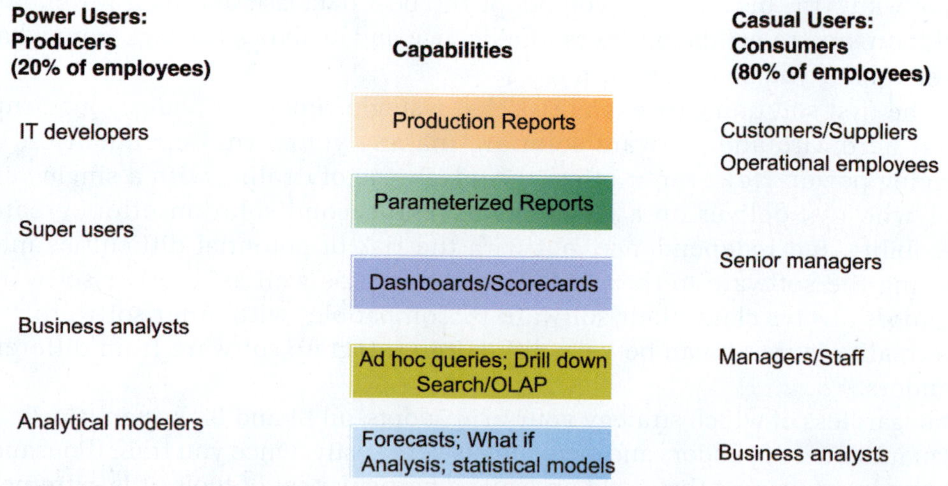

Power Users: Producers (20% of employees)	Capabilities	Casual Users: Consumers (80% of employees)
IT developers	Production Reports	Customers/Suppliers Operational employees
Super users	Parameterized Reports	
	Dashboards/Scorecards	Senior managers
Business analysts	Ad hoc queries; Drill down Search/OLAP	Managers/Staff
Analytical modelers	Forecasts; What if Analysis; statistical models	Business analysts

Casual users are consumers of BI output, while intense power users are the producers of reports, new analyses, models, and forecasts.

TABLE 12.6 EXAMPLES OF MIS APPLICATIONS

COMPANY	MIS APPLICATION
California Pizza Kitchen	Inventory Express application "remembers" each restaurant's ordering patterns and compares the amount of ingredients used per menu item to predefined portion measurements established by management. The system identifies restaurants with out-of-line portions and notifies their managers so that corrective actions will be taken.
Black & Veatch	Intranet MIS tracks construction costs for various projects across the United States.
Taco Bell	Total Automation of Company Operations (TACO) system provides information on food, labor, and period-to-date costs for each restaurant.

a specific territory fall below an anticipated level or employees have exceeded their spending limits in a dental care plan. Table 12.6 provides some examples of MIS for business intelligence.

Support for Semi-structured Decisions

Some managers are "super users" and keen business analysts who want to create their own reports and use more sophisticated analytics and models to find patterns in data, to model alternative business scenarios, or to test specific hypotheses. Decision-support systems (DSS) are the BI delivery platform for this category of users, with the ability to support semi-structured decision making.

DSS rely more heavily on modeling than MIS, using mathematical or analytical models to perform what-if or other kinds of analysis. "What-if" analysis, working forward from known or assumed conditions, allows the user to vary certain values to test results to predict outcomes if changes occur in those values. What happens if we raise product prices by 5 percent or increase the advertising budget by $1 million? **Sensitivity analysis** models ask what-if questions repeatedly to predict a range of outcomes when one or more variables are changed multiple times (see Figure 12.5). Backward sensitivity analysis helps decision makers with goal seeking: If I want to sell 1 million product units next year, how much must I reduce the price of the product?

FIGURE 12.5 SENSITIVITY ANALYSIS

Total fixed costs	19000					
Variable cost per unit	3					
Average sales price	17					
Contribution margin	14					
Break-even point	1357					
				Variable Cost per Unit		
Sales	1357	2	3	4	5	6
Price	14	1583	1727	1900	2111	2375
	15	1462	1583	1727	1900	2111
	16	1357	1462	1583	1727	1900
	17	1267	1357	1462	1583	1727
	18	1188	1267	1357	1462	1583

This table displays the results of a sensitivity analysis of the effect of changing the sales price of a necktie and the cost per unit on the product's break-even point. It answers the question "What happens to the break-even point if the sales price and the cost to make each unit increase or decrease?"

Chapter 6 described multidimensional data analysis and OLAP as key business intelligence technologies. Spreadsheets have a similar feature for multidimensional analysis called a **pivot table**, which manager "super users" and analysts employ to identify and understand patterns in business information that may be useful for semi-structured decision making.

Figure 12.6 illustrates a Microsoft Excel pivot table that examines a large list of order transactions for a company selling online management training videos and books. It shows the relationship between two dimensions: the sales region and the source of contact (web banner ad or e-mail) for each customer order. It answers the question: Does the source of the customer make a difference in addition to region? The pivot table in this figure shows that most customers come from the West and that banner advertising produces most of the customers in all the regions.

One of the Hands-On MIS projects for this chapter asks you to use a pivot table to find answers to a number of other questions using the same list of transactions for the online training company as we used in this discussion. The complete Excel file for these transactions is available in MyMISLab. We have also added a Learning Track on creating pivot tables using Excel.

In the past, much of this modeling was done with spreadsheets and small stand-alone databases. Today these capabilities are incorporated into large enterprise BI systems where they are able to analyze data from large corporate databases. BI analytics include tools for intensive modeling, some of which we described earlier. Such capabilities help Progressive Insurance identify the best customers for its products. Using widely available insurance industry data, Progressive defines small groups of customers, or "cells," such as motorcycle riders age 30 or above with college educations, credit scores over a certain level, and no accidents. For each "cell," Progressive performs a regression analysis to identify factors most closely

FIGURE 12.6 A PIVOT TABLE THAT EXAMINES CUSTOMER REGIONAL DISTRIBUTION AND ADVERTISING SOURCE

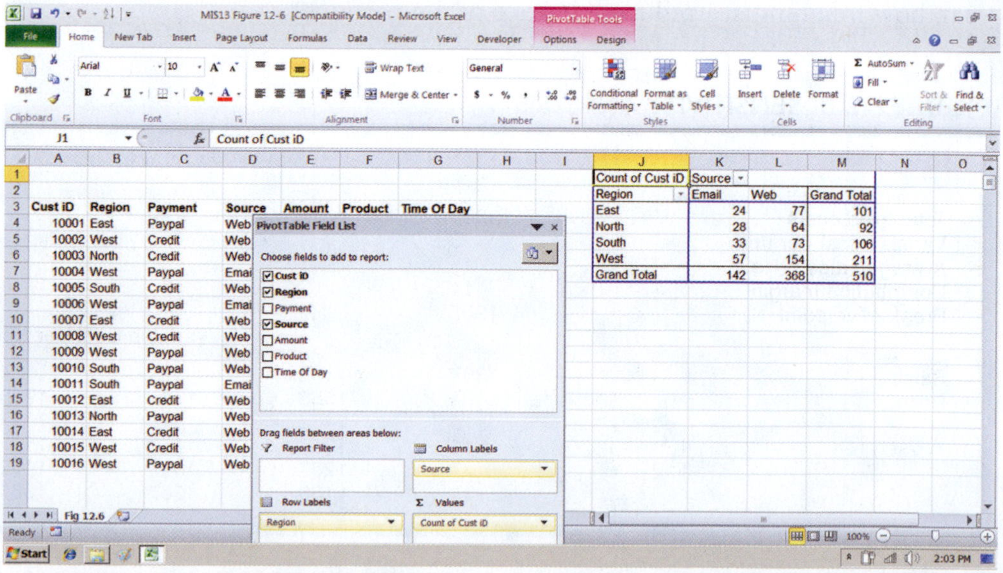

In this pivot table, we are able to examine where an online training company's customers come from in terms of region and advertising source.

Chapter 12 Enhancing Decision Making   **475**

correlated with the insurance losses that are typical for this group. It then sets prices for each cell and uses simulation software to test whether this pricing arrangement will enable the company to make a profit. These analytic techniques make it possible for Progressive to profitably insure customers in traditionally high-risk categories that other insurers would have rejected.

Decision Support for Senior Management: Balanced Scorecard and Enterprise Performance Management Methods

The purpose of executive support systems (ESS), introduced in Chapter 2, is to help C-level executive managers focus on the really important performance information that affects the overall profitability and success of the firm. There are two parts to developing ESS. First, you will need a methodology for understanding exactly what is "the really important performance information" for a specific firm that executives need, and second, you will need to develop systems capable of delivering this information to the right people in a timely fashion.

Currently, the leading methodology for understanding the really important information needed by a firm's executives is called the **balanced scorecard method** (Kaplan and Norton, 1992, 2004). The balanced scorecard is a framework for operationalizing a firm's strategic plan by focusing on measurable outcomes on four dimensions of firm performance: financial, business process, customer, and learning and growth (Figure 12.7).

FIGURE 12.7 THE BALANCED SCORECARD FRAMEWORK

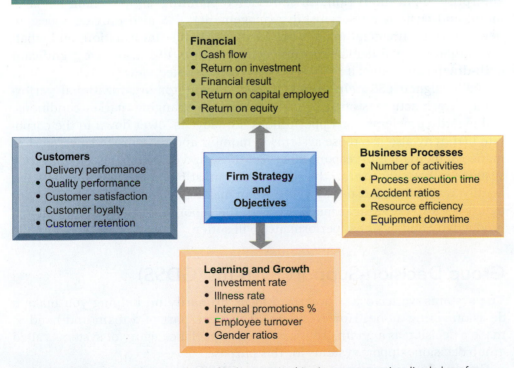

In the balanced scorecard framework, the firm's strategic objectives are operationalized along four dimensions: financial, business process, customer, and learning and growth. Each dimension is measured using several KPIs.

Performance on each dimension is measured using **key performance indicators (KPIs)**, which are the measures proposed by senior management for understanding how well the firm is performing along any given dimension. For instance, one key indicator of how well an online retail firm is meeting its customer performance objectives is the average length of time required to deliver a package to a consumer. If your firm is a bank, one KPI of business process performance is the length of time required to perform a basic function like creating a new customer account.

The balanced scorecard framework is thought to be "balanced" because it causes managers to focus on more than just financial performance. In this view, financial performance is past history—the result of past actions—and managers should focus on the things they are able to influence today, such as business process efficiency, customer satisfaction, and employee training. Once a scorecard is developed by consultants and senior executives, the next step is automating a flow of information to executives and other managers for each of the key performance indicators. There are literally hundreds of consulting and software firms that offer these capabilities, which are described below. Once these systems are implemented, they are often referred to as ESS.

Another closely related popular management methodology is **business performance management (BPM)**. Originally defined by an industry group in 2004 (led by the same companies that sell enterprise and database systems like Oracle, SAP, and IBM), BPM attempts to systematically translate a firm's strategies (e.g., differentiation, low-cost producer, market share growth, and scope of operation) into operational targets. Once the strategies and targets are identified, a set of KPIs are developed that measure progress toward the targets. The firm's performance is then measured with information drawn from the firm's enterprise database systems. BPM uses the same ideas as the balanced scorecard but with a stronger strategy flavor.

Corporate data for contemporary ESS are supplied by the firm's existing enterprise applications (enterprise resource planning, supply chain management, and customer relationship management). ESS also provide access to news services, financial market databases, economic information, and whatever other external data senior executives require. ESS also have significant **drill-down** capabilities if managers need more detailed views of data.

Well-designed ESS help senior executives monitor organizational performance, track activities of competitors, recognize changing market conditions, and identify problems and opportunities. Employees lower down in the corporate hierarchy also use these systems to monitor and measure business performance in their areas of responsibility. For these and other business intelligence systems to be truly useful, the information must be "actionable"—it must be readily available and also easy to use when making decisions. If users have difficulty identifying critical metrics within the reports they receive, employee productivity and business performance will suffer.

Group Decision-Support Systems (GDSS)

The systems we have just described focus primarily on helping you make a decision acting alone. However, what if you are part of a team and need to make a decision as a group? You would use a special category of systems called group decision-support systems for this purpose.

Group decision-support systems (GDSS) are interactive computer-based systems that facilitate the solution of unstructured problems by a set of decision makers working together as a group in the same location or in different locations. Originally, GDSS required dedicated conference rooms with special hardware and software tools for documenting and ranking ideas. GDSS capabilities have evolved along with the power of desktop PCs, the explosion of mobile computing, and the rapid expansion of bandwidth on Wi-Fi and cellular networks. Dedicated rooms for collaboration can be replaced with much less expensive and flexible virtual collaboration rooms that can connect mobile employees with colleagues in the office sitting at desktops in a high-quality video and audio environment. We introduced some of these contemporary collaboration environments in Chapter 2.

Cisco's Collaboration Meeting Rooms Hybrid (CMR) allows groups of employees to meet using any device via WebEx video software, which does not require any special network connections, special displays, or complex software. The software to run CMR can be hosted on company servers or in the cloud. This allows even customers to participate in group meetings. The meetings can be scheduled by employees whenever needed. CMR can handle up to 500 participants in a meeting, but that is quite rare. Skype began deploying a similar cloud-based collaboration environment called Skype for Business to support online meetings, sharing of documents, audio, and video. Skype for Business is integrated into Microsoft Office 365, which will make Skype for Business an integral part of office life in the near future.

Review Summary

12-1 *What are the different types of decisions, and how does the decision-making process work?*

The different levels in an organization (strategic, management, operational) have different decision-making requirements. Decisions can be structured, semi-structured, or unstructured, with structured decisions clustering at the operational level of the organization and unstructured decisions at the strategic level. Decision making can be performed by individuals or groups and includes employees as well as operational, middle, and senior managers. There are four stages in decision making: intelligence, design, choice, and implementation.

12-2 *How do information systems support the activities of managers and management decision making?*

Early classical models of managerial activities stress the functions of planning, organizing, coordinating, deciding, and controlling. Contemporary research looking at the actual behavior of managers has found that managers' real activities are highly fragmented, variegated, and brief in duration and that managers shy away from making grand, sweeping policy decisions.

Information technology provides new tools for managers to carry out both their traditional and newer roles, enabling them to monitor, plan, and forecast with more precision and speed than ever before and to respond more rapidly to the changing business environment. Information systems have been most helpful to managers by providing support for their roles in disseminating information, providing liaisons between organizational levels, and allocating resources. However, information systems are less successful at supporting unstructured decisions. Where information systems are useful, information quality, management filters, and organizational culture can degrade decision making.

12-3 *How do business intelligence and business analytics support decision making?*

Business intelligence and analytics promise to deliver correct, nearly real-time information to decision makers, and the analytic tools help them quickly understand the information and take action. A business intelligence environment consists of data from the business environment, the BI infrastructure, a BA toolset, managerial users and methods, a BI delivery platform (MIS, DSS, or ESS), and the user interface. There are six analytic functionalities that BI systems deliver to achieve these ends: predefined production reports, parameterized reports, dashboards and scorecards, ad hoc queries and searches, the ability to drill down to detailed views of data, and the ability to model scenarios and create forecasts.

12-4 *How do different decision-making constituencies in an organization use business intelligence, and what is the role of information systems in helping people working in a group make decisions more efficiently?*
Operational and middle management are generally charged with monitoring the performance of their firm. Most of the decisions they make are fairly structured. Management information systems (MIS) producing routine production reports are typically used to support this type of decision making. For making unstructured decisions, middle managers and analysts will use decision-support systems (DSS) with powerful analytics and modeling tools, including spreadsheets and pivot tables. Senior executives making unstructured decisions use dashboards and visual interfaces displaying key performance information affecting the overall profitability, success, and strategy of the firm. The balanced scorecard and business performance management are two methodologies used in designing executive support systems (ESS). Group decision-support systems (GDSS) help people working together in a group arrive at decisions more efficiently.

Key Terms

Balanced scorecard method, 475	Intelligence, 457
Behavioral models, 459	Interpersonal role, 459
Business performance management (BPM), 476	Key performance indicators (KPIs), 476
Choice, 457	Managerial roles, 459
Classical model of management, 459	Location analytics, 469
Data visualization, 464	Operational intelligence, 466
Decisional role, 459	Pivot table, 474
Design, 457	Predictive analytics, 465
Drill down, 476	Semi-structured decisions, 456
Geographic information systems (GIS), 469	Sensitivity analysis, 473
Group decision-support systems (GDSS), 476	Structured decisions, 456
Implementation, 457	Unstructured decisions, 456
Informational role, 459	

MyMISLab

To complete the problems with the MyMISLab, go to the EOC Discussion Questions in MyMISLab.

Review Questions

12-1 What are the different types of decisions, and how does the decision-making process work?

- List and describe the different levels of decision making and decision-making constituencies in organizations. Explain how their decision-making requirements differ.
- Distinguish between an unstructured, semi-structured, and structured decision.
- List and describe the stages in decision making.

12-2 How do information systems support the activities of managers and management decision making?

- Compare the descriptions of managerial behavior in the classical and behavioral models.
- Identify the specific managerial roles that can be supported by information systems.

12-3 How do business intelligence and business analytics support decision making?

- Define and describe business intelligence and business analytics.

- List and describe the elements of a business intelligence environment.
- List and describe the analytic functionalities provided by BI systems.
- Compare two different management strategies for developing BI and BA capabilities.

12-4 How do different decision-making constituencies in an organization use business intelligence, and what is the role of information systems in helping people working in a group make decisions more efficiently?

- List each of the major decision-making constituencies in an organization and describe the types of decisions each makes.
- Describe how MIS, DSS, or ESS provide decision support for each of these groups.
- Define and describe the balanced scorecard method and business performance management.
- Define a group decision-support system (GDSS) and explain how it differs from a DSS.

Discussion Questions

12-5 MyMISLab As a manager or user of information systems, what would you need to know to participate in the design and use of a DSS or an ESS? Why?

12-6 MyMISLab If businesses used DSS, GDSS, and ESS more widely, would managers and employees make better decisions? Why or why not?

12-7 MyMISLab How much can business intelligence and business analytics help companies refine their business strategy? Explain your answer.

Hands-On MIS Projects

The projects in this section give you hands-on experience identifying opportunities for DSS, using a spreadsheet pivot table to analyze sales data, and using online retirement planning tools for financial planning. Visit MyMISLab's Multimedia Library to access this chapter's Hands-On MIS Projects.

Management Decision Problems

12-8 Dealerships for Subaru and other automobile manufacturers keep records of the mileage of cars they sell and service. Mileage data are used to remind customers of when they need to schedule service appointments, but they are used for other purposes as well. What kinds of decisions does this piece of data support at the local level and at the corporate level? What would happen if this piece of data were erroneous, for example, showing mileage of 130,000 instead of 30,000? How would it affect decision making? Assess its business impact.

12-9 Applebee's is the largest casual dining chain in the world, with more than 1,800 locations throughout the United States and also in 20 other countries. The menu features beef, chicken, and pork items as well as burgers, pasta, and seafood. Applebee's CEO wants to make the restaurant more profitable by developing menus that are tastier and contain more items that customers want and are willing to pay for despite rising costs for gasoline and agricultural products. How might business intelligence help management implement this strategy? What pieces of data would Applebee's need to collect? What kinds of reports would be useful to help management make decisions on how to improve menus and profitability?

Improving Decision Making: Using Pivot Tables to Analyze Sales Data

Software skills: Pivot tables
Business skills: Analyzing sales data

12-10 This project gives you an opportunity to learn how to use Excel's PivotTable feature to analyze a database or data list. Use the data file for Online Management Training Inc. described earlier in the chapter. This is a list of the sales transactions at OMT for one day. You can find this spreadsheet file at MyMISLab. Use Excel's PivotTable to help you answer the following questions:

- Where are the average purchases higher? The answer might tell managers where to focus marketing and sales resources, or pitch different messages to different regions.
- What form of payment is the most common? The answer could be used to emphasize in advertising the most preferred means of payment.
- Are there any times of day when purchases are most common? Do people buy more products while at work (likely during the day) or at home (likely in the evening)?
- What's the relationship between region, type of product purchased, and average sales price?

We provide instructions on how to use Excel PivotTables in our Learning Tracks.

Improving Decision Making: Using a Web-Based DSS for Retirement Planning

Software skills: Internet-based software
Business skills: Financial planning

12-11 This project will help develop your skills in using web-based DSS for financial planning.

The websites for CNN Money and Kiplinger feature web-based DSS for financial planning and decision making. Select either site to plan for retirement. Use your chosen site to determine how much you need to save to have enough income for your retirement. Assume that you are 50 years old and single and plan to retire in 17 years. You have $100,000 in savings. Your current annual income is $85,000. Your goal is to be able to generate an annual retirement income of $60,000, including social security benefit payments.

Use the website you have selected to determine how much money you need to save to help you achieve your retirement goal. If you need to calculate your estimated social security benefit, use the Quick Calculator at the Social Security Administration website

Critique the site—its ease of use, its clarity, the value of any conclusions reached, and the extent to which the site helps investors understand their financial needs and the financial markets.

Collaboration and Teamwork Project

Investigating Data-Driven Analytics in Sports

12-12 With three or four of your classmates, select a sport, such as football, baseball, basketball, or soccer. Use the web to research how the sport uses data and analytics to improve team performance or increase ticket sales to events. If possible, use Google Docs and Google Drive or Google Sites to brainstorm, organize, and develop a presentation of your findings for the class.

GE Bets on the Internet of Things and Big Data Analytics
CASE STUDY

General Electric (GE) is one of the world's largest industrial companies with products ranging from turbines to jet engines to medical equipment, but it may not be much longer. The company is transitioning to a much more technology-centric business strategy and business model. GE is selling off its division that makes refrigerators and microwave ovens along with most of GE Capital financial services to focus on electric power generators, jet engines, locomotives, and oil-refining gear and software to connect these devices to the cloud. Leading software companies such Oracle, SAP, and Microsoft have traditionally been focused on providing technology for the back office. In contrast, GE is putting its money on the technology that controls and monitors industrial machines as well as software-powered, cloud-based services for analyzing and deriving value from the data. GE hopes this strategy will turn it into a major software company.

GE is using sensor-generated data from industrial machines to help customers monitor equipment performance, prevent breakdowns, and assess the machines' overall health. This new technology is opening new opportunities for GE customers while also helping to transform GE from a traditional manufacturer to a modern digital business. GE has committed $1 billion to installing sensors on gas turbines, jet engines, and other machines; connecting them to the cloud; and analyzing the resulting data to identify ways to improve machine productivity and reliability. In other words, GE is betting its future on software and the Internet of Things (IoT).

In a number of industries, improving the productivity of existing assets by even a single percentage point can generate significant benefits. This is true of the oil and gas sector, where average recovery rate of an oil well is 35 percent. That means 65 percent of a well's potential is left in the earth because available technology makes it too expensive to extract. If technology can help oil extraction companies raise the recovery rate from 35 to 36 percent, the world's output will increase by 80 billion barrels—the equivalent of three years of global supply.

The oil and gas industry is also deeply affected by unplanned downtime, when equipment cannot operate because of a malfunction. A single unproductive day on a platform can cost a liquified natural gas (LNG) facility as much as $25 million, and an average midsized LNG facility experiences about five down days a year. That's $125 to $150 million lost. Minimizing downtime is critical, especially considering declining revenues from lower energy prices. GE sees a $1 billion opportunity for its IoT software.

The foundation for all of GE's Industrial Internet (IoT) applications is Predix, a software platform launched in 2015 to collect data from industrial sensors and analyze the information in the cloud. Predix can run on any cloud infrastructure. The platform has open standards and protocols that allow customers to more easily and quickly connect their machines to the Industrial Internet. The platform can accommodate the size and scale of industrial data for every customer at current levels of use, but it also has been designed to scale up as demand grows. Predix can offer apps developed by other companies as well as GE, is available for on-premises or cloud-based deployment, and can be extended by customers with their own data sources, algorithms, and code. Customers may develop their own custom applications for the Predix platform. GE is also building a developer community to create apps that can be hosted on Predix. Predix is not limited to industrial applications. It could be used for analyzing data in healthcare systems, for example. GE now has a Health Cloud running on Predix. Data security is embedded at all platform application layers, and this is essential for companies linking their operations to the Internet.

GE currently uses Predix to monitor and maintain its own industrial products, such as wind turbines, jet engines, and hydroelectric turbine systems. Predix is able to provide GE corporate customers' machine operators and maintenance engineers with real-time information to schedule maintenance checks, improve machine efficiency, and reduce downtime. Helping customers collect and use this operational data proactively would lower costs in GE service agreements. When GE agrees to provide service for a customer's machine, it often comes with a performance guarantee. Proactive identification of potential issues that also takes the cost out of shop visits helps the customer and helps GE.

In early 2013, GE began to use Predix to analyze data across its fleet of machines. By identifying what made one machine more efficient or downtime-prone than another, GE could more tightly manage its operations. For example, by using high-performance analytics, GE learned that some of its jet aircraft engines were beginning to require more frequent unscheduled maintenance. A single engine's operating data will only tell you there's a problem with that engine. But by collecting massive amounts of data and analyzing the data across its entire fleet of machines, GE was able to cluster engine data by operating environment. The company found that the hot and harsh environments in the Middle East and China caused engines to clog, heat up, and lose efficiency, so they required more maintenance. GE found that engines had far fewer of these problems if they were washed more frequently. Fleet analytics helped GE increase engine lifetime and reduce engine maintenance. The company thinks it can save its customers an average of $7 million of jet airplane fuel annually because their engines will be more efficient. Predix's robust data and analytics platform made it possible for GE to use data across every GE engine all over the world and cluster fleet data.

Predix is starting to provide solutions for GE customers. Irish Power is an early Predix user. The company adopted GE's predictive analytics tool suite Reliability Excellence based on the Predix platform.

Irish Power started out by using operational data analytics to improve the efficiency of its Whitegate plant, a 445-megawatt gas combined-cycle power plant located 25 miles east of the city of Cork, Ireland. Irish Power plans to roll out a module for process optimization and will connect plant performance to the real-time energy marketplace. These analytics help Irish Power and customers identify ways of lowering production costs, increasing plant capability, and improving system reliability. Applying analytics built on the Predix platform can enable GE to offer customers like Irish Power anomaly detection or enable cost savings by reducing the need for preventative maintenance thanks to the visibility of the operational data GE can now provide.

British oil and gas company BP plc had been using its own software to monitor conditions in its oil wells. Recently, however, BP management decided to get out of the software business and became a GE customer. By the end of 2015, BP equipped 650 of its thousands of oil wells with GE sensors linked to Predix. Each well was outfitted with 20 to 30 sensors to measure pressure and temperature, transmitting 500,000 data points to the Predix cloud every 15 seconds. BP hopes to use the data to predict well flows and the useful life of each well and ultimately to obtain an enterprise-wide view of its oil fields' performance.

GE identified pipeline risk management as a major challenge for the oil and gas industry. There are 2 million miles of transmission pipe throughout the globe, moving liquid oil or gas from its point of extraction to refining, processing, or market. About 55 percent of transmission pipeline in the United States was installed before 1970. Pipeline spills are not frequent, but when they occur, they cause serious economic and environmental damage as well as bad publicity for pipeline operators and energy companies. Pipeline operators are always anxious to know where their next rupture will be, but they typically lacked the data to measure pipeline fitness. Operators had no way of integrating multiple sources of data into one place so they could see and understand the risk in their pipelines.

GE developed a pipeline-management software suite for accessing, managing, and integrating critical data for the safe management of pipelines, including a risk assessment tool to monitor aging infrastructure. GE's risk-assessment solution combines internal and external factors (such as flooding) to provide an accurate, up-to-the minute visual representation of where risk exists in a pipeline. This risk assessment tool enables pipeline operators to see how recent events affect their risk and make real-time decisions about where field service crews should be deployed along the pipeline. The risk assessment tool visualization and analytics capabilities run on Predix.

GE is also pulling data from weather systems and dig-reporting services to provide a more comprehensive view of a pipeline network. Weather has a sizable impact on risk for pipelines in areas prone to seismic activity, waterways, and washouts. Checking weather patterns along thousands of miles of pipe for rain or flood zones, and integrating those data with other complex pipeline data sets is very difficult to perform manually. But by bringing all relevant together data in one place, GE gives pipeline operators easier access to information to help them address areas with the greatest potential impact.

GE expects customers to benefit immediately from having all of their data integrated. But it wants them to be able to do more. In addition to being able to examine all current risk, pipeline operators would benefit from a "what-if" calculation tool to model hypothetical scenarios, such as assessing the impact of adjusting operating pressures or addressing particular areas of corrosive pipe. GE would give them the tools for a color-coded view of how those actions affect pipeline risk.

In addition, GE wants to go beyond helping its customers manage the performance of their GE machines to managing the data on all of the machines in their entire operations. Many customers use GE equipment alongside of equipment from competitors. The customer cares about running the whole plant, not just GE turbines, for example, and 80 percent of the equipment in these facilities is not from GE. If, for example, if an oil and gas customer has a problem with a turbo compressor, a heat exchanger upstream from that compressor may be the source of the problem, so analyzing data from the turbo compressor will only tell part of the story. Customers therefore want GE to analyze non-GE equipment and help them keep their entire plant running. GE is in discussions with some customers about managing sensor data from all of the machine assets in their operation.

If a customer purchases a piece of GE equipment such as a gas turbine or aircraft engine, GE often enters into a 10- to 15-year contractual services agreement that allows GE to connect to and monitor that machine, perform basic maintenance and diagnostics, and provide scheduled repairs. GE receives a bonus payment for keeping the equipment running at a specified threshold. GE may now be able to apply such outcome-based pricing to coverage of non-GE machines.

GE CEO Jeffrey Immelt wants GE to become a top 10 software company by 2020. In order to do this, GE needs to sell vast amounts of applications and Predix-based analytics. Although few businesses have the capital or infrastructure to operate a platform for integrating and analyzing their IoT data, GE faces competition from many sources. Amazon, Google, IBM, and Microsoft are all getting into Internet of Things platforms, and dozens of start-ups have similar ambitions. The biggest question is whether other large industrial companies will turn to GE or to another cloud platform to manage their information. And if you're a manufacturer of some size and sophistication, will you allow GE to "own" the data on your business, or will you manage and analyze the data yourself?

Sources: Laura Winig, "GE's Big Bet on Data and Analytics," *MIT Sloan Management Review,* February 2016; Devin Leonard and Rick Clough, "How GE Exorcised the Ghost of Jack Welch to Become a 124-Year-Old Startup," *Bloomberg Businessweek,* March 21, 2016; www.ge.com, accessed May 19, 2016; Holly Lugassy,"GE Leverages Pivotal Cloud Foundry to Build Predix, First Cloud for Industry,"

CloudFoundry.org, May 11, 2016; Kurt Marko, "AWS IoT Platform Connects Devices to Cloud Services," techtarget.com, accessed May 24, 2016; Cliff Saran, "GE Predictive Analytics Optimises Irish Power Electricity Production," *Computer Weekly,* July 13, 2015; Charles Babcock, "GE Predix Cloud: Industrial Support for Machine Data," *Information Week,* August 6, 2015; and "GE: IoT Makes Power Plants $50M More Valuable," *Information Week,* September 29, 2015.

CASE STUDY QUESTIONS

12-13 How is GE changing its business strategy and business model? What is the role of information technology in GE's business?

12-14 On what business functions and level of decision making is GE focusing?

12-15 Describe three kinds of decisions that can be supported using Predix. What is the value to the firm of each of those decisions? Explain.

12-16 To what extent is GE becoming a software company? Explain your answer.

12-17 Do you think GE will become one of the top 10 U.S. software companies? Why or why not?

MyMISLab

Go to the Assignments section of MyMISLab to complete these writing exercises.

12-18 Identify and describe three factors that prevent managers from making good decisions.

12-19 Give three examples of data used in location analytics and explain how each can help businesses.

Chapter 12 References

Bell, Peter C. "Sustaining an Analytics Advantage." *MIT Sloan Management Review* (Spring 2015).

Bhandari, Rishi, Marc Singer, and Hiek van der Scheer. "Using Marketing Analytics to Drive Superior Growth." McKinsey & Co. (June 2014).

Chen, Daniel Q, David S. Preston, and Morgan Swink. "How the Use of Big Data Analytics Affects Value Creation in Supply Chain Management." *Journal of Management Information Systems* 32, No. 4 (2015).

Clark, Thomas D., Jr., Mary C. Jones, and Curtis P. Armstrong. "The Dynamic Structure of Management Support Systems: Theory Development, Research Focus, and Direction." *MIS Quarterly* 31, No. 3 (September 2007).

Davenport, Thomas H. "Analytics 3.0." *Harvard Business Review* (December 2013).

_____ *Big Data at Work*: *Dispelling the Myths, Uncovering the Opportunities*. Harvard Business Review Press (2014).

Davenport, Thomas H. and Jill Dyche. "Big Data in Big Companies." International Institute of Analytics (May 2013).

Davenport, Thomas H., Jeanne G. Harris, and Robert Morison. *Analytics at Work: Smarter Decisions, Better Results*. Boston: Harvard Business Press (2010).

De la Merced, Michael J. and Ben Protess. "A Fast-Paced Stock Exchange Trips over Itself." *New York Times* (March 23, 2012)

Dennis, Alan R., Jay E. Aronson, William G. Henriger, and Edward D. Walker III. "Structuring Time and Task in Electronic Brainstorming." *MIS Quarterly* 23, No. 1 (March 1999).

Fogarty, David and Peter C. Bell. "Should You Outsource Analytics?" *MIT Sloan Management Review* (Winter 2014).

Gallupe, R. Brent, Geraldine DeSanctis, and Gary W. Dickson. "Computer-Based Support for Group Problem-Finding: An Experimental Investigation." *MIS Quarterly* 12, No. 2 (June 1988).

Grau, Jeffrey. "How Retailers Are Leveraging 'Big Data' to Personalize Ecommerce." *eMarketer* (2012).

Harris, Jeanne G. and Vijay Mehrotra. "Getting Value from Your Data Scientists." *MIT Sloan Management Review* (Fall 2014).

Hurst, Cameron with Michael S. Hopkins and Leslie Brokaw. "Matchmaking with Math: How Analytics Beats Intuition to Win Customers." *MIT Sloan Management Review* 52, No. 2 (Winter 2011).

Jensen, Matthew, Paul Benjamin Lowry, Judee K. Burgoon, and Jay Nunamaker. "Technology Dominance in Complex Decision Making." *Journal of Management Information Systems* 27, No. 1 (Summer 2010).

Kahneman, Daniel. *Thinking, Fast and Slow*. New York: Farrar, Straus and Giroux (2011).

Kaplan, Robert S. and David P. Norton. "The Balanced Scorecard: Measures That Drive Performance." *Harvard Business Review* (January–February 1992).

Kaplan, Robert S. and David P. Norton. *Strategy Maps: Converting Intangible Assets into Tangible Outcomes.* Boston: Harvard Business School Press (2004).

Kiron, David, Pamela Kirk Prentice, and Renee Boucher Ferguson. "Raising the Bar with Analytics." *MIT Sloan Management Review* (Winter 2014).

Lauricella, Tom and Scott Patterson. "With Knight Wounded, Traders Ask If Speed Kills." *Wall Street Journal* (August 2, 2012).

LaValle, Steve, Eric Lesser, Rebecca Shockley, Michael S. Hopkins and Nina Kruschwitz. "Big Data, Analytics, and the Path from Insights to Value." *MIT Sloan Management Review* 52, No. 2 (Winter 2011).

Leidner, Dorothy E., and Joyce Elam. "The Impact of Executive Information Systems on Organizational Design, Intelligence, and Decision Making." *Organization Science* 6, No. 6 (November–December 1995).

Luca, Michael, Jon Kleinberg, and Sendhil Mullainathan. "Algorithms Need Managers, Too." *Harvard Business Review* (January–February 2016).

Marchand, Donald A. and Joe Peppard. "Why IT Fumbles Analytics." *Harvard Business Review* (January–February 2013).

Mintzberg, Henry."Managerial Work: Analysis from Observation." Management Science 18 (October 1971).

Nichols, Wes. "Advertising Analytics 2.0." *Harvard Business Review* (March 2013).

"The New Science of Sales Performance." *Harvard Business Review Analytic Services* (March 5, 2015).

Parenteau, Josh, Rita L. Sallam, Cindi Howson, Joao Tapadinhas, Kurt Schlegel, and Thomas W. Oestreich. "Magic Quadrant for Business Intelligence and Analytics Platforms." Gartner, Inc. (February 4, 2016).

Ransbotham, Sam, David Kiron, and Pamela Kirk Prentice. "Minding the Analytics Gap." *MIT Sloan Management Review* (Spring 2015).

Simon, H. A. *The New Science of Management Decision*. New York: Harper & Row (1960).

Tversky, Amos and Daniel Kahneman. "Rational Choice and the Framing of Decisions." *Journal of Business* (1986).

Building and Managing Systems

PART FOUR shows how to use the knowledge acquired in earlier chapters to analyze and design information system solutions to business problems. This part answers questions such as these: How can I develop a solution to an information system problem that provides genuine business benefits? How can the firm adjust to the changes introduced by the new system solution? What alternative approaches are available for building system solutions?

13 Building Information Systems

Learning Objectives

After reading this chapter, you will be able to answer the following questions:

13-1 How does building new systems produce organizational change?

13-2 What are the core activities in the systems development process?

13-3 What are the principal methodologies for modeling and designing systems?

13-4 What are alternative methods for building information systems?

13-5 What are new approaches for system building in the digital firm era?

MyMISLab™

Visit **mymislab.com** for simulations, tutorials, and end-of-chapter problems.

CHAPTER CASES

Angostura Builds a Mobile Sales System
Fujitsu Selects a SaaS Solution to Simplify the Sales Process
Developing Mobile Apps: What's Different
ConAgra's Recipe for a Better Human Resources System

VIDEO CASES

IBM: Business Process Management in a SaaS Environment
IBM Helps the City of Madrid with Real-Time BPM Software
Instructional Videos:
BPM Business Process Management Customer Story
Workflow Management Visualized

Angostura Builds a Mobile Sales System

House of Angostura (also known as Angostura Limited), headquartered in Laventille, Trinidad, is one of the Caribbean's leading rum producers and the world market leader for bitters used in many cocktails. Angostura has 330 full-time employees and annual revenue of approximately $100 million.

Angostura still takes care of local distribution of its products in Trinidad and Tobago, with a team of 16 sales representatives taking orders out in the field. Although this arrangement worked well in the past, the process was heavily manual, tedious, and time-consuming and sometimes produced inaccurate orders.

Each day, the 16 sales reps in the field had to copy the orders on paper and return to the office to hand off the order forms to a customer service representative, who would then manually input the order data into Angostura's SAP enterprise resource planning (ERP) system. Because the orders were handwritten, information could be read and entered incorrectly, which could result in the wrong goods being sent to a customer. Such inaccurate orders were often returned, creating more paperwork and higher costs. Angostura also used manual processes for reporting and tracking invoices and accounts receivable information, which could create additional delays and errors.

© TristanBM/Fotolia

The sales representatives were also working with data on product availability that might be out of date. If the sales reps were away from the office, they would not be able to tell whether an order could actually be fulfilled. They would have to call Angostura's warehouse to find out if an order was possible.

In 2012 Angostura's management decided that the sales process needed to be more streamlined and efficient and that it should use mobile technology. The company identified a set of detailed information requirements for the improved sales process and spent more than a year evaluating system solutions from five mobile vendors. One important requirement was that the application should be able to automatically update the availability of purchased products from the company's overall inventory and integrate with the firm's back-end SAP ERP system. Another requirement was that the mobile system be able to operate offline so that a sales representative could still input an order on a mobile device even if there was no online connectivity. Once online, the device could then send the order through to the ERP system.

The vendor selected was the one that could best develop the mobile application to the company's specifications and stay within the budget established by management. In 2013 Angostura partnered with IDS Scheer and itCampus consultants to develop a mobile sales solution running on Apple iPads. The solution includes an offline customer database, product catalog, customer-specific pricing, order entry, order preview, and integration with Bluetooth printers. It was quickly created using SAP NetWeaver Gateway technology to connect various devices and platforms to SAP software. A pilot application was ready for testing that June, and the entire application went live January 2014.

Each of Angostura's 16 sales representatives was issued an iPad that includes not only the order application but other mobile apps to make the sales process more efficient, such as email, Google Maps, and a video and PDF document uploader to display the Angostura product line. The sales application integrates with the corporate ERP system, providing the sales reps with up-to-date information on the availability of products in the warehouse.

With the Angostura Mobile Sales App, an order can be created in less than 30 seconds, depending on the size of the order, making the ordering process two times faster. There is a 20 percent time savings per salesperson because the sales reps now have the ability to send orders through as they place them rather than waiting until they return to the office. The amount of time customer service representatives would typically spend on data entry—which was considerable—has been reduced by 75 percent, freeing up time for more useful tasks. Returned orders have been reduced by 30 percent.

Sources: Natalie Miller, "Generations-Old Company with a Modern Twist on Sales," SAP Insider Profiles, January 2016; www.angostura.com, accessed February 10, 2016; and IDS Scheer Consulting Group, "Angostura's iPad-Based SAP Mobile Sales Solution," 2014.

Angostura's experience illustrates some of the steps required to design and build new information systems. Building a new system for mobile sales orders entailed analyzing the organization's problems with existing systems, assessing information requirements, selecting appropriate technology, and redesigning business processes and jobs. Management had to oversee the systems-building effort and evaluate benefits and costs. The information requirements were incorporated into the design of the new system, which represented a process of planned organizational change.

The chapter-opening case calls attention to important points raised by this case and this chapter. Angostura's ability to handle sales orders was hampered by outdated and inefficient manual processes, which raised costs, slowed down work, and limited the company's ability to serve its customers.

The solution was to redesign the sales order process to use mobile devices and software and allow orders to be entered through iPads and transmitted to the firm's back-end ERP system. Angostura's information requirements were incorporated into the system design. The solution encompassed not just the

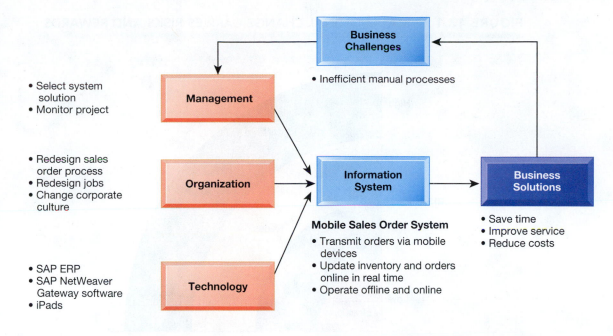

Business
Challenges

• Inefficient manual processes

Management

• Select system
  solution
• Monitor project

Organization

• Redesign sales
  order process
• Redesign jobs
• Change corporate
  culture

Technology

• SAP ERP
• SAP NetWeaver
  Gateway software
• iPads

Information
System

Mobile Sales Order System

• Transmit orders via mobile
  devices
• Update inventory and orders
  online in real time
• Operate offline and online

Business
Solutions

• Save time
• Improve service
• Reduce costs

application of new technology but changes to corporate culture, business processes, and job functions. Angostura's sales operations have become much more efficient and cost-saving.

Here are some questions to think about: How did Angostura's Mobile Sales App meet its information requirements? How effective a solution was Angostura's Mobile Sales App? Why? How much did the new system change the way Angostura ran its business?

13-1 How does building new systems produce organizational change?

Building a new information system is one kind of planned organizational change. The introduction of a new information system involves much more than new hardware and software. It also includes changes in jobs, skills, management, and organization. When we design a new information system, we are redesigning the organization. System builders must understand how a system will affect specific business processes and the organization as a whole.

Systems Development and Organizational Change

Information technology can promote various degrees of organizational change, ranging from incremental to far-reaching. Figure 13.1 shows four kinds of structural organizational change that are enabled by information technology: (1) automation, (2) rationalization, (3) business process redesign, and (4) paradigm shifts. Each carries different risks and rewards.

The most common form of IT-enabled organizational change is **automation**. The first applications of information technology involved assisting employees with performing their tasks more efficiently and effectively. Calculating paychecks and payroll registers, giving bank tellers instant access to customer deposit records, and developing a nationwide reservation network for airline ticket agents are all examples of early automation.

FIGURE 13.1 ORGANIZATIONAL CHANGE CARRIES RISKS AND REWARDS

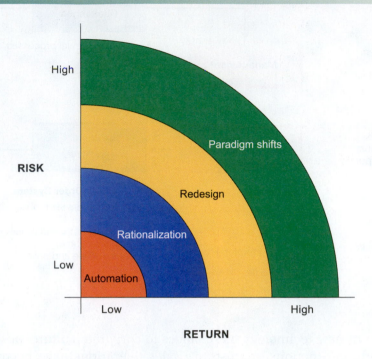

The most common forms of organizational change are automation and rationalization. These relatively slow-moving and slow-changing strategies present modest returns but little risk. Faster and more comprehensive change—such as redesign and paradigm shifts—carries high rewards but offers substantial chances of failure.

A deeper form of organizational change—one that follows quickly from early automation—is **rationalization of procedures**. Automation frequently reveals new bottlenecks in production and makes the existing arrangement of procedures and structures painfully cumbersome. Rationalization of procedures is the streamlining of standard operating procedures. For example, Angostura's new mobile order system is effective not only because it uses computer technology but also because the company simplified its business processes for this function. Fewer manual steps are required.

Rationalization of procedures is often found in programs for making a series of continuous quality improvements in products, services, and operations, such as total quality management (TQM) and six sigma. **Total quality management (TQM)** makes achieving quality an end in itself and the responsibility of all people and functions within an organization. TQM derives from concepts developed by American quality experts such as W. Edwards Deming and Joseph Juran, but it was popularized by the Japanese. **Six sigma** is a specific measure of quality, representing 3.4 defects per million opportunities. Most companies cannot achieve this level of quality but use six sigma as a goal for driving ongoing quality improvement programs.

A more powerful type of organizational change is **business process redesign**, in which business processes are analyzed, simplified, and redesigned. Business process redesign reorganizes workflows, combining steps to cut waste and eliminate repetitive, paper-intensive tasks. (Sometimes the new design eliminates jobs as well.) It is much more ambitious than rationalization of procedures, requiring a new vision of how the process is to be organized.

A widely cited example of business process redesign is Ford Motor Company's invoiceless processing, which reduced head count in Ford's North American Accounts Payable organization of 500 people by 75 percent. Accounts payable clerks used to spend most of their time resolving discrepancies between purchase orders, receiving documents, and invoices. Ford redesigned its accounts payable process so that the purchasing department enters a purchase order into an online database that can be checked by the receiving department when the ordered items arrive. If the received goods match the purchase order, the system automatically generates a check for accounts payable to send to the vendor. There is no need for vendors to send invoices.

Rationalizing procedures and redesigning business processes are limited to specific parts of a business. New information systems can ultimately affect the design of the entire organization by transforming how the organization carries out its business or even the nature of the business. For instance, the long-haul trucking and transportation firm Schneider National used new information systems to change its business model. Schneider created a new business managing logistics for other companies. This more radical form of business change is called a **paradigm shift**. A paradigm shift involves rethinking the nature of the business and the nature of the organization.

Paradigm shifts and business process redesign often fail because extensive organizational change is so difficult to orchestrate (see Chapter 14). Why, then, do so many corporations contemplate such radical change? Because the rewards are equally high (see Figure 13.1). In many instances, firms seeking paradigm shifts and pursuing reengineering strategies achieve stunning, order-of-magnitude increases in their returns on investment (or productivity). Some of these success stories, and some failure stories, are included throughout this book.

Business Process Redesign

Like Angostura, described in the chapter-opening case, many businesses today are trying to use information technology to improve their business processes. Some of these systems entail incremental process change, but others require more far-reaching redesign of business processes. To deal with these changes, organizations are turning to business process management. **Business process management (BPM)** provides a variety of tools and methodologies to analyze existing processes, design new processes, and optimize those processes. BPM is never concluded because process improvement requires continual change. Companies practicing business process management go through the following steps:

1. **Identify processes for change:** One of the most important strategic decisions that a firm can make is not deciding how to use computers to improve business processes but understanding what business processes need improvement. When systems are used to strengthen the wrong business model or business processes, the business can become more efficient at doing what it should not do. As a result, the firm becomes vulnerable to competitors who may have discovered the right business model. Considerable time and cost may also be spent improving business processes that have little impact on overall firm performance and revenue. Managers need to determine what business processes are the most important and how improving these processes will help business performance.

2. **Analyze existing processes:** Existing business processes should be modeled and documented, noting inputs, outputs, resources, and the sequence of activities. The process design team identifies redundant steps, paper-intensive tasks, bottlenecks, and other inefficiencies.

Figure 13.2 illustrates the "as-is" process for purchasing a book from a physical bookstore. Consider what happens when a customer visits a physical bookstore and searches its shelves for a book. If he or she finds the book, that person takes it to the checkout counter and pays for it via credit card, cash, or check. If the customer is unable to locate the book, he or she must ask a bookstore clerk to search the shelves or check the bookstore's inventory records to see if it is in stock. If the clerk finds the book, the customer purchases it and leaves. If the book is not available locally, the clerk inquires about ordering it for the customer from the bookstore's warehouse or from the book's distributor or publisher. Once the ordered book arrives at the bookstore, a bookstore employee telephones the customer with this information. The customer would have to go to the bookstore again to pick up the book and pay for it. If the bookstore is unable to order the book for the customer, the customer would have to try another bookstore. You can see that this process has many steps and might require the customer to make multiple trips to the bookstore.

3. **Design the new process:** Once the existing process is mapped and measured in terms of time and cost, the process design team will try to improve the process by designing a new one. A new streamlined "to-be" process will be documented and modeled for comparison with the old process.

Figure 13.3 illustrates how the book-purchasing process can be redesigned by taking advantage of the Internet. The customer accesses an online bookstore over the Internet from his or her computer. He or she searches the bookstore's online catalog for the book he or she wants. If the book is available, the customer orders the book online, supplying credit card and shipping address information, and the book is delivered to the customer's home. If the online bookstore does not carry the book, the customer selects another online bookstore and searches for the book again. This process has far fewer steps than that

FIGURE 13.2   AS-IS BUSINESS PROCESS FOR PURCHASING A BOOK FROM A PHYSICAL BOOKSTORE

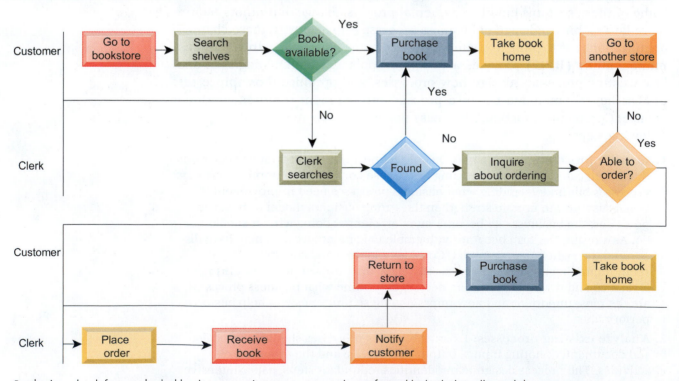

Purchasing a book from a physical bookstore requires many steps to be performed by both the seller and the customer.

FIGURE 13.3 REDESIGNED PROCESS FOR PURCHASING A BOOK ONLINE

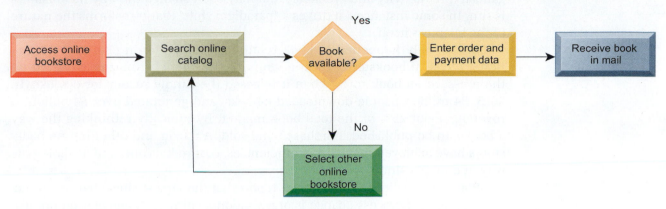

Using Internet technology makes it possible to redesign the process for purchasing a book so that it requires fewer steps and consumes fewer resources.

for purchasing the book in a physical bookstore, requires much less effort on the part of the customer, and requires less sales staff for customer service. The new process is therefore much more efficient and time-saving.

The new process design needs to be justified by showing how much it reduces time and cost or enhances customer service and value. Management first measures the time and cost of the existing process as a baseline. In our example, the time required for purchasing a book from a physical bookstore might range from 15 minutes (if the customer immediately finds what he or she wants) to 30 minutes if the book is in stock but has to be located by sales staff. If the book has to be ordered from another source, the process might take one or two weeks and another trip to the bookstore for the customer. If the customer lives far away from the bookstore, the time to travel to the bookstore would have to be factored in. The bookstore will have to pay the costs for maintaining a physical store and keeping the book in stock, for sales staff on site, and for shipment costs if the book has to be obtained from another location.

The new process for purchasing a book online might only take several minutes, although the customer might have to wait several days or a week to have the book delivered and will have to pay a shipping charge. But the customer saves time and money by not having to travel to the bookstore or make additional visits to pick up the book. Booksellers' costs are lower because they do not have to pay for a physical store location or for local inventory.

4. **Implement the new process:** Once the new process has been thoroughly modeled and analyzed, it must be translated into a new set of procedures and work rules. New information systems or enhancements to existing systems may have to be implemented to support the redesigned process. The new process and supporting systems are rolled out into the business organization. As the business starts using this process, problems are uncovered and addressed. Employees working with the process may recommend improvements.

5. **Continuous measurement:** Once a process has been implemented and optimized, it needs to be continually measured. Why? Processes may deteriorate over time as employees fall back on old methods, or they may lose their effectiveness if the business experiences other changes.

Although many business process improvements are incremental and ongoing, there are occasions when more radical change must take place. Our example of a physical bookstore redesigning the book-purchasing process so that it can be carried out online is an example of this type of radical, far-reaching change.

When properly implemented, business process redesign produces dramatic gains in productivity and efficiency and may even change the way the business is run. In some instances, it drives a "paradigm shift" that transforms the nature of the business itself.

This actually happened in book retailing when Amazon challenged traditional physical bookstores with its online retail model. Amazon racheted up the pressure on bookstores when it released the Kindle reader for e-books. In 2015, 84 million people downloaded e-books, and generated over $4 billion in revenue, about 25% of the total book market. By radically rethinking the way a book can be published, purchased and sold, Amazon and other online bookstores have achieved remarkable efficiencies, cost reductions, and a whole new way of doing business.

BPM poses challenges. Executives report that the largest single barrier to successful business process change is organizational culture. Employees do not like unfamiliar routines and often try to resist change. This is especially true of projects where organizational changes are very ambitious and far-reaching. Managing change is neither simple nor intuitive, and companies committed to extensive process improvement need a good change management strategy (see Chapter 14).

Tools for Business Process Management

More than 100 software firms provide tools for various aspects of BPM, including IBM, Oracle, and TIBCO. These tools help businesses identify and document processes requiring improvement, create models of improved processes, capture and enforce business rules for performing processes, and integrate existing systems to support new or redesigned processes. BPM software tools also provide analytics for verifying that process performance has been improved and for measuring the impact of process changes on key business performance indicators.

Some BPM tools document and monitor business processes to help firms identify inefficiencies using software to connect with each of the systems a company uses for a particular process to identify trouble spots. Another category of tools automate some parts of a business process and enforce business rules so that employees perform that process more consistently and efficiently.

For example, American National Insurance Company, which offers life insurance, medical insurance, property casualty insurance, and investment services, used Pega BPM workflow software to streamline customer service processes across four business groups. The software built rules to guide customer service representatives through a single view of a customer's information that was maintained in multiple systems. By eliminating the need to juggle multiple applications simultaneously to handle customer and agent requests, the improved process increased customer service representative workload capacity by 192 percent.

A third category of tools helps businesses integrate their existing systems to support process improvements. They automatically manage processes across the business, extract data from various sources and databases, and generate transactions in multiple related systems.

13-2 What are the core activities in the systems development process?

New information systems are an outgrowth of a process of organizational problem solving. A new information system is built as a solution to some type of problem or set of problems the organization perceives it is facing. The problem may be one in which managers and employees realize that the organization is not performing as well as expected or that the organization should take advantage of new opportunities to perform more successfully.

The activities that go into producing an information system solution to an organizational problem or opportunity are called **systems development**. Systems development is a structured kind of problem solved with distinct activities. These activities consist of systems analysis, systems design, programming, testing, conversion, and production and maintenance.

Figure 13.4 illustrates the systems development process. The systems development activities depicted usually take place in sequential order. But some of the activities may need to be repeated or some may take place simultaneously depending on the approach to system building that is being employed (see Section 13-4).

Systems Analysis

Systems analysis is the analysis of a problem that a firm tries to solve with an information system. It consists of defining the problem, identifying its causes, specifying the solution, and identifying the information requirements that must be met by a system solution.

The systems analyst creates a road map of the existing organization and systems, identifying the primary owners and users of data along with existing hardware and software. The systems analyst then details the problems of existing systems. By examining documents, work papers, and procedures, observing system operations, and interviewing key users of the systems, the analyst can identify the problem areas and objectives a solution would achieve. Often, the solution requires building a new information system or improving an existing one.

The systems analysis also includes a **feasibility study** to determine whether that solution is feasible, or achievable, from a financial, technical, and organizational standpoint. The feasibility study determines whether the proposed system is expected to be a good investment, whether the technology needed for

FIGURE 13.4 THE SYSTEMS DEVELOPMENT PROCESS

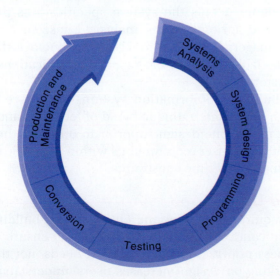

Building a system can be broken down into six core activities.

the system is available and can be handled by the firm's information systems specialists, and whether the organization can handle the changes introduced by the system.

Normally, the systems analysis process identifies several alternative solutions that the organization can pursue and assess the feasibility of each. A written systems proposal report describes the costs and benefits, and the advantages and disadvantages, of each alternative. It is up to management to determine which mix of costs, benefits, technical features, and organizational impacts represents the most desirable alternative.

Establishing Information Requirements

Perhaps the most challenging task of the systems analyst is to define the specific information requirements that must be met by the chosen system solution. At the most basic level, the **information requirements** of a new system involve identifying who needs what information, where, when, and how. Requirements analysis carefully defines the objectives of the new or modified system and develops a detailed description of the functions that the new system must perform. Faulty requirements analysis is a leading cause of systems failure and high systems development costs (see Chapter 14). A system designed around the wrong set of requirements will either have to be discarded because of poor performance or will need to undergo major modifications. Section 13-3 describes alternative approaches to eliciting requirements that help minimize this problem.

Some problems do not require an information system solution but instead need an adjustment in management, additional training, or refinement of existing organizational procedures. If the problem is information-related, systems analysis still may be required to diagnose the problem and arrive at the proper solution.

Systems Design

Systems analysis describes what a system should do to meet information requirements, and **systems design** shows how the system will fulfill this objective. The design of an information system is the overall plan or model for that system. Like the blueprint of a building or house, it consists of all the specifications that give the system its form and structure.

The systems designer details the system specifications that will deliver the functions identified during systems analysis. These specifications should address all of the managerial, organizational, and technological components of the system solution. Table 13.1 lists the types of specifications that would be produced during systems design.

Like houses or buildings, information systems may have many possible designs. Each design represents a unique blend of technical and organizational components. What makes one design superior to others is the ease and efficiency with which it fulfills user requirements within a specific set of technical, organizational, financial, and time constraints.

The Role of End Users

User information requirements drive the entire system-building effort. Users must have sufficient control over the design process to ensure that the system reflects their business priorities and information needs, not the biases of the technical staff. Working on design increases users' understanding and acceptance of the system. As we describe in Chapter 14, insufficient user involvement

TABLE 13.1 SYSTEM DESIGN SPECIFICATIONS

OUTPUT	PROCESSING	DOCUMENTATION
Medium	Computations	Operations documentation
Content	Program modules	Systems documentation
Timing	Required reports	User documentation
INPUT	Timing of outputs	CONVERSION
Origins	MANUAL PROCEDURES	Data conversion rules
Flow	What activities	Testing method
Data entry	Who performs them	Conversion strategy
USER INTERFACE	When	TRAINING
Simplicity	How	Training techniques
Efficiency	Where	Training modules
Logic	CONTROLS	ORGANIZATIONAL CHANGES
Feedback	Input controls (characters, limit, reasonableness)	Task redesign
Errors	Processing controls (consistency, record counts)	Job design
DATABASE DESIGN	Output controls (totals, samples of output)	Process design
Logical data model	Procedural controls (passwords, special forms)	Organization structure design
Volume and speed requirements	SECURITY	Reporting relationships
File organization and design	Access controls	
Record specifications	Catastrophe plans	
	Audit trails	

in the design effort is a major cause of system failure. However, some systems require more user participation in design than others, and Section 13-4 shows how alternative systems development methods address the user participation issue.

Completing the Systems Development Process

The remaining steps in the systems development process translate the solution specifications established during systems analysis and design into a fully operational information system. These concluding steps consist of programming, testing, conversion, production, and maintenance.

Programming

During the **programming** stage, system specifications that were prepared during the design stage are translated into software program code. Today, many organizations no longer do their own programming for new systems. Instead, they purchase the software that meets the requirements for a new system from external sources such as software packages from a commercial software vendor, software services from a software service provider, or outsourcing firms that develop custom application software for their clients (see Section 13-4).

Testing

Exhaustive and thorough **testing** must be conducted to ascertain whether the system produces the right results. Testing answers the question "Will the system produce the desired results under known conditions?" As Chapter 5 noted, some companies are starting to use cloud computing services for this work.

The amount of time needed to answer this question has been traditionally underrated in systems project planning (see Chapter 14). Testing is time-consuming: Test data must be carefully prepared, results reviewed, and corrections made in the system. In some instances, parts of the system may have to be redesigned. The risks resulting from glossing over this step are enormous.

Testing an information system can be broken down into three types of activities: unit testing, system testing, and acceptance testing. **Unit testing**, or program testing, consists of testing each program separately in the system. It is widely believed that the purpose of such testing is to guarantee that programs are error-free, but this goal is realistically impossible. Testing should be viewed instead as a means of locating errors in programs, focusing on finding all the ways to make a program fail. Once they are pinpointed, problems can be corrected.

System testing tests the functioning of the information system as a whole. It tries to determine whether discrete modules will function together as planned and whether discrepancies exist between the way the system actually works and the way it was conceived. Among the areas examined are performance time, capacity for file storage and handling peak loads, recovery and restart capabilities, and manual procedures.

Acceptance testing provides the final certification that the system is ready to be used in a production setting. Systems tests are evaluated by users and reviewed by management. When all parties are satisfied that the new system meets their standards, the system is formally accepted for installation.

The systems development team works with users to devise a systematic test plan. The **test plan** includes all of the preparations for the series of tests we have just described.

Figure 13.5 shows an example of a test plan. The general condition being tested is a record change. The documentation consists of a series of test plan screens maintained on a database (perhaps a PC database) that is ideally suited to this kind of application.

FIGURE 13.5 A SAMPLE TEST PLAN TO TEST A RECORD CHANGE

Procedure	Address and Maintenance "Record Change Series"		Test Series 2		
	Prepared By:	Date:	Version:		
Test Ref.	Condition Tested	Special Requirements	Expected Results	Output On	Next Screen
2.0	Change records				
2.1	Change existing record	Key field	Not allowed		
2.2	Change nonexistent record	Other fields	"Invalid key" message		
2.3	Change deleted record	Deleted record must be available	"Deleted" message		
2.4	Make second record	Change 2.1 above	OK if valid	Transaction file	V45
2.5	Insert record		OK if valid	Transaction file	V45
2.6	Abort during change	Abort 2.5	No change	Transaction file	V45

When developing a test plan, it is imperative to include the various conditions to be tested, the requirements for each condition tested, and the expected results. Test plans require input from both end users and information systems specialists.

Conversion

Conversion is the process of changing from the old system to the new system. Four main conversion strategies can be employed: the parallel strategy, the direct cutover strategy, the pilot study strategy, and the phased approach strategy.

In a **parallel strategy**, both the old system and its potential replacement are run together for a time until everyone is assured that the new one functions correctly. This is the safest conversion approach because, in the event of errors or processing disruptions, the old system can still be used as a backup. However, this approach is very expensive, and additional staff or resources may be required to run the extra system.

The **direct cutover strategy** replaces the old system entirely with the new system on an appointed day. It is a very risky approach that can potentially be more costly than running two systems in parallel if serious problems with the new system are found. There is no other system to fall back on. Dislocations, disruptions, and the cost of corrections may be enormous.

The **pilot study strategy** introduces the new system to only a limited area of the organization, such as a single department or operating unit. When this pilot version is complete and working smoothly, it is installed throughout the rest of the organization, either simultaneously or in stages.

The **phased approach strategy** introduces the new system in stages, either by functions or by organizational units. If, for example, the system is introduced by function, a new payroll system might begin with hourly workers who are paid weekly, followed six months later by adding salaried employees (who are paid monthly) to the system. If the system is introduced by organizational unit, corporate headquarters might be converted first, followed by outlying operating units four months later.

Moving from an old system to a new one requires that end users be trained to use the new system. Detailed **documentation** showing how the system works from both a technical and end-user standpoint is finalized during conversion time for use in training and everyday operations. Lack of proper training and documentation contributes to system failure, so this portion of the systems development process is very important.

Production and Maintenance

After the new system is installed and conversion is complete, the system is said to be in **production**. During this stage, the system will be reviewed by both users and technical specialists to determine how well it has met its original objectives and to decide whether any revisions or modifications are in order. In some instances, a formal **post-implementation audit** document is prepared. After the system has been fine-tuned, it must be maintained while it is in production to correct errors, meet requirements, or improve processing efficiency. Changes in hardware, software, documentation, or procedures to a production system to correct errors, meet new requirements, or improve processing efficiency are termed **maintenance**.

Approximately 20 percent of the time devoted to maintenance is used for debugging or correcting emergency production problems. Another 20 percent is concerned with changes in data, files, reports, hardware, or system software. But 60 percent of all maintenance work consists of making user enhancements, improving documentation, and recoding system components for greater processing efficiency. The amount of work in the third category of maintenance problems could be reduced significantly through better systems analysis and design practices. Table 13.2 summarizes the systems development activities.

TABLE 13.2 SYSTEMS DEVELOPMENT

CORE ACTIVITY	DESCRIPTION
Systems analysis	Identify problem(s)
	Specify solutions
	Establish information requirements
Systems design	Create design specifications
Programming	Translate design specifications into program code
Testing	Perform unit testing
	Perform systems testing
	Perform acceptance testing
Conversion	Plan conversion
	Prepare documentation
	Train users and technical staff
Production and maintenance	Operate the system
	Evaluate the system
	Modify the system

13-3 What are the principal methodologies for modeling and designing systems?

There are alternative methodologies for modeling and designing systems. Structured methodologies and object-oriented development are the most prominent.

Structured Methodologies

Structured methodologies have been used to document, analyze, and design information systems since the 1970s. **Structured** refers to the fact that the techniques are step by step, with each step building on the previous one. Structured methodologies are top-down, progressing from the highest, most abstract level to the lowest level of detail—from the general to the specific.

Structured development methods are process-oriented, focusing primarily on modeling the processes, or actions that capture, store, manipulate, and distribute data as the data flow through a system. These methods separate data from processes. A separate programming procedure must be written every time someone wants to take an action on a particular piece of data. The procedures act on data that the program passes to them.

The primary tool for representing a system's component processes and the flow of data between them is the **data flow diagram (DFD)**. The data flow diagram offers a logical graphic model of information flow, partitioning a system into modules that show manageable levels of detail. It rigorously specifies the processes or transformations that occur within each module and the interfaces that exist between them.

Figure 13.6 shows a simple data flow diagram for a mail-in university course registration system. The rounded boxes represent processes, which portray the transformation of data. The square box represents an external entity, which is an originator or receiver of information located outside the boundaries of the system being modeled. The open rectangles represent data stores, which

FIGURE 13.6 DATA FLOW DIAGRAM FOR MAIL-IN UNIVERSITY REGISTRATION SYSTEM

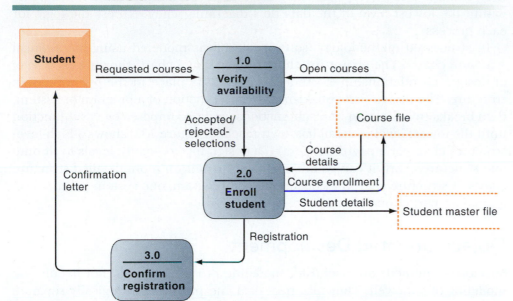

The system has three processes: Verify availability (1.0), Enroll student (2.0), and Confirm registration (3.0). The name and content of each of the data flows appear adjacent to each arrow. There is one external entity in this system: the student. There are two data stores: the student master file and the course file.

are either manual or automated inventories of data. The arrows represent data flows, which show the movement between processes, external entities, and data stores. They contain packets of data with the name or content of each data flow listed beside the arrow.

This data flow diagram shows that students submit registration forms with their name, their identification number, and the numbers of the courses they wish to take. In process 1.0, the system verifies that each course selected is still open by referencing the university's course file. The file distinguishes courses that are open from those that have been canceled or filled. Process 1.0 then determines which of the student's selections can be accepted or rejected. Process 2.0 enrolls the student in the courses for which he or she has been accepted. It updates the university's course file with the student's name and identification number and recalculates the class size. If maximum enrollment has been reached, the course number is flagged as closed. Process 2.0 also updates the university's student master file with information about new students or changes in address. Process 3.0 then sends each student applicant a confirmation of registration letter listing the courses for which he or she is registered and noting the course selections that could not be fulfilled.

The diagrams can be used to depict higher-level processes as well as lower-level details. Through leveled data flow diagrams, a complex process can be broken down into successive levels of detail. An entire system can be divided into subsystems with a high-level data flow diagram. Each subsystem, in turn, can be divided into additional subsystems with second-level data flow diagrams, and the lower-level subsystems can be broken down again until the lowest level of detail has been reached.

Another tool for structured analysis is a data dictionary, which contains information about individual pieces of data and data groupings within a system (see Chapter 6). The data dictionary defines the contents of data flows and data stores so that systems builders understand exactly what pieces of data they contain. **Process specifications** describe the transformation occurring within the lowest level of the data flow diagrams. They express the logic for each process.

In structured methodology, software design is modeled using hierarchical structure charts. The **structure chart** is a top-down chart, showing each level of design, its relationship to other levels, and its place in the overall design structure. The design first considers the main function of a program or system, then breaks this function into subfunctions, and decomposes each subfunction until the lowest level of detail has been reached. Figure 13.7 shows a high-level structure chart for a payroll system. If a design has too many levels to fit onto one structure chart, it can be broken down further on more detailed structure charts. A structure chart may document one program, one system (a set of programs), or part of one program.

Object-Oriented Development

Structured methods are useful for modeling processes but do not handle the modeling of data well. They also treat data and processes as logically separate entities, whereas in the real world such separation seems unnatural. Different modeling conventions are used for analysis (the data flow diagram) and for design (the structure chart).

Object-oriented development addresses these issues. Object-oriented development uses the **object** as the basic unit of systems analysis and design. An object combines data and the specific processes that operate on those data. Data encapsulated in an object can be accessed and modified only by the operations, or methods, associated with that object. Instead of passing data to procedures, programs send a message for an object to perform an operation that is already embedded in it. The system is modeled as a collection of objects and the relationships among them. Because processing logic resides within objects rather than in separate software programs, objects must collaborate with each other to make the system work.

Object-oriented modeling is based on the concepts of *class* and *inheritance*. Objects belonging to a certain class, or general category of similar objects, have the features of that class. Classes of objects in turn can inherit all the structure and behaviors of a more general class and then add variables and behaviors unique to each object. New classes of objects are created by choosing an

FIGURE 13.7 HIGH-LEVEL STRUCTURE CHART FOR A PAYROLL SYSTEM

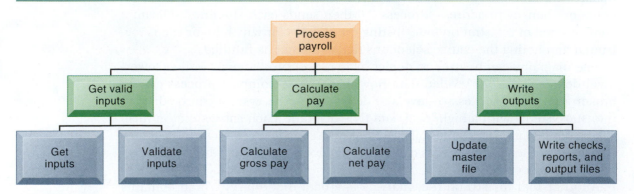

This structure chart shows the highest or most abstract level of design for a payroll system, providing an overview of the entire system.

existing class and specifying how the new class differs from the existing class instead of starting from scratch each time.

We can see how class and inheritance work in Figure 13.8, which illustrates the relationships among classes concerning employees and how they are paid. Employee is the common ancestor, or superclass, for the other three classes. Salaried, Hourly, and Temporary are subclasses of Employee. The class name is in the top compartment, the attributes for each class are in the middle portion of each box, and the list of operations is in the bottom portion of each box. The features that are shared by all employees (ID, name, address, date hired, position, and pay) are stored in the Employee superclass, whereas each subclass stores features that are specific to that particular type of employee. Specific to hourly employees, for example, are their hourly rates and overtime rates. A solid line from the subclass to the superclass is a generalization path showing that the subclasses Salaried, Hourly, and Temporary have common features that can be generalized into the superclass Employee.

Object-oriented development is more iterative and incremental than traditional structured development. During analysis, systems builders document the functional requirements of the system, specifying its most important properties and what the proposed system must do. Interactions between the system and its users are analyzed to identify objects, which include both data and processes. The object-oriented design phase describes how the objects will behave and how they will interact with one another. Similar objects are grouped together to form a class, and classes are grouped into hierarchies in which a subclass inherits the attributes and methods from its superclass.

The information system is implemented by translating the design into program code, reusing classes that are already available in a library of reusable software objects, and adding new ones created during the object-oriented design phase. Implementation may also involve the creation of an object-oriented database. The resulting system must be thoroughly tested and evaluated.

FIGURE 13.8 CLASS AND INHERITANCE

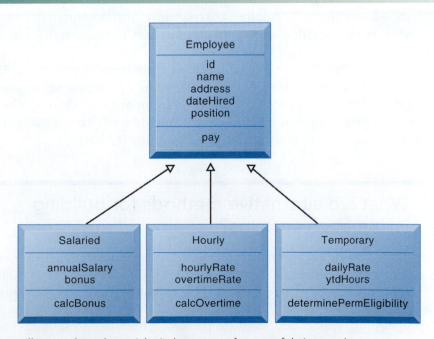

This figure illustrates how classes inherit the common features of their superclass.

Because objects are reusable, object-oriented development could potentially reduce the time and cost of writing software because organizations can reuse software objects that have already been created as building blocks for other applications. New systems can be created by using some existing objects, changing others, and adding a few new objects. Object-oriented frameworks have been developed to provide reusable, semicomplete applications that the organization can further customize into finished applications.

Computer-Aided Software Engineering

Computer-aided software engineering (CASE)—sometimes called *computer-aided systems engineering*—provides software tools to automate the methodologies we have just described to reduce the amount of repetitive work the developer needs to do. CASE tools also facilitate the creation of clear documentation and the coordination of team development efforts. Team members can share their work easily by accessing each other's files to review or modify what has been done. Modest productivity benefits can also be achieved if the tools are used properly.

CASE tools provide automated graphics facilities for producing charts and diagrams, screen and report generators, data dictionaries, extensive reporting facilities, analysis and checking tools, code generators, and documentation generators. In general, CASE tools try to increase productivity and quality by:

- Enforcing a standard development methodology and design discipline
- Improving communication between users and technical specialists
- Organizing and correlating design components and providing rapid access to them using a design repository
- Automating tedious and error-prone portions of analysis and design
- Automating code generation and testing and control rollout

CASE tools contain features for validating design diagrams and specifications. CASE tools thus support iterative design by automating revisions and changes and providing prototyping facilities. A CASE information repository stores all the information defined by the analysts during the project. The repository includes data flow diagrams, structure charts, entity-relationship diagrams, data definitions, process specifications, screen and report formats, notes and comments, and test results.

To be used effectively, CASE tools require organizational discipline. Every member of a development project must adhere to a common set of naming conventions and standards as well as to a development methodology. The best CASE tools enforce common methods and standards, which may discourage their use in situations where organizational discipline is lacking.

13-4 What are alternative methods for building information systems?

Systems differ in terms of their size and technological complexity and in terms of the organizational problems they are meant to solve. A number of systems-building approaches have been developed to deal with these differences. This section describes these alternative methods: the traditional systems life cycle, prototyping, application software packages, end-user development, and outsourcing.

Traditional Systems Life Cycle

The **systems life cycle** is the oldest method for building information systems. The life cycle methodology is a phased approach to building a system, dividing systems development into formal stages, as illustrated in Figure 13.9. Systems development specialists have different opinions on how to partition the systems-building stages, but they roughly correspond to the stages of systems development we have just described.

The systems life cycle methodology maintains a formal division of labor between end users and information systems specialists. Technical specialists, such as systems analysts and programmers, are responsible for much of the systems analysis, design, and implementation work; end users are limited to providing information requirements and reviewing the technical staff's work. The life cycle also emphasizes formal specifications and paperwork, so many documents are generated during the course of a systems project.

The systems life cycle is still used for building large complex systems that require a rigorous and formal requirements analysis, predefined specifications, and tight controls over the system-building process. However, the systems life cycle approach can be costly, time-consuming, and inflexible. Although systems builders can go back and forth among stages in the life cycle, the systems life cycle is predominantly a "waterfall" approach in which tasks in one stage are completed before work for the next stage begins. Activities can be repeated, but volumes of new documents must be generated and steps retraced if requirements and specifications need to be revised. This encourages freezing of specifications relatively early in the development process. The life cycle approach is also not suitable for many small desktop systems, which tend to be less structured and more individualized.

FIGURE 13.9 THE TRADITIONAL SYSTEMS DEVELOPMENT LIFE CYCLE

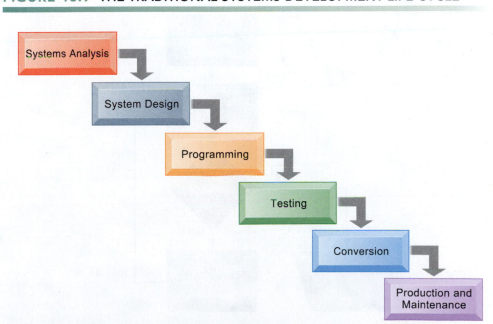

The systems development life cycle partitions systems development into formal stages, with each stage requiring completion before the next stage can begin.

Prototyping

Prototyping consists of building an experimental system rapidly and inexpensively for end users to evaluate. By interacting with the prototype, users can get a better idea of their information requirements. The prototype endorsed by the users can be used as a template to create the final system.

The **prototype** is a working version of an information system or part of the system, but it is meant to be only a preliminary model. Once operational, the prototype will be further refined until it conforms precisely to users' requirements. Once the design has been finalized, the prototype can be converted to a polished production system.

The process of building a preliminary design, trying it out, refining it, and trying again has been called an **iterative** process of systems development because the steps required to build a system can be repeated over and over again. Prototyping is more explicitly iterative than the conventional life cycle, and it actively promotes system design changes. It has been said that prototyping replaces unplanned rework with planned iteration, with each version more accurately reflecting users' requirements.

Steps in Prototyping

Figure 13.10 shows a four-step model of the prototyping process, which consists of the following:

Step 1: *Identify the user's basic requirements.* The systems designer (usually an information systems specialist) works with the user only long enough to capture the user's basic information needs.

FIGURE 13.10 **THE PROTOTYPING PROCESS**

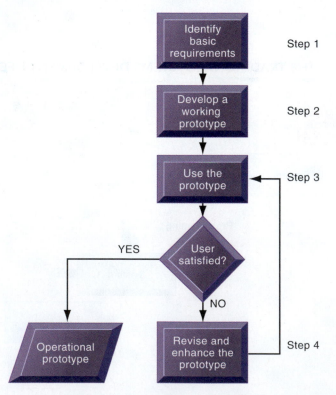

The process of developing a prototype can be broken down into four steps. Because a prototype can be developed quickly and inexpensively, systems builders can go through several iterations, repeating steps 3 and 4, to refine and enhance the prototype before arriving at the final operational one.

Step 2: Develop an initial prototype. The systems designer creates a working prototype quickly, using tools for rapidly generating software.

Step 3: Use the prototype. The user is encouraged to work with the system to determine how well the prototype meets his or her needs and to make suggestions for improving the prototype.

Step 4: Revise and enhance the prototype. The system builder notes all changes the user requests and refines the prototype accordingly. After the prototype has been revised, the cycle returns to Step 3. Steps 3 and 4 are repeated until the user is satisfied.

When no more iterations are required, the approved prototype then becomes an operational prototype that furnishes the final specifications for the application. Sometimes the prototype is adopted as the production version of the system.

Advantages and Disadvantages of Prototyping

Prototyping is most useful when there is some uncertainty about requirements or design solutions and often used for designing an information system's **end-user interface** (the part of the system with which end users interact, such as online display and data entry screens, reports, or web pages). Because prototyping encourages intense end-user involvement throughout the systems development life cycle, it is more likely to produce systems that fulfill user requirements.

However, rapid prototyping can gloss over essential steps in systems development. If the completed prototype works reasonably well, management may not see the need for reprogramming, redesign, or full documentation and testing to build a polished production system. Some of these hastily constructed systems may not easily accommodate large quantities of data or a large number of users in a production environment.

End-User Development

End-user development allows end users, with little or no formal assistance from technical specialists, to create simple information systems, reducing the time and steps required to produce a finished application. Using user-friendly query languages and reporting, website development, graphics, and PC software tools, end users can access data, create reports, and develop simple applications on their own with little or no help from professional systems analysts or programmers. A **query language** is a software tool that provides immediate online answers to questions that are not predefined, such as "Who are the highest-performing sales representatives?" Query languages are often tied to data management software (see Chapter 6).

For example, Yellow Pages (YP), a digital media and marketing solutions company serving 260,000 small and medium-sized Canadian businesses, used Information Builders WebFOCUS to build a user-friendly analytics application that helps customers measure return on their advertising dollars and track the success of their campaigns. The system, called YP Analytics, features a user-friendly dashboard to track interactions and measure key performance indicators focused on ROI and revenue. YP Analytics users can track important metrics such as visitors, visits, page views, and interactions/clicks as well as calls, in-shop walk-ins, digital contacts, and other performance indicators, and they can customize the outputs they want (Information Builders, 2015).

On the whole, end-user-developed systems can be completed more rapidly than those developed through the conventional systems life cycle. Allowing users to specify their own business needs improves requirements gathering and often leads to a higher level of user involvement and satisfaction with the system. However, end-user software tools still cannot replace conventional tools for some business applications because they cannot easily handle the processing of large numbers of transactions or applications with extensive procedural logic and updating requirements.

End-user computing also poses organizational risks because it occurs outside of traditional mechanisms for information systems management and control. When systems are created rapidly without a formal development methodology, testing and documentation may be inadequate. Control over data can be lost in systems outside the traditional information systems department. To help organizations maximize the benefits of end-user applications development, management should control the development of end-user applications by requiring cost justification of end-user information system projects and by establishing hardware, software, and quality standards for user-developed applications.

Application Software Packages, Software Services, and Outsourcing

Chapter 5 points out that much of today's software is not developed in-house but is purchased from external sources. Firms can rent the software from an online software service provider, they can purchase the software from a commercial vendor as a package to run in-house, or they can have a custom application developed by an outside outsourcing firm.

Application Software Packages and Cloud Software Services

Today many systems are based on commercially available application software packages or cloud software as a service (SaaS). For example, companies can choose to implement Oracle enterprise resource planning, supply chain management, or human capital management software in-house or pay to use this software running on the Oracle Cloud platform. Microsoft Office desktop productivity software comes in both desktop and cloud (Office 365) versions. Many applications are common to all business organizations—for example, payroll, accounts receivable, general ledger, or inventory control. For such universal functions with standard processes that do not change a great deal over time, a more generic system will fulfill the requirements of many organizations.

If a commercial software package or cloud software service can fulfill most of an organization's requirements, the company does not have to write its own software (see the Interactive Session on Organizations). The company can save time and money by using the prewritten, predesigned, pretested software programs from the software vendor. Package and SaaS vendors supply much of the ongoing maintenance and support for the system, including enhancements to keep the system in line with ongoing technical and business developments. When a package or SaaS solution is pursued, end users will be responsible for supplying the business information requirements for the system, and information systems specialists will provide technical requirements.

INTERACTIVE SESSION: ORGANIZATIONS

Fujitsu Selects a SaaS Solution to Simplify the Sales Process

If you surf the web, stream video on your phone, or watch cable TV in North America, equipment from Fujitsu Network Communications most likely keeps you connected. Fujitsu Network Communications Inc., based in Richardson, Texas, provides optical and wireless networking equipment, including servers, storage products, client computing devices, scanners, printers, and displays. It is a leading patent-holder in optical networking.

Fujitsu network equipment provides optical transport solutions to major telecommunications carriers across North America. There are more than 450,000 Fujitsu network elements, including shelves and cards that house connectivity hardware, signaling and routing setup, and management provisioning. The company's numerous products contain thousands of parts and innumerable configuration scenarios. A single product, for example, might be priced differently for 600 separate customers because pricing is determined by a customer's unique configurations concerning network sites, geographic locations, and distances between sites. Additionally, each of the various sites in a network involves a multitude of setup configurations concerning power supply, labeling, and rules for communication. Just think how difficult the process of configuring, pricing, and quoting orders for products and services might be for a 40-site network, which is not uncommon.

For many years, Fujitsu sales teams had trouble handling all this complexity in the sales and ordering processes. They had to use individual spreadsheets to configure, price, and quote (CPQ) solutions for their customers. The company had no centralized repository for price quotes, records of offerings, or capability for integrating quotes with the ordering process. Even though Fujitsu had an ERP system to maintain its enterprise-wide master pricing and materials master data, the CPQ process still took days and resulted in quoting errors and countless hours of corrections and rework.

A system solution was in order. Dave Hawkins, Fujitsu's Vice President of Sales Engineering, Sales Operations, and Commercial Management, and his team issued a request for proposal (RFP) for a solution that would produce quotes quickly and reduce quoting errors and rework. The most critical requirements were the ability to centralize and control all of the quoting that was going on, ensure accurate pricing, and ensure that the parts being configured were all available.

A rigorous selection process identified FPX's software as a service (SaaS) CPQ quote solution as the best choice. FPX is a leading vendor of cloud-based configure-price-quote (CPQ) software and a certified SAP Independent Software Vendor (ISV) partner. Only the FPX solution had the ability to integrate with Fujitsu's front-end Salesforce lead management and forecasting software and also with data from the company's back-end ERP system—and it ran on a cloud computing platform.

FPX CPQ automatically configures all sales orders, even when they are based on extremely complex business rules. The software validates all selections of products and services to eliminate costly rework and helps preserve profit margins by requiring approval for discounts that exceed preapproved levels.

For Fujitsu, FPX CPQ automates all of the company's complex pricing rules and requirements and integrates them in nearly real time with the quoting system so that quotes and orders are able to immediately capture any change to product and materials master data. Pricing that used to take Fujitsu's sales teams days to calculate now just takes seconds. And by centralizing this information, one does not have to pore through individual spreadsheets to see how pricing is being done. When a change is made, it no longer is buried in one or a handful of spreadsheets maintained by individual sales staff.

FPX CPQ can also automatically recognize additional opportunities based on changing the placement of a product in a specific location. This feature eliminates the cumbersome manual process of cross-checking a configuration against a promotion list and eliminates the need to make post-sale concessions to customers who did not initially receive the lowest-cost option. Within six months of implementing FPX CPQ, Fujitsu was already achieving business benefits. A single cloud-based platform for CPQ replaced multiple quoting systems for configuring multishelf and multislot networking platforms. Pricing errors were reduced 80 percent, which in turn significantly reduced rework and write-downs (reductions in the value of an asset). The overall cycle time (total time from beginning to end of a process) decreased as well. Moreover, automating the CPQ enterprise-wide made it possible to see more important information about sales, services, and what customers were requesting.

Every time a change is made, such as a new price, new product availability, or a change in a product description, all users can see that change as soon as they access the system and look at their quotes. If a quote is in the process of being generated, Fujitsu can also update that quote with such changes. End users can be out in the field with customers and show them real-time visual representations of solutions, make changes to configurations, and instantly obtain accurate-up-to-the-minute prices.

The new CPQ system enables Fujitsu to streamline the sales process by placing a significant portion of the product data and configuration rules directly within the quoting application. The sales team is able to operate more independently and to focus on selling.

Sources: Ken Murphy, "Fujitsu Untangles Sales Complexities," SAP Insider Profiles, July 6, 2015; "FPX: Single Application Platform for Multi-Channel Management," cioreview.com, accessed February 20, 2016; www.fpx.com, accessed February 20, 2016; and www.fujitsu.com, accessed February 20, 2016.

CASE STUDY QUESTIONS

1. What were Fujitsu's problems with its existing systems for the CPQ process? What was the business impact of these problems?

2. List and describe the most important information requirements you would expect to see in Fujitsu's RFP.

3. Why was the FPX CPQ solution selected? Was it a good choice? Why or why not?

4. Why would software as a service be an appropriate solution for Fujitsu? Should Fujitsu have built its own CPQ system in-house?

5. How much did FPX CPQ change the way Fujitsu ran its business?

If an organization has unique requirements that the package does not address, many packages include capabilities for customization. **Customization** features allow a commercial software package or cloud-based software to be modified to meet an organization's unique requirements without destroying the integrity of the software. If a great deal of customization is required, additional programming and customization work may become so expensive and time-consuming that they negate many of the advantages of software packages and services.

When a system is developed using an application software package or a cloud software service, systems analysis will include a formal evaluation of the software package or service in which both end users and information systems specialists will participate. The most important evaluation criteria are the functions provided by the software, flexibility, user-friendliness, hardware requirements, database requirements, installation and maintenance efforts, documentation, vendor quality, and cost. The package or software service evaluation process often is based on a **request for proposal (RFP)**, which is a detailed list of questions submitted to software vendors.

When software from an external source is selected, the organization no longer has total control over the systems design process. Instead of tailoring the systems design specifications directly to user requirements, the design effort will consist of trying to mold user requirements to conform to the features of the package or software service. If the organization's requirements conflict with the way the package or software service works and this software cannot be customized, the organization will have to adapt to the package or software service and change its procedures.

Outsourcing

If a firm does not want to use its internal resources to build or operate information systems, it can outsource the work to an external organization that specializes in providing these services. Cloud computing and software as a service (SaaS) providers, which we described in Chapter 5, are one form of outsourcing. Subscribing companies use the software and computer hardware provided by the service as the technical platform for their systems. In another form of outsourcing, a company could hire an external vendor to design and create the software for its system, but that company would operate the system on its own computers. The outsourcing vendor might be domestic or in another country.

Domestic outsourcing is driven primarily by the fact that outsourcing firms possess skills, resources, and assets that their clients do not have. Installing a new supply chain management system in a very large company might require hiring an additional 30 to 50 people with specific expertise in supply chain management software, licensed from a vendor. Rather than hire permanent new employees, most of whom would need extensive training in the new software, and then release them after the new system is built, it makes more sense, and is often less expensive, to outsource this work for a 12-month period.

In the case of **offshore outsourcing**, the decision is much more cost-driven. A skilled programmer in India or Russia earns about $10,000–$30,000 per year compared with about $60,000–$120,000 per year for a comparable programmer in the United States. The Internet and low-cost communications technology have drastically reduced the expense and difficulty of coordinating the work of global teams in offshore locations. In addition to cost savings, many offshore outsourcing firms offer world-class technology assets and skills. Wage inflation outside the United States has recently eroded some of these advantages, and some jobs have moved back to the United States. Firms generally do not outsource the conception, systems analysis, and design of IT systems to offshore firms, but often do outsource programming, testing, maintenance, and daily operation of IT systems.

There is a very strong chance that at some point in your career, you'll be working with offshore outsourcers or global teams. Your firm is most likely to benefit from outsourcing if it takes the time to evaluate all the risks and to make sure outsourcing is appropriate for its particular needs. Any company that outsources its applications must thoroughly understand the project, including its requirements, method of implementation, anticipated benefits, cost components, and metrics for measuring performance.

Many firms underestimate costs for identifying and evaluating vendors of information technology services, for transitioning to a new vendor, for improving internal software development methods to match those of outsourcing vendors, and for monitoring vendors to make sure they are fulfilling their contractual obligations. Companies will need to allocate resources for documenting requirements, sending out RFPs, handling travel expenses, negotiating contracts, and project management. Experts claim it takes from three months to a full year to fully transfer work to an offshore partner and make sure the vendor thoroughly understands your business.

Outsourcing offshore incurs additional costs for coping with cultural differences that drain productivity and dealing with human resources issues, such as terminating or relocating domestic employees. All of these hidden costs undercut some of the anticipated benefits from outsourcing. Firms should be especially cautious when using an outsourcer to develop or to operate applications that give it some type of competitive advantage.

FIGURE 13.11 TOTAL COST OF OFFSHORE OUTSOURCING

TOTAL COST OF OFFSHORE OUTSOURCING				
Cost of outsourcing contract			$10,000,000	
Hidden Costs	Best Case	Additional Cost ($)	Worst Case	Additional Cost ($)
1. Vendor selection	0%	20,000	2%	200,000
2. Transition costs	2%	200,000	3%	300,000
3. Layoffs & retention	3%	300,000	5%	500,000
4. Lost productivity/cultural issues	3%	300,000	27%	2,700,000
5. Improving development processes	1%	100,000	10%	1,000,000
6. Managing the contract	6%	600,000	10%	1,000,000
Total additional costs		1,520,000		5,700,000
	Outstanding Contract ($)	Additional Cost ($)	Total Cost ($)	Additional Cost
Total cost of outsourcing (TCO) best case	10,000,000	1,520,000	11,520,000	15.2%
Total cost of outsourcing (TCO) worst case	10,000,000	5,700,000	15,700,000	57.0%

If a firm spends $10 million on offshore outsourcing contracts, that company will actually spend 15.2 percent in extra costs even under the best-case scenario. In the worst-case scenario, where there is a dramatic drop in productivity along with exceptionally high transition and layoff costs, a firm can expect to pay up to 57 percent in extra costs on top of the $10 million outlay for an offshore contract.

General Motors Corporation (GM) had outsourced 90 percent of its IT services, including its data centers and application development. The company recently decided to bring 90 percent of its IT infrastructure in-house, with only 10 percent managed by outsourcers. Lowering costs is important, but GM's primary reason for cutting back outsourcing is to take back control of its information systems, which it believes were preventing the company from responding quickly to competitive opportunities. Bringing information systems in-house will make it easier for GM standardize and streamline its systems and data centers. Figure 13.11 shows best- and worst-case scenarios for the total cost of an offshore outsourcing project. It shows how much hidden costs affect the total project cost. The best case reflects the lowest estimates for additional costs, and the worst case reflects the highest estimates for these costs. As you can see, hidden costs increase the total cost of an offshore outsourcing project by an extra 15 to 57 percent. Even with these extra costs, many firms will benefit from offshore outsourcing if they manage the work well.

13-5 What are new approaches for system building in the digital firm era?

In the digital firm environment, organizations need to be able to add, change, and retire their technology capabilities very rapidly to respond to new opportunities, including the need to provide applications for mobile platforms. Companies are starting to use shorter, more informal development processes that provide fast solutions. In addition to using software packages and online software services, businesses are relying more heavily on fast-cycle techniques such as rapid application development, joint application design, agile development, and reusable standardized software components that can be assembled into a complete set of services for e-commerce and e-business.

Rapid Application Development (RAD), Agile Development, and DevOps

Object-oriented software tools, reusable software, prototyping, and tools for automating program code generation are helping systems builders create working systems much more rapidly than they could using traditional systems-building methods and software tools. The term **rapid application development (RAD)** is used to describe this process of creating workable systems in a very short period of time with some flexibility to adapt as a project evolves. RAD also involves close teamwork among end users and information systems specialists as well as among the IT groups developing and operating the systems. Simple systems often can be assembled from prebuilt components. The process does not have to be sequential, and key parts of development can occur simultaneously.

Sometimes a technique called **joint application design (JAD)** is used to accelerate the generation of information requirements and to develop the initial systems design. JAD brings end users and information systems specialists together in an interactive session to discuss the system's design. Properly prepared and facilitated, JAD sessions can significantly speed up the design phase and involve users at an intense level.

Agile development focuses on rapid delivery of working software by breaking a large project into a series of small subprojects that are completed in short periods of time using iteration and continuous feedback. Each mini-project is worked on by a team as if it were a complete project. Improvement or addition of new functionality takes place within the next iteration as developers clarify requirements. This helps to minimize the overall risk and allows the project to adapt to changes more quickly. Agile methods emphasize face-to-face communication over written documents, encouraging people to collaborate and make decisions quickly and effectively.

DevOps

DevOps builds on agile development principles as an organizational strategy to create a culture and environment that further promote rapid and agile development practices. *DevOps* stands for "development and operations" and emphasizes close collaboration between the software developers who create applications and the IT operational staff who run and maintain the applications. Traditionally, in a large enterprise, an application development team would be in charge of gathering business requirements for an application, designing the application, and writing and testing the software. The operations team would run and maintain the software once it was put into production. Problems arise when the development team is unaware of operational issues that prevent the software from working as expected, requiring additional time and rework to fix the software.

DevOps tries to change this relationship by promoting better and more frequent communication and collaboration between systems development and operations groups and a fast and stable workflow throughout the entire application development life cycle. With this type of organizational change along with agile techniques, standardized processes, and more powerful automated software creation and testing tools, it is possible to release more reliable applications more rapidly and more frequently.

For example, Netflix has a cloud-based IT infrastructure where hundreds of software changes are made each day. Its website consists of hundreds of small software services that communicate with each other. Each service is maintained by a dedicated DevOps team. Netflix developers can automatically create software code for web images with features and services that can be tested in the production environment, integrated with Netflix's existing infrastructure, and monitored automatically to make sure nothing goes wrong. Netflix's use of DevOps and automated processes makes it possible to update its production systems with new software within hours. Most companies would require months (Bossert, Ip, and Starikova, 2015).

Component-Based Development and Web Services

We have already described some of the benefits of object-oriented development for building systems that can respond to rapidly changing business environments, including web applications. To further expedite software creation, groups of objects have been assembled to provide software components for common functions such as a graphical user interface or online ordering capability that can be combined to create large-scale business applications. This approach to software development is called **component-based development**, and it enables a system to be built by assembling and integrating existing software components. Increasingly, these software components are coming from cloud services. Businesses are using component-based development to create their e-commerce applications by combining commercially available components for shopping carts, user authentication, search engines, and catalogs with pieces of software for their own unique business requirements.

Web Services and Service-Oriented Computing

Chapter 5 introduced *web services* as loosely coupled, reusable software components using Extensible Markup Language (XML) and other open protocols and standards that enable one application to communicate with another with no custom programming required to share data and services. In addition to supporting internal and external integration of systems, web services can be used as tools for building new information system applications or enhancing existing systems. Because these software services use a universal set of standards, they promise to be less expensive and less difficult to weave together than proprietary components.

Web services can perform certain functions on their own, and they can also engage other web services to complete more complex transactions, such as checking credit, procurement, or ordering products. By creating software components that can communicate and share data regardless of the operating system, programming language, or client device, web services can provide significant cost savings in systems building while opening up new opportunities for collaboration with other companies.

Mobile Application Development: Designing for A Multiscreen World

Today, employees and customers expect, and even demand, to be able to use a mobile device of their choice to obtain information or perform a transaction anywhere and at any time. To meet these needs, companies will need to develop mobile websites, mobile apps, and native apps as well as traditional information systems.

Once an organization decides to develop mobile apps, it has to make some important choices, including the technology it will use to implement these apps (whether to write a native app or mobile web app) and what to do about a mobile website. A **mobile website** is a version of a regular website that is scaled down in content and navigation for easy access and search on a small mobile screen. (Access Amazon's website from your computer and then from your smartphone to see the difference from a regular website.)

A **mobile web app** is an Internet-enabled app with specific functionality for mobile devices. Users access mobile web apps through their mobile device's web browser. The web app resides primarily on a server, is accessed via the Internet, and doesn't need to be installed on the device. The same application can be used by most devices that can surf the web, regardless of their brand.

A **native app** is a standalone application designed to run on a specific platform and device. The native app is installed directly on a mobile device. Native apps can connect to the Internet to download and upload data, and they can also operate on these data even when not connected to the Internet. For example, an e-book reading app such as Kindle software can download a book from the Internet, disconnect from the Internet, and present the book for reading. Native mobile apps provide fast performance and a high degree of reliability. They are also able to take advantage of a mobile device's particular capabilities, such as its camera or touch features. However, native apps are expensive to develop because multiple versions of an app must be programmed for different mobile operating systems and hardware.

Developing applications for mobile platforms is quite different from development for PCs and their much larger screens. The reduced size of mobile devices makes using fingers and multitouch gestures much easier than typing and using keyboards. Mobile apps need to be optimized for the specific tasks they are to perform, they should not try to carry out too many tasks, and they should be designed for usability. The user experience for mobile interaction is fundamentally different from using a desktop or laptop PC. Saving resources—bandwidth, screen space, memory, processing, data entry, and user gestures—is a top priority.

When a full website created for the desktop shrinks to the size of a smartphone screen, it is difficult for the user to navigate through the site. The user must continually zoom in and out and scroll to find relevant material. Therefore, companies need to design websites specifically for mobile interfaces and create multiple mobile sites to meet the needs of smartphones, tablets, and desktop browsers. This equates to at least three sites with separate content, maintenance, and costs. Currently, websites know what device you are using because your browser will send this information to the server when you log on. Based on this information, the server will deliver the appropriate screen.

One solution to the problem of having multiple websites is to use **responsive web design**. Responsive web design enables websites to change layouts automatically according to the visitor's screen resolution, whether on a desktop, laptop, tablet, or smartphone. Responsive design uses tools such as flexible grid-based layouts, flexible images, and media queries to optimize the design for different viewing contexts. This eliminates the need for separate design and development work for each new device. HTML5, which we introduced in Chapter 5, is also used for mobile application development because it can support cross-platform mobile applications.

The Interactive Session on Technology describes how some companies have addressed the challenges of mobile development we have just identified.

Developing Mobile Apps: What's Different

Just about all businesses today want to deploy mobile apps. Studies show that mobile consumers look at their phones an average of 1,500 times each week and spend 177 minutes on their phone per day. With every swipe, tap, and zoom, customers are coming to expect the same experience in all their dealings with businesses. Businesses today know they must respond, and they want mobile apps developed in a very short time frame. That's not so easy.

Developing successful mobile apps poses some unique challenges. The user experience on a mobile device is fundamentally different from that on a PC. There are special features on mobile devices such as location-based services that that give firms the potential to interact with customers in meaningful new ways. Firms need to be able to take advantage of those features while delivering an experience that is appropriate to a small screen. There are multiple mobile platforms to work with, including iOS, Android, and Windows 10, and a firm may need a different version of an application to run on each of these. System builders need to understand how, why, and where customers use mobile devices and how these mobile experiences change business interactions and behavior. You can't just port a website or desktop application to a smartphone or tablet. It's a different systems development process.

Alex and Ani learned this when developing mobile app for employees in its stores to help customers make selections and then complete the purchase transaction. Alex and Ani, founded in 2004, designs, produces, and sells high-quality, eco-friendly jewelry in the United States using artisanal techniques and is dedicated to helping its customers find inner peace and positive energy. Having customers in Alex and Ani stores wait in long checkout lines ran counter to the company's philosophy and brand image.

Working with Mobiquity, a developer of enterprise mobile solutions, Alex and Ani created a mobile point-of-sale and payment solution where Alex and Ani's Bangle Bartenders can swipe credit cards, scan bar codes, and print, allowing customers to sign and receive a copy of the credit card receipt at the time of purchase while they are in the store aisles. They do not have to wait in line for a cashier. The mobile app helps store sales staff to be more attentive to customers while reducing time to pay for purchases. This enhances the in-store customer experience,

improves brand perception, and provides better customer service, thereby increasing sales revenues.

The starting point for developing a mobile app is to identify the mobile moments (occasions when someone would pull out a mobile device to get something done) where a mobile app would be especially helpful. Alex and Ani's chief technology officer Joe Lezon and head of retail operations Susan Soards mapped out the mobile moments where employees interact with customers. They then specified the context—the situation, preferences, and attitudes of customers and employees in these mobile moments. Lezon and Soards determined where physically in the store mobile moments occur, how long they last, the stage of the checkout process, what information is available, and customer expectations.

The second step is to design the mobile engagement. Businesspeople, designers, and app developers get together to decide how to engage a customer during mobile moments and which moments benefit both the customer and the company. A mobile app for moments that benefit both customers and the company is more likely to be successful. Alex and Ani had a small team draw pictures to design the mobile engagement, mapping out exactly how an employee would use an iPod Touch application and a credit card reader/printer linked directly to the company's point-of-sale system to engage customers. The design specifications included screen layouts, the sequence of events, and transactions needed at each step.

The third step is to engineer people, processes, and platforms to deliver the mobile experience. An effective mobile app often requires changing the firm's internal systems, such as those for inventory management, customers, and reservations. Changes such as new APIs and tuning the systems to respond more quickly to requests account for 80 percent of the cost of most mobile projects. (*API* stands for "application program interface," a set of routines, protocols, and tools for building software applications, specifying how software components should interact.) Alex and Ani connected their mobile app to the company's point-of-sale systems as well as to systems with detailed product information.

The fourth, final step is to monitor performance and improve outcomes. Alex and Ani analyzed its mobile retail application to determine how much the length of time for checkouts decreased and which customers completed transactions. The new mobile system gave Bangle Bartenders more time to spend with customers, eliminated customer lines, and helped increase holiday sales by more than 300 percent. Alex and Ani was able to increase the number of checkout points from four to 10 in most of its 28 U.S. stores.

Mobile apps should not be built for the sake of going mobile but for genuinely helping the company become more successful. The mobile app must be connected in a meaningful way to the systems that power the business. Chicago-based TTX, which provides rail cars and freight rail management services to the railroad industry, found that the most critical aspect of its mobile application development project was having a firm idea of what it was trying to accomplish with the app. In 2014 the company developed a mobile app to improve billing accuracy and boost the productivity of its maintenance crews in its 50 maintenance shops that operate along the railroads. The app took about six months to design and build in-house.

The purpose of the app was to improve record-keeping involved in TTX's maintenance work, which takes place in rough outdoor conditions where connectivity is spotty or nonexistent and is performed by employees who often wear gloves. Maintenance crews had used paper and pencil to record their notes on the rail car repairs. The mobile application was based on a Windows platform for a plastic-encased PC with a touchscreen. TTX CIO and Vice President Bruce Schinelli and his systems development team recognized that what the app needed to do was to replace pen and paper, and it had to work that well in the field. That early understanding of how the mobile app would provide value to the business drove the entire system design and implementation. Schinelli believes that if a company makes the wrong assumptions about the purpose of its mobile application, it will have to do a lot of rework. For TTX, the hard work was making sure its system builders knew exactly how the mobile app would work out in the field.

Sources: Mary K. Pratt, "As Mobile Apps for Employees Proliferate, CIOs Get Involved," searchCIO.com, accessed February 10, 2016; Alex and Ani, "Alex and Ani mPOS," www.mobiquity.com, accessed February 22, 2016; Linda Tucci, "Enterprise Mobile App Development: No Easy Answers," searchCIO.com, accessed February 22, 2016; and Brian Solis, "Mobile Is Eating the World," Sitecore Corporation, February 2016.

CASE STUDY QUESTIONS

1. What management, organization, and technology issues need to be addressed when building a mobile application?

2. How does user requirement definition for mobile applications differ from traditional systems analysis?

3. Describe how Alex and Ani's sales process before and after the mobile application was deployed.

Review Summary

13-1 *How does building new systems produce organizational change?*

Building a new information system is a form of planned organizational change. Four kinds of technology-enabled change are (1) automation, (2) rationalization of procedures, (3) business process redesign, and (4) paradigm shift, with far-reaching changes carrying the greatest risks and rewards. Many organizations are using business process management to redesign workflows and business processes in the hope of achieving dramatic productivity breakthroughs. Business process management is also useful for promoting total quality management (TQM), six sigma, and other initiatives for incremental process improvement.

13-2 *What are the core activities in the systems development process?*

The core activities in systems development are systems analysis, systems design, programming, testing, conversion, production, and maintenance. Systems analysis is the study and analysis of problems of existing systems and the identification of requirements for their solutions. Systems design provides the specifications for an information system solution, showing how its technical and organizational components fit together.

13-3 *What are the principal methodologies for modeling and designing systems?*

The two principal methodologies for modeling and designing information systems are structured methodologies and object-oriented development. Structured methodologies focus on modeling processes and data separately. The data flow diagram is the principal tool for structured analysis, and the structure chart is the principal tool for representing structured software design. Object-oriented development models a system as a collection of objects that combine processes and data. Object-oriented modeling is based on the concepts of class and inheritance.

13-4 *What are alternative methods for building information systems?*

The oldest method for building systems is the systems life cycle, which requires that information systems be developed in formal stages. The stages must proceed sequentially and have defined outputs; each requires formal approval before the next stage can commence. The systems life cycle is useful for large projects that need formal specifications and tight management control over each stage of systems building, but it is very rigid and costly.

Prototyping consists of building an experimental system rapidly and inexpensively for end users to interact with and evaluate. Prototyping encourages end-user involvement in systems development and iteration of design until specifications are captured accurately. The rapid creation of prototypes can result in systems that have not been completely tested or documented or that are technically inadequate for a production environment.

Using a software package or online software services (SaaS) reduces the amount of design, programming, testing, installation, and maintenance work required to build a system. Application software packages or SaaS are helpful if a firm does not have the internal information systems staff or financial resources to custom develop a system. To meet an organization's unique requirements, packages may require extensive modifications that can substantially raise development costs.

End-user development is the development of information systems by end users, either alone or with minimal assistance from information systems specialists. End user–developed systems can be created rapidly and informally using user-friendly software tools. However, end-user development may create information systems that do not necessarily meet quality assurance standards and that are not easily controlled by traditional means.

Outsourcing consists of using an external vendor to build (or operate) a firm's information systems instead of the organization's internal information systems staff. Outsourcing can save application development costs or enable firms to develop applications without an internal information systems staff. However, firms risk losing control over their information systems and becoming too dependent on external vendors. Outsourcing also entails hidden costs, especially when the work is sent offshore.

13-5 *What are new approaches for system building in the digital firm era?*

Companies are turning to rapid application design (RAD), joint application design (JAD), agile development, and reusable software components to accelerate the systems development process. RAD uses object-oriented software, visual programming, prototyping, and tools for very rapid creation of systems. Agile development breaks a large project into a series of small subprojects that are completed in short periods of time using iteration and continuous feedback. Component-based development expedites application development by grouping objects into suites of software components that can be combined to create large-scale business applications. DevOps emphasizes close collaboration between the software developers who create applications and the IT operational staff who run and maintain the applications. Web services provide a common set of standards that enable organizations to link their systems regardless of their technology platform through standard plug-and-play architecture. Mobile application development must pay attention to simplicity, usability, and the need to optimize tasks for tiny screens.

Key Terms

Acceptance testing, 498
Agile development, 513
Automation, 489
Business process management (BPM), 491
Business process redesign, 490
Component-based development, 514
Computer-aided software engineering (CASE), 504
Conversion, 499
Customization, 510
Data flow diagram (DFD), 500
DevOps, 513
Direct cutover strategy, 499
Documentation, 499
End-user development, 507
End-user interface, 507
Feasibility study, 495
Information requirements, 496
Iterative, 506
Joint application design (JAD), 513
Maintenance, 499
Mobile web app, 515
Mobile website, 515
Native app, 515
Object, 502
Object-oriented development, 502
Offshore outsourcing, 511
Paradigm shift, 491

Parallel strategy, 499
Phased approach strategy, 499
Pilot study strategy, 499
Post-implementation audit, 499
Process specifications, 502
Production, 499
Programming, 497
Prototype, 506
Prototyping, 506
Query languages, 507
Rapid application development (RAD), 513
Rationalization of procedures, 490
Request for proposal (RFP), 510
Responsive web design, 515
Six sigma, 490
Structure chart, 502
Structured, 500
Systems analysis, 495
Systems design, 496
Systems development, 495
Systems life cycle, 505
System testing, 498
Test plan, 498
Testing, 497
Total quality management (TQM), 490
Unit testing, 498

MyMISLab

To complete the problems with the MyMISLab, go to the EOC Discussion Questions in MyMISLab.

Review Questions

13-1 How does building new systems produce organizational change?

- Describe each of the four kinds of organizational change that can be promoted with information technology.

- Define business process management and describe the steps required to carry it out.

13-2 What are the core activities in the systems development process?

- Distinguish between systems analysis and systems design. Describe the activities for each.

- Define information requirements and explain why they are difficult to determine correctly.

- Explain why the testing stage of systems development is so important. Name and describe the three stages of testing for an information system.

- Describe the role of programming, conversion, production, and maintenance in systems development.

13-3 What are the principal methodologies for modeling and designing systems?

- Compare object-oriented and traditional structured approaches for modeling and designing systems.

13-4 What are alternative methods for building information systems?

- Define the traditional systems life cycle. Describe its advantages and disadvantages for systems building.

- Define information system prototyping. Describe its benefits and limitations. List and describe the steps in the prototyping process.

- Define an application software package. Explain the advantages and disadvantages of developing information systems based on software packages.

- Define end-user development and describe its advantages and disadvantages. Name some policies and procedures for managing end-user development.

- Describe the advantages and disadvantages of using outsourcing for building information systems.

13-5 What are new approaches for system building in the digital firm era?

- Define rapid application development (RAD), agile development, and DevOps and explain how they can speed up system building.

- Explain how component-based development and web services help firms build and enhance their information systems.

- Explain the features of mobile application development and responsive web design.

Discussion Questions

13-6
MyMISLab
Why is selecting a systems development approach an important business decision? Who should participate in the selection process?

13-7
MyMISLab
Some have said that the best way to reduce systems development costs is to use application software packages or user-friendly tools. Do you agree? Why or why not?

13-8
MyMISLab
Why is it so important to understand how a business process works when trying to develop a new information system?

Hands-On MIS Projects

The projects in this section give you hands-on experience analyzing business processes, designing and building a customer system for auto sales, and analyzing website information requirements.

Management Decision Problems

13-9 For an additional fee, a customer purchasing a Sears Roebuck appliance, such as a washing machine, can purchase a three-year service contract. The contract provides free repair service and parts for the specified appliance using an authorized Sears service provider. When a person with a Sears service contract needs to repair an appliance, such as a washing machine, he or she calls the Sears Repairs & Parts department to schedule an appointment. The department makes the appointment and gives the caller the date and approximate time of the appointment. The repair technician arrives during the designated time frame and diagnoses the problem. If the problem is caused by a faulty part, the technician either replaces the part if he or she is carrying the part or orders the replacement part from Sears. If the part is not in stock at Sears, Sears orders the part and gives the customer an approximate time when the part will arrive. The part is shipped directly to the customer. After the part has arrived, the customer must call Sears to schedule a second appointment for a repair technician to replace the ordered part. This process is very lengthy. It may take two weeks to schedule the first repair visit, another two weeks to order and receive the required part, and another week to schedule a second repair visit after the ordered part has been received.

- Diagram the existing process.

- What is the impact of the existing process on Sears's operational efficiency and customer relationships?

- What changes could be made to make this process more efficient? How could information systems support these changes? Diagram the improved process.

13-10 Management at your agricultural chemicals corporation has been dissatisfied with production planning. Production plans are created using best guesses of demand for each product, which are based on how much of each product has been ordered in the past. If a customer places an unexpected order or requests a change to an existing order after it has been placed, there is no way to adjust production plans. The company may have to tell customers it can't fill their orders, or it may run up extra costs maintaining additional inventory to prevent stock-outs.

At the end of each month, orders are totaled and manually keyed into the company's production planning system. Data from the past month's production and inventory systems are manually entered into the firm's order management system. Analysts from the sales department and from the production department analyze the data from their respective systems to determine what the sales targets and production targets should be for the next month. These estimates are usually different. The analysts then get together at a high-level planning meeting to revise the production and sales targets to take into account senior management's goals for market share, revenues, and profits. The outcome of the meeting is a finalized production master schedule.

The entire production planning process takes 17 business days to complete. Nine of these days are required to enter and validate the data. The remaining days are spent developing and reconciling the production and sales targets and finalizing the production master schedule.

- Draw a diagram of the existing production planning process.
- Analyze the problems this process creates for the company.
- How could an enterprise system solve these problems? In what ways could it lower costs? Diagram what the production planning process might look like if the company implemented enterprise software.

Improving Decision Making: Using Database Software to Design a Customer System for Auto Sales

Software skills: Database design, querying, reporting, and forms
Business skills: Sales lead and customer analysis

13-11 This project requires you to perform a systems analysis and then design a system solution using database software.

Ace Auto Dealers specializes in selling new vehicles from Subaru in Portland, Oregon. The company advertises in local newspapers and is listed as an authorized dealer on the Subaru website and other major websites for auto buyers. The company benefits from a good local word-of-mouth reputation and name recognition.

Ace does not believe it has enough information about its customers. It cannot easily determine which prospects have made auto purchases, nor can it identify which customer touch points have produced the greatest number of sales leads or actual sales so it can focus advertising and marketing more on the channels that generate the most revenue. Are purchasers discovering Ace from newspaper ads, from word of mouth, or from the web?

Prepare a systems analysis report detailing Ace's problem and a system solution that can be implemented using PC database management software. Then use database software to develop a simple system solution. In MyMISLab, you will find more information about Ace and its information requirements to help you develop the solution.

Achieving Operational Excellence: Analyzing Website Design and Information Requirements

Software skills: Web browser software
Business skills: Information requirements analysis, website design

13-12 Visit the website of your choice and explore it thoroughly. Prepare a report analyzing the various functions provided by that website and its information requirements. Your report should answer these questions: What functions does the website perform? What data does it use? What are its inputs, outputs, and processes? What are some of its other design specifications? Does the website link to any internal systems or systems of other organizations? What value does this website provide the firm?

Collaboration and Teamwork Project

Preparing Website Design Specifications

13-13 With three or four of your classmates, select a system described in this text that uses the web. Review the website for the system you select. Use what you have learned from the website and the description in this book to prepare a report describing some of the design specifications for the system you select. If possible, use Google Docs and Google Drive or Google Sites to brainstorm, organize, and develop a presentation of your findings for the class.

ConAgra's Recipe for a Better Human Resources System
CASE STUDY

Do you have Chef Boyardee Ravioli or Orville Redenbacher popcorn in your pantry or Healthy Choice or Banquet chicken nuggets in your freezer? If so, you're one of the 99 percent of U.S. households that use ConAgra food products. ConAgra Foods Inc., headquartered in Omaha, Nebraska, is one of North America's largest food companies, providing quick, convenient meals, tasty treats, and snacks with brands such as Libbys, Banquet, LaChoy, Hunts, Healthy Choice, and Blue Bonnet. Thirty-two of ConAgra's brands account for more than $100 million in annual retail sales.

ConAgra relies on 33,000 employees to ensure that supermarket and grocery shelves are stocked with its products, and management considers its human resources to be an essential ingredient for its success. Like many forward-looking companies, ConAgra recognizes the importance of human resources to overall corporate success and the ability of the firm to have the right people in place as it pursues its business strategy. Technology is expected to play an even larger role going forward in helping the company recruit, retain, develop, and manage the workers it needs.

Until recently, ConAgra did not have the right technology in place to obtain maximum value from the talents and expertise of its salaried and hourly employees. It had a core system for basic human resources (HR) functions, but it also had disparate siloed systems for HR functions such as employee compensation, development, recruiting, succession planning, and talent review. These systems produced fragmented information and could not support companywide views of the employee or human resources processes. Some of these systems were based on commercial business software products, and others were homegrown. These systems worked well but only up to a point because they were not integrated. That meant that data from one system could not be combined easily with data from another for more insightful reporting and talent analysis or for obtaining a complete picture of employees. There was no central system to house and manage the data so HR staff often had to extract information from multiple systems and piece reports together manually. The company also had to pay for multiple information systems teams to support these systems.

That all changed in 2013 when the company decided to retire most of its existing HR systems and implement a comprehensive talent management system that was integrated with its on-premises core HR system. The talent management system consisted of integrated modules that ran on a cloud-based platform. ConAgra called the project to build the new talent management system "My Recipe."

A major objective of My Recipe was to store and share all workforce data in a single central, integrated cloud-based system. Another was to reduce data redundancies, complexity, and operational efficiencies by centralizing the data so they appeared to be coming from one source. Another was to provide user-friendly tools and processes that made it easier for managers and employees to have meaningful conversations about performance and career growth. Another requirement was the ability to provide a snapshot of ConAgra's current talent pool and show how it was developing to meet future business needs. Such a system was expected to better engage employees and managers, provide more useful data to HR staff, improve talent management, and increase productivity.

After a thorough vendor evaluation process, ConAgra narrowed the search to three vendors and then selected SuccessFactors. SuccessFactors is an SAP-owned global provider of cloud-based software for human capital management. Its human capital management application suite features a learning management system (LMS), performance management, recruiting software, applicant tracking software, succession planning, talent management, and HR analytics along with social business and collaboration tools to help organizations maximize employee growth and performance. Management believed SuccessFactors was superior because it provided an easy-to-use and customizable user interface that would support employee and management self-service using the system. SuccessFactors also integrated with other SAP products and third-party products.

ConAgra implemented My Recipe in three phases over a 15-month period. During the first phase, completed in mid-2013, ConAgra upgraded the overall user interface and implemented the SuccessFactors Learning and Succession & Development modules. In phase two, completed in late 2013, the firm implemented SAP SuccessFactors Workforce Analytics, Workforce Planning, Recruiting Marketing, and Recruiting Management modules. In the final phase, completed in mid-2014, ConAgra implemented a SuccessFactors Compensation module and an update to SuccessFactors Performance & Goals, including the functionality for performance rating calibration. (Calibration is a process for gaining greater consistency in how performance evaluation ratings are delivered.) The new SuccessFactors system replaced eight legacy human resource systems, substantially reduced the amount of HR data stored in manual files, and provided new tools for managers and employees to obtain information and reports directly from the system on their own.

The My Recipe team selected implementation target dates that coincide with the time of year the specified processes were typically performed. For example, the rollout of the SuccessFactors Succession & Development software was timed for when the company conducted its annual talent review. Rolling out the system in stages kept the project alive and relevant, and staff were able to easily understand how one module built upon the next. The project timelines also facilitated adoption of the system because users were exposed from early on to a one-stop shop for human resources and became increasingly interested in seeing the system completed. System log records show that the average HR user accesses some aspect of the SuccessFactors solution about 100 times per year. When ConAgra had fragmented HR systems, there was never that amount of manager and employee interactions with those systems.

Once fully implemented, My Recipe made it possible for ConAgra to capture, store and share succession planning, talent review, and other data that were previously inaccessible and impossible to share. It empowered employees to proactively track tasks, performance, career growth, and opportunities on their own, and it standardized HR business processes throughout the employee life cycle. The new system makes it possible for HR staff to focus on workforce planning issues instead of on tactical day-to-day employee management and recordkeeping. My Recipe also eliminated eight legacy HR systems and their associated administrative burdens and inefficiencies.

One of the new system improvements is the ability to link an employee's payroll records (which are processed in ConAgra's core HR system) to a tile on the SuccessFactors home screen, allowing employees to view their payroll records directly from My Recipe. Other home screen tiles, which can be easily customized, provide access to employee performance and career data in a way that is easy to understand. Ease of use is further promoted by built-in reminders. For instance, a manager viewing an employee's objectives might be alerted that the employee has an upcoming talent review. By centralizing employee data and making the data more easily available, the company is able to see how each employee fits into to individual, team, and companywide plans involving performance, succession, and development. In other words, the system makes it possible for human resources to operate more strategically and align ConAgra's workforce more precisely with the overall goals of the firm.

It was not easy to develop a fully integrated system with common companywide processes. ConAgra had to spend considerable time identifying and evaluating its existing processes and deciding which should be kept and which would need to be changed. The processes had to be mapped against the business processes supported by the SuccessFactors software. It was important to know what each of ConAgra's processes would look like when the SuccessFactors system was implemented and the new system ran in the cloud.

Another challenge was dealing with analytics and reporting. Reporting was difficult when ConAgra's systems were fragmented because it was so difficult to assemble the required data from so many different sources. When the company realized how much more useful and retrievable human resources data the new system would produce, the project was redirected to pay more attention to reporting and analytics and to make sure the system was designed to deliver the data required for this purpose.

ConAgra harnessed the expertise of PricewaterhouseCoopers (PwC) consultants for the implementation. They were able to quickly learn about ConAgra's needs and apply that knowledge along with their expertise to the project. For example, PwC made themselves experts in ConAgra's compensation structure and used that knowledge to configure the system accordingly. They also brought to bear their expertise in cloud systems projects.

How much has the new SuccessFactors system helped ConAgra? According to KC Bradley, ConAgra's Director of Talent Management, SuccessFactors has helped take HR to the next level at her firm. The system has helped facilitate conversations between managers and employees and has armed managers with information they can articulate to higher management about how each employee contributes to the organization's business goals and affects the bottom line. Everyone is now able to see if the right people are in place throughout the organization.

Sources: Ken Murphy, "ConAgra Foods Fine-Tunes Recipe for Enhanced HR," SAP Insider Profiles, October 1, 2015; www. conagra.com, accessed February 21, 2016; www.successfactors. com, accessed February 21,2016; and "ConAgra Foods: Food Leader Finds Right Recipe to Drive Change Management with SuccessFactors Solutions,"SAP, 2015.

CASE STUDY QUESTIONS

13-14 Analyze ConAgra's problems with its old systems. What management, organization, and technology factors were responsible for these problems? What was the business impact of these problems?

13-15 List and describe the information requirements of My Recipe.

13-16 What types of systems-building methods and tools did ConAgra use for building its system?

13-17 What steps did ConAgra take to make sure the My Recipe was successful?

13-18 What were the benefits of the new system? How did it change operational activities and decision making at ConAgra ? How successful was this system solution?

MyMISLab

Go to the Assignments section of MyMISLab to complete these writing exercises.

13-19 Describe four system conversion strategies.

13-20 Describe the role of end users in developing systems using the traditional systems life cycle, prototyping, application software packages, and end-user development.

Chapter 13 References

"5 DevOps Trends Businesses Should Adopt this Year." Itbusinessedge.com, accessed March 31, 2016.

Armstrong, Deborah J. and Bill C. Hardgrove. "Understanding Mindshift Learning: The Transition to Object-Oriented Development." *MIS Quarterly* 31, No. 3 (September 2007).

Aron, Ravi, Eric K.Clemons, and Sashi Reddi. "Just Right Outsourcing: Understanding and Managing Risk." *Journal of Management Information Systems* 22, No. 1 (Summer 2005).

Ashrafi, Noushin and Hessam Ashrafi. *Object-Oriented Systems Analysis and Design*. Upper Saddle River, NY: Prentice-Hall (2009).

Baily, Martin N. and Diana Farrell. "Exploding the Myths of Offshoring." *McKinsey Quarterly* (July 2004).

Benaroch, Michael, Yossi Lichtenstein, and Lior Fink. "Contract Design Choices and the Balance of Ex Ante and Ex Post Transaction Costs in Software Development Outsourcing." *MIS Quarterly* 40 No. 1 (March 2016).

Bossert, Oliver, Chris Ip, and Irina Starikova. "Beyond Agile: Reorganizing IT for Faster Software Delivery." McKinsey & Company (2015).

Cao, Lan, Kannan Mohan, Balasubramaniam Ramesh, and Sumantra Sarkar. "Evolution of Governance: Achieving Ambidexterity in IT Outsourcing." *Journal of Management Information Systems* 30, No. 3 (Winter 2014).

DeMarco, Tom. *Structured Analysis and System Specification*. New York: Yourdon Press (1978).

Dibbern, Jess, Jessica Winkler, and Armin Heinzl. "Explaining Variations in Client Extra Costs between Software Projects Offshored to India." *MIS Quarterly* 32, No. 2 (June 2008).

Edberg, Dana T., Polina Ivanova, and William Kuechler. "Methodology Mashups: An Exploration of Processes Used to Maintain Software." *Journal of Management Information Systems* 28, No. 4 (Spring 2012).

El Sawy, Omar A. *Redesigning Enterprise Processes for E-Business*. McGraw-Hill (2001).

Feeny, David, Mary Lacity, and Leslie P. Willcocks. "Taking the Measure of Outsourcing Providers." *MIT Sloan Management Review* 46, No. 3 (Spring 2005).

Gefen, David and Erran Carmel. "Is the World Really Flat? A Look at Offshoring in an Online Programming Marketplace." *MIS Quarterly* 32, No. 2 (June 2008).

Goo, Jahyun, Rajive Kishore, H. R. Rao, and Kichan Nam. "The Role of Service Level Agreements in Relational Management of Information Technology Outsourcing: An Empirical Study." *MIS Quarterly* 33, No. 1 (March 2009).

Hahn, Eugene D., Jonathan P. Doh, and Kraiwinee Bunyaratavej. "The Evolution of Risk in Information Systems Offshoring: The Impact of Home Country Risk, Firm Learning, and Competitive Dynamics." *MIS Quarterly* 33, No. 3 (September 2009).

Hammer, Michael and James Champy. *Reengineering the Corporation*. New York: HarperCollins (1993).

Hoehle, Hartmut and Viswanath Venkatesh. "Mobile Application Usability: Conceptualization and Instrument Development." *MIS Quarterly* 39, No. 2 (June 2015).

Information Builders. "Yellow Pages Uses WebFOCUS to Demonstrate ROI to Advertisers." www.informationbuilders.com, accessed March 30, 2015.

Ivari, Juhani, Rudy Hirscheim, and Heinz K. Klein. "A Dynamic Framework for Classifying Information Systems Development Methodologies and Approaches." *Journal of Management Information Systems* 17, No. 3 (Winter 2000–2001).

Kendall, Kenneth E. and Julie E. Kendall. *Systems Analysis and Design* (9th ed.). Upper Saddle River, NJ: Prentice Hall (2014).

Kindler, Noah B., Vasantha Krishnakanthan, and Ranjit Tinaikar. "Applying Lean to Application Development and Maintenance." *McKinsey Quarterly* (May 2007).

Kotlarsky, Julia, Harry Scarbrough, and Ilan Oshri. "Coordinating Expertise Across Knowledge Boundaries in Offshore-Outsourcing Projects: The Role of Codification." *MIS Quarterly* 38 No. 2 (June 2014).

Levina, Natalia and Jeanne W. Ross. "From the Vendor's Perspective: Exploring the Value Proposition in Information Technology Outsourcing." *MIS Quarterly* 27, No. 3 (September 2003).

Majchrzak, Ann, Cynthia M. Beath, and Ricardo A. Lim. "Managing Client Dialogues During Information Systems Design to Facilitate Client Learning." *MIS Quarterly* 29, No. 4 (December 2005).

Mani, Deepa, Anitesh Barua, and Andrew Whinston. "An Empirical Analysis of the Impact of Information Capabilities Design on Business Process Outsourcing Performance." *MIS Quarterly* 34, No. 1 (March 2010).

Mani, Deepa and Anitesh Barua. "The Impact of Firm Learning on Value Creation in Strategic Outsourcing Relationships." *Journal of Management Information Systems* 32 No. 1 (2015).

Mocker, Martin, Jeanne Ross, and Craig Hopkins." How USAA Architected Its Business for Life Event Integration." *MIS Quarterly Executive* 14, No. 4 (2015).

Nelson, H. James, Deborah J. Armstrong, and Kay M. Nelson. "Patterns of Transition: The Shift from Traditional to Object-Oriented Development." *Journal of Management Information Systems* 25, No. 4 (Spring 2009).

Overby, Stephanie. "The Hidden Costs of Offshore Outsourcing," *CIO Magazine* (September 1, 2003).

Ozer, Muammer and Doug Vogel. "Contextualized Relationship Between Knowledge Sharing and Performance in Software Development." *Journal of Management Information Systems* 32, No. 2 (2015).

Pollock, Neil and Sampsa Hyysalo. "The Business of Being a User: The Role of the Reference Actor in Shaping Packaged Enterprise System Acquisition and Development." *MIS Quarterly* 38, No. 2 (June 2014).

Saunders, Adam and Erik Brynjolfsson. "Valuing Information Technology Related Intangible Assets." *MIS Quarterly* 40 No. 1 (March 2016).

Sircar, Sumit, Sridhar P. Nerur, and Radhakanta Mahapatra. "Revolution or Evolution? A Comparison of Object-Oriented and Structured Systems Development Methods." *MIS Quarterly* 25, No. 4 (December 2001).

Su, Ning, Natalia Levina, and Jeanne W. Ross. "The Long-Tail Strategy for IT Outsourcing." *MIT Sloan Management Review* (Winter 2016).

Valacich, Joseph A. and Joey George. *Modern Systems Analysis and Design* (7th ed.). Upper Saddle River, NJ: Prentice-Hall (2014).

Yourdon, Edward and L. L. Constantine. *Structured Design*. New York: Yourdon Press (1978).

14 Managing Projects

Learning Objectives

After reading this chapter, you will be able to answer the following questions:

14-1 What are the objectives of project management, and why is it so essential in developing information systems?

14-2 What methods can be used for selecting and evaluating information systems projects and aligning them with the firm's business goals?

14-3 How can firms assess the business value of information systems?

14-4 What are the principal risk factors in information systems projects, and how can they be managed?

MyMISLab™

Visit **mymislab.com** for simulations, tutorials, and end-of-chapter problems.

CHAPTER CASES

Intuit Counts on Project Management

Can the National Health Service Go Paperless?

Snohomish County Public Utility District Implements a New Human Resources System

The Philly311 Project: The City of Brotherly Love Turns Problems into Opportunities

VIDEO CASES

Blue Cross Blue Shield: Smarter Computing Project

NASA Project Management Challenges

Intuit Counts on Project Management

Intuit is a leading provider of financial management software and tools for consumers and business professionals such as TurboTax, QuickBooks, Quicken, and Mint.com. Selling these tools and providing customer service generate a great deal of valuable data. Intuit had no problem gathering and storing such data, but it did face hurdles deriving useful insights from all of its data. That's why Intuit launched the Intuit Analytics Cloud (IAC) project to turn lakes of data into pools of information.

In the past, Intuit had a number of data teams and multiple data silos maintained in isolation of each other. Despite many positive outcomes the arrangement produced within the enterprise or within the infrastructures for the individual products, Intuit was unable to utilize its data effectively for the entire organization or for all of its customers. Management wanted a more holistic approach so that the company could better use data to serve its customers and customers could have better experiences from the data and better insight about themselves.

The IAC project differed from the way projects were handled at Intuit in two major ways: first, Intuit's Analytics Cloud wasn't designed for a specific business use. Instead, it was supposed to be a general (holistic) platform serving the entire company for business units to use in any way they chose. Second, IAC was less structured than a traditional database so that the data could be used more flexibly. (In a traditional database, one designs and organizes the database before entering any data.) A data lake, such as IAC, is quite the opposite, dumping data into a big Hadoop repository without designing a data model beforehand. This approach provides tools for people to analyze the data along with a high-level definition of what data exists in the lake. People build various views into the data as they go along.

© Lucadp/Fotolia

The Intuit IAC project required cooperation across the entire company because it incorporated all of the company's enterprise data, its product data, and third-party data into a single platform. IAC project leaders moved a number of functional teams from the data engineering group to production work for the project.

The project team was very sensitive to deadlines and the project budget. One of the key steps was breaking down the project into easy-to-handle pieces. Organizing a large project into "bite-sized" pieces makes it possible to deliver demonstrable results as the project progresses. The IAC project was a multiyear endeavor, and a "big bang" approach wasn't operationally or politically feasible. Creating a series of smaller deliverables rather than a single large end product made the project more manageable for the project teams. Additionally, executives authorizing project expenditures would be pleased by a series of demonstrable results as well. The success of the smaller project "bites" meant that project leaders didn't have to work hard to convince business unit leaders to participate in the project. Intuit's IAC project has been so successful that internal business units are jostling to use the new enterprise analytics cloud.

Sources: www.intuit.com, accessed January 16, 2016; Curtis Franklin Jr.,"Intuit CIO: Changing the Way Projects Are Managed," *Information Week*, December 17, 2015; Vindu Goel, "Intuit Sheds Its PC Roots and Rises as a Cloud Software Company," *New York Times*, April 10, 2016; and Robert L. Mitchell, "Eight Big Trends in Big Data Analytics," *Computerworld*, October 23, 2014.

One of the principal challenges posed by information systems is ensuring they deliver genuine business benefits. There is a very high failure rate among information systems projects because organizations have incorrectly assessed their business value or because firms have failed to manage the organizational change surrounding the introduction of new technology. Projects to build or improve information systems require special managerial and organizational techniques to make them effective.

Intuit's management realized this when it undertook its Intuit Analytics Cloud (IAC) project. The new technology involved changes to important business processes (and use of data) as well as new software. Intuit succeeded with this project because its management clearly understood that strong project management and attention to organizational issues were essential to success.

The chapter-opening diagram calls attention to important points raised by this case and this chapter. Intuit's future growth called for more intensive companywide use of internal and external data. Outdated file organization and legacy systems made internal operations inefficient, preventing the company from providing the high level of service to customers that management desired. Management wisely assembled a project team and established desired outcomes and deadlines. It chose to break this very large project down into manageable chunks, each with a deliverable, which made the project more manageable and also garnered support from top management and from the business units that wanted to use the IAC.

Here are some questions to think about: Why was this project successful? Why was it important to break down the project into smaller chunks?

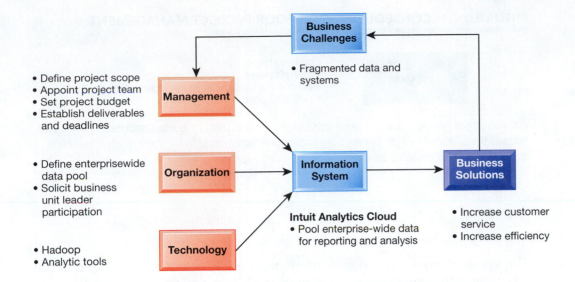

14-1 What are the objectives of project management, and why is it so essential in developing information systems?

There is a very high failure rate among information systems projects. In nearly every organization, information systems projects take much more time and money to implement than originally anticipated, or the completed system does not work properly. When an information system does not meet expectations or costs too much to develop, companies may not realize any benefit from their information system investment, and the system may not be able to solve the problems for which it was intended. The development of a new system must be carefully managed and orchestrated, and the way a project is executed is likely to be the most important factor influencing its outcome. That's why it's essential to have some knowledge about managing information systems projects and the reasons why they succeed or fail.

Runaway Projects and System Failure

How badly are projects managed? On average, private sector projects are underestimated by half in terms of budget and time required to deliver the complete system promised in the system plan. Many projects are delivered with missing functionality (promised for delivery in later versions). A joint study by McKinsey and Oxford University found that large software projects on average run 66 percent over budget and 33 percent over schedule; as many as 17 percent of projects turn out so badly that they can threaten the existence of the company (Chandrasekaran, Gudlavalleti, and Kaniyar, 2014). Between 30 and 40 percent of all software projects are "runaway" projects that far exceed the original schedule and budget projections and fail to perform as originally specified.

As illustrated in Figure 14.1, a systems development project without proper management will most likely suffer these consequences:

- Costs that vastly exceed budgets
- Unexpected time slippage

FIGURE 14.1   CONSEQUENCES OF POOR PROJECT MANAGEMENT

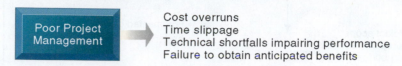

Poor Project Management → Cost overruns
Time slippage
Technical shortfalls impairing performance
Failure to obtain anticipated benefits

Without proper management, a systems development project takes longer to complete and most often exceeds the allocated budget. The resulting information system most likely is technically inferior and may not be able to demonstrate any benefits to the organization.

- Technical performance that is less than expected
- Failure to obtain anticipated benefits

The systems produced by failed information projects are often not used in the way they were intended or are not used at all. Users often have to develop parallel manual systems to make these systems work. According to a 2015 report by 1E, which develops software solutions for managing and reducing IT costs, 37 percent of all software installed is not being used, wasting $30 billion in the United States alone (1E, 2016).

The actual design of the system may fail to capture essential business requirements or improve organizational performance. Information may not be provided quickly enough to be helpful, it may be in a format that is impossible to digest and use, or it may represent the wrong pieces of data.

The way in which nontechnical business users must interact with the system may be excessively complicated and discouraging. A system may be designed with a poor user interface. The **user interface** is the part of the system with which end users interact. For example, an online input form or data entry screen may be so poorly arranged that no one wants to submit data or request information. System outputs may be displayed in a format that is too difficult to comprehend.

Websites may discourage visitors from exploring further if the web pages are cluttered and poorly arranged, if users cannot easily find the information they are seeking, or if it takes too long to access and display the web page on the user's computer.

Additionally, the data in the system may have a high level of inaccuracy or inconsistency. The information in certain fields may be erroneous or ambiguous, or it may not be organized properly for business purposes. Information required for a specific business function may be inaccessible because the data are incomplete.

Project Management Objectives

A **project** is a planned series of related activities for achieving a specific business objective. Information systems projects include the development of new information systems, enhancement of existing systems, or upgrade or replacement of the firm's information technology (IT) infrastructure.

Project management refers to the application of knowledge, skills, tools, and techniques to achieve specific targets within specified budget and time constraints. Project management activities include planning the work, assessing risk, estimating resources required to accomplish the work, organizing the work, acquiring human and material resources, assigning tasks, directing activities, controlling project execution, reporting progress, and analyzing the results. As in other areas of business, project management for information systems must deal with five major variables: scope, time, cost, quality, and risk.

Scope defines what work is or is not included in a project. For example, the scope of a project for a new order processing system might be to include new modules for inputting orders and transmitting them to production and accounting but not any changes to related accounts receivable, manufacturing, distribution, or inventory control systems. Project management defines all the work required to complete a project successfully and should ensure that the scope of a project does not expand beyond what was originally intended.

Time is the amount of time required to complete the project. Project management typically establishes the amount of time required to complete major components of a project. Each of these components is further broken down into activities and tasks. Project management tries to determine the time required to complete each task and establish a schedule for completing the work.

Cost is based on the time to complete a project multiplied by the cost of human resources required to complete the project. Information systems project costs also include the cost of hardware, software, and work space. Project management develops a budget for the project and monitors ongoing project expenses.

Quality is an indicator of how well the end result of a project satisfies the objectives specified by management. The quality of information systems projects usually boils down to improved organizational performance and decision making. Quality also considers the accuracy and timeliness of information produced by the new system and ease of use.

Risk refers to potential problems that would threaten the success of a project. These potential problems might prevent a project from achieving its objectives by increasing time and cost, lowering the quality of project outputs, or preventing the project from being completed altogether. Section 14.4 describes the most important risk factors for information systems.

14-2 What methods can be used for selecting and evaluating information systems projects and aligning them with the firm's business goals?

Companies typically are presented with many different projects for solving problems and improving performance. There are far more ideas for systems projects than there are resources. Firms will need to select from this group the projects that promise the greatest benefit to the business. Obviously, the firm's overall business strategy should drive project selection. How should managers choose among all the options?

Management Structure for Information Systems Projects

Figure 14.2 shows the elements of a management structure for information systems projects in a large corporation. It helps ensure that the most important projects are given priority.

At the apex of this structure is the corporate strategic planning group and the information system steering committee. The corporate strategic planning group is responsible for developing the firm's strategic plan, which may require the development of new systems. Often, this group will have developed objective measures of firm performance (called *key performance indicators*, introduced in Chapter 12) and choose to support IT projects that can make a substantial

FIGURE 14.2 MANAGEMENT CONTROL OF SYSTEMS PROJECTS

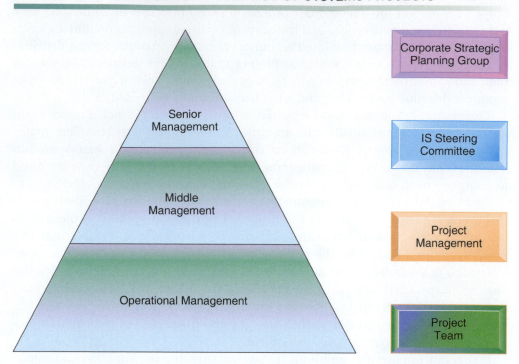

Each level of management in the hierarchy is responsible for specific aspects of systems projects, and this structure helps give priority to the most important systems projects for the organization.

improvement in one or several key performance indicators. These performance indicators are reviewed and discussed by the firm's board of directors.

The information systems steering committee is the senior management group with responsibility for systems development and operation. It is composed of department heads from both end-user and information systems areas. The steering committee reviews and approves plans for systems in all divisions, seeks to coordinate and integrate systems, and occasionally becomes involved in selecting specific information systems projects. This group also has a keen awareness of the key performance indicators decided on by higher-level managers and the board of directors.

The project team is supervised by a project management group composed of information systems managers and end-user managers responsible for overseeing several specific information systems projects. The project team is directly responsible for the individual systems project. It consists of systems analysts, specialists from the relevant end-user business areas, application programmers, and perhaps database specialists. The mix of skills and the size of the project team depend on the specific nature of the system solution.

Linking Systems Projects to The Business Plan

In order to identify the information systems projects that will deliver the most business value, organizations need to develop an **information systems plan** that supports their overall business plan and in which strategic systems are incorporated into top-level planning. The plan serves as a road map indicating the direction of systems development (the purpose of the plan), the rationale, the state of current systems, new developments to consider, the management strategy, the implementation plan, and the budget (see Table 14.1).

TABLE 14.1 INFORMATION SYSTEMS PLAN

1. Purpose of the Plan
   Overview of plan contents
   Current business organization and future organization
   Key business processes
   Management strategy

2. Strategic Business Plan Rationale
   Current situation
   Current business organization
   Changing environments
   Major goals of the business plan
   Firm's strategic plan

3. Current Systems
   Major systems supporting business functions and processes
   Current infrastructure capabilities
   - Hardware
   - Software
   - Database
   - Telecommunications and Internet
   Difficulties meeting business requirements
   Anticipated future demands

4. New Developments
   New systems projects
   - Project descriptions
   - Business rationale
   - Applications' role in strategy
   New infrastructure capabilities required
   - Hardware
   - Software
   - Database
   - Telecommunications and Internet

5. Management Strategy
   Acquisition plans
   Milestones and timing
   Organizational realignment
   Internal reorganization
   Management controls
   Major training initiatives
   Personnel strategy

6. Implementation Plan
   Anticipated difficulties in implementation
   Progress reports

7. Budget Requirements
   Requirements
   Potential savings
   Financing
   Acquisition cycle

The plan contains a statement of corporate goals and specifies how information technology will support the attainment of those goals. The report shows how general goals will be achieved by specific systems projects. It identifies specific target dates and milestones that can be used later to evaluate the plan's progress in terms of how many objectives were actually attained in the time frame specified in the plan. The plan indicates the key management decisions concerning hardware acquisition; telecommunications; centralization/decentralization of authority, data, and hardware; and required organizational change. Organizational changes are also usually described, including management and employee training requirements, recruiting efforts, changes in business processes, and changes in authority, structure, or management practice.

In order to plan effectively, firms will need to inventory and document all of their information system applications and IT infrastructure components. For projects in which benefits involve improved decision making, managers should try to identify the decision improvements that would provide the greatest additional value to the firm. They should then develop a set of metrics to quantify the value of more timely and precise information on the outcome of the decision. (See Chapter 12 for more detail on this topic.)

Information Requirements and Key Performance Indicators

To develop an effective information systems plan, the organization must have a clear understanding of both its long- and short-term information requirements. A strategic approach to information requirements, strategic analysis, or critical success factors argues that an organization's information requirements are determined by a small number of key performance indicators (KPIs) of managers. KPIs are shaped by the industry, the firm, the manager, and the broader environment. For instance, KPIs for an automobile firm might be unit production costs, labor costs, factory productivity, rework and error rate, customer brand recognition surveys, J.D. Power quality rankings, employee job satisfaction ratings, and health costs. New information systems should focus on providing information that helps the firm meet these goals implied by key performance indicators.

Portfolio Analysis

Once strategic analyses have determined the overall direction of systems development, **portfolio analysis** can be used to evaluate alternative systems projects. Portfolio analysis inventories all of the organization's information systems projects and assets, including infrastructure, outsourcing contracts, and licenses. This portfolio of information systems investments can be described as having a certain profile of risk and benefit to the firm (see Figure 14.3) similar to a financial portfolio.

Each information systems project carries its own set of risks and benefits. (Section 14-4 describes the factors that increase the risks of systems projects.) Firms would try to improve the return on their portfolios of IT assets by balancing the risk and return from their systems investments. Although there is no ideal profile for all firms, information-intensive industries (e.g., finance) should have a few high-risk, high-benefit projects to ensure that they stay current with technology. Firms in non-information-intensive industries should focus on high-benefit, low-risk projects.

FIGURE 14.3 A SYSTEM PORTFOLIO

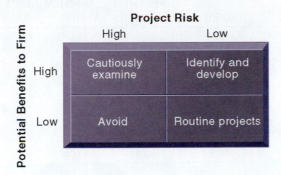

Companies should examine their portfolio of projects in terms of potential benefits and likely risks. Certain kinds of projects should be avoided altogether and others developed rapidly. There is no ideal mix. Companies in different industries have different profiles.

Most desirable, of course, are systems with high benefit and low risk. These promise early returns and low risks. Second, high-benefit, high-risk systems should be examined; low-benefit, high-risk systems should be totally avoided; and low-benefit, low-risk systems should be reexamined for the possibility of rebuilding and replacing them with more desirable systems having higher benefits. By using portfolio analysis, management can determine the optimal mix of investment risk and reward for their firms, balancing riskier high-reward projects with safer lower-reward ones. Firms where portfolio analysis is aligned with business strategy have been found to have a superior return on their IT assets, better alignment of IT investments with business objectives, and better organization-wide coordination of IT investments (Jeffrey and Leliveld, 2004).

Scoring Models

A **scoring model** is useful for selecting projects where many criteria must be considered. It assigns weights to various features of a system and then calculates the weighted totals. Using Table 14.2, the firm must decide among two alternative enterprise resource planning (ERP) systems. The first column lists the criteria that decision makers will use to evaluate the systems. These criteria are usually the result of lengthy discussions among the decision-making group. Often the most important outcome of a scoring model is not the score but agreement on the criteria used to judge a system.

Table 14.2 shows that this particular company attaches the most importance to capabilities for sales order processing, inventory management, and warehousing. The second column in Table 14.2 lists the weights that decision makers attached to the decision criteria. Columns 3 and 5 show the percentage of requirements for each function that each alternative ERP system can provide. Each vendor's score can be calculated by multiplying the percentage of requirements met for each function by the weight attached to that function. ERP System B has the highest total score.

As with all "objective" techniques, there are many qualitative judgments involved in using the scoring model. This model requires experts who understand the issues and the technology. It is appropriate to cycle through the scoring model several times, changing the criteria and weights, to see how sensitive the outcome is to reasonable changes in criteria. Scoring models are used most commonly to confirm, to rationalize, and to support decisions rather than as the final arbiters of system selection.

TABLE 14.2 EXAMPLE OF A SCORING MODEL FOR AN ERP SYSTEM

CRITERIA	WEIGHT	ERP SYSTEM A %	ERP SYSTEM A SCORE	ERP SYSTEM B %	ERP SYSTEM B SCORE
1.0 Order Processing					
1.1 Online order entry	4	67	268	73	292
1.2 Online pricing	4	81	324	87	348
1.3 Inventory check	4	72	288	81	324
1.4 Customer credit check	3	66	198	59	177
1.5 Invoicing	4	73	292	82	328
Total Order Processing			1,370		1,469
2.0 Inventory Management					
2.1 Production forecasting	3	72	216	76	228
2.2 Production planning	4	79	316	81	324
2.3 Inventory control	4	68	272	80	320
2.4 Reports	3	71	213	69	207
Total Inventory Management			1,017		1,079
3.0 Warehousing					
3.1 Receiving	2	71	142	75	150
3.2 Picking/packing	3	77	231	82	246
3.3 Shipping	4	92	368	89	356
Total Warehousing			741		752
Grand Total			3,128		3,300

14-3 How can firms assess the business value of information systems?

Even if a systems project supports a firm's strategic goals and meets user information requirements, it needs to be a good investment for the firm. The value of systems from a financial perspective essentially revolves around the issue of return on invested capital. Does a particular information system investment produce sufficient returns to justify its costs?

Information System Costs and Benefits

Table 14.3 lists some of the more common costs and benefits of systems. **Tangible benefits** can be quantified and assigned a monetary value. **Intangible benefits**, such as more efficient customer service or enhanced decision making, cannot be immediately quantified but may lead to quantifiable gains in the long run. Transaction and clerical systems that displace labor and save space always produce more measurable, tangible benefits than management information systems, decision-support systems, and computer-supported collaborative work systems (see Chapters 2 and 11).

TABLE 14.3 COSTS AND BENEFITS OF INFORMATION SYSTEMS

COSTS

Hardware
Telecommunications
Software
Services
Personnel

TANGIBLE BENEFITS (COST SAVINGS)

Increased productivity
Lower operational costs
Reduced workforce
Lower computer expenses
Lower outside vendor costs
Lower clerical and professional costs
Reduced rate of growth in expenses
Reduced facility costs

INTANGIBLE BENEFITS

Improved asset utilization
Improved resource control
Improved organizational planning
Increased organizational flexibility
More timely information
More information
Increased organizational learning
Legal requirements attained
Enhanced employee goodwill
Increased job satisfaction
Improved decision making
Improved operations
Higher client satisfaction
Better corporate image

Chapter 5 introduced the concept of total cost of ownership (TCO), which is designed to identify and measure the components of information technology expenditures beyond the initial cost of purchasing and installing hardware and software. However, TCO analysis provides only part of the information needed to evaluate an information technology investment because it does not typically deal with benefits, cost categories such as complexity costs, and "soft" and strategic factors discussed later in this section.

Capital Budgeting for Information Systems

To determine the benefits of a particular project, you'll need to calculate all of its costs and all of its benefits. Obviously, a project where costs exceed benefits should be rejected. But even if the benefits outweigh the costs, additional financial analysis is required to determine whether the project represents a good return on the firm's invested capital. **Capital budgeting** models are one of several techniques used to measure the value of investing in long-term capital investment projects.

Capital budgeting methods rely on measures of cash flows into and out of the firm; capital projects generate those cash flows. The investment cost for information systems projects is an immediate cash outflow caused by expenditures for hardware, software, and labor. In subsequent years, the investment may cause additional cash outflows that will be balanced by cash inflows resulting from the investment. Cash inflows take the form of increased sales of more products (for reasons such as new products, higher quality, or increasing market share) or reduced costs in production and operations. The difference between cash outflows and cash inflows is used for calculating the financial worth of an investment. Once the cash flows have been established, several alternative methods are available for comparing different projects and deciding about the investment.

. The principal capital budgeting models for evaluating IT projects are the payback method, the accounting rate of return on investment (ROI), net present value, and the internal rate of return (IRR). You can find out more about how these capital budgeting models are used to justify information system investments in the Learning Tracks for this chapter.

Limitations of Financial Models

The traditional focus on the financial and technical aspects of an information system tends to overlook the social and organizational dimensions of information systems that may affect the true costs and benefits of the investment. Many companies' information systems investment decisions do not adequately consider costs from organizational disruptions created by a new system, such as the cost to train end users, the impact that users' learning curves for a new system have on productivity, or the time managers need to spend overseeing new system-related changes. Intangible benefits such as more timely decisions from a new system or enhanced employee learning and expertise may also be overlooked in a traditional financial analysis.

14-4 What are the principal risk factors in information systems projects, and how can they be managed?

We have already introduced the topic of information system risks and risk assessment in Chapter 8. In this chapter, we describe the specific risks to information systems projects and show what can be done to manage them effectively.

Dimensions of Project Risk

Systems differ dramatically in their size, scope, level of complexity, and organizational and technical components. Some systems development projects are more likely to create the problems we have described earlier or to suffer delays because they carry a much higher level of risk than others. The level of project risk is influenced by project size, project structure, and the level of technical expertise of the information systems staff and project team.

- *Project size*. The larger the project—as indicated by the dollars spent, the size of the implementation staff, the time allocated for implementation, and the number of organizational units affected—the greater the risk. Very large-scale systems projects have a failure rate that is 50 to 75 percent higher than that for other projects because such projects are complex and difficult to control. The organizational complexity of the system—how many units and groups use it and how much it influences business processes—contributes to the complexity of large-scale systems projects just as much as technical characteristics, such as the number of lines of program code, length of project, and budget. In addition, there are few reliable techniques for estimating the time and cost to develop large-scale information systems.

- *Project structure.* Some projects are more highly structured than others. Their requirements are clear and straightforward, so outputs and processes can be easily defined. Users know exactly what they want and what the system should do; there is almost no possibility of the users changing their minds. Such projects run a much lower risk than those with relatively undefined, fluid, and constantly changing requirements; with outputs that cannot be fixed easily because they are subject to users' changing ideas; or with users who cannot agree on what they want.

- *Experience with technology.* The project risk rises if the project team and the information system staff lack the required technical expertise. If the team is unfamiliar with the hardware, system software, application software, or database management system proposed for the project, it is highly likely that the project will experience technical problems or take more time to complete because of the need to master new skills.

Although the difficulty of the technology is one risk factor in information systems projects, the other factors are primarily organizational, dealing with the complexity of information requirements, the scope of the project, and how many parts of the organization will be affected by a new information system. The Interactive Session on Management about the UK National Health Service's move toward paperless recordkeeping illustrates a project with some of these risks.

Change Management and the Concept of Implementation

The introduction or alteration of an information system has a powerful behavioral and organizational impact. Changes in the way that information is defined, accessed, and used to manage the organization's resources often lead to new distributions of authority and power. This internal organizational change breeds resistance and opposition and can lead to the demise of an otherwise good system.

A very large percentage of information systems projects stumble because the process of organizational change surrounding system building was not properly addressed. Successful system building requires careful **change management**.

The Concept of Implementation

To manage the organizational change surrounding the introduction of a new information system effectively, you must examine the process of implementation. **Implementation** refers to all organizational activities working toward the adoption, management, and routinization of an innovation, such as a new information system. In the implementation process, the systems analyst is a **change agent**. The analyst not only develops technical solutions but also redefines the configurations, interactions, job activities, and power relationships of various

INTERACTIVE SESSION: MANAGEMENT

Can the National Health Service Go Paperless?

The National Health Service (NHS) is the United Kingdom's publicly funded national healthcare system. Funded primarily by taxation, NHS provides free or low-cost healthcare to all legal residents of the United Kingdom. NHS services include hospitals, family doctors, specialists, dentists, chemists (pharmacists), opticians, and ambulance service. Medications are subsidized as well. Specific policies vary among England, Scotland, Wales, and Northern Ireland.

The UK Department of Health oversees the NHS. Patient records are maintained by healthcare providers, who must ensure confidentiality of patient data and compliance with regulatory standards. Like other healthcare systems, such as in the United States, patient records were primarily paper-based. Physician and hospital offices had shelves full of folders and papers devoted to the storage of medical records, making patient and treatment information very difficult to access or share. Just pulling the notes for NHS patients to be seen in the morning was a nightmare.

In January 2013 Health Secretary Jeremy Hunt called for making the NHS paperless by 2018 to save billions, improve services, and help meet the challenges of an aging population. Hunt and many others believe that patients should have compatible digital records so their health information can follow them around the health and social care system. Whether patients need a general practitioner (GP), hospital, or care home, the professionals involved in their treatment should be able to see their history at the touch of a button and share crucial information. Improved use of technology would allow health professionals to spend more time with patients and help patients take control of their own care, saving more than £4 billion.

Hunt announced the following goals:

- Paperless referrals: Instead of sending a letter to the hospital when referring a patient, the GP can send an e-mail instead.
- Secure linking of the electronic health and care records wherever they are held, so there is as complete a record as possible of the care someone receives.
- Ability of those records to be able to follow individuals, with their consent, to any part of the NHS or social care system.
- Ability of individuals to get online access to their own health records held by their GP by March 2015.

- Digital information fully available across NHS and social care services by April 2018 unless individuals opt out.

Paperless solutions can lead to a reduction in treatment/medication errors, quicker time to diagnosis, shorter time to treatment, more collaborative diagnostics (allowing a wider range of specialists to be involved), and better overall patient care.

However, many working in the NHS and private sectors—including those within the technology industry—believe that a paperless NHS is not achievable within a five-year time frame. This is an extremely ambitious target, and critics question how much this will really improve NHS services, if it's worth the cost of implementing new IT systems, and if it's even achievable.

According to S. A. Mathieson, an EHI Intelligence analyst, the English NHS is made up of several hundred organizations with greatly differing IT capabilities as well as thousands of independent GPs. All of them would have to acquire new software and hardware and convert their paper records to digital form. To make the new system effective, they would also have to change their procedures (business processes) to take advantage of the new technology. Answering patient phone calls, examining patients, and writing prescriptions will need to incorporate procedures for accessing and updating electronic medical records; paper-based records will have to be converted into electronic form, most likely with codes assigned for various treatment options and data structured to fit the record's format. Training can take up to 20 hours of a doctor's time, and doctors are extremely time-pressed. In order to get the system up and running, physicians themselves may have to enter some of the data, taking away time they could be spending with their patients. When the United States tried to implement electronic medical records in healthcare nationwide, many physicians complained about the time and effort required to make these changes. NHS has experienced some of this resistance.

The UK doctors' union, the British Medical Association (BMA), says there are several challenges to be overcome in order to make the NHS paperless and is skeptical about the extent of the benefits such a system can offer. According to the BMA, the biggest challenges to making the NHS paperless by 2018 are funding, resources, prioritization, and the choice of systems in secondary care. As well as ongoing hardware and software funding, sufficient resources will be required to support training of users and IT specialists to use the paperless system and to provide IT support and administrative support. Although there may potentially be some efficiencies, technology alone will not necessarily create very large cost savings.

Currently, 40 percent of a clinician's time is spent waiting for relevant information or making decisions based on information that is inaccurate or unreliable, and digitization needs to tackle these problems as well.

The House of Commons Public Accounts Committee warned that making the NHS paperless requires significant additional investments in IT and business transformation. Yet the Department of Health had not even set aside a specific budget for this purpose. The department said it was investing £1 billion (approximately $1.5 billion) in the paperless project—half from the central government and the rest from local health and care budgets.

A report by a Public Accounts Committee (PAC) recently said that changes made toward a digital NHS system "has not gone to plan," and some are saying it has been an "expensive waste of time." For any large organization, going paperless is a challenge, but when it is cash strapped and under intense public scrutiny and has a dismal history of IT failure (including unsuccessful earlier efforts to digitize patient records), the task looks like mission impossible, observes Michael Cross, news editor at *The Law Society Gazette*. Can the health service meet that deadline? Or will the NHS just end up with less paper than it did when the paperless project started?

Sources: Kat Hall, "NHS IT Projects Worth £5bn at 'High Risk' of Failure, Warns HSCIC," *The Register,* December 8, 2015; Clare McDonald, "What Is Standing in the Way of a Paperless NHS?" *Computer Weekly,* September 2015; S. A. Mathieson, "How Can IT Contribute to NHS Efficiency?" *Computer Weekly,* September 2015; Michael Cross, "NHS Chases a Paperless Tiger," *Raconteur,* April 29, 2014; Claire Read, "Barriers to a Paperless NHS: Are You Ready for Your Screen Test?" *HSJ,* March 14, 2014; Ben Rossi, "Going Paperless: The Clash Between IT Staff and NHS Trust Heads," *Information Age,* February 18, 2014; Department of Health and the Rt Hon Jeremy Hunt MP, "NHS Challenged to Go Paperless by 2018," www.gov.uk, accessed January 4, 2016; "The Paperless NHS…?" *Computacenter,* April 12, 2013.

CASE STUDY QUESTIONS

1. Why is paperless NHS a risky project? Identify the key risk factors.

2. What management, organization, and technology problems is the paperless NHS likely to encounter?

3. What steps should be taken to make the paperless NHS more successful?

organizational groups. The analyst is the catalyst for the entire change process and is responsible for ensuring that all parties involved accept the changes created by a new system. The change agent communicates with users, mediates between competing interest groups, and ensures that the organizational adjustment to such changes is complete.

The Role of End Users

System implementation generally benefits from high levels of user involvement and management support. User participation in the design and operation of information systems has several positive results. First, if users are heavily involved in systems design, they have more opportunities to mold the system according to their priorities and business requirements and more opportunities to control the outcome. Second, they are more likely to react positively to the completed system because they have been active participants in the change process. Incorporating user knowledge and expertise leads to better solutions.

The relationship between users and information systems specialists has traditionally been a problem area for information systems implementation efforts.

TABLE 14.4 THE USER DESIGNER COMMUNICATIONS GAP

USER CONCERNS	DESIGNER CONCERNS
Will the system deliver the information we need for our work?	What demands will this system put on our servers?
Can we access the data on our iPhones, BlackBerrys, tablets, and PCs?	What kind of programming demands will this place on our group?
What new procedures do we need to enter data into the system?	Where will the data be stored? What's the most efficient way to store them?
How will the operation of the system change employees' daily routines?	What technologies should we use to secure the data?

Users and information systems specialists tend to have different backgrounds, interests, and priorities. This is referred to as the **user-designer communications gap**. These differences lead to divergent organizational loyalties, approaches to problem solving, and vocabularies.

Information systems specialists, for example, often have a highly technical, or machine, orientation to problem solving. They look for elegant and sophisticated technical solutions in which hardware and software efficiency is optimized at the expense of ease of use or organizational effectiveness. Users prefer systems that are oriented toward solving business problems or facilitating organizational tasks. Often the orientations of both groups are so at odds that they appear to speak in different tongues.

These differences are illustrated in Table 14.4, which depicts the typical concerns of end users and technical specialists (information systems designers) regarding the development of a new information system. Communication problems between end users and designers are a major reason why user requirements are not properly incorporated into information systems and why users are driven out of the implementation process.

Systems development projects run a very high risk of failure when there is a pronounced gap between users and technical specialists and when these groups continue to pursue different goals. Under such conditions, users are often driven away from the project. Because they cannot comprehend what the technicians are saying, users conclude that the entire project is best left in the hands of the information specialists alone.

Management Support and Commitment

If an information systems project has the backing and commitment of management at various levels, it is more likely to be perceived positively by both users and the technical information services staff. Both groups will believe that their participation in the development process will receive higher-level attention and priority. They will be recognized and rewarded for the time and effort they devote to implementation. Management backing also ensures that a systems project receives sufficient funding and resources to be successful. Furthermore, to be enforced effectively, all the changes in work habits and procedures and any organizational realignments associated with a new system depend on management backing. If a manager considers a new system a priority, the system will more likely be treated that way by his or her subordinates. According to the Project Management Institute, executive sponsors who are actively engaged is the leading factor in project success (Kloppenborg and Tesch, 2015; Project Management Institute, 2013).

Change Management Challenges for Business Process Reengineering, Enterprise Applications, and Mergers and Acquisitions

Given the challenges of innovation and implementation, it is not surprising to find a very high failure rate among enterprise application and business process reengineering (BPR) projects, which typically require extensive organizational change and which may require replacing old technologies and legacy systems that are deeply rooted in many interrelated business processes. A number of studies have indicated that 70 percent of all business process reengineering projects fail to deliver promised benefits. Likewise, a high percentage of enterprise applications fail to be fully implemented or to meet the goals of their users even after three years of work.

Many enterprise application and reengineering projects have been undermined by poor implementation and change management practices that failed to address employees' concerns about change. Dealing with fear and anxiety throughout the organization, overcoming resistance by key managers, and changing job functions, career paths, and recruitment practices have posed greater threats to reengineering than the difficulties companies faced visualizing and designing breakthrough changes to business processes. All of the enterprise applications require tighter coordination among different functional groups as well as extensive business process change (see Chapter 9).

Projects related to mergers and acquisitions have a similar failure rate. Mergers and acquisitions are deeply affected by the organizational characteristics of the merging companies as well as by their IT infrastructures. Combining the information systems of two different companies usually requires considerable organizational change and complex systems projects to manage. If the integration is not properly managed, firms can emerge with a tangled hodgepodge of inherited legacy systems built by aggregating the systems of one firm after another. Without a successful systems integration, the benefits anticipated from the merger cannot be realized, or, worse, the merged entity cannot execute its business processes effectively.

Controlling Risk Factors

Various project management, requirements gathering, and planning methodologies have been developed for specific categories of implementation problems. Strategies have also been devised for ensuring that users play appropriate roles throughout the implementation period and for managing the organizational change process. Not all aspects of the implementation process can be easily controlled or planned. However, anticipating potential implementation problems and applying appropriate corrective strategies can increase the chances for system success.

The first step in managing project risk involves identifying the nature and level of risk confronting the project. Implementers can then handle each project with the tools and risk management approaches geared to its level of risk. Not all risks are identifiable in advance, but with skilful project management, most are. Frequent communication and a culture of collaboration will help project teams adapt to unforeseen problems that arise (Browning and Ramasesh, 2015; Laufer et al., 2015; McFarlan, 1981).

Managing Technical Complexity

Projects with challenging and complex technology to master benefit from **internal integration tools**. The success of such projects depends on how well their technical complexity can be managed. Project leaders need both heavy technical and administrative experience. They must be able to anticipate problems and develop smooth working relationships among a predominantly technical team. The team should be under the leadership of a manager with a strong technical and project management background, and team members should be highly experienced. Team meetings should take place frequently. Essential technical skills or expertise not available internally should be secured from outside the organization.

Formal Planning and Control Tools

Large projects benefit from appropriate use of **formal planning tools** and **formal control tools** for documenting and monitoring project plans. The two most commonly used methods for documenting project plans are Gantt charts and PERT charts. A **Gantt chart** lists project activities and their corresponding start and completion dates. The Gantt chart visually represents the timing and duration of different tasks in a development project as well as their human resource requirements (see Figure 14.4). It shows each task as a horizontal bar whose length is proportional to the time required to complete it.

Although Gantt charts show when project activities begin and end, they don't depict task dependencies, how one task is affected if another is behind schedule, or how tasks should be ordered. That is where **PERT charts** are useful. *PERT* stands for "Program Evaluation and Review Technique," a methodology developed by the U.S. Navy during the 1950s to manage the Polaris submarine missile program. A PERT chart graphically depicts project tasks and their interrelationships. The PERT chart lists the specific activities that make up a project and the activities that must be completed before a specific activity can start, as illustrated in Figure 14.5.

The PERT chart portrays a project as a network diagram consisting of numbered nodes (either circles or rectangles) representing project tasks. Each node is numbered and shows the task, its duration, the starting date, and the completion date. The direction of the arrows on the lines indicates the sequence of tasks and shows which activities must be completed before the commencement of another activity. In Figure 14.5, the tasks in nodes 2, 3, and 4 are not dependent on each other and can be undertaken simultaneously, but each is dependent on completion of the first task. PERT charts for complex projects can be difficult to interpret, and project managers often use both techniques.

These project management techniques can help managers identify bottlenecks and determine the impact that problems will have on project completion times. They can also help systems developers partition projects into smaller, more manageable segments with defined, measurable business results. Standard control techniques can successfully chart the progress of the project against budgets and target dates, so deviations from the plan can be spotted.

Increasing User Involvement and Overcoming User Resistance

Projects with relatively little structure and many undefined requirements must involve users fully at all stages. Users must be mobilized to support one of many possible design options and to remain committed to a single design. **External integration tools** consist of ways to link the work of the implementation team to users at all organizational levels. For instance, users can become active members of the project team, take on leadership roles, and take charge of installation and training. The implementation team can demonstrate its responsiveness to users, promptly answering questions, incorporating user feedback, and showing their willingness to help.

FIGURE 14.4 A GANTT CHART

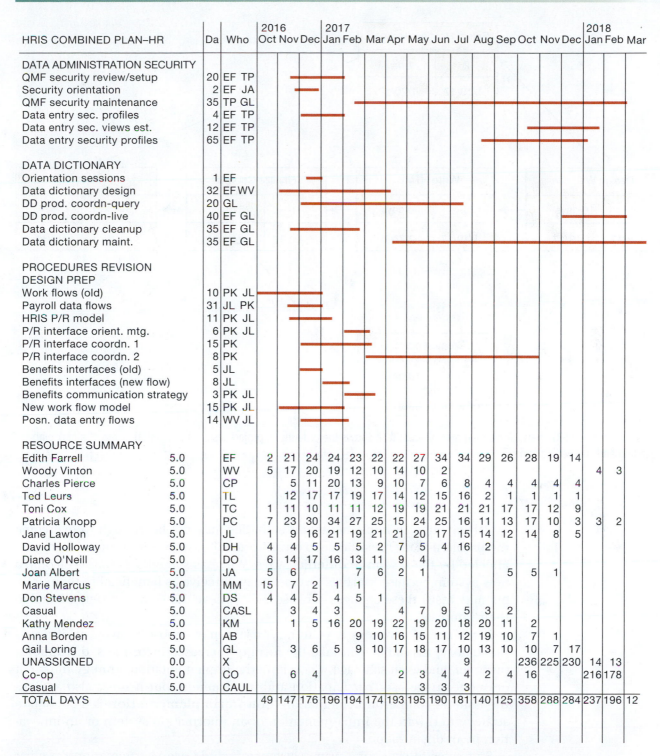

HRIS COMBINED PLAN–HR	Da	Who	2016 Oct	Nov	Dec	2017 Jan	Feb	Mar	Apr	May	Jun	Jul	Aug	Sep	Oct	Nov	Dec	2018 Jan	Feb	Mar
DATA ADMINISTRATION SECURITY																				
QMF security review/setup	20	EF TP																		
Security orientation	2	EF JA																		
QMF security maintenance	35	TP GL																		
Data entry sec. profiles	4	EF TP																		
Data entry sec. views est.	12	EF TP																		
Data entry security profiles	65	EF TP																		
DATA DICTIONARY																				
Orientation sessions	1	EF																		
Data dictionary design	32	EF WV																		
DD prod. coordn-query	20	GL																		
DD prod. coordn-live	40	EF GL																		
Data dictionary cleanup	35	EF GL																		
Data dictionary maint.	35	EF GL																		
PROCEDURES REVISION DESIGN PREP																				
Work flows (old)	10	PK JL																		
Payroll data flows	31	JL PK																		
HRIS P/R model	11	PK JL																		
P/R interface orient. mtg.	6	PK JL																		
P/R interface coordn. 1	15	PK																		
P/R interface coordn. 2	8	PK																		
Benefits interfaces (old)	5	JL																		
Benefits interfaces (new flow)	8	JL																		
Benefits communication strategy	3	PK JL																		
New work flow model	15	PK JL																		
Posn. data entry flows	14	WV JL																		

RESOURCE SUMMARY

		Who	Oct	Nov	Dec	Jan	Feb	Mar	Apr	May	Jun	Jul	Aug	Sep	Oct	Nov	Dec	Jan	Feb	Mar
Edith Farrell	5.0	EF	2	21	24	24	23	22	22	27	34	34	29	26	28	19	14			
Woody Vinton	5.0	WV	5	17	20	19	12	10	14	10	2								4	3
Charles Pierce	5.0	CP		5	11	20	13	9	10	7	6	8	4	4	4	4	4			
Ted Leurs	5.0	TL		12	17	17	19	17	14	12	15	16	2	1	1	1	1			
Toni Cox	5.0	TC	1	11	10	11	11	12	19	19	21	21	21	17	17	12	9			
Patricia Knopp	5.0	PC	7	23	30	34	27	25	15	24	25	16	11	13	17	10	3	3	2	
Jane Lawton	5.0	JL	1	9	16	21	19	21	21	20	17	15	14	12	14	8	5			
David Holloway	5.0	DH	4	4	5	5	5	2	7	5	4	16	2							
Diane O'Neill	5.0	DO	6	14	17	16	13	11	9	4										
Joan Albert	5.0	JA	5	6			7	6	2	1				5	5	1				
Marie Marcus	5.0	MM	15	7	2	1	1													
Don Stevens	5.0	DS	4	4	5	4	5	1												
Casual	5.0	CASL		3	4	3			4	7	9	5	3	2						
Kathy Mendez	5.0	KM		1	5	16	20	19	22	19	20	18	20	11	2					
Anna Borden	5.0	AB				9	10	16	15	11	12	19	10	7	1					
Gail Loring	5.0	GL		3	6	5	9	10	17	18	17	10	13	10	10	7	17			
UNASSIGNED	0.0	X											9		236	225	230	14	13	
Co-op	5.0	CO		6	4				2	3	4	4	2	4	16			216	178	
Casual	5.0	CAUL								3	3	3								
TOTAL DAYS			49	147	176	196	194	174	193	195	190	181	140	125	358	288	284	237	196	12

The Gantt chart in this figure shows the task, person-days, and initials of each responsible person as well as the start and finish dates for each task. The resource summary provides a good manager with the total person-days for each month and for each person working on the project to manage the project successfully. The project described here is a data administration project.

FIGURE 14.5 A PERT CHART

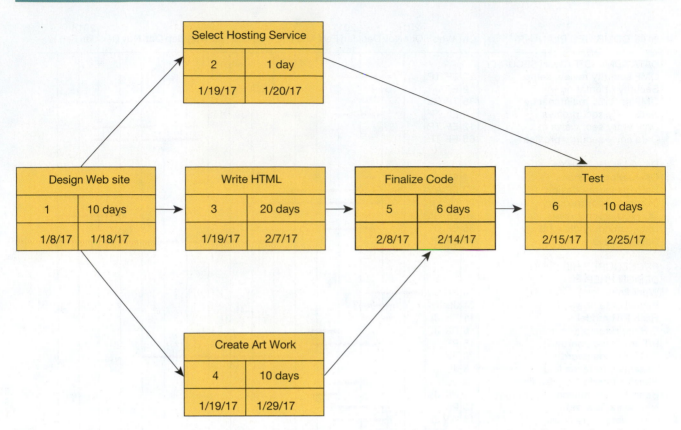

This is a simplified PERT chart for creating a small website. It shows the ordering of project tasks and the relationship of a task with preceding and succeeding tasks.

Participation in implementation activities may not be enough to overcome the problem of user resistance to organizational change. Different users may be affected by the system in different ways. Whereas some users may welcome a new system because it brings changes they perceive as beneficial to them, others may resist these changes because they believe the shifts are detrimental to their interests.

If the use of a system is voluntary, users may choose to avoid it; if use is mandatory, resistance will take the form of increased error rates, disruptions, turnover, and even sabotage. Therefore, the implementation strategy must not only encourage user participation and involvement, but it must also address the issue of counterimplementation. **Counterimplementation** is a deliberate strategy to thwart the implementation of an information system or an innovation in an organization.

Strategies to overcome user resistance include user participation (to elicit commitment as well as to improve design), user education and training, management edicts and policies, and better incentives for users who cooperate. The new system can be made more user-friendly by improving the end-user interface. Users will be more cooperative if organizational problems are solved prior to introducing the new system.

You can see some of these project management strategies at work in the Interactive Session on Organizations, which describes how the Snohomish County Public Utility District (PUD) implemented a new human resources system.

INTERACTIVE SESSION: ORGANIZATIONS

Snohomish County Public Utility District Implements a New Human Resources System

Snohomish County Public Utility District (PUD) in Washington State provides electric power to 330,000 households and also provides water to 19,000 homes throughout a territory covering 2,200 square miles. In 2013, the Everett, Washington-based company took a hard look at its 1,100-strong workforce, which had many highly experienced and capable employees. However, more than 35 percent were eligible to retire within five years. This impending staff turnover and concomitant need to recruit engineers, IT staff, and other technical positions spurred Snohomish PUD to scrutinize its Employee Resources department and recruitment systems.

An aging human resources (HR) system had been used for employee data and benefits, with access restricted to HR employees. Managers in other departments could not make changes to employee data or obtain information for their employees. Outdated processes included paper-based performance appraisals and manually conveying employee data that originated in HR into the payroll system. Bogged down with routine day-to-day tasks, PUD's Employee Resources department could not concentrate on the career development and talent recruitment needed for future success.

CIO Benjamin Beberness and Employee Resources Director Kristi Treckeme began searching for a self-service system that would enable employees to access and update their own data. Employees today, accustomed to instant smartphone access to all manner of personal data, are put off by having to contact the HR department every time a minor issue arises. What's more, high-tech employees today expect to be able to access information whenever and however necessary to perform their jobs.

PUD decided to upgrade its SAP ERP system to consolidate and create a single system of record for the organization and to use SAP's cloud version to maintain its HR records because SAP had such a strong commitment to cloud technology. PUD also decided to implement in parallel SuccessFactors, SAP's cloud-based human capital management (HCM) suite, which features modules for workforce planning and workforce analytics.

Because both crews in the field and in-house employees would be able to access data from the cloud on any device from any location, a major

challenge was assuring them that their data would be safe. A key component of end-user training had to outline SuccessFactors' built-in security measures for protecting employee personally identifiable information and meeting the privacy requirements of the Health Insurance Portability and Accountability Act (HIPAA).

To implement SuccessFactors, the project team used a wave approach in which pieces of software were released to employees in stages so they could gradually get comfortable with the new system. The Project Preparation stage began in March 2014. All fundamental business processes were examined and a business process design settled upon. Next, in the Business Blueprint stage, a detailed description of the business processes and system requirements was outlined to produce the project structure and documentation.

By May the team was ready to launch the first wave of the Realization stage. ADP Payroll and two SuccessFactors modules, Employee Central and Learning, were rolled out along with Benefitfocus, a benefits administration package. Employee Central is the core self-service human resources system in which employees can enter data about their skills, accomplishments, areas of concentration, and proficiencies and where managers can enter information such as promotions, salary changes, and terminations. Employee Central is linked to Learning, the talent management module in which curriculum can be developed, deployed, and managed.

From November 2014 to March 2015, the second wave rolled out SAP Jam, the social collaboration tool, and SuccessFactors modules for compensation management, performance and goals, succession management, career development and planning, and the competency framework. The third and final wave took place in August of 2015, deploying SuccessFactors modules for recruiting management, recruiting marketing, onboarding, workforce planning and analytics, and advanced reporting. The Realization phase concluded when all business process requirements had been implemented.

In the Final Preparation stage, the SAP ERP system was integrated with SuccessFactors to complete the final configuration. All HR data were now linked to security access controls, all processes for employee time tracking, and ADP payroll. The Go Live & Support phase began in September 2015.

The wave rollout created a climate of persistently building on success. This and the meticulously assembled project team propelled the project forward. Headed by a functional lead from the Employee Resources department and assisted by several strategic subject matter experts (SMEs) who rotated in and out to perform system and end-user acceptance testing, the team also included SAP specialists from Deloitte Consulting.

As with any project, however, there were a few hiccups. Despite the full support of management, including the utility's board of commissioners, the project struggled with improper resource allocation. With all departments naturally having to maintain normal operations, transferring team members in and out sometimes resulted in understaffing either departmentally or on the project team. Key Employee Resources staff members helped to navigate these rough waters with their thorough knowledge of HR processes and complete familiarity with SuccessFactors.

Change management was addressed upfront and consistently emphasized. From the start, the project was presented as a company transformation as opposed to simply an IT initiative to foster an atmosphere of shared commitment. The Deloitte partners recommended a "change champion" process. Groups of employees were inserted in various departments to make sure that their colleagues understood the system. They served as trainers, trouble shooters, helpers, and cheerleaders. Assisted by "super users," they used SuccessFactors' Learning module to make sure that all employees would be ready when Go Live day arrived. Each and every employee in the Employee Resources department participated in

testing so that they were well versed in every aspect of the new system and capable of helping their fellow employees. A dedicated internal corporate communications team reinforced and encouraged these efforts.

Project objectives and targets were successfully met, in part because each core business process was assigned to a senior leader. These business process "owners" had developed backup procedures. This freed team members to make on-the-spot system implementation decisions without worrying about business process interruptions. It also meant that it was predominantly broader issues that were shuttled up the executive decision-making chain.

Centralized, transparent employee data have resulted not only in astonishing time savings but also in a noticeable companywide morale boost. Managers and employees can monitor goal setting and performance evaluations, enter feedback, and respond to comments in real time as opposed to the cumbersome paper system previously used. A number of antiquated HR systems and their attendant maintenance costs were eliminated. Employee Resources personnel are no longer dependent on the IT department to run reports and perform analytics. All HR business processes have been consolidated into a single stream that follows employees through their careers and beyond. Next up is optimizing the career development and succession planning tools so that when positions are vacated, whether through promotion, resignation, or retirement, a ready and able replacement is internally available.

Sources: Lauren Bonneau, "This Is Not Your Grandfather's Utility," *SAP Insider Profiles*, October–December 2015; "SAP SuccessFactors: SAP JAM, SAP SuccessFactors: Learning, and SAP SuccessFactors: Employee Central," www.successfactors.com, accessed February 10, 2016; and Craig Powers, "Snohomish PUD Went to the Cloud for HR: The Result? Success," asugnews.com, May 14, 2015.

CASE STUDY QUESTIONS

1. How important was the human resources project for Snohomish PUD? Why?

2. Classify and describe the management, organization, and technology issues the project had to address in order to implement the new system successfully. How did the project team deal with these issues?

3. Describe the composition of the project team. How important was this? Why?

4. Why do you think the implementation of Snohomish PUD's new human resource system was successful? Explain your answer.

Designing for the Organization

Because the purpose of a new system is to improve the organization's performance, information systems projects must explicitly address the ways in which the organization will change when the new system is installed, including installation of mobile and web applications. In addition to procedural changes, transformations in job functions, organizational structure, power relationships, and the work environment should be carefully planned.

Areas where users interface with the system require special attention, with sensitivity to ergonomics issues. **Ergonomics** refers to the interaction of people and machines in the work environment. It considers the design of jobs, health issues, and the end-user interface of information systems. Table 14.5 lists the organizational dimensions that must be addressed when planning and implementing information systems.

Although systems analysis and design activities are supposed to include an organizational impact analysis, this area has traditionally been neglected. An **organizational impact analysis** explains how a proposed system will affect organizational structure, attitudes, decision making, and operations. To integrate information systems successfully with the organization, thorough and fully documented organizational impact assessments must be given more attention in the development effort.

Sociotechnical Design

One way of addressing human and organizational issues is to incorporate **sociotechnical design** practices into information systems projects. Designers set forth separate sets of technical and social design solutions. The social design plans explore different workgroup structures, allocation of tasks, and the design of individual jobs. The proposed technical solutions are compared with the proposed social solutions. The solution that best meets both social and technical objectives is selected for the final design. The resulting sociotechnical design is expected to produce an information system that blends technical efficiency with sensitivity to organizational and human needs, leading to higher job satisfaction and productivity.

Project Management Software Tools

Commercial software tools that automate many aspects of project management facilitate the project management process. Project management software typically features capabilities for defining and ordering tasks, assigning resources to tasks, establishing starting and ending dates to tasks, tracking

TABLE 14.5 ORGANIZATIONAL FACTORS IN SYSTEMS PLANNING AND IMPLEMENTATION

Employee participation and involvement
Job design
Standards and performance monitoring
Ergonomics (including equipment, user interfaces, and the work environment)
Employee grievance resolution procedures
Health and safety
Government regulatory compliance

progress, and facilitating modifications to tasks and resources. Many automate the creation of Gantt and PERT charts and provide communication, collaboration, and social tools.

Some of these tools are large sophisticated programs for managing very large projects, dispersed work groups, and enterprise functions. These high-end tools can manage very large numbers of tasks and activities and complex relationships. The most widely used project management tool today is Microsoft Project, but there are also lower-cost tools for smaller projects and small businesses, such as Zoho Projects and Teamwork Projects, which are available in the cloud as are some versions of Microsoft Project. Many project management applications are now cloud-based to enable project team members to access project management tools and their data wherever they are working. Huddle, Clarizen, and Citrix Podio are other examples (Reisinger, 2016).

While project management software helps organizations track individual projects, the resources allocated to them, and their costs, **project portfolio management software** helps organizations manage portfolios of projects and dependencies among them. Project portfolio management software helps managers compare proposals and projects against budgets and resource capacity levels to determine the optimal mix and sequencing of projects that best achieves the organization's strategic goals.

Review Summary

14-1 *What are the objectives of project management, and why is it so essential in developing information systems?*

Good project management is essential for ensuring that systems are delivered on time and on budget and provide genuine business benefits. Project management activities include planning the work, assessing the risk, estimating and acquiring resources required to accomplish the work, organizing the work, directing execution, and analyzing the results. Project management must deal with five major variables: scope, time, cost, quality, and risk.

14-2 *What methods can be used for selecting and evaluating information systems projects and aligning them with the firm's business goals?*

Organizations need an information systems plan that describes how information technology supports the attainment of their business goals and documents all their system applications and IT infrastructure components. Large corporations will have a management structure to ensure the most important systems projects receive priority. Key performance indicators, portfolio analysis, and scoring models can be used to identify and evaluate alternative information systems projects.

14-3 *How can firms assess the business value of information systems?*

To determine whether an information systems project is a good investment, one must calculate its costs and benefits. Tangible benefits are quantifiable, and intangible benefits that cannot be immediately quantified may provide quantifiable benefits in the future. Benefits that exceed costs should be analyzed using capital budgeting methods to make sure a project represents a good return on the firm's invested capital.

14-4 *What are the principal risk factors in information systems projects, and how can they be managed?*

The level of risk in a systems development project is determined by (1) project size, (2) project structure, and (3) experience with technology. IS projects are more likely to fail when there is insufficient or improper user participation in the systems development process, lack of management support, and poor management of the implementation process. There is a very high failure rate among projects involving business process reengineering, enterprise applications, and mergers and acquisitions because they require extensive organizational change.

Implementation refers to the entire process of organizational change surrounding the introduction of a new information system. User support and involvement and management support and control of the implementation process are essential, as are mechanisms for dealing with the level of risk in each new systems project. Project risk factors can be brought under some control by a contingency approach to project management. The risk level of each project determines the appropriate mix of external integration tools, internal integration tools, formal planning tools, and formal control tools to be applied.

Key Terms

Capital budgeting, 537
Change agent, 539
Change management, 539
Counterimplementation, 546
Ergonomics, 549
External integration tools, 544
Formal control tools, 544
Formal planning tools, 544
Gantt chart, 544
Implementation, 539
Information systems plan, 532
Intangible benefits, 536
Internal integration tools, 543

Organizational impact analysis, 549
PERT chart, 544
Portfolio analysis, 534
Project, 530
Project management, 530
Project portfolio management, 550
Scope, 531
Scoring model, 535
Sociotechnical design, 549
Tangible benefits, 536
User-designer communications gap, 542
User interface, 530

MyMISLab

To complete the problems with the MyMISLab, go to the EOC Discussion Questions in MyMISLab.

Review Questions

14-1 What are the objectives of project management, and why is it so essential in developing information systems?

- Describe information system problems resulting from poor project management.

- Define project management. List and describe the project management activities and variables addressed by project management.

14-2 What methods can be used for selecting and evaluating information systems projects and aligning them with the firm's business goals?

- Name and describe the groups responsible for the management of information systems projects.

- Describe the purpose of an information systems plan and list the major categories in the plan.

- Explain how key performance indicators, portfolio analysis, and scoring models can

be used to select information systems projects.

14-3 How can firms assess the business value of information systems?

- List and describe the major costs and benefits of information systems.

- Distinguish between tangible and intangible benefits.

14-4 What are the principal risk factors in information systems projects, and how can they be managed?

- Identify and describe each of the principal risk factors in information systems projects.

- Explain why builders of new information systems need to address implementation and change management.

- Explain why eliciting support of management and end users is so essential for successful implementation of information systems projects.

- Explain why there is such a high failure rate for implementations involving enterprise applications, business process reengineering, and mergers and acquisitions.
- Identify and describe the strategies for controlling project risk.

- Identify the organizational considerations that should be addressed by project planning and implementation.
- Explain how project management software tools contribute to successful project management.

Discussion Questions

14-5 How much does project management impact the success of a new information system?
MyMISLab

14-6 It has been said that most systems fail because systems builders ignore organizational behavior problems. Why might this be so?
MyMISLab

14-7 What is the role of end users in information systems project management?
MyMISLab

Hands-On MIS Projects

The projects in this section give you hands-on experience evaluating information systems projects, using spreadsheet software to perform capital budgeting analyses for new information systems investments, and using web tools to analyze the financing for a new home. Visit MyMISLab's Multimedia Library to access this chapter's Hands-on MIS Projects.

Management Decision Problems

14-8 The U.S. Census launched an IT project to arm its census takers in the field with high-tech handheld devices that would save taxpayer money by directly beaming population data to headquarters from census takers in the field. Census officials signed a $600 million contract with Harris Corporation in 2006 to build 500,000 devices but still weren't sure which features they wanted included in the units. Census officials did not specify the testing process to measure the performance of the handheld devices. As the project progressed, 400 change requests to project requirements were added. Two years and hundreds of millions of taxpayer dollars later, the handhelds were far too slow and unreliable to be used for the 2010 U.S. census. What could Census Bureau management and the Harris Corporation have done to prevent this outcome?

14-9 Caterpillar is the world's leading maker of earth-moving machinery and supplier of agricultural equipment. Caterpillar wants to end its support for its Dealer Business System (DBS), which it licenses to its dealers to help them run their businesses. The software in this system is becoming outdated, and senior management wants to transfer support for the hosted version of the software to Accenture Consultants so it can concentrate on its core business. Caterpillar never required its dealers to use DBS, but the system had become a de facto standard for doing business with the company. The majority of the 50 Cat dealers in North America use some version of DBS, as do about half of the 200 or so Cat dealers in the rest of the world. Before Caterpillar turns the product over to Accenture, what factors and issues should it consider? What questions should it ask? What questions should its dealers ask?

Improving Decision Making: Using Spreadsheet Software for Capital Budgeting for a New CAD System

Software skills: Spreadsheet formulas and functions
Business skills: Capital budgeting

14-10 This project provides you with an opportunity to use spreadsheet software to use the capital budgeting models discussed in this chapter and its Learning Tracks to analyze the return on an investment for a new computer-aided design (CAD) system.

Your company would like to invest in a new computer-aided design (CAD) system that requires purchasing hardware, software, and networking technology as well as expenditures for installation, training, and support. MyMISLab contains tables showing each cost component for the new system as well as annual maintenance costs over a five-year period, along with a Learning Track on capital budgeting models. You believe the new system will reduce the amount of labor required to generate designs and design specifications, thereby increasing your firm's annual cash flow.

- Using the data provided in these tables, create a worksheet that calculates the costs and benefits of the investment over a five-year period and analyzes the investment using the four capital budgeting models presented in this chapter's Learning Track.
- Is this investment worthwhile? Why or why not?

Improving Decision Making: Using Web Tools for Buying and Financing a Home

Software skills: Internet-based software
Business skills: Financial planning

14-11 This project will develop your skills using web-based software for searching for a home and calculating mortgage financing for that home.

You would like to purchase a home in Fort Collins, Colorado. Ideally, it should be a single-family house with at least three bedrooms and one bathroom that costs between $170,000 and $300,000 and financed with a 30-year fixed rate mortgage. You can afford a down payment that is 20 percent of the value of the house. Before you purchase a house, you would like to find out what homes are available in your price range, find a mortgage, and determine the amount of your monthly payment. Use the Realtor.com site to help you with the following tasks:

- Locate homes in Fort Collins, Colorado, that meet your specifications.
- Find a mortgage for 80 percent of the list price of the home. Compare rates from at least three sites (use search engines to find sites other than Yahoo).
- After selecting a mortgage, calculate your closing costs and the monthly payment.

When you are finished, evaluate the whole process. For example, assess the ease of use of the site and your ability to find information about houses and mortgages, the accuracy of the information you found, and the breadth of choice of homes and mortgages.

Collaboration and Teamwork Project

Identifying Implementation Problems

Form a group with three or four other students. Write a description of the implementation problems you might expect to encounter in one of the systems described in the Interactive Sessions or chapter-ending cases in this text. Write an analysis of the steps you would take to solve or prevent these problems. If possible, use Google Docs and Google Drive or Google Sites to brainstorm, organize, and develop a presentation of your findings for the class.

The Philly311 Project: The City of Brotherly Love Turns Problems into Opportunities
CASE STUDY

Philly311 is the City of Philadelphia government's centralized non-emergency contact center that is accessible to all residents, businesses, and visitors. Using Philly311, you can find out how to start a business, contact your local police district, obtain a smoke alarm, and issue requests for services such as fixing broken traffic signals, repairing potholes, or removing graffiti. You can also use Philly311 to report abandoned vehicles, unsafe/improper housing conditions, and complaints. Philly311 can be contacted by phone, by visiting its website, or by using a mobile app. Philly311 receives more than a million calls each year.

Requests for service through 311 generally have expected time frames for action or resolution. After receiving a request for service, Philly311 will provide a citizen with a reference number to track the status of that request as it moves through different departments by calling the Philly311 Call Center, visiting the Philly311 website, or using the mobile app. Residents can relay photos to city officials for more effective response to service calls and receive real-time updates on their requests. The city is able to mine data from the Philly311 system to identify trends that will help city employees to discover and address the needs of citizens. Philly311 also features a Neighborhood Community portal that allows citizens to engage with fellow residents on shared concerns and interact with each other and city departments and officials directly. The system includes GPS integrative mapping so the public and city government can view service requests by location.

Philly311 has been extremely popular with citizens, earning a customer satisfaction rate of 98 percent. Moreover, Philly311 is much, much more than a traditional government call center. Residents can connect with Philly311 by telephone, e-mail, mail, a walk-in center, or the Philly Mobile App. Philly311 has also extended its service through social media. The Philly311 Facebook and Twitter accounts are managed by an experienced agent who responds to questions and enters service requests based on user interaction. Since the beginning of 2012, Philly311 has seen a 360 percent increase in its social media followers.

Philly311 started out as a traditional 311 call center. (The telephone number *3-1-1* is a special telephone number used by many communities in Canada and the United States to provide access to non-emergency municipal services.) The first version of Philly311 was designed to provide the public with quick, easy phone access to all city services and information.

When Mayor Michael A. Nutter came into office in 2007, he called for a more transparent and efficient government, increasing integrity, more open data practices, and improving government accountability. The Nutter administration wanted to empower Philadelphians and work with them on government-related issues that citizens care most about. According to Rosetta Lue, Philadelphia's Chief Customer Service Officer, the customer may always be right, but that only goes so far if the customer can't be heard. Philadelphia's citizens are its customers, and city government should use the best tools possible to make sure every citizen is connected and can be

heard loud and clear. In the past, when Philadelphians called 311 with a service request, such as a pothole they wanted fixed, they would have no idea when the city would get around to addressing it, which led to frustration for residents and repeated calls to the city.

The project timeline for upgrading Philly311 was ambitious, aiming for making the new center operational by the end of 2008. Managers Jeffrey Friedman and Patrick Morgan engaged an external consulting group to develop a plan and scope for the 311 system. In June 2008, Mayor Nutter and City Managing Director and Executive Sponsor Camille Barnett approved the implementation strategy. Lue joined the Philly311 project team in May 2008. The team worked collectively to develop civil service testing requirements for contact center agents. Thirty representatives from various city departments helped populate the Philly311 knowledge base with more than 2,000 articles about city services and municipal information.

In September 2008, the national financial crisis caused a drastic cut in Philly311's budget, affecting the Philly311 implementation. At the same time, however, the crisis created an opportunity to improvise creatively by developing a fairly low-cost solution using established city services and technologies. Instead of implementing new software for a customer relationship management (CRM) system, the Philly311 project team worked with the city's Department of Technology to implement a less expensive web-based solution with CRM functions. This web-based system was integrated with other systems so, for example, agents were able to look up municipal information and directly enter service requests into the integrated work systems of servicing departments. Philly311's new budget constraints also put a brake on hiring and head count. Instead of hiring experienced contact center agents, Philly311 hired internal transfers and employees who would have been laid off due to budget cutbacks. Delays in the implementation timetable gave Lue and her team more time to study the problem and develop a sound solution.

Lue wanted to make sure that the system would be easy for customers to use, so local citizens were involved in the new Philly311 design from the beginning. Bringing users in early in the process also saved time during system implementation and rollout. They were able to bring together about 100 people from different city departments to say what they liked and what they didn't like about the technology and new business processes. They had a chance to see how data were coming in, how they would be used, and how Philadelphia could be more efficient and effective.

The Philly311 project had full executive support from Mayor Nutter and the city's managing director. The upgraded call center opened on December 31, 2008, and the new Philly311 website went online in January 2009. The website had many of the same functions as the call center: customers could connect with 311, report an issue, or ask about public services through e-mail. To make Philly311 even more accessible to citizens through multiple channels, the city launched a social media campaign and expanded its public reach through social media in October 2009. Philly311 established a Twitter account that provided citizens a new way to receive information.

With a city as large as Philadelphia, which has an above-average percentage of residents living below the poverty line, city leaders realized they needed to work on establishing trust within individual communities to educate and provide access to Philly311. The city hired a community engagement coordinator to address community concerns and to oversee the Neighborhood Liaison Program (NLP), which trains volunteers to record items discussed during community meetings and encourages standout community leaders to bring their neighbors' public service concerns straight to Philly311. In the program's first year, 600 neighborhood liaisons were trained, and two years after the program's launch, the number of neighborhood liaisons had doubled.

Philly311 launched its mobile application in 2012. The app provides another way for residents to connect to Philly311, and it also allows customers to add on-site and real-time images to their service requests. The app is free to the public and can be downloaded onto a smartphone. Add-on widgets, such as a widget for election days and after-school programs, can be incorporated when needed. The mobile Philly311 app was the first 311 app to be offered in 16 different languages. This app now accounts for 18 percent of the requests Philly311 receives.

Philly311's traffic volume steadily increased, and by the end of 2012, Philly311 had taken its 5 millionth call. The popularity of the service demonstrates the tremendous benefit and popularity of the system, but it also created operational strain. In 2011, an independent gap analysis found that the existing system did not have the capacity to continue supporting Philadelphia's growing service requirements. The system was not built to handle very large volumes of data, nor could it easily archive data about citizen calls, complaints, and follow-ups.

These technology limitations prevented the city from crunching data or from changing business processes to improve workforce efficiency.

The time had come to invest in new technology to keep pace with current demands and to position the city for future technology and business developments. After months of planning, a solution was finalized: The project planning process took special care to define a detailed set of business and technical requirements for the new system. The solution selected contained several modules, allowing city management to pick and choose which features were most critical. One called the Neighborhood Community portal allows citizens to communicate with neighbors and like-minded residents about concerns and issues relevant to them. Mayor Nutter finally obtained $120 million in funding for capital investment projects to upgrade technology infrastructure and chose Philly311 as one of those investments.

After a rigorous RFP selection process, Unisys was chosen to lead the IT implementation for this project, and Salesforce's cloud computing platform was selected as the underlying technology for the system. Unisys had implemented similar 311 systems on the Salesforce platform for Hampton, Virginia, and Elgin, Illinois. The city chose Salesforce.com in part because of its capabilities as a platform. In addition to full-featured CRM functionality, Salesforce.com has its own app store and cloud platform for building and running apps. That way, the city can leverage its investment to take advantage of other apps that work on the Salesforce platform.

The new CRM system, released in December 2014, is much more robust, integrating the city's knowledge base, service departments' work order systems, and community engagement programs in a single customer portal. The system improves the city's ability to share knowledge and work interdepartmentally and creates a social platform that facilitates conversations between neighbors and stakeholders who want to collaborate, share best practices, and organize events to improve their community. The new Philly311 helps the city capitalize on a variety of communications, including social media data, to better understand the needs of its citizen customers.

Philly311 has been widely embraced by Philadelphia residents, and has received numerous accolades. It was selected as a winner of the 2015 Government Computer News Awards for IT excellence. In 2015, Philly311 became a finalist for the United Nations' Public Service Award for demonstrating attention to its international audience, and in

2013 Philly311 was named an ICMI Global Call Center award finalist. The system has expanded its reach and has even become a resource and example for those outside of Philadelphia. Philly311 has helped build a more reliable city government and make Philadelphia a welcoming and connected city.

Sources: Rosetta Carrington Lue and Cory Fleming with Amanda V. Wagner, "Creating a Welcoming and Connected City: The Philadelphia Experience," www.phila.gov, accessed January 11, 2016; Derek Major, "Philly 311: Innovation That Was Worth the Wait," *Government Computer News,* October 15, 2015; Jake Williams, "Philadelphia Rolls Out Innovation Blueprint, 311 Upgrade," statescoop.com, February 19, 2015; City of Philadelphia, "Mayor Nutter Announces Successful Launch of New Philly 311 System," February 18, 2015; and Lauren Hertzler, "Philadelphia Unveils Enhanced 311 System at Innovation Summit," bizjournals.com, February 19, 2015.

CASE STUDY QUESTIONS

14-12 Assess the importance of the Philly311 project for the city of Philadelphia and its citizens.

14-13 Why was the Philly311 project so successful? What management, organization, and technology factors contributed to its success?

14-14 What risk mitigation strategies did Philadelphia use for its Philly311 project? How did they help?

MyMISLab

Go to the Assignments section of MyMISLab to complete these writing exercises.

14-15 Identify and describe three methods for helping managers select information systems projects.

14-16 Compare the two major types of planning and control tools.

Chapter 14 References

1E. "The Real Cost of Unused Software." www.1E.com, accessed February 5, 2016.

Appan, Radha and Glenn J. Browne. "The Impact of Analyst-Induced Misinformation on the Requirements Elicitation Process." *MIS Quarterly* 36, No 1 (March 2012).

Banker, Rajiv. "Value Implications of Relative Investments in Information Technology." Department of Information Systems and Center for Digital Economy Research, University of Texas at Dallas, January 23, 2001.

Barki, Henri, Suzanne Rivard, and Jean Talbot. "An Integrative Contingency Model of Software Project Risk Management." *Journal of Management Information Systems* 17, No. 4 (Spring 2001).

Bloch, Michael, Sen Blumberg, and Jurgen Laartz. "Delivering Large-Scale IT Projects on Time, on Budget, and on Value." *McKinsey Quarterly* (October 2012).

Brock, Jon Tamim Saleh and Sesh Iyer. "Large-Scale IT Projects: From Nightmare to Value Creation." Boston Consulting Group (May 20, 2015).

Browning, Tyson, R. and Ranga V. Ramasesh. "Reducing Unwelcome Surprises in Project Management." *MIT Sloan Management Review* (Spring 2015).

Brynjolfsson, Erik and Lorin M. Hitt. "Information Technology and Organizational Design: Evidence from Micro Data." (January 1998).

Ditmore, Jim. "Why Do Big IT Projects Fail So Often?" *Information Week* (October 29, 2013).

Dubravka Cecez-Kecmanovic, Karlheinz Kautz, and Rebecca Abrahall. "Reframing Success and Failure of Information Systems: A Performative Perspective." *MIS Quarterly* 38, No. 2 (June 2014).

Chandrasekaran, Sriram, Sauri Gudlavalleti, and Sanjay Kaniyar. "Achieving Success in Large Complex Software Projects." *McKinsey Quarterly* (July 2014).

Clement, Andrew and Peter Van den Besselaar. "A Retrospective Look at PD Projects." *Communications of the ACM* 36, No. 4 (June 1993).

Delone, William H. and Ephraim R. McLean. "The Delone and McLean Model of Information Systems Success: A Ten-Year Update. *Journal of Management Information Systems* 19, No. 4 (Spring 2003).

Flyvbjerg, Bent and Alexander Budzier. "Why Your IT Project May Be Riskier Than You Think." *Harvard Business Review* (September 2011).

He Jun and William R. King. "The Role of User Participation In Information Systems Development: Implications from a Meta-Analysis." *Journal of Management Information Systems* 25, No. 1 (Summer 2008).

Hitt, Lorin, D. J. Wu, and Xiaoge Zhou. "Investment in Enterprise Resource Planning: Business Impact and Productivity Measures." *Journal of Management Information Systems* 19, No. 1 (Summer 2002).

Housel, Thomas J., Omar El Sawy, Jianfang Zhong, and Waymond Rodgers. "Measuring the Return on e-Business Initiatives at the Process Level: The Knowledge Value-Added Approach." ICIS (2001).

Jeffrey, Mark and Ingmar Leliveld. "Best Practices in IT Portfolio Management." *MIT Sloan Management Review* 45, No. 3 (Spring 2004).

Jiang, James J., Jamie Y. T. Chang, Houn-Gee Chen, Eric T. G. Wang, and Gary Klein. "Achieving IT Program Goals with Integrative Conflict Management." *Journal of Management Information Systems* 31, No. 1 (Summer 2014).

Karhade, Prasanna, Michael J. Shaw, and Ramanath Subramanyam. "Patterns in Information Systems Portfolio Prioritization: Evidence from Decision Tree Induction." *MIS Quarterly* 39, No.2 (June 2015).

Keen, Peter W. "Information Systems and Organizational Change." *Communications of the ACM* 24 (January 1981).

Keil, Mark, H. Jeff Smith, Charalambos L. Iacovou, and Ronald L. Thompson. "The Pitfalls of Project Status Reporting." *MIT Sloan Management Review* 55, No. 3 (Spring 2014).

Keil, Mark, Joan Mann, and Arun Rai. "Why Software Projects Escalate: An Empirical Analysis and Test of Four Theoretical Models." *MIS Quarterly* 24, No. 4 (December 2000).

Kim, Hee Woo and Atreyi Kankanhalli. "Investigating User Resistance to Information Systems Implementation: A Status Quo Bias Perspective." *MIS Quarterly* 33, No. 3 (September 2009).

Kloppenborg, Timothy J. and Debbie Tesch. "How Executive Sponsors Influence Project Success." *MIT Sloan Management Review* (Spring 2015).

Kolb, D. A. and A. L. Frohman. "An Organization Development Approach to Consulting." *Sloan Management Review* 12 (Fall 1970).

Lapointe, Liette and Suzanne Rivard. "A Multilevel Model of Resistance to Information Technology Implementation." *MIS Quarterly* 29, No. 3 (September 2005).

Laudon, Kenneth C. "CIOs Beware: Very Large Scale Systems." Center for Research on Information Systems, New York University Stern School of Business, working paper (1989).

Laufer, Alexander, Edward J. Hoffman, Jeffrey S. Russell, and W. Scott Cameron. "What Successful Project Managers Do." *MIT Sloan Management Review* (Spring 2015).

Lee, Jong Seok, Mark Keil, and Vijay Kasi. "The Effect of an Initial Budget and Schedule Goal on Software Project Escalation." *Journal of Management Information Systems* 29, No. 1 (Summer 2012).

Li, Xitong and Madnick, Stuart E. "Understanding the Dynamics of Service-Oriented Architecture Implementation." *Journal of Management Information Systems* 32, No. 2 (2015).

Liang, Huigang, Zeyu Peng, Xue Zeyu, Guo Yajiong, and Wang Xitong. "Employees' Exploration of Complex Systems: An Integrative View." *Journal of Management Information Systems* 32 No. 1 (2015).

Liang, Huigang, Nilesh Sharaf, Qing Hu, and Yajiong Xue. "Assimilation of Enterprise Systems: The Effect of Institutional Pressures and the Mediating Role of Top Management." *MIS Quarterly* 31, No. 1 (March 2007).

Mastrogiacomo, Stefano, Stephanie Missonier, and Riccardo Bonazzi. "Talk Before It's Too Late: Reconsidering the Role of Conversation in Information Systems Project Management." *Journal of Management Information Systems* 31, No. 1 (Summer 2014).

McFarlan, F. Warren. "Portfolio Approach to Information Systems." *Harvard Business Review* (September–October 1981).

Mumford, Enid and Mary Weir. *Computer Systems in Work Design*: *The ETHICS Method*. New York: John Wiley (1979).

Polites, Greta L. and Elena Karahanna. "Shackled to the Status Quo: The Inhibiting Effects of Incumbent System Habit, Switching Costs, and Inertia on New System Acceptance." *MIS Quarterly* 36, No. 1 (March 2012).

Project Management Institute. *A Guide to the Project Management Body of Knowledge* (5th ed.). Newtown Square, PA: Project Management Institute (2013).

_____"The High Cost of Low Performance." (2016).

Ramasubbu, Narayan, Anandhi Bharadwaj, and Giri Kumar Tayi. "Software Process Diversity: Conceptualization, Measurement, and Analysis of Impact on Project Performance." *MIS Quarterly* 39, No. 4 (December 2015).

Reisinger, Don. "10 Cloud-Based Project Management Tools to Serve Every Company's Needs." *eWeek* (March 10, 2016).

Rivard, Suzanne and Liette Lapointe. "Information Technology Implementers' Responses to User Resistance: Nature and Effects." *MIS Quarterly* 36, No. 3 (September 2012).

Ross, Jeanne W. and Cynthia M. Beath. "Beyond the Business Case: New Approaches to IT Investment." *Sloan Management Review* 43, No. 2 (Winter 2002).

Ryan, Sherry D., David A. Harrison, and Lawrence L Schkade. "Information Technology Investment Decisions: When Do Cost and Benefits in the Social Subsystem Matter?" *Journal of Management Information Systems* 19, No. 2 (Fall 2002).

Schmidt, Roy, Kalle Lyytinen, Mark Keil, and Paul Cule. "Identifying Software Project Risks: An International Delphi Study." *Journal of Management Information Systems* 17, No. 4 (Spring 2001).

Schwalbe, Kathy. *Information Technology Project Management* (8th ed.). Cengage (2016).

Sharma, Rajeev and Philip Yetton. "The Contingent Effects of Training, Technical Complexity, and Task Interdependence on Successful Information Systems Implementation." *MIS Quarterly* 31, No. 2 (June 2007).

Smith, H. Jeff, Mark Keil, and Gordon Depledge. "Keeping Mum as the Project Goes Under." *Journal of Management Information Systems* 18, No. 2 (Fall 2001).

Sting, Fabian J., Christoph H. Loch, and Dirk Stempfhuber. "Accelerating Projects by Encouraging Help." *MIT Sloan Management Review* (Spring 2015).

Swanson, E. Burton. *Information System Implementation*. Homewood, IL: Richard D. Irwin (1988).

Sykes, Tracy Ann. "Support Structures and Their Impacts on Employee Outcomes: A Longitudinal Field Study of an Enterprise System Implementation." *MIS Quarterly* 39, No. 2 (June 2015).

Tornatsky, Louis G., J. D. Eveland, M. G. Boylan, W. A. Hetzner, E. C. Johnson, D. Roitman, and J. Schneider. *The Process of Technological Innovation: Reviewing the Literature*. Washington, DC: National Science Foundation (1983).

Vaidyanathan, Ganesh. *Project Management: Process, Technology and Practice*. Upper Saddle River, NJ: Prentice Hall (2013).

Wang, Eric T. G., Gary Klein, and James J. Jiang. "ERP Misfit: Country of Origin and Organizational Factors." *Journal of Management Information Systems* 23, No. 1 (Summer 2006).

Westerman, George. "IT Is from Venus, Non-IT Is from Mars." *Wall Street Journal* (April 2, 2012).

Xue, Yajion, Huigang Liang, and William R. Boulton. "Information Technology Governance in Information Technology Investment Decision Processes: The Impact of Investment Characteristics, External Environment, and Internal Context." *MIS Quarterly* 32, No. 1 (March 2008).

Yin, Robert K. "Life Histories of Innovations: How New Practices Become Routinized." *Public Administration Review* (January–February 1981).

Zhu, Kevin and Kenneth L. Kraemer. "E-Commerce Metrics for Net-Enhanced Organizations: Assessing the Value of e-Commerce to Firm Performance in the Manufacturing Sector." *Information Systems Research* 13, No. 3 (September 2002).

15

Managing Global Systems

Learning Objectives

After reading this chapter, you will be able to answer the following questions:

15-1 What major factors are driving the internationalization of business?

15-2 What are the alternative strategies for developing global businesses?

15-3 What are the challenges posed by global information systems and management solutions for these challenges?

15-4 What are the issues and technical alternatives to be considered when developing international information systems?

MyMISLab™

Visit **mymislab.com** for simulations, tutorials, and end-of-chapter problems.

Dunlop Aircraft Tyres Takes Off Worldwide with Customer Relationship Management

Based in Birmingham, UK, Dunlop Aircraft Tyres Ltd specializes in manufacturing aircraft tires and tubes from design thorough to delivery, using the most sophisticated precision and manufacturing and retreading techniques available. The company is the world's only dedicated aircraft tire manufacturer and retreader. Dunlop Aircraft Tyres can supply tires for more than 300 different types of aircraft in the civil and military aviation market, and its comprehensive product range is backed by service 24 hours a day, all year round. Dunlop's customers include major international airlines, aircraft constructors, wheel and brake manufacturers, and maintenance facilities throughout the world. This firm is committed to providing airplane operators around the globe with new or retreaded airplane tires of the highest quality and customer service of the highest standard.

Over the past decade the company's global presence has increased rapidly. It has opened an aircraft retread and distribution business in China and in the United States. At present, Dunlop exports more than 80 percent of the products it makes in Birmingham, but it would like to expand operations globally so that it can pursue a strategy of localizing aircraft tire production and retreading. Dunlop's business as a supplier to the aircraft industry requires a high degree of personalization and attention in communications with customers and prospects.

© Trekandshoot/Shutterstock

In order to do this, Dunlop had to replace some of its legacy systems with a more robust scalable system and sales platform that could enhance visibility, rigor, and consistency across global sales and customer-related functions and provide access to timely and accurate information on prospects and customers. Processes, strategies, and communication tools needed to be aligned across each location. Dunlop had been trying to make do with a combination of ERP, separate databases, and spreadsheets, and these systems were not sufficiently integrated to do the job.

After analyzing customer relationship management offerings from Infor, Microsoft Dynamics, and Salesforce the company selected Infor CRM for its system solution. Infor CRM best met Dunlop's information requirements, was available as a cloud service, and complemented the company's existing ERP system, which was also from Infor. Implementing the system as a cloud service proceeded rapidly.

Infor CRM offers a complete view of every customer touch point across sales, marketing, customer service, and support teams. Companies using Infor CRM are able to maximize the impact of every interaction across the entire customer life cycle, whether in the office or out in the field. The CRM system features industry-specific capabilities, deep integration, functionality for mobile devices, and options for running systems in the cloud, on premises, or both.

Dunlop's new global CRM system is being used to support market segmentation and increase alignment with customer service teams in various locations. The system provides a complete picture of the customer life cycle, including historical and production data to help increase customer service and satisfaction. According to Dunlop Marketing Manager Stuart Hawker, Infor CRM has given the company a set of best practices for its sales and CRM activities, utilizing an accurate and consistent set of data in a timely and user-friendly manner to make better decisions. Managers are able to streamline operations and manage in multiple time zones with automated processes that synchronize data across the business worldwide.

Sources: www.aviationpros.com, accessed January 10, 2016; www.dunlop.com, accessed January 9, 2016; "Dunlop Aircraft Tyres: A Case Study on CRM and Geographic Expansion," November. 30, 2015; and Infor, "Dunlop Aircraft Tyres Takes Off with Infor," June 1, 2015.

Dunlop Aircraft Tyres's efforts to create global customer relationship management systems identify some of the issues that organizations need to consider if they want to operate worldwide. Like many large, multinational firms, Dunlop has operating units and sales offices in a number of different countries. These units had their own systems, business processes, and reporting standards. As a result, Dunlop Group was unable to effectively coordinate global operations and relationships with customers across multiple countries and regions. The company's systems were unable to provide the information for personalization, attention to customers, and coordination of localized operations that business strategy required.

The chapter-opening diagram calls attention to important points raised by this case and this chapter. To improve global management and customer-facing business processes, Dunlop Aircraft Tyres implemented a new global system based on Infor CRM software. The system integrated customer and other information from different business locations around the globe. Dunlop's new CRM system, hosted in the cloud, provides managers and employees with enterprise-wide information on operations, customers, and prospects so that the company can more easily manage and coordinate sales times around the globe. This helps the company operate more efficiently and effectively around the world and also pursue its global growth strategy.

Here are some questions to think about: How did information technology improve operations and decision making at Dunlop Aircraft Tyres? How would the company's new CRM system facilitate its business strategy?

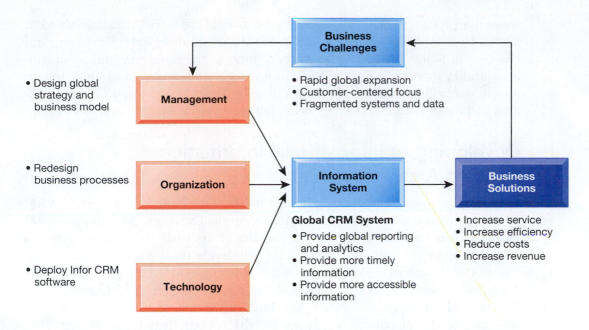

15-1 What major factors are driving the internationalization of business?

In earlier chapters, we describe the emergence of a global economic system and global world order driven by advanced networks and information systems. The new world order is sweeping away many national corporations, national industries, and national economies controlled by domestic politicians. Many localized firms will be replaced by fast-moving networked corporations that transcend national boundaries. The growth of international trade has radically altered domestic economies around the globe.

Consider the path to market for an iPhone, which is illustrated in Figure 15.1. The iPhone was designed by Apple engineers in the United States, sourced with

FIGURE 15.1 APPLE IPHONE'S GLOBAL SUPPLY CHAIN

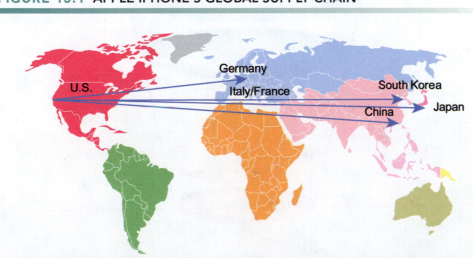

Apple designs the iPhone in the United States and relies on suppliers in the United States, Germany, Italy, France, Japan, and South Korea for other parts. Final assembly occurs in China.

more than 100 high-tech components from around the world, and assembled in China. Companies in Taiwan, South Korea, Japan, France, Italy, Germany, and the United States provided components such as the case, camera, processor, accelerator, gyroscope, electronic compass, power management chip, touch-screen controller, and high-definition display screen. Foxconn, a Chinese division of Taiwan's Hon Hai Group, is in charge of manufacturing and assembly.

Developing an International Information Systems Architecture

This chapter describes how to go about building an international information systems architecture suitable for your international strategy. An **international information systems architecture** consists of the basic information systems required by organizations to coordinate worldwide trade and other activities. Figure 15.2 illustrates the reasoning we follow throughout the chapter and depicts the major dimensions of an international information systems architectue.

The basic strategy to follow when building an international system is to understand the global environment in which your firm is operating. This means understanding the overall market forces, or business drivers, that are pushing your industry toward global competition. A **business driver** is a force in the environment to which businesses must respond and that influences the direction of the business. Likewise, examine carefully the inhibitors or negative factors that create *management challenges*—factors that could scuttle the development of a global business. Once you have examined the global environment, you will need to consider a corporate strategy for competing in that environment. How will your firm respond? You could ignore the global market and focus on domestic competition only, sell to the globe from a domestic base, or organize production and distribution around the globe. There are many in-between choices.

FIGURE 15.2 INTERNATIONAL INFORMATION SYSTEMS ARCHITECTURE

The major dimensions for developing an international information systems architecture are the global environment, the corporate global strategies, the structure of the organization, the management and business processes, and the technology platform.

After you have developed a strategy, it is time to consider how to structure your organization so it can pursue the strategy. How will you accomplish a division of labor across a global environment? Where will production, administration, accounting, marketing, and human resource functions be located? Who will handle the systems function?

Next, you must consider the management issues in implementing your strategy and making the organization design come alive. Key here will be the design of business processes. How can you discover and manage user requirements? How can you induce change in local units to conform to international requirements? How can you reengineer on a global scale, and how can you coordinate systems development?

The last issue to consider is the technology platform. Although changing technology is a key driving factor leading toward global markets, you need to have a corporate strategy and structure before you can rationally choose the right technology.

After you have completed this process of reasoning, you will be well on your way toward an appropriate international information systems portfolio capable of achieving your corporate goals. Let's begin by looking at the overall global environment.

The Global Environment: Business Drivers and Challenges

Table 15.1 lists the business drivers in the global environment that are leading all industries toward global markets and competition.

The global business drivers can be divided into two groups: general cultural factors and specific business factors. Easily recognized general cultural factors have driven internationalization since World War II. Information, communication, and transportation technologies have created a *global village* in which communication (by telephone, television, radio, or computer network) around the globe is no more difficult and not much more expensive than communication down the block. The cost of moving goods and services to and from geographically dispersed locations has fallen dramatically.

The development of global communications has created a global village in a second sense: A **global culture** created by television, the Internet, and other globally shared media such as movies now permits different cultures and peoples to develop common expectations about right and wrong, desirable and undesirable, heroic and cowardly. The collapse of the Eastern bloc has accelerated the growth of a world culture enormously, increased support for capitalism and business, and reduced the level of cultural conflict in Europe considerably.

TABLE 15.1 THE GLOBAL ENVIRONMENT: BUSINESS DRIVERS AND CHALLENGES

GENERAL CULTURAL FACTORS	SPECIFIC BUSINESS FACTORS
Global communication and transportation technologies	Global markets
Development of global culture	Global production and operations
Emergence of global social norms	Global coordination
Political stability	Global workforce
Global knowledge base	Global economies of scale

A last factor to consider is the growth of a global knowledge base. At the end of World War II, knowledge, education, science, and industrial skills were highly concentrated in North America, Western Europe, and Japan, with the rest of the world euphemistically called the *Third World*. This is no longer true. Latin America, China, India, southern Asia, and Eastern Europe have developed powerful educational, industrial, and scientific centers, resulting in a much more democratically and widely dispersed knowledge base.

These general cultural factors leading toward internationalization result in specific business globalization factors that affect most industries. The growth of powerful communications technologies and the emergence of world cultures lay the groundwork for *global markets*—global consumers interested in consuming similar products that are culturally approved. Coca-Cola, American sneakers (made in Korea but designed in Los Angeles), and Cable News Network (CNN) programming can now be sold in Latin America, Africa, and Asia.

Responding to this demand, global production and operations have emerged with precise online coordination between far-flung production facilities and central headquarters thousands of miles away. At Maersk, a major global shipping company based in Copenhagen, Denmark, shipping managers at Copenhagen and other locations can watch the loading of ships in Rotterdam online, check trim and ballast, and trace packages to specific ship locations as the activity proceeds. This is all possible through an international satellite link.

The new global markets and pressure toward global production and operation have called forth whole new capabilities for global coordination. Production, accounting, marketing and sales, human resources, and systems development (all the major business functions) can be coordinated on a global scale.

Frito-Lay, for instance, can develop a marketing sales force automation system in the United States and, once provided, may try the same techniques and technologies in Spain. Micromarketing—marketing to very small geographic and social units—no longer means marketing to neighborhoods in the United States but to neighborhoods throughout the world! Internet-based marketing means marketing to individuals and social networks throughout the world. These new levels of global coordination permit for the first time in history the location of business activity according to comparative advantage. Design should be located where it is best accomplished, as should marketing, production, and finance.

Finally, global markets, production, and administration create the conditions for powerful, sustained global economies of scale. Production driven by worldwide global demand can be concentrated where it can best be accomplished, fixed resources can be allocated over larger production runs, and production runs in larger plants can be scheduled more efficiently and precisely estimated. Lower-cost factors of production can be exploited wherever they emerge. The result is a powerful strategic advantage to firms that can organize globally. These general and specific business drivers have greatly enlarged world trade and commerce.

Not all industries are similarly affected by these trends. Clearly, manufacturing has been much more affected than services that still tend to be domestic and highly inefficient. However, the localism of services is breaking down in telecommunications, entertainment, transportation, finance, law, and general business. Clearly, those firms within an industry that can understand the internationalization of the industry and respond appropriately will reap enormous gains in productivity and stability.

Business Challenges

Although the possibilities of globalization for business success are significant, fundamental forces are operating to inhibit a global economy and to disrupt international business. Table 15.2 lists the most common and powerful challenges to the development of global systems.

At a cultural level, **particularism**, making judgments and taking action on the basis of narrow or personal characteristics, in all its forms (religious, nationalistic, ethnic, regionalism, geopolitical position) rejects the very concept of a shared global culture and rejects the penetration of domestic markets by foreign goods and services. Differences among cultures produce differences in social expectations, politics, and ultimately legal rules. In certain countries, such as the United States, consumers expect domestic name-brand products to be built domestically and are disappointed to learn that much of what they thought of as domestically produced is in fact foreign made.

Different cultures produce different political regimes. Among the many different countries of the world are different laws governing the movement of information, information privacy of their citizens, origins of software and hardware in systems, and radio and satellite telecommunications. Even the hours of business and the terms of business trade vary greatly across political cultures. These different legal regimes complicate global business and must be considered when building global systems.

For instance, European countries have different laws concerning transborder data flow and privacy than those in the United States. **Transborder data flow** is defined as the movement of information across international boundaries in any form. In 1998 the European Union adopted a Data Protection Directive that broadened and standardized privacy protection in E.U. nations, and allowed for the transfer of personal data to systems located in the United States and under nations under a "safe harbor" provision. As long as systems in the United States met European privacy standards, the data could be transferred to and processed by U.S. systems. This agreement was replaced with a new agreement known as the E.U.-U.S. Privacy Shield in July 2016. Privacy Shield provides additional privacy protection for European citizens. Over 4,000 U.S. firms are registered with European privacy regulators allowing them to process personal information of European citizens in the United States. Privacy Shield also protects European citizens from certain surveillance activities of U.S. national security agencies. U.S. firms are changing their practices to ensure their systems comply with Privacy Shield.

TABLE 15.2 CHALLENGES AND OBSTACLES TO GLOBAL BUSINESS SYSTEMS

GLOBAL	SPECIFIC
Cultural particularism: Regionalism, nationalism, language differences	Standards: Different Electronic Data Interchange (EDI), e-mail, telecommunications standards
Social expectations: Brand-name expectations, work hours	Reliability: Phone networks not uniformly reliable
Political laws: Transborder data and privacy laws, commercial regulations	Speed: Different data transfer speeds, many slower than United States
	Personnel: Shortages of skilled consultants

Cultural and political differences profoundly affect organizations' business processes and applications of information technology. A host of specific barriers arise from the general cultural differences, everything from different reliability of phone networks to the shortage of skilled consultants.

National laws and traditions have created disparate accounting practices in various countries, which affects the ways profits and losses are analyzed. German companies generally do not recognize the profit from a venture until the project is completely finished and they have been paid. Conversely, British firms begin posting profits before a project is completed, when they are reasonably certain they will get the money.

These accounting practices are tightly intertwined with each country's legal system, business philosophy, and tax code. British, U.S., and Dutch firms share a predominantly Anglo-Saxon outlook that separates tax calculations from reports to shareholders to focus on showing shareholders how fast profits are growing. Continental European accounting practices are less oriented toward impressing investors, focusing rather on demonstrating compliance with strict rules and minimizing tax liabilities. These diverging accounting practices make it difficult for large international companies with units in different countries to evaluate their performance.

Language remains a significant barrier. Although English has become a kind of standard business language, this is truer at higher levels of companies and not throughout the middle and lower ranks. Software may have to be built with local language interfaces before a new information system can be successfully implemented.

Currency fluctuations can play havoc with planning models and projections. A product that appears profitable in Mexico or Japan may actually produce a loss because of changes in foreign exchange rates.

These inhibiting factors must be taken into account when you are designing and building international systems for your business. For example, companies trying to implement "lean production" systems spanning national boundaries typically underestimate the time, expense, and logistical difficulties of making goods and information flow freely across different countries.

State of the Art

One might think, given the opportunities for achieving competitive advantages as outlined previously and the interest in future applications, that most international companies have rationally developed marvelous international systems architectures. Nothing could be further from the truth. Most companies have inherited patchwork international systems from the distant past, often based on concepts of information processing developed in the 1960s—batch-oriented reporting from independent foreign divisions to corporate headquarters, manual entry of data from one legacy system to another, with little online control and communication. Corporations in this situation increasingly face powerful competitive challenges in the marketplace from firms that have rationally designed truly international systems. Still other companies have recently built technology platforms for international systems but have nowhere to go because they lack global strategy.

As it turns out, there are significant difficulties in building appropriate international architectures. The difficulties involve planning a system appropriate to the firm's global strategy, structuring the organization of systems and business units, solving implementation issues, and choosing the right technical platform. Let's examine these problems in greater detail.

15-2 What are the alternative strategies for developing global businesses?

Three organizational issues face corporations seeking a global position: choosing a strategy, organizing the business, and organizing the systems management area. The first two are closely connected, so we discuss them together.

Global Strategies and Business Organization

Four main global strategies form the basis for global firms' organizational structure. These are domestic exporter, multinational, franchiser, and transnational. Each of these strategies is pursued with a specific business organizational structure (see Table 15.3). For simplicity's sake, we describe three kinds of organizational structure or governance: centralized (in the home country), decentralized (to local foreign units), and coordinated (all units participate as equals). Other types of governance patterns can be observed in specific companies (e.g., authoritarian dominance by one unit, a confederacy of equals, a federal structure balancing power among strategic units, and so forth).

The **domestic exporter** strategy is characterized by heavy centralization of corporate activities in the home country of origin. Nearly all international companies begin this way, and some move on to other forms. Production, finance/accounting, sales/marketing, human resources, and strategic management are set up to optimize resources in the home country. International sales are sometimes dispersed using agency agreements or subsidiaries, but even here, foreign marketing relies on the domestic home base for marketing themes and strategies. Caterpillar Corporation and other heavy capital-equipment manufacturers fall into this category of firm.

The **multinational** strategy concentrates financial management and control out of a central home base while decentralizing production, sales, and marketing operations to units in other countries. The products and services on sale in different countries are adapted to suit local market conditions. The organization becomes a far-flung confederation of production and marketing facilities in different countries. Many financial service firms, along with a host of manufacturers, such as General Motors, Chrysler, and Intel, fit this pattern.

Franchisers are an interesting mix of old and new. On the one hand, the product is created, designed, financed, and initially produced in the home country but for product-specific reasons must rely heavily on foreign personnel for further production, marketing, and human resources. Food franchisers such as McDonald's, Mrs. Fields Cookies, and KFC fit this pattern. McDonald's created a new form of fast-food chain in the United States and continues to rely largely

TABLE 15.3 GLOBAL BUSINESS STRATEGY AND STRUCTURE

BUSINESS FUNCTION	DOMESTIC EXPORTER	MULTINATIONAL	FRANCHISER	TRANSNATIONAL
Production	Centralized	Dispersed	Coordinated	Coordinated
Finance/accounting	Centralized	Centralized	Centralized	Coordinated
Sales/marketing	Mixed	Dispersed	Coordinated	Coordinated
Human resources	Centralized	Centralized	Coordinated	Coordinated
Strategic management	Centralized	Centralized	Centralized	Coordinated

on the United States for inspiration of new products, strategic management, and financing. Nevertheless, because the product must be produced locally—it is perishable—extensive coordination and dispersal of production, local marketing, and local recruitment of personnel are required.

Generally, foreign franchisees are clones of the mother country units, but fully coordinated worldwide production that could optimize factors of production is not possible. For instance, potatoes and beef can generally not be bought where they are cheapest on world markets but must be produced reasonably close to the area of consumption.

Transnational firms are the stateless, truly globally managed firms that may represent a larger part of international business in the future. Transnational firms have no single national headquarters but instead have many regional headquarters and perhaps a world headquarters. In a **transnational** strategy, nearly all the value-adding activities are managed from a global perspective without reference to national borders, optimizing sources of supply and demand wherever they appear, and taking advantage of any local competitive advantages. Transnational firms take the globe, not the home country, as their management frame of reference. The governance of these firms has been likened to a federal structure in which there is a strong central management core of decision making but considerable dispersal of power and financial muscle throughout the global divisions. Few companies have actually attained transnational status.

Information technology and improvements in global telecommunications are giving international firms more flexibility to shape their global strategies. Protectionism and a need to serve local markets better encourage companies to disperse production facilities and at least become multinational. At the same time, the drive to achieve economies of scale and take advantage of short-term local advantage moves transnationals toward a global management perspective and a concentration of power and authority. Hence, there are forces of decentralization and dispersal as well as forces of centralization and global coordination.

Global Systems to Fit the Strategy

Information technology and improvements in global telecommunications are giving international firms more flexibility to shape their global strategies. The configuration, management, and development of systems tend to follow the global strategy chosen. Figure 15.3 depicts the typical arrangements. By *systems*

FIGURE 15.3 GLOBAL STRATEGY AND SYSTEMS CONFIGURATIONS

SYSTEM CONFIGURATION	Strategy			
	Domestic Exporter	Multinational	Franchiser	Transnational
Centralized	X			
Duplicated			X	
Decentralized	x	X	x	
Networked		x		X

The large Xs show the dominant patterns, and the small Xs show the emerging patterns. For instance, domestic exporters rely predominantly on centralized systems, but there is continual pressure and some development of decentralized systems in local marketing regions.

we mean the full range of activities involved in building and operating information systems: conception and alignment with the strategic business plan, systems development, and ongoing operation and maintenance. For the sake of simplicity, we consider four types of systems configuration. *Centralized systems* are those in which systems development and operation occur totally at the domestic home base. *Duplicated systems* are those in which development occurs at the home base but operations are handed over to autonomous units in foreign locations. *Decentralized systems* are those in which each foreign unit designs its own unique solutions and systems. *Networked systems* are those in which systems development and operations occur in an integrated and coordinated fashion across all units.

As can be seen in Figure 15.3, domestic exporters tend to have highly centralized systems in which a single domestic systems development staff develops worldwide applications. Multinationals offer a direct and striking contrast: Here, foreign units devise their own systems solutions based on local needs with few if any applications in common with headquarters (the exceptions being financial reporting and some telecommunications applications). Franchisers have the simplest systems structure: Like the products they sell, franchisers develop a single system usually at the home base and then replicate it around the world. Each unit, no matter where it is located, has identical applications. Last, the most ambitious form of systems development is found in transnational firms: Networked systems are those in which there is a solid, singular global environment for developing and operating systems. This usually presupposes a powerful telecommunications backbone, a culture of shared applications development, and a shared management culture that crosses cultural barriers. The networked systems structure is the most visible in financial services where the homogeneity of the product—money and money instruments—seems to overcome cultural barriers.

Reorganizing the Business

How should a firm organize itself for doing business on an international scale? To develop a global company and information systems support structure, a firm needs to follow these principles:

1. Organize value-adding activities along lines of comparative advantage. For instance, marketing/sales functions should be located where they can best be performed for least cost and maximum impact; likewise with production, finance, human resources, and information systems.

2. Develop and operate systems units at each level of corporate activity—regional, national, and international. To serve local needs, there should be *host country systems units* of some magnitude. *Regional systems units* should handle telecommunications and systems development across national boundaries that take place within major geographic regions (European, Asian, American). *Transnational systems units* should be established to create the linkages across major regional areas and coordinate the development and operation of international telecommunications and systems development (Roche, 1992).

3. Establish at world headquarters a single office responsible for development of international systems—a global chief information officer (CIO) position.

Many successful companies have devised organizational systems structures along these principles. The success of these companies relies not only on the proper organization of activities but also on a key ingredient—a management team that can understand the risks and benefits of international systems and that can devise strategies for overcoming the risks. We turn to these management topics next.

15-3 What are the challenges posed by global information systems and management solutions for these challenges?

Table 15.4 lists the principal management problems posed by developing international systems. It is interesting to note that these problems are the chief difficulties managers experience in developing ordinary domestic systems as well. But these are enormously complicated in the international environment.

A Typical Scenario: Disorganization on a Global Scale

Let's look at a common scenario. A traditional multinational consumer-goods company based in the United States and operating in Europe would like to expand into Asian markets and knows that it must develop a transnational strategy and a supportive information systems structure. Like most multinationals, it has dispersed production and marketing to regional and national centers while maintaining a world headquarters and strategic management in the United States. Historically, it has allowed each of the subsidiary foreign divisions to develop its own systems. The only centrally coordinated system is financial controls and reporting. The central systems group in the United States focuses only on domestic functions and production.

The result is a hodgepodge of hardware, software, and telecommunications. The e-mail systems between Europe and the United States are incompatible. Each production facility uses a different manufacturing resources planning system (or a different version of the same ERP system) and different marketing, sales, and human resource systems. Hardware and database platforms are wildly different. Communications between different sites are poor, given the high cost of European intercountry communications.

What do you recommend to the senior management leaders of this company, who now want to pursue a transnational strategy and develop an information systems architecture to support a highly coordinated global systems environment? Consider the problems you face by reexamining Table 15.4. The foreign divisions will resist efforts to agree on common user requirements; they have never thought about much other than their own units' needs. The systems groups in American local sites, which have been enlarged recently and told to focus on local needs, will not easily accept guidance from anyone recommending a transnational strategy. It will be difficult to convince local managers anywhere in the world that they should change their business procedures to align with other units in the world, especially if this might interfere with their local performance. After all, local managers are rewarded in this company for

TABLE 15.4 MANAGEMENT CHALLENGES IN DEVELOPING GLOBAL SYSTEMS

Agreeing on common user requirements
Introducing changes in business processes
Coordinating applications development
Coordinating software releases
Encouraging local users to support global systems

meeting local objectives of their division or plant. Finally, it will be difficult to coordinate development of projects around the world in the absence of a powerful telecommunications network and, therefore, difficult to encourage local users to take on ownership in the systems developed.

Global Systems Strategy

Figure 15.4 lays out the main dimensions of a solution. First, consider that not all systems should be coordinated on a transnational basis; only some core systems are truly worth sharing from a cost and feasibility point of view. **Core systems** support functions that are absolutely critical to the organization. Other systems should be partially coordinated because they share key elements, but they do not have to be totally common across national boundaries. For such systems, a good deal of local variation is possible and desirable. A final group of systems is peripheral, truly provincial, and needed to suit local requirements only.

Define the Core Business Processes

How do you identify core systems? The first step is to define a short list of critical core business processes. Business processes are defined and described in Chapter 2, which you should review. Briefly, business processes are sets of logically related tasks to produce specific business results, such as shipping out correct orders to customers or delivering innovative products to the market. Each business process typically involves many functional areas, communicating and coordinating work, information, and knowledge.

FIGURE 15.4 LOCAL, REGIONAL, AND GLOBAL SYSTEMS

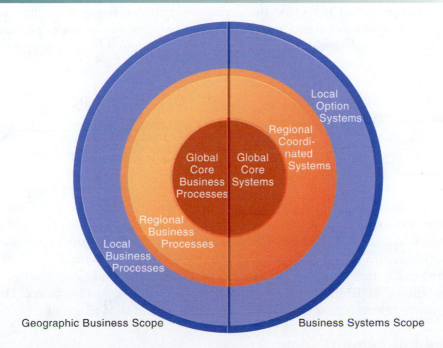

Agency and other coordination costs increase as the firm moves from local option systems toward regional and global systems. However, transaction costs of participating in global markets probably decrease as firms develop global systems. A sensible strategy is to reduce agency costs by developing only a few core global systems that are vital for global operations, leaving other systems in the hands of regional and local units.

Source: From *Managing Information Technology in Multinational Corporations* by Edward M. Roche, © 1993. Adapted by permission of Prentice Hall, Inc., Upper Saddle River, NJ.

The way to identify these core business processes is to conduct a business process analysis. How are customer orders taken, what happens to them once they are taken, who fills the orders, and how are they shipped to the customers? What about suppliers? Do they have access to manufacturing resource planning systems so that supply is automatic? You should be able to identify and set priorities in a short list of 10 business processes that are absolutely critical for the firm.

Next, can you identify centers of excellence for these processes? Is the customer order fulfillment superior in the United States, manufacturing process control superior in Germany, and human resources superior in Asia? You should be able to identify some areas of the company, for some lines of business, where a division or unit stands out in the performance of one or several business functions.

When you understand the business processes of a firm, you can rank-order them. You then can decide which processes should be core applications, centrally coordinated, designed, and implemented around the globe and which should be regional and local. At the same time, by identifying the critical business processes, the really important ones, you have gone a long way to defining a vision of the future that you should be working toward.

Identify the Core Systems to Coordinate Centrally

By identifying the critical core business processes, you begin to see opportunities for transnational systems. The second strategic step is to conquer the core systems and define these systems as truly transnational. The financial and political costs of defining and implementing transnational systems are extremely high. Therefore, keep the list to an absolute minimum, letting experience be the guide and erring on the side of minimalism. By dividing off a small group of systems as absolutely critical, you divide opposition to a transnational strategy. At the same time, you can appease those who oppose the central worldwide coordination implied by transnational systems by permitting peripheral systems development to progress unabated with the exception of some technical platform requirements.

Choose an Approach: Incremental, Grand Design, Evolutionary

A third step is to choose an approach. Avoid piecemeal approaches. These surely will fail for lack of visibility, opposition from all who stand to lose from transnational development, and lack of power to convince senior management that the transnational systems are worth it. Likewise, avoid grand design approaches that try to do everything at once. These also tend to fail because of an inability to focus resources. Nothing gets done properly, and opposition to organizational change is needlessly strengthened because the effort requires extraordinary resources. An alternative approach is to evolve transnational applications incrementally from existing applications with a precise and clear vision of the transnational capabilities the organization should have in five years. This is sometimes referred to as the "salami strategy," or one slice at a time.

Make the Benefits Clear

What is in it for the company? One of the worst situations to avoid is to build global systems for the sake of building global systems. From the beginning, it is crucial that senior management at headquarters and foreign division managers clearly understand the benefits that will come to the company as well as to individual units. Although each system offers unique benefits to a particular budget, the overall contribution of global systems lies in four areas.

Global systems—truly integrated, distributed, and transnational systems—contribute to superior management and coordination. A simple price tag cannot be put on the value of this contribution, and the benefit will not show up in any capital budgeting model. It is the ability to switch suppliers on a moment's notice from one region to another in a crisis, the ability to move production in response to natural disasters, and the ability to use excess capacity in one region to meet raging demand in another.

A second major contribution is vast improvement in production, operation, and supply and distribution. Imagine a global value chain with global suppliers and a global distribution network. For the first time, senior managers can locate value-adding activities in regions where they are most economically performed.

Third, global systems mean global customers and global marketing. Fixed costs around the world can be amortized over a much larger customer base. This will unleash new economies of scale at production facilities.

Last, global systems mean the ability to optimize the use of corporate funds over a much larger capital base. This means, for instance, that capital in a surplus region can be moved efficiently to expand production of capital-starved regions; that cash can be managed more effectively within the company and put to use more effectively.

These strategies will not by themselves create global systems. You will have to implement what you strategize.

The Management Solution: Implementation

We now can reconsider how to handle the most vexing problems facing managers developing the global information systems architectures that were described in Table 15.4.

Agreeing on Common User Requirements

Establishing a short list of the core business processes and core support systems will begin a process of rational comparison across the many divisions of the company, develop a common language for discussing the business, and naturally lead to an understanding of common elements (as well as the unique qualities that must remain local).

Introducing Changes in Business Processes

Your success as a change agent will depend on your legitimacy, your authority, and your ability to involve users in the change design process. **Legitimacy** is defined as the extent to which your authority is accepted on grounds of competence, vision, or other qualities. The selection of a viable change strategy, which we have defined as evolutionary but with a vision, should assist you in convincing others that change is feasible and desirable. Involving people in change, assuring them that change is in the best interests of the company and their local units, is a key tactic.

Coordinating Applications Development

Choice of change strategy is critical for this problem. At the global level there is far too much complexity to attempt a grand design strategy of change. It is far easier to coordinate change by making small incremental steps toward a larger vision. Imagine a five-year plan of action rather than a two-year plan of action, and reduce the set of transnational systems to a bare minimum to reduce coordination costs.

Coordinating Software Releases

Firms can institute procedures to ensure that all operating units convert to new software updates at the same time so that everyone's software is compatible.

Encouraging Local Users to Support Global Systems

The key to this problem is to involve users in the creation of the design without giving up control over the development of the project to parochial interests. The overall tactic for dealing with resistant local units in a transnational company is cooptation. **Cooptation** is defined as bringing the opposition into the process of designing and implementing the solution without giving up control over the direction and nature of the change. As much as possible, raw power should be avoided. Minimally, however, local units must agree on a short list of transnational systems, and raw power may be required to solidify the idea that transnational systems of some sort are truly required.

How should cooptation proceed? Several alternatives are possible. One alternative is to permit each country unit the opportunity to develop one transnational application first in its home territory and then throughout the world. In this manner, each major country systems group is given a piece of the action in developing a transnational system, and local units feel a sense of ownership in the transnational effort. On the downside, this assumes the ability to develop high-quality systems is widely distributed and that a German team, for example, can successfully implement systems in France and Italy. This will not always be the case.

A second tactic is to develop new transnational centers of excellence, or a single center of excellence. There may be several centers around the globe that focus on specific business processes. These centers draw heavily from local national units, are based on multinational teams, and must report to worldwide management. Centers of excellence perform the initial identification and specification of business processes, define the information requirements, perform the business and systems analysis, and accomplish all design and testing. Implementation, however, and pilot testing are rolled out to other parts of the globe. Recruiting a wide range of local groups to transnational centers of excellence helps send the message that all significant groups are involved in the design and will have an influence.

Even with the proper organizational structure and appropriate management choices, it is still possible to stumble over technology issues. Choices of technology platforms, networks, hardware, and software are the final element in building transnational information systems architectures.

15-4 What are the issues and technical alternatives to be considered when developing international information systems?

Once firms have defined a global business model and systems strategy, they must select hardware, software, and networking standards along with key system applications to support global business processes. Hardware, software, and networking pose special technical challenges in an international setting.

One major challenge is finding some way to standardize a global computing platform when there is so much variation from operating unit to operating unit and from country to country. Another major challenge is finding specific software applications that are user-friendly and that truly enhance the productivity of international work teams. The universal acceptance of the Internet around the globe has greatly reduced networking problems. But the mere presence of the Internet does not guarantee that information will flow seamlessly throughout the global organization because not all business units use the same applications, and the quality of Internet service can be highly variable (just as with the telephone service). For instance, German business units may use an open source collaboration tool to share documents and communicate, which is incompatible with American headquarters teams, which use Microsoft solutions. Overcoming these challenges requires systems integration and connectivity on a global basis.

Computing Platforms and Systems Integration

The development of a transnational information systems architecture based on the concept of core systems raises questions about how the new core systems will fit in with the existing suite of applications developed around the globe by different divisions and different people and for different kinds of computing hardware. The goal is to develop global, distributed, and integrated systems to support digital business processes spanning national boundaries. Briefly, these are the same problems faced by any large domestic systems development effort. However, the problems are magnified in an international environment. Just imagine the challenge of integrating systems based on the Windows, Linux, Unix, or proprietary operating systems running on IBM, Oracle Sun, HP, and other hardware in many different operating units in many different countries!

Moreover, having all sites use the same hardware and operating system does not guarantee integration. Some central authority in the firm must establish data standards as well as other technical standards with which sites are to comply. For instance, technical accounting terms such as the beginning and end of the fiscal year must be standardized (review the earlier discussion of the cultural challenges to building global businesses) as well as the acceptable interfaces between systems, communication speeds and architectures, and network software.

Connectivity

Truly integrated global systems must have connectivity—the ability to link together the systems and people of a global firm into a single integrated network just like the phone system but capable of voice, data, and image transmissions. The Internet has provided an enormously powerful foundation for providing connectivity among the dispersed units of global firms. However, many issues remain. The public Internet does not guarantee any level of service (even in the United States). Few global corporations trust the security of the Internet and generally use private networks to communicate sensitive data and Internet virtual private networks (VPNs) for communications that require less security. Not all countries support even basic Internet service that requires obtaining reliable circuits, coordinating among different carriers and the regional telecommunications authority, and obtaining standard agreements for the level of telecommunications service provided. Table 15.5 lists the major challenges posed by international networks.

While private networks have guaranteed service levels and better security than the Internet, the Internet is the primary foundation for global corporate networks when lower security and service levels are acceptable. Companies

TABLE 15.5 CHALLENGES OF INTERNATIONAL NETWORKS

Quality of service
Security
Costs and tariffs
Network management
Installation delays
Poor quality of international service
Regulatory constraints
Network capacity

can create global intranets for internal communication or extranets to exchange information more rapidly with business partners in their supply chains. They can use the public Internet to create global networks using VPNs from Internet service providers, which provide many features of a private network using the public Internet (see Chapter 7). However, VPNs may not provide the same level of quick and predictable response as private networks, especially during times of the day when Internet traffic is very congested, and they may not be able to support large numbers of remote users.

The high cost of PCs and low incomes limit access to Internet service in many developing countries (see Figure 15.5). Where an Internet infrastructure exists in less-developed countries, it often lacks bandwidth capacity and is unreliable in part due to power grid issues. The purchasing power of most people in developing countries makes access to Internet services very expensive in local currencies. In the case of India, uneven Internet service and an undeveloped infrastructure for distributing and paying for goods have hampered the growth of e-commerce (see the Interactive Session on Organizations).

FIGURE 15.5 INTERNET POPULATION IN SELECTED COUNTRIES

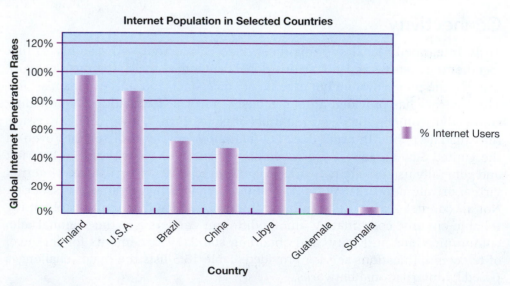

The percentage of the total population using the Internet in developing countries is much smaller than in the United States and Europe, but it is growing rapidly.

Source: Based on data from Internerworldstats.com, 2015; Pew Global Attitudes Project, 2015; and authors.

INTERACTIVE SESSION: ORGANIZATIONS

Indian E-commerce: Obstacles to Opportunity

After China, India has the world's second-largest number of Internet users, more than 400 million by the end of 2015. Rising smartphone ownership, with 4G networks rapidly replacing 3G in urban centers and slower, more affordable data plans in rural areas, has made this possible. Still, this represents only 32 percent of India's population of 1.25 billion. E-commerce in India is expected to surge in the next five years, but it faces some hefty challenges.

For example, a government initiative to lay fiber-optic cable and connect hundreds of thousands of villages to the national Internet backbone formulated in 2011 has stalled due to inaccessibility of remote areas, unwillingness of the large telecoms to invest (even with government financing) in non-lucrative sparsely populated areas, and red tape engendered by overlapping authority between governmental bodies in India's seven union territories, 29 states, and numerous districts and smaller administrative divisions.

Because standard infrastructure in India is primitive—including poor and even nonexistent roads and bridges—less than 5 percent of the planned million miles of cable had been completed by the end of 2015. What's more, India's electrical grid is woefully inadequate, many villages lack sufficient power lines, and electrical service is spotty at best. Bureaucratic right-of-way conflicts stalled work in 15 percent of villages scheduled to be connected, while a duct shortage and glitches with government-developed technology to connect the cables to their endpoints caused additional delays.

Prime Minister Narenda Modi is determined to hook up 600 million rural Indians, including schools, community centers, and hospitals, by 2019. Along with healthcare, educational, and other government services, he wants to ensure that online banking and e-commerce are universally available. Modi has tried to reduce intergovernmental body red tape and to curb corrupt state border officials, and he has also created the Committee on the National Fibre Optic Network to jump-start state government and private sector cooperation in both construction and maintenance and wrest control from state-owned giants.

The picture is mixed. In 2015, 94 percent of Internet usage was conducted by 276 million mobile phone users. Uber rival Ola, restaurant search site Zomato, and the What's App messaging service are rapidly gaining followers, but only 25 percent of urban dwellers and 5 percent of rural Indians have made an online purchase. Pending completion of Modi's broadband superhighway, growth will still be driven by falling smartphone and mobile data plan prices, with two-thirds of the projected 11 million new 2016 users accessing the Internet via portable device.

E-commerce travel sites are especially popular. MakeMytrip.com, Yatra.com, and Indian Railways' IRCTC website along with a number of smaller players account for 75 to 80 percent of all e-commerce purchases. Another top sector is digital downloads, including e-books, music, and content subscriptions, also traditionally a breakthrough sector. The remaining 20 percent of the business-to-consumer (B2C) e-commerce market is composed of durable goods, financial instruments such as online bill payment services and insurance products, and online classified ads, including job, dating, and matrimonial services driven by a growing middle class with rising disposable incomes.

The rush to capitalize on the projected $70 billion in online purchases by 2020 has been led by online giants Amazon and eBay. Amazon is following an unconventional path in India with Junglee.com, a transaction facilitator site that connects buyers and sellers while providing product and price comparison services, making it unambiguously a direct competitor to eBay India. eBay India was a pioneer, setting up shop in 2005. Credit card adoption is still in its infancy, and eBay had to pave the way in gaining consumer trust. The Indian iteration of PayPal, Paisa Pay, remits payment to the seller only after the buyer has received the item and refunds payment if the item is not shipped within three days. (Two days is the goal.) Coupons, a guarantee of full refund or replacement within 30 days if the buyer is not satisfied, and a Power Ship service have aided eBay's efforts. About 30,000 domestic and 15,000 worldwide sellers, mostly small, many artisans, and some from the poorest areas of the country, sell 16 products every minute to 128 million buyers in more than 30 countries. The key to this success was appreciating the unique nature of Indian consumers and tailoring the shopping experience and transaction flow to satisfy their needs.

Still, not all the kinks have been ironed out. Some states insist on requiring buyers to complete a form that must be sent to the seller before the product can ship. Less than 2 percent of Indian consumers own credit cards, so most e-commerce sites must offer a cash-on-delivery (COD) payment option. In 2015 60 to 70 percent of Indian e-commerce purchases were cash-on-delivery. About 45 percent of customers reject these COD orders at the point of delivery, making this a very expensive and probably unsustainable business model. Making matters worse, many e-tailers offer free shipping to acquire and retain customers. The national Indian poverty rate runs between 22 and 25 percent depending on how the rate is measured.

All retailers face steep costs for warehouses and logistics systems to overcome poor transportation infrastructure, bad roads, and traffic congestion. Until India's infrastructure catches up, the e-commerce war is likely to be won by those competitors with the best mobile app. On low-price smartphones feasible for most Indian consumers, many apps come preinstalled, and there is little space on the phone for additional app storage. In this emerging market, profits are yet to be realized, and market consolidation is ongoing. Developing a strong brand and effective customer service and, for some companies, cultivating a vibrant market niche will be the keys to survival.

Sources: Sean McLain and Newley Purnell, "India Startups Vie to Win E-Commerce Battle," *Wall Street Journal*, October 22, 2015; Joanna Sugden, "In 'Digital India,' a 15-Minute Wait for Email," *Wall Street Journal*, August 20, 2015; Sean McLain, "India to Become World's Second-Largest Internet User Base," *Wall Street Journal*, November 17, 2015; "The Quest for E-commerce Dominance in India," *Bloomberg News*, July 31, 2015; Arun Shroff, "E-Commerce in India: Trends, Opportunities and Challenges," India Advisory Board, February 1, 2013; Ramnath Subbu, "Indian E-commerce Market Is Nowhere Near Maturity—eBay India MD," *The Hindu*, April 21, 2014.

CASE STUDY QUESTIONS

1. Describe the technical, cultural, and organizational obstacles to e-commerce growth in India.

2. How do these factors hamper companies from doing business in India or setting up Indian e-commerce sites?

3. Will non-Indian companies like Amazon.com and eBay flourish in India? Explain.

In addition, many countries monitor transmissions. Governments in China, Singapore, Iran, and Saudi Arabia monitor Internet traffic and block access to websites considered morally or politically offensive. On the other hand, the rate of growth in the Internet population is far faster in Asia, Africa, and the Middle East than in North America and Europe, where the Internet population is growing slowly if at all. Therefore, in the future, Internet connectivity will be much more widely available and reliable in less-developed regions of the world, and it will play a significant role in integrating these economies with the world economy.

Software Localization

The development of core systems poses unique challenges for application software: How will the old systems interface with the new? Entirely new interfaces must be built and tested if old systems are kept in local areas (which is common). These interfaces can be costly and messy to build. If new software must be created, another challenge is to build software that can be realistically used by multiple business units from different countries given that business units are accustomed to their unique business processes and definitions of data.

Aside from integrating the new with the old systems, there are problems of human interface design and functionality of systems. For instance, to be truly

INTERACTIVE SESSION: MANAGEMENT

Steelcase Designs Goes for Global Talent Management

You may not have heard of Steelcase Designs, but if you work in a modern office, you may very well have used one of its chairs or interactive whiteboards. Steelcase produces office furniture and architectural and technology products for office environments and the education and healthcare industries and is the largest office furniture manufacturer in the world. It has facilities, offices, and factories in the Americas, Asia, the Middle East, and Australia with 10,000 employees and more than 800 dealers. Steelcase's fiscal 2015 revenue was $3.1 billion.

The company started in 1912 as the Metal Office Furniture Company in Grand Rapids, Michigan, and is noted for its innovations. Steelcase's first patent in 1914 was for a strong, low-cost fireproof steel wastebasket, considered a major breakthrough at a time when many people smoked at work.

Steelcase is also noted for its close attention to people issues. If you go to the Steelcase website, you'll see articles about employee engagement, productivity, technology-empowered learning, and how Steelcase products help people work more comfortably, unlock creative potential, and support social, economic, and environmental sustainability.

Steelcase tries to similarly nurture its own employees, realizing that the company's continuing innovation and success depend on their skills and insights. Employees are its greatest asset. Until a few years ago, management felt this asset was underutilized, especially on the global level. Management questioned whether the company's information systems were supporting company goals of promoting innovation, global integration, and attracting and retaining world-class employees in all of the company's locations around the globe.

Like other organizations expanding globally, Steelcase needed to manage its global workforce and talent pool as well as its relationships with customers and suppliers worldwide. Management needed to understand the needs of the company's skilled global workforce and align business processes with local customs and practices. In addition to maintaining accurate job information on a worker, Steelcase wanted to keep track of future career opportunities and ensure proper planning from a worker engagement and budgetary perspective.

When the company evaluated its systems in 2014, it found that it needed more capabilities for talent management. Talent management involves planning to align the firm's human resources with its business strategy so that the firm has the quantity and quality of employees with the skills it needs to improve business performance and reach its goals. Human resources talent management includes capabilities for recruiting, developing, retaining, and rewarding employees as well as strategic workforce planning.

Steelcase had been using SAP's ERP HCM (Human Capital Management) software, but it was too out of date and required workarounds for the talent management functionality that it needed. The old system was not able to define jobs in enough detail to address the level of workforce planning and development management desired.

Fortunately, Steelcase did not have to discard its SAP system entirely. SAP's HCM version 6.0 featured new talent management functionality that would meet its needs, such as being able to define jobs by job family, task functionality, and the functional area of the business to create a variety of ways to combine work. The new system's ability to organize data by career level, type, and talent group helps the Steelcase HR team create better services, such as career planning for employees. Employees can match their current skill sets against any job in the company and know what competencies will be required and how their current performance evaluations compare with what will be required in future roles they are interested in.

To take advantage of new talent management capabilities to support global operations, Steelcase needed much more standardization than in the past. Simply searching for a name or term is very different depending on the country or the region in terms of how the name is entered in the system. Steelcase faced a challenge in trying to standardize what that looks like and how it is used globally as well as understanding the definitions of common ways to identify the workforce. For example, terms like *salary* and *hourly*, which are used for classifying and determining pay for employees in the United States, don't exist on a global scale. Other countries define their workforce differently. For reporting or analytics, Steelcase needed to define, collect, and use data in a way that is uniform across the globe.

The SAP ERP HCM software enables Steelcase to create an enterprise-wide talent profile, which maintains data for each employee on external job experience as well as their work within Steelcase; showcases their achievements from one job to the next; and notes aspirations and future career goals. Managers can use the system to review assessments, qualification skill sets, and training demands. Steelcase's HR team can now assign the company's high-potential talent to a specific talent group and create a learning and development curriculum for them. Without these capabilities, Steelcase had difficulty showcasing the skills of its workforce.

Steelcase recently contracted with SuccessFactors, an SAP company, to implement SAP SuccessFactors Performance & Goals and take succession planning to the cloud. (Succession planning is the process of identifying and developing employees with the potential to fill key business leadership positions in the company.) Steelcase will be using this capability to complete organizational talent reviews of its workforce and issue employee ratings based on overall performance and leadership potential as a way of identifying high-potential talent. These assessments are more strategically oriented than a typical annual employee performance review and can determine potential risk and bench strength (the competence of employees ready to fill vacant leadership and other positions). When staffing positions worldwide, Steelcase can identify roles and career paths to match its high-potential talent and segment them for promotion.

For the future, Steelcase is looking more toward the cloud and most likely will adopt a hybrid cloud model. According to Lucinda Pick, Steelcase's Global Workforce Strategy Consultant, the company wants to bring the results from the SAP SuccessFactors talent review back to the on-premises core system to analyze core demographic data and use some of the on-premises capabilities for talent management. That way, when HR is analyzing talent review data on performance and future leadership potential, it can see how many high-potential employees the company has according to region, gender, or age group. All those data reside in the core SAP system. Another plan is to integrate talent profiles with learning management to support Steelcase's goal of fostering a learning culture.

According to Pick, for talent management to be effective, Steelcase needs to be able to match the employee with the right skills to a complete set of job requirements. With the new SAP ERP HCM and SuccessFactors systems, the company can now do that. Competition for talent is great. The more Steelcase can automate its business processes and the more it understands its workforce market, the more it can make sound and timely decisions.

Sources: www.steelcase.com, accessed January 3, 2016; www.sap.com, accessed January 4, 2016; and Natalie Miller, "Steelcase Designs Form-Fitting Talent Management," SAP Insider Profiles, October 17, 2015.

CASE STUDY QUESTIONS

1. Why are human resources and talent management so important at Steelcase?

2. Identify the problem described in this case. What management, organization and technology factors contributed to this problem? What role did globalization play?

3. Describe the capabilities of the SAP ERP HCM and SuccessFactors systems that were helpful to Steelcase. How did these systems improve global operations and decision making?

useful for enhancing productivity of a global workforce, software interfaces must be easily understood and mastered quickly. Graphical user interfaces are ideal for this but presuppose a common language—often English. When international systems involve knowledge workers only, English may be the assumed international standard. But as international systems penetrate deeper into management and clerical groups, a common language may not be assumed and human interfaces must be built to accommodate different languages and even conventions. The entire process of converting software to operate in a second language is called **software localization**.

What are the most important software applications? Many international systems focus on basic transaction and management reporting systems. Increasingly, firms are turning to supply chain management and enterprise resource planning systems to standardize their business processes on a global basis and to create coordinated global supply chains and workforces (see the Interactive Session on Management). However, these cross-functional systems are not always compatible with differences in languages, cultural heritages, and business processes in other countries (Accenture, 2014;). Company units in countries that are not technically sophisticated may also encounter problems trying to manage the technical complexities of enterprise applications.

Electronic Data Interchange (EDI) systems and supply chain management systems are widely used by manufacturing and distribution firms to connect to suppliers on a global basis. Collaboration systems, e-mail, and videoconferencing are especially important worldwide collaboration tools for knowledge- and data-based firms, such as advertising firms, research-based firms in medicine and engineering, and graphics and publishing firms. Internet-based tools will be increasingly employed for such purposes.

Review Summary

15-1 *What major factors are driving the internationalization of business?*

The growth of inexpensive international communication and transportation has created a world culture with stable expectations or norms. Political stability and a growing global knowledge base that is widely shared also contribute to the world culture. These general factors create the conditions for global markets, global production, coordination, distribution, and global economies of scale.

15-2 *What are the alternative strategies for developing global businesses?*

There are four basic international strategies: domestic exporter, multinational, franchiser, and transnational. In a transnational strategy, all factors of production are coordinated on a global scale. However, the choice of strategy is a function of the type of business and product.

There is a connection between firm strategy and information systems design. Transnational firms must develop networked system configurations and permit considerable decentralization of development and operations. Franchisers almost always duplicate systems across many countries and use centralized financial controls. Multinationals typically rely on decentralized independence among foreign units with some movement toward development of networks. Domestic exporters typically are centralized in domestic headquarters with some decentralized operations permitted.

15-3 *What are the challenges posed by global information systems and management solutions for these challenges?*

Global information systems pose challenges because cultural, political, and language diversity magnifies differences in organizational culture and business processes and encourages proliferation of disparate local information systems that are difficult to integrate. Typically, international systems have evolved without a conscious plan. The remedy is to define a small subset of core business processes and focus on building systems to support these processes. Tactically, managers will have to co-opt widely dispersed foreign units to participate in the development and operation of these systems, being careful to maintain overall control.

15-4 *What are the issues and technical alternatives to be considered when developing international information systems?*

Implementing a global system requires an implementation strategy that considers both business design and technology platforms. The main hardware and telecommunications issues are systems integration and connectivity. The choices for integration are to go either with a proprietary architecture or with open systems technology. Global networks are extremely difficult to build and operate. Firms can build their own global networks or they can create global networks based on the Internet (intranets or virtual private networks). The main software issues concern building interfaces to existing systems and selecting applications that can work with multiple cultural, language, and organizational frameworks.

Key Terms

Business driver, 564
Cooptation, 576
Core systems, 573
Domestic exporter, 569
Franchisers, 569
Global culture, 565
International information systems architecture, 564

Legitimacy, 575
Multinational, 569
Particularism, 567
Software localization, 582
Transborder data flow, 567
Transnational, 570

MyMISLab

To complete the problems with the MyMISLab, go to EOC Discussion Questions in MyMISLab.

Review Questions

15-1 What major factors are driving the internationalization of business?

- List and describe the five major dimensions for developing an international information systems architecture.

- Describe the five general cultural factors leading toward growth in global business and the four specific business factors. Describe the interconnection among these factors.

- List and describe the major challenges to the development of global systems.

- Explain why some firms have not planned for the development of international systems.

15-2 What are the alternative strategies for developing global businesses?

- Describe the four main strategies for global business and organizational structure.

- Describe the four different system configurations that can be used to support different global strategies.

15-3 What are the challenges posed by global information systems and management solutions for these challenges?

- List and describe the major management issues in developing international systems.

- Identify and describe three principles to follow when organizing the firm for global business.

- Identify and describe three steps of a management strategy for developing and implementing global systems.

- Define cooptation and explain how can it be used in building global systems.

15-4 What are the issues and technical alternatives to be considered when developing international information systems?

- Describe the main technical issues facing global systems.

- Identify some technologies that will help firms develop global systems.

Discussion Questions

15-5 If you were a manager in a company that operates in many countries, what criteria would you use to determine whether an application should be developed as a global application or as a local application?

15-6 Describe ways the Internet can be used in international information systems.

Hands-On MIS Projects

The projects in this section give you hands-on experience conducting international market research, analyzing international systems issues for an expanding business, and building a job posting database and web page for an international company. Visit MyMISLab's Multimedia Library to access this chapter's Hands-on MIS Projects.

Management Decision Problems

15-7 United Parcel Service (UPS) has been expanding its package delivery and logistics services in China, serving both multinational companies and local businesses. UPS drivers in China need to use UPS systems and tools such as its handheld Delivery Information Acquisition Device for capturing package delivery data. UPS wants to make its WorldShip, CampusShip, and other shipping-management services accessible to Chinese and multinational customers via the web. What are some of the international systems issues UPS must consider in order to operate successfully in China?

15-8 Your company manufactures and sells tennis racquets and would like to start selling outside the United States. You are in charge of developing a global web strategy, and the first countries you are thinking of targeting are Brazil, China, Germany, Italy, and Japan. Using the statistics in the *CIA World Factbook* and other online sources, which of these countries would you target first? What criteria did you use? What other considerations should you address in your web strategy? What features would you put on your website to attract buyers from the countries you target?

Achieving Operational Excellence: Building a Job Database and Web Page for an International Consulting Firm

Software skills: Database and web page design
Business skills: Human resources internal job postings

15-9 Companies with many overseas locations need a way to inform employees about available job openings in these locations. In this project you'll use database software to design a database for posting internal job openings and a web page for displaying this information.

KTP Consulting operates in various locations around the world. KTP specializes in designing, developing, and implementing enterprise systems for medium- to large-size companies. KTP offers its employees opportunities to travel, live, and work in various locations throughout the United States, Europe, and Asia. The firm's human resources department has a simple database that enables its staff to track job vacancies. When an employee is interested in relocating, she or he contacts the human resources department for a list of KTP job vacancies. KTP also posts its employment opportunities on the company website.

What type of data should be included in the KTP job vacancies database? What information should not be included in this database? Based on your answers to these questions, build a job vacancies database for KTP. Populate the database with at least 20 records. You should also build a simple web page that incorporates job vacancy data from your newly created database. Submit a copy of the KTP database and web page to your professor.

Improving Decision Making: Conducting International Marketing and Pricing Research

Software skills: Internet-based software
Business skills: International pricing and marketing

15-10 In this project you'll use the web to research overseas distributors and customs regulations and use Internet-based software to calculate prices in foreign currencies.

You are in charge of marketing for a U.S. manufacturer of furniture that has decided to enter the international market. You want to test the market by contacting a European office furniture retailer to offer it a specific desk that you have to sell at about $125. Using the web, locate the information needed to locate and contact this firm and to find out how many euros you would get for the chair in the current market. One source for locating European companies is Europages. In addition, consider using a universal currency converter website, which determines the value of one currency expressed in other currencies. Obtain both the information needed to contact the firm and the price of your chair in its local currency. Then locate and obtain customs and legal restrictions on the products you will export from the United States and import into the country of the retailer you have selected. Finally, locate a company that will represent you as a customs agent and gather information on shipping costs.

Collaboration and Teamwork Project

Identifying Technologies for Global Business Strategies

15-11 With a group of students, identify an area of information technology and explore how this technology might be useful for supporting global business strategies. For instance, you might choose e-mail, smartphones, virtual private networks, enterprise systems, collaboration software, or the web. It will be necessary to identify a business scenario to discuss the technology. You might choose an automobile parts franchise or a clothing franchise, such as Express, as example businesses. Which applications would you make global, which core business processes would you choose, and how would the technology be helpful? If possible, use Google Docs and Google Drive or Google Sites to brainstorm, organize, and develop a presentation of your findings for the class.

Crocs Clambers to Global Efficiency

CASE STUDY

Crocs, Inc. is a world leader in innovative casual footwear for men, women and children. From the first mall kiosk in 2004, Crocs has grown to more than 500 branded retail locations around the world. It has outlets in more than 30 countries including Australia, New Zealand, China, Japan, South Korea, the United Kingdom, France, Germany, and the Netherlands but sells footwear in more than 90. The company now produces more than 300 four-season styles including boots, wedges, flip-flops, sandals, loafers, slippers, rain boots, and sneakers.

Rapid expansion from 2005 through 2007 was amplified by the acquisitions of footwear companies Ocean Minded and Bite Footwear, Dutch messenger bag company Tagger, South African third-party distributor Tidal Trade, and Jibbitz, a manufacturer of charms that snap into the holes of the classic clogs. Unsurprisingly, this resulted in a number of disparate IT systems. To keep pace with short-term growth, Crocs purchased best-of-breed systems in a variety of categories for order management, warehouse management, retail merchandising and reporting, and Electronic Data Interchange (EDI) functions. The problem with this approach is that while dedicated systems often perform better within their specialized niche, without an integrated system, enterprise-wide connectivity is compromised and maintenance needs exacerbated.

Regionally, this meant that highly customized systems evolved in order to integrate functions. This in turn meant that integration across regions became increasingly difficult if not impossible. Basic business functions such as closing the books required manually collating and reconciling spreadsheets from multiple countries and regions, punctuated by multiple phone calls and e-mails in pursuit of missing or incorrectly formatted data. Order entry began in numerous locales but had to proceed through three different systems before the order was placed. What's more, points of failure were unwieldy to locate.

By 2011, it became clear that Crocs's patchwork system was unsustainable. Cross-currency and multilanguage orders were unmanageable, and local or country-specific business regulations had to be managed manually. Crocs began scrutinizing and revamping its business processes and embarked on an enterprise-level IT project named Sunlight. Only after all vital business processes had been re-envisioned to support and serve the way the company did business did management begin searching for an enterprise resource planning (ERP) system to fit those needs. In this way, a companywide transformation was undertaken.

When management began to search for a solution to implement the standardized global processes it had outlined, SAP Apparel and Footwear was quickly chosen. It is one of a number of SAP Consumer Products solutions that tailor the SAP Enterprise Resource Planning (ERP) platform for specific industries. With its main goal of avoiding customizations uppermost, Crocs was further persuaded by the three-way size grid function and many other features custom-made for footwear sellers. Materials master data now store all size, color, and style information, reducing the number of SKUs (stock-keeping units) by an astonishing 40 percent. In fact, according to Dennis Sheldon, Senior Vice President of Global Distribution, the grid function in SAP Apparel and Footwear was instrumental in excising the surfeit of SKUs that had been driving the numerous system customizations at the regional level, shackling global integration. With shoe size, the key demand variable in the footwear industry, driving the grid, data requirements plummeted, business processes were streamlined, and at least 24 legacy systems were shed.

Phase one of the global rollout began in Australia in November 2012. The objectives were to modify the core product as minimally as possible, validate best practices, and discover areas in need of improvement while problems were confined to a single region. Phased ERP rollouts are often functional, rolling out modules for essential business functions (daily operations) enterprise-wide and gradually adding more modules and functionality. Alternatively, a rollout can be implemented by business unit, starting perhaps in the Human Resources department and then moving on to Accounting, Finance, and so on. For Crocs, neither of these approaches was tenable due to the fragmented state of its systems; thus, a phased global rollout was chosen.

SAP's general methodology for implementation of any project follows five steps. Phase I, Project Preparation, is the initial planning and preparation stage. Phase II is the Business Blueprint stage in which a detailed description of the business processes and system requirements is compiled producing the project structure and documentation that will be used in the next two phases.

A hierarchical structure of business scenarios, business processes, and process steps is created, and transactions are assigned to each process step. Phase III, Realization, is when all business process requirements are implemented and the system configuration is outlined at two levels: the baseline (major scope) configuration and the final (remaining scope) configuration. Phase IV is the Final Preparation stage in which testing, end-user training, system management, and cutover activities are performed

and any unresolved critical issues are ironed out. Phase V is the Go Live & Support stage in which the project moves from a project-oriented, preproduction operation to a live production undertaking.

During the Business Blueprint phase, Crocs worked with an implementation partner, which helped it with development and data conversion. In total, the Blueprint, Realization, and Final Preparation stages took just 17 months, with Crocs's Australia division going live in April 2014.

Because Crocs also implemented a full suite of other SAP products, including SAP BusinessObjects (a Business Intelligence product), SAP BW (Business Warehouse), a B2B Internet sales application, SAP solutions for GRC (Governance, Risk, and Compliance), and SAP Business Planning and Consolidation to interface with the ERP system, it could use its Australian rollout to discover and implement any necessary modifications in a complete system before it proceeded to the next region, which it did within two months.

However, when Crocs took its Japan division (a six-times-larger business—$120 million as opposed to $20 million) live, it ran into language and cultural barriers that even advance training with a change management consulting firm could not forestall. Change management (CM) focuses on the human side of change—how to guide people through major organizational changes, including those brought about by information systems. Nevertheless, despite having to navigate several unforeseen cultural hurdles, the Japan rollout saw fewer data migration problems, and in short order, the company announced a target date of January 7, 2015, for its full global rollout.

To meet this goal, Crocs built regional "readiness" teams of subject matter experts (SMEs) from the different functional departments by immersing them in the training, development, and testing of the system. This eased adoption and bolstered the change management side of the equation. Often, companies will fly in IT department project managers and/or vendor project managers to train employees and oversee system implementation. Instead, Crocs made sure that known quantities familiar with local culture, business practices, and habits guided the process. These resident teams proved invaluable in troubleshooting and crisis management during the Go Live & Support phase.

With more than 100 of these "readiness" team leaders and SMEs on the ground and, equally as importantly, an enterprise-wide buy-in and broad understanding of the project goals, 1,400 users successfully finalized the launch across 32 countries, speaking 15 different languages and using 23 different currencies. What's more, Crocs could not have been more pleased that only 25 customizations were required, and those were to satisfy local legal and regulatory stipulations.

Crocs now administers the automation of purchasing, delivery tracking, inventory segmentation, chargebacks, and nearly every other aspect of the design, manufacture, and distribution of its footwear in SAP Apparel and Footwear. With business processes streamlined, sales are now outstanding for fewer days, and the fill, or demand satisfaction rate—percent of orders satisfied from inventory on hand—has significantly improved. Freight costs, nonproduction selling expenses, and SG&A (selling, general, and administrative) expenditures, which combine salaries, commissions, and travel expenses for executives and salespeople, advertising costs, and payroll expenses, have all been substantially reduced.

Perhaps even more noteworthy, whereas data were formerly regarded with a dubious eye, managers now have confidence in the numbers and can immediately proceed to data analysis. Order location, order status, and inventory availability are readily discernible, making order fulfillment both easier and faster.

In the year following implementation, Crocs kept a close eye on its users to make sure that they did not slip back into old habits, maintaining a strict prohibition on regionally based spreadsheets and insisting on meticulous conformance with revamped business processes. Analytics solutions working with SAP Apparel and Footwear are providing greater visibility into the business at the enterprise level. Operational efficiencies have provided improved control over Crocs's global supply chain from raw materials purchase to product delivery around the world. Its numerous design and style variations, seasonal offerings, and customer value–added services such as Jibbitz personalization generate very large quantities of data that can now be efficiently managed.

Though Crocs experienced a company shakeup in 2014 that included 70 jobs lost, 100 store closings, scaling back some of its newer, fashion-seeking styles to concentrate on its casual styles, and reducing investment in some smaller markets to concentrate on just six countries—the United States, the United Kingdom, Germany, South Korea, Japan, and China—its financial difficulties were not attributed to its IT investment. Rather, the slowdown was ascribed to changing customer tastes for a brand that has perennially suffered slings and arrows for its unattractive form.

Refocusing on its footwear's five key attributes—colorful, relaxed, comfortable, distinctive, and fun—Crocs was able to revive business back up to $9.7 million in 2015 (a 3.7 percent increase from the previous year) after Crocs had become a billion-dollar company in 2012.

Though some dissatisfaction with supply chain efficiency that resulted in poor customer service was noted by President and Principal Executive Officer Andrew Rees at the end of the third quarter of 2015, SAP Footwear and Apparel had only been up and running for those three quarters, and full functionality of the integrated analytics software had likely not yet been reached.

It is unlikely that without Crocs's forward-thinking commitment to revamping and streamlining its business processes, reducing costs, and improving order fulfillment efficiency the downturn of 2014 would have been navigated so seamlessly. The company was able to reduce its SKU count to simplify product development, forecasting, and inventory management. Crocs had identified reducing its direct-ship model as crucial. It had always permitted very low minimum order quantities and direct order placement with factories, but this was becoming unwieldy, creating needless complexity in the factory order management process. With its new systems, the company could now easily increase the minimum order quantity to industry standards enterprise-wide.

Crocs also decided to bring its value-added services more in line with industry standards to make it easier to package orders and move them through distribution centers. Once again, without an integrated global system, achieving this goal would have been significantly more problematic. Order location, order status, and inventory availability are all now easily obtainable, making global supply chain management easier. Finally, Crocs developed its management team, adding leaders from several key areas to ensure that its IT investment was used to its fullest potential. Project Sunlight should continue to reap benefits in 2016 and beyond.

Sources: www.company.crocs.com, accessed February 3, 2016; Ken Murphy, "Crocs Climbs New Business Heights," SAP Insider Profiles, July 6, 2015; Natalie Rinn, "Finding My Fun: A Thorough Examination of Crocs, the Most-Hated Shoe in America," racked. com, May 14, 2015; Jamie Grill-Goodman, "Crocs' E-commerce Business Grows Despite Inventory, Supply Chain Issues," Consumer Goods Technology, November 6, 2015; and "Crocs Discovers Multichannel Growth, Rolls Out ERP," *Retail Info Systems News*, February 26, 2013.

CASE STUDY QUESTIONS

15-12 What management problems typical of global systems was Crocs experiencing? What management, organization, and technology factors were responsible for those problems?

15-13 How did Crocs's new systems and use of SAP Apparel and Footwear support its business strategy? How effective was the solution chosen by the company?

15-14 How did Crocs's new systems improve operations and management decision making?

15-15 What influence does the global business environment have on Crocs, and how does that affect its choice of systems?

MyMISLab

Go to the Assignments section of MyMISLab to complete these writing exercises.

15-16 Identify and describe solutions to the five management challenges of developing global systems.

15-17 Identify and describe five problems of international networks that prevent companies from developing effective global systems.

Chapter 15 References

Accenture. "Technology Not Widely Used in Global Companies' Emerging Market Supply Chains, Study Says." (September 16, 2014).

Bisson, Peter, Elizabeth Stephenson, and S. Patrick Viguerie. "Global Forces: An Introduction." *McKinsey Quarterly* (June 2010).

Burtch, Gordon, Anindya Ghose, and Sunil Watta. "Cultural Differences and Geography as Determinants of Online Prosocial Lending." *MIS Quarterly* 38, No. 3 (September 2014).

Davison, Robert. "Cultural Complications of ERP." *Communications of the ACM* 45, No. 7 (July 2002).

Deans, Candace P. and Michael J. Kane. *International Dimensions of Information Systems and Technology*. Boston, MA: PWS-Kent (1992).

Dewhurst, Martin, Jonathan Harris, and Suzanne Heywood. "The Global Company's Challenge." *McKinsey Quarterly* (June 2012).

Dou, Eva. "Timeline of China's Social Media Crackdowns." *Wall Street Journal* (August 8, 2014).

Ghislanzoni, Giancarlo, Risto Penttinen, and David Turnbull. "The Multilocal Challenge: Managing Cross-Border Functions." *McKinsey Quarterly* (March 2008).

Ives, Blake and Sirkka Jarvenpaa. "Applications of Global Information Technology: Key Issues for Management." *MIS Quarterly* 15, No. 1 (March 1991).

Ives, Blake, S. L. Jarvenpaa, and R. O. Mason. "Global Business Drivers: Aligning Information Technology to Global Business Strategy." *IBM Systems Journal* 32, No. 1 (1993).

King, William R. and Vikram Sethi. "An Empirical Analysis of the Organization of Transnational Information Systems." *Journal of Management Information Systems* 15, No. 4 (Spring 1999).

Kirsch, Laurie J. "Deploying Common Systems Globally: The Dynamic of Control." *Information Systems Research* 15, No. 4 (December 2004).

Krishna, S., Sundeep Sahay, and Geoff Walsham. "Managing Cross-Cultural Issues in Global Software Outsourcing." *Communications of the ACM* 47, No. 4 (April 2004).

Martinsons, Maris G. "ERP In China: One Package Two Profiles," *Communications of the ACM* 47, No. 7 (July 2004).

Meyer, Erin. "When Culture Doesn't Translate." *Harvard Business Review* (October 2015).

McKinsey & Company. "Lions Go Digital: The Internet's Transformative Potential in Africa. (November 2013).

Pew Research Global Attitudes Project. "Emerging Nations Embrace Internet, Mobile Technology." (February 13, 2014).

Quelch, John A. and Lisa R. Klein. "The Internet and International Marketing." *Sloan Management Review* (Spring 1996).

Roche, Edward M. *Managing Information Technology in Multinational Corporations*. New York: Macmillan (1992).

Su, Ning. "Cultural Sensemaking in Offshore Information Technology Service Suppliers: A Cultural Frame Perspective." *MIS Quarterly* 39, No. 4 (December 2015).

Tractinsky, Noam and Sirkka L. Jarvenpaa. "Information Systems Design Decisions in a Global Versus Domestic Context." *MIS Quarterly* 19, No. 4 (December 1995).

Waxer, Cindy. "Cross-Border Data Blues." *Computerworld Digital Magazine* (May 2016).

Glossary

3-D printing   Uses machines to make solid objects, layer by layer, from specifications in a digital file. Also known as additive manufacturing.

3G networks   Cellular networks based on packet-switched technology with speeds ranging from 144 Kbps for mobile users to more than 2 Mbps for stationary users, enabling users to transmit video, graphics, and other rich media in addition to voice.

4G networks   The next evolution in wireless communication is entirely packet switched and capable of providing between 1 Mbps and 1 Gbps speeds; up to 10 times faster than 3G networks.

acceptable use policy (AUP)   Defines acceptable uses of the firm's information resources and computing equipment, including desktop and laptop computers, wireless devices, telephones, and the Internet, and specifies consequences for noncompliance.

acceptance testing   Provides the final certification that the system is ready to be used in a production setting.

accountability   The mechanisms for assessing responsibility for decisions made and actions taken.

advertising revenue model   Website generating revenue by attracting a large audience.

affiliate revenue model   An e-commerce revenue model in which websites are paid as "affiliates" for sending their visitors to other sites in return for a referral fee.

agency theory   Economic theory that views the firm as a nexus of contracts among self-interested individuals who must be supervised and managed.

agent-based modeling   Modeling complex phenomena as systems of autonomous agents that follow relatively simple rules for interaction.

agile development   Rapid delivery of working software by breaking a large project into a series of small sub-projects that are completed in short periods of time using iteration and continuous feedback.

analytic platform   Preconfigured hardware-software system that is specifically designed for high-speed analysis of large datasets.

analytical CRM   Customer relationship management applications dealing with the analysis of customer data to provide information for improving business performance.

Android   A mobile operating system developed by Android, Inc. (purchased by Google) and later the Open Handset Alliance as a flexible, upgradeable mobile device platform.

antivirus software   Software designed to detect, and often eliminate, malware from an information system.

application controls: Specific controls unique to each computerized application that ensure that only authorized data are completely and accurately processed by that application.

application server   Software that handles all application operations between browser-based computers and a company's back-end business applications or databases.

apps   Small pieces of software that run on the Internet, on your computer, or on your cell phone and are generally delivered over the Internet.

artificial intelligence (AI)   The effort to develop computer-based systems that can behave like humans, with the ability to learn languages, accomplish physical tasks, use a perceptual apparatus, and emulate human expertise and decision making.

attribute   A piece of information describing a particular entity.

augmented reality (AR)   A technology for enhancing visualization. Provides a live direct or indirect view of a physical real-world environment whose elements are augmented by virtual computer-generated imagery.

authentication   The ability of each party in a transaction to ascertain the identity of the other party.

automation   Using the computer to speed up the performance of existing tasks.

backward chaining   A strategy for searching the rule base in an expert system that acts like a problem solver by beginning with a hypothesis and seeking out more information until the hypothesis is either proved or disproved.

balanced scorecard method   Framework for operationalizing a firm's strategic plan by focusing on measurable financial, business process, customer, and learning and growth outcomes of firm performance.

bandwidth   The capacity of a communications channel as measured by the difference between the highest and lowest frequencies that can be transmitted by that channel.

behavioral models   Descriptions of management based on behavioral scientists' observations of what managers actually do in their jobs.

behavioral targeting   Tracking the click-streams (history of clicking behavior) of individuals across multiple websites for the purpose of understanding their interests and intentions, and exposing them to advertisements which are uniquely suited to their interests.

benchmarking   Setting strict standards for products, services, or activities and measuring organizational performance against those standards.

best practices   The most successful solutions or problem-solving methods that have been developed by a specific organization or industry.

big data   Data sets with volumes so huge that they are beyond the ability of typical relational DBMS to capture, store, and analyze. The data are often unstructured or semi-structured.

biometric authentication   Technology for authenticating system users that compares a person's unique characteristics such as fingerprints, face, or retinal image against a stored set profile of these characteristics.

bit   A binary digit representing the smallest unit of data in a computer system. It can only have one of two states, representing 0 or 1.

blog   Popular term for "weblog," designating an informal yet structured website where individuals can publish stories, opinions, and links to other websites of interest.

blogosphere   Totality of blog-related websites.

Bluetooth   Standard for wireless personal area networks that can transmit up to 722 Kbps within a 10-meter area.

botnet   A group of computers that have been infected with bot malware without users' knowledge, enabling a hacker to use the amassed resources of the computers to launch distributed denial-of-service attacks, phishing campaigns, or spam.

broadband   High-speed transmission technology. Also designates a single communications medium that can transmit multiple channels of data simultaneously.

bugs   Software program code defects.

bullwhip effect Distortion of information about the demand for a product as it passes from one entity to the next across the supply chain.

business continuity planning Planning that focuses on how the company can restore business operations after a disaster strikes.

business driver A force in the environment to which businesses must respond and that influences the direction of business.

business ecosystem Loosely coupled but interdependent networks of suppliers, distributors, outsourcing firms, transportation service firms, and technology manufacturers.

business functions Specialized tasks performed in a business organization, including manufacturing and production, sales and marketing, finance and accounting, and human resources.

business intelligence Applications and technologies to help users make better business decisions.

business model An abstraction of what an enterprise is and how the enterprise delivers a product or service, showing how the enterprise creates wealth.

business performance management (BPM) Attempts to systematically translate a firm's strategies (e.g., differentiation, low-cost producer, market share growth, and scope of operation) into operational targets.

business process management (BPM) An approach to business which aims to continuously improve and manage business processes.

business process redesign Type of organizational change in which business processes are analyzed, simplified, and redesigned.

business processes The unique ways in which organizations coordinate and organize work activities, information, and knowledge to produce a product or service.

business-to-business (B2B) electronic commerce Electronic sales of goods and services among businesses.

business-to-consumer (B2C) electronic commerce Electronic retailing of products and services directly to individual consumers.

BYOD Stands for "bring your own device," and refers to employees using their own computing devices in the workplace.

byte A string of bits, usually eight, used to store one number or character in a computer system.

cable Internet connections Internet connections that use digital cable lines to deliver high-speed Internet access to homes and businesses.

capital budgeting The process of analyzing and selecting various proposals for capital expenditures.

carpal tunnel syndrome (CTS) Type of RSI in which pressure on the median nerve through the wrist's bony carpal tunnel structure produces pain.

case-based reasoning (CBR) Artificial intelligence technology that represents knowledge as a database of cases and solutions.

change agent In the context of implementation, the individual acting as the catalyst during the change process to ensure successful organizational adaptation to a new system or innovation.

change management Managing the impact of organizational change associated with an innovation, such as a new information system.

chat Live, interactive conversations over a public network.

chatbot Software agent designed to simulate a conversation with one or more human users via textual or auditory methods.

chief data officer (CDO) Responsible for enterprise-wide governance and utilization of information to maximize the value the organization can realize from its data.

chief information officer (CIO) Senior manager in charge of the information systems function in the firm.

chief knowledge officer (CKO) Senior executive in charge of the organization's knowledge management program.

chief privacy officer (CPO) Responsible for ensuring the company complies with existing data privacy laws.

chief security officer (CSO) Heads a formal security function for the organization and is responsible for enforcing the firm's security policy.

choice Simon's third stage of decision making, when the individual selects among the various solution alternatives.

Chrome OS Google's lightweight computer operating system for users who do most of their computing on the Internet; runs on computers ranging from netbooks to desktop computers.

churn rate Measurement of the number of customers who stop using or purchasing products or services from a company. Used as an indicator of the growth or decline of a firm's customer base.

classical model of management Traditional description of management that focused on its formal functions of planning, organizing, coordinating, deciding, and controlling.

click fraud Fraudulently clicking on an online ad in pay per click advertising to generate an improper charge per click.

client The user point-of-entry for the required function in client/server computing. Normally a desktop computer, workstation, or laptop computer.

client/server computing A model for computing that splits processing between clients and servers on a network, assigning functions to the machine most able to perform the function.

cloud computing Model of computing in which computer processing, storage, software, and other services are provided as a shared pool of virtualized resources over a network, primarily the Internet.

collaboration Working with others to achieve shared and explicit goals.

community provider A website business model that creates a digital online environment where people with similar interests can transact (buy and sell goods); share interests, photos, videos; communicate with like-minded people; receive interest-related information; and even play out fantasies by adopting online personalities called avatars.

communities of practice (COPs) Informal social networks of professionals and employees within and outside the firm who have similar work-related activities and interests and share their knowledge.

competitive forces model Model used to describe the interaction of external influences, specifically threats and opportunities, that affect an organization's strategy and ability to compete.

complementary assets Additional assets required to derive value from a primary investment.

component-based development Building large software systems by combining preexisting software components.

computer abuse The commission of acts involving a computer that may not be illegal but are considered unethical.

computer crime The commission of illegal acts through the use of a computer or against a computer system.

computer forensics The scientific collection, examination, authentication, preservation, and analysis of data held on or retrieved from computer storage media in such a way that the information can be used as evidence in a court of law.

computer hardware Physical equipment used for input, processing, and output activities in an information system.

computer literacy Knowledge about information technology, focusing on understanding of how computer-based technologies work.

computer software Detailed, preprogrammed instructions that control and coordinate the work of computer hardware components in an information system.

computer virus Rogue software program that attaches itself to other software programs or data files in order to be executed, often causing hardware and software malfunctions.

computer vision syndrome (CVS) Eyestrain condition related to computer display screen use; symptoms include headaches, blurred vision, and dry and irritated eyes.

computer-aided design (CAD) Information system that automates the creation and revision of designs using sophisticated graphics software.

computer-aided software engineering (CASE)   Automation of step-by-step methodologies for software and systems development to reduce the amounts of repetitive work the developer needs to do.

consumer-to-consumer (C2C)   Consumers selling goods and services electronically to other consumers.

consumerization of IT   New information technology originating in the consumer market that spreads to business organizations.

controls   All of the methods, policies, and procedures that ensure protection of the organization's assets, accuracy and reliability of its records, and operational adherence to management standards.

conversion   The process of changing from the old system to the new system.

cookies   Tiny file deposited on a computer hard drive when an individual visits certain websites. Used to identify the visitor and track visits to the website.

cooptation   Bringing the opposition into the process of designing and implementing a solution without giving up control of the direction and nature of the change.

copyright   A statutory grant that protects creators of intellectual property against copying by others for any purpose for a minimum of 70 years.

core competency   Activity at which a firm excels as a world-class leader.

core systems   Systems that support functions that are absolutely critical to the organization.

cost transparency   The ability of consumers to discover the actual costs merchants pay for products.

counterimplementation   A deliberate strategy to thwart the implementation of an information system or an innovation in an organization.

cross-selling   Marketing complementary products to customers.

crowdsourcing   Using large Internet audiences for advice, market feedback, new ideas, and solutions to business problems. Related to the "wisdom of crowds" theory.

culture   The set of fundamental assumptions about what products the organization should produce, how and where it should produce them, and for whom they should be produced.

customer lifetime value (CLTV)   Difference between revenues produced by a specific customer and the expenses for acquiring and servicing that customer minus the cost of promotional marketing over the lifetime of the customer relationship, expressed in today's dollars.

customer relationship management (CRM)   Business and technology discipline that uses information systems to coordinate all of the business processes surrounding the firm's interactions with its customers in sales, marketing, and service.

customer relationship management systems   Information systems that track all the ways in which a company interacts with its customers and analyze these interactions to optimize revenue, profitability, customer satisfaction, and customer retention.

customization   The modification of a software package to meet an organization's unique requirements without destroying the package software's integrity.

customization   In e-commerce, changing a delivered product or service based on a user's preferences or prior behavior.

cybervandalism   Intentional disruption, defacement, or destruction of a website or corporate information system.

cyberwarfare   State-sponsored activity designed to cripple and defeat another state or nation by damaging or disrupting its computers or networks.

data   Streams of raw facts representing events occurring in organizations or the physical environment before they have been organized and arranged into a form that people can understand and use.

data administration   A special organizational function for managing the organization's data resources, concerned with information policy, data planning, maintenance of data dictionaries, and data quality standards.

data cleansing   Activities for detecting and correcting data in a database or file that are incorrect, incomplete, improperly formatted, or redundant. Also known as data scrubbing.

data definition   DBMS capability that specifies the structure and content of the database.

data dictionary   An automated or manual tool for storing and organizing information about the data maintained in a database.

data element   A field.

data flow diagram (DFD)   Primary tool for structured analysis that graphically illustrates a system's component process and the flow of data between them.

data governance   Policies and processes for managing the availability, usability, integrity, and security of the firm's data.

data inconsistency   The presence of different values for same attribute when the same data are stored in multiple locations.

data management technology   Software governing the organization of data on physical storage media.

data manipulation language   A language associated with a database management system that end users and programmers use to manipulate data in the database.

data mart   A small data warehouse containing only a portion of the organization's data for a specified function or population of users.

data mining   Analysis of large pools of data to find patterns and rules that can be used to guide decision making and predict future behavior.

data quality audit   A survey and/or sample of files to determine accuracy and completeness of data in an information system.

data redundancy   The presence of duplicate data in multiple data files.

data visualization   Technology for helping users see patterns and relationships in large amounts of data by presenting the data in graphical form.

data warehouse   A database, with reporting and query tools, that stores current and historical data extracted from various operational systems and consolidated for management reporting and analysis.

data workers   People such as secretaries or bookkeepers who process the organization's paperwork.

database   A group of related files.

database (rigorous definition)   A collection of data organized to service many applications at the same time by storing and managing data so that they appear to be in one location.

database administration   Refers to the more technical and operational aspects of managing data, including physical database design and maintenance.

database management system (DBMS)   Special software to create and maintain a database and enable individual business applications to extract the data they need without having to create separate files or data definitions in their computer programs.

database server   A computer in a client/server environment that is responsible for running a DBMS to process SQL statements and perform database management tasks.

decisional roles   Mintzberg's classification for managerial roles where managers initiate activities, handle disturbances, allocate resources, and negotiate conflicts.

decision-support systems (DSS)   Information systems at the organization's management level that combine data and sophisticated analytical models or data analysis tools to support semi-structured and unstructured decision making.

deep packet inspection (DPI)   Technology for managing network traffic by examining data packets, sorting out low-priority data from higher priority business-critical data, and sending packets in order of priority.

demand planning   Determining how much product a business needs to make to satisfy all its customers' demands.

denial-of-service (DoS) attack Flooding a network server or web server with false communications or requests for services in order to crash the network.

design Simon's second stage of decision making, when the individual conceives of possible alternative solutions to a problem.

DevOps Organizational strategy to create a culture and environment to promote rapid and agile development practices by emphasizing close collaboration between software developers and the IT operational staff.

digital asset management systems Classify, store, and distribute digital objects such as photographs, graphic images, video, and audio content.

digital certificate An attachment to an electronic message to verify the identity of the sender and to provide the receiver with the means to encode a reply.

digital dashboard Displays all of a firm's key performance indicators as graphs and charts on a single screen to provide one-page overview of all the critical measurements necessary to make key executive decisions.

digital divide Large disparities in access to computers and the Internet among different social groups and different locations.

digital firm Organization where nearly all significant business processes and relationships with customers, suppliers, and employees are digitally enabled, and key corporate assets are managed through digital means.

digital goods Goods that can be delivered over a digital network.

Digital Millennium Copyright Act (DMCA) Adjusts copyright laws to the Internet Age by making it illegal to make, distribute, or use devices that circumvent technology-based protections of copyrighted materials.

digital subscriber line (DSL) A group of technologies providing high-capacity transmission over existing copper telephone lines.

direct cutover strategy A risky conversion approach where the new system completely replaces the old one on an appointed day.

direct goods Goods used in a production process.

disaster recovery planning Planning for the restoration of computing and communications services after they have been disrupted.

disintermediation The removal of organizations or business process layers responsible for certain intermediary steps in a value chain.

disruptive technologies Technologies with disruptive impact on industries and businesses, rendering existing products, services, and business models obsolete.

distributed denial-of-service (DDoS) attack Numerous computers inundating and overwhelming a network from numerous launch points.

documentation Descriptions of how an information system works from either a technical or end-user standpoint.

domain name English-like name that corresponds to the unique 32-bit numeric Internet Protocol (IP) address for each computer connected to the Internet.

Domain Name System (DNS) A hierarchical system of servers maintaining a database enabling the conversion of domain names to their numeric IP addresses.

domestic exporter Form of business organization characterized by heavy centralization of corporate activities in the home county of origin.

downtime Period of time in which an information system is not operational.

drill down The ability to move from summary data to lower and lower levels of detail.

drive-by download Malware that comes with a downloaded file a user intentionally or unintentionally requests.

due process A process in which laws are well-known and understood and there is an ability to appeal to higher authorities to ensure that laws are applied correctly.

dynamic pricing Pricing of items based on real-time interactions between buyers and sellers that determine what a item is worth at any particular moment.

e-government Use of the Internet and related technologies to digitally enable government and public sector agencies' relationships with citizens, businesses, and other arms of government.

efficient customer response system System that directly links consumer behavior back to distribution, production, and supply chains.

electronic business (e-business) The use of the Internet and digital technology to execute all the business processes in the enterprise. Includes e-commerce as well as processes for the internal management of the firm and for coordination with suppliers and other business partners.

electronic commerce (e-commerce) The process of buying and selling goods and services electronically involving transactions using the Internet, networks, and other digital technologies.

electronic data interchange (EDI) The direct computer-to-computer exchange between two organizations of standard business transactions, such as orders, shipment instructions, or payments.

email The computer-to-computer exchange of messages.

employee relationship management (ERM) Software dealing with employee issues that are closely related to CRM, such as setting objectives, employee performance management, performance-based compensation, and employee training.

encryption The coding and scrambling of messages to prevent their being read or accessed without authorization.

end-user development The development of information systems by end users with little or no formal assistance from technical specialists.

end-user interface The part of an information system through which the end user interacts with the system, such as online screens and commands.

end users Representatives of departments outside the information systems group for whom applications are developed.

enterprise applications Systems that can coordinate activities, decisions, and knowledge across many different functions, levels, and business units in a firm. Include enterprise systems, supply chain management systems, and knowledge management systems.

enterprise content management (ECM) Help organizations manage structured and semi-structured knowledge, providing corporate repositories of documents, reports, presentations, and best practices and capabilities for collecting and organizing email and graphic objects.

enterprise software Set of integrated modules for applications such as sales and distribution, financial accounting, investment management, materials management, production planning, plant maintenance, and human resources that allow data to be used by multiple functions and business processes.

enterprise systems Integrated enterprise-wide information systems that coordinate key internal processes of the firm.

enterprise-wide knowledge management systems General-purpose, firmwide systems that collect, store, distribute, and apply digital content and knowledge.

entity A person, place, thing, or event about which information must be kept.

entity-relationship diagram A methodology for documenting databases illustrating the relationship between various entities in the database.

ergonomics The interaction of people and machines in the work environment, including the design of jobs, health issues, and the end-user interface of information systems.

e-tailer Online retail stores from the giant Amazon to tiny local stores that have websites where retail goods are sold.

ethical no-free-lunch rule Assumption that all tangible and intangible objects are owned by someone else, unless there is a specific declaration otherwise, and that the creator wants compensation for this work.

ethics Principles of right and wrong that can be used by individuals acting as free moral agents to make choices to guide their behavior.

evil twins Wireless networks that pretend to be legitimate to entice participants to log on and reveal passwords or credit card numbers.

exchange Third-party Net marketplace that is primarily transaction oriented and that connects many buyers and suppliers for spot purchasing.

executive support systems (ESS) Information systems at the organization's strategic level designed to address unstructured decision making through advanced graphics and communications.

expert system Knowledge-intensive computer program that captures the expertise of a human in limited domains of knowledge.

explicit knowledge Knowledge that has been documented.

Extensible Markup Language (XML) General-purpose language that describes the structure of a document and can perform presentation, communication, and storage of data, allowing data to be manipulated by the computer.

external integration tools Project management technique that links the work of the implementation team to that of users at all organizational levels.

extranet Private intranet that is accessible to authorized outsiders.

Fair Information Practices (FIP) A set of principles originally set forth in 1973 that governs the collection and use of information about individuals and forms the basis of most U.S. and European privacy laws.

fault-tolerant computer systems Systems that contain extra hardware, software, and power supply components that can back a system up and keep it running to prevent system failure.

feasibility study As part of the systems analysis process, the way to determine whether the solution is achievable, given the organization's resources and constraints.

feedback Output that is returned to the appropriate members of the organization to help them evaluate or correct input.

field A grouping of characters into a word, a group of words, or a complete number, such as a person's name or age.

File Transfer Protocol (FTP) Tool for retrieving and transferring files from a remote computer.

file A group of records of the same type.

firewall Hardware and software placed between an organization's internal network and an external network to prevent outsiders from invading private networks.

foreign key Field in a database table that enables users find related information in another database table.

formal control tools Project management technique that helps monitor the progress toward completion of a task and fulfillment of goals.

formal planning tools Project management technique that structures and sequences tasks, budgeting time, money, and technical resources required to complete the tasks.

forward chaining A strategy for searching the rule base in an expert system that begins with the information entered by the user and searches the rule base to arrive at a conclusion.

franchiser Form of business organization in which a product is created, designed, financed, and initially produced in the home country, but for product-specific reasons relies heavily on foreign personnel for further production, marketing, and human resources.

free/fremium revenue model An e-commerce revenue model in which a firm offers basic services or content for free while charging a premium for advanced or high-value features.

fuzzy logic Rule-based AI that tolerates imprecision by using nonspecific terms called membership functions to solve problems.

Gantt chart Visually representats the timing, duration, and resource requirements of project tasks.

general controls Overall control environment governing the design, security, and use of computer programs and the security of data files in general throughout the organization's information technology infrastructure.

genetic algorithms Problem-solving methods that promote the evolution of solutions to specified problems using the model of living organisms adapting to their environment.

geoadvertising services Delivering ads to users based on their GPS location.

geographic information system (GIS) System with software that can analyze and display data using digitized maps to enhance planning and decision-making.

geoinformation services Information on local places and things based on the GPS position of the user.

geosocial services Social networking based on the GPS location of users.

global culture The development of common expectations, shared artifacts, and social norms among different cultures and peoples.

Golden Rule Putting oneself in the place of others as the object of a decision.

Gramm-Leach-Bliley Act Requires financial institutions to ensure the security and confidentiality of customer data.

green computing (green IT) Refers to practices and technologies for designing, manufacturing, using, and disposing of computers, servers, and associated devices such as monitors, printers, storage devices, and networking and communications systems to minimize impact on the environment.

group decision-support system (GDSS) An interactive computer-based system to facilitate the solution to unstructured problems by a set of decision makers working together as a group.

hacker A person who gains unauthorized access to a computer network for profit, criminal mischief, or personal pleasure.

Hadoop Open source software framework that enables distributed parallel processing of huge amounts of data across many inexpensive computers.

hertz Measure of frequency of electrical impulses per second, with 1 Hertz equivalent to 1 cycle per second.

HIPAA Law outlining rules for medical security, privacy, and the management of healthcare records.

hotspot A specific geographic location in which an access point provides public Wi-Fi network service.

HTML5 Next evolution of HTML, which makes it possible to embed images, video, and audio directly into a document without add-on software.

hubs Very simple devices that connect network components, sending a packet of data to all other connected devices.

hybrid AI systems Integration of multiple AI technologies into a single application to take advantage of the best features of these technologies.

hybrid cloud Computing model where firms use both their own IT infrastructure and also public cloud computing services.

Hypertext Markup Language (HTML) Page description language for creating web pages.

Hypertext Transfer Protocol (HTTP) The communications standard used to transfer pages on the web. Defines how messages are formatted and transmitted.

identity management Business processes and software tools for identifying the valid users of a system and controlling their access to system resources.

identity theft Theft of key pieces of personal information, such as credit card or Social Security numbers, in order to obtain merchandise and services in the name of the victim or to obtain false credentials.

Immanuel Kant's categorical imperative A principle that states that if an action is not right for everyone to take it is not right for anyone.

implementation   All the organizational activities surrounding the adoption, management, and routinization of an innovation, such as a new information system.

in-memory computing   Technology for very rapid analysis and processing of large quantities of data by storing the data in the computer's main memory rather than in secondary storage.

indirect goods   Goods not directly used in the production process, such as office supplies.

inference engine   The strategy used to search through the rule base in an expert system; can be forward or backward chaining.

information   Data that have been shaped into a form that is meaningful and useful to human beings.

information asymmetry   Situation where the relative bargaining power of two parties in a transaction is determined by one party in the transaction possessing more information essential to the transaction than the other party.

information density   The total amount and quality of information available to all market participants, consumers, and merchants.

information policy   Formal rules governing the maintenance, distribution, and use of information in an organization.

information requirements   A detailed statement of the information needs that a new system must satisfy; identifies who needs what information, and when, where, and how the information is needed.

information rights   The rights that individuals and organizations have with respect to information that pertains to themselves.

information system   Interrelated components working together to collect, process, store, and disseminate information to support decision making, coordination, control, analysis, and visualization in an organization.

information systems audit   Identifies all the controls tht govern individual information systems and assesses their effectiveness.

information systems department   The formal organizational unit that is responsible for the information systems function in the organization.

information systems literacy   Broad-based understanding of information systems that includes behavioral knowledge about organizations and individuals using information systems as well as technical knowledge about computers.

information systems managers   Leaders of the various specialists in the information systems department.

information systems plan   A road map indicating the direction of systems development: the rationale, the current situation, the management strategy, the implementation plan, and the budget.

information technology (IT)   All the hardware and software technologies a firm needs to achieve its business objectives.

information technology (IT) infrastructure   Computer hardware, software, data, storage technology, and networks providing a portfolio of shared IT resources for the organization.

informational roles   Mintzberg's classification for managerial roles where managers act as the nerve centers of their organizations, receiving and disseminating critical information.

informed consent   Consent given with knowledge of all the facts needed to make a rational decision.

input   The capture or collection of raw data from within the organization or from its external environment for processing in an information system.

instant messaging   Chat service that allows participants to create their own private chat channels so that a person can be alerted whenever someone on his or her private list is online to initiate a chat session with that particular individual.

intangible benefits   Benefits that are not easily quantified; they include more efficient customer service or enhanced decision making.

intellectual property   Intangible property created by individuals or corporations that is subject to protections under trade secret, copyright, and patent law.

intelligence   The first of Simon's four stages of decision making, when the individual collects information to identify problems occurring in the organization.

intelligent agent   Software program that uses a built-in or learned knowledge base to carry out specific, repetitive, and predictable tasks for an individual user, business process, or software application.

intelligent techniques   Technologies that aid human decision makers by capturing individual and collective knowledge, discovering patterns and behaviors in large quantities of data, and generating solutions to problems that are too large and complex for human beings to solve on their own.

internal integration tools   Project management technique that ensures that the implementation team operates as a cohesive unit.

international information systems architecture   The basic information systems required by organizations to coordinate worldwide trade and other activities.

Internet   Global network of networks using universal standards to connect millions of different networks.

Internet of Things   Pervasive web in which each object or machine has a unique identity and is able to use the Internet to link with other machines or send data. Also known as the Industrial Internet.

Internet Protocol (IP) address   Four-part numeric address indicating a unique computer location on the Internet.

Internet service provider (ISP)   A commercial organization with a permanent connection to the Internet that sells temporary connections to subscribers.

Internet2   Research network with new protocols and transmission speeds that provides an infrastructure for supporting high-bandwidth Internet applications.

interorganizational systems   Information systems that automate the flow of information across organizational boundaries and link a company to its customers, distributors, or suppliers.

interpersonal roles   Mintzberg's classification for managerial roles where managers act as figureheads and leaders for the organization.

intranet   An internal network based on Internet and World Wide Web technology and standards.

intrusion detection system   Tools to monitor the most vulnerable points in a network to detect and deter unauthorized intruders.

iOS   Operating system for the Apple iPad, iPhone, and iPod Touch.

IPv6   New IP addressing system using 128-bit IP addresses. Stands for Internet Protocol version 6.

IT governance   Strategy and policies for using information technology within an organization, specifying the decision rights and accountabilities to ensure that information technology supports the organization's strategies and objectives.

iterative   A process of repeating over and over again the steps to build a system.

Java   Programming language that can deliver only the software functionality needed for a particular task, such as a small applet downloaded from a network; can run on any computer and operating system.

joint application design (JAD)   Process to accelerate the generation of information requirements by having end users and information systems specialists work together in intensive interactive design sessions.

just-in-time strategy   Scheduling system for minimizing inventory by having components arrive exactly at the moment they are needed and finished goods shipped as soon as they leave the assembly line.

key field   A field in a record that uniquely identifies instances of that record so that it can be retrieved, updated, or sorted.

key performance indicators   Measures proposed by senior management for understanding how well the firm is performing along specified dimensions.

keylogger   Spyware that records every keystroke made on a computer to steal personal information or passwords or to launch Internet attacks.

knowledge   Concepts, experience, and insight that provide a framework for creating, evaluating, and using information.

knowledge base   Model of human knowledge that is used by expert systems.

knowledge discovery   Identification of novel and valuable patterns in large databases.

knowledge management   The set of processes developed in an organization to create, gather, store, maintain, and disseminate the firm's knowledge.

knowledge management systems   Systems that support the creation, capture, storage, and dissemination of firm expertise and knowledge.

knowledge workers   People such as engineers or architects who design products or services and create knowledge for the organization.

knowledge work systems   Information systems that aid knowledge workers in the creation and integration of new knowledge into the organization.

learning management system (LMS)   Tools for the management, delivery, tracking, and assessment of various types of employee learning.

legacy system   A system that has been in existence for a long time and that continues to be used to avoid the high cost of replacing or redesigning it.

legitimacy   The extent to which one's authority is accepted on grounds of competence, vision, or other qualities.

liability   The existence of laws that permit individuals to recover the damages done to them by other actors, systems, or organizations.

Linux   Reliable and compactly designed operating system that is an offshoot of UNIX and that can run on many different hardware platforms and is available free or at very low cost. Used as alternative to UNIX.

local area network (LAN)   A telecommunications network that requires its own dedicated channels and that encompasses a limited distance, usually one building or several buildings in close proximity.

location-based services   GPS map services available on smartphones.

location analytics   Ability to gain insights from the location (geographic) component of data, including loation data from mobile phones, output from sensors or scanning devices, and data from maps.

long tail marketing   Refers to the ability of firms to profitably market goods to very small online audiences, largely because of the lower costs of reaching very small market segments (people who fall into the long tail ends of a Bell curve).

machine learning   Study of how computer programs can improve their performance without explicit programming.

mainframe   Largest category of computer, used for major business processing.

maintenance   Changes in hardware, software, documentation, or procedures to a production system to correct errors, meet new requirements, or improve processing efficiency.

malware   Malicious software programs such as computer viruses, worms, and Trojan horses.

managed security service provider (MSSP)   Company that provides security management services for subscribing clients.

management information systems (MIS)   Specific category of information system providing reports on organizational performance to help middle management monitor and control the business.

management information systems (MIS):   The study of information systems focusing on their use in business and management.

managerial roles   Expectations of the activities that managers should perform in an organization.

market creator   An e-commerce business model in which firms provide a digital online environment where buyers and sellers can meet, search for products, and engage in transactions.

market entry costs   The cost merchants must pay to bring their goods to market.

marketspace   A marketplace extended beyond traditional boundaries and removed from a temporal and geographic location.

mashups   Composite software applications that depend on high-speed networks, universal communication standards, and open source code.

mass customization   The capacity to offer individually tailored products or services using mass production resources.

massive open online course (MOOC)   Online course made available via the web to very large numbers of participants.

menu costs   Merchants' costs of changing prices.

metropolitan area network (MAN)   Network that spans a metropolitan area, usually a city and its major suburbs. Its geographic scope falls between a WAN and a LAN.

microblogging   Blogging featuring very short posts, such as using Twitter.

micropayment systems   Payment for a very small sum of money, often less than $10.

middle management   People in the middle of the organizational hierarchy who are responsible for carrying out the plans and goals of senior management.

minicomputer   Middle-range computer used in systems for universities, factories, or research laboratories.

mobile commerce (m-commerce)   The use of wireless devices, such as smartphones or tablets to conduct both business-to-consumer and business-to-business e-commerce transactions over the Internet.

mobile web app   Internet-enabled app with specific functionality for mobile devices that is accessed through a mobile device's web browser.

mobile website   Version of a regular website that is scaled down in content and navigation for easy access and search on a small mobile screen.

modem   A device for translating a computer's digital signals into analog form for transmission over analog networks or for translating analog signals back into digital form for reception by a computer.

Moore's Law   Assertion that the number of components on a chip doubles each year.

multicore processor   Integrated circuit to which two or more processors have been attached for enhanced performance, reduced power consumption, and more efficient simultaneous processing of multiple tasks.

multinational   Form of business organization that concentrates financial management, and control out of a central home base while decentralizing production, sales and marketing.

multitiered (N-tier) client/server architecture   Client/server network which the work of the entire network is balanced over several different levels of servers.

multitouch   Interface that features the use of one or more finger gestures to manipulate lists or objects on a screen without using a mouse or keyboard.

nanotechnology   Technology that builds structures and processes based on the manipulation of individual atoms and molecules.

native advertising   Placing ads within social network newsfeeds or traditional editorial content, such as a newspaper article.

native app   Standalone application designed to run on a specific platform and device and is installed directly on the mobile device

near field communication (NFC)   Short-range wireless connectivity standard that uses electromagnetic radio fields to enable two compatible devices to exchange data when brought within a few centimeters of each other.

net marketplace   A single digital marketplace based on Internet technology linking many buyers to many sellers.

network   The linking of two or more computers to share data or resources, such as a printer.

network economics   Model of strategic systems at the industry level based on the concept of a network where adding another participant entails zero marginal costs but can create much larger marginal gains.

network operating system (NOS)   Special software that routes and manages communications on the network and coordinates network resources.

networking and telecommunications technology   Physical devices and software that link various computer hardware components and transfer data from one physical location to another.

neural network   Hardware or software that attempts to emulate the processing patterns of the biological brain.

non-relational database management system   Database management system for working with large quantities of structured and unstructured data that would be difficult to analyze with a relational model.

nonobvious relationship awareness (NORA)   Technology that can find obscure hidden connections between people or other entities by analyzing information from many different sources to correlate relationships.

normalization   The process of creating small stable data structures from complex groups of data when designing a relational database.

object   Software building block that combines data and the procedures acting on the data.

object-oriented development   Approach to systems development that uses the object as the basic unit of systems analysis and design. The system is modeled as a collection of objects and the relationship between them.

offshore outsourcing   Outsourcing systems development work or maintenance of existing systems to external vendors in another country.

on-demand computing   Firms off-loading peak demand for computing power to remote, large-scale data processing centers, investing just enough to handle average processing loads and paying for only as much additional computing power as the market demands. Also called utility computing.

online analytical processing (OLAP)   Capability for manipulating and analyzing large volumes of data from multiple perspectives.

online transaction processing   Transaction processing mode in which transactions entered online are immediately processed by the computer.

open source software   Software that provides free access to its program code, allowing users to modify the program code to make improvements or fix errors.

operating system   Software that manages the resources and activities of the computer.

operational CRM   Customer-facing applications, such as sales force automation, call center and customer service support, and marketing automation.

operational intelligence   Business analytics that delivers insight into data, streaming events and business operations.

operational management   People who monitor the day-to-day activities of the organization.

opt-in   Model of informed consent permitting prohibiting an organization from collecting any personal information unless the individual specifically takes action to approve information collection and use.

opt-out   Model of informed consent permitting the collection of personal information until the consumer specifically requests that the data not be collected.

organization (behavioral definition)   A collection of rights, privileges, obligations, and responsibilities that are delicately balanced over a period of time through conflict and conflict resolution.

organization (technical definition)   A stable, formal, social structure that takes resources from the environment and processes them to produce outputs.

organizational and management capital   Investments in organization and management such as new business processes, management behavior, organizational culture, or training.

organizational impact analysis   Study of the way a proposed system will affect organizational structure, attitudes, decision making, and operations.

organizational learning   Creation of new standard operating procedures and business processes that reflect organizations' experience.

output   The distribution of processed information to the people who will use it or to the activities for which it will be used.

outsourcing   The practice of contracting computer center operations, telecommunications networks, or applications development to external vendors.

packet switching   Technology that breaks messages into small, fixed bundles of data and routes them in the most economical way through any available communications channel.

paradigm shift   Radical reconceptualization of the nature of the business and the nature of the organization.

parallel strategy   A safe and conservative conversion approach where both the old system and its potential replacement are run together for a time until everyone is assured that the new one functions correctly.

particularism   Making judgments and taking action on the basis of narrow or personal characteristics, in all its forms (religious, nationalistic, ethnic, regionalism, geopolitical position).

partner relationship management (PRM)   Automation of the firm's relationships with its selling partners using customer data and analytical tools to improve coordination and customer sales.

password   Secret word or string of characters for authenticating users so they can access a resource such as a computer system.

patch   Small pieces of software to repair the software flaws without disturbing the proper operation of the software.

patent   A legal document that grants the owner an exclusive monopoly on the ideas behind an invention for 20 years; designed to ensure that inventors of new machines or methods are rewarded for their labor while making widespread use of their inventions.

peer-to-peer   Network architecture that gives equal power to all computers on the network; used primarily in small networks.

personal area network (PAN)   Computer network used for communication among digital devices that are close to one person.

personalization   Ability of merchants to target marketing messages to specific individuals by adjusting the message for a person's name, interests, and past purchases.

PERT chart   Network diagram depicting project tasks and their interrelationships.

pharming   Phishing technique that redirects users to a bogus web page, even when an individual enters the correct web page address.

phased approach   Introduces the new system in stages either by functions or by organizational units.

phishing   Form of spoofing involving setting up fake websites or sending email messages that resemble those of legitimate businesses that ask users for confidential personal data.

pilot study strategy   A strategy to introduce the new system to a limited area of the organization until it is proven to be fully functional; only then can the conversion to the new system across the entire organization take place.

pivot table   Spreadsheet tool for reorganizing and summarizing two or more dimensions of data in a tabular format.

platform   Business providing information systems, technologies, and services that thousands of other firms in different industries use to enhance their own capabilities.

podcasting   Publishing audio broadcasts via the Internet so that subscribing users can download audio files onto their personal computers or portable music players.

portal   Web interface for presenting integrated personalized content from a variety of sources. Also refers to a website service that provides an initial point of entry to the web.

portfolio analysis   An analysis of the portfolio of potential applications within a firm to determine the risks and benefits, and to select among alternatives for information systems.

post-implementation audit   Formal review process conducted after a system has been placed in production to determine how well the system has met its original objectives.

predictive analytics   The use of data mining techniques, historical data, and assumptions about future conditions to predict outcomes of events, such as the probability a customer will respond to an offer or purchase a specific product.

predictive search   Part of a search alogrithm that predicts what a user query is looking as it is entered based on popular searches.

price discrimination   Selling the same goods, or nearly the same goods, to different targeted groups at different prices.

price transparency   The ease with which consumers can find out the variety of prices in a market.

primary activities   Activities most directly related to the production and distribution of a firm's products or services.

primary key   Unique identifier for all the information in any row of a database table.

privacy   The claim of individuals to be left alone, free from surveillance or interference from other individuals, organizations, or the state.

private cloud   A proprietary network or a data center that ties together servers, storage, networks, data, and applications as a set of virtualized services that are shared by users inside a company.

private exchange   Another term for a private industrial network.

private industrial networks   Web-enabled networks linking systems of multiple firms in an industry for the coordination of trans-organizational business processes.

process specifications   Describe the logic of the processes occurring within the lowest levels of a data flow diagram.

processing   The conversion, manipulation, and analysis of raw input into a form that is more meaningful to humans.

product differentiation   Competitive strategy for creating brand loyalty by developing new and unique products and services that are not easily duplicated by competitors.

production   The stage after the new system is installed and the conversion is complete; during this time the system is reviewed by users and technical specialists to determine how well it has met its original goals.

production or service workers   People who actually produce the products or services of the organization.

profiling   The use of computers to combine data from multiple sources and create electronic dossiers of detailed information on individuals.

program-data dependence   The close relationship between data stored in files and the software programs that update and maintain those files. Any change in data organization or format requires a change in all the programs associated with those files.

programmers   Highly trained technical specialists who write computer software instructions.

programming   The process of translating the system specifications prepared during the design stage into program code.

project   Planned series of related activities for achieving a specific business objective.

project management   Application of knowledge, tools, and techniques to achieve specific targets within a specified budget and time period.

project portfolio management   Helps organizations evaluate and manage portfolios of projects and dependencies among them.

protocol   A set of rules and procedures that govern transmission between the components in a network.

prototype   The preliminary working version of an information system for demonstration and evaluation purposes.

prototyping   The process of building an experimental system quickly and inexpensively for demonstration and evaluation so that users can better determine information requirements.

public cloud   A cloud maintained by an external service provider, accessed through the Internet, and available to the general public.

public key encryption   Uses two keys: one shared (or public) and one private.

public key infrastructure (PKI)   System for creating public and private keys using a certificate authority (CA) and digital certificates for authentication.

pull-based model   Supply chain driven by actual customer orders or purchases so that members of the supply chain produce and deliver only what customers have ordered.

push-based model   Supply chain driven by production master schedules based on forecasts or best guesses of demand for products, and products are "pushed" to customers.

quantum computing   Use of principles of quantum physics to represent data and perform operations on the data, with the ability to be in many different states at once and to perform many different computations simultaneously.

query language   Software tool that provides immediate online answers to requests for information that are not predefined.

radio frequency identification (RFID)   Technology using tiny tags with embedded microchips containing data about an item and its location to transmit short-distance radio signals to special RFID readers that then pass the data on to a computer for processing.

ransomware   Malware that extorts money from users by taking control of their computers or displaying annoying pop-up messages.

Rapid Application Development (RAD)   Process for developing systems in a very short time period by using prototyping, state-of-the-art software tools and close teamwork among users and systems specialists.

rationalization of procedures   The streamlining of standard operating procedures, eliminating obvious bottlenecks, so that automation makes operating procedures more efficient.

record   A group of related fields.

referential integrity   Rules to ensure that relationships between coupled database tables remain consistent.

relational DBMS   A type of logical database model that treats data as if they were stored in two-dimensional tables. It can relate data stored in one table to data in another as long as the two tables share a common data element.

Repetitive stress injury (RSI)   Occupational disease that occurs when muscle groups are forced through repetitive actions with high-impact loads or thousands of repetitions with low-impact loads.

Request for proposal (RFP)   A detailed list of questions submitted to vendors of software or other services to determine how well the vendor's product can meet the organization's specific requirements.

responsibility   Accepting the potential costs, duties, and obligations for the decisions one makes.

responsive web design   Ability of a website to automatically change screen resolution and image size as a user switches to devices of different sizes, such as a laptop, tablet computer, or smartphone. Eliminates the need for separate design and development work for each new device.

revenue model   A description of how a firm will earn revenue, generate profits, and produce a return on investment.

richness   Measurement of the depth and detail of information that a business can supply to the customer as well as information the business collects about the customer.

risk assessment   Determining the potential frequency of the occurrence of a problem and the potential damage if the problem were to occur. Used to determine the cost/benefit of a control.

Risk aversion principle   Principle that one should take the action that produces the least harm or incurs the least cost.

router   Specialized communications processor that forwards packets of data from one network to another network.

routines   Precise rules, procedures and practices that have been developed to cope with expected situations.

RSS   Technology using aggregator software to pull content from websites and feed it automatically to subscribers' computers.

safe harbor   Private self-regulating policy and enforcement mechanism that meets the objectives of government regulations but does not involve government regulation or enforcement.

sales revenue model   Selling goods, information, or services to customers as the main source of revenue for a company.

Sarbanes-Oxley Act   Law passed in 2002 that imposes responsibility on companies and their management to protect investors by safeguarding the accuracy and integrity of financial information that is used internally and released externally.

scalability   The ability of a computer, product, or system to expand to serve a larger number of users without breaking down.

scope   Defines what work is and is not included in a project.

scoring model   A quick method for deciding among alternative systems based on a system of ratings for selected objectives.

search costs   The time and money spent locating a suitable product and determining the best price for that product.

search engine   A tool for locating specific sites or information on the Internet.

search engine marketing   Use of search engines to deliver in their results sponsored links, for which advertisers have paid.

search engine optimization (SEO)   The process of changing a website's content, layout, and format in order to increase the ranking of the site on popular search engines and to generate more site visitors.

Secure Hypertext Transfer Protocol (S-HTTP)   Protocol used for encrypting data flowing over the Internet; limited to individual messages.

Secure Sockets Layer (SSL)   Enables client and server computers to manage encryption and decryption activities as they communicate with each other during a secure web session.

security   Policies, procedures, and technical measures used to prevent unauthorized access, alteration, theft, or physical damage to information systems.

security policy   Statements ranking information risks, identifying acceptable security goals, and identifying the mechanisms for achieving these goals.

semantic search   Search technology capable of understanding human language and behavior.

semi-structured decisions   Decisions in which only part of the problem has a clear-cut answer provided by an accepted procedure.

senior management   People occupying the topmost hierarchy in an organization who are responsible for making long-range decisions.

sensitivity analysis   Models that ask "what-if" questions repeatedly to determine the impact of changes in one or more factors on the outcomes.

sentiment analysis   Mining text comments in an email message, blog, social media conversation, or survey form to detect favorable and unfavorable opinions about specific subjects.

server   Computer specifically optimized to provide software and other resources to other computers over a network.

service level agreement (SLA)   Formal contract between customers and their service providers that defines the specific responsibilities of the service provider and the level of service expected by the customer.

service-oriented architecture (SOA)   Software architecture of a firm built on a collection of software programs that communicate with each other to perform assigned tasks to create a working software application

shopping bot   Software with varying levels of built-in intelligence to help electronic commerce shoppers locate and evaluate products or service they might wish to purchase.

six sigma   A specific measure of quality, representing 3.4 defects per million opportunities; used to designate a set of methodologies and techniques for improving quality and reducing costs.

smart card   A credit-card-size plastic card that stores digital information and that can be used for electronic payments in place of cash.

smartphone   Wireless phone with voice, text, and Internet capabilities.

sniffer   Type of eavesdropping program that monitors information traveling over a network.

social business   Use of social networking platforms, including Facebook, Twitter, and internal corporate social tools, to engage employees, customers, and suppliers.

social CRM   Tools enabling a business to link customer conversatins, data, and relationships from social networking sites to CRM processes.

social engineering   Tricking people into revealing their passwords by pretending to be legitimate users or members of a company in need of information.

social graph   Map of all significant online social relationships, comparable to a social network describing offline relationships.

social networking sites   Online community for expanding users' business or social contacts by making connections through their mutual business or personal connections.

social search   Effort to provide more relevant and trustworthy search results based on a person's network of social contacts.

social shopping   Use of websites featuring user-created web pages to share knowledge about items of interest to other shoppers.

sociotechnical design   Design to produce information systems that blend technical efficiency with sensitivity to organizational and human needs.

sociotechnical view   Seeing systems as composed of both technical and social elements.

Software as a service (SaaS)   Services for delivering and providing access to software remotely as a web-based service.

software-defined networking (SDN)   Using a central control program separate from network devices to manage the flow of data on a network.

software-defined storage (SDS)   Software to manage provisioning and management of data storage independent of the underlying hardware.

software localization   Process of converting software to operate in a second language.

software package   A prewritten, precoded, commercially available set of programs that eliminates the need to write software programs for certain functions.

spam   Unsolicited commercial email.

spoofing   Tricking or deceiving computer systems or other computer users by hiding one's identity or faking the identity of another user on the Internet.

spyware   Technology that aids in gathering information about a person or organization without their knowledge.

SQL injection attack   Attacks against a website that take advantage of vulnerabilities in poorly coded SQL (a standard and common database software application) applications in order to introduce malicious program code into a company's systems and networks.

strategic transitions   A movement from one level of sociotechnical system to another. Often required when adopting strategic systems that demand changes in the social and technical elements of an organization.

streaming   A publishing method for music and video files that flows a continuous stream of content to a user's device without being stored locally on the device.

structure chart   System documentation showing each level of design, the relationship among the levels, and the overall place in the design structure; can document one program, one system, or part of one program.

structured   Refers to the fact that techniques are carefully drawn up, step by step, with each step building on a previous one.

structured decisions   Decisions that are repetitive and routine and have a definite procedure for handling them.

structured knowledge   Knowledge in the form of structured documents and reports.

Structured Query Language (SQL)   The standard data manipulation language for relational database management systems.

subscription revenue model   Website charging a subscription fee for access to some or all of its content or services on an ongoing basis.

supply chain   Network of organizations and business processes for procuring materials, transforming raw materials into intermediate and finished products, and distributing the finished products to customers.

supply chain execution systems   Systems to manage the flow of products through distribution centers and warehouses to ensure that products are delivered to the right locations in the most efficient manner.

supply chain management systems   Information systems that automate the flow of information between a firm and its suppliers in order to optimize the planning, sourcing, manufacturing, and delivery of products and services.

supply chain planning systems   Systems that enable a firm to generate demand forecasts for a product and to develop sourcing and manufacturing plans for that product.

support activities   Activities that make the delivery of a firm's primary activities possible. Consist of the organization's infrastructure, human resources, technology, and procurement.

switch   Device to connect network components that has more intelligence than a hub and can filter and forward data to a specified destination.

switching costs   The expense a customer or company incurs in lost time and expenditure of resources when changing from one supplier or system to a competing supplier or system.

system testing   Tests the functioning of the information system as a whole in order to determine if discrete modules will function together as planned.

systems analysis   The analysis of a problem that the organization will try to solve with an information system.

systems analysts   Specialists who translate business problems and requirements into information requirements and systems, acting as liaison between the information systems department and the rest of the organization.

systems design   Details how a system will meet the information requirements as determined by the systems analysis.

systems development   The activities that go into producing an information systems solution to an organizational problem or opportunity.

systems life cycle   A traditional methodology for developing an information system that partitions the systems development process into formal stages that must be completed sequentially with a very formal division of labor between end users and information systems specialists.

T lines   High-speed guaranteed service level data lines leased from communications providers, such as T-1 lines (with a transmission capacity of 1.544 Mbps).

tablet computer   Mobile handheld computer that is larger than a mobile phone and operated primarily by touching a flat screen.

tacit knowledge   Expertise and experience of organizational members that has not been formally documented.

tangible benefits   Benefits that can be quantified and assigned a monetary value; they include lower operational costs and increased cash flows.

taxonomy   Method of classifying things according to a predetermined system.

teams   Formal groups whose members collaborate to achieve specific goals.

teamware   Group collaboration software that is customized for teamwork.

technology standards   Specifications that establish the compatibility of products and the ability to communicate in a network.

telepresence   Telepresence is a technology that allows a person to give the appearance of being present at a location other than his or her true physical location.

Telnet   Network tool that allows someone to log on to one computer system while doing work on another.

test plan   Prepared by the development team in conjunction with the users; it includes all of the preparations for the series of tests to be performed on the system.

testing   The exhaustive and thorough process that determines whether the system produces the desired results under known conditions.

text mining   Discovery of patterns and relationships from large sets of unstructured data.

token   Physical device similar to an identification card that is designed to prove the identity of a single user.

total cost of ownership (TCO)   Designates the total cost of owning technology resources, including initial purchase costs, the cost of hardware and software upgrades, maintenance, technical support, and training.

total quality management (TQM)   A concept that makes quality control a responsibility to be shared by all people in an organization.

touch point   Method of firm interaction with a customer, such as telephone, email, customer service desk, conventional mail, or point-of-purchase.

trade secret   Any intellectual work or product used for a business purpose that can be classified as belonging to that business, provided it is not based on information in the public domain.

transaction costs   Costs incurred when a firm buys on the marketplace what it cannot make itself.

transaction cost theory   Economic theory stating that firms grow larger because they can conduct marketplace transactions internally more cheaply than they can with external firms in the marketplace.

transaction fee revenue model   An online e-commerce revenue model where the firm receives a fee for enabling or executing transactions.

transaction processing systems (TPS)   Computerized systems that perform and record the daily routine transactions necessary to conduct the business; they serve the organization's operational level.

transborder data flow   The movement of information across international boundaries in any form.

Transmission Control Protocol/Internet Protocol (TCP/IP)   Dominant model for achieving connectivity among different networks. Provides a universally agreed-on method for breaking up digital messages into packets, routing them to the proper addresses, and then reassembling them into coherent messages.

transnational   Truly global form of business organization with no national headquarters; value-added activities are managed from a global perspective without reference to national borders, optimizing sources of supply and demand and local competitive advantage.

Trojan horse   A software program that appears legitimate but contains a second hidden function that may cause damage.

tuple   A row or record in a relational database.

two-factor authentication   Validating user identity with two means of identification, one of which is typically a physical token, and the other of which is typically data.

Unified communications   Integrates disparate channels for voice communications, data communications, instant messaging, email, and electronic conferencing into a single experience where users can seamlessly switch back and forth between different communication modes.

unified threat management (UTM)   Comprehensive security management tool that combines multiple security tools, including firewalls, virtual private networks, intrusion detection systems, and web content filtering and anti-spam software.

uniform resource locator (URL)   The address of a specific resource on the Internet.

unit testing   The process of testing each program separately in the system. Sometimes called program testing.

Unix   Operating system for all types of computers, which is machine independent and supports multiuser processing, multitasking, and networking. Used in high-end workstations and servers.

unstructured decisions   Nonroutine decisions in which the decision maker must provide judgment, evaluation, and insights into the problem definition; there is no agreed-upon procedure for making such decisions.

user interface   The part of the information system through which the end user interacts with the system; type of hardware and the series of on-screen commands and responses required for a user to work with the system.

user-designer communications gap   The difference in backgrounds, interests, and priorities that impede communication and problem solving among end users and information systems specialists.

utilitarian principle   Principle that assumes one can put values in rank order of utility and understand the consequences of various courses of action.

value chain model   Model that highlights the primary or support activities that add a margin of value to a firm's products or services where information systems can best be applied to achieve a competitive advantage.

value web   Customer-driven network of independent firms who use information technology to coordinate their value chains to collectively produce a product or service for a market.

virtual company   Organization using networks to link people, assets, and ideas to create and distribute products and services without being limited to traditional organizational boundaries or physical location.

virtual private network (VPN)   A secure connection between two points across the Internet to transmit corporate data. Provides a low-cost alternative to a private network.

Virtual Reality Modeling Language (VRML)   A set of specifications for interactive three-dimensional modeling on the World Wide Web.

virtual reality systems   Interactive graphics software and hardware that create computer-generated simulations that provide sensations that emulate real-world activities.

virtualization   Presenting a set of computing resources so that they can all be accessed in ways that are not restricted by physical configuration or geographic location.

visual web   Refers to web linking visual sites such as Pinterest where pictures replace text socuents and where users search on pictures and visual characteristics.

Voice over IP (VoIP)   Facilities for managing the delivery of voice information using the Internet Protocol (IP).

war driving   Technique in which eavesdroppers drive by buildings or park outside and try to intercept wireless network traffic.

Web 2.0   Second-generation, interactive Internet-based services that enable people to collaborate, share information, and create new services online, including mashups, blogs, RSS, and wikis.

Web 3.0   Future vision of the web where all digital information is woven together with intelligent search capabilities.

web beacons   Tiny objects invisibly embedded in email messages and web pages that are designed to monitor the behavior of the user visiting a website or sending email.

web browser   An easy-to-use software tool for accessing the World Wide Web and the Internet.

web hosting service   Company with large web server computers to maintain the websites of fee-paying subscribers.

web mining   Discovery and analysis of useful patterns and information from the World Wide Web.

web server   Software that manages requests for web pages on the computer where they are stored and that delivers the page to the user's computer.

web services   Set of universal standards using Internet technology for integrating different applications from different sources without time-consuming custom coding. Used for linking systems of different organizations or for linking disparate systems within the same organization.

website   All of the World Wide Web pages maintained by an organization or an individual.

Wi-Fi   Stands for "wireless fidelity" and refers to the 802.11 family of wireless networking standards.

wide area network (WAN)   Telecommunications network that spans a large geographical distance. May consist of a variety of cable, satellite, and microwave technologies.

wiki   Collaborative website where visitors can add, delete, or modify content, including the work of previous authors.

WiMax   Popular term for IEEE Standard 802.16 for wireless networking over a range of up to 31 miles with a data transfer rate of up to 75 Mbps. Stands for Worldwide Interoperability for Microwave Access.

Windows   Microsoft family of operating systems for both network servers and client computers.

Windows 10   Most recent Microsoft Windows client operating system.

Wintel PC   Any computer that uses Intel microprocessors (or compatible processors) and a Windows operating system.

wireless sensor networks (WSNs)   Networks of interconnected wireless devices with built-in processing, storage, and radio frequency sensors and antennas that are embedded into the physical environment to provide measurements of many points over large spaces.

wisdom   The collective and individual experience of applying knowledge to the solution of problems.

wisdom of crowds   The belief that large numbers of people can make better decisions about a wide range of topics or products than a single person or even a small committee of experts.

World Wide Web   A system with universally accepted standards for storing, retrieving, formatting, and displaying information in a networked environment.

worms   Independent software programs that propagate themselves to disrupt the operation of computer networks or destroy data and other programs.

zero-day vulnerabilities   Security vulnerabilities in software, unknown to the creator, that hackers can exploit before the vendor becomes aware of the problem.

Index

Name Index

A
Agnifilo, Karen Friedman, 229
Alden, Rick, 337
Archuleta, Katherine, 332

B
Barnett, Camille, 554
Bayer, Thomas, 331
Beane, Billy, 467
Beberness, Benjamin, 547
Bingham, Elizabeth, 448
Bonner, Brett, 4
Bradley, KC, 523
Brin, Sergey, 272
Brynjolfsson, Erik, 151

C
Camp, Garrett, 371
Carr, Nicholas, 153
Carson, Ryan, 92
Cochrane, James, 211–212
Cook, Tim, 288
Cortadellas, Xavi, 103
Cox, Michael, 36
Cross, Michael, 541

D
Dean, Jeff, 440
Deming, W. Edwards, 490

E
Ellison, Larry, 73

F
Fayol, Henri, 459
Filo, David, 271
Ford, Henry, 58
Friedman, Jeffrey, 554
Friedman, Thomas, 11

G
Ganenthiran, Nilam, 404
Gates, Bill, 58
Goelman, Aitan, 313

H
Hackenberg, Ulrich, 151
Hatz, Wolfgang, 151
Hawker, Stuart, 562
Hawkins, Dave, 509
Hevesi, Patrick, 326
Hsieh, Tony, 92
Hunt, Jeremy, 540

I
Immelt, Jeffrey, 483

J
Jennings, Ken, 447
Jobs, Steve, 58
Juran, Joseph, 490

K
Kalanick, Travis, 371
Kesanupalli, Ramesh, 331
Khan, Iftekhar, 207
Kris, Mark, 449

L
Lamonica, Sam, 207
Lampert, Eddie, 118
Leibbrandt, Gottfried, 294
Lezon, Joe, 516
Lue, Rosetta, 554

M
Martinez, Arthur, 116
Mathieson, S. A., 540
McAfee, Andrew P., 151
Mehta, Apoorva, 403
Metcalfe, Robert, 175
Minihan, Colin, 326
Mintzberg, Henry, 88, 459–460
Modi, Narenda, 579
Monash, Curt, 449
Montgomery, Tom, 92
Moore, Gordon, 173
Morgan, Patrick, 554

N
Nadella, Satya, 397
Neusser, Heinz-Jakob, 151
Ng, Andrew Y., 440
Nutter, Michael A., 554–555

O
Obama, Barack, 263, 332
O'Donnell, Glenn, 189
Olson, Sara, 36
Oxley, Michael, 308
Ozment, Andy, 331

P
Page, Larry, 272
Pick, Lucinda, 582
Porter, Michael, 95

Q
Quy Huy, 92

R
Rees, Andrew, 588
Rogers, Michael S., 331
Rometty, Virginia, 449
Routh, Jim, 326
Rutter, Brad, 447

S
Sarao, Navinder, 311–312
Sarbanes, Paul, 308
Schinelli, Bruce, 517
Seymour, Donna, 331–332
Sidhu, Suresh, 357
Simon, H. A., 457
Snowden, Edward, 137
Soards, Susan, 516
Sopkin, Rob, 471

T
Torvalds, Linus, 193
Treckeme, Kristi, 547
Triplett, Clifton, 332

V
Vance, Cyrus, Jr., 228

W
Watson, Michael, 92
Watson, Thomas J., 447
Wheeler, Tom, 263
Winterkorn, Martin, 150–151
Wotus, Ron, 467

Y
Yang, Jerry, 271
Yarbrough, Brian, 411

Z
Zeidman, Steven, 229
Zuckerberg, Mark, 159, 290

Organizations Index

A
ABB, 41–44, 433
Accenture, 91, 182, 311, 367
Acronis, 314
Advanced Micro Design (AMD), 11, 179
Airbnb, 107, 372, 376, 387, 402
Airborne Express, 23
AirWatch, 326
Alcoa, 342–343
Alex and Ani, 516–517
Allot Communications, 322
Amazon, 272, 303, 383, 385, 386, 401, 405,
    411–413, 439, 483, 494, 579
Amazon.com, 45, 95, 173
American Airlines, 110, 306
American Bar Association (ABA), 133
American Medical Association (AMA), 133
American National Insurance Company
    (ANCO), 494
America Online (AOL), 80, 140, 266, 385, 391
Angostura, 487–489

Subject Index

INTEGRATING BUSINESS WITH TECHNOLOGY

By completing the projects in this text, students will be able to demonstrate business knowledge, application software proficiency, and Internet skills. These projects can be used by instructors as learning assessment tools and by students as demonstrations of business, software, and problem-solving skills to future employers. Here are some of the skills and competencies students using this text will be able to demonstrate:

Business Application skills: Use of both business and software skills in real-world business applications. Demonstrates both business knowledge and proficiency in spreadsheet, database, and web page/blog creation tools.

Internet skills: Ability to use Internet tools to access information, conduct research, or perform online calculations and analysis.

Analytical, writing and presentation skills: Ability to research a specific topic, analyze a problem, think creatively, suggest a solution, and prepare a clear written or oral presentation of the solution, working either individually or with others in a group.

Business Application Skills

BUSINESS SKILLS	SOFTWARE SKILLS	CHAPTER
Finance and Accounting		
Financial statement analysis	Spreadsheet charts	Chapter 2*
	Spreadsheet formulas	Chapter 10
	Spreadsheet downloading and formatting	
Pricing hardware and software	Spreadsheet formulas	Chapter 5
Technology rent vs. buy decision Total Cost of Ownership (TCO) analysis	Spreadsheet formulas	Chapter 5*
Analyzing telecommunications services and costs	Spreadsheet formulas	Chapter 7
Risk assessment	Spreadsheet charts and formulas	Chapter 8
Retirement planning	Spreadsheet formulas and logical functions	Chapter 11
Capital budgeting	Spreadsheet formulas	Chapter 14
		Chapter 14*
Human Resources		
Employee training and skills tracking	Database design Database querying and reporting	Chapter 13*
Job posting database and Web page	Database design Web page design and creation	Chapter 15
Manufacturing and Production		
Analyzing supplier performance and pricing	Spreadsheet date functions Database functions Data filtering	Chapter 2
Inventory management	Importing data into a database Database querying and reporting	Chapter 6
Bill of materials cost sensitivity analysis	Spreadsheet data tables Spreadsheet formulas	Chapter 12*
Sales and Marketing		
Sales trend analysis	Database querying and reporting	Chapter 1

Customer reservation system	Database querying and reporting	Chapter 3
Improving marketing decisions	Spreadsheet pivot tables	Chapter 12
Customer profiling	Database design Database querying and reporting	Chapter 6*
Customer service analysis	Database design Database querying and reporting	Chapter 9
Sales lead and customer analysis	Database design Database querying and reporting	Chapter 13
Blog creation and design	Blog creation tool	Chapter 4

Internet Skills

Using online software tools for job hunting and career development	Chapter 1
Using online interactive mapping software to plan efficient transportation routes	Chapter 2
Researching product information and evaluating websites for auto sales	Chapter 3
Analyzing web browser privacy protection	Chapter 4
Researching travel costs using online travel sites	Chapter 5
Searching online databases for products and services	Chapter 6
Using web search engines for business research	Chapter 7
Researching and evaluating business outsourcing services	Chapter 8
Researching and evaluating supply chain management services	Chapter 9
Evaluating e-commerce hosting services	Chapter 10
Using shopping bots to compare product price, features, and availability	Chapter 11
Using online software tools for retirement planning	Chapter 12
Analyzing website design and information requirements	Chapter 13
Researching real estate prices	Chapter 14
Researching international markets and pricing	Chapter 15

Analytical, Writing and Presentation Skills*

BUSINESS PROBLEM	CHAPTER
Management analysis of a business	Chapter 1
Value chain and competitive forces analysis	Chapter 3
Business strategy formulation	
Formulating a corporate privacy policy	Chapter 4
Employee productivity analysis	Chapter 7
Disaster recovery planning	Chapter 8
Locating and evaluating suppliers	Chapter 9
Developing an e-commerce strategy	Chapter 10
Identifying knowledge management opportunities	Chapter 11
Identifying international markets	Chapter 15

*Dirt Bikes Running Case on MyMISLab